CHINA
CONFIDENTIAL

CHINA
CONFIDENTIAL

AMERICAN DIPLOMATS
AND SINO-AMERICAN RELATIONS,
1945–1996

Compiled and edited with introductions and conclusion by

Nancy Bernkopf Tucker

Published in cooperation with the
Association for Diplomatic Studies and Training
Foreign Affairs Oral History Program,
and the ADST-DACOR Diplomats and Diplomacy Series

COLUMBIA UNIVERSITY PRESS
NEW YORK

Columbia University Press
Publishers Since 1893
New York Chichester, West Sussex

Library of Congress Cataloging-in-Publication Data
Tucker, Nancy Bernkopf.
China confidential : American diplomats and Sino-American
relations since 1945 / Nancy Bernkopf Tucker
p. cm.
Includes bibliographical references (p.) and index.
ISBN 0–231–10630–0 (acid free paper) —
ISBN 0–231–10631–9 (pbk. : acid-free paper)
1. United States—Foreign relations—China.
2. China—Foreign relations—United States.
3. United States—Foreign relations—1945–1989.
4. United States—Foreign relations—1989–.
5. Diplomats—United States—History—20th century.
6. Diplomats—China—History—20th century.
I. Title.
E183.8.C5 T835 2000
327.73051—dc21   00–040445

Casebound editions of Columbia University Press books are
printed on permanent and durable acid-free paper.
Printed in the United States of America
c 10 9 8 7 6 5 4 3 2 1
p 10 9 8 7 6 5 4 3 2 1

An Association for Diplomatic Studies and Training (ADST)/
Diplomatic and Consular Officers, Retired (DACOR) Book

To Gisl
whose remembrance of things past shaped my world

and Warren
who has given me so much to remember

THIS WAS TO HAVE BEEN ONE of those quick books done in between other, more taxing projects. As always, time passed and the book lingered. I want, therefore, to begin by thanking several people and organizations for their patience: Kate Wittenberg, my editor, who remained encouraging even after I exceeded deadlines; the Woodrow Wilson International Center for Scholars, where I began the project while a resident fellow writing a different book; and, of course, my husband, Warren I. Cohen, who sacrificed many an outing to my all too hectic schedule.

I owe to Warren as well an intellectual debt for his careful reading of the manuscript, his enthusiasm for its contents, and suggestions for revisions. Six other scholars also deserve gratitude for reading the proposal and/or manuscript. Unfortunately, four remain anonymous, allowing me to thank only George C. Herring and Richard H. Immerman. Editing oral history is not the same as writing history and I am grateful to Don Ritchie, associate historian of the U.S. Senate, who has made this relatively new field more accessible to novices like me and who encouraged me to go ahead with the project.

The Association for Diplomatic Studies and Training, housed at Georgetown University and the National Foreign Affairs Training Center, collected all but one of the interviews I have used. They compose a small fraction of the more than eleven hundred currently in the constantly growing collection covering all parts of the world. Ambassador Steven Low, at the time serving as president of the association, cleared the way through copyright agreements for the project to begin. Charles Stuart Kennedy, director of the ADST Oral History Program, conducted most of the interviews, although a few were done by others, including myself, and the late Marshall Green, who contributed not only his own reflections and interviewing talents, but also some of the funding for the ADST effort. For the single non-ADST interview, I thank the Bancroft Library of the University of California, Berkeley which graciously shared the recollections of John S. Service with me.

At Georgetown University, the staff of the Department of History, most especially Larry Fields and Elizabeth English, rendered continuing support, even while laughing at my lack of computer skills and constant warfare with the copying machine. The School of Foreign Service gave me time off at the beginning of the project and down the road supported the transcription of the Winston Lord interview.

Finally, I want to thank the diplomats whose words I have captured in this history of U.S.-China relations. They have made a unique contribution with their obvious effort to look back thoughtfully at their lives and record the difficult, amusing, and significant moments they experienced in the field and in Washington while dealing with Chinese affairs between 1945 and 1996. As a result of my own brief service in the Office of Chinese Affairs at the Department of State and the U.S. Embassy in Beijing, as well as my participation in continuing China policy discussions in Washington, D.C. over the past decade, I have been fortunate to know many of these individuals personally. They are in real life every bit as dedicated and insightful as they appear in the book. Their interest in the betterment of U.S.-China-Taiwan relations and their concern for the future of Hong Kong continues in most cases beyond their government service. In particular, I must thank Paul Kriesberg, who sadly did not live to see the volume published, and Winston Lord, both of whom were especially generous with their time.

(only China-related positions are listed)

Donald Anderson
Chinese Language Training, Department of State and Taichung, Taiwan, 1958–1961; Consular Officer/Political Officer, Consulate General, Hong Kong, 1962–1965; Interpreter Training, Taichung, Taiwan, 1965–1966; China Desk/Warsaw Talks, Department of State, 1966–1970; Talks with Chinese Embassy, Paris, France, 1972–1973; Political Officer, Liaison Office, Beijing, 1973–1975; Political Officer, Consulate General, Hong Kong, 1975–1977; Office of Chinese Affairs, Department of State, 1977–1980; Consul General, Consulate General, Shanghai, 1980–1983; Director, Office of Chinese Affairs, Department of State, 1983–1985; Consul General, Consulate General, Hong Kong, 1986–1990

Robert Anderson
Vice-Consul, Consulate General, Shanghai, 1946–1947; Political Officer, Nanjing, 1947–1949

Oscar Armstrong
Officer, Consulate General, Guangzhou, 1946–1947; Embassy, Beijing, 1947–1950; Consulate General, Hong Kong, 1954–1957; INR—Chinese Affairs, Department of State, 1957–1961; Deputy Principal Officer, Hong Kong, 1964–1966; East Asia Bureau/Public Affairs, Department of State, 1966–1968; Taiwan Affairs, Department of State, 1968–1971; Director, Office of Chinese Affairs, 1973–1976

Willis Armstrong
Assistant Secretary of State for Economic and Business Affairs, 1972–1973

Leonard Bacon

Officer, Consulate, Hankou, 1947–1948; Embassy, Nanjing, 1949–1950; Deputy Director, Office of Northeast Asian Affairs, Department of State, 1961–1963; Acting Director, East Asian Affairs, Department of State, 1964

Natale Bellocchi

Administrative Assistant, Consulate General, Hong Kong, 1960–1962; Chinese Language Training, Taichung, Taiwan, 1963–1965; Assistant Commercial Attaché, Embassy, Taipei, Taiwan, 1965–1967; Chief, Commercial Unit, Consulate General, Hong Kong, 1968–1969; Deputy Principal Officer, Consulate General, Hong Kong, 1979–1981; Director, American Institute in Taiwan, 1990–1995

Robert R. Bowie

Director, Policy Planning Staff, Department of State, 1953–1955; Assistant Secretary for Policy Planning, Department of State, 1955–1957

Marshall Brement

Staff Assistant, East Asian Affairs, Department of State, 1956–1957; Chinese Language Training, Department of State and Taiwan, 1958–1960; Political Officer, Consulate General, Hong Kong, 1960–1963

Frank Burnet

Chinese Language Training, Department of State, Taichung, Taiwan, 1955–1957; Staff Assistant, Far East Bureau, Department of State, 1961–1963; Political Counselor, Embassy, Taipei, Taiwan, 1975–1979

Ralph Clough

Vice Consul, Consulate, Kunming, 1945; Embassy, Chongqing, 1945–1946; Embassy, Nanjing, 1946; Language Officer, Embassy, Beijing, 1946–1947; Chinese Secretary, Embassy, Nanjing, 1947–1950; Political Officer, Consulate General, Hong Kong, 1950–1954; Deputy Director, Office of Chinese Affairs, Department of State, 1955–1957; Director, Office of Chinese Affairs, Department of State, 1958; Advisor, Negotiations with Chinese Poland, Switzerland, Great Britain, 1958–1961; Deputy Chief of Mission, Embassy, Taipei, Taiwan, 1961–1965; Policy Planning Staff, Department of State, 1966–1967

David Dean
Chinese language training, Taichung, Taiwan, 1957–1959; Consulate General, Hong Kong, 1959–1962; Officer in Charge of Mainland China Affairs, Office of Asian Communist Affairs, Department of State, 1962–1965; Deputy Director, Office of Asian Communist Affairs, Department of State, 1965–1966; Political Counselor and Chargé, Embassy, Taipei, 1966–1969; Deputy Principal Officer, Consulate General, Hong Kong, 1970–1974; Deputy Chief of Mission, Beijing, 1976–1978; Head, Office of East Asian Affairs, Intelligence and Research Bureau, Department of State, 1978; Board of Directors, American Institute in Taiwan (AIT), 1979–1995; Chairman, AIT/Washington, 1979–1987; Director, AIT/Taipei, 1987–1989

Willard Devlin
Chief of Consular Section, Consulate General, Hong Kong, 1974–1976

Robert S. Dillon
Operations with Nationalist Chinese, Taiwan, 1951–1954

Everett Drumright
Vice Consul, Consulate, Hankou, 1931–1932; Chinese Language Training Beijing, 1932–1934; Officer, Consulate General, Shanghai, 1934–1937; Political Officer, Consulate General, Hankou, 1937–1938; Political Officer, Embassy, Chongqing, 1938–1941; Internment Shanghai, 1941–1942; Consul, Consulate, Chengdu and Xi'an, 1943–1944; Political Officer, Embassy, Chongqing, 1944–1945; Office of Chinese Affairs, Department of State, 1945–1946; Office of Chinese Affairs, Department of State, 1953–1954; Consul General, Consulate General, Hong Kong, 1954–1958; Ambassador, Embassy, Taipei, Taiwan, 1958–1962

Eldon B. Erickson
Clerk, Consulate General Mukden, 1948–1950

Charles W. [Chas] Freeman, Jr.
American Interpreter for Nixon Trip, 1972; Visiting Fellow, East Asian Legal Research Center, Harvard, 1974–1975; Deputy Director, Taiwan Affairs, 1975–1978; Director, Office of Chinese Affairs, Department of State, 1979–1981; Deputy Chief of Mission, Embassy, Beijing, 1982–1985; Assistant Secretary of Defense, Pentagon, 1993–1994

Lindsey Grant

Officer, Consulate General, Hong Kong, 1950–1952, 1955–1958; Economic Officer, Taipei, Taiwan, 1958–1961; Officer in Charge of Mainland Chinese Affairs, Department of State, 1962–1964; Acting Director, Office of Asian Communist Affairs, Department of State, 1964; Director, Office of Asian Communist Affairs, Department of State, 1964–1965

Marshall Green

Regional Planning Advisor for Far East Affairs, Department of State, 1956–1959; Acting Deputy Assistant Secretary for Far East, Department of State, 1959–1960; Consul General, Consulate General, Hong Kong, 1961–1963; Deputy Assistant Secretary for Far East, Department of State, 1963–1965; Assistant Secretary, East Asian Affairs, Department of State, 1969–1973

John Holdridge

Chinese Language Training, American Universities, 1948–1951; Political Officer, Consulate General, Hong Kong, 1953–1956; Political Officer, Office of Chinese Affairs, Department of State, 1958–1962; Political Officer, Consulate General, Hong Kong, 1962–1966; Deputy Director , Office of Research and Analysis for East Asia, INR, Department of State, 1966–1968; National Security Council, White House, 1969–1973; Deputy Chief of Mission, Liaison Office, Beijing, 1973–1975; Assistant Secretary, East Asian Affairs, Department of State, 1981–1982

Jerome Holloway

Officer, Consulate General, Shanghai, 1949–1950; Political Officer, Consulate General, Hong Kong, 1952–1957

Herbert Horowitz

Consular Officer/Chinese Language Student/Economic Officer, Embassy, Taipei, Taiwan, 1957–1962; Office of Chinese Affairs , Department of State, 1962–1964; Chief, Economic Section, Consulate General, Hong Kong, 1965–1969; Office of Chinese Affairs, Department of State, 1972–1973; Economic Counselor, Liaison Office, Beijing, 1973–1975; Director, Office of Research, East Asia, Department of State, 1975–1978; Deputy Chief of Mission, Embassy, Beijing, 1985–1986

Arthur W. Hummel, Jr.
Beijing, 1930s; Internment by Japanese, 1941–1944; Life with Partisans in North China, 1944–1945; Liaison Officer, UNRRA, Tianjin, 1945–1946; Deputy Public Affairs Officer, Consulate General, Hong Kong, 1952; Public Affairs Officer, Consulate General, Hong Kong, 1953–1955; Deputy Chief of Mission, Embassy, Taipei, Taiwan, 1965–1967; Deputy Assistant Secretary for Far Eastern and Pacific Affairs, Department of State, 1971–1975; Assistant Secretary for Far Eastern Affairs, 1976–1977; Ambassador, Embassy, Beijing, 1981–1985

Walter Jenkins
Training Chinese Army, 1943–1945; Office of Chinese Affairs, Department of State, 1948–1950; Political Officer, Embassy, Taipei, Taiwan, 1952–1955; Talks with Chinese in Poland, Embassy, Warsaw, Poland 1969

Richard E. Johnson
Office of Chinese Affairs, Department of State, 1947–1951; Economic Officer, Consulate General, Hong Kong, 1951–1954

John Wesley Jones
Head of Political Section, Embassy, Nanjing, 1948–1949

Ralph Kartosh
U.S. Military Assistance Group, Taipei, Taiwan, 1950–1951

Paul Kreisberg
Chinese Language Training, Taiwan, 1955–1956; Political Officer, Consulate General, Hong Kong, 1956–1959; INR—Chinese Affairs, Department of State, 1960–1962; Deputy Director, Senior Adviser to Warsaw Talks and then Director, Office of Asian Communist Affairs, 1965–1970; Senior Deputy Director, Policy Planning Staff, Department of State, 1977–1981

Ruth Kurzbauer
Chinese Language Training, 1982–1983; American Institute in Taiwan, Taipei, Taiwan, 1983–1984; Assistant Press Officer, Embassy, Beijing, 1984–1986

John A. Lacey

U.S. Navy Chongqing/Beijing, 1944–1945; Analyst, Intelligence and Research Bureau, Department of State, 1950–1956; Economic Officer, Embassy, Taipei, Taiwan, 1956–1960; Economic Officer, Consulate General, Hong Kong, 1960–1964

James Leonard

Chinese Language Training/Political Officer, Embassy, Taipei, Taiwan, 1957–1963; INR, Department of State, 1964–1966

Herbert Levin

Chinese Language Training, Taichung, Taiwan, 1959–1961; Economic Officer, Consulate General, Hong Kong, 1961–1964; Political Officer, Embassy, Taipei, 1964–1967; National Security Council, 1970–1971; Assistant National Intelligence Officer for East Asia, 1981–1983; Policy Planning Council, Department of State, 1983–1985

James R. Lilley

Quingdao, 1930s; CIA Station, Hong Kong, 1969–1970; China Operations Division, CIA, 1971–1973; CIA Station Chief, Liaison Office, Beijing, 1973–1975; National Intelligence Officer for China, 1975–1978; Senior East Asia Specialist, National Security Council, 1981–1982; Director, American Institute in Taiwan, 1982–1984; Consultant, International Security Affairs, Department of Defense, 1984–1985; Deputy Assistant Secretary for East Asia, Department of State, 1985–1986; Ambassador, Embassy, Beijing, 1989–1991; Assistant Secretary of Defense for International Security Affairs, 1991–1993

Winston Lord

National Security Council, 1969–1973; Special Assistant to the Assistant to the President for National Security Affairs, 1970–1973; Director, Policy Planning Staff, Department of State, 1973–1977; Ambassador, Embassy, Beijing, 1985–1989; Assistant Secretary for East Asian and Pacific Affairs, Department of State, 1993–1997

Larue R. Lutkins

Chinese Language Training, Department of State and Beijing, 1946–1948; Consulate, Kunming, 1948–1949; Political Officer, Consulate General,

Hong Kong, 1954–1957; Deputy Director and Acting Director, Office of Chinese Affairs, Department of State, 1957–1961

Richard McCarthy
Information Officer, Embassy, Beijing, 1947–1950; Consulate General, Hong Kong, 1950–1956; Embassy, Taipei, Taiwan, 1958–1962

Philip Manhard
Chinese Languages Training, Beijing, 1947–1949; Vice Consul, Consulate, Tianjin, 1949–1950

Edwin W. Martin
Chinese Language Training, Yale, Beijing, 1945–1948; Officer, Consulate, Hankou, 1948–1949; Economic Officer, Embassy, Taipei, Taiwan 1949–1950; Political Officer, Office of Chinese Affairs, Department of State 1951–1955; Political Advisor to Talks with Chinese at Panmunjon, Korea, 1953–1954 and Geneva, Switzerland, 1955; Director, Office of Chinese Affairs, Department of State, 1958–1961; Consul General, Consulate General, Hong Kong, 1967–1970

John Melby
Political Officer, Embassy, Chongqing/Nanjing, 1945–1948; China White Paper, Department of State, 1949

James Moceri
Information Officer, Embassy, Taipei, Taiwan, 1956–1959

Robert L. Nichols
Chinese Language Training, Department of State, Taiwan, 1959–1961; Information Officer, Consulate General, Hong Kong, 1962–1965; Chinese Programs, Voice of America, Washington, D.C., 1966–1968; Public Affairs Officer, Embassy, Taipei, Taiwan, 1969–1971

David Osborn
Information Office, Tainan, Taiwan, 1949–1953; Office of Chinese Affairs (Taiwan), Department of State/Geneva Talks, 1954–1957; Consul General, Consulate General, Hong Kong, 1970–1974

Elizabeth Raspolic
Chinese Language Training, Department of State and Taiwan, 1981–1983; Chief of Consular Section, Consulate General, Guangzhou, 1983–1986; Consul General, Embassy, Beijing, 1986–1988

David Reuther
Office of Chinese Affairs, Department of State, 1979–1981; Chinese Language Training, Washington and Taipei, 1981–1983; Chief, General Affairs Section, American Institute in Taiwan, Taipei, 1983–1985; Deputy, Economic Section, Embassy, Beijing, 1987–1989; Taiwan Desk Officer while seconded to Office of Asian-Pacific Affairs, Office of the UnderSecretary of Defense, 1994–1995

John S. Service
Clerk/Vice Consul, Kunming, 1933–1935; Language Attaché, Beijing, 1935–1937; Vice Consul, Shanghai, 1938–1941; Political Officer, Chongqing, 1941–1945; General Joseph Stilwell Staff, 1943–1945; Amerasia Affair, Washington, D.C., 1945

Thomas P. Shoesmith
Officer, Consulate General, Hong Kong, 1956–1958; Taiwan Desk, Department of State, 1966; Officer in Charge of ROC Affairs, Department of State, 1967–1971; Consul General, Consulate General, Hong Kong, 1977–1981; Deputy Assistant Secretary, East Asian Bureau, Department of State, 1981–1983

Gaston Sigur
Special Assistant to the President for National Security Affairs, National Security Council, 1982–1986; Assistant Secretary, East Asian Affairs, Department of State, 1986–1989

Richard Solomon
National Security Council, 1971–1976; Director, Policy Planning Staff, Department of State, 1986–1989; Assistant Secretary, East Asian and Pacific Affairs, Department of State, 1989–1992

William N. Stokes
Vice Consul, Mukden 1946–1950

Harry E. T. Thayer
Officer, Consulate General, Hong Kong, 1957–1959; East Asian Bureau, Department of State, 1959–1961; Chinese Language Training, Department of State/Taiwan, 1961–1963; Political Officer, Embassy, Taipei, Taiwan, 1963–1966; Taiwan Desk, Department of State, 1966–1970; East Asia Advisor, United Nations Mission, New York City, 1971–1975; Deputy Chief of Mission, Embassy, Beijing, 1975–1976; Director, Office of Chinese Affairs, Department of State, 1976–1979; Director, American Institute in Taiwan, Taipei, Taiwan, 1984–1986

Hendrick Van Oss
Officer, Consulate General, Shanghai, 1948–1950

Earl Wilson
Information Officer, Consulate General, Shanghai, 1947–1949; Consulate General, Hong Kong, 1961–1964

AIT: American Institute in Taiwan

APEC: Asia Pacific Economic Cooperation Forum

CIA: Central Intelligence Agency

CHICOM: Chinese Communist

CHINAT: Chinese Nationalist

DCM: Deputy Chief of Mission

DIA: Defense Intelligence Agency

DSB: Diplomatic Security Bureau

EAP: East Asian and Pacific Affairs Bureau, Department of State

ESD: External Survey Detachment

GIMO: Generalissimo Chiang Kai-shek

INR: Intelligence and Research Bureau, Department of State

IPR: Intellectual Property Rights

MAAG: Military Assistance and Advisory Group

MTCR: Missile Technology Control Regime

NSA: National Security Agency

OSS: Office of Strategic Services, predecessor to CIA

PLA: People's Liberation Army

R&R: Rest and Recreation

TRA: Taiwan Relations Act

USIS/USIA: U.S. Information Service/U.S. Information Agency

USTR: U.S. Trade Representative

VOA: Voice of America

Map of China showing the places discussed by
the diplomats interviewed in the volume

CHINA
CONFIDENTIAL

Introduction

SINO-AMERICAN RELATIONS have fluctuated wildly over the five decades explored in these pages. Chinese and Americans suffered war, famine, inflation, and revolution. Through good times and bad they displayed a variable mixture of friendship, compassion, ruthlessness, and antipathy toward one another, making the exercise of diplomacy a complex and sometimes fruitless pursuit.

The Chinese had worried about contacts with alien peoples long before Westerners arrived, and had fashioned a system designed to allow for domination over, distance from, or, when necessary, appeasement of outsiders. Traditionally known as the tribute system, it required neighboring states to bring gifts to the Chinese emperor in exchange for the privileges of borrowing Chinese culture, conducting limited trade and, on occasion, securing China's protection. At times, tributary relations consisted of little more than nominal submission to the throne, a pretense of hierarchy through which the Chinese could disguise their weakness. When the Westerners arrived, it seemed natural to the Chinese to incorporate these new barbarians into the existing mold. Even after China accepted the idea that the western barbarians were different and were strong enough to demand a more formal and active commercial network, suspicion and distaste remained. Above all, the Chinese wanted to believe themselves to be the center of the world, and they felt little need to know much about the periphery.

Americans shared some of China's reservations about the outside world and the dangers of intimate association with decadent peoples. George Washington, who tried to shape his countrymen's views of foreign affairs in his hallowed 1795 Farewell Address, warned against entanglements, observing that "the nation which indulges toward another an habitual hatred or an habitual fondness is in some degree a slave." But the caution demonstrated by the United States with regard to international relations extended to political, *not* commercial, intercourse. Americans quickly came to believe that open markets abroad held out the promise of rapid growth and prosperity at home. The United States dispatched its first merchant ship to China as early as 1784. In fact, although Washington had asserted that "our commercial policy should . . . [be conducted] by gentle means . . . forcing nothing," the United States compelled China to sign the first bilateral Sino-American treaty in 1844 (the Treaty of Wangxia), never hesitating to capitalize on Britain's military victory in the Opium War (1839–1842).

By the 1930s, these contrasting principles and the often painful lessons of history had created a framework for relations of inequality. The Americans clearly belonged to the community of imperialists who enjoyed legal immunities and preferential trade terms. Although those same Americans liked to think of themselves as more generous and less opportunistic than their European or Japanese counterparts, the differences were often lost on the Chinese who felt victimized by the unequal treaty system. The Second Sino-Japanese War, formally launched in 1937, would eventually improve Sino-American relations as Washington felt compelled to aid the Chinese. But before the United States aligned itself with China, there were years of American indifference and even trade in war matériel with Japan. When assistance did materialize, it came not from a searching reappraisal of the needs of the Chinese, but rather from the confluence of war in Europe and Asia as Washington sought to assist allies in the European theater by preventing Japan from striking out at the Russians. Tons of equipment, food, and funds flowed and Washington renounced unequal privileges in China. But the United States never considered employing the kind of force in China that it deployed on the European continent, investing only enough in Chiang Kai-shek's war effort to keep him on the battlefield.

The experiences delineated here follow directly from these strikingly different legacies: Americans interpreting their encroachment as beneficial, Chinese feeling victimized. For the most part, these particular Americans approached China with sympathy and the desire to improve conditions for individual and national survival. Their routes into the Foreign Service of the United States, and the China service in particular, varied considerably, but were not perceived as opportunities to exploit or control China. Everett Drumright, eventually U.S. ambassador to China, clearly found the country as captivating as did so many American missionaries and business-men. "I had found the China that I had gotten to know [in the early 1930s] . . . charming. I found the Chinese to be an interesting and enjoyable peo-ple. And, on that basis, I decided I would, perhaps, try to make China my career. I found the study of the Chinese language to be incredibly difficult, but I stayed with it. In fact, one time I was ordered by doctors to leave [Bei-jing] for a month because of my health. But I came back."

Others joined through inadvertence. Ralph Clough remembers, "When I was a freshman at the University of Washington, I applied for and received an award for an exchange scholarship at Lingnan University in Guangzhou (Canton), China. I hadn't particularly been interested in China before that—I had been studying Spanish. I was majoring in foreign trade . . . and hoped to get into business with Latin America. But suddenly came this offer to go abroad, and I was interested in traveling. It happened to be China; it could have been Argentina or Germany or whatever. So I went off to China . . . and . . . I was hooked."

The exposure to things Chinese occurred, in not a few cases, before conscious choice intervened. Donald Anderson recalled that "when I was in the third grade, my school teacher was a former Chinese missionary. She used to read us stories about China and show us all of the things that she had brought back from China." For quite a number of China diplomats, the decision to spend a lifetime addressing the relationship followed from their missionary backgrounds. Arthur Hummel, an ambassador to China after normalization, spoke about those early roots at some length:

> I was born in China, and spent my early years mostly in Peking. I left when I was eight years old. Missionaries were normally on a seven-year cycle, six years followed by a year of furlough. We left early because Chiang Kai-shek and his troops were moving North, mopping up the war lords, and unifying the country for the first time on the Northern Expedition of 1927.[1] Whenever he took over a place, there was quite a bit of turmoil, unrest, and shooting—as well as anti-foreign actions by his troops.
>
> Like a number of missionary kids coming back to the States it was traumatic and I sort of put all that away and didn't even want to speak Chinese anymore. As a matter of fact, because of the Chinese servants and the fact that my parents were practicing their own Chinese, I spoke Chinese before I spoke English, but that withered away considerably

because I refused to speak it, which, I understand, is not too unusual among kids born abroad who want to be like other Americans.

My father moved to Washington where, being more of a scholar than a missionary, he was asked to be the head of the Library of Congress Oriental Division. Then my father was invited to go back to Peking for a book buying and research stint of several months, so my parents decided to take me with them and sent me ahead. I arrived in September 1940 [when I was 20]. The tense and worsening situation between the United States and Japan caused their trip to be canceled. So there I was, a young bachelor all alone in Beijing. My Chinese came back with a rush. I learned 40 times faster than anybody else in this language school, the same school where my father had been part of the faculty and where I used to live as a child, the Peking Language School. I was working as an English teacher in a Chinese high school, a Catholic mission high school. I was too dumb to leave before Pearl Harbor, even though the embassy and my parents were all urging me to leave. So I was interned by the Japanese.

The war shaped the careers of a number of men who became diplomats. For John Holdridge, wartime conditions comprised an introduction to China, "My father was an Army officer stationed in the Philippines. I was eleven. We went to Beijing via Tianjin . . . in 1937 . . . on a Japanese ship serving as a troop transport from Osaka. It was just loaded to the gunnels with Japanese troops. In the city of Beijing itself you could feel a sort of tenseness. One of my early memories of that place was seeing the Japanese troops marching through the old city walls for exercises." John Lacey, a little older, found himself putting his college degree in Chinese literature to use when "Pearl Harbor changed . . . the lives of many, many millions of Americans. . . . I immediately quit schooling. I tried to get into the government service . . . fighting those dirty Japs. The best I could do immediately was to join the Office of Censorship in the Chicago branch, where my Chinese enabled me to censor Chinese mail that was picked up, intercepted."

Art Hummel, meanwhile, watched the war first from occupied Beijing, then from a Japanese internment camp along with 3,000 other enemy aliens, and finally as part of a Nationalist Chinese guerrilla unit on the North China plain. His escape from the camp, engineered through bribing camp workers, landed him with a group that offered to come in with large forces and do away with the Japanese guards. They would quickly construct an air field, the Americans would come and fly us all away to Free China. This, of course, was a hare-brained idea—not practical, for many different reasons. However, eventually, it was decided by the prisoners' camp government that two people would be given authorization to escape and go to these guerrillas and establish contact with Chongqing, presumably. The camp would then have a liaison base outside. We had a small ladder which we used to get over a brick wall. We put a stepping stool outside, stood on that, jumped over the barbed wire, and we were out.

We were considered valuable assets. We sent a couple of messengers back by land, who eventually arrived in Chongqing and contacted the Office of Strategic Services (OSS) detachment there. Plans were being made, right at the end of the war, for a large air drop of ammunition and a small unit of OSS troops—Americans—to drop into our guerrilla area. The thinking was that it seemed possible then that American troops might be landing somewhere on the coast of China and it could turn out very useful to have some Americans in place. Unfortunately, the weather was bad the day that the air drop was supposed to come, and the planes flew back to Chongqing. Our unit was of course Nationalist, rather than Communist. There were also Communist guerrillas nearby, who had clear lines of communications all the way back to Yan'an, their headquarters. By accident, we had been contacted by Nationalists. If we had wound up with the Communists, we could have walked out through Communist territory and gotten back to Chongqing, had we chosen to do so.

The guerrilla outfit was very interesting and very self sufficient and very patriotic. It was one of the very few such efficient and patriotic Nationalist guerrilla outfits. From time to time the guerrillas would receive a warning that Japanese or Chinese puppet troops were advancing on the border of our area. We would pack up everything that we could pack up and become mobile. There was no point in a frontal battle, which is what the Japanese were trying to force them into. Fundamentally, the Japanese would sweep back and forth through our area, sometimes for as long as two weeks, trying to capture the guerrilla headquarters and leaders. But there wasn't any running around and riding horses in mountain forests. It was a typical North China plains area, densely populated.

As the war dragged on, mutual hostilities were commonplace between Communist and Nationalist units and antipathies were high. In fact there was a three-cornered war going on, and it was difficult to say which side was more at fault. As the Japanese looked more and more like losers, the Communists in Shandong systematically started to wipe out Nationalist guerrilla areas one by one, with an eye on occupying more of the territory at the time the war ended.[2]

Conditions in China became more chaotic as world war was replaced by a renewed civil war. American Foreign Service officers found themselves in the vortex of revolution, aligned with one side and yet aware that the other side appeared increasingly likely to win. When these premonitions proved accurate, American representatives left the Chinese mainland and did not return for twenty years. During those two decades, they observed developments in the new People's Republic of China from afar, never sure that they understood the internal dynamics, always uncertain as to the external implications of growing Chinese power.

While the Chinese mainland remained closed to American representatives, the Foreign Service officers interviewed here watched Communist China from Hong Kong, analyzed its behavior in Washington, or conducted relations with the competing Nationalist Chinese regime on the island of Taiwan. In Hong Kong, they found themselves deeply immersed in pursuing cases of visa corruption, enforcing trade sanctions against China, and attempting to gauge agricultural production in the PRC by examining the size of hogs sold in Hong Kong markets. American policy mandated that the diplomatic corps pretend that the Taipei government represented all Chinese and insist that Taiwan retain the Chinese seats in the United Nations General Assembly and Security Council. In Washington, this meant endless hours lobbying allies to stand with the United States in annual admission contests that depleted political capital in increasingly useless battles.

When not arrayed against the mainland or other foes of American policy, these Foreign Service officers found they also had to struggle with their allies in Taiwan. Although ties could be very close when confronting artillery fire in the Taiwan Straits, different goals and values produced antagonism and even rioting that destroyed the American Embassy in 1957. In the midst of political and military turmoil, however, Taiwan also underwent an economic development miracle that accentuated not just indigenous talent, but also the virtues of American aid and technical cooperation.

Eventually, Washington and Beijing found that they needed each other (far more than Washington needed Taipei), and they set their relationship on a new course. The opening for this reversal of fortunes came with developments in the United States and the Soviet Union. Richard Nixon sought a China opening to help negotiate a way out of Vietnam, and manipulate Moscow into living up to détente. At the same time, Soviet leaders were dealing with disarray in the communist bloc and, as they suppressed dissent in Czechoslovakia, they issued the Brezhnev Doctrine, which claimed the right to rescue bloc regimes from destabilization. In Beijing, this was seen as a threat. Subsequent fighting along the Sino-Soviet border, coupled with the advantages of reconciliation with Washington such as open markets and access to technology, led Chinese leaders, most especially Zhou Enlai, to see advantages in an opening to the United States. Given the stakes, neither side allowed Taiwan and the Nationalist Chinese regime to get in the way.

Into these uncharted waters, American diplomacy was piloted largely by a new generation of Foreign Service officers. These people could claim to be more professional than their predecessors. No longer primarily the sons of missionaries, like Arthur Hummel or John S. Service, they came to the China field through study of the language and history, hoping that someday they would be able to serve in the country rather than on the periphery, but never certain that that time would come. Their delight in living among the Chinese is apparent from their words recorded here.

Once Americans and Chinese came into regular contact, however, the common interest in opposing the Soviet Union could not completely divert officers from routine problems occasioned by political, cultural, and economic differences. Friction became even more obvious after the Soviet Union ceased to exist and conflicting viewpoints and goals of earlier years reemerged without the constraints imposed by the old Cold War. Indeed, suspicion and misunderstanding characterized the end of the period under scrutiny here as it had characterized the beginning.

Similarly, in the last days of the twentieth century, as at the close of World War II, the American public remained largely indifferent to foreign relations and focused almost entirely on domestic issues. When they did look abroad they continued, as had been true from the 1940s to the 1990s, to be preoccupied with Atlantic affairs and to demonstrate apathy with regard to Asia. These realities could not help but have a powerful influence on how these diplomats carried out their responsibilities and saw their contributions. John Lacey, for instance, noted his frustration with American ignorance as he enlisted in the U.S. Navy and his superiors decided to put his Asian studies background to use, ordering him to learn Japanese. "When I protested that I knew nothing about Japanese [being a China specialist], the answer was, `Well, they are more or less the same.' " Even as American trade with Asia soared and the most serious challenges to American national security could be found in Asia, such unawareness and indifference remained endemic.

ABOUT THE TEXT

Given the nature of this project, it should be obvious to the reader that this is not a balanced investigation into the events of the years between 1945 and 1996. It is an account from one side, lacking a Chinese voice. It would be important and exciting to hear the reminiscences of Chinese diplomats and America specialists confronted with identical problems and similar experiences. Some Chinese diplomats have written useful memoirs such as Wang Bingnan.[3] One can only hope that some day Chinese scholars will be able to have the broad access to oral history collections comparable to those in the United States and that someone will then compile a book like this in China.

Meanwhile, it is crucial in reading the words of these American diplomats to keep in mind that their perception of reality in China, however sympathetic to the Chinese they may have been, remained an American perspective on China. In the course of their service, they did become composite beings no longer quite like their brethren who stayed at home and shunned things foreign. Some acclimated so much as to be called China hands or find themselves accused of clientitis. Nevertheless, they could not and did not forsake their American culture, attitudes, or values.[4]

The purpose of this volume is to provide context for understanding diplomatic interaction between the United States and China. By drawing on the reminiscences of a wide range of American diplomats, I have tried to give the memoranda, cables, and dispatches that shaped the formal relationship broader meaning and greater nuance. These interviews also provide insight into the circumstances under which difficult and crucial decisions were reached and reveal the background and biases of the people who made and carried out those policies.

Oral history is to some extent an art form. Memories can be erratic, interviewers know more or less about different subjects raised in a session, some participants are expansive and others laconic, and there is the insidious problem of bias in both subject and questioner. A further problem in this volume is that the interviews were conducted by a number of different people, sometimes involving more than one interviewer for the same interviewee.[5] In the pages that follow I have tried to flag or eliminate errors, but have not tampered with strong points of view, nor have I been able to compensate for gaps in the interviews. Inevitably, you will think of important issues about which the interviewers, who were not China specialists, did not ask. Be assured that I share your frustration. To provide as much continuity and coverage as possible, I have grouped portions of interviews around particular issues and have arranged them loosely in a chronological sequence. This has meant blurring the lines between separate interviews conducted at different times.

A few additional points regarding the editing are in order. The goal in assembling this material was to retain the words of individuals who experienced these events so far as possible. I have, however, sought to make the material readable and, to this end, eliminated repetition, omitted extraneous observations, and jettisoned the occasional inarticulate lapses. Also, in virtually all cases, I dropped interjections such as "I think" or "I believe," because the entire interview represents the accumulated recollections and interpretation of the individual speaking. Further, I have sometimes dropped the questions addressed to the interviewees, sometimes rewritten them, and in rare instances added a comment (in brackets) or question not in the original transcript. This was always done without changing the substance or thrust of the interview and solely in order to clarify the meaning or context of the response.

The romanization system used here is the Pinyin system, with the exception of a few names that are far more familiar in other renderings, such as Chiang Kai-shek rather than Jiang Jieshi. In addition, the names for China's capital are used by various interviewers interchangeably: Beijing, Peking, and the civil war-era Peiping, which is discussed in the text.

War Ends, War Begins

IN THE 1930S AND 1940S, Americans dealt with a China riven by civil war and foreign intervention. As communists labored to seize and transform China, the Japanese sought to expand their empire on the mainland of Asia. Complicating the situation further, the government of China under Chiang Kai-shek appeared increasingly ineffective, corrupt, and uncooperative. Although the American public tended to be apathetic toward foreign relations and ignorant about Asia, the United States had no choice but to confront the challenges that the forces of aggression and revolution posed. At the forefront were the diplomats, who struggled with the realities of war on the ground in China, seeking to protect American interests and work with authorities who often resented American advice while demanding American aid.

The United States had grown accustomed to a certain degree of chaos in China. After the fall of the Qing dynasty in 1911, the Chinese political scene changed rapidly and often. Hopes for a democratic government quickly dissipated as Sun Yat-sen, the revolutionary leader who had traveled in the United States and been hailed as the George Washington of China, was pushed aside. Eventually, his successor Chiang Kai-shek built a political coalition and mounted a military campaign to reunify the country. His Northern Expedition, which defeated or coopted rival holders of power, known as warlords, succeeded in 1928, but not without provoking Japan and driving the Chinese Communists into armed rebellion.

Japanese aggression worried Washington more than the Chinese opposition, which did not seem a significant force at the time. Japan saw control of China as essential to its great power status. When Chinese nationalism threatened to undermine this vision, the Japanese tried to thwart it by deploying troops in North China to stop the Guomindang's consolidation of victory. Washington had long been aware of Japanese ambitions in the region and had intervened ineffectually on various occasions to try to limit Tokyo's reach. But the United States had never been concerned enough to devote the attention and resources necessary to circumscribe Japanese activities effectively, so in the 1920s and 1930s, when Japan stepped up its military maneuvers, the United States objected but did nothing.

Failing initially to stop reunification, the Japanese took more vigorous and decisive action in Manchuria in 1931, in the so-called Mukden Incident. Fabricating an attack on the South Manchuria Railway, Japanese troops marched into the area in force to undo the attempt of the local warlord Zhang Xueliang (Chang Hsueh-liang) to integrate China's three northeastern provinces into the newly created Republic of China. The rapid conquest of China's northeast followed with the establishment of a puppet regime called Manchukuo in 1932. Thereafter, Japan's troops launched repeated incursions onto the North China plain. Chiang Kai-shek hoped to avoid or at least delay war and made a series of concessions, but the Japanese were not satisfied. Ultimately, in the wake of the Luguoqiao (Marco Polo Bridge) Incident of July 1937, in which Japanese and Chinese forces exchanged fire, public pressure inside China forced the Guomindang to resist Japan.

Meanwhile, China's leaders had to confront the domestic insurgency by the Chinese Communist Party (CCP) as well. After establishment of the party in 1921, there had been attempts to unify and reform China through a "united front" between the Communists and the Guomindang. But at Shanghai in 1927, Chiang betrayed his erstwhile allies, fearing their growing power, and with the support of bankers, gangsters, and the foreign community, sought to eradicate communist organizers and the labor movement in the city. Thereafter the Guomindang waged a series of suppression campaigns that failed to eliminate the Communists but distracted Chiang from the more popular effort to counter the Japanese.

Finally, in 1934, Chiang managed to drive the Communists out of central China and temporarily isolated them in the far northwest. His success proved short-lived, however, because from Yan'an the CCP made contact with Zhang Xueliang and his refugee Manchurian troops who wanted to fight the Japanese rather than fellow Chinese. Together, in 1936, they kidnapped Chiang at Xi'an and forced him to suspend the civil conflict and focus national attention on Japan. As a result, when the Japanese assault occurred in July 1937, instead of taking his preferred and easy route of concession, Chiang resisted. War followed.

The United States and its representatives in China found their options severely limited in the face of these conflicts. Washington repeatedly refused to risk war against the Japanese to succor China. After the Mukden Incident, Secretary of State Henry Stimson ineffectually declared in his 1932 Stimson Doctrine that the United States would not recognize developments in Manchuria that would circumscribe American rights and interests there. Similarly, the United States took no clear position against Japanese encroachments in North China even after full-fledged war began. The United States continued to sell the Japanese war supplies such as oil, iron, and steel, and insisted on conducting trade with China under onerous treaty terms that compromised China's economy. When the United States entered the war, it did so not because of China's desperation, but because the Japanese had attacked Pearl Harbor. Wartime propaganda would suggest that the war was caused by Japanese aggression in China and the American determination to save the Chinese. In fact, Washington's real preoccupation centered upon the fate of Europe's colonial possessions in Asia whose resources helped fuel the anti-Nazi war effort, the continued fighting that British Commonwealth soldiers would do in the European theater, and prevention of a Japanese attack on the Soviet Union that could undermine the Eastern front against Hitler. After December 7, 1941, while Chiang's followers danced in the streets of his wartime capital Chongqing in relief that Washington would now defeat Japan for them, the U.S. military kept its focus on Europe. The Pacific War remained a secondary battlefront and only enough supplies and support went to Chiang to keep China in the war.

To improve the fighting capabilities and the morale of the Chinese national army, Roosevelt sent Chiang a special adviser who, the Americans anticipated, would train the troops and purge the incompetent officer corps. But the Americans did not understand that Chiang demanded loyalty above talent and did not want a military force that placed defeat of the Japanese above defense against his Communist rivals. Thus Chiang clashed almost immediately with the American representative, General Joseph Stilwell. Of course, it did not help that the abrasive Stilwell, known as "Vinegar Joe," took an early dislike to Chiang, who he called "the Peanut." Chiang was, after all, a head of state, and Roosevelt refused to confront him directly and risk the stability of his regime. Stilwell had to go. Thereafter, American strategic planners shifted away from the idea of using bases in China to defeat Japan to an island hopping strategy and then, finally, to dropping the atomic bomb to end the war.

American intervention on the political front proved no more successful. American officials urged Chiang Kai-shek to devote his attention to defeating the common enemy Japan rather than saving his best men and weapons for a postwar struggle with the CCP. To many Americans, communism remained a fearsome threat, but the world war made it essential to put aside ideological battles. If Washington could join with Joseph Stalin to fight the Nazis, then Chiang had little excuse not to work with Mao Zedong to vanquish the Japanese.

American diplomats based in Chongqing grew increasingly disillusioned with both Chiang's refusal to fight Japan wholeheartedly and the venality, inefficiency, and incompetence of the Guomindang regime. Increasingly they argued that contact with the Communist Chinese would allow for more effective prosecution of the war because Communist guerrillas ranged behind Japanese lines in large parts of the Chinese countryside, able to assist downed American pilots or cooperate in a final assault on the Japanese home islands. The United States dispatched an observer group to Yan'an (the Dixie Mission) in the summer of 1944 and decided that if Washington could broker an understanding between the Guomindang and the Communists, the war effort would be enhanced and China might avoid a return to civil conflict when the Pacific War ended.

To realize this effort Franklin Roosevelt embarked upon direct bargaining with the Soviet Union and sent General Patrick Hurley as his special representative to China. The president undertook his personal diplomacy at Yalta in February 1945, where he purchased Stalin's agreement to enter the Pacific War with economic and territorial concessions from China. In exchange, Stalin pledged to support Chiang Kai-shek's government instead of the CCP. Later, when the Yalta agreements became public, Roosevelt's Yalta legacy would be attacked as a betrayal of China, which it was, and a give-away to the Russians, which it was not because there was little American forces could have done to stop Soviet troops from advancing in Manchuria.[1]

The appointment of Hurley, a Republican and former secretary of war, to find a solution to the Chinese civil war despite his ignorance of Chinese affairs was indicative of Roosevelt's domestic political agenda and his fundamental indifference to China. Hurley negotiated with Mao and reached an agreement to integrate Communist forces into a national coalition that would grant the Communist Party legitimacy. Chiang, horrified by what the naive and uninformed Hurley had done, rejected the compromise. Hurley's triumph undone, he sought targets for his frustration. Those he found among the Foreign Service officers stationed in Chongqing who had been critical of his activities and of Chiang's regime. Hurley denounced them as soft on the Communists and persuaded the State Department to remove them from China. This proved to be but the first in a series of accusations made against American diplomats for "losing China" to the Communists. Late in 1945, Hurley himself would resign in exhaustion from the effort to be both a mediator and an exponent of one side in the contest for power.[2]

In the final days of the war both the Guomindang and the Communists maneuvered to strengthen their positions for the new contest ahead. Chiang's government signed a treaty with Moscow that promised that Stalin would abandon the CCP in return for concessions of raw materials, ports, and railways to Soviet control in Xinjiang and Manchuria. Although the Chinese Communists were distraught and angry upon hearing of this betrayal, they had never been puppets of Moscow and their determination to win the looming civil war was not altered by Stalin's deal. Their energies were, at that very moment, focused on dispersal across northern China, where they intended to accept the surrender of Japanese troops despite international agreements designating Chiang's forces in that role. Although exhausted by the war just ended, Chinese of all political persuasions understood that the respite would be brief.

The abrupt end of the Pacific War in August 1945, when the United States dropped atomic bombs on Hiroshima and Nagasaki and the Soviet Union invaded Manchuria meant new priorities for Americans in China. The most pressing of these was to assist Chiang's Nationalist forces in reclaiming territory from the Japanese before the Chinese Communists could seize it. Americans also were concerned about the rehabilitation of a country devastated by the decade long depredations of a foreign conqueror, not to mention the earlier civil struggles among warlords and between the Nationalists and Communists. Above all, Washington wanted to avoid a new civil war.

To prevent resumption of fighting, Harry Truman sent a trusted World War II hero, General George Catlett Marshall, to mediate, replacing Patrick Hurley. Marshall had initial success, proving able to arrange a cease-fire and limited cooperation between government and Communist officials in January and February 1946. In this effort he worked with John Leighton Stuart, president of a leading American university in China, who he named ambassador, and a diverse group of Foreign Service officers who hoped to avert conflict. It quickly became apparent to these Americans that neither side genuinely wanted to resolve the underlying problems and create an enduring coalition government. The Communists were somewhat more cooperative, recognizing that they needed a respite before they could mount a new offensive. The Nationalists, however, believed that they could capitalize on American support and press the advantage they had in numbers of soldiers and quality of equipment. Indeed, throughout the negotiations, American aid continued to flow into Nationalist coffers. As a result, Chiang ignored Marshall's advice and overextended his lines into Manchuria where, because of Soviet occupation, the Communists had the advantage. At the same time, he refused to compromise on any real power-sharing. Not surprisingly, the Communists concluded that Marshall's mediation was biased and that there would be no alternative to war. Marshall left China in frustration in 1947, condemning both sides.

By this time, full-scale warfare again engulfed China. What became apparent was that, although the Nationalists enjoyed superficial superiority in fighting capabilities, the Communists could call upon better military minds, more motivated troops, and greater popular support. Far faster than anyone, even Mao Zedong, imagined, Communist forces swept the Nationalists aside as they scored victory upon victory during 1948 and 1949.

Corrupt, inept, and brutish governance by the Guomindang contributed to making this rapid triumph possible. Rather than liberating the areas oppressed by Japanese forces, the Nationalists descended like locusts, plundering and terrorizing the population whom they dismissed as collaborators for remaining behind Japanese lines. Chiang neither carried out necessary reforms nor promoted competent officials, producing economic disarray illustrated most graphically in unbridled inflation.

American diplomats observed the military and economic decline and lamented the increasingly inevitable outcome. Even those critical of Chiang Kai-shek did not look forward to Communist control. Those who championed Chiang's cause, although unhappy with Truman administration policies, saw little hope for the Nationalists without massive American aid, including an unthinkable large-scale infusion of American armed forces. For the United States, that degree of involvement could not be justified, given China's fundamental unimportance to American national interests.

Also militating against intervention was the hope that Mao might not marry China to the Soviet Union. American officials hoped for Titoism in

China, meaning that Mao, like his Yugoslav Communist colleague, might wish to assert his autonomy and refuse Moscow's dictation. Signs of friction between Chinese and Russian communists had been noted in Washington and Secretary of State Dean Acheson made a point of emphasizing Soviet occupation of Chinese land and control of Chinese resources at every opportunity.

To explain what was happening in China and make the case that the United States could not have prevented the outcome, the Truman administration released the China White Paper in August 1949. This fifteen-hundred-page volume revealed embarrassing details about the ineptitude of Chiang's rule and attested to American generosity. In his letter of transmittal, moreover, Acheson underlined American regrets regarding the likely Communist victory and spoke of American hopes that in the future a democratic opposition would reemerge among the Chinese people.

The reaction to the White Paper illustrated the problems that the administration faced in crafting a China policy. Domestically, the document was attacked by disparate friends of Chiang Kai-shek, including members of Congress, journalists, and businessmen (usually identified as the China Lobby), which felt that Chiang had been betrayed by this revelation of confidential information and the devastating portrait of the Nationalists that it drew. Republican Party stalwarts, determined to embarrass Truman and terminate the Democratic hold upon the presidency, supported all the scurrilous China Lobby attacks. In China, the document was also assailed by Mao Zedong, who saw it as confirmation of American perfidy in trying to thwart Chinese aspirations for dignity, sovereignty, and socialism.

Mao had, in any case, already declared his intention to lean to the side of the Soviet Union in the international contest between the communist and capitalist camps in a June 1949 speech. On October 1, 1949, he mounted the gates of the imperial palace in Beijing and established the People's Republic of China. During the following weeks his armies erased the few remaining remnants of opposition on the mainland.

By then the real quarry had escaped to the island of Taiwan, a mere 100 miles off the coast but an irretrievable distance, given the Communists' lack of amphibious capabilities. Chiang Kai-shek had begun preparations for a retreat to the island sanctuary as early as 1946. He had asserted Guomindang control, precipitating a rebellion on February 28, 1947, in response to his harsh measures. The subsequent crackdown led to a massacre of the island elite. Thereafter, the sullen population could not be counted upon to withstand a Communist assault or sabotage. Nevertheless, in 1949, Chiang sent the Nationalist regime's stocks of gold, crates of art treasures, and units of loyal troops to Taiwan, where he set up his own government dedicated to the idea of recapturing the mainland.

For Washington the unavoidable question became whether to continue diplomatic relations with Chiang Kai-shek's regime or recognize the new Chinese Communist authorities. Acheson had seriously contemplated the possibility of establishing relations with the Communists, keeping Stuart and part of the American embassy in Nanjing when Communist forces took the city in May 1949, even as the Soviet ambassador fled south with the Guomindang. Various modest gestures followed from Communist officials who believed that commercial relations with the Americans would be important in stabilizing the economy after the civil war ended. But neither the Chinese Communists nor the Americans were prepared to make any bold moves to overcome mutual suspicion. Moreover, the civil war created a volatile situation in which some Americans were attacked and beaten, or placed under house arrest, or charged with espionage. The most notorious instances were the Mukden hostage case of Angus Ward and the beating of a Shanghai consulate official William Olive.

The administration still tried to keep its options open. Acheson noted that the attacks on Americans had been few and relatively mild for a situation of revolutionary anarchy. The signing of the Sino-Soviet Treaty of Friendship in February 1950, although clearly demonstrating Mao's plans to align with Moscow, did not make trade relations impossible. Even the decision to close American diplomatic posts in China as a result of the requisition of American embassy facilities in Beijing was not seen as a final judgment. In fact, in January 1950, Harry Truman announced that the United States would not intervene further in the Chinese civil war and would not prevent Taiwan from falling to the Communists when they attacked. In December, Acheson had warned his diplomatic corps worldwide to prepare for the collapse of the Guomindang regime, and in January, he placed Taiwan and Korea outside the American defensive perimeter in Asia. American intelligence sources predicted that the Communists would attack and take over Taiwan in the summer of 1950. Acheson believed that it might then be possible to establish relations with Beijing after the November congressional elections.

Thus on June 25, 1950, American policy remained one of watchful waiting.

IMMEDIATE POSTWAR PERIOD

In the immediate aftermath of the war, various agencies, American and international, tried to provide assistance to a war-devastated China. But politics overwhelmed humanitarian consideration and little of the aid was distributed outside Guomindang-controlled areas. Moreover, continuing instability meant that help never graduated from crisis prevention and rehabilitation to construction and development.

HUMMEL: I was so enamored by China [even after the internment and living with the guerrillas] that I stayed on an extra year [after the end of the war], working for the United Nations relief program, UNRRA [United Nations Relief and Rehabilitation Administration]. I was doing survey trips, mostly into Chinese Communist areas, to find out what was needed for relief there. This was during the Civil War, the ceasefire mission, and the Marshall Mission. Of course, as it turned out, we never turned over practically any relief supplies to the Communists. It was all sent to help the Nationalists. This was one of the reasons why I became disgusted and went home. Not that I liked the Communists, but I didn't think that it was the right policy.

How was UNRRA run in China at that time?

HUMMEL: Headquarters was in Tianjin, about 60 or 70 miles east of Beijing and near the sea coast. They sent me to investigate reports that relief supplies were being stolen in a Nationalist-controlled area. They sent me into an area that was entirely flooded out, in southern Hubei Province. The Communists had breached the dikes and flooded the fields right up to the brick and mud walls of the county seat. The Nationalist government in Beijing was air-dropping huge gunny sacks of bread. They killed about four people and damaged quite a few houses with these bread sacks. However, they were sustaining life inside the city. I negotiated an agreement, which was promptly broken by the Communists, under which they would allow the purchase from outside of a certain amount of wheat and wheat products, cooking oil, and so on.

I went to OSS headquarters in Shanghai a couple of times and to see other people in Shanghai. It was quite obvious to me that the

Chiang Kai-shek, Madame Chiang, and Chiang Ching-kuo (the Generalissimo's son). *Courtesy of the Government Information Office, Taipei, Taiwan.*

Nationalists were messing up the situation in so many ways in their attitude. They treated the people not as liberated brothers, but as dastardly collaborators with the Japanese, quite unnecessarily alienating people and ripping them off, right and left. There was a lot of corruption.

What kind of attitude did you and your colleagues in the U.S. Navy group stationed in China have towards the Chiang government?

LACEY: We were by then rather down on the Chiang government. It was well known that, first and foremost, the country was saddled with impossible inflation. I can remember having a dinner in Shanghai where the four of us paid for a dinner that cost us seven million plus local currency. Inflation was so bad that people would carry money around in wheel barrows. In suitcases. Well, they would bag it up and carry it openly. That was one obvious sign of maladministration. But the worst thing that we all felt—at least my colleagues and I felt—was that Chiang's generals were most interested in lining their own pockets. Chiang's senior minister of finance, T.V. Soong, was well known to have milked China dry. None of us felt very kindly toward the Soong clan, including Madame Chiang Kai-shek, who was a Soong girl.[3]

What about the Communists at that stage? What kind of attitude or knowledge did you have of the Chinese Communists?

LACEY: I may have had a better knowledge of the Chinese Communists than did the boys in Washington. Remember, Roosevelt's policies were still prevalent. The Yalta hangover enabled Stalin to send his own forces into the Far East before the war finally ended. It was a belated gesture to show that Stalin and Russia also had a stake in the treaty of peace in Japan. In the meantime, what actually was the case was the Russian Communist forces were commanding almost all of North China, and as they retreated, they turned over their arms and their territory not to Chiang Kai-shek but to Mao Zedong. I could see that going on right within the perimeter of Beijing.

SERVICE: The terrible thing was that the Yalta agreement was founded on such completely erroneous reasoning and assumptions. It was based on the idea that if we made a deal with Stalin, the Chinese Communists would very nicely and quietly go along with what Stalin told them to do, which was the exact opposite of what all of us in the field were busily reporting. Who advised Roosevelt and how he came to the idea is still a mystery. But it guaranteed the civil war, which was what we all had been working so hard to prevent. We knew a civil war would not only be a long, drawn out, disastrous civil war, but it would result in a Communist victory. I must say by this time some of us weren't sure that was a bad thing, but for American policy it was certainly a bad thing.

LACEY: At that time under Mao's leadership the Chinese Communist forces unquestionably were well disciplined. Unlike the Nationalist forces, the Chinese Communist troops would take over cities and towns, and instead of raping the women and looting precious stores, they would take off their shirts and work in the fields. It was a majestic example of how good propaganda can be a partner of diplomacy.

Along with motivating people, they inherited all of the five- and ten-year plans which the Chinese government under Chiang Kai-shek had been developing. I've heard from many different sources—they had blueprints of bridges to be built, of roadways to be repaired, of dams to be erected which fell into their hands. This was a primary reason why initially the Chinese Communists were so successful. They just put into place plans that had already been made.[4]

What was your impression of the Communists you dealt with at that time?

HUMMEL: Very straightforward, stern—not hostile but very military and very disciplined. They were also very tricky. Perhaps I shouldn't say that, as every human being is capable of deceit. In other words, they were capable of breaking their word. When people are told to break their word by higher authority, that's what they do. But I was impressed with them. They were businesslike.

CLOUGH: In the beginning, when I was in Chongqing, I would say the prevailing view in the embassy was that if we could not work out a coalition agreement (and people were rather pessimistic that we could) between the Nationalists and the Communists, then China was in for a long period of civil war. Very long. People did not think the Nationalists could be defeated. On the other hand, they didn't think that they could defeat the Communists, and therefore it would drag on and on. No one, in 1945 or '46, would have predicted that by 1949 these huge Nationalists armies with all their equipment and so on, so much superior in material terms to the Communists, would be reeling back in total defeat.

LACEY: Chiang Kai-shek's soldiers and generals were vainly trying to hold ground. Against the advice of General George Marshall, who was sent to China as a presidential advisor, the Nationalist forces went into Manchuria and tried to regain that territory.

DRUMRIGHT: The Chinese Government actually made a big mistake in sending their main forces into Manchuria to try to seize it from the Chinese Communists, who were being put in place there by the Soviet Russians, and handed over all the Japanese military equipment that had been left there. This did not succeed, with the result that the [Nationalist] Chinese suffered some serious military defeats there. This led, eventually, to their being driven off the mainland.

MARSHALL MISSION

Americans were determined to settle the conflict between the Nationalists and Communists through negotiation, averting more bloodshed. Part of the impetus was to repatriate Japanese soldiers quickly to prevent conditions in which the Soviets could extend their influence in China. Marshall's initial orders were that if the Communists would compromise and the Nationalists proved recalcitrant, he should threaten Chiang Kai-shek with an end to American aid. However, neither the president nor his secretary of state, James F. Byrnes (1945–1946) were comfortable with those instructions. Before Marshall left Washington they backtracked and told him that, in fact, no matter how stubborn Chiang became, Washington would stick with him. In the field, Marshall found little maneuvering room. The Chinese Communist Party made repeated concessions, but remained suspicious. Chiang simply wouldn't cooperate. Marshall continued to try, enlisting John Leighton Stuart to use his connections in both Chinese camps to resolve problems, but civil war resumed.

CLOUGH: The first change was the employment of General Marshall, who came in December of '45 as a result of Truman's decision for the United States to mediate between the Communists and the Nationalists and try to work out some sort of coalition government. It wasn't a normal period. Our own Air Force was engaged in transferring Nationalist troops across Communist-held areas into Beijing, Tianjin, into Manchuria. There was a unit of U.S. Marines stationed in Beijing and in Tianjin also, and they were responsible for the safety of that rail line, which was attacked by the Communists from time to time.

There were these negotiations going on at the top level. Zhou Enlai with Chiang Kai-shek. They had this elaborate Executive Headquarters set up in Beijing, with a large number of field grade officers whose job was to go out in groups of three—American, Nationalist, Communist—and check on reports of clashes between Nationalist and Communist forces.

We had particular contacts, as usually happens, with the Chinese who thought like we did about democracy in China, people in the Democratic League.[5] We had contacts with the Communists as well. Zhou Enlai had an office in Chongqing. The embassy moved down from Chongqing to Nanjing in early '46.

[Political Officers] were generally rather pessimistic about the way things were going, The war was continuing sporadically here and there. The Executive Headquarters system had not successfully created a cease-fire. Both sides were throwing accusations at each other.

DRUMRIGHT: Now I was on the China Desk at the time, and I took the position that trying to work out a compromise between those two groups was futile. It would not work and it would probably redound to the disadvantage of the government. My position was that we should assist the government in reclaiming all of occupied China, including Manchuria. But we chose to send the Marshall Mission out with the objective of getting a settlement between the Chinese government of Chiang Kai-shek and the Chinese Communists. General Marshall worked hard on that for about a year out there. He met and was charmed by Leighton Stuart. We had not had an ambassador out there during that critical time after the departure of Pat Hurley. Marshall had been very much impressed with Stuart, and his background, and his talk about China. And he, therefore, recommended that Stuart be appointed ambassador. Stuart went to Nanjing, took over the embassy, and there he worked with Marshall. And as I said, they worked hard to try to achieve a settlement. I think Stuart, in his own mind, felt that it was not very likely that one could be achieved, but he went along with it. But it failed.[6]

Did Marshall have much to do with the embassy?

MELBY: He had nothing to do with the embassy. Literally. We were around, and we briefed him from time to time. Initially, of course, we did a great deal more than we did later on. After he got to know his way around, he really had nothing to do with us at all.

CLOUGH: Walter Robertson was the chargé d'affaires when I arrived. He had been in Chongqing as economic counselor. He was a former Richmond banker. When General Hurley left, he became chargé, and was chargé for several months until General Marshall arrived. I remember Robertson saying, when he read the instructions about the U.S. function in mediating and trying to set up a coalition government, "Well, we have a variety of means by which we can put pressure on the GMD, but I don't see any way we can put pressure on the Communists." So he was rather pessimistic about the future, although he worked at it. He was named by General Marshall as director of the Executive Headquarters in Beijing, later on when the operation moved up there. He tended to blame the Communists more than the Nationalists when negotiations broke down.

HUMMEL: Walter Robertson was the civilian deputy to General George Marshall at Ceasefire Headquarters in Beijing. Robertson asked me, first off, to give my views on the prospects for getting the Chinese Communists and Nationalists together in a coalition arrangement in North China to avert a civil war. I said that there was virtually no prospect of success. I had seen both sides. There was too much mutual hatred. It was hard for me to imagine that they could ever work together. If they ever did work together, temporarily, they would split apart again. I said that both sides had strong reasons for wanting to break any agreements, if they could get some territorial advantage out of it. I don't think that I even got that far, when Robertson jumped up from the breakfast table—there were just the two of us—and stomped around the room, berating me for my lack of patriotism! He said that they were going to make a coalition government work and that I shouldn't say that it wouldn't function.

Robertson, of course, became assistant secretary of state for Far Eastern Affairs during the Eisenhower administration. He was a great supporter of Chiang Kai-shek.

HUMMEL: He was part of what people loosely called, "The China Lobby."

Who was the new ambassador? How did he operate?

MELBY: John Leighton Stuart. He'd been a missionary in China for 50 years. The last 20 or 25 years, he'd been president of Yenching University, which was one of the model universities of China. General Marshall asked him to be ambassador because most of the leaders, prominent people, not only the Guomindang, but the Communists, too, had all been students of his. And considering the special Chinese relationship between teacher and student, the general thought that perhaps Dr. Stuart could persuade the Chinese to sit down and talk to each other, and maybe this way you could work out their differences.

And Dr. Stuart agreed with him. He thought it was worth the

chance. So he took the job. He didn't know anything about American foreign policy. He couldn't care less! He was interested in China. He wanted to see the fighting, civil war ended in China. It just killed him to see what the Chinese were doing to each other. He never moved into the chancery. He never had an office there [even though all the] telegrams or dispatches were always signed by the ambassador. But that was the way the embassy worked. That didn't mean he'd seen it, let alone read it. All that was done in the chancery. Sometimes our initials would be on it, and sometimes [they] wouldn't. But it all looked as though it was Dr. Stuart. [That explains why in the historical record] Dr. Stuart's views don't seem to be consistent, about China and so on.

What was Leighton Stuart like as an ambassador?

BACON: He had been appointed, not because of any diplomatic skills really. He was very well liked by the Chinese, he was born in Hankou. Many of the leading figures—not the top figures—but many of the non-military figures had been former students of his, and he believed that he had a gateway to the communist government through them, that he could, if not get things done, at least find out what was going on and what they were thinking. This turned out to be a considerable mistake.

CLOUGH: For example, the head of the Alien Affairs Office in Nanjing City was a man named Huang Hua, who had been a student of Leighton Stuart at Yenching University and then gone over to the Communists and worked his way up in the ranks. He had meetings with Huang Hua on several occasions.[7]

Did you have much contact at that time with the Guomindang government?

MELBY: Oh, sure. Continually. Day to day. As a matter of fact, Dr. Stuart's Chinese secretary, who had been with him for many, many years, Philip Fugh, was very close to Chiang Kai-shek. This was one reason that we didn't encourage the old gentleman to go around the chancery, because we knew that the minute Dr. Stuart got a telegram, he would show it to Philip. And the first thing Philip would do would be to read it, and then call for a car and go over to Chiang Kai-shek's office and show it to him!

The world's worst security leak was going on, and Marshall knew it and [W. Walton] Butterworth [minister-counselor at the embassy] knew it. In order to protect ourselves, insofar as we could, we just simply got where we didn't show the old gentleman any telegrams. Or Walt would take the telegrams over to him and let him read them, and then he'd take them back. He wouldn't leave them with him. Dr. Stuart knew why he was doing it and was kind of amused by it.

What contacts were there with the Communist Chinese?

MELBY: The Communists had had an office in Chongqing and one in Nanjing. We all used to see them quite regularly. I knew Zhou Enlai very well. He was the head of the Communist office. They were quite open, frankly. No problem. It was easier to talk with them than with the Nationalists. You knew the Nationalists were lying most of the time. The communists never lied.

Marshall left in January '47. Marshall issued a statement of a "plague on both your houses," and came back to the U.S.[8] Later [in January], he was appointed secretary of state. The summer of '47, Chiang Kai-shek outlawed the Communist Party. All their offices in Nationalist China closed. From then on, we had no contact whatsoever.

CIVIL WAR

When efforts at mediation failed, Americans found themselves in the midst of renewed civil war. The U.S. government funneled some $2 billion in aid to the Guomindang, much of which was squandered. Chiang did not carry out requisite reforms and increasingly lost the loyalty of his troops, who were ineptly led, poorly paid, and brutally treated.[9] As is evident from their commentary here, Americans sought to influence values and institutions to combat the growing influence of the Communists. But, amidst the inflation, corruption, and renewed fighting, they lost hope.

CLOUGH: [As a language student in 1946 and 1947 in Beijing, I] spent time with students at the universities. Generally speaking, the students were very critical of the GMD. They were also critical of the United States. There was a famous case of an alleged rape of a Chinese student by an American Marine, and that occupied the newspapers for quite a while.[10] There was a widespread feeling among the students that the United

States and the GMD were in the wrong, and that we were not really backing democracy.

The Communists had considerable appeal. They were seen as more upright, less corrupt. And they had this vision for the future: a peoples' China that would not be at the service of the compradors[11] and the rich people, the Kungs and the Soongs.

MARTIN: I did a thing which none of my language officer colleagues did that gave me a rather interesting entree into Peking University.[12] I audited a course taught in Chinese. It was a course in diplomatic history, really—Chinese relations with foreign governments. It was an eye-opener to me, because it was obviously from the Chinese point of view, and none of the stuff I had read before was from the Chinese point of view.

But perhaps the main value of this to me was that as a student who sat there at a desk with other students, all of whom were Chinese, and I was a little older than most of them but not that much older, I had a chance to become acquainted with a number of Chinese students. I visited them in their dormitories and had some over to the house. My wife was born and brought up in China, and her Chinese accent is beautiful, so that was a great help in talking to people. Certainly the strong impression I had of the Chinese students was that as far as the Guo-mindang was concerned, it was just beyond the pale; there was no hope for it really. This was due, in part, to the fact that the economic situation was very bad, and they had very poor prospects for getting jobs. On the other hand, a number of the students actually left the university and went over the hill to the Communists, where they got some sort of a job. I used to have arguments with these people. Of course, they were very critical of American policy, which was seen as supportive of the Guo-mindang. We used to have arguments about that and whether American democracy and the capitalist system was applicable to China. They generally felt that it wasn't, that socialism was the only way for China to go. As far as I could tell, the students that I knew and talked to on a very friendly basis were not doctrinaire Marxists; in fact, they were fairly illiterate, as far as Marxist literature was concerned, but they looked at it from a point of view of nationalism. To them, the Communists represented Chinese nationalism more than the Nationalists. They also represented what they felt was a hope for the future; but the idea that China would be independent, stand up and be a power in the world was the main attraction, and they felt the Communists offered that more than the Nationalists did at that particular time. Their view was, it seemed to me, very nationalistic. In terms of their own future, they felt that the Communists offered them, as young people, a future, whereas the Guomindang offered them no jobs, depression, and an appearance of weakness, corruption, and really sort of doing the bidding of the United States.

WILSON: I'll give an example of how the Communists were operating. Their cells in the universities and the schools were a very important part of their apparatus. Students held innumerable strikes and demonstrations, demanding the Nationalist government to stop fighting the Communists, for example. But in 1948, they shifted their line and began to demonstrate against American imperialism, alleging that we were rearming Japan for reconquest of China. This propaganda campaign started one night at the American School, where my daughter, April, was a student. We went there for a program depicting the birth of the United Nations. The school had 50 nationalities, so they had a lot of native costumes. Just as the program started, a grotesque figure suddenly appeared on the stage as Uncle Sam, wearing a suit covered with dollar signs. Then another figure came on the stage dressed in a baggy Japanese Army officer's uniform, carrying a large bag covered with dollar signs. It took only a moment. Uncle Sam put an affectionate arm around the servile Japanese, while slipping him dollars. A third figure dressed as a Chinese peasant armed with a stick dashed out and drove Uncle Sam back in confusion. Then someone pulled the light switch.

In the various universities, suddenly there was an exhibit of photographs. At Episcopal St. John's University in Shanghai, one of the best, there was one on the theme of America imperialism rearming Japan. University authorities ordered the exhibit removed. Demonstrations broke out there and at universities across the country, carefully orchestrated, spreading like a prairie fire. The students were able, at St. John's, to force the resignation of the president of the university. These demonstrations peaked in Shanghai with a gigantic anti-American parade. Americans were told to stay off the streets.

From the perspective of our embassy in Nanjing from '47 to '50, what was the situation?

CLOUGH: We were looking for rays of light, I suppose, in this gloom that surrounded the political situation. The negotiations were not progressing.

MELBY: [In the Embassy in Nanjing] they saw the situation and said, "It's hopeless." All the career officers, without exception, agreed that the Communists were going to win. Didn't mean they looked on it with any great favor. On the other hand, they just thought the Nationalists were hopeless. They were corrupt beyond measure. They were going to get worse.[13]

CLOUGH: And this was the worst period of inflation. People were scrambling to try to make ends meet. I can recall how the embassy had to send a truck to the bank to get a truckload of currency. Each of us got an allowance of local currency, as part of our salary, in order to pay our servants and to buy things that we needed on the local market. We'd line up at the accounting office in the embassy and each of us would get a mail sack full of bundles of notes.

I understand at that period of time nobody bothered to unbundle notes.

CLOUGH: That's right. I don't know how many million each bundle stood for. But I'd take my sack back to the house, and I would pass out the appropriate amount to each of the servants, and they would rush off to the market to buy something before the currency lost any more of its value. They'd try to turn it promptly into rice or cloth or gold coins.

BACON: Inflation was enormous. The consulate had difficulty getting the money out to pay the staff every week. At one time the plane from Shanghai, which carried the money, failed to arrive and the Hankou police didn't get paid. What they did was to take direct action, which didn't get them any money either, but they went to the branch of the Bank of China and demolished it. They simply tore it down, leveled it to the ground. There was almost no support for the Guomindang except as something that might stave off the Communists for a while. But in the course of the year even that changed, where people looked forward to the arrival of Communists as putting an end to an almost impossible life that they were leading.

CLOUGH: Now the political situation was simply going from bad to worse, because in the middle of '46, the civil war broke out in full scale. The Nationalists, at first, made an advance. They captured Yan'an up in

Shaanxi Province. They seemed to be making progress, but it was an illusion, because they had disregarded Marshall's advice about Manchuria. He had felt that they couldn't maintain themselves in Manchuria. They had Shenyang and Changchun, several cities, but the countryside was mostly controlled by the Communists. He felt they simply couldn't keep their supply lines open, which turned out to be the case. Gradually they lost the battle for Manchuria and then the battle for North China.[14] But we could see it coming, you know. We'd go into the embassy and our Military Attaché would put a map up and give us a briefing on the latest military situation. Any layman could see it was going badly for the Nationalists.

Were we making any effort that you know of to make contact with the democratic groups?

CLOUGH: Oh, yes, we had contact with those people all along. But as always happens in a situation when you have two strong antagonists fighting each other, the people in the middle tend to be very small in number and very weak. They wanted something which the Americans approved of very much, they wanted some democratic, peaceful arrangement. But the two sides who held the power weren't interested in what these people were peddling. They wanted their own views to prevail.

VAN OSS: In 1948, in Shanghai, I was the main liaison with what they called the Third Force. They were the liberal non-Communist Chinese who we hoped would be friendly to us and a bridge between what we thought even then certainly would become a Communist government and the United States. There was one fellow, Carson Chang, for example, who was the chairman of one of these third parties. He was an old man, a scholar. I remember his house was just filled with books. The rooms were like the stacks in a library. You had to weave your way between shelves of books. I used to go to see him and get his views on what was happening.[15] There was another liberal leader, Lo Longji, who had tuberculosis. We were keeping him alive by sending him antibiotics. He was kept under detention by the Nationalist government in a hospital, and we would visit him from time to time to deliver the antibiotics and find out what was going on with him.

MARTIN: The so-called Third Force people there around the universities tended to be fairly optimistic about the possibility of doing business [with the Communists] or setting up some sort of a coalition government.

Did you have the impression that the group that you worked with or the official staff there in Beijing placed much confidence with the Third Force groups?

MARTIN: I would say that we had more faith in them—that's a strong word, faith. We had more hope about the possibility of some sort of a coalition with these chaps than was justified by subsequent events.

Could you describe how the embassy was reacting to this civil war that was moving, seemingly slowly, but in an unstoppable way, towards Nanjing?

MELBY: Fatalism. "It's coming." It just felt like the grave-watchers, watching the whole civilization, two thousand years of history going down the drain.

You reported it as you saw it? Nobody was saying, "These reports aren't going very well"?

MELBY: We knew they weren't going over very well, but we did it, anyway. We recorded what we saw, and the people to whom we were reporting had, at one time, been in the embassy and knew as much about China as anyone.

Were there any repercussions from bad reports about the situation with Chiang Kai-shek or his officials saying, "What do you mean, reporting that we're corrupt?"

MELBY: The Nationalists didn't do that, because they knew that what we were reporting was the truth. And in a sense, they didn't care. The way the corruption was going, it was every man for himself, anyway.

MARTIN: My first post in China as a reporting officer, was in Hankou, now part of Wuhan. Hankou is on the Yangzi River, about 600 miles up the river. There I had sort of a grassroots view of what was going on in China. The consular district consisted of five provinces in Central China. They had a population of about 100 million people. To put things in perspective, how many countries in the world in 1948–49 had a population of 100 million? But this was just part of China. I was the only political reporting officer covering that territory.

I might say that in China political reporting from the consulates was more important than in most countries, because it was a country where power had been in the hands of warlords and of regional political factions. Even as late as 1948, when I went to Hankou, there was a faction in control of Central China—not in control of it, but it was very important there, namely the Guangxi clique, sometimes called the Li-Bai clique, lead by Li Zongren and Bai Chongxi. Bai and Li, of course, were not the best of friends with Chiang Kai-shek, and we had the feeling that Chiang was often reluctant to call on Bai for support.[16]

How did you view Madame Chiang Kai-shek?

MELBY: I didn't take quite as dim a view of her as a lot of people did. I felt kind of sorry for her. I didn't know her at all well. She belonged to two worlds. She had been educated in the States, southern-belle type. Chinese didn't trust her, because they thought she was too westernized. Westerners thought she was still too Chinese. She really didn't have many friends. She had a few old Chinese missionary ladies—biddies— who used to come around to tea. But otherwise, she was pretty isolated.

However, the GIMO [Generalissimo Chiang Kai-shek] did trust her, in the sense that he relied on her as interpreter. He didn't speak a word of English. He didn't even speak Mandarin, for that matter. He had to conduct cabinet meetings with an interpreter, because his dialect was Fujian [actually Zhejiang], which is a hillbilly dialect, if there ever was one! But she was very useful to him, that way. I know that General Marshall thought that the GIMO really relied on her a great deal. And he, too—although he didn't much like her—in a way, felt kind of sorry for her. Even though he was a fairly austere kind of person, he softened up a bit with her. She didn't fool him. She was an impossible woman. Very demanding, like all the Soongs. The whole clan were like that. But she was a very beautiful woman. Very interesting to see her. When she was with Chinese, she was the demure Chinese lady, with the high dressed neck, and flat-chested, and so on. When she was with Westerners, she suddenly was all full-bosomed and so on, and her skirts were slit up to her hip. She had very good-looking legs, too. She was very adept at using her feminine wiles. The only one who was never affected by her, was General [Albert C.] Wedemeyer [who succeeded Joseph Stilwell as Chiang's chief of staff]. He really didn't like her.

LUTKINS: It wasn't so much that we were hostile to or critical of the national government, the Guomindang government. They faced extraordinarily difficult problems. The war had weakened them badly. It forced them into the interior, where they lost their foundation with western middle-class roots and were forced back into the old China, depending on warlordism. Inflation was rampant, which again was not by any means entirely their fault; it was just a wartime situation. The bottom line to all this was that the regime was very obviously weak, it lacked control over much of the country. There was the usual traditional Chinese corruption, both in the military and in the civil government. The regime really lacked the ability to do anything effective economically on behalf of either the middle class, to which it really owed most of its support, or to the peasantry around the country.

And then, contrasted with this, you had the Communists under Mao Zedong who, whatever their methods, seemed to have a real conviction and spirit, and to be, at that time at least, fairly self-sacrificing in making efforts to do something on behalf of the people and not merely being interested in enriching themselves. So one couldn't help be rather skeptical of the claims of the national government that it was reasserting its control, and also a little pessimistic as to how things were going to go.

BACON: Our government was slow in fulfilling its undertakings [regarding aid to the Nationalists]. I'm not so sure that it would have made any difference at all anyway. The cash did come, but very little of it ever got out of the hands of the Chinese hierarchy. Much of what we sent was never used, much that was used was either wasted or simply lost and abandoned to the Communists as the Communists came forward. The people we thought we could rely upon would give us assurances without having any intention of carrying them out. There was a general feeling of despair really, that since the whole thing was going down the chute, the best thing to do was to look after yourself and your family. Generally in China it's true the family does come first. Your first loyalty is to your family, your parents, and your descendants.

In addition to the political struggle, there was also a cultural struggle going on in China in the 1940s.

WILSON: In 1947, we still had USIS [United States Information Service] offices in Nanjing, Peking, Mukden, Chongqing, Hankou, Guangzhou, and Taipei. The Associated Press was servicing less than 30 percent of the estimated 600 daily newspapers in China and the United Press reached about 70 percent [most of which] were concentrated in the Shanghai-Nanjing area. Of course, the Guomindang Central News Agency subscribed to AP, but through quite a filter. USIS was trying to take up the slack.

We also had a Chinese newsletter, made up of reprints of American magazine articles. The press section put this out periodically. I thought it very unappealing, so I brightened it up, gave it a cover, made it like a magazine, with line drawings and so on. We began to reach 13,000 schools, universities, selected groups, and 75 percent of that material was reprinted.

In Shanghai, fourth largest city in the world, there was only one free library, and that was ours. It had American books and magazines available for free loan. Of course, we had libraries in various branch posts. Also, we had a grant from the American Library Association of $100,000 to buy books for Chinese libraries and universities. The first Fulbright Agreement was signed with China, the first in the world. They had $20 million to send American teachers and students to that country, and Chinese to our country.

During the war, the Office of War Information [OWI] sent to Chongqing, among other things, high-speed leaflet presses. One of these later came to USIS in Shanghai. We had a lot of press capacity left over. So the thought occurred to me, why not make posters, with captions in English and Chinese, [with] some relevancy to Chinese problems. The first exhibit was about American elections and voting in a democracy. China had adopted its first constitution in five thousand years. They were about to hold their first national election. So I got an OWI booklet, and we copied the excellent drawings and diagrams on the American system. We began to reach more millions of people. These posters were being put up all over the country.

MCCARTHY: In the presidential election in 1948, Dewey versus Truman, the Nationalists, who still held on very tenuously to Peking, saw the handwriting on the wall if the Democrats continued in office. So to a man, they were all pulling very vigorously for Tom Dewey. USIS had a big election chart on the outer wall of our premises in Peking to chart the returns as they came in over the Voice of America. The crowd was so big that it eventually blocked traffic on the street outside. Most of the crowd was composed of university students, Nationalist military officers, and government officials who all had a personal stake in the selection. They cheered at the early returns which showed Dewey in the lead, and they were very much crestfallen when Harry Truman eventually turned out to be the winner.

The military situation for the GMD deteriorated sharply in the last months of 1948, as the battle for Manchuria turned against them. That was followed closely by disastrous losses in Central China. At what point did the U.S. embassy and consulate officers decide to evacuate Americans?

MELBY: We had a lot of trouble in Shanghai. The mobs got out of control. We evacuated people. We were under a lot of pressure from the GIMO. "Please don't evacuate! Don't do it, because it will just give the advantage to the Communists." Finally, it got to the point, in October 1948, where I just had to make the decision, "Look, I'm sorry, but we've got to do it." We warned Americans, private citizens, to get out. Which meant mostly missionaries. Most of the business community had left. As usual, missionaries didn't do it. They never want to go. And then they get into trouble, and start yelling because the embassy doesn't get them out of trouble.[17]

HOLLOWAY: You have to distinguish in the missionary movement between the headquarters group, let's say, in Shanghai, and the missionaries out in the field. They were two different breeds of cats. The missionaries in Shanghai, the headquarters, were pretty sophisticated, politically astute people, who were well aware of the power they had behind them in Washington. The missionaries in the field tended to be good-hearted, somewhat naive, but certainly men of good will. I talked to a lot of them when they came into Shanghai, after they lost their churches and the Chinese had turned on them. They were quite shocked. I remember one doctor saying he was going back [to the United States] and go to work for the UMW, the United Mine Workers. They needed doctors. "I'll treat Americans now. I won't treat any more Chinese." There was a profound disillusionment. The Catholics were a little different. I knew Bishop Walsh, who, of course, stayed for twenty-one years.

Yes. In jail, mostly.[18]

HOLLOWAY: They had no families, of course, and they looked upon it as just a cross to bear, if I could put it that way.

MELBY: What finally decided me [about calling for evacuation] was we weren't getting very good information out of Manchuria. I decided to go up to Mukden again and have a look at it myself. I was going up with Dave Barrett, who was assistant military attaché. The planes started shuttling in from Mukden, unloading. Dave Barrett just looked at them and said, "John, I don't have to go to Mukden. When the generals start to evacuate the gold bars and concubines, the flap is on."

I got there, and it was clear that Mukden was going to fall. And once Manchuria was gone, then you knew that all China was gone. Traditionally, he who controls Manchuria, controls China. It's always been the case. I got out on one of the last planes out of Mukden. I went right back to Nanjing and issued the evacuation order: "Get the people out and get them out fast."

VAN OSS: Mind you, I don't want to go into all the business of whether the Communists would win or lose, because this was much more of an issue at home in the U.S. than it was in China. Over there there was no question about the fact that the Communists were winning. The arms and materials we were sending to support the Nationalists were being wasted. They were given to troops which eventually surrendered with all their weapons, so the Communists probably had more of our stuff than the Nationalists had.

So it was quite evident from the time I arrived that it was just a question of a few months. It wasn't just I who felt that way. It was evident to all of us, including the consul general. Of course we had to be a little careful how we expressed this view, because there was a very powerful China lobby at home and a number of U.S. Congressmen were very much interested and very strong supporters of Chiang Kai-shek and the Nationalists. We couldn't just make it appear that we were selling him short. So we couldn't report as frankly as I am talking to you, although we found ways of expressing our views.

What was the feeling in Washington at the time about the Communists and the Nationalists—who was going to win, what American interests were?

WALTER JENKINS: We were not all of one mind, but as these dispatches came in from the China posts, we began to see the Nationalist side disintegrating and contemplated what could be done about it. For instance, on the military side, Chiang had taken away command of 10 divisions—American-equipped and trained in China during World War II—from Sun Liren, who was a VMI [Virginia Military Institute] graduate but just too objective—and gave the troops and command to Fu Zuoyi, who had been a warlord. Fu eventually defected, with the 10 divisions, to the Communists. And then you began to see warlord cliques develop and split off. One was the Guangxi Clique, led by Li Zongren, who was vice president to Chiang Kai-shek at the time. And you got a feeling from the reporting that the Guangxi Clique was trying to join hands with Fu Zuoyi and Governor Long Yun of Yunnan to provide an alternative to Chiang.

And so you could see three alternatives, at least I could, and you could see people thinking about them. Should there be a support of alternative groupings the Guangxi Clique and other factions? "Look, the Chinese Communists are obviously winning." Others would say, "Why not establish contact with them, establish diplomatic relations, and wean them away from the worldwide, monolithic communist movement?" And then you had the viewpoint, represented by the China Lobby, "Follow through with Chiang to the very end, even though he had retired to Taiwan, and someday we'll return to the mainland," which became the slogan.

CHINA LOBBY

As the fortunes of Chiang Kai-shek declined in China, pro-Chiang interests in the United States pressed harder for increased aid to the Guomindang. The motives of this China Lobby were mixed. There were those who cared about building a democratic China, and others who had lucrative business investments at stake. However, they all agreed that the Truman administration had not done enough and was losing China. Among the main targets of such criticism were American diplomats whose support for Chiang did not appear sufficiently strong or unquestioning.

CLOUGH: Those of us who were in the embassy and in touch with our American military were strongly opposed to getting any more deeply involved. General Wedemeyer was sent out on a mission to tour China [in 1947] and see what might be done. He went with Phil Sprouse, who was the director for Chinese affairs at the time. The Wedemeyer report was so negative to the Nationalists that it was not published for a considerable period of time. It became one of the political footballs back here in the United States. Wedemeyer's judgment was that it would have required an enormous investment of American military to maintain the Nationalists in China. And in the opinion of those of us in the embassy, it was not worth it. We couldn't support this collapsing structure.[19]

I recall one occasion when Congressman Walter Judd came out. We had an evening session with Judd, and he kept saying "What can we do? What can we do?" And none of the embassy officers had any very good ideas. It was a gloomy session, and I think he came away with the feeling that those China specialists in Nanjing are not much good, they can't think of any useful things for the United States to do at this critical point. Of course he was a missionary in China for years and years.

He was a missionary and then a very influential congressman on China issues.

CLOUGH: He was a very strong pro-Nationalist, along with Senator [William] Knowland from California. Those two were the outstanding ones.[20]

Could you describe your impression of Henry Luce? He too was a powerful figure trying to shape China policy as a publisher of Time *and* Life *magazines.*

MELBY: I had only met him once on the street in Nanjing. He was headed in to see Dr. Stuart. He stopped me—he knew who I was—and we talked about China. He was giving me a pathetic lament. I believe he said, "Those of you who criticize people like me for our stand in support of the Nationalists, you've got to remember that we were born here. This is all we've ever known. We had made a lifetime commitment to the advancement of Christianity in China. And now you're attacking us for it. You're asking us to say that all our lives have been wasted; they've been futile. They've been lived for nothing."

Henry Luce was a very troubled man. I think he was beginning to have real doubts—this was in the fall of 1947—as to what had happened in China, and had he been wrong after all. Particularly he had them when he was in China. He'd go back to New York and he'd revert back to the old China Lobby syndrome.[21]

Did any of the members of the conservative wing of the Republican Party come and visit during this period? Or was their criticism pretty much limited to being back in Washington?

MELBY: No, they used to come out. In the summer of 1947, we had some 40 or 50 congressmen who came out. Walter Judd was always dropping in.

Did you get any feel for this battle back in the States?

HOLLOWAY: No. We saw very few newspapers. The English-language papers in China were very careful about what they printed. We relied on the Voice of America and the BBC. But we didn't have any idea about the virulence of the China Lobby fight. The Republicans, having lost the '48 election, decided to win the Chinese revolution instead. There was tremendous pressure on the administration to do something to save the Chinese Nationalists.

WARD INCIDENT

Believing that the American consulate general in Mukden operated a spy ring in Manchuria, the Chinese Communists placed Consul General Angus Ward and his staff under house arrest in November 1948. They remained in detention until November 1949, when the Communists put Ward on trial, found him guilty, and expelled him from China. During the tense months of imprisonment, officials in Washington thought about taking military action to free Ward but hesitated to take such a risk. In fact, although hotly denied at the time, the Mukden consulate *was* the center of an espionage operation.

STOKES: Mukden turned out to be everything that I had hoped for in terms of strife and struggle. In the period immediately following VJ Day and the Japanese surrender, when I arrived, the civil war was in full tilt. The Chinese armies were the American-trained crack armies from the Burma road, the Stilwell trainees, and American equipped armies, and the Chinese Communists were not yet fully understood to be as redoubtable as they later proved to be. As our staff dwindled, I was really the right hand, or in effect if the consulate has a deputy chief of mission [DCM] to Angus Ward.

So the consulate was the only official American presence.

STOKES: Yes, except for this shadowy External Survey Detachment [ESD], which was we can all guess what it was.[22] In any case, Secretary Acheson had wanted to seek a modis vivendi or explore the possibilities of a modis vivendi with the Chinese Communists. So we were all secretly asked if we wanted to volunteer to remain behind in case the city should fall to the Communists. And I volunteered.

ERICKSON: The Communists came in on the first of November. We were very apprehensive. [The Nationalist Army had] just evaporated. They were nowhere to be seen. We went up to the roof of the consulate and watched the Communists start taking over the communications building, which was about two blocks down. Then they came up to our area. I remember there was an old lady that they just shot and went right on. They saw us looking over the top of the building and they started shooting at us.

STOKES: In pursuit of our instructions from the secretary to try to make an opening to the Communist authorities as soon as the hubbub died down, I telephoned, and to my astonishment they accepted the offer of the consul general to call on the mayor. When the consul general and I arrived there, we were ushered into a waiting room and we saw on the couch opposite us the head of the Soviet Trade Commission and his deputy, who was the senior Soviet official there. There were a lot of cigarette butts around, showing that they'd been there a long time. Well, the door opened to the mayor's office, and the Russians all stood up, and the man in the mayor's office walked right by them as though they didn't exist. I could hardly look at the Russians as I went by because they'd have spit nails if they could have. The mayor said yes, we are interested in a reasonable, mutually respectful relationship. We have to rebuild this country, most of the equipment is Japanese, you are occupying Japan. The reality is we need to get along. So the consul general pressed his luck and talked about a diplomatic courier, and talked about the rights of American businessmen, and there was a reasonable response to all of this. So when we came back to the consulate we could hardly contain our euphoria. We sent off reports of just exactly what had been said. Then the phone rang. To my astonishment the mayor wanted to pay a return call on the consulate. And he did come. The conversation continued. The next day, we wanted local currency, so I went down to the central bank and asked to speak to the new head to the central bank. He gave us more of the economic reasons for collaboration and promised to expedite our reasonable needs.

So when we went back to the consulate we were making all kinds of plans. In came a special messenger with a notification from the garrison commander to surrender all of our radio equipment. We thought, well, you know, that's in the context of what's happening, this is nothing threatening, but we sent the proper reply as requested but explained that we could not release the equipment because it was the property of the U.S. government and we needed to ask instructions and see that this was the right thing to do—following which came a phone call telling us that the former consul general must appear within 30 minutes before the garrison commander, who turned out to be Wu Xiuquan, later [vice] foreign minister of the Communist government and the man who at Lake Success threw the riot act.[23] He looked at the consul general. "You have one hour to have all the radio equipment in your office in the hands of my staff." The garrison commander got up and walked out.

We had guidance, but Consul General Ward was not really interested in following it. Mr. Ward had made the friendship of [Ambassador] William Bullitt during the Hoover relief mission in Russia [1921–1923]. Mr. Bullitt was Thomas Dewey's choice to be secretary of state, and Mr. Ward expected to be the leader of the department under Bullitt. Mr. Ward's consul generalship sort of was a constant running battle with the department and the embassy over a whole range of things, including matters of policy. Mr. Ward represented the conservative wing of the Republican Party, which felt more that the national government should be strengthened at all costs. There were divisions within the consulate over this, of course. Mr. Ward was the boss, but the young officers' view was [different]. With the defeat of Dewey he rather lost interest in what was going on.

So we were informed that we were violating the laws, we were under house arrest. And there began 13 months incommunicado. The lights went out, the telephones went dead, the water stopped, and there we were, 75 people in an office building: Chinese, foreigners, locals, Americans, anyone who was there. If you came near the window a sentry would point a rifle at you and arm the device. They took out the Chinese one by one and gave them a going over, and finally ordered them all under pain of whatnot not to have anything to do with us. So at that point I had to do all of the interpreting between the Chinese and consul general who didn't know any Chinese.

Were there any anti-American demonstrations?

ERICKSON: Oh yes. Every single day. Singing and parades all along the side of our compound. I still can sing their little chant—without communism there will be no China. Two or three hours every day in the beginning. Another thing that was rather terrifying in the beginning was that every night we were bombed by the Nationalists. That was ironic, too. Here we were being bombed by our own planes. We were hit one evening, quite a few of the windows blown out.

Did you get the feeling that nobody cared or knew the situation?

ERICKSON: Yes. We had no knowledge otherwise. It was an eerie sensation. It went on and on. We had no fuel. You couldn't take a bath because there was no hot water. You just put on layers of clothing like the Chinese did. But it was really the cold that I remember the worst. It would get 40 below, and that was really cold. Then the pump would freeze. We didn't have any running water, of course. We would bake bread and the cockroaches would practically line the bread pans as it was rising. We would bake it with the cockroaches in it and then just slice the sides off. . . . They didn't get inside the bread. We played bridge. We didn't have any electricity and nights start very early in the winter. We did get candles, and that was all we had. The vegetables— carrots and cabbage—we got most of the time, meat, from time to time, but it would be full of straw and dirt. However, we would just wash it up and boil it well. We were never hungry. And I think that is important in maintaining at least a modicum of morale. If you are cold and hungry, that is a lot worse then being just cold.

STOKES: So just about this time an old Chinese who had been caught asleep by the consul general and was ordered out to some remote part of the consulate came in one day to ask for his retirement money. Ward went out and took him by the ear and led him down the stairs. The Chinese was frightened and began screaming. When Ward got to the bottom of the stairs, there was the mass Chinese staff confronting the consul general. The door then burst open and in came the Chinese guards. They arrested Ward and any Americans that were close to him, carried him off to jail. They wanted some kind of pretext in order to get rid of us. There was then a trial, the consul general was sentenced to 10 years at hard labor.

WILLIS ARMSTRONG: Those of us who knew Angus and had served with him in Moscow were sure that he had beaten those Chinese to an inch of their lives. He was a rough man.

STOKES: And there was a trial of personnel who were allegedly left behind by the external survey detachment. They had masses of Army/Navy type transmitters and camouflage gear and everything else you could imagine. The attempt was made to link the consulate to this work.

MANHARD: Mukden was out of communication. No one knew their condition, what was happening. At that point we were totally dependent on what we could pick up, at least as far as I knew, in Tianjin from the local Chinese-language press. I followed that closely. There was a trial before what they called then the People's Court, and they [Ward and several others] were finally convicted of sabotaging the revolution and were sentenced to execution. Shortly thereafter, it was announced in the press again that due to the lenient policy of the Chinese Communist regime, that their sentence was being commuted to deportation.

At that point, the first thing that seemed obvious to me, my own personal speculation, was that they had no way of physically carrying out the sentence of deportation from [the] China Mainland unless they had the cooperation of the United States or some other foreign power. They had no aircraft, there was no commercial transportation coming in or out of North China. So I decided that I'd take the initiative to go down to see the head of the Public Safety Bureau in the Chinese Communist regime, which was the equivalent of the internal and external *Gestapo*.

I asked him first if his government intended to deport them via the Soviet Union. I asked that question clearly because I personally believed that the Chinese Communists were having great difficulties with their relationship with the Soviet Union. There had been a lot of discussion in some quarters about the Soviet rape of Manchuria, cleaning out materials, taking people, and so forth. Whether that was entirely the opinion of Chinese Nationalist officials and their government's attitude, or whether this was shared by the Chinese Communists, of course, no one knew for sure. But I just detected an atmosphere and undercurrent of restiveness and unhappiness toward the Soviets. He glowered and bristled and said, "Certainly not. Absolutely not." So my parting shot at that point was simply, "Well, I trust you and your superiors realize that there is no way you can carry out the order of your court unless you have the cooperation of the United States. We are prepared."

A week or so later, two of the Chinese staff came to me very ceremoniously and very seriously, and said, "Mr. Manhard, we're sorry to say that we have just received a call from the Public Safety Bureau, asking us to tell you that they request that you come to their office right away." I said, "Fine, I'll do so." They said, "Oh, no, please don't." As is typical in China, they said, "We have a cousin who has another relative, who has a relative who works in that office. They tell us that once you get there, you are going to be put in prison as an example to the rest of this office, just like Angus Ward and his party were treated in Mukden." I went down there, and I was very surprised to see the head of the Public Safety Bureau seated behind his desk, slightly to the rear of two much younger men with very high quality cloth uniforms, neither of whom had insignia. They did not give their name or rank or title. They wanted to inform me that they represented the central government in Peking, and wanted me to know that what had happened to Mr. Ward— they still didn't use the title—and his group in Mukden did not reflect the policy of the Central Committee of the Chinese Communist Government. They went so far as to say that what had happened in Mukden was unfortunate.

I was very surprised, because that was about as close to an official apology as any American official could ever get from the Chinese at that point under those circumstances. They said, "However, this case has gone too far. There is nothing we can do to change what has happened in Mukden now, but we wish to cooperate with the United States in every way possible to make some smooth arrangements for him to leave China with your help and assistance."

Later I also suggested to my consul, "I think that this indicates to me that there is a serious split at the Chinese Communist Party Central Committee at the top level about policy toward the United States." Because they repeated this twice, about, "We want you to understand clearly that what happened to Angus Ward and his party in Manchuria do not reflect the policy of the central government in Peking." I was turned down from sending cables, because my boss, I guess, felt that it was only my personal speculation and I really had nothing more to go on.

CHINESE COMMUNIST VICTORY—BEIJING AND NANJING

The Chinese civil war moved toward a Communist victory far more quickly than anyone had imagined. Americans repeatedly caught in the chaos of retreating Nationalist forces surprised themselves by anxiously anticipating the arrival of Communist forces that would impose order. Once behind Communist lines, they had to accommodate to new conditions in which the authorities did not recognize their status because Washington had no diplomatic relations with the Communists.

MCCARTHY: The final year in Peking under the Nationalist regime was a fairly hairy one, partly because Nationalist troops, several hundred thousand strong, poured into Peking after they were defeated up north. They were under no discipline, they hadn't been paid, they were ragged, and most of them became marauders. Eventually Peking was surrounded by the Mao Zedong forces. The only means of communication into the city was by an air strip built on the old polo field inside the city walls.

So we weren't quite sure what was going to happen, but six of the consular officers, including myself, were asked to stay after the Liberation. I can recall going down to one of the main avenues and watching the Communist forces move in. I guess at that point at least 80 percent of the population was delighted to see them come on, because they figured that nothing could be worse than what they'd gone through in the last couple of years.

What were your impressions of the initial impact of the Chinese Communists taking over in Beijing in January 1949?

OSCAR ARMSTRONG: Well, in the first place the takeover was not by military action. The Communists had been moving down into the area, and eventually the [Nationalist] Chinese general commanding the armies in the area, Fu Zuoyi, in effect defected with all of his forces. So Beijing was under siege for a while, but it was not shelled. A lot of the younger people, students, etc., had already been slipping out through the Nationalist lines, joining with the Communists, probably not knowing too much about communism, but they wanted a change. They didn't see a change being promised by the Nationalist regime. I have always felt that Chiang Kai-shek lost China partly because of some serious military mistakes he, himself, made, but basically he did not have and was unable to project a vision of a changed China. Many, many Chinese did not want the old China, the old corrupt regime. So whether you call it political, or ideological, or what, he was just unable to break away from the way he had done things in the past or the circle of people he had around him.

Going back to the Beijing takeover, it was rather a complex mixture of relief that they were not going to be caught up in the fighting, and hope that some sort of change was going to occur. This was at a time when the Communists were still talking about what they called "new democracy." They were not implementing, whenever they got to a city, the harsher measures they adopted later. They essentially took over the administrations and kept them doing what they were doing, etc. So, some hope for some change, but also some concern because they didn't know much about these people.

MCCARTHY: After the Liberation [of Beijing], USIS did continue in business for a while, and there was a very brief honeymoon period of several months when we maintained our normal operations. Eventually, subtle pressures and some not so subtle pressures began to be exerted upon students. I worked a great deal with students. In fact, I taught an English class at one of the local universities. They were afraid to come around and see us because the military posted guards at the door, and people had to show their residence permits when they entered, which discouraged a great many of them from coming to see us. We ended up pretty much isolated. However, we stuck it out, which was a marvelous chance to see a new communist government established first-hand.

MELBY: The battle of Huai Hai had already started, which was the final engagement, which I happened to witness because I'd taken one last trip to Beijing, mid-December 1948. It was a clear day and we flew high over the battle of Huai Hai, over the China plain. You could see exactly what Lin Biao [the great CCP military strategist] was doing. This huge enveloping movement was broken up into literally hundreds, maybe thousands of small pincer movements. Each one moving in, pinching off one group of Nationalist troops after another. It was magnificent! It was fascinating. At the same time, it was horrible. You could imagine the death and destruction that was going on as villages were burning and people were dying. And when it was over—that particular campaign lasted for two months—there was no Nationalist Army left. The Communists had destroyed them all. Some they captured; there was something like 900,000 prisoners before it was all over, living prisoners, to say nothing of those who had been killed. It was the only real conventional battle the Communists fought in the civil war.

CLOUGH: We could see that the Communists were winning the civil war. It was very evident, particularly as the Huai Hai battle developed and the Nationalists began to use desperation measures to try to shore up this place with airlifts and that place. It was obvious they weren't going to be able to do it. Therefore, the government was going to have to move, because Nanjing would be immediately threatened once they couldn't hold the ground to the north. So we had to divide the embassy. The government prepared to move. It was going down to Guangzhou. We sent the larger part of our embassy in late '48. Lewis Clark, who was the minister counselor, headed the group that went down to Guangzhou. Leighton Stuart stayed on, along with all the other ambassadors in Nanjing, with the exception of the Soviet ambassador who moved down to Guangzhou.

BACON: The Nationalist army had the idea that if they could hold the cities they could eventually tire out the Communists. But this had been a failing policy for years and years, and frequently instead of holding the cities, they would abandon them at the approach of the Communists. This happened, of course, at Nanjing. It was generally supposed that the Yangzi River, being a mile wide, would be an absolutely impossible barrier if there were any kind of defense at all. Well there wasn't any defense, and I recall very well the morning when we discovered that the Communists were already in town, in April 1949. The walls of Nanjing were over 20 miles in circumference, 30 to 40 feet high—of course, they're made of bricks, so they could have been blown up, but there was no need to do that. The gates were left open, the Communists walked in. The Chinese government and the police had left town the night before knowing what was going to happen.

Some of [the] looting that went on was rather comical. I remember seeing some poor Chinese coming away from the chief of police's house with a water closet [a toilet] on his shoulders—absolutely no use to him, he had no water supply, but it was a pretty impressive object.

JOHN WESLEY JONES: The thing that was the greatest danger was not the incoming Communist troops who had already crossed the Yangzi, but looters. I remember standing on the high ground just inside the embassy compound wall looking out over the city of Nanjing and being horrified at all of the fires that had been set, most of them in empty houses belonging to officials of the Chiang Kai-shek government who had fled to Guangzhou leaving their houses with some provisions and some furniture but empty and unoccupied. And after the local populace had ravaged these houses and looted them, they then set fire to them. So, every 15 minutes or every half hour or whenever it seemed appropriate, the Marine guards would shoot their guns off into the air to let prospective looters know that this was not a place that was easy to attack. Because it was occupied and because it was armed, we were really never in any danger of looters coming near because they had so many other unoccupied places that they could go to. I never would have thought that I would welcome the advent of Communist troops into a city where I was living, but I can assure you that it was with some joy that I saw the Communist troops come into Nanjing the next day. Order was very quickly restored.

BACON: What was really comical was that a few weeks later in the fall, the Communist government decided to make a historical event out of the capture of Nanjing. We could see the cameras being placed on the top of the walls, the army approaching with scaling ladders, soldiers climbing up and getting on top of the wall, waving the flag. None of which, of course, had ever happened. They just walked in.

CLOUGH: When the Communist troops came in, they were very orderly, and they informed us that we had to stay in our compounds. For the first few days they posted sentries at the gates and wouldn't allow the foreigners out. But within a few days we got a notice from this Alien Affairs Office, which had been set up.

You have to remember that in April of '49 there was no central government. The People's Republic of China had not yet been established. This was simply a military government, and the Alien Affairs Office was the office that was set up to deal with the foreigners. We assumed that we could function in a consular capacity, as we had done in Manchukuo. After the Japanese took Manchuria, we never recognized Manchukuo. We never had any diplomatic relations with that government, but we kept our consuls there, and we dealt with the local government on a consular basis. Never had any serious problems. The Japanese accepted that. That's what we had done throughout Latin America. When there was a change of government, we'd keep our consular officers on, and we'd deal with the successor, whoever it was. So we thought we could do that in China, but the Chinese Communists took a different attitude.

They sent a notice around to all the embassies in Nanjing, saying: "You people have no official status whatsoever. You're just ordinary citizens, and you're not allowed to leave the city without permission from the Public Security Bureau. There's an eight o'clock curfew. No one is allowed on the streets after eight o'clock. And if you have any business, you have to deal with this office and present your business in the form of a written statement in so many copies in Chinese and English, or Chinese and a foreign language, whatever your language is."[24]

ROBERT ANDERSON: So they split the embassy in half. And seeing that I was young, single, and expendable, I guess, I was told to stay behind [in Nanjing]. When we tried to go to the office a couple of times, they'd ram bayonets through the radiators of our cars. A couple of us were dumb enough to say the heck with this, and we'd creep around and go through back alleys, because we wanted to get over the chancery so we could send a telegram or two.

CLOUGH: We did have this incident involving Leighton Stuart's quarters. Early on, the first few days of the occupation, some soldiers wandered into his house early in the morning before he was out of bed. They intimidated the servants, and they bulled their way upstairs into his bedroom, where he spoke to them in Chinese and explained that this was foreign government premises, that they were violating the law by coming there and so on. But they didn't pay much attention.

One of my jobs was to go to the Alien Affairs Office and make a protest of this invasion of our ambassador's quarters by soldiers. So we wrote it all out, and I went down to the Alien Affairs Office. The first problem I had was to get in, because you had to fill out a form at the gate, all this in Chinese, saying who you were, what your position was, what your business was, who you wanted to see. So I filled this all out, saying that I was the second secretary of the American Embassy. The gatekeeper said, "No, you're not. You have to say you're the *former* second secretary of the American Embassy." And I argued with him. I said, "No, as far as *my* government is concerned, I *still am* the second secretary of the American Embassy." So we argued awhile, and then he took the paper and wrote "former" in front of it and took it in.

I went in, and I made my protest to the appropriate official. In fact, this was Huang Hua [director of the Office and Zhou Enlai protégé] himself. He lambasted me. He said, "You have no right to make a protest. You have no status. You're just an ordinary citizen." We found out later that these soldiers were tracked down and they were punished. We heard indirectly, but they wouldn't acknowledge our protest.[25]

Why did the United States hang on there?

CLOUGH: The theory was (and this was a theory widely shared among the foreign ambassadors in Nanjing at that time) that the Nationalists were on the way out, that they were losing the civil war, that they were going to be driven off the mainland, and that the best way to make the adjustment to the new government that was taking over was to keep our ambassadors there so we would have some representation. We could begin a dialogue and work out the arrangements. That was the theory, but in fact it turned out to be much more difficult than anybody anticipated.

We were doing useful things. We were reporting on the situation in Nanjing. After the first few days, we could move fairly freely around the town. Not outside the walls, but within the town. We could talk to people, and we could report on what the newspapers were saying. They had taken over the former *Central Daily News* and turned it into the *Xinhua Ribao*, the new China daily published in Nanjing. We also got newspapers, sometimes, from other parts of the country. We could analyze what they were saying, what campaigns were going on. We had our own radio. We had our own broadcasting, transmitting set, encoding equipment. We operated entirely by radio. For months, we didn't get any pouches in or out.

BACON: We were having labor troubles, of course. The USIA staff, who, not really voluntarily, were used as a front, were demanding tremendous settlements in lieu, or in anticipation of, their retirement allowances. It became apparent that the Communists wanted partly to demonstrate to the population that they were in charge, they could make the Americans jump over hoops, and call them to account for whatever they'd been doing. Also, they wanted hard currency any way they could get it, trying to levy fines on us for this and that.

Did you feel that this was a transition period and that there were signs that the Communist authorities were probably going to open up?

CLOUGH: Yes, we were optimistic. We drafted a telegram, I guess probably the summer of '49, to the effect that the Nationalists were losing the civil war, that it was important for us to maintain some connection. We expressed the view that, in time, strains would develop between the Soviet Union and China, in spite of the lean-to-one-side views expressed by Mao on July 1, and that we should wait for that time, take advantage of what we felt then would be a growing division between the Soviet Union and China.

CHINESE COMMUNIST VICTORY—SHANGHAI

The CCP takeover of Shanghai was an important test because it was the largest, most complex, urban center in China at that time. Many Americans had dismissed the Communists as uncouth peasants who could not hope to govern such an enclave and were astonished at the relatively smooth transition. Incidents, of course, did occur given the large size of the foreign community. For instance, in the case of one American consular officer, William Olive, the cultural and political clash turned violent. Olive resisted arrest, reportedly lashing out at the authorities, who then beat him. They saw him as an arrogant imperialist. The Foreign Service officers recalling the incident here see Olive in a more sympathetic light.

VAN OSS: Shanghai, the Consulate General, was a huge post. I think only Paris and London were larger. Shanghai was an important city. A cosmopolitan city. The Communists later said it was an excrescence or goiter on the body of China proper. It was different from any other Chinese city, except that there were a lot of Chinese there, of course. There were also lots and lots of non-Chinese. There were many German Jewish refugees, White Russian refugees, Iraqi Jewish refugees. It was a polyglot and fast moving city. A naughty city. A wicked city. A busy city.

We were worried about what would happen in the interim between the time that Chiang Kai-shek left and pulled out his troops from Shanghai and the time that the Communists came in. The specter that hovered over our heads was the thought that the Chinese in the old city, all the Chinese poor people and everybody would rise up and plunder the wealthier parts of the city. We were all issued carbines. A lot of what [Consul] Sabin Chase and I were doing was trying to make contact with forces in Shanghai that would be able to exercise some form of control. Sabin did most of this work because he spoke fluent Chinese and I did not. He formed a contact with a Chinese colonel who had close contacts with the so-called Red Gang of Shanghai.

It is quite well known that there were secret societies in Shanghai, generally referred to as the Triad. The most powerful group was called the Green Gang, and that was headed by a person called Du Yuesheng, a mysterious figure who controlled crime, drugs, the underground, and who was one of the powers behind the political scene in Shanghai. A sort of "godfather." He was also close to Chiang Kai-shek and his henchmen.[26] There was a rival underground group, which we called the Red Gang. I can't remember the name of its leader. But the colonel whom Sabin Chase had contacted was in deep with the Red Gang leader and we arranged through him after a long process of negotiation that the Red Gang would take over and have its men out to keep things under control, prevent rioting, etc.

As it turned out, the turnover was relatively quiet. The end of all this was typically Chinese. I think it was about the 23rd of May when the Nationalist leader Chiang Kai-shek held a "victory" march, in which he paraded all his troops through the streets of Shanghai with their weapons. There were dancers, bands, and all sorts of noisemakers. So he had his face saving victory march and then pulled out. The only fighting that took place was between the Communists and the Nationalists at the point of embarkation where the Nationalists were getting on ships to retreat to Formosa [Taiwan].

WILSON: The old China hands were mystified by the behavior of the Communists. First of all, they had never really thought they had good troops. Over night, right after they took over, the city was plastered with thousands of posters, reassuring the populace that their property would be protected, and it was. Unlike the Nationalists, the Communist soldiers slept on the sidewalks rather than intrude into any home or building. They refused to accept so much as a cigarette without paying for it. There was no doubt, given the turbulence of the past, when the Nationalists soldiers did exactly the opposite, that many people in the city were happy to see the Communists come as a promise of peace and order.

What happened commercially? Did stores stay open, was food available?

VAN OSS: The economic situation in Shanghai had become deplorable during the last months of the Nationalists' regime. Inflation was just terrible. The rate would go from say one million yuan to one American dollar one day, to two million to one the next day. At one time Chiang Kai-shek put his son Chiang Ching-kuo in charge of Shanghai. Ching-kuo put in a new exchange rate and forced everybody to turn over gold in exchange for this new currency. He shot a couple of reputable businessmen who patronized the black market in currency. Of course by doing that it meant that nobody could buy anything in Shanghai because the shelves were empty since merchants could get more money by selling their products outside the city at black market rates than inside at the official rate. Eventually Chiang Ching-kuo was forced to lift the limits on the currency and inflation zoomed again.

When the Communists came in they tied the currency to the price at any one time of basic commodities—rice, cotton, tobacco, and gold. So if you put a certain amount of money in the bank on a given day, you were credited with the amount of rice, cotton, etc., that that original amount of money could buy. So no matter what happened to the actual currency exchange rate you could always get the same quantity of the basic commodities as you were credited with when you had originally deposited. That pretty well did away with inflation within a very short time.

Another thing the Communists did: they put a severe tax on all vehicles, so we sent our cars home and had to take pedicabs. That really was one of the best things we ever did because we saw more of Shanghai that way than we ever would have seen in a car. In those days the Foreign Service spent a great deal of time dealing with other officials, driving in cars and living with the upper crust with very little idea of how the peasants, the poor, the lower classes lived. We dealt mainly with the people who could give us the information we wanted and didn't worry too much about wandering about in the villages. And, of course, with the Communist war going on we couldn't travel very far beyond city limits.

Did the Communists make any efforts to keep you from contact with the people?

VAN OSS: No, I don't think they made any conscious efforts, but we had to have permission for any travel. And, of course, many of our contacts were afraid to come to us. Many of our contacts were genuinely trying to get along with the new government, so they wouldn't have phoned us. They began to accuse us of the same things the government was accusing us of doing.

What about the men in the street, the peasant class, did they seem to welcome this new government?

VAN OSS: Anything was better for most of them than what they had under the Nationalist government.

Except nothing did become better for them.

VAN OSS: Well, I don't know that I could dogmatically say that. Probably economically they were better off in some ways. China was not Europe; its average standard of living was much worse than Europe's. The average person in China was poor. There certainly were many poor in the cities. In Shanghai after a typical winter's night the authorities collected bodies off the street of people who had to sleep out and had frozen to death. We saw a bundle in the street outside our house one time coming back from a walk. Our dog started sniffing at it. I went over to see what it was. It was a dead baby. The watchman at our place said it was probably a baby girl that the poor family had not wanted and had thrown out on the street.

There were wealthy businessmen who did very well under the Nationalists, but the man in the street didn't. So I can't say dogmatically that the peasants were worse off under the Communists. They were worse off in the sense that their lives were controlled; they had to obey regulations and couldn't do what they wanted to do, but they couldn't do everything they wished under the Nationalists, either. Don't forget Chiang Kai-shek's GMD party structure was very similar to the Communist Party structure. Chiang Ching-kuo, Chiang's son, was trained in Moscow. The people who were affected adversely under the Communists, of course, were those who had money and owned land.

HOLLOWAY: But the question was, what's going to happen? Here's Shanghai, one of the world's largest cities, a very complex city. It was the biggest city in the communist world, bigger than Moscow. How was this going to be run by these people who had come out of caves in the northwest of China? We all made a mistake, the old China hands in particular, in thinking that they couldn't run this, that they weren't sophisticated enough. Fortunately for them, there was a very, very low level of economic activity, because the Nationalists claimed to have mined the Yangzi. And then, of course, they had a blockade, or port closing as they called it—self-blockade, I guess you would call it in international law. So that economic activity slowed, and this made Shanghai easier to run. They had many, many handicaps. They had a bias against cities. They'd been out in the boondocks for 10 years, and they thought cities were sinkholes and cesspools.

But we were not planning to close Shanghai?

VAN OSS: As of the moment we are talking about—May 1949—we still hoped that we could find some way of making contact with the new government, and seeing if we couldn't repair relations. We had hoped that for a long time, but as the Communists advanced Mao Zedong had become increasingly anti-American in his pronouncements. One of their big slogans was "leaning to one side." This meant leaning towards the Soviets; that became a big thing with them.

WILSON: For a while, we were able to run a restricted USIS program. Communist soldiers would visit our library. But in July 1949, we had to close up. The bamboo curtain had fallen. The U.S. was going to be the main target for vilification. Propaganda techniques were varied. In the press, for one thing, letters were planted asking straightforward questions, like, "Why can't newspapers continue printing AP and UP stories?" And the Communist answer, in part, "Because they are the mouthpieces of imperialism." The Communist Press and Publications Department of the Cultural and Educational Control Committee called a meeting of key Shanghai editors for a discussion forum. They were told that news and feature stories produce ideological and political effects, and the role of newspapers and magazines under the Communists is to serve the interest of the people.

They had an editorial in one of the papers, commenting on USIS. It said we had been ordered to cease our activities, and although on the surface USIS looked like a cultural liaison in public relations such as movie shows, library services, concerts, photo exhibits, giving advice to students going to America, the article said that in fact, the center of work was the dissemination of official news dispatches and the gathering of information concerning public opinion reaction to America. Our posts were filled with Secret Service men trained by the FBI, and we were just megaphones of imperialism.

The radio editors of Shanghai were called in for a lecture. They didn't understand how things worked under Communists. Worst of all, some of them were still relaying the Voice of America. That was a no-no. Motion picture people and producers were called in and told their films had to reflect the policy of the government, that films should educate the people, reform their thoughts, encourage production. American commercial films had been very popular. Now they had the movie industry workers union demand that the government immediately impose censorship on the poisonous American-made pictures. As these movies disappeared, it was announced that 200 Russian films with Chinese lip sync had been imported. Anything American was erased. Street names, like Wedemeyer Road, named after the American general, were changed; brand names, products, soaps, cigarettes. In every element of society, the Communist control mechanism was taking over.

VAN OSS: The interesting thing about this whole experience was that it gave me an insight into just what it is like to be in a communist country where the communist government starts from scratch. There are various impressions that I have. One of them is the noise factor. There were loudspeakers on every street corner and they were turned on incessantly. If it wasn't Chinese music and opera, it was propaganda. We had propaganda in loud Mandarin at all times during the day or night.

Another impression I have is the extreme thoroughness of the Communists. They intruded into every walk of life. They made people attend infinite numbers of political meetings at which Communist officials talked for countless hours repeating endlessly the same slogans and general theories.

The early stages of the Communist takeover didn't have much impact on us except for the fact that our government didn't recognize them and we thus had no official status. But we were not molested, cursed, or pelted with mud. On the other hand, we had to be very careful because one of the things they did early in the game was to take measures to inform foreigners, white men if you will, that they were no longer on a pedestal, were no better than anyone else. In fact, they were a little bit worse than the citizens of China. Where this comes into play is that there were still quite a few beggars in Shanghai. The beggars were a nuisance even for the Communists. They would come up to you and would clutch you and do just anything you would allow them to get away with. In the old days you sometimes were forced to push them aside and go about your business. Once the Communists had taken over this was no longer possible. The minute you so much as touched a beggar, no matter what he did to you, a policeman would appear and you would be taken into custody. This didn't happen to me but it did happen to a number of Americans and other foreigners. The routine was that they would be hauled before a political commissar, not a judge, and would be asked why they had molested a peaceful citizen of China. Then they would give their case. After that they would be fined or told to write a letter of apology and then allowed to go. But this was unpleasant.

WILSON: There was another aspect of their propaganda against foreigners. They felt the Chinese man in the street had too much respect for foreigners. They wanted to break this up, so they began picking different nationalities to create an incident on which to focus. They got a Frenchman, accused him of knocking a Communist officer from his bicycle, made him spend two weeks sweeping the streets, pay a fine, medical expenses, public apologies, wear a sign around his neck, all that. Then it was the American turn. We had a young vice consul by the name of Bill Olive. He was a very slight, unassuming man.

VAN OSS: On the day the Chinese Communists held their victory parade (without prior notice)—about a month after the takeover—Bill Olive happened to be in his car to get gas. Two soldiers jumped out at Bill Olive. They held up their hands. He either ignored them or didn't see them. This was the last we saw of Bill Olive for a while. We didn't know where he was, he had just disappeared.

Eventually we found out that he had been taken to jail. All was well. He explained what he was doing. A police officer quizzed him. He asked if he could call the consulate, and just then the police officer was joined by one of these political commissars. The latter took over and claimed that Bill was trying to brush past guards of the People's Republic of China and interfere with the victory parade. By this time Bill was a little nervous and asked again to call the consulate. The commissar said something like, there isn't a consulate any more, he couldn't call. Then he told Olive that they were going to retain him for a night or two. Olive protested vigorously, and the commissar ordered the guards to take him away. Bill struggled and grabbed the bench in front of the desk and knocked over a bottle of ink, which, I guess, spilled onto the political commissar. He was then pulled back, thrown to the ground and beaten severely by the armed guards.

WILSON: He was locked in a cell without food, water, or medical attention, while two guards kept bayonets thrust through the bars at his throat. He wasn't permitted to move a muscle, and then every few hours they'd take him out, put him in front of a blinding light, and harangue him. They wanted him to write a confession, which he wrote. They'd look at them, crumble them up, throw them back in his face, and say, "Write a better one." And so he wrote, under their tutelage, a confession, which then was published on the front page of the newspapers, which included such things as saying, "I am grateful to the People's Government for the consideration given my case, for the lenient and kind treatment accorded me."

VAN OSS: They wouldn't let him sleep. They kept the light on and kept taking him out for interrogation. This turned out to be the first instance of "brainwashing" that any of us had heard about first hand. They told him that the United States was worse than Nazi Germany and had committed grievous sins against the People's Republic of China. He, Bill Olive, as a representative of the U.S. government, was just as guilty as that government. The grilling went on incessantly for several days. By the end of those days he was so beaten down he almost believed he was as guilty as they told him he was. He was in pretty bad shape at that point. This was a rather ominous event.

So our diplomats were really in a very precarious situation?

VAN OSS: The Olive case was the only episode of that sort at the time, and you could say that the authorities had some flimsy excuse because he did ignore their original instruction to stop his car.[27] Later on, of course, after we Americans had left, the British stayed behind and were subjected to all kinds of embarrassing experiences. They were jailed, forced to kowtow, frog hop across the room, and so on. Terribly humiliating.

BOMBING BY NATIONALISTS

Although Americans remained on the ground in China, the Nationalists utilized American planes and ammunition to bomb Shanghai in 1949, enforcing their blockade and damaging industrial plants and electric power generation capacity. Diplomats reported that the bombing was not limited to military targets. Nevertheless, protests from the American government were half-hearted and the Nationalists ignored them. Ironically, Americans were also blamed for the destruction because of the provenance of the weaponry being used. Washington also refused to interfere with the Nationalist blockade of the China coast.

HOLLOWAY: It got a little dicey when the Nationalists started air raids on Shanghai. These were American planes, American bombs, American gasoline. They were B-24s; that's a fairly potent plane. The Nationalist Air Force, which had never shown any capacity for accurate bombing in the fighting, suddenly became crack bombers, bombardiers! They hit the American power plant in Shanghai. American Foreign Power had a plant at Riverside, a big plant. They knocked out the French power plant, which meant there was no light or heat in Shanghai in the winter.
VAN OSS: I wouldn't put too much stress on the bombing, it didn't amount to very much. It wasn't nearly as severe as the shelling just before the city fell, for example, although the Communists didn't have any planes

so there was no bombing from the sky. After Shanghai fell to the Communists, the Nationalists sent over a few planes periodically to drop a few bombs. But we used to go down to the coffee bar in the basement of our consulate office and use that as our bomb shelter when the siren went off.

WILSON: Meanwhile, from Taiwan, the Nationalists claimed they had mined the Yangzi River entrance. They sent bombers over with 500-pound bombs. The Communists, as a counter-propaganda move, put machine guns—they didn't have any aircraft—on the roofs of the buildings, so that when these planes were up there, all of a sudden the machine guns would go off, and you'd have to watch out for falling lead. Then the newspapers would claim the "bandit" planes had been driven away by the valiant troops.

HOLLOWAY: Isbrantsen shipping line ships were fired on and hit and put on fire by the Chinese Nationalists outside of Shanghai. Our Navy would do nothing to help them. Isbrantsen and Acheson got into a newspaper war, taking ads out, insulting each other. In the end, Acheson got the Coast Guard to, in effect, say that the masters were hazarding their ships by going into Shanghai, and if they went in they might lose their ticket. The department said—it's now been published in *Foreign Relations*—that we would take no action which would lessen the effect of the Nationalist blockade of Shanghai.[28]

CHINA WHITE PAPER

In the spring of 1949, President Truman endorsed the writing of an official document that would absolve his administration of responsibility for the fall of Chiang Kai-shek while clarifying the events in China for the American public.

MELBY: I was asked to take charge of the White Paper. It took about five months to do. The White Paper was a decision on the part of the department, secretary of state, with the approval of the president, who was enthusiastic about it, to write the record of our relationship with China with special reference to the period 1944–1949. [We were to] set forth the record, and set it straight, no matter who got hurt. It was not to be a propaganda job, presenting one side.

I must have gone over several hundred thousand documents, picking out essential ones, and writing it, and getting people—I wrote about half of the White Paper myself. Other people wrote other chapters. We worked on it 18 hours a day, from March until August. We produced this fifteen-hundred-page document, which came out August 8, 1949. George Kennan, who at this point had gone to the hospital with another attack of his stomach ulcers, took the White Paper with him to the hospital and read it straight through. He said that it was the greatest state document ever produced by the American government!

The purpose was to call the dogs off from the China Lobby. It didn't work. The China Lobby, insofar as you can define it, was the antecedent of the so-called Committee of One Million.[29] It was composed of people from a whole political spectrum, from the far right to the far left, who had only one thing in common: for whatever their reasons, they were in complete support of Chiang Kai-shek and the Nationalists. That was the only thing they were united on because of anti-communism. The American obsession with communism.

You produced this paper, and then it just didn't seem to have the desired effect.

MELBY: It was just the opposite. It just accrued more fuel for the fire. I thought, "Well, at least the communists are going to be able to say there's something to it. Maybe they'll like it, and so what." And so help me God, Mao Zedong read the damn thing and proceeded to write five editorials for the official Communist newspaper attacking it as proof of how imperialistic American policy had been. So I figured, "Yes, you can't win."

SERVICE: In hindsight it's remarkable that intelligent and experienced men in the department, people like Dean Acheson and so on, had so little realization of what a hot topic China was. They should have known, because China had been a hot topic since '45, and all through the Chinese civil war the department had been under tremendous pressure. Before Truman was elected [1948], and then particularly after Truman was elected, he was bitterly attacked. The critics charged, "We're letting China go down the drain."

By the summer of '49, it was apparent that [Guomindang] China was finished. All through the civil war we had abstained from anything which could be interpreted as being critical of the central government, Chiang

Kai-shek. We couldn't appear to push him out of China. By the summer of '49, the administration had had enough of criticism. They were going to counterattack and defend themselves, prove that they had done everything they could to support Chiang, that it was not our fault that the Communists were winning. It was Chiang's own failings. The administration decided to put out a White Paper, but they didn't foresee what the effect was going to be, how this would really boomerang, which it did.

ATTACK ON THE FOREIGN SERVICE

Chiang's fall provided the occasion for a brutal attack on American diplomats. Initiated by Patrick Hurley in 1945, the assault became far more vicious with Senator Joseph McCarthy's discovery of the China issue. McCarthy unscrupulously made China policy a central element of his attack on the Truman administration for alleged softness on communism. Foreign Service officers who had predicted the end of Guomindang rule, like Fulton (Tony) Freeman, were forced out of the Asia arena or, like John (Jack) Stewart Service, out of the State Department entirely. Academic China specialists also suffered in the McCarthy era, including Owen Lattimore, who endured years of expensive legal battles.[30]

LACEY: Then and now, the top echelon was more motivated by domestic political considerations than they were by U.S.-foreign developments. The China Lobby was a very potent force. It still was for a long time. Pro-Taiwan was built into U.S. policy towards the two Chinas. I disagreed with it then, and I take issue even now with a black-white view of China. My colleagues, the rank and file working officer, more familiar with the facts of the two Chinas, were inclined towards . . . well, I would guess that seven out of ten of such people would have opted for Communist China at the time.

Did the careers of those who were correct in their evaluation of the strengths of the Chinese regime prosper, or did they suffer as a result of having a view that diverged from American policy?

LACEY: Ralph Clough's name comes to mind. He is a long-standing China watcher, a real expert. Such is his stature as a scholar that he has been able to not only write effectively about Taiwan, but Communist China as well. Bill Gleysteen also comes to mind. Bill was a outspoken critic of Chiang Kai-shek, and yet he rose rapidly in the service, indeed became ambassador to Korea.

Were you feeling any particular pressure on you? Was there pressure to "think right"?

LUTKINS: The constraints were felt more by people in Washington than they were in the field. There was no effort, certainly from Washington, to dictate to us what we should be saying. And no complaints about what we were reporting that I recall.

WALTER JENKINS: No, there was objectivity from my point of view. I felt we were getting excellent balanced reporting out of China. But in the broader political environment you did have the feeling of pressure from the Judds and the Knowlands that we mustn't be "traitors," and you began to feel that Jack Service and others were not exactly welcome in this environment. As a junior officer focusing on the military I was perhaps less aware of the siege. But I had a feeling that Edmund Clubb, Service, and others, and maybe my two bosses, Phil Sprouse and Tony Freeman, were feeling this pressure a lot more than I was. Of course we all know what happened to Service; John Paton Davies was another.[31] Tony Freeman, who was one of the best China language officers I've ever known, left the Far East and became ambassador to Mexico eventually. And Phil Sprouse did go out to Cambodia eventually. But their careers with China or anything important in that region were ended. And you could sort of feel that by 1950.

LACEY: Almost all of them were not only discredited but left the service. I remember reporting on March 3 in 1950 to a Joe Yager, who was then chief of the China branch of intelligence research for the Far East. Joe Yager was a godsend to me. Joe was a very stubborn, tough-minded analyst. He insisted that nothing leave his office that he hadn't personally examined. Joe insisted that we call them as the shots fell, but he always made certain that we worded our analysis in such a way that it wouldn't offend McCarthy. I am always grateful for that. On the other hand, some of our best people were dragged through the McCarthy grinder and had to leave the government. It was a very uneasy period, a shameful period in terms of our democratic process.

MANHARD: Tony Freeman had to have two-thirds of his stomach removed for a bleeding ulcer, he was under such emotional stress.

RICHARD E. JOHNSON: I was in the Office of Chinese Affairs, and of course these were McCarthy days, so that, in a way, conditioned the mood in the State Department, which was a very cautious one and one of considerable concern, even seeping down to the lower levels in the Civil Service. You never knew when you were going to show up on some list for some crime you really didn't commit. I worked for a time for several old China hands who were hit by McCarthy, and their careers were seriously damaged. They later recovered and they're now highly respected as Sinologists, but, at that time, McCarthy had succeeded in creating a good deal of fear in the ranks.

SINO-SOVIET RELATIONS

Frictions between the Chinese and Soviets were apparent to American diplomats in China, as was the fact that few Chinese really understood communism in these early years. In Washington, officials debated the relative importance of communism and nationalism in motivating Mao Zedong's behavior, hoping that he might prove to be as independent of Moscow's control as Tito in Yugoslavia.

MARTIN: Naturally, [in discussions with students about China's future] I tried to put forth the merits of the American system, which they generally would not argue about, except that they would say, "Well, it's all right for America, but it really doesn't apply to China and our situation." I wouldn't say that any of them were strongly pro-Soviet; neither were they strongly anti-Soviet.

STOKES: While we were hostages [in Mukden], Mao made his famous visit to Moscow for his meeting with Stalin [December 1949–February 1950]. Stalin treated him very shabbily and the agreement that came out of that was even worse for the Communist government than the agreement in 1945 that Stalin had negotiated with Chiang Kai-shek.[32] So the myth of Chinese/Russian solidarity and eternal friendship under the banner of communism was to my mind absolutely unraveled by the time all of this experience had come to a head. There is and always has been a latent hostility between the Chinese and the Russians. It's cultural, it's visceral. It goes way back. Just before we arrived there, the Russians seized all kinds of Japanese assets and transferred them to Russian ownership, put Russian signs on them, and tried to keep it as property. Factory equipment they stole. Mao was prepared to swallow all of this until his confrontation with Stalin. And then when he came back, of course, it was such a loss of face.

Was there a line in Washington that felt if you started talking about different types of communism, this would make you look soft on communism?

MANHARD: In 1950, I got the impression from INR [the State Department's Intelligence and Research Bureau] and others who had made a specialty of studying, analyzing, and researching China, that at that time this was an absolute fantasy, ridiculous, absolutely impossible to conceive of any difference of view between China and the Soviet Union, because the conventional wisdom at that time all over Washington, as far as I could make of it, military, civilian, State Department, CIA, whatever, was, "It's a monolithic communist bloc," and anybody who had a different opinion was way out in left field. I had a different opinion and found nobody who agreed with me.[33] Oh, yes. The Chinese poured out a tremendous quantity of propaganda characterized by such expressions as "lean to one side," and "learn from the example of the Soviet Union." But underneath it, the human relations, the personal feelings and attitudes of their own officials was quite different. I saw that.

GREEN: Chiang Kai-shek, even when I saw Chiang for the next to the last time in 1969—1969!—long after we all knew that the Sino-Soviet rift was real and vicious and all the rest of it, he told me that he believed that this was a ruse that was being pulled off by both Beijing and Moscow, that they were trying to delude the West into thinking there was a split, so that it would cause splits in our ranks and weaken our ranks, whereas they were solid, and we were being galled and lured.

I'm saying that because obviously it's wrong, but it shows that that was the line of the Chinese Nationalists that this was all a monolith. The Chinese Nationalists had a tremendous power in Washington, the so-called China Lobby. Of course, it weakened over time, but at the time we're talking about, back in 1950–52, they were very strong. So the line was coming through very hard from Taipei that this was the situation.

MANHARD: However, going back to this incident [the detention of] Angus Ward, the conclusion I personally draw from that experience was that the last thing the Russians wanted to see was, they were afraid of a flexible policy by the United States toward the new regime in Beijing as a potential attempt by us to wean the Chinese Communist regime away from Soviet influence. Anything that would potentially be a threat to that total untrammeled domination by the Soviet Union, they tried their best to undermine.

The media just leaped on this thing. This played into the hands of people with a very conservative view of foreign policy in the Congress and in Washington, that even if certain people in the State Department, for instance, Acheson or Butterworth, even if they'd been inclined to adopt what I'd call a more pragmatic approach to the new Beijing regime, this kind of incident provided a lot of fodder for the grist mills of agitation about, "This is how they're treating official Americans in this regime." If the Russians had expected to have some irritating effect both in Beijing and in the United States, it worked very beautifully.

DEPARTURE

Americans in China faced problems staying or going as the civil war ended and Communist forces emerged triumphant. The final event that led to evacuation was the decision by the Communists to seize official American consulate property in Beijing in early 1950. The land, originally ceded under the 1901 Boxer Protocol, had been intended for garrisoning American troops. Although the United States had long since converted the buildings to office space, the Chinese Communists sought to erase the humiliation of the Boxer era. They may also have been trying to force foreign recognition of the new Chinese government. When neither the Americans nor the Chinese would compromise, the Americans left China.

LUTKINS: Governor Lu Han, plus the political-economic elite in Kunming and in Yunnan, very strongly favored the central government against the Communists. But, of course, they weren't dumb; they knew what was going on and were a little worried about what was going to happen to them if the Communists succeeded in defeating the Nationalists and taking over. And they also, of course, were uncertain as to what the attitude of the United States would be. I was approached by a leading local citizen, who obviously was speaking on behalf of the local power structure, including the governor, asking if they could count on American support if they tried to resist the Communists, and whether we'd be willing to put in any military forces, and so forth. The expected reply came back that under no circumstances would we be prepared to do that. The day before our scheduled departure the local Yunnanese power structure staged a coup against what remained of the rather limited national government force there.

WILSON: The Communists did not have the technical expertise to run the factories and do many things associated with Shanghai. They wanted the foreigners to stay around and run these places until they could properly take over. They didn't want to drop everything overnight. They wouldn't let anybody out. That was part of the problem—it was *the* problem.

Meanwhile, they were telling employees to demand various things. Our military had let their Chinese employees go. They formed a group to demand higher separation settlements than they were entitled to under our regulations. Consul General John Cabot said he would negotiate with a committee, not with all of them. They turned that down, blocked the entrances. We were prisoners inside our own consulate. It was blackmail, and in the end, the U.S. had to pay these people to get them off our back.

In August 1949, the Communists said they would begin giving 25 applications a day for exit visas. They knew thousands wanted to leave. At night, around two o'clock in the morning, there would be long lines waiting. The first time I went, I waited eight hours in the rain. The Communists also wanted the populace to see the spectacle of foreigners lined up, sort of begging, especially the Americans. So we decided we could play that game another way. We began to go downtown late at night with camp stools, cards, magazines, sandwiches, coffee, and just sit around and enjoy ourselves. The Chinese have a good sense of humor, and many of them were amused to see us out there gossiping, munching on sandwiches, as though at a picnic. So the Communists were losing face.

Were you getting instructions that were trickling down to you from the Department of State?

HOLLOWAY: No. I got the impression—again, I was very low on the totem pole—and the impression was confirmed when I got back to Washington, the State Department was in a state of shock, and they just didn't know what to do. They had people in a half a dozen posts in China, and they just had to get them out. The amount of guidance they were getting from the secretary or the president was minimal, because the administration was under fairly heavy fire from the China lobby.

MANHARD: The major event that bore on that for all of us in China in the autumn of 1949 was a telegram from the department signed by Acting Secretary Lovett, telling everybody in China that we were the indispensable eyes and ears, we could not be replaced, that China policy was still under very serious debate in Washington, and they wanted us to stay at all costs, and only those with a dire emergency should ask permission to return to the United States.

Approximately a week later, just after the first of January, we get another telegram to all the China posts saying, "Get out and get out immediately." So evidently, at the very end of December or the first few days of January 1950, policy had been decided that we were not going to recognize Communist China and, "We'd better get people out. We don't want any more potential hostages in China." Immediately, the next day, I took the lead, since I was dealing with all the local officials on leaving. I walked in first to the customs office. There was a very gentlemanly, probably non-Party member, as head of that office, whose specialty was dealing with foreigners leaving. So I said, "I would like to request the customs forms for our belongings and so forth we want to take with us." He said, "Why?" I said, "Because our entire office is leaving China as soon as possible." He looked like he'd been hit by a thunderbolt. He was very alarmed, unhappy, and I could only interpret his reaction to mean, "Oh, my God, are we going to go to war?" He was well into his sixties, I would estimate, and he'd been through a lot, the Japanese occupation and everything else, and he'd seen war conditions. He said, "Are you sure you're not going to stay?" He didn't say, "I hope you'll stay," but he implied that.

So after maybe two or three weeks, we got another telegram from the department, "What are you doing to get out of China? Why aren't you obeying our directives?" We tried to patiently explain that we were trying to obey it, but there were certain serious problems that we could not leave without permission of the Chinese Communist authorities, which didn't seem to be very well understood in Washington.

HOLLOWAY: The final act came when the Beijing authorities attempted to requisition French, British, Dutch, and American property, which had been turned over as a consequence of the Boxer conventions at the turn of the century, for military barracks.[34] And they wanted them back. We claimed they were confiscating American government property, and if they were going to do this, we were going to withdraw our consuls from China. Now, frankly, the political sophistication that came up with that kind of an argument is pretty low. The British, Dutch, and French figured a way to finesse it. We chose to make a stand on that issue. Acheson was a lawyer, and he fought a good legal case. But it was a very bad political case. On the other hand, given our backing of the Nationalists, it was obvious there was nothing for us to do.

VAN OSS: From that time on, just about all of our activities were related to closing down the consulate general and arranging for our evacuation. We also announced to all American citizens in China that the bell had now rung and if they wanted to leave China we would take them out with us. Once we were gone we couldn't guarantee the safety of or be responsible for any Americans remaining in China. We couldn't answer for what might happen to them afterwards. Some of the missionaries announced to us they would stay. As things turned out, they too had to leave eventually.

The business of trying to leave certainly was not easy. Once you got your exit permit you had to put an advertisement in the paper stating that you were going to leave on such and such a date. You had to have an exact departure date. This advertisement was supposed to indicate to anybody who had any claim whatsoever on you that you were going to leave and that you would settle all claims. Now this wasn't as easy as it sounded, because a lot of servants held their masters up and forced them to pay a year's separation pay and so on. A lot of the businessmen were being very brutally treated by their labor force. Kept awake all night bargaining, etc. Fortunately we didn't have that trouble because we were on good terms with our cook and amah and gave them as much as we could.

VAN OSS: If the ship, or whatever it was we hoped to go out on, didn't arrive, then we had to redo the whole business every month. So we had to go through roughly the same procedure on a monthly basis. This was a rather painful process.

BACON: Since everybody was likely to have some claims outstanding, possible claims by Chinese employees, personal employees, possible debts to local suppliers, everybody of course, paid up—it didn't amount to much. But the Communists demanded that a guarantor be provided for each person departing who could be held liable for any claims that might arise after the member departed. I was chosen to be the guarantor. I signed altogether upwards of 30 such, but when they finally wanted us all out, bingo. Nothing more was said about these things. A few [foreigners], necessarily, in Shanghai and Guangzhou for trade, but otherwise the whole of China was going to be a closed box, with no foreigners except Soviets admitted.

How did you get a departure date?

VAN OSS: Well now this was another laborious process. It wasn't very easy because the Nationalists had imposed a naval blockade on Shanghai and were bombing Shanghai in a rather desultory fashion. They would send a plane or two over every day and drop one or two or five or six bombs. They had armed ships out beyond the harbor entrance to enforce the blockage. And, what was worst in our eyes, was that our own government didn't want to break the blockade even to help get us out. They were on the side of the Nationalists. We were sort of annoyed. We felt that our lives and welfare should have been uppermost in our government's mind and that it should have insisted that an evacuation ship be allowed to enter. Finally we worked out, after a long hard negotiation, a scheme whereby we were to go by train to Tianjin, leave Tianjin harbor by barge, which would take us out over the bar where we would transfer from the barge to the *General Gordon*. The exodus finally took place in April 1950.

Does that mean that everyone was gone? The embassy was closed?

VAN OSS: All the official personnel were out. I would say almost all of the American citizens were out. But some were not. Some of the businessmen stayed. For example, there was a man named Bill Orchard who was head of the American Express bank in Shanghai. He had to stay because many Chinese had deposited money in his bank years before. In the meantime inflation had taken its toll. The bank wanted to return to them the actual amount they had originally deposited. But they said they wanted what the original deposit was worth now. So they wouldn't let him leave.

Were we trying to get the missionaries out?

HOLLOWAY: Yes. After we were leaving, we pointed out that we could no longer protect them. Not that we could protect them very much when we were there. We advised Americans to leave China. Obviously, some businessmen stayed. Chase and National City kept on functioning to a limited extent. Many of these men, of course, this was their lives. They didn't have an institution like the State Department to go back to which would send you out to another job.

CLOUGH: The British, in January 1950, recognized the People's Republic of China, which had been established on the first of October 1949. But they were not allowed, immediately, to set up an embassy in Beijing, which was the new capital. The British had to send a negotiating team to Beijing to negotiate the terms under which they would establish a mission there after they had recognized. They had a special problem that nobody else had. They had a consulate in Tamsui in Taiwan, which they didn't close down. Taiwan, of course, was still under the control of the Nationalists. The Communists wanted them to close that down, and they refused. As a result, the British were not able to send an ambassador to Beijing for about 20 years, until the early '70s, when they finally closed their Tamsui consulate. They had only a chargé d'affaires in Beijing.

HOLLOWAY: This was, of course, the big question, where were we split with the British and where the split was to continue for years. Do you stay and try to do business with these people, or do you declare them beyond the pale and get out? The British, who had never gotten along with the Nationalists as well as we had, they thought the Communists might work out [and formally recognized the PRC on January 6, 1950]. We thought otherwise.

But as you know, we were left there after the thing, after the capture, with the hope that there might be some eventual development. So that had there been any political will to reach an agreement with the Chinese Communists, we had plenty of time. Shanghai fell in May—May 24th, 1949. The People's Republic was proclaimed on October 1, '49. So we had plenty of time to make up our minds whether we wanted to recognize them. We chose not to; we were going to let the dust settle, as Dean Acheson said. It was all, of course, tied up with the China Lobby politics in the United States, and it became politically impossible for Truman to take that step.

DEVELOPMENTS IN TAIWAN

With the end of the Pacific War, the island of Taiwan reverted to Chinese control by agreement of the wartime allies at Cairo (1943), Teheran (1944), and Potsdam (1945). The Nationalists, however, reclaimed Taiwan as an occupying rather than liberating force, treating the people as collaborators with their Japanese overlords and indiscriminately looting the island. They excluded the Taiwanese from political participation and introduced inflation, corruption, and disease. American Foreign Service officers were pessimistic about the ability of the Nationalists to sustain their rule under such circumstances.

OSBORN: The situation in China was disintegrating badly in 1949. It was becoming obvious that the government of Chiang Kai-shek—the GMD—would very likely end up going to Taiwan; or at least that was a strong possibility. So it was of interest to the United States, and the Department of State, whether the situation in Taiwan would be stable enough to allow Chiang to take refuge there. The GMD's misrule in Taiwan, in 1947, had already provoked an uprising there, in which some thousands of people were killed [the February 28 Incident]; and there was some possibility that the Taiwanese might not exactly welcome Chiang Kai-shek.[35]

At any rate, the Department of State wanted to get a fix on the situation in Taiwan. Now the people in Taiwan, at that time, spoke Japanese. They had been through the Japanese educational system, and it was possible to communicate with them in Japanese. I happened to be, probably, the most available Japanese language speaker at that time, so I was sent to Taiwan.

We were all—on Taiwan—debating the pros and cons of a United States commitment to Taiwan; the argument being between those who felt that the United States had been pouring sand down a rat hole in trying to help the forces of Chiang Kai-shek, and the forces of the China

Lobby who argued that we had never aided Chiang Kai-shek enough, and we should now do more. This debate was so powerful that we all became engaged in it.

The old China hands had—during the war—tended to favor working toward some kind of mutual understanding with the Chinese Communists, which would avoid conflict there. Whereas there were many people who assumed that conflict between us and Communist China eventually was inevitable, and that we should simply prepare ourselves for it. These debates were going back and forth, and that's how the Strait issue assumed its most urgent form.

MARTIN: What I do remember about that fall of '49, particularly, was several things. One was the fact that the Communists failed to take Jinmen [Quemoy]. That is something you can't blow up too much, but perhaps hasn't been given enough attention. That was a real morale boost. After all, the Nationalists, in the last six months, had been swept so easily away. But the Communists obviously underestimated the will to fight—maybe it was the combination of will to fight plus the difficulty of making this rather short but still amphibious attack. They were beaten back, and they didn't try it again.

Another interesting thing that happened during that period in Taiwan was a rather ambiguous message which came from the State Department at the end of October, which we were supposed to go to Chiang Kai-shek with, which said, in effect, that we thought that the Nationalists had enough materiel and equipment and so forth on Taiwan to defend the island adequately. The message was sort of mixed, because on the one hand, it was the first communication we had sent from Washington to Chiang Kai-shek since he'd retired.[36] It was sort of an acknowledgment that he was the head man, although at that time he had not yet actually reassumed his title. So in a sense, it was a kind of a boost for him. On the other hand, it wasn't a very clear-cut statement of just what we were going to do.

Ambassador [Philip] Jessup came over.[37] It was in January of '50. It was right around in there. He had an interview with Chiang Kai-shek, in which I was present. Chiang did most of the talking. He thought it was a matter of time before Japan went communist, and Southeast Asia was bound to go the same way. War between the U.S. and the Soviet Union was inevitable. Conclusion: the U.S. must support his anti-communist fight. Our own military estimates were that it was just a matter of time before the communists would attack Taiwan and that they would be able to conquer it. There was a lot of reporting about the fact that the Communists were massing junks on the Fujian coast. Another indication of what the State Department anticipated was that we evacuated dependents, especially families with children, and we cut down on the staff in anticipation that there would be an invasion.

VAN OSS: Another policy aim [for the Communists], of course, was to go across to Taiwan, defeat the Nationalist forces and capture the "running dog," Chiang Kai-shek. Little kindergarten kids, instead of playing ring-around-the-rosy, performed little skits about rowing across the Straits, catching Chiang Kai-shek, and then pretending to beat up the child playing the part of Chiang with pillows.

Why do you think the Communists did not actually attack Taiwan during that period?

MARTIN: They were, as I said, surprised by their failure on Jinmen, and this was a heck of a lot bigger operation. They needed to accumulate a lot of transport and get a lot more training and perhaps try to get air superiority.

Another reason might have been that, after all, they had launched their offensive across the Yangzi at Nanjing in April of 1949, and in the next six months they had taken all of South China, and by the fall of 1949, late fall, they had taken most of West China as well. It was enormous territory. And then they had set up their government. It was set up on the first of October 1949. In other words, they had a lot of things that were preoccupying them, and having been set back at Jinmen, they probably just hadn't been able to organize and prepare well enough.

Were you puzzled at the time by American policy?

MARTIN: Yes, I remember that we were puzzled. We didn't really know what the signal was supposed to be. It was sort of, "We wish you all sorts of success, and we think you can defend the island. You've got enough matériel here and so forth," but we were very cautious about any kind of support we were going to commit ourselves to. We felt rather unhappy that we were getting such mixed signals, that we were not getting more clear-cut—it sort of left us in a difficult position.

Did you feel you were in any position to influence policy from Washington at this time?

MARTIN: Well, Bob Strong [Robert C. Strong, chargé d'affaires] was in charge, and was a person who was quite outspoken. Strong was very skeptical of the capabilities of the GRC [Government of the Republic of China] to do any better and to hold out. He had very little faith that Taiwan would last. So the mood, in other words, is well reflected in Truman's statement that the U.S. would keep hands off Taiwan.[38]

Did you formulate an impression of how well or badly the Guomindang was administering Taiwan?

MARTIN: Well, we didn't feel that they were administering it too well, but there was an improvement as compared to the time of Governor Ch'en Yi, which was in '47, when they had the riots and so forth. You still got overtones of that from the Taiwanese. But in fact, due in large part to our stimulus, under Governor Ch'en Ch'eng (who was the governor in '49, replaced by K.C. Wu about the end of that year or beginning of '50) there was a land reform program going on there which was one of the best land reform programs that I know of anywhere in that part of the world. Under this land reform program, large landowners were deprived of the land which they had over a reasonable minimum. They were compensated partly in rice and partly in industrial bonds. This was administered by a joint Chinese-U.S. organization, the Joint Commission on Rural Reconstruction [JCRR].[39] The Chinese side's man was Chiang Mon-lin. He was the chairman. On the U.S. side Ray Moyer was the principal member. It gave the Taiwanese a stake in the industrialization of Taiwan, and we all know how successful that's been in the long run. It led also to an increase in agricultural production in Taiwan.

GRANT: Chiang Mon-lin was really one of the great men I've ever dealt with, and earned the faith of the Taiwan peasant. They did all the things that are needed to make land reform work, setting up marketing cooperatives, credit cooperatives, seed purchasing organizations. In other words, really mobilizing the farm sector. That was a tremendous advantage for Chiang Kai-shek. The Taiwanese anti-Guomindang movement, the people who were trying to get the Guomindang out of Taiwan, had very little support in the countryside because of Chiang Mon-lin.

MARTIN: The program was well administered, and it was probably because the Nationalists were fairly desperate then. Certainly land reform on the mainland, if it had been carried out like this, might have been quite decisive in the future of China. But by the time we came to Taiwan, the Nationalists were more amenable to do what we advised. Also, Taiwan's a small place, and it's much easier to do it there than it was in a very large land mass with a huge population.

Under the Japanese, of course, Taiwan had become more developed than probably any single province in China. I remember being impressed when I first went there by the fact that electricity was very widely available in small towns and that it was so cheap that people would keep the lights burning in their little shops all day. You have to be very cautious about saying, "Well, if they'd only done this on the mainland." It was a lot easier in Taiwan. But they did do it; I think that's important.

You got to know Chiang Ching-kuo.

MARTIN: Yes. Chiang Ching-kuo was an enigma in a way. He came there from Shanghai with a rather bad reputation. He was a fairly young guy. He had studied in Russia and he had a Russian wife. I didn't have a great deal of business to take up with him, but I found him fairly easy to talk to and less dogmatic than his father seemed to be, although I can't say I ever got really well acquainted with Chiang Kai-shek. Ching-kuo was a person that seemed to me to be more realistic about going back to the mainland. Naturally, that was the line, and nobody was going to undercut it, but he struck me as being a fairly down-to-earth, practical sort of guy. Obviously, he was prepared to execute people, and he did. But he wasn't a dogmatic tyrannical person at all. That was not my impression of him.

ON THE EVE OF THE KOREAN WAR

During the early months of 1950, as Mao Zedong labored to consolidate his new government, Kim Il Sung confronted a far less favorable environment. Although he had assistance from the Soviet Union, he contended with political rivals in North Korea and a determined foe to the south—a foe who's lack of domestic popularity was offset by support from the United States.

But it appeared that Washington's aid would not extend to the battlefield, and so Kim was able, after repeated attempts, to persuade Stalin and Mao to agree to let him wage a campaign to reunify Korea. Mao may have been reluctant to risk distraction from his own internal agenda, but could not say no to Kim, so China offered encouragement and took measures to put troops in place to protect China and rescue Kim should that prove necessary.

MANHARD: [A mysterious neighbor in Tianjin told me] "There will be very soon, we don't know exactly when, an all out offensive against South Korea. There will be more Chinese forces coming through Tianjin en route to Manchuria. We don't know whether they will participate in the initial offensive against South Korea with the North Korean troops, whether the North Korean troops alone will conduct the initial offensive with the Chinese troops in backup positions within North Korea, or whether the Chinese troops in that case would be held on the Chinese side in a back position in the case of need. Please tell my friend Mr. Freeman." On the fourth of June, boiling hot, opening of business on Monday morning, I went straight to see Tony Freeman. A week later he said, "I checked it out with the Korean desk, and they said there was nothing to that because there's no indication of anything happening in North Korea, and our main problem now is to prevent Syngman Rhee [president of the Republic of Korea] from marching north. That's our main problem in Korea." What could I do?

GREEN: What I can't remember historically is exactly what the line was that we were about to take in the time when the Korean War broke out. I think we were beginning to consider quite seriously at that time whether we shouldn't move our policy towards recognizing the realities of Mainland China, that the Chinese had taken over, and that they did represent one-quarter of humanity, and that we had to have some kind of relationship with them. I think Acheson was thinking that way. I'm sure that this was a line of thought that was widely shared. I'm sure that men like Walton Butterworth, who was the assistant secretary of state for East Asian Affairs at that time, thought that way. I was very close to him. I was working on Japanese affairs; that's why I'm not completely clear as to what all the details were. But had the war in Korea not intervened, it is possible that our China policy could have moved in a different direction.

1950s

THE NORTH KOREAN attack across the 38th parallel came as a surprise to the American government and the public even though there were warning signs, some reported by Foreign Service officers in China. President Truman concluded immediately that the assault demonstrated the malevolence of the communist bloc, which seemed suddenly to be more of a monolith than many had thought. The immediate government reaction was to rally its forces and the world community in opposition. Truman promptly sent in air and naval units, quickly followed by ground troops. The United Nations Security Council approved an American-sponsored resolution on June 25, calling for an end to hostilities and withdrawal of North Korean forces. On June 27, it urged military resistance. The Security Council proved able to act quickly because Moscow was at the time boycotting the UN in protest against Chiang Kai-shek's continued possession of the Chinese seat.

Communist troops did not stop their advance and soon had driven South Korean and United Nations soldiers to a tiny foothold at the southern end of the peninsula at Pusan. But the international coalition, dominated by the United States, fought its way back until, in September 1950, the American commander of UN troops, General Douglas MacArthur, staged a risky but brilliant maneuver at Inchon and then charged across the 38th parallel, determined to reunify Korea under free world auspices. Late in November, he mounted a final offensive designed to have American boys home by Christmas.

Beijing had long since warned against such campaigns, broadly hinting that it would intervene, and in October it sent its men across the Yalu River. The United States did not heed its initial probing attacks, and Beijing unloosed full-scale warfare against exposed American forces in November, again driving United States/United Nations forces south. Eventually the fighting stabilized along the 38th parallel, and after the death of Joseph Stalin, exhausted Chinese officials accepted an armistice agreement that Washington imposed upon reluctant South Korean authorities.

The result of all this for Sino-American relations, not surprisingly, was an era of hostility. American hopes for a semi-independent China disappeared into the swift moving currents of anti-communism, to be revived only cautiously and indecisively during the Eisenhower administration. With American soldiers dying on Korean battlefields under the guns of Red Chinese "hordes," Washington abruptly abandoned interest in bettering relations with Beijing. The decision to place the U.S. Seventh Fleet in the Taiwan Strait in the first hours of the Korean conflict, moreover, although designed to be a temporary effort to prevent expansion of the war, grew into a tighter commitment to the preservation of the Nationalist Chinese regime. From China's perspective, therefore, the Americans had not only threatened security in the industrial northeast, taking a significant toll on Chinese troops in the war, depleting China's already weak economy, and preventing concentration on rehabilitation, but it had also thwarted completion of the civil war and reunification of the nation.

During the 1950s, Chiang Kai-shek, with considerable American assistance, proved able to consolidate control over the island of Taiwan. Carrying out changes that had seemed impossible on the mainland, particularly land reform, the Nationalists slowly constructed a more efficient and effective government, which, while repressing the political rights of the Taiwanese majority,[1] gave them scope to launch an economic revival. These were not yet days of miraculous growth. Among other impediments were the huge military budgets that sapped limited resources. Chiang remained determined to recover the mainland and sustained an unrealistically large military establishment dedicated to that proposition. Nevertheless, behind the shield that American forces provided, Taiwan prospered.

During the 1950s, the shield also became more formal. In 1953, among his first acts as president, Dwight Eisenhower "unleashed" Chiang, announcing that U.S. naval ships in the Strait would protect Taiwan from Chinese Communist attack but would not inhibit Nationalist operations against the mainland. In fact, although this was public policy, privately American leaders made clear to Chiang that they would not sanction any large scale attack on China that might drag the United States into war. The provocative rhetoric of Secretary of State John Foster Dulles aimed at protecting the administration against the right wing of his own Republican party rather than at altering the behavior of Beijing officials.

But the administration's policies frightened and angered Beijing. Chinese officials believed that American policies were designed to encircle and isolate China, as well as to sever Taiwan from the mainland permanently. Determined to try to convince Washington that its support for Chiang and increasing involvement in the region would bring it nothing but trouble, in 1954, Mao Zedong initiated the shelling of two groups of offshore islands, Jinmen (Quemoy) and Mazu (Matsu). Mao specifically objected to creation of the Southeast Asia Treaty Organization and a rumored alliance treaty with the Nationalists. Ironically, although welcoming the multilateral security arrangement in southeast Asia, Dulles had been trying to avoid an alliance with Taiwan. Early in 1954, he delayed consideration of a pact by claiming it would interfere with the Geneva Conference on Korea and Indochina scheduled for the spring, preferring to maintain his flexibility and suspicious of Chiang's willingness to involve Washington in a new war. But the offshore island attacks and the need to take the issue to the UN for resolution forced Dulles to capitulate to Chiang on a defense treaty to prevent his use of a Security Council veto. Further, the crisis in the Strait prompted Congress to vote for the Formosa Resolution in 1955, which empowered the president to use American forces to protect Taiwan. This mandate would be employed in 1958 when Beijing again shelled the islands and took the United States and China once more to the brink of war.

In analyzing each of these Taiwan Straits crises as they occurred, American policy makers feared that the Chinese Communists hoped to seize the offshore islands as a first step in capturing Taiwan itself. Dulles tried repeatedly to persuade Chiang to evacuate his forces from Jinmen lest their loss seriously undermine his power and the morale of his people. But Mao may not have intended to seize these islands, and also was not yet powerful enough to attempt the capture of Taiwan. Domestic developments, such as the suppression of the Hundred Flowers Campaign [1956–1957] and the initiation of the Great Leap Forward [1958–1961], played a role in encouraging a bold policy facilitating mobilization of the public. Documents released in recent years suggest that Mao sought to challenge Chiang and to further tensions between Taipei and Washington but did not want to take the offshore islands because that would risk promoting Taiwan independence and furthering Dulles' unacceptable "two Chinas" policy.

Dulles did hope to initiate a new policy in which the United States would be able to deal with both the China based on Taiwan and the authorities dominating the mainland. He distrusted and disliked Chiang and found the association with Nationalist China uncomfortable. He was willing to be a bit more tractable toward Communist China and explored possible ways of getting China into the United Nations without having to throw Taiwan out. But the policy had no future as neither Taipei nor Beijing would accept it.

The approach was also opposed at home by the China Lobby, which grew in strength during the decade. At first the attacks on American policy came most stridently from Senator Joseph McCarthy as he denounced the presence of alleged communists in the government and berated officials for the loss of China. Even after his malign influence waned, however, the coalition of pro-Chiang members of Congress, the press, academia, and the business community continued to attack any potential weakening of established China policy, focusing on preventing American recognition of the Communist government and keeping Beijing out of the UN. In these areas they proved quite successful, forcing the administration to expend considerable effort to keep its friends and allies around the world committed to a UN exclusion strategy increasingly objectionable in foreign capitals. At the same time, China Lobby activism discouraged realistic analysis of Sino-Soviet relations and delayed realization that a serious rift had developed between the erstwhile allies.

Throughout the 1950s, paralleling the crises that kept relations tenuous, the United States and China talked to each other in a series of negotiations that produced few tangible agreements, but kept the channels of communication open and may have contributed to avoiding armed conflict. The first discussions at Panmunjom regarding a Korean War settlement taxed the patience and resolve of the American team and never yielded a peace treaty. At the Geneva Conference on Korea and Indochina in the spring of 1954, American officials appeared as concerned about not promoting China's international prestige as they were about reaching any agreements on Korea. But, despite their reluctance to deal with the Chinese, Americans found themselves committed to continuing negotiations directly with Beijing, initially in hopes of securing the release of Americans imprisoned in China, and later to effect a renunciation of force in the Taiwan Strait. The bilateral ambassadorial talks, first at Geneva and later at Warsaw, although held irregularly, provided the United States better access to Chinese officials than was given to many countries whose representatives resided in Beijing.

The breakdown in Sino-American relations occasioned by the communist victory in the Chinese civil war and Washington's refusal to recognize that victory elevated the importance of areas on the periphery of Mainland China: Hong Kong, Taiwan, and overseas Chinese communities in southeast Asia. American Foreign Service officers who would have been posted to China in normal times found themselves looking in from a distance, trying to assess developments in a rapidly changing society. The consulate general in Hong Kong, for instance, grew tremendously in size and devoted much of its energies to gauging China's economic performance, its military capabilities, and the satisfaction/dissatisfaction of its people. These activities became especially significant at times of crisis inside China, as during the Hundred Flowers Campaign and the Great Leap Forward, when China was in tumult. Further, these diplomats had to deal with repercussions of such upheavals, including the influx of refugees from China and the efforts of many to find ways to emigrate to the United States. In Southeast Asia, China specialists were posted to countries having large overseas Chinese populations to monitor sentiment toward the Chinese Communists and assist Taiwan in winning the struggle for hearts and minds.

In Taiwan itself, American efforts to encourage growth and change did not always meet with government appreciation or public approval. In 1957, in what was probably a choreographed response to a racist verdict in an American military court, rioters sacked the U.S. Embassy and USIA headquarters. The outburst caught the American ambassador by surprise and forced Washington to accept that its ally resented some of the advice being proffered so liberally, especially American opposition to plans to return to the mainland.

KOREA

The Korean War led to tougher U.S. policies in Europe and Asia. Washington concluded that a massive communist conspiracy was at work. In the European theater of the Cold War, the United States rapidly militarized NATO. What flexibility there may have been regarding relations with the new communist regime in China evaporated.

OSBORN: In 1950, the Korean War broke out. This had the effect of freezing the positions on both sides of the Taiwan Strait. We feared an attack, so we put the Seventh Fleet in the Strait. The Chinese on the mainland saw the action as a United States declaration of hostility towards China, as a step towards seizing Taiwan. It's important to note that from the Chinese Communist standpoint, we put the Seventh Fleet in the Strait before they had challenged our position on Taiwan, militarily certainly. We put the fleet there in anticipation of a Chinese Communist threat to Taiwan. So that was the origin of the question, from the Chinese Communist side. From our side the question also had a strong domestic-political component. That is to say, people were still arguing whether we were doing the right thing to support Chiang Kai-shek, or whether we should write him off as a bad bet.

Did the Korean War, which started in June 1950, change much of what you were doing?

JOHNSON: Yes, it intensified the battle between those who were in support of Chiang Kai-shek and felt we should demonstrate that support by large aid programs, and the more conservative forces that didn't see much benefit for the U.S. in further supporting the GIMO. I say that because when General MacArthur came back from Korea, a great deal of this sentiment coalesced around him. He was a very strong exponent for helping Chiang Kai-shek, because he felt that was a good hope for getting at the Chinese Communists.[2]

HUMMEL: It changed a lot of things for the China specialists, because there was no longer any lingering hope that we could find a way to live with Mao Zedong. We were at war with him. We had suspended all aid—both military and civilian—to Chiang Kai-shek in 1949, in an effort to build a relationship with the Communists, to no avail.[3] A lot of people have forgotten that. We didn't reinstate aid to Taiwan until the attack on the Republic of Korea in June 1950. The whole mood of our country changed. After all, there was a Sino-Soviet bloc, and there was reason to believe that the whole Soviet bloc was testing us out in Korea. It was a matter of life and death, not only for Koreans, but also for American foreign policy in general.

By the way, conditions were pretty grim [in China]. The Chinese Communists were knocking off landlords and other "undesirable class elements" or "class enemies." It was no longer a question of whether we should speak out about what was going to happen in China. That stage had passed. Nobody knew what was going to happen in China. There was no possibility of a rapprochement with the Chinese Communists.

GRANT: We were listening to missionaries and other Americans, White Russians, foreigners, who were now being chased out of China by these so-called work teams, teams of young fanatics that the Communists were sending in to consolidate their control of the countryside. They were getting rid of everybody that represented an alternative source of authority. One of the sources of authority might very well be the missionaries. So they were setting them up, charging them with all manner of things, organizing the peasants to go by, and show themselves sufficiently pro-Communist by spitting on the poor missionaries and so on. It was a rough experience, and they were coming out very shaken. We were beginning to learn both of the roughness of the regime and also to recognize how totally they were extirpating any source of challenge.[4]

How did you feel about the permanence of Chiang Kai-shek and the GMD on Taiwan?

CLOUGH: We didn't have a lot of confidence in the future of the GMD on Taiwan. Of course, once Truman had made the decision to put the Seventh Fleet in the Taiwan Strait, then it was obvious that the Communists didn't have the military capability of overcoming that kind of obstacle. So, in that sense, the GMD was safe. But I don't think those of us who had been associated with the GMD in China had any confidence that they could turn things around the way they actually did. It was quite a remarkable feat.

Did you worry about the Chinese getting involved in Korea?

CLOUGH: We had reports of the Chinese moving troops from south to north, toward Manchuria. These were rather persistent and rather well established. That was the main question coming at us from Washington. They wanted any information that we could get on what the Chinese attitude toward Korea was. We scrambled around to pick up every scrap of information we could.[5]

In late September, Zhou Enlai made a speech in which he warned that they couldn't tolerate the destruction of a neighboring country, or something to that effect. At about the same time [October 3], we got a warning through Ambassador [K.M.] Panikkar, the Indian ambassador in Beijing, from Zhou Enlai, to the effect that we should take this seriously.[6] And there began to be reports then of an occasional Chinese being captured in northern Korea.

The question then was: Were the Chinese serious? Were they going to come in, in force, or were they just trying to intimidate us or deter us? MacArthur decided, on the basis of his intelligence, that it was the latter, and he issued his famous statement about getting the boys out of the trenches by Christmas.[7] Went ploughing full steam ahead. The Inchon landing was September 15, and they moved north quite rapidly over the 38th Parallel. The question was whether they should go all the way to the Yalu. I had one White Russian informant in Hong Kong who had lived in Manchuria, and he would get messages from time to time. He told me that the Chinese were having people put tape on their windows in the event of bombing, a suggestion that perhaps they were expecting to get involved in the war in Korea.

The most notable incident was when we had a Chinese who came down from Beijing. He had been known to the consulate general there. He turned up one day in Hong Kong, and told us that there had just been a very important meeting in Beijing at which all of the members of the Democratic League and the other so-called democratic parties had been called in, and they had been told that there was a new slogan: "Resist America. Help Korea." There was going to be a full-scale campaign on this all over China.[8]

I should say that that message from Panikkar, the Indian ambassador, was not taken as seriously in Washington as it turned out it should have been, largely because of Panikkar's own views. He was known in Nanjing as being very pro-Communist, and he wasn't regarded as an entirely reliable intermediary. I've often thought afterwards that if Zhou Enlai had given that message to, say, the Norwegian ambassador in Beijing, instead of the Indian ambassador, it might have been taken more seriously.[9]

MANHARD: My next assignment was in Pusan, Korea. INR [Intelligence and Research Bureau at the State Department] gave orders to me to go interrogate Chinese prisoners of war in our camps in South Korea, early 1951 to early 1953. Many of the Chinese—this is low level, mostly illiterate, uneducated, peasant people, who were captured during the war in

Korea—had been in Chinese Nationalist units captured by the Communists, converted and integrated into the Chinese Communist Army after they occupied the mainland. Many of them had been stationed with units in the lower Yangzi River area. They had been told—this is just shortly after the Korean War started—that their training mission, including practicing landing craft going across the Yangzi River, was to go liberate Taiwan, and that was what they thought they were getting trained for. But suddenly, without any preparation or warning, they were told, "Get on a train. Your unit is going to the Northeast." When they crossed the Yalu River, they realized that they were going to fight in Korea. It came as a great surprise to these young men, they said. The Chinese communist priority was Taiwan; Korea was not. When some decision at some level was made to go and pull the fat out of the fire in Korea, it was, in my opinion, more logically a Soviet priority than a Chinese priority.[10]

Were you seeing anything about getting ready to go into Korea?

CLOUGH: I remember from time to time we sort of added up the pros and cons as to whether the Chinese were planning to come on a large scale. We came down on the side that they probably weren't. I think that was based on a misreading of the Chinese. A feeling that, after all, their government was less than a year old. They still were in the process of consolidating their rule in China. They were poor. They had a long road ahead of them. Was this the time to get involved in a full-scale war with a country like the United States, which was the most powerful military state in the world?

After brutal fighting and heavy losses, the war reached a stalemate. How was this received in China?

HOLDRIDGE: Well, the Chinese were, of course, cock-a-hoop, if you will. They had defeated the Americans, or so it would seem. It was a stalemate. But just holding back American power was sufficient for them. It gave them an enormous shot in the arm, psychologically speaking.

MARTIN: I was the only person that was involved in the Panmunjom [peace talks], the Geneva, and the Warsaw talks. So I was in at the very ground floor, you might say, of our first diplomatic contacts with the Chinese Communists after the Korean War.

The thing that struck me rather strongly when we got together with Arthur Dean, who was leader [of the UN delegation] and a New York corporation lawyer, not a diplomat, (although he had diplomatic assignments before) was that he was very strongly convinced that we must get an agreement with the Chinese for the sake of the Eisenhower administration.[11] I thought that our chances were very slim. He was telling the press we could do it in two weeks. Well, he finally walked out of the talks. He walked out in December, and I don't think he ever forgave me for being right about that. It wasn't that I wanted them to fail, it's just that I didn't think the situation was one in which the Chinese had that much flexibility. This particularly was true because, after all, we were negotiating there in the DMZ, and also going on in the DMZ were these prisoner interrogations. It was pretty obvious, once the prisoners began to opt not to return to China, that the Chinese couldn't let this go on, so there were all sorts of disturbances which prevented the interrogation. Finally, the prisoners were released. They were told, "That's the way south; that's the way north," and most of them went south.[12]

Well, all during this hassle in the fall of '53, where the Chinese and the North Koreans were accusing us of sabotaging the armistice, it was just not the kind of atmosphere where they're going to reach an agreement implementing the armistice agreement.

What kind of agreement was Dean actually hoping to reach? Was it a peace treaty with the Chinese?

MARTIN: No, no. This was very limited. This was a very limited negotiation, and maybe that was why he felt we could accomplish it. Under Paragraph 60 of the armistice agreement, the two sides were to meet, to discuss the future of Korea, and arrive at some political settlement. Well, our negotiations in Panmunjom were merely to make arrangements to set up the conference: it was not the conference itself. As far as we were concerned, there were only two things to talk about: when would the conference be held and where would it be held. The Chinese and the North Koreans wanted to discuss the composition of the conference. We felt the composition of the conference had already been settled by Paragraph 60, and actually, that language about the two sides was originally introduced by the Communist side. So one wouldn't expect that they would make an issue of this, but they did. They wanted to have neutral countries, and they wanted to have the Soviet Union there. We said, "We don't object to the Soviet Union being there, but we can't call it neutral. It's completely on your side." So this is what we wrangled about, and we never got anywhere on that. But it should be pointed out that in Berlin, in January '54, an agreement was reached to have a conference on Korea and on Indochina to convene in Geneva in April of 1954.[13] But anyway, that Panmunjom exercise was an exercise in complete futility.

Our main problem at the Korean end of the Geneva conference (and that's why I was an advisor to the U.S. delegation, because of my experience in Panmunjom), was, as it often was, of getting the South Koreans to go along and to present a united front. We finally succeeded in getting a position which we could offer as the UN side's position, and it was rejected by the Communists, which wasn't surprising, and the conference went on to deal with Indochina, where they really did something. So it's not surprising that people forget about the Korean part because nothing came out of it at all.

The South Koreans actually had not signed the armistice.

MARTIN: No, they had not signed the armistice, that's true. And we didn't want them to denounce our proposal [at Geneva], because it would look very poor: the Communists could always come back and say, "Well, look, the South Koreans don't agree to this."

Can you tell us something about Zhou Enlai who you saw in action in Geneva?

MARTIN: Well, he had been a Chinese opera actor as a student, you know, so he was a dramatic fellow, and he had this high-pitched voice which was perhaps a little . . .

Women's parts.

MARTIN: Yes, perhaps that's why he did women's parts. But that came across when he was making his points. What he said was pretty much to be expected.

U.S. CHINA POLICY I

China policy under the Eisenhower administration has often been seen as far tougher than policy in the Truman years. The Foreign Service officers speaking here, however, generally agree, toughness was more illusion than reality. Policy changed little between the two administrations. The Korean War and developments inside China were more important in changing American perceptions than American politics. Belligerent rhetoric, on the other hand, did serve the purpose of fending off attacks on the White House and the State Department.

MARTIN: The difference between the China policy under Truman in his last year and the Eisenhower policy toward China was very little. It was mainly cosmetic, and I can illustrate that point. My first job was chief of political section [Office of Chinese Affairs], and that was during the Truman year [1952]. The next year I became deputy director. It had nothing to do with the change in administration; it was just internal bureaucratic things. We drafted an NSC paper on China policy in that last year [of Truman]. It was as many NSC papers are. There was nothing basically new in it, but it reflected accurately what the policy was [in 1952]. And for some reason or other, it never got through the whole NSC process until [1953], which was the Eisenhower administration. This business about Chiang Kai-shek being "unleashed" by Eisenhower. That was simply when the Eisenhower administration said, "We will no longer prevent them from attacking the mainland." Well, as you can find in the documents, actually we made very sure that the Chinese on Taiwan understood that we would not support them and we would very much oppose their going to the mainland without our approval, and we had no intention of approving it.

Having been in the department and on the China desk during that particular transition period, the rhetoric got a lot tougher, but the basic policies, there wasn't much we could change. It was because our China policy had been set by the Korean War and by our response to the Korean War, basically, and especially after the Chinese intervened. I mean, we were already committed by Truman to defend Taiwan. I never saw any indication that Mr. Dulles, let alone President Eisenhower, were willing to back any kind of mainland invasion. But getting somebody like Walter Robertson in there, who was a very nice guy but a fairly hard-liner, not an extremist by any means, you had somebody who could go down there and talk to the right-wingers who were pretty strong in the Senate at that time.

What was the role of Walter Robertson?

BOWIE: Well, Robertson was quite genuinely a Southern gentleman. He was really the soul of courtesy and a very decent, fine person. He was absolutely committed to the support for Chiang Kai-shek and to the conviction that the Chinese Communists were a source of evil. He dedicated himself to whatever could be done to maintain the position and American support for Chiang and to oppose anything which in any way suggested or implied acceptance of Communist China. And those were the guidelines which he pursued whatever the situation. And of course he was really dedicated to this cause. But Robertson was too decent a person to be a real zealot. For example, he knew very well that from time to time I'd taken a different view about China. Not that I had illusions about China, I didn't think we were going to have a friendship with China at that stage, but it was just a question of how much resources you devoted and how much you still nurtured what to me was the total illusion about Chiang's real role. I saw no reason either why we should abandon Chiang or Taiwan, but still it was a question really of perception, of what was the role, what was the future. He was just as strong in his convictions as many of these right-wing people in the Republican Party. But as a human being he was a good deal more attractive.

GREEN: Walter Robertson dominated the China field. He was very much of a Sino-centric when it came to East Asian policy, a great man, but a very, very strong, ardent supporter of Chiang Kai-shek, and had absolutely no use for the more balanced view that some of us took with regard to Chinese issues. However, he was very much the voice of the administration at that time and had the strong support of the China Lobby. I found that, while writing speeches for him, they would only pass muster if I pledged allegiance to Chiang Kai-shek.

HOLDRIDGE: I can remember Walter Robertson always talking about the Chinese Communists and how they had killed 20 million people. This was the era of the Committee of One Million in the United States, Congressman Walter Judd, Senator [William] Knowland from Oakland,

California, and Admiral [Arthur W.] Radford [commander-in-chief, Pacific (CINCPAC) until July 1953 and thereafter chairman of the Joint Chiefs of Staff]. This is the environment in which we labored. Of course, McCarthy was floating around in the background.

BREMENT: Walter Robertson was quite a desk-banger, and could handle a meeting better than anybody I've ever seen in the U.S. government. In terms of getting his way, he almost always did.

MARTIN: I do think that in the mid-50s—and this is pure speculation— that under Dulles and Robertson and Eisenhower, our response to some Chinese overtures was tougher than it might have been under another administration. But since China policy was a political issue on the Hill, the Republicans had to do whatever they could to make it look like they were pursing a different policy.

Did McCarthy affect what was going on in the Far East Bureau?

HUMMEL: Not particularly. When the Communists took over in 1949, they showed themselves not to be agrarian reformers, and they showed that they were not abiding by their promises to have a multiparty system and accommodate other parties. Also, because of the well-documented killing of landlords and class enemies, there wasn't anybody who wanted to do anything differently in American policy; particularly after the Korean War started there was no occasion for dissent. Our relations with China, whatever they were, did not leave room for anybody to be thinking about conciliation or advancing heretical views about American policy. We were all polarized by these events.

Were you getting any corridor talk about: Boy, watch this McCarthyism business?

CLOUGH: Oh, yes. We were getting quite a lot of that. Not formally, but through the back door. It worried us, because, after all, we were China specialists, we were China language people. But we were not caught up in it, because we were not in responsible positions at the time that China was lost. All of us, who were trained after the war, were the new generation, and we were reasonably confident that nothing serious would happen to us, because the whole attitude of the United States toward China had changed. Of course, we heard the rumblings of all the

McCarthy attacks on Foreign Service officers. We were concerned, but I never found that that affected our reporting particularly. Perhaps we were in a more fortunate position, because we were in the period of war with China, and everybody was hostile to China.

Did you feel that one had really to watch what one said about China?

THAYER: Some older Foreign Service officers in Hong Kong did feel that they needed to pull some punches specifically because of concern about the psychology of Washington. I don't think it meant not reporting facts, it's just that one was cautious. And I remember at about the same time, there was some concern about being seen reading a communist publication on the bus, for example.

HOLLOWAY: I'll show you the sort of clumsy thing they did. The security officer would come around [in Hong Kong in 1952–1957] and start asking me about a fellow I'd served with in Shanghai. And then the next day, he'd go to that fellow, who was working in say the political section, and say, "Now, you served with Jerry Holloway in Shanghai. What did he do there? What was his ideology? Did he have any Chinese girlfriends or anything like that?" It was very clumsy, but enough to make things uneasy. And there were some incidents that were not very pretty. There seemed to be—I wouldn't say an attempt to set us against each other, but Big Brother was looking over your shoulder in a way that he didn't used to.

Did you have any feeling that you'd better not make your reports too positive?

HOLLOWAY: For instance, there was this organization called ECAFE, the Economic Commission for Asia and the Far East, which was a UN subsidiary. It put out an annual economic report on Asia. The State Department arranged so that we had a veto. We went over it in draft, to take out anything too favorable to the People's Republic. As you know, our policy was, as Walter Robertson, expressed it, to keep pressure on the mainland in the hope that a revolt would ensue there, of which we or the Nationalists could take advantage. Dulles spoke quite openly. You can read it in Ridgway's memoirs,[14] of how to invade China through Korea. This was part of the purpose of keeping Li Mi and the Chinese Nationalist Divisions in Burma resupplied.[15] It was our aim—we were hoping for the overthrow of the Chinese Communist government, and to suggest that this government was fairly permanent was to fly in the face of policy.

NEGOTIATION WITH THE PRC

Although the United States and the People's Republic of China did not have diplomatic relations, beginning in 1954, they talked more frequently than Beijing did with the representatives of virtually any other nation. The early Geneva negotiations did solve some of the prisoner problems arising from the Chinese civil war and the Korean War, but few other concrete accomplishments resulted. This seemed generally to be the case because the two sides were never flexible at the same time. Nevertheless, the simple fact of meeting face-to-face, first in Geneva and later in Warsaw, had a positive impact in helping to avoid war, as became apparent at the time of the 1958 Taiwan Straits Crisis.

KREISBERG: We were aware—although some of us later than others—of what had been happening in Geneva with Alex Johnson,[16] specifically proposing normalization to John Foster Dulles in his bathroom. A great bathroom story. At one point during the Geneva talks when—what was it, '54–'55—Dulles was in his bathroom taking a bath, and Alex Johnson came in to describe the conversation he had been having with [Ambassador] Wang Bingnan.[17] He essentially said that the Chinese were willing to strike a deal on normalization, which would involve release of prisoners and meeting of virtually all the conditions that we had set. He recommended to Dulles that we accept it and begin the negotiations on that. And Dulles categorically and said, "No, we will not do it." I love the image of Dulles lying in his bathtub while Ambassador Johnson is sitting on the toilet. It was obviously one of these large Swiss bathrooms. It would have meant that we would have broken our relations with Taiwan, or that we would have some other kind of association with Taiwan. Conceivably where we are now except twenty years earlier.

Did Dulles give any reasons for not being willing to explore it?

KREISBERG: No. One could reconstruct what all of his reasons would have been. Having refused to shake Zhou Enlai's hand [at the conference], it is not surprising that he would not be interested in normalization.[18]

MARTIN: Of course, the thing that interested me as far as our relations with China were concerned at the Geneva conference, was that we sat down and had bilateral discussions with the Chinese on the question of the Americans detained in China and the Chinese who had not been allowed to leave the United States. Those two issues really weren't comparable, because we had never imprisoned any Chinese. There had been some who had been refused permission to leave because they knew secrets. But certainly after the Korean War it was no longer valid, so we had no interest whatsoever in keeping them. In subsequent years we even went to prisons to try to get Chinese that had been convicted of crimes to say they'd go back to the mainland if we let them go. We just couldn't find anybody. They'd rather stay in this country. We didn't force anybody, obviously, but if they wanted to, even if they were in jail, they could return.[19]

Having bilateral discussions with the PRC at Geneva was a breakthrough. Dulles, by that time, had left the Geneva conference, and [Walter] Bedell Smith, the under secretary, was in charge, and Robertson was still there. I drafted the telegram which went back to the department, saying, "We're either going to talk to the Chinese or we're not going to get anywhere on the prisoner issue. It's not going to read very well at home, you know, if you say, 'These guys are detaining our citizens and we refuse to talk to them about it.' " We wanted to try to do it through the British, as we'd done before, but the Chinese would have none of it. We brought in [Humphrey] Trevelyan, the British chargé [in Beijing] at that time, as sort of an umpire to begin with, but then we wound up with bilateral talks. So that was the beginning. Dulles seemed to be a little reluctant, but he did eventually agree.

What was the reluctance, in your judgment, on the part of Dulles?

MARTIN: Well, it was because of the background of the Geneva conference. It was agreed at Berlin that the Chinese would be there. Beijing played it up: "This shows we're now a great power. We're sitting down with the Soviet Union, the United States, Britain, and France." The PRC at that time was trying to get as much as it could in gestures of recognition from the United States. Our policy was very rigid on that. People like Walter McConaughy [director of the Office of Chinese

Affairs, State Department] and others would make speeches saying, "Just because we're sitting down with them in a conference with a lot of other people doesn't mean we're recognizing them." But sitting down with them bilaterally might seem like a step forward to recognition, at least an appearance of an acceptance, of the PRC. That's why we tried to get the British involved. The PRC did release some of our people. Then the talks sort of petered out.

HOLDRIDGE: Zhou Enlai was the instigator or initiator of [renewed talks] at the Bandung Conference in April 1955.[20] He proposed that the United States and China get together to resolve their differences—to talk about resolving them, anyway. The ambassadorial-level talks went on, off and on, between 1955 and 1970. The idea was to try to keep some degree of contact with the Chinese Communists.

CLOUGH: Johnson and Wang met in Geneva amid great press attention. I was sent to be the advisor to Alex Johnson at those talks in Geneva, and I was there for probably two and a half months. We reached our first agreement with the Chinese on the return of civilians who were detained in Communist China, which was, from our point of view, the number one object on the agenda. We signed that agreement in September. Some of them were missionaries who had been there a long time. Many of them had been arrested at the time of the Korean War. And there were also 13 American Air Force people who had been shot down. The Chinese announced, on the day that Wang arrived in Geneva, that they were releasing the 13 military people. As Wang put it, to create a good atmosphere for the talks. Which it did.

GREEN: *Wang Bingnan, what kind of a person was he? Alex seemed to rather like him. [NOTE: Marshall Green is both interviewer and subject in some chapters.]*

CLOUGH: He was a very correct, professional diplomat. He did his job. He repeated whatever he was told to say at the meetings, but there was a little give around the edges. At one point in these talks about the civilians, before we reached agreement, we'd come to a sticking point, and so he and Alex Johnson arranged to have dinner together without the advisors, just an interpreter and themselves, to talk about this, and then they made some progress. It was a very complex negotiation; took about six weeks. A number of these imprisoned Americans were released, came home, but not all of them. The Chinese then wanted to go on to other subjects. They wanted a foreign ministers meeting. They wanted exchange of correspondents between the United States and China. They wanted lifting of the American economic embargo on China.

OSBORN: The Chinese were urging the United States to permit American newsmen to go to China—to permit the exchange of newsmen. Favoring the exchange of information was the popular side of this issue, so we and the Chinese jockeyed for position on it. We feared that dropping the bars would tend to erode domestic support for our own position on China. The Chinese were looking for leverage on Taiwan.

Was this all bad news from Taiwan's viewpoint?

CLOUGH: Oh, yes. Even the fact that we had sat down to talk with the Chinese Communists was bad news from Chiang Kai-shek's viewpoint. They were very nervous about what was going on in Geneva, because it was kept very secret. After the first few meetings, when some scraps of the proceedings leaked out in Washington, Dulles clamped down and restricted all of the correspondence to and from the State Department and Geneva to a very small number of people in Washington so that this wouldn't happen again. We kept Chiang Kai-shek generally informed, but, of course, he wasn't confident that we were telling him everything, which we probably weren't.

GREEN: And then Beijing tried to make use of this to expand our relationship. Knowing the discomfiture this would cause in Taipei.

CLOUGH: Not only discomfiture, but eventually, they hoped, a shift of our diplomatic relations from Taipei to Beijing. But they made a mistake in that they wouldn't release all the Americans. They had evidence that some of them actually were spies. Most of them were accused of being spies. Those cases lingered on, and we took the position that we couldn't go on to talk about other things in Geneva until they had released all the Americans. They had to fulfill their first and only agreement with the United States before we could talk seriously about closer relations.

We soon moved on to the Taiwan issue, and we demanded a renunciation of force with respect to Taiwan, which they would not give. Their position was that the Taiwan issue was composed of two parts: a domestic part and an international part. The domestic part was their own problem, and they didn't want any foreign interference. That was the problem of reunifying China, ending the civil war, bringing Taiwan under PRC control. The international part was what they called the U.S. occupation of Taiwan, American interference in Chinese internal affairs, interference in the civil war. Civil war was not over, because Chiang Kai-shek had not been totally defeated and he still occupied a piece of Chinese territory. So they wanted to separate the two. And they said they could not renounce the use of force against Taiwan so long as the United States was interfering there.

CLOUGH: It went on for years. We exchanged drafts on this issue of renunciation of force. They were willing to sign a general renunciation of force with the United States—they wouldn't use force against the United States—but not with respect to Taiwan.

MARTIN: No, the Chinese weren't about to do this. They felt that this was an internal affair because Taiwan was part of China, so they could not enter formally into an international agreement, renouncing force against their own territory. So it was a built-in, total impasse there.

CLOUGH: So as time went on, the intervals between meetings got longer. We had less to talk about. We were just repeating what we'd said in previous meetings.

What was the job of the Bureau, to write the instructions?

CLOUGH: Yes. In fact, when I came back to Washington, that was my principal job, to draft the instructions to Geneva for the talks. Then Walter McConaughy and I would take them to a meeting with Dulles and the legal advisor, Herman Phleger, and Walter Robertson. Usually there were just the five of us in those meetings. Dulles himself went over the instructions line by line, made changes here and there, and approved it. Then the telegram would go out.

Could you give a feeling for the atmospherics when you would sit down for instructions with Dulles, Walter Robertson, McConaughy, and Phleger? What was their attitude towards these talks?

CLOUGH: They took them very seriously as a way to keep in touch with a very important adversary of ours at that period, with the hope that the effort to at least promote a more peaceful atmosphere in the Taiwan Strait would be successful. I don't know what Dulles had in mind as sort of long term, whether he thought these might lead eventually to a diplomatic relationship with Beijing. He might have.

OSBORN: By 1957, the Chinese had become fed up with the lack of progress on Taiwan. This coincided with powerful frustrations in China's domestic programs and its relations with Russia.[21] China put us on hold and decided to try other means of attaining its objectives. Putting it another way, the Chinese lost faith in our good faith in seeking an answer to the Taiwan question. But they didn't want to abandon the talks because they still had hopes that at some future time it would be possible to resume progress toward a solution to the Taiwan issue. So they didn't drop the talks altogether.

Now we—for our part—wanted the talks to keep going, as a kind of mailbox, where we could drop messages to the Chinese when we felt the need to communicate with them. This helped us to withstand political pressures at home. When people demanded that we negotiate with the Chinese, we could say, "Well, we're talking to them at Geneva"—or Warsaw, after the venue was shifted—without any of the pitfalls of actual negotiating, which would have been difficult politically because of our right-wing in the United States.

CLOUGH: It got so that really the only thing we'd agree on at the end of each meeting was the date for the next meeting. Even that dwindled off, because by the winter of '57 the State Department wanted to transfer Alex Johnson from Czechoslovakia to Thailand, make him ambassador to Thailand. Obviously, it wouldn't be convenient to commute from Thailand to Geneva for talks, so they wanted to have Ed Martin, who had been his advisor and had the rank of first secretary at the embassy in London, represent the United States against a Chinese of appropriate rank to continue the talks.

MARTIN: So the Chinese said, "These are ambassadorial talks, and we like Mr. Martin, but we can't accept him because he's not an ambassador." We had deliberately tried to downgrade the talks; there's no question about it. We felt we weren't getting anywhere. After returning to London, I had some correspondence with the Chinese side, trying to get talks going at my level, but it didn't work out. The only significance of that is that we and the Chinese both decided that these Geneva talks were getting nowhere. We were the ones that took the initiative. I don't know whether they honestly thought in Washington that the Chinese would accept the downgrading of talks; I never thought they would.

CLOUGH: So we had no agreement, and the talks were de facto suspended about December of '57, and there were no talks in the early part of '58. About June, I was by this time the director for Chinese Affairs, we decided that we ought to try to get the talks started again. We looked around Europe for an appropriate ambassador, and we decided on Jake Beam, who was ambassador at Warsaw at that time. It would be convenient to have him deal with the Chinese ambassador at Warsaw, it wouldn't involve commuting. Jake was also a Soviet specialist, a person who knew something about communism, and had also served in Indonesia, so he knew something about East Asia. He seemed to be the logical choice. So we were just about to make the proposal in late June of '58, when the Chinese came out with a blast against us for suspending these talks. That caused us to hold off on making the proposal. We didn't want to seem to be reacting to this kind propaganda rhetoric.

The next response we got was the August 23 commencement of the bombarding of Jinmen. So that brought the idea of talks right into center stage. Dulles made his speech at Portsmouth [Newport, Rhode Island, on September 4], then Zhou Enlai made his proposal [September 6] that talks be resumed, and we agreed on Warsaw.[22] And it was about the tenth or sixteenth of September [September 15] when we sat down in Warsaw to have the first talks. The shooting was still going on.

There was one thing about the meetings in Warsaw that we had considered when I was still on the desk in Washington. We knew that if we selected a Polish building in which to meet, it would be bugged. The Poles would listen in. And we assumed that what the Poles heard, they would pass on to the Soviets. That didn't bother us too much. We thought it was useful for the Soviets to know what we were saying to the Chinese, and what they were saying to us, at this particular point.

With your background in China you must have had a great many subjects to discuss with Wang Bingnan's assistant or others on that delegation. Did you have any such talks?

CLOUGH: No. There was no outside contact, and that was the difficulty. It was a very formal sort of set up. Occasionally, we might exchange a few words before or after a meeting, but not much. In Warsaw, we were given the Mysliwiecki Palace by the Polish government as a place where we could meet. It was nicely arranged for this purpose, because we had separate entrances, and we had little rooms where we could gather and consult about our tactics and so on before we went in. Then the meeting room was in the center. We'd go in from opposite ends.

GREEN: *Having worked for both Alex and for Jake, did you notice any major differences in their style of approach to the problem? Were they equally effective? Alex, for one thing, tends to be quite talkative; Jake tends to be rather taciturn. And I was wondering whether the differences in their personalities and the way they articulated made much difference in terms of their negotiating capacities.*

CLOUGH: It's hard to judge, because the situations were so different. In 1955, there was no fighting going on. It was relatively calm. The Chinese Communists were in a period just after the famous Bandung Conference, where Zhou Enlai had taken a rather mild attitude toward the United States, so that things were more relaxed. In Warsaw, when we began in 1958, it was very tense. Nobody knew how far this war [the Taiwan Strait crisis] was going to spread, or what the intentions of the Chinese or the Soviets were at that point. My impression of Alex Johnson was that he was more broad-gauge. He had a sort of broader view of the negotiations, and he did more of the actual drafting of reports on meetings and recommendations for the next meeting. Jake left more of that work to me. I was in Warsaw with Jake Beam for three years, from '58 to '61.[23]

Did you, sitting in Hong Kong, have any sense that there was a real danger of a larger war with China during the 1958 Straits Crisis?

KREISBERG: No. None of us saw any possibility of a larger war. In fact, it may well have been closer than any of us thought it was. But at the time, we didn't see it.

HONG KONG

The American consulate general in the British colony of Hong Kong quickly became the primary listening post in efforts to understand what was happening inside the People's Republic of China. The staff mushroomed and virtually all resources were directed to various monitoring and diagnostic programs, including surveys of the Chinese press. When American diplomats in Hong Kong were not analyzing pork production in some distant province, they tended to be caught up in the other major issue of the period in Hong Kong. This was the refugee question and the related effort on the part of the Chinese in Hong Kong to migrate to the United States through whatever means necessary.

How did you view the Korean War at the post in Hong Kong?

CLOUGH: The most immediate question was whether the Communists would stop at the border of Hong Kong, because there was no way of defending Hong Kong militarily. So we had a rather tense period there in which American dependents were advised to leave, [although] the British did not advise their people to leave.

GRANT: The situation we were in was pretty dicey from a number of standpoints. One, you had this great unknown beast on the mainland that might or might not want to forcibly communize the world as fast as it could. You had in the United States the beginnings of the 1952 election, in which the Republicans were running in part on the charge that the Democrats were soft on communism, had lost China to the communists. This assumes, of course, we ever had it. The result was that those of us reporting—I can remember feeling this very acutely—figured it was our obligation to tell Washington that what we were seeing was a regime that was establishing itself very effectively in power, even though it was not a very attractive one in many ways. At the same time, you wondered whether your dispatch might suddenly turn up on the Senate floor being quoted or misquoted, quoted out of context by Senator McCarthy. Although I don't think any of us trimmed—I certainly don't remember any trimming—we wrote our dispatches with great care, and what we were saying was: "We feel this crowd is very rough"—I think I overestimated the degree to which they were communist, and underestimated that they were also Chinese—"but they are going to stay there."

Did the end of the Korean War in 1953 make any difference at all?

HUMMEL: Yes, it did. The end of that war calmed everybody down. British investors and traders began to come back to Hong Kong. The tension and sense of impermanence virtually disappeared. At that time, too, the British government decided that it was worthwhile to put a lot more money into social services in Hong Kong.

How did the consulate general get information from China, or was there a group of Cold Warriors really hunkered down at that time?

JOHNSON: It was the principal listening post for China. It was one of the very largest American posts in the world at that time, larger than most embassies. We had 42 vice consuls, just vice consuls alone.

LUTKINS: That was *the* place to be to try to follow what was going on, interpret what was going on inside China, even with governments like the British and the Dutch who had relations with the Chinese Communists and an office in Peking.

HOLDRIDGE: Quite a few of the Chinese analysts and interpreters/translators, who had been with the consulate general in Beijing and even in Shanghai, were able to make it out. They set up shop with the American consulate general in Hong Kong. We had, in effect, an institutional memory.

GREEN: We really had a tremendous wealth of information about what was going on in China, which was probably superior to anything outside of China anywhere in the world.

HOLDRIDGE: We were able to keep up with the internals and some of the problems quite well, even though it was like the old Chinese doctor treating one of the emperor's concubines. He couldn't see the woman directly, but he sat behind a screen and she described her symptoms to him. Then he had this little carved ivory doll which he could use.

LEVIN: The Chinese prefer to eat fresh rather than frozen pork, and therefore you had railroad carloads of live pigs coming into Hong Kong. When there were suggestions that there were food shortages and crop failures in China, you could see what provinces the carloads of pigs were coming from, whether they were thinner or fatter. This gave you some idea of what was going on in different parts of China which supplied food to Hong Kong.

There were literally hundreds of thousands of Chinese in Hong Kong who were exchanging letters with their families all over China. There were also visits of Hong Kong Chinese who were Cantonese to nearby parts of China, which was always relatively easy. Visits to the

North in those days were a bit more difficult, but nevertheless there was an enormous flow of people, mail, and information between China and Hong Kong.

What were you getting from our "China watchers"? Could you describe how they operated at that time and how effective they were in terms of their point of view?

HUMMEL: Well, there was an active corps of nongovernment people who were journalists, "China watchers," scholars, as well as staff members of the consulate general. Obviously, the Political Section of the consulate general was very interested in anything that was going on in Mainland China. Word of a new refugee who had come out of Communist China who was a particularly good source would spread quickly through this community.

LUTKINS: The Chinese press, of course, was a major source. Some of it was readily available, other publications we obtained by a clandestine procurement program.

BREMENT: In my first year in Hong Kong I was in charge of the unit which published the *Survey of the China Mainland Press*, which was the standard source of reference both for the government and for the academic community on current developments in China. I had 10 translators and 20 typists and we had a subscription list of about 600 and we turned out 60 or 70 single-spaced sheets of paper a day.

Why would the press be useful? I mean, supposedly this was a tightly controlled regime where everybody was spouting the party line.

LUTKINS: There was a great deal of work done in trying to read fine nuances into what was being said in the press and if one paper differed slightly from another. Of course, you had the major organs controlled by the Chinese Party, but then you had one by the military, and theoretically, a youth paper and so forth, and you could pick up interesting little tidbits. And, in any case, we were relying on it not only for major trends but for factual information as to what the regime itself was saying in terms of statistical information on production and that sort of thing. And then it was also extremely important when they were engaged in one of their major campaigns.

HOLDRIDGE: If you kept on reading the Chinese press, day after day you began to understand some of the lines of thinking and policies of the time. If something came up that was different, it immediately rang bells. For example, in 1956, I noticed that they were celebrating the anniversary of the establishment of the Chinese Communist Party, which was July 1921. There were remarks about many of the cadres having lost faith in the leadership of the party. "This will have to be rectified, we have to bring these people around." You could see that inside China there were severe problems.

LUTKINS: I might mention another source of information we had. We were in very close contact with the representatives of other governments, particularly the British, French, Dutch, Australian, Japanese. Both on a day-to-day basis and in regular evening sessions, we would get together in a sort of informal group. And that included people from the press as well. There was quite a large press presence there. A certain number of academics, such as a fellow named Doak Barnett,[24] an eminent authority on China, who happened to be there part of the time. We were all trying to exchange ideas, pick each other's minds. And we did see some foreign government reports. Particularly I recall the British reports written by their embassy in Peking, which they made available to us.

The British authorities in Hong Kong were also debriefing the Chinese refugees who were coming in, weren't they? Did you have access to their information?

HOLDRIDGE: Yes. Since it is 30 years and more since that time, I can say that we cooperated quite fully.

Were their assessments of what was happening inside of China very different from American views, since their policy towards China was different?

KREISBERG: No, I don't think so. The general assessment of the community tended to come together around a fairly common center '56 to '59. There began to be some divergence after '59 over what had been responsible for the turn to the left and the crackdown by Deng Xiaoping and Mao on the rightists and then the movement toward the Great Leap Forward.[25] There was a lot of uncertainty as to what one could believe about the Great Leap Forward. At that time, the viewpoints really began to diverge quite widely. It centered around what people's own personal ideologies were in part. But what you really have to remember is that we in Hong Kong knew what was going on in Chinese foreign policy from our reading of what the Chinese were telling the rest of the world. So none of us had any sense of confidence as to the accuracy of our interpretation of Chinese foreign policy. It was obviously what the Chinese wanted us to know. There were other places where people had better information on Chinese foreign policies, or thought they had, in different embassies—Delhi, Paris.

From local contacts?

KREISBERG: Yes. Hong Kong was really far away from Beijing. It wasn't really used by China as its center for international foreign policy activities.

Did you have any contacts in Hong Kong with people known to be from the mainland who were attempting in any way to . . .

KREISBERG: No. We were instructed to stay far from them, and they were instructed to stay far from us. One of the great moments in U.S.-Chinese diplomatic relations was when permission was given—I think this was in the mid-1960s—for someone from the consulate to meet with the publisher of the Communist-controlled *Ta Kung Po* newspaper in Hong Kong. The degree of isolation that was imposed was almost complete. We knew no one and were supposed to know no one from the Bank of China or from New China News Agency. It was a period of great ideological intensity. Not as great as between 1950 and 1955, but the instructions were still, "You will not have contact with, discuss, shake hands with anybody from the People's Republic of China."

Was there concern that Mainlanders were trying to cause trouble in Hong Kong?

KREISBERG: Shortly after I arrived in 1955, there were major demonstrations, rioting in Kowloon directed at foreigners and at the British, and in which it was assumed that the Chinese Communists had played a major role. The interpretation that the British encouraged, and that we accepted at the time, was that China wanted to make life as uncomfortable for the British as possible in the hope that this would increase the willingness of the British to negotiate an early withdrawal from Hong Kong.

In watching these major developments going on in China, was there a feeling that the Chinese government was going to be so destabilized that there might be a change or that anything of that magnitude was going to happen?

KREISBERG: Never. Nor from any interviews that we ever got.

In addition to following and publicizing negative developments on the mainland, did the consulate have a cultural program designed to promote an anti-PRC agenda.

MCCARTHY: Those were the days of the China Reporting Program, where we were producing material in English and other languages for worldwide consumption about what was happening on the China Mainland. We also started a very successful Chinese-language publication for Taiwan and Chinese and Southeast Asia called *World Today* magazine, which lasted for over 25 years. We ran a very extensive book translation program. At one point we did around 60 titles in a single year. We did achieve some publishing success in English. We discovered Eileen Chang, who many people regard as probably one of the two or three top Chinese writers of the second half of the twentieth century. She wrote a book for us called *Rice Sprout Song*, which was published in the United States and had some critical acclaim.[26]

We also did a fair amount of work supporting filmmakers who were producing anti-communist pictures in Hong Kong, and Chinese language pictures in Southeast Asia. So we were very much involved in the Chinese motion picture industry. Raymond Chow, who became one of the principal movie tycoons of Asia, ran an outfit called Golden Harvest, is the man who is largely responsible for the craze in kung fu movies. He was the one who discovered Bruce Lee. Raymond was our VOA reporter until the bright lights and a lot of money beckoned. Very, very capable guy.

You were mentioning that you were getting some glimmers of statistics and all coming out of Hong Kong. Could you talk about the reporting?

GRANT: During my first tour in Hong Kong, 1950–52, there were really no data on China. The Chinese Communists themselves had only the crudest of data. We didn't know how little they knew at the time. When I went back, 1955–58, and was doing economic reporting, I guess the two things that one quickly learned is that the Chinese use statistics for political purposes. They admit it. They say, "Statistics must serve politics." They have a propaganda output which you do well to take very much askance.

By the mid-1950s, the Chinese—I think it was December of 1955—put out the first tiny, slim volume of economic statistics. I put all hands to work translating it and getting it to Washington. We were also getting enough Chinese materials, like provincial newspapers for domestic consumption, not the propaganda stuff, which would give you an idea as to what the rations were in the market towns for pork, cotton, things like that. From this we began to construct some idea as to how the Chinese were doing. They were doing better than our official estimates admitted. We had been too much misled by hope and by some old anti-communist reporting people, including our Chinese locals, who hated the communists, into thinking that the Chinese were doing much worse than we finally concluded.

But the other thing we were also beginning to learn was that the official data did not necessarily mean what they claimed. Just after I left in 1958, the Great Leap Forward started. I got back to Washington and found a lot of people believing their claims. I remember saying at the time—I was horrified—"They can't do it that way—that simplistic effort to mobilize labor—these people are putting out these data because they're trying to create a bandwagon." They claimed that they doubled wheat production in a year and things like that. We understood this in Hong Kong earlier than a lot of people in Washington did.

CLOUGH: The Chinese were reluctant, particularly in those early years, to put out any reliable statistics that an economist could use to put together what was really going on. So it was rather impressionistic, what we learned in Hong Kong. And there were also a large number of peddlers of information, who wanted to sell it, who wanted to gain access to American visas or something. They were very troublesome, because there were so many phonies. And it wasn't always easy to spot the phony.

The CIA was very new in those years. We had a small unit of CIA people in the consulate general, whose job was to gather covert intelligence. They had money to pay people for intelligence. We didn't.

LILLEY: [There were] people who manufactured intelligence in Hong Kong allegedly from big mainland networks. The quick fix, the easy way. A hundred thousand bucks, here's the information you want. [The CIA] got stung on that. This lasted till roughly the late '50s and then they begin to mature in the Far East.

Hong Kong acted as a base for espionage by both sides and for smuggling in defiance of trade restrictions on the PRC.[27]

JOHNSON: In Hong Kong we had very intensive controls to prevent goods from Communist China getting into the United States, and, conversely, to prevent U.S. exports from getting into Communist China. It even got kind of amusing, the depth of our concerns. For example, in trying to prevent Chinese Communist products from arriving in the United States, we got into some very detailed definitions of what is a Chinese product. There are a lot of Chinese products based on egg and chicken, food products that were exported to the U.S. traditionally. And, of course, exports from Hong Kong we were happy to let in, because this was a friendly British colony, but nothing from Communist China. Well, the border between Hong Kong and Communist China runs through a swamp, and there were a lot of Chinese vegetable goods produced in that swamp, on both sides of the border, and there was no way of detecting, for example, a litchi nut produced in Hong Kong from one produced in China. And it got even more technical when you got into egg products. It was clear that if the egg had been hatched in Communist China, even though the egg was brought into Hong Kong for processing, it was a communist product. But how about if the chicken comes from Communist China and is brought across the border into Hong Kong live and lays the egg on the Hong Kong side, is that then a communist product?

These were matters of debate?

JOHNSON: These were matters that had to be answered, defined, because we were policing this sort of thing. And there was a tremendous effort to keep U.S. goods from getting into Communist China. In the commercial section I did a lot of export checking, where you try to decide what will happen to this particular product—if it's brought in, will it be reexported? That was really a battle of wits in Hong Kong, because a Chinese company that was importing and perhaps did intend to send it to Communist China, would find all sorts of ways of evading these eager-beaver American vice consuls. I remember particularly one export check that I was asked to make on, of all things, prophylactic rubbers. And the question was: What are Hong Kong's requirements for prophylactic rubbers? And I had to go all around Hong Kong, talking to importers of prophylactic rubbers and asking: How many do you think Hong Kong uses? And how many are reexported to China? And I wrote about a 10- or 12-page airgram, which received commendations from Washington. Then I got a further communication saying, "Please update this carefully. We have heard that the Chinese Communists are using prophylactic rubbers to protect the muzzles of their guns from moisture." They said this is being done in Korea. And so I was double checking, and then I got another telegram from the Pentagon that said, "Forget all about it. Our experts have said that if you do try to protect your gun muzzles that way, it will simply rust and pit out the muzzles themselves because moisture will collect, there is no air in the muzzle. So any prophylactic rubbers that want to go to Communist China, okay."

So you didn't look at the strategic value of trying to keep the Chinese population down?

JOHNSON: No, that wasn't part of that check. So that was challenging, but a tremendous expense of time and effort. We had some concern that maybe the British patrols that were designed to prevent smuggling from Hong Kong to China were not sufficiently efficient. To reassure us, they said I could ride on British patrols at night and watch them intercepting junks smuggling—steel plate was a big item and tires—to Guangzhou. I spent several very exciting nights patrolling Hong Kong waters. They'd pull junks over and go aboard and search for contraband. A few of these junks tried to evade the patrols.

Were the Chinese in Hong Kong seen as a potential "fifth column" at that time?

HUMMEL: Most people felt that the Chinese in Hong Kong were there because they didn't want to be under communist domination. While, no doubt, the British Special Branch had plenty of work to do, a large amount of that work was centered on making sure that the Chinese Nationalists—people controlled by Taiwan—were not being provocative to the PRC in an unacceptable way.

HOLDRIDGE: In Hong Kong, we all thought of the Guomindang as sort of an annoyance, frankly. What the Guomindang was trying to do was to organize resistance groups to infiltrate back across the Chinese border, and the British hated that and kept on picking these guys up. We didn't have a great deal of respect for the Guomindang because they seemed to be so ineffective and inefficient. Frankly, we stayed away from them like the plague because we didn't want to get mixed up in the minds of our Chinese friends with the Guomindang.

Did the Chinese in Hong Kong and the refugees from the mainland get along?

HUMMEL: I wouldn't say that there was friction, but they were completely different groups and operated socially in different circles. Quite a few of the very rich people from Shanghai managed to get their money out of the mainland—or at least part of it—and quite often became the entrepreneurs in Hong Kong. That caused a certain amount of friction with the local Cantonese entrepreneurs. At first the Hong Kong sharpies managed to strip the fortunes of several of the Shanghai newcomers, who had thought that they were smarter than any of these local people. However, I think it is fair to say that production activity in Hong Kong remained in the hands of the refugees who had come to Hong Kong. This was true, for example, of the whole textile industry, which had been transplanted from Shanghai. Previously, there was very little manufacturing going on in Hong Kong. However, entrepreneurial Shanghai investors and other people from elsewhere on the mainland brought with them the skills and the desire to engage in manufacturing.

Could you give a little idea of the atmosphere of what a visa officer was doing?

THAYER: There was a study done a year or two before I arrived, which included a calculation that about 85 percent of the cases we were working with were fraudulently based. That is to say, the petitioners in the States had come in on phony slots opened by their alleged parents' declaration to the Immigration Service that they had a certain number of sons back in China. But they had sold off those slots. This next generation was filing petitions in turn, for their wives and children.

DONALD ANDERSON: Basically, the origins of the passport fraud was in the late nineteenth century, early twentieth century. There was a tremendous amount of, not immigration, but travel by people from Guangdong Province just across the border from Hong Kong, to the United States, largely working on the railroads as laborers. This group of people actually came almost entirely from two or three counties. Their practice was generally to leave the wife back in the village, and go earn enough money that they were prosperous by Chinese standards; then they would come home and maybe spend a year, and then go back and work some more. During that time they would sire children. And, of course, the desirable thing to have was boys, because they would then grow up and as soon as they were eligible they would go to the United States and work to continue this process of sending money back to the village. If your brother who had stayed back in China had a son, and you came back and your wife produced a daughter, your brother's son would become your son for immigration purposes. They developed an intricate network of fraud.

THAYER: When I was there, the consulate was in the second year of a million dollar anti-fraud program. So there was an atmosphere of suspicion and distrust that exceeds the situation in most places. I went on a raid in Macao with one of our investigative officers and his Chinese local investigator. We literally charged up the back stairs of a rickety old house to raid an apartment on the third or fourth floor, where we tore the place apart looking for documents demonstrating the real identity of applicants that were before us applying for visas. We had no warrant. We had nothing at all. I went along as an observer. But my moral outrage at what we were doing only came in retrospect. At the time, I wasn't sensitive to this.

JOHNSON: The base of the problem was that, in China, at least then, they didn't have civil documents. There was no such thing as an official birth certificate or an official marriage certificate. So you had to rely on informal evidence to prove that you were the son of a Chinese father in the States and therefore entitled to nonquota entry. And the "son" would come in with what was called informal evidence. This would be, oh, say, badly worn letters from "Dad," sent to this kid supposedly when he was such and such an age—but sometimes the ink wouldn't be too dry on them. Or they would unroll a beautiful certificate, and you'd say, "What is that thing?" And he'd say, "That is the announcement of the marriage of Mom and Dad, and it's signed down here by the Chinese gentleman who presided at the wedding." And you'd feel it and say, "This paper feels pretty new. This doesn't look like the certificate that was used when your father was married." And then he'd pull out a photograph of him with old "Dad" alongside, to prove the relationship. And you'd say, "Why is it that the left-hand side of this photograph is light, whereas the right-hand side is so dark? Looks almost as though something had been pasted together here."

Sometimes the effort was based principally on his trying to prove that he was born in a certain village at a certain time. He would come into the consulate with a "witness," a friend from the same village. And both of them had been very carefully coached at a school set up in Hong Kong to brief guys who were appearing before the U.S. consul so they would know what to say. The examination consisted of getting a piece of paper and drawing a sort of an informal map of the village. And the examiner would say, "Now in your village where was the, let's say, the place where the gentlemen bathed themselves?" And you'd ask them separately. The witness would come in and say it was over here; and the applicant would put it over here. And you'd say, "Well, you two don't seem to be from the same town really." Tremendous detail. If you passed this oral quizzing, there was a place in Hong Kong where you could buy healthy, warm stools before you came in for your physical exam. Colorful assignment.

Then they developed blood testing as a means of tripping things up. Because, of course, a blood test can prove that by anything known to medical science you cannot be the result of the union of these two people. "Mother," of course, was often a part of this. She would come in with this alleged son, to testify that yes, I remember well when Jimmy here was born, and his father is, sure enough, this guy in San Francisco. And you'd take a blood test on all three, and it would come out that Jimmy just couldn't be the son of this union. And you'd not only have to turn him down, but you'd—this was the hardest, really the hardest thing I had to do in all my consular work—you'd have to turn down this poor, aging woman because she had lied under oath. And you'd have to tell her that under no circumstances could she rejoin her husband. And that is just a real, real hard thing.

Somebody at one point figured that there were very few Chinese women before the 1906 San Francisco earthquake and each one of them had to have produced something like 200 children in order to produce the numbers who claim American citizenship.

HOLLOWAY: You mention the San Francisco earthquake. These Chinese knew every town in the West where the courthouse had burned town and there would be no records! "Oh, I'm from so and so, Montana, 1923." "Oh, that burned down. We don't have any records."

THAYER: I and I think most of my colleagues went through stages—initially of sympathy, then of outrage at being lied to day after day after day, and ultimately passing through that sense of outrage to a feeling of resignation and compassion. It created a certain degree of arrogance, a colonialist mentality. And in those days, Hong Kong was very much a colony. People called Chinese "boys." While there were friendships, certainly close friendships between many of the consulate employees and the Chinese, the Chinese intellectuals and their senior local employees and so forth, there was, on the visa front, a different set of relationships, and they were, in many respects, mutually hostile—the visa officer angry at being exploited himself and his country being exploited from his perspective; the visa applicant, as is still the case, simply anxious one way or the other, ethics be damned, to get to the States.

When you were in Hong Kong from 1954–1957, the consul general, Everett Drumright, had very fixed ideas about China policy. What sort of pressures were on your reporting?

LUTKINS: There were only minimal constraints. And, although I disagreed with Mr. Drumright on his basic outlook, to his credit he never tried to tell us that we should report differently. He may have reported under separate channels himself. If so, I wasn't aware of it. I don't, frankly, think he did.

DRUMRIGHT: My assignment in the State Department was on the China desk [1953–1954]. We began to have increasing tensions with the Chinese. And in those, I usually took a fairly strong line, stronger than some of my superiors liked. So after about a year in Washington I was reassigned to Hong Kong as consul general.

LUTKINS: I remember one rather amusing little thing that involves a Chinese nuance between the two names for the Chinese city: one, being Peking and the other, Peiping. Traditionally it was Peking, which means, in Chinese, "Northern Capital." And during the Nationalist days, in the late '20s and '30s, when they moved the capital down to Nanjing, which means "Southern Capital," Peking became Peiping, because they couldn't have two capitals, so it was "Northern Peace," Peiping. It was a corollary of our support of the Nationalist government, even after they moved to Taiwan, that when the Chinese Communists took over and restored the name of Peking, we refused to call it Peking. We called it Peiping. I thought this was a little silly, so when I got posted to Hong Kong, in charge of the reporting there, I started calling it Peking in our telegrams, which Mr. Harrington, the consul general, didn't object to. Washington didn't object to it. But as soon as Mr. Drumright got there, he said, "In Washington, we call it Peiping, not Peking." So we had to go back to the old method. As I said, it's not important at all, but it shows the Washington mindset at the time.

Allen Whiting [who served on the Policy Planning Staff] has said that it could be perilous to your career within the State Department if you could be heard speaking of Peking or Beijing rather than calling it Peiping. So that was true in the field as well?

KREISBERG: Yes, if you used it in written reports. My recollection is that in the office we often used Beijing simply because so much of the material we worked on used that form.

LUTKINS: There was one other thing involving policy, when they were going to have a conference down in Indonesia, the Bandung Conference. We felt that it would be desirable to give Washington the benefit of our views on what our attitude and position should be at this conference, particularly because we knew that Chinese Communists were going to be involved there. Art Hummel and I suggested that we send out a joint message from the consulate general giving our views. Everett Drumright nixed the idea. But there are more ways than one to skin a cat, so Art Hummel, through his own channels, contacted Washington and had them send out a message requesting that we should send them a telegram with our views. So we were able to get one in to Washington as desired.

THAYER: I remember asking Consul General Drumright did he ever think we would go back to China during my professional lifetime. And he said, "Oh, yes." He said, "I have no doubt that we'll go back. The Chinese will become democratic again, or at least the Communists will fall, and we'll reopen the same number of posts that we used to have."

DEVELOPMENTS IN TAIWAN I

Americans initially feared that the Nationalist authorities on Taiwan would not be able to overcome the poor governing practices that had contributed to their downfall on the mainland. In fact, the Guomindang did reform itself and conducted a thoroughgoing land reform program that not only satisfied the peasant desire for land, but also created a group of former landlords with disposable income who proceeded to invest in industry. Thus Americans found themselves advising an economically more flexible and effective regime, although they still lamented the pervasive political repression.

KARTOSH: Chiang Kai-shek left the mainland and arrived in Taiwan with absolutely nothing.[28] The United States government agreed to set up a purchasing commission in the Department of the Army which would furnish the Chinese government certain people who were expert in buying and selling things the Chinese would need to establish themselves in Taiwan. U.S. personnel also would go to Taiwan and organize the Nationalist military remnants, which were disorganized. Believe me, it was a mess. There were about 30 of us and we packed off to Taiwan in 1950–51. The State Department had an excellent attitude for dealing with Chiang at that time. The basis of our policy was, "Look fellow, we will protect you on Taiwan, but we are going to support you only to a degree that will allow this protection to be realistic. You have got to do the rest." Lo and behold, Chiang Kai-shek did it.

In the midst of this Chiang Kai-shek was apparently trying to use the Korean War to his advantage. There was an offer of "give us the training, the equip-

ment, and the money and we will put so many divisions into Korea." How did you all respond to this sort of talk?

KARTOSH: Not a chance. That was strictly propaganda. Propaganda even in Chiang's eyes. His army when it came off the mainland was absolutely worthless, and in 1951–53, he couldn't put together two divisions that would go anywhere. They had no uniforms, a minimum amount of ammunition, no artillery, no transport. They just had rifles, and some of the troops didn't even have that.[29]

What was your impression of the Chinese officialdom that you dealt with?

KARTOSH: There were some brilliant exceptions, particularly the younger men educated in the United States, as well as some of the older businessmen. The military was hopeless, except for two or three generals who would fight. The military was still very corrupt, the troops had as yet no real stake in survival of the Chinese Nationalist government other than, for whatever reason, they would be shot if they defected to the Communists. Taiwan was the only refuge available to them.

By 1955 that began to change. The older group was moving out. Some of the younger men were taking the middle-level positions. The army was beginning to induct younger people, even Taiwanese, at the enlisted level, not yet the officer level. We had a Military Assistance Advisory Group there and it was beginning to have an effect. It was a very small group, I don't think more than 20 officers.[30] They made sure that the Nationalist troops had uniforms, received pay, food, and medical care. To the Chinese soldier at that point of history, this was very important, this was good living. A better living than many of the peasants. Then we, the U.S., re-equipped the Chinese Air Force. Also a cadre was organized and trained for the Chinese Navy. So from about 1955 on, they became a more reliable force. But prior to 1955 they were absolutely worthless, really.

DILLON: During the Korean War, I was recruited by a U.S. government agency for a program in Taiwan that assisted Chinese Nationalist irregular forces. They were looking for civilians or for officers who could be seconded to a civilian status, so that there would be no direct connection with the American military services.

We went through training and then to Taiwan. I spent the last year

of the war on one of the small offshore islands on the China coast—
Dachen. Others went to Jinmen and Mazu. My island was the most
northern one near the mouth of the Hangzhou Bay. We trained and
advised Chinese irregulars in raiding operations along the China coast.
The idea was to deflect the Chinese Communist Army from Korea. Half
of us were civilian and half were serving military officers. There were
no distinctions among the group. We all wore Chinese military uniforms; our counterparts were Chinese officers.

What was your impression of the Nationalist irregulars?

DILLON: We were all very young—I was one of the youngest. I was not
greatly impressed by the Nationalist officers. They were scornful and
inconsiderate of their troops. The troops were brave and suffered hard-
ships with extraordinary good nature. I always think of the Chinese soldier as a little guy walking up a steep hill with a big mortar plate on his
back. His officer walked up the hill, breathing heavily, staggering under
the weight of a sidearm.

We quickly became very cynical about political statements that we
would hear. We were not of course very sophisticated, but we would
hear unrealistic statements about how the Chinese Nationalists were
prepared to unleash these mighty forces. Many of these statements
came from American Republican conservatives. General MacArthur
talked about landing a couple of divisions on the mainland. My group
was involved on the ground, and indeed, in combat, with irregular Chinese Nationalist troops. It was our considered judgment—coming from
a bunch of men the ages of 23 to 31 (we considered the latter to be a very
old man)—that no Nationalist intervention would have any effect on
Mainland China, except perhaps to get us into a lot more trouble than
we were in already. None of us believed that the Nationalist government really wanted to fight.

One interesting aspect of our little operation was that we spent a lot
of time trying to persuade the Chinese to do battle. Once when we did
succeed in convincing a general to attack a truly significant target, our
troops took a terrific beating. It was disaster, primarily due to the tactical incompetence of the officers who led the attack. They landed on the
wrong beach. The reconnaissance was faulty, the maps were wrong. We
landed on a sandbar across the river from our target and became

exposed to enemy fire without cover. The Nationalists took a lot of casualties. This confirmed to them that it was dumb to do anything the Americans suggested.

The Korean War ended in July 1953, and that gave the Americans an opportunity to end these irregular operations. It was then that the Nationalists became very active. Indeed, the largest raid conducted by the Nationalist irregulars occurred after the war in August 1953. No Americans participated directly in that operation; it was disaster despite the bravery of the troops involved. The Nationalists were afraid that peace would break out.

What was your impression of the Chinese Nationalist government at that time?

HUMMEL: I made several trips to Taiwan, partly because the [USIS] materials that we were producing [in Hong Kong] were also being used in Taiwan. I was quite impressed with the way in which the Nationalist government had pulled up its socks and eliminated many, if not most, of the ills that had caused its downfall on the mainland.

Corruption was one of the major ones.

HUMMEL: Corruption was one of them. When the Nationalist Chinese took over the areas which had been occupied by the Japanese, they quite often treated the local Chinese population as if they had all been collaborators with the Japanese. They did a good many stupid things in the early years of their control of Taiwan. However, they had a very serious self-examination within the Guomindang Party to diagnose what had gone wrong. They did a pretty fair job of it. Among other things, they prohibited the rich Nationalists who had come over from the mainland from monopolizing the various industries and economic power. Moreover, they carried out a very effective land reform program. Today the big, big businessmen, the richest people in Taiwan are Taiwanese, these Taiwanese ex-landlords—not Mainlanders. [But] political power was very carefully kept in the hands of the Guomindang Party.

WALTER JENKINS: Also, there was internal tension. Chiang Ching-kuo, the older son [by Chiang Kai-shek's first wife], was having a struggle with Madame Chiang and her son, Chiang Wei-kuo [he was, in fact, not her son but was Chiang's second son], for a position of power and influence on Chiang Kai-shek. And it had its impact on the diplomatic corps, too. For example, when Madame Chiang organized a fashion show, supported by Wei-kuo, and invited all the diplomats there, Ching-kuo surreptitiously got his bully boys to disrupt the fashion show, turn over diplomats' vehicles, while appealing to the public that the fashion show was a frivolous event at the time of serious civil and Korean wars with the communists.

Also, Sun Li-jen, the VMI-educated [Virginia Military Institute] general who trained the troops that finally opened up the Burma Road during W.W.II, was put under house arrest in 1954.[31] Two of his generals were sent to Green Island, a detention re-education camp for political prisoners. I remember going to Green Island with a U.S. Army colleague and Chiang Ching-kuo, who controlled security for the Nationalist Government. During the tour of the camp he pointed out that they were reforming the resident political dissidents, and that 95 percent of them, after re-education in the Three People's Principles, returned to Taiwan.[32] Well, that was interesting so my colleague and I asked, "Well, what happens to the other 5 percent?"

Oh, we don't hurt them. No, actually, we give them a boat, food supplies, and a radio, and send them back to the Chinese mainland. And after three or four days, we start sending radio messages to them asking: " 'When are you going to report?' And the Communists take care of them." Well, he was a very, very clever man. But he was also very clever in a more positive sense: he cultivated the Taiwanese and supported their involvement, developing close relation with them, and not relying exclusively on the Mainlanders resident on Taiwan.

What was your impression of Chiang Kai-shek, Madame Chiang and all, as far as their grasp of how to run the government? Was there a reform going on within their ranks at that time?

WALTER JENKINS: Well it's a very strange source of reform, but Chiang's older son, Ching-kuo, who was, after all, educated in Moscow, took all of the communist techniques, developed them for the Guomindang against the communists. Now that's one side of him. But under his influence there was a tendency, demonstrated by the JCRR land reform,

A 1955 airfield discussion between (from left to right) Assistant Secretary of State Walter Robertson, Chairman of the Joint Chiefs of Staff Admiral Arthur W. Radford, Ambassador to the ROC Karl Rankin, and Chief of the Military Assistance Advisory Group Major General William C. Chase. Courtesy of the U.S. Navy and National Archives.

to compensate the Taiwanese with economic prosperity in exchange for maintaining Guomindang political and military control.

Karl Rankin was the ambassador. What was your impression of him?

WALTER JENKINS: He was a nice, even-handed person, and he was like several other ambassadors with whom I have served, believing that you don't muddy up the waters. I mean they emphasize that this is the policy—the way we're going to do it. To illustrate, I recall one fascinating report prepared jointly by officers of the Political Section. It was a dispatch analyzing the feasibility of a military "return to the mainland," concluding that it was most unlikely. It was drafted by FSO China-language experts and sent up to the ambassador. He recognized a problem with the China Lobby now pretty much in control in the department. He left the analysis intact but changed the conclusions—this was his report. But the underlying message stood out when it got back to the department, because the analysis was still there. Ambassador Rankin tried to be fair to his reporting officers and at the same time avoid rocking the boat in Washington. All copies of the report were recalled from distribution by the department

Was there any feeling at the time, particularly when you got into the political-military side, that this idea of returning to the mainland just was a nonstarter from the very beginning?

WALTER JENKINS: Yes, most of the political officers, economic officers, and most everyone in the embassy felt the same way; but "return to the mainland," like many other slogans of autocratic leaders, seemed to help hold things together. They had their impressive military parades, and we trained them and gave them equipment to maintain the unified posture. So while the analysts thought it was a nonstarter, it had its politically unifying purpose among the Mainlanders. We had pretty close associations with some people like General Sun Li-jen and others we had known back during the war, and they didn't seem to believe in the feasibility of a military return to the mainland. But you didn't discuss such things with Chiang Ching-kuo or other inside members of the government.

In the period where you were in Taiwan studying language from 1954 to 1955, what were your impressions of Taiwan?

KREISBERG: Well, first was that it was a period of intense public propaganda. Everywhere that you went, there were posters and signs to support the government in Taiwan, to oppose the People's Republic of China, to "Gloriously Return to the Mainland." There was a considerable degree of tension between Taiwanese and Mainlanders, very little speaking of Mandarin in the streets. We never saw any overt expression of that tension.

Your contacts were mainly Taiwanese, then?

KREISBERG: Those were the people who were in Taichung. The concept that the embassy had was they would put us into a place where there were not a lot of foreigners, so our Chinese would not be polluted. But they hadn't really thought about the fact that there weren't many Mainlanders there either. So in the main good Mandarin was being spoken at the language school.

It, of course, was a period of very low development in town. Very few cars. Most people rode bicycles or bicycle-driven rickshaws. The outskirts of the town, where the language school sat at the edge of a rice paddy, was about half a mile from the very center of town. The whole population of Taichung at that point was probably under a 100,000. It was, of course, very difficult, and absolutely illegal, to listen to Radio Beijing or any of the other Chinese Communist radio stations. It was illegal to have materials from China. We weren't able to look at the *People's Daily*. We weren't able to have FBIS [Foreign Broadcast Information Service] there. So my knowledge of what was happening in China was sharply curtailed. I picked it up only when I went up to the embassy.

What did you think from '52 to '57, about the survivability of the Nationalists?

HOLLOWAY: Whatever was going to happen in Communist China, there wasn't one of us who had any illusions about the Nationalists. Even those who served in Taipei. They weren't going back to the mainland. They had not improved a great deal over their performance on the mainland. Now, this was not held by many of the top folks, particularly the ambassador in Taipei. No, nobody was going to tell him—we weren't going to say the Nationalists were hopeless.

Did you have any problems with the Nationalists on Taiwan, "looking over your shoulder" at your magazine or other publications?

HUMMEL: Occasionally, they felt that we weren't anti-communist enough. We were, of course, catering to a somewhat different audience than they were. We were trying to sell a magazine on the newsstands, and publishing translations of American books that we hoped would sell, and producing a daily newsfile. Some of the Nationalists would have preferred straight out anti-communist propaganda, calling everybody on the mainland a "Communist bandit," which was the cliché they used.

OFFSHORE ISLANDS

Among the main events of the decade were the two offshore islands, or Taiwan Straits, crises of 1954–1955 and 1958. They revolved around island groups off the coast of China that the Nationalists continued to hold and garrison. Nationalist harassment made shipping more difficult for the Communists. The islands also served as platforms for espionage. Perhaps as important, the inability to seize them and put an end to such activities was humiliating to the new government on the mainland.

For American diplomats, the offshore islands crises were difficult to deal with because they occurred at the intersection of public opinion and high policy. Military leaders focused so narrowly on avoiding embarrassment and the fall of Taiwan that they ignored both the lack of strategic value and the indefensibility of islands that were so close to the PRC coast that American military ships could not be arrayed between them and the mainland batteries. Instead, officials talked seriously, privately and publicly, about the use of nuclear weapons. But, in the end, the United States did no more than escort shipping and keep the Nationalists supplied. John Foster Dulles tried and failed to convince Chiang to remove his garrison from the islands. He did eventually coerce Chiang into renouncing the use of force to try to recover the mainland. Washington had avoided war, but not by much.

KARTOSH: The Chinese Communists tried to take Jinmen soon after Chiang left the mainland [actually attempted October 1949]. An old [Nationalist] Chinese general, one of the few good ones, beat them back. Jinmen is in Xiamen harbor, and it is like holding Manhattan against the United States Army. The Chinese Communists didn't try to take Jinmen all through the Korean War, which surprised many of us in the area at the time.

There was just enough of the Chinese Air Force left on Taiwan and just enough of our fleet in the Formosa [Taiwan] Straits—at that time we had a policy of physically separating the two sides—to force the Chinese Communists to keep a good number of their divisions in Fujian and Zhejiang Province. On the offshore islands the Nationalists built up a guerrilla force, which raided the China coast and captured small Chinese Communist and other flag merchant vessels. There was a rather effective blockade of Fuzhou and other Fujianese ports. Butterfield and Swire [a major British merchant company] used to love to run blockade runners into the Taiwan Straits and try to cut into Xiamen or Fuzhou on a dark night. The Chinese Nationalist guerrillas would bring these ships to one of the offshore islands and steal their cargo and send the ships back to Hong Kong saying, "Don't try it again." The guerrillas on the islands would take the cargo that they stole to Hong Kong and sell it. They were fully self-supporting.

The British complained to us that the situation was getting expensive and they didn't want to confront the Chinese Nationalists or us with a military escort for these ships. They wanted us to tell the [Nationalist] Chinese to back off. Eisenhower did and that silliness, up to a point, ceased. But at the same time the people on the offshore islands became even more dependent on Taiwan, because most of those islands are not self-sufficient, particularly if you have more than the basic population in residence. If there is a military unit or guerrillas, then you have to send additional supplies to the islands.

In [September] 1954, the first heavy Chinese Communist bombardment occurred. They didn't invade, but they bombarded it quite severely. They could do that because of the location of the island.

CLOUGH: In January of '55, the Chinese Communists attacked and occupied Yijiangshan Island, which was one of the Dachens, and then we assisted the Nationalists in withdrawing their troops and civilians.

KARTOSH: China retook the Dachens, the northernmost of the Nationalists' island chain to free up any nonsense around the Shanghai approaches and Zhejiang ports.[33]

CLOUGH: They launched a very effective amphibious assault. In '55, our military operation was designed to help the Nationalists withdraw 10,000 or more people from those islands, because they were considered too far away. And in exchange for Chiang Kai-shek's agreement to withdraw, it involved, at least implicitly, a greater commitment by us to the other offshores, the bigger ones, Jinmen and Mazu particularly.

But it was still left unclear as to whether we would defend those islands if they were attacked?

CLOUGH: That's right. We would never give an ironclad commitment. What we got from the Congress was the Formosa Resolution, in February of '55, authorizing the president to intervene in any attack on off-shore islands, which he considered to be part of or preliminary to an attack on Taiwan.

Did the policy planning staff ever seriously consider the nuclear option?

BOWIE: Well, the one case I can remember where this became a real possibility was at the time of Jinmen and Mazu, in 1954. Chiang Kai-shek had put a very large part of his forces on the islands and saw them as symbols of his determination to return to the mainland. It was very clear the United States did not take his return to the mainland at all as a serious possibility. But when the Chinese began to shell the islands and seemed to threaten the possibility that they might try to take the islands, this was seen as a test of containment—as to whether or not they would by force be able to throw out Western power or a power supported by the West from these small islands. And in the discussions of what to do, the Air Force said, well, the way to deal with this is to drop small nuclear weapons on the airfields, the Chinese mainland airfields, which would be necessary to achieve air dominance or air cover in the case of any attempt at an invasion of the islands.

This was not a specific action to be taken at the moment, because they had not invaded the islands, but this was at least the proposed way of reacting to that if it occurred.[34] I was very concerned by the implications of this because this was an area which was heavily populated, and while the Air Force claimed that it could make surgical strikes on the airfields, I felt sure that the amount of casualties would be very serious. So I arranged for a presentation to be made based on the weapons' effects which were determined by the Atomic Energy Commission. They had made studies of weapons' effects in terms of the various circles of effect—impact from blast and heat and radiation. So we took the size of weapons, which was quite small by most standards, and we got from the CIA the Chinese population distribution in the area involved. And we plotted to show what would be the consequences of these various airstrikes in terms of casualties. It ran into the millions.

So I had this presented to Dulles to be sure that he fully understood the implications of this course and how horrifying it would be that for the protection of these small islands you would be inflicting these very large numbers of casualties. He never said what the consequence was in his mind of this presentation, but I always had the feeling that it certainly made him extremely reluctant to move in that direction. But I will simply say that as far as policy and planning was concerned, we were doing everything to show that this was not a wise policy.

MCCARTHY: In August of 1958, the thing started when the Chinese Communists began shelling Nationalist supply vessels going in to resupply the Jinmen garrison. We decided that the offshore islands were essential to American interests, so we announced that we were going to escort these Nationalist supply ships into this very narrow body of water.

GREEN: The administration made the declaration that this was the first step towards Taiwan, and thereby gave Dulles the ammunition he needed for invoking the agreement we had with the Republic of China with regard to defense.

CLOUGH: That's right, although we still did not intervene militarily in defense of the offshore islands. We moved the Seventh Fleet in. We convoyed the supply ships to within three miles, but we did not engage in combat, nor did we agree to the bombing of mainland airfields by the ROC Air Force.

MCCARTHY: I was down in the atomic bomb-proofed command center with Drumright, the senior Chinese military commanders, Vice Admiral [Roland N.] Smoot [commander, U.S. Taiwan Defense Command/Military Assistance Advisory Group], who was running an American carrier task force, which was ready to go. We sent several destroyers in with the Nationalist supply vessels and all up and down the China coast, the Chinese Air Force sent up fighters. We had three carriers on the other side of the island of Taiwan, on the east side, away from the mainland. We launched fighters, and they patrolled back and forth for several hours before the Chinese fighters landed to refuel, and they did not come up again. And the Communist forces did not fire on the American vessels.

GREEN: Of course, when you say "blockade," you're really talking about an artillery interdiction. We were receiving these reports from CIA, largely from their people on Jinmen, that depicted the island as just about running out of supplies and obviously of the Howitzer shells and things like that that they had expended, so that we were at the point ourselves, almost, of yielding and calling for some kind of international approach to it. Dulles had gone up to New York to call for a UN resolution calling for the neutralization of the offshore islands, which I thought was a crazy idea, but it was that desperate.[35]

HOLDRIDGE: Marshall Green was very much involved in this one as regional planning adviser. I have to give Marshall credit for an enormous contribution to American foreign policy, and that was the Dulles-Chiang Kai-shek communiqué that came out in October of 1958 [October 23]. This is the one in which the wording was something along the lines that Taiwan was the repository, in effect, of the values of the Chinese people. It went on to say that we supported Chiang Kai-shek's ambitions to restore freedom to the people on the mainland, but this was to be accomplished mainly by political means and not the use of force.[36]

GREEN: Dulles was about to go out on a trip to Taiwan at what appeared to be the end of the firing on the offshore islands. There had been a complete lull. He was going to sign a communiqué with Chiang Kai-shek. What kind of language could we put into this communiqué that would be acceptable to Taiwan? Also, we wanted to make clear that we just didn't see Taiwan as a separate appendage hanging out there in the distance and that it was unrelated to China. It was very important that it be regarded as an integral part of China.

GRANT: The Chinese Communists, if they could humiliate the Nationalists, they might begin to create enough political instability in Taiwan to get the Guomindang to fall or at least become more amenable to some role for them in Taiwan.

Several things became very clear. The Nationalists had been taking Americans on tours of Jinmen and saying, "This is impregnable. We could last forever." As soon as the shelling started, they said, "We have just so many weeks left of shells and supplies. If you don't get in there and help us, it will go down. It will be terrible." This was a lesson, but I don't think that the administration of Eisenhower and Dulles was particularly anxious to lose Taiwan, having said what they had about the Democrats. First off, we began to put pressure on the Nationalists to force them to do as much of their own supply as they could, but we did start moving to give them enough protection so they could save the island. When the Communists saw the U.S. coming into this close proximity, memories of Korea were very clear on both their side and ours, and neither one of us wanted it repeated. They lifted the bombardment, without admitting it, away from the beaches so that we could get the supplies in, so that a crisis was not precipitated.

Meanwhile, we had finally to face the anomalies of our own position. Dulles had to say publicly what had always been privately clear, and that was we did not commit ourselves to the Chinese Nationalists retaking the mainland, nor even to them forever. In some very tough arm-twisting, before he left the island, he forced the Generalissimo to sign a joint statement saying that the Guomindang would rely primarily on political means to recover the mainland. In other words, "Don't rock the boat." This was very important, because then it finally got us off this rollback syndrome. We couldn't talk rollback after that and the Hungarian Revolution in 1956.[37]

In which we did not intervene, although there had been a lot of rhetoric about rolling back communism.

GRANT: Precisely. So in a way, both we and the Chinese Communists had to learn to live publicly with the realities of the situation. You asked me whether this was generally the "school answer" in the embassy, and I would say no. I don't remember anybody drawing that publicly. Certainly with Everett Drumright, he was not about ready to make that leap personally.

There were a lot of people in Taiwan who were delighted with that communiqué. One thing happened within weeks. We began to notice people started fixing up their residences. They obviously had read it and they said, "Uncle Sam ain't gonna put us back there. We are not going to be able to get back on our own. We're going to be here." That movement was just palpable. It went right through the community. Even for the hardest bitten return-to-the-mainland types, they began to recognize that they'd better make their peace with Taiwan.

OSBORN: I recall particularly one thing about Secretary Dulles' visit of October 1958 [to Taiwan]. This was toward the end of the Strait Crisis. When Dulles talked to Chiang, the GIMO urged him to take a very stern military posture against the Chinese Communists. According to accounts circulating within the embassy, Secretary Dulles said to him, "Well, you know there's a limit to what we can do against them, without the possibility of having to use nuclear weapons, and of course, nobody wants that." Reportedly, from the GIMO's lack of reaction against this suggestion, Secretary Dulles got the impression that Chiang Kai-shek was not averse to contemplating this possibility—if necessary.[38] Dulles was quite taken aback by that. At any rate, from about that time on, we put increasing pressure on the Taiwan Chinese to accept their position in Taiwan with good grace, and to stop continually harping on returning to the mainland. The Chinese Nationalists—for their part—while they accepted the position, and did not really try to attack the mainland, or really seriously threaten to do so—they would not commit themselves to accepting what they considered a two-Chinas situation. They became very strongly committed to maintaining their identity, as the one sole government of China.

DRUMRIGHT: The heavy bombardment of Jinmen in September of 1958 went on continuously for over two weeks. In that case, I am glad to say that President Eisenhower and Secretary of State Dulles presented a very firm front. I recall that President Eisenhower made a visit [June 1960]. He was very warmly received in Taiwan, probably one of the warmest receptions he ever received anywhere. We assisted the Chinese as we could, but they did most of the defending there and with the result that, after four to six weeks, the Chinese Communists pulled back and stopped their bombardment.

Tell me why was this energetic defense of Jinmen undertaken?

DRUMRIGHT: Well, it's mainly symbolic. They held onto all the territory that they could. And they still have it today.

KREISBERG: In Hong Kong what we were doing is, essentially, reporting on, analyzing, and picking up through intelligence and interviews information on the Chinese intentions during the Jinmen-Mazu crisis. Our judgments were that they, in fact, did not intend to seize the island—that the effort was to try to frighten the GMD off the island. Politically, if there had been a severance of the offshore islands from Taiwan, it would probably have intensified the probability of a political separation of Taiwan from the mainland. What the islands represented was the link of China with Taiwan. So it was a question of intimidation.

Then the question is what Beijing would have done had the GMD actually decided to pull out. We could never quite figure out where that was going to take them. And, of course, it was never clear to us precisely why they were running this risk. There is some evidence, which came out later, but I don't think we thought it at the time, there were differences inside the party over this whole exercise between the minister of defense, Peng Dehuai, and Lin Biao and Mao.[39]

GREEN: *Do you think that the Warsaw Talks had anything to do with what actually eventuated in the resolution of the Taiwan Strait crisis of 1958?*

CLOUGH: Ken Young gives them considerable credit (I think more than they are actually due) in his book on negotiating with the Chinese Communists.[40] I've always felt that what really impressed the Chinese was the rapid massing of the Seventh Fleet in the vicinity of the Taiwan Strait, and the fact that we were willing to convoy ships. We took a very hard line. Their effort against the offshore islands was, in part, a probe to see where the United States stood. Mao Zedong had just come back from Moscow the previous year, where he had talked about the East Wind prevailing over the West Wind.[41] In '58, they were getting their Great Leap Forward started. They were in a period of high confidence, and I think he wanted to test the United States on the Taiwan issue.

GREEN: I was handling this Taiwan Straits Crisis as Dulles's principal assistant, working on the problem. I would tend to agree with you, as opposed to Ken Young, with regard to the impact of the Warsaw channel in the resolution of this issue. The U.S. military commitment and our apparent willingness to go pretty far had a little bit of impact. When we brought these two large LSTs [tank landing ship] on station, with all the small craft that could swim out of them, which were manned by "Chinats," as we called them [Chinese Nationalists], it was clear that we had the capacity to resupply the islands. They wanted to take the initiative and not be seen as having lost out, and that's when they came out with their first announcement.

Were there concerns about any Soviet involvement at the time?

KREISBERG: All that we were able to see was what the Soviets were actually saying. Our interpretation from what the Soviets *were* saying was that their support was very lukewarm.

ARMSTRONG: There were some who felt we had edged towards nuclear war. I never felt that way. Partly because the Soviets, although giving a reasonable amount of support to the Chinese, didn't come out with their real sort of vigorous support and threatening language vis-à-vis the West until it became apparent that the whole thing was going to calm down. Many years later we learned that one of the problems of the Sino-Soviet relationship was the failure of the Soviets to give China as much support as China thought it should have.

GREEN: The Soviets had supplied the artillery and most of the shells that were being expended on the islands by what we used to call the "Chicoms." The Soviets had the capacity for turning off the supply of these shells, and therefore it could have been a factor in the decision of the Chinese to call off the shelling. But we didn't know much about the depth of the Sino-Soviet breach. We knew that there were tensions, but the full flavor of the Sino-Soviet split didn't become manifest for another two or three years.

CLOUGH: I've always felt that, in respect to the Sino-Soviet relations, the evidence that we had broken the blockade was of vital importance. Because if you look at the dates of Khrushchev's first message to us and his second message, which was the more intemperate one and the one which the president refused to accept, the more intemperate one was sent after the blockade had been broken. I've always felt that the Soviets felt they weren't taking as much risk then, because the actual fighting was going to diminish.[42]

DEVELOPMENTS IN TAIWAN II

As time passed, conditions in Taiwan improved notably. This happened particularly after the Nationalists accepted in practice, though certainly not in rhetoric or ambition, that their sojourn on the island would be prolonged and possibly permanent.

LACEY: Whereas [in the mid-'50s] the embassy's political section was a prisoner of Chiang Kai-shek's foreign office, I and my colleagues [in economics] were free to wander afield and to really see what was going on and to really report on developments affecting U.S. policies. That was a fascinating experience, including a friendship which I still enjoy with a Martin Wong, who was then in Taipei, the chief of the China-U.S. Administration (CUSA), a Chinese government-U.S. collaboration to administer economic aid. It was the senior office in China concerned with the administration of U.S. economic aid. Economic aid and military are so closely intertwined that Martin Wong wisely had invited to attend his weekly meeting a General Chiang Ching-kuo, who represented the Chinese government military side of the aid program. His main title, at the time, may have been chief of the veterans program [actually deputy secretary general, National Defense Council]. That involved a very major source of U.S. assistance, as well as the military side of it. Anyway, that was my first [extended] exposure to Chiang Ching-kuo. And I didn't like him one bit. I was prejudiced beforehand because of my prejudice against his father. I saw him as a thick-necked Gauleiter, a strong-arm man, not one that I would particularly like to associate with.

Did you see the base being laid down for the kind of prosperity Taiwan has come to enjoy?

LACEY: Yes, I did. And the base was the very multimillion dollar, multibillion dollar aid program that the U.S. government had with Taiwan. Taiwan, at the time and for some while afterwards, was our major aid recipient in the world.[43]

I was appointed the senior officer in charge of U.S. technical relations with the ROC. Our job was to "wean away" Taiwan or the Republic of China from U.S. aid programs. My mandate was to, first of all, find somebody in the technological community who would be willing to go to Taipei in a special capacity as scientific advisor. Not in the conventional sense of science attaché to the ambassador, but science advisor to the whole of the republic in terms of his ability to acquire contacts with various centers of technological expertise in America. He [Bruce Billings] introduced something as simple as computers, which back in those days, was still an unknown, an uncharted field.

DRUMRIGHT: After Hong Kong, much to my delight, I was assigned to Taiwan, where I knew the Chinese officials from Chiang Kai-shek on down, and where I felt there was some opportunity for advancement of Chinese aims. I arrived there in March 1958.

MOCERI: Not very long after that, the question of Drumright's appointment as ambassador to Taipei came up. The Chinese government had given its *agrément* to his appointment, but he made some unfortunate remarks in Hong Kong, before coming to Taipei. Reportedly he had indicated that the Nationalists would not find him the soft touch that Rankin had been. They'd find him very hard to deal with. They certainly weren't going to get the fighter planes that they'd asked for and that Rankin had promised them. Rankin was great at delaying tactics and he just kept delaying, delaying, delaying, which was proper because they couldn't take offense at that. He'd cite complications, difficulties, bureaucratic procedures. Well, obviously, the Chinese in Taipei got wind of what was being said in Hong Kong. The editor of the *Chinese Post*, which was the local English-language paper, and other informal emissaries came to me to express their dismay and their disappointment.

HOLLOWAY: Drumright was very right wing, very conservative, and was a strong believer in Robertson's policies. But he was also intellectually interested in the problems. He had no sympathy for the Chinese Communists, but he was certainly not prepared to say they don't exist.

KREISBERG: My relations with Drumright were not good. He was an aloof and chilly person, intensely anti-communist and anti-PRC. Very rigid. He ran things absolutely by the book. Very conservative. He, of course, had been one of the staunchest opponents of the Communists and strongest supporters of the GMD government while he was in Nanjing. The man became a strong policy enemy, and not a personal friend of any of the China officers who subsequently were dismissed, or cast into oblivion, by Senators McCarthy and [Pat] McCarran [D-NV].[44]

I violated his instructions [earlier] in Bombay by allowing an American newspaperman to return to the United States via Europe even though we had been instructed to amend his passport so he would have to go directly back to Washington in order to testify before the McCarran Committee. He had been suspected of spying for the Chinese Communists or the Soviets. Amos Landman and his wife Lynn had written a book together in Shanghai in the late 1940s, and were being accused of having had connections with a Soviet agent in Shanghai at the time. [The book referred to is *Profile of Red China* (New York: Simon and Schuster, 1951).] I thought this was probably absurd. Drumright and I had a big fight about that. The newspaperman was eventually cleared but the experience dramatically affected his later career.

GRANT: I was doing economic reporting and I was tremendously impressed. How did Chiang Kai-shek, with his dismal record on the mainland, do so well in Taiwan? The fact is that Chiang Kai-shek was a lot more astute than people thought. He was inarticulate in any language, including Chinese, but he did know that he had to make Taiwan work. The Chinese government had basically been frozen into immobility during the anti-Japanese war. On Taiwan he had a free hand, and he knew it had to work, and he appointed some brilliant guys.

They had a brilliant financial man, K.Y. Yin. He was the one who forced an honest system of foreign exchange control on Taiwan. He dismantled the preferential rates that encouraged those who could get their hands on money to get it out. He made it very difficult to move money out of Taiwan, and he priced the Taiwan NTU (new Taiwan dollar) at a level that made Taiwan competitive economically. That's when their export drive began, based at first on processed agricultural goods.

I remember they learned about mushrooms, and their exports of mushrooms to the United States went from something like a couple of hundred thousand in one year up to about $6 million the next year. Kennett Square—the mushroom town in Pennsylvania—was beginning to scream to their congressmen. I remember going to the Chinese and saying, "Listen, cool it. Move out. Diversify so you won't generate these resistances." But agricultural policy and the financial policy, along with a very educable and hard-working people, is what started what we see now.

MOCERI: The Taiwanese population, at that point, was being held down very, very firmly. On the other hand, there were taking root within that society a number of rather important democratic practices. These became possible because Chinese Mainlanders were carrying out in Taiwan what they failed to do on the mainland: a very aggressive and effective land reform program, and setting up agricultural cooperatives, because no peasant could own more than approximately three acres of land.

The agricultural economy had to have credits if it was to rise above the subsistence level, feed a burgeoning population, and generate foreign exchange. Through the cooperatives, the farmers themselves started pressing for measures. They needed credits. They needed fertilizer. They needed seed and tools. Pressuring the Chinese government—the Chiang Kai-shek government—brought them such returns. This was democracy in action at that level. It was shaping the practice of democratic discussion and debate and the arts of exerting pressures on governmental entities. I regarded that as something that had to come

out of the soil of Taiwan itself. It was not something any USIS operator was going to instruct a foreign populace about.

Was the Chiang Kai-shek government at all responsive to those pressures?

MOCERI: They had to be, because they needed the food supplies and they
needed the export earnings. And that is why the Taiwanese nationalists,
who called for the overthrow of the government, all from the safe haven
of the Japanese islands, were off base. Democratic practice cannot be
imposed even by an exile movement, because the democratic practice
has to have grass roots. It has to be born in the soil and be nurtured in
the soil, in the land and the spirit of a nation. And in Taiwan of the
fifties it was slowly forming.

Not all U.S. programs were focused on economic reform.

MCCARTHY: The most notable thing about the time I was there, which
was from August of 1958 to July of 1962, was the work that we did with
young writers and artists. We sponsored and, indeed, worked upon a
large number of English-language translations of the work of younger
Chinese writers. We published books of art by the more advanced avant
garde Chinese and Taiwanese painters in Taiwan. One reason for doing
this was competition with the outpouring of works in English translation, art work from the Foreign Languages Press in Peiping. This stuff
was designed for distribution to the rest of the world, some of it
through commercial channels, some of it through USIS posts elsewhere.

Another reason was that we were particularly anxious to get to know
the younger generation in Taiwan, which was composed partly of
Mainlanders and partly of Taiwanese. We learned fairly rapidly that at
least among the people we were dealing with, the real battle wasn't
between Taiwanese and the Mainland Chinese; the main battle was
between the generation that held power, somewhat disparagingly called
"the long gowns" by these younger people. The student generation,
both Mainland Chinese and Taiwanese, was pretty much united by the
fact that they felt held back and restrained by the older generation.
They were a force for change, a force for progress. We did identify

some very capable people. A great many of them went to the United States to study writing, many at the University of Iowa international writing program.

What about the effect of this very large standing military force on Taiwan? Was this tolerated or was this a problem?

GRANT: They were getting so old that they finally had to retire. You'd see old sergeants that looked like they were in their fifties and sixties, and some of them were. Some of them began to melt into the countryside. I remember picking one up—way back in a little village where I'd been out walking—and taking him back to his base. He was a funny little character. He had a wife and a family in that village and was favorably known. I'm sure as soon as he could get out, he just retired to his village. There were a lot of old soldiers. There were hundreds of thousands. The Chinese, again, approached this rather well in some respects, under Chiang Ching-kuo. Ching-kuo was a wonderful politician and nobody's fool. He realized that you had to do something with these servicemen as they grew old. They created an employment system for retired servicemen. They put them to work in the mountains, for instance, building roads, logging. They settled wherever they could find some niche for them, yet kept them in a group context in a barracks-type existence. They kept the people from becoming totally a drag on the society. They kept them, on the other hand, from competing too directly. So it was an effective operation. They had a loyal cadre that they could still turn back to if they needed. It probably minimized the cost. Sure, to carry several hundred thousand soldiers on an island economy of 15 million people was very difficult. But it was a burden that they succeeded in handling very well.

LEVIN: Getting to Taichung in 1959, ten years after Chiang Kai-shek's government had evacuated to Taiwan, it was quite clear that Chiang was not going "to reconquer the mainland," the phrase in use then. At the same time, many of the people who came from the mainland didn't have any other rationale for their preferred position. They felt they had moved a national government to Taiwan. In their eyes, to dissolve a national government and to turn it over to the local provincial Taiwanese Chinese was both legally and personally anathema. Some of them were motivated by selfish reasons. They wished to retain their politically justified positions which provided them with authority and money. Others were motivated by a kind of patriotism. They thought that communism was bad and that they should hold out an alternative for China. After all, who knew what opportunities the future would bring the Chinese people.

Others felt that the Nationalist—Guomindang—government of Chiang on the mainland had done a bad job. It had been corrupt, it had been inefficient, it had been warlord ridden, and so forth, and they would show in a different place, in a different time, when they weren't fighting the Japanese, that non-Communist China could do a good job with the local people. So among the Mainland Chinese in Taiwan, there was a whole range of rationales for their situation.

The Taiwanese majority viewed things differently. In the nineteenth century, the Chinese in Taiwan had not liked being ruled from Beijing. Then they were under the Japanese, who had been an efficient but not a cruel colonial regime the way they were in Korea. And since 1945, they were again under the mainland, so the Taiwanese had a long history of adjusting to people from outside their province ruling them. Many of them resented this but historically there were relatively few Taiwanese martyrs in these situations. Perhaps more a demonstration of adaptability than cowardice.

Taiwan was a relatively prosperous place. After the economy got going in Taiwan, due both to a great deal of American aid and a lot of educated, highly motivated people who were anti-communist from the mainland, both Taiwanese and Mainlanders saw their daily lives improving. Also, the people from the mainland were not a monolith. In addition to the Guomindang there were a lot of other minor political parties and individuals who came from the mainland to Taiwan who were anti-communist but were also highly critical of the Nationalists. Foreign Service officers whose reports suggested the possibility of a benign democratic outcome received much less attention than those predicting Taiwanese-Mainlanders violence like that which occurred in 1948 [actually 1947], or a communist invasion, or other dramatic events.

GREEN: [In Washington] the focus was so much on Taiwan. China almost meant Taiwan in those days. In the bureau most of the officers were working on Taiwan.

HOLDRIDGE: Well, we were defending the integrity of Taiwan. I hate to think of how many thousands of man-hours went into defending Taiwan's position in the United Nations and other international organizations, as well as making sure that the budget carried a sufficient amount of military assistance for Taiwan. We also had the AID program going, which was remarkably successful development assistance and which eventually reached the point where Taiwan became self-sufficient, economically speaking.

TAIWAN RIOT

American support for the Chinese Nationalist government in Taiwan did not always proceed smoothly. In the mid-1950s, Washington pressured Chiang to reduce his military establishment and focus on developing Taiwan rather than planning for a return to the mainland. On May 24, 1957, dissatisfaction with American policy led to an assault on the American Embassy and USIS headquarters in Taipei. Although allegedly a popular demonstration triggered by an unjust verdict in a court case, many believed, and circumstantial evidence suggested, that the government, perhaps even Chiang Ching-kuo, had been responsible. For Washington and the American ambassador the event was unexpected and deeply disturbing.

OSBORN: There was an incident in Taiwan called "Black Friday," in which Chinese demonstrators sacked our embassy, and rioted and destroyed USIS. It was a sensational affair, because the Chinese on Taiwan had been considered—by everyone, ourselves included—to be model clients of ours. No one could imagine why they were doing this, especially since the Department of State had not received any adequate forewarning from the embassy in Taipei.

HOLLOWAY: The ambassador was in our staff meeting, visiting Hong Kong, telling us that, "Oh, our relations with the Nationalists are fine. Everything is great." And one of the clerks came in and called him out. There was a message that the Nationalists had just broken into his embassy and, among other things, had dropped the safe on his car!

This was after an incident of—

HOLLOWAY: An Air Force sergeant, named [Robert G.] Reynolds, was acquitted of murdering a Chinese. And the ambassador Karl Rankin was there telling us that this was all going to pass and blow over! And at that moment, his embassy was on fire!

MOCERI: The incident had its origin in an event that had occurred a very few weeks before: an American sergeant had shot and killed a "Peeping Tom" Chinese coolie. Publicly, it appeared to be a commonplace, minor tabloid story with only two mildly titillating aspects, a glimpse of sex and the resulting confrontation of a white American soldier and a nondescript Chinese male. The facts were quite different: the Chinese was a colonel in the intelligence organization headed by Chiang Ching-kuo, son of the president, and he had been shot in the back, probably as a result of a quarrel over the division of spoils from an illegal activity. I argued for a two-step solution: first, the embassy should make a formal apology to the Chinese government, extend its deepest regrets to the widow of the colonel, and offer an appropriate monetary compensation in accordance with Chinese tradition and practice; and second, the American should be tried as soon as possible in an American court-martial in Taipei, found guilty of murder, removed immediately from Taiwan, and at an appropriate time allowed to appeal the verdict in another military jurisdiction. The ambassador seemed at least interested in my proposal, but the military present rejected it in the most vehement terms, draping themselves in the honor of the American flag and the military code of justice.

Within a very short time the court-martial, open to the public, was convened. A verdict of "not guilty" was brought in. The Americans, the great majority of the public present, rose to their feet and cheered. According to all reports, the few Chinese present maintained a stunned silence. The next day, Black Friday, the Chinese authorities took their revenge or, as I put it then, taught a lesson the Americans could neither ignore nor forget. At about ten that Friday morning a group of about 20 stalwart Chinese males, armed with crowbars, entered the embassy building and proceeded to smash everything in sight. A few Americans who tried to hide in the building rather than attempting escape were injured. In the meantime a large, orderly, and very quiet crowd of Chinese gathered around the perimeter of the embassy ground to watch the unfolding spectacle. For that day and the entire weekend the American community was rife with reports of a rioting Chinese mob in the tradition of the anti-foreign Chinese riots around the turn of the century. The American media, as far as I could tell, indulged the same fantasy. There was not a shred of evidence of any rioting anywhere in the city.

On hearing of the activity at the embassy, I decided to keep the USIS facilities open as long as possible without endangering the staff or Chinese in our facility. Late that afternoon, at about four o'clock I was informed that the Chinese "wrecking squad" was leaving the embassy and apparently was headed in the direction of our building. Quietly I ordered our office closed, sent everyone home, secured the building, and left the premises at four-thirty. Half an hour later the wrecking crew arrived, accomplished its mission, and vanished. It could hardly escape my attention that the USAID building was not a target. The following week I began an intensive search for photographic evidence of the behavior of the Chinese crowd at the Embassy. I soon had a collection of 20 or 25 photos, collected from various sources. From that evidence the only conclusion that could be drawn was that a group of perhaps two hundred Chinese men, women, and children had gathered or been gathered to watch—without the slightest sign of emotion—an interesting spectacle.[45]

WALTER JENKINS: It was the same group that was turning over the diplomats' cars at the fashion show, and it was Ching-kuo who was a little bit behind that, too.

GREEN: That's right, and scattering all these officials papers around the streets, picked up, spuriously, by a newspaper in Bombay which printed all these things. They were very incriminating, but they were false documents. But we couldn't tell the world that they were false documents, because in proving that they were, we'd be giving away some of our secrets. So we just had to live with this situation.

MCCARTHY: When I arrived in 1958, the year after the riot, USIS was housed in a private residence, a rather dilapidated private residence. Not even the screens worked very effectively, and we didn't have air-conditioning. It was something of a slap in the face to us, because the house had previously been occupied by General Sun Li-jen, who was in deep disfavor with the Chinese National government. In fact, I think at that point he was under house arrest someplace outside of Taipei. So the staff was a bit demoralized. Several people had been hurt in the riot.

SINO-SOVIET SPLIT

American diplomats found the idea of a Sino-Soviet split difficult to credit. In examining the thoughts of Foreign Service officers during the 1950s, it becomes clear that different people and different agencies of the government accepted the fact of a rift between Moscow and Beijing at different times and dated it to different events.

BOWIE: NSC 162/2, which was prepared in October 1953, was the document that took account of the Solarium exercise and was the first so-called National Security Strategy Paper or something of that order.[46] It was essentially a presentation of our broader set of purposes but also in particular our approach to the Soviet Union. It was a pretty balanced approach. Essentially it took the view that the Soviet Union was not at all likely to launch any aggressive war in Europe, that it had very substantial military capabilities but it would try to use them politically to extend its influence; that it was engaged in trying broadly to extend its influence wherever it could; that it was on the whole cautious in its pursuit of that purpose but nevertheless unflagging; that its control of the satellites at that point was firm and was not likely to be disrupted, because of its military capability to put down any uprisings. The paper carried forward the basic concept of containment as formulated in the Truman Administration but modified to incorporate the "New Look."[47]

   With respect to China, it took the view that its relation with the USSR then was close and cooperative but that over time it seemed unlikely that this would be able to persist, that there were almost sure to be cleavages because of the somewhat different interests of the Soviet Union and China, and that it was quite likely that over time there would be a fissure in that relationship. Not predicting any time, but simply taking the view that it was not forever a solid kind of relationship.

CLOUGH: Soviet-Chinese relations, as far as we could see, were getting stronger and stronger, because of the close military relationship, the supply of large amounts of tanks and planes and all kinds of military equipment, which continued after the [Korean] war.

   For at least several years after that, we were concerned about the next move on the part of the Sino-Soviet bloc; it was still a bloc in '54. It was evident that they were already beginning to strengthen the Vietminh. The Chinese had been extending their railroads down to the border so they could get equipment down more easily. That was our main concern, this and a lot of the propaganda that was coming out. In '54, the Huk movement was still quite active in the Philippines.[48] The various Burmese civil wars were going full tilt and the communists in Malaysia were still fighting very vigorously. Northeast Thailand had its own communist rebellion. There were communist rebellions all around. So we were very much concerned with what seemed to us to be a Sino-Soviet advance into Southeast Asia, the next move by communism.

I recall one occasion, maybe the spring of '54, [the popular reporter and columnist] Joe Alsop came through. He had written a big article for the *Saturday Evening Post*, in which he had a new theory. At the rate that the Soviets were building up the Chinese military forces by a certain date, about a year from then, a year, maybe two years, they would have enough force on the southern border of China so that they could just overwhelm Thailand, Indochina, it would all become part of China.[49]

I argued with him. I said, "You know, if the Chinese wanted to do that, they wouldn't have to have all this Russian equipment. They've got manpower to burn compared with these countries. They could go down there and take them over. You're building up a house of cards here, based upon a lot of calculations, which really don't. . . . It's the intention of the Chinese that's important, not what they happen to have in the way of military equipment." But he brushed that aside. He'd made up his mind and wasn't going to listen to anybody out there.

BOWIE: As I said to you earlier, as early as October '53, the analysis in NSC 162/2 was that while the alliance between China and the Soviet Union at that point was strong, in the longer run there was going to be friction and tension and perhaps more. The policy was to put pressure on China, partly for the purpose of forcing it to depend on the Soviet Union. In other words, it was felt that to the extent the Chinese had to make demands on the Soviet Union, they would be more of a burden on the Soviet Union, and that the Soviets would not be able fully to meet the demands and therefore that the possibility of increasing tensions was there, although one couldn't be sure what form they would take. I don't think there was any expectation or hope that this would produce any short-run consequences, but it was going to add to the possibility of gradual cleavages, gradual tensions, gradual emergence of differences in national interest.

And that was the basis on which there was an effort to keep China out of the UN and also keep the COCOM restrictions: the restrictions on strategic trade with China were more stringent than they were on the Soviet Union.[50] The result was that the Chinese had to get whatever they wanted through the USSR. We understood that they could get it through the Soviet Union, but inevitably that made them dependent on the Soviets and made them more demanding of the Soviets.

Did you view the communists as a great monolithic brotherhood?

HOLLOWAY: No, no. Our original policy was very sophisticated. We said that Mao was going to be a Tito. This was done at the very highest levels in Washington. Afterward, you get into the mid-'50s, you had to start asking yourself, "Haven't we pushed the Chinese into the Soviet's arms?" But we certainly did [not] think of them as monolithic.

But you didn't see any sort of rift coming between the Soviets and . . .

HOLLOWAY: No, except for these reports that the Soviet advisors couldn't get along with the Chinese. The foreigners [coming out of China to Hong Kong] were more interesting [than the Chinese], particularly the White Russians, most of whom spoke Chinese and had gotten some fairly good insights. We were hearing that the Chinese and the communists and the Soviet advisors were not getting along from '53 on. They would detail arguments in this factory or that factory, where the Soviets said "Do it that way," and the Chinese said. . . . Now this turns out to be indicative of much deeper disagreements.

How did you, and the people around you, view the China-Soviet bloc?

LUTKINS: We very much saw it as a monolith at that particular point. I guess we should have been alert. Maybe it was because not enough of us had been steeped in Chinese studies and Chinese history to remember that there had been very long-lasting and bitter relations between China and Russia that predated communism, and that the Chinese resented the Russians taking over territory that they regarded as Chinese and that was subject to Chinese suzerainty. But, probably because of the Korean War and pressures on Vietnam and whatnot, we definitely regarded the Sino-Soviet alliance as a pretty firm and fixed thing. I don't recall before 1961, any of us who had enough sense to have second thoughts.

At what point did the Sino-Soviet split begin to be a serious consideration in the minds of American analysts of China?

KREISBERG: Well, we began thinking about the serious problems in Sino-Soviet relations back in 1956. There had been a widespread assumption that Sino-Soviet relations were strained as early as 1952, coming out of the Gao [Gang]-Rao [Shushi] case,[51] in which it was widely assumed there was Soviet involvement. Before that there was an assumption among professionals, but not at a high political level in the U.S. government, that something had gone wrong between Mao and Stalin in the long Mao stay in Moscow in 1950–1951.[52]

Certainly the degree of involvement by the Chinese in the eastern European crisis in 1956 suggested to us that there was likely to be considerable tension between the Chinese and the Soviets over that issue, even though Zhou Enlai was supporting the Soviet Union in its effort to regain control, both in Hungary and in Poland.[53]

GRANT: The thing that legitimized the extreme anti-communist positions in the United States [was] that they really did talk as though they wanted to take over the world. This does encourage an adversarial relationship. Even after I should have recognized it—it was much later—it must have been about 1959 or '60 that I finally said to myself, "These guys, the Russians and the Chinese, really hate each other." And yet the schism really came when Mao went to Moscow [in 1957] and said to Khrushchev, "We can't afford your liberalization. We've got to keep the whip, got to keep discipline." And Khrushchev went ahead and did it his way.

This triggered the schism, but in a sense, aside from a deep sense of cultural antipathy, the Chinese looked down on the Russians, as they looked down on other people, and felt themselves the civilized people on earth. At the same time, the Russians had the techniques and the Chinese had to use them. Even their economic organizational techniques were very much in the Russian mode. It was only when that schism became evident, even to the slowest reader, that there was any real chance of American policy moving.

Where did you see the Sino-Soviet monolith developing? Looking back on it,
it's hard to believe these two very dissimilar states, basically enemies, thought
that they were working in absolute lockstep.

GREEN: The conventional wisdom is that they were pretty much in lock-
step, certainly in their foreign policies, and that the first evidences of the
split between Moscow and Peking occurred in 1957 after the Sputnik
was put up, and when the Chinese sent two delegations to Moscow to try
to benefit and participate in this breakthrough, getting certain kinds of
technical support from the Russians. But the Russians gave them the
cold shoulder.

HOLDRIDGE: The first sign of [a rift] was in 1959, during the anniversary
of Lenin's birthday. In Beijing's media, out comes this big editorial on
"Long Live Leninism."[54] This, in effect, took to task the "modern revisionists" for having deviated from the true course, saying that it was
impossible to really bring about the victory of communism by peaceful
means, that there had to be bloodshed. Later on, we found that he had
also said elsewhere, in another context, that if 20 million Chinese died
in the course of a nuclear war, there would be many, many more Chinese to carry on the tradition.[55] This was a real break with the Soviet
Union. The [Chinese said they were attacking] Yugoslav modern revisionism to begin with. It was only later that they dropped the
"Yugoslav" and began to attack the Soviets directly. A lot of people,
when this editorial came out, couldn't believe it. They thought that the
cohesive factors are more important than the divisive factors in the
Sino-Soviet relationship. It didn't work out that way.

You mentioned earlier the problems with having Walter Robertson at the helm.
Was he one of those who shared that sense that it was all a fraud?

KREISBERG: Yes. He just shrugged his shoulders and said, "These guys
just don't understand." There is an ideological affinity. They are arguing, but that doesn't change the fact that there is a Sino-Soviet conspiracy. There was this cabal of Drumright, McConaughy, Rankin, Robertson, and Rusk. There were the five of them who really dominated
American policy toward Asia between 1950 and 1968. It was only after
that group passed from the scene that it became possible even to begin
talking about a change in policy.

U.S. CHINA POLICY II

Toward the end of the decade relations entered into one of those periods that recurred, in which one side in the dispute appeared willing to try to improve relations while the other side was distracted or under severe political pressures. At this point, the Eisenhower administration softened somewhat toward China, for instance, by easing trade controls, but Chinese internal politics made even modest reconciliation impossible.

HOLDRIDGE: We always had this feeling in the back of our minds that we didn't want to foreclose any opportunities which might open in the future. We wanted some kind of a relationship. In addition to that, Dulles was very upset by the second offshore-islands crisis, and the fact that Chiang Kai-shek insisted on keeping a large percentage of his forces on those highly exposed islands. This was a strong temptation for the Chinese Communists to knock them out. In so doing, they could destroy effectively all the will to resist on the part of all of Taiwan. It was a pawn that the Chinese Communists could take advantage of. Therefore, there was a great deal of disagreement and problems that we had with Chiang Kai-shek over the disposition of his forces, and their unwillingness to withdraw them. Dulles said, "Never again are we going to get ourselves involved in one of these things."[56]

This began to have another effect of making us more and more wary of becoming too much the protagonist for the causes of the Chinese Nationalists, and not taking a broader view of the total problem of China. Dulles, who had been one of the strongest pro-Chiang Kai-shek types when he first came aboard in the State Department, by the time he died in 1959, he had a rather different view of the problem—a much more comprehensive understanding of the total China problem.[57]

CLOUGH: I felt that China was a huge country we were going to have to deal with one way or another, whether we liked it or not. I felt that the economic policies followed by the Communists in the late '50s were going to be disastrous for them. If you looked at their demography, if you looked at the very small proportion of budget they were putting in agriculture, it was clear they were going to have food problems. And, of course, within a few years, they did.

OSCAR ARMSTRONG: I took over the China Office in INR 1957–61. Then you had the Great Leap Forward in '58, one of the world's craziest experiments. China needed land reform because you had 80 percent of the Chinese working the land who were deeply in debt to the landlords, etc. The Chinese carried it out in a very violent manner. Nobody really knows how many people were killed, but I suspect the figure is in the millions. They did distribute the land. Then gradually they started with mutual aid teams, then cooperatives, then collectives, and eventually they moved into communes, by which time the peasants had lost all the land. They had no land or implements to work with, everything had been communalized. And the system didn't work. Together with the Great Leap Forward, the commune system, and some bad weather, China came closer to the type of traditional famine for which China was infamous than any other time of the Communist rule. That would have been '58, '59 and the really bad year was 1960–61. The Chinese popular parlance still refers to it as the Bad Years. Nobody really knows how serious the problem really was. One demographer later said that China should have 28 million more than they seem to have. That doesn't mean 28 million died, but there were many deaths through starvation and malnutrition. Infant morality rate was very high.[58]

But there was a conviction that China was going to be a continuing presence and that you would have to go on dealing with China?

KREISBERG: Absolutely. A broad consensus among most of the professionals that the sooner the United States began dealing with China, the better. The question was always how we were going to be able to create a strategy that would enable us to achieve this. But with Walter Robertson as the assistant secretary of state, it was a subject that one could not possibly put in writing.

BOWIE: The policy of the administration was to isolate China, to contain China, to put pressures of whatever sort you could on China, without undue hopes or expectations. The only aspect I differed on that was that it seemed to me that we were using up an enormous amount of effort to keep China out of the UN every year. We had to try to twist arms so that they could never get a majority in order to get in the UN. My view was that it made more sense from our point of view not to use up all this political capital but essentially to try to cut a deal with the other countries that we would not object to the Chinese coming into the General

Assembly but that the position of Taiwan was not to be disturbed. And I thought that the Chinese would then say, well, we're not going to come in on that basis and therefore the situation would relax. But if they did come in it wouldn't make any difference.

This, however, was strongly opposed by Walter Robertson. When I tried to raise this in the Planning Board of the NSC as a subject to discuss, he insisted that he and I talk about it with Dulles before I went further with it. And Dulles decided that he would prefer that I did not pursue it in the Planning Board, so I dropped it.

My own feeling was that this involved the relations with the right wing of the Republican Party, which was absolutely committed to Chiang. But they had also the supposed backing of quite a large pressure group in the population generally which they had mobilized. My sense of it was that Dulles and Eisenhower tried to keep these people quiet by throwing them verbal bones and acquiescing in certain things which neither Eisenhower nor Dulles thought were terribly important, so as to have a free hand to deal with the other things which they did feel important. And this decision of Dulles about China may partly have been based on his strategy of trying to keep pressure on China: maybe forcing them to use the Soviets as their spokesmen in the UN may have been part of that. But also a factor was that he didn't think this was terribly important to American foreign policy. If he in any way indicated some acceptance of China by letting them in the UN, even though it was purely pragmatic, he thought he would stir the right wing people up and get them on his neck. I'm not saying he shared my view, and he may well have thought it was a mistake for substantive reasons, but on top of that there surely was the element that this was simply going to bring down a lot of trouble on him and wasn't worth it.

How did you personally feel about the two Chinas?

BOWIE: Certainly as far as the Policy Planning Staff was concerned, they took it for granted that the Communist regime on the mainland was in charge and solidly in control. There was no expectation that Chiang would be able to return to the mainland or take over all of China. It was understood that this stance was merely one that was for morale of the Chinese Nationalists.

How did you see China? Where were they going? How was the thing working?

LUTKINS: As I saw it at that time, and as I reported it (and this ran against the wishful thinking of certain people back in Washington, and even to that of our consul general, Mr. Drumright, who wanted to really believe that the Chinese Communist regime was only a temporary aberration, a temporary phenomenon and that it wouldn't last) it seemed to me definitely that the new government had entrenched itself pretty securely. That by and large it governed with the support of the mass of the people. That it had brought some improvements, which were not necessarily due to communism but to the mere fact that it did exercise authority over the whole country for the first time in fifty years or more, and therefore was in the position to take purposeful action in terms of preventing famine, in getting supplies from one area of the country to the other, in getting production back in shape after a period of the war years in which everything was disrupted.

And, what was possibly more important, the people in charge of the government showed no signs whatever of either disunity or lack of confidence in their ability to govern. This all pointed to the fact that they were there to stay for the foreseeable future. It seemed to be a fairly stable, secure government enjoying popular support. And we reported that to Washington. In Washington they were still trying to deny that picture and to work for the undermining and downfall of the communist regime.

Those of us who were on the spot during the period recognized that it takes two to tango, and that we couldn't just automatically recognize the Chinese Communists. There would have to be some negotiations and some terms involved. But most of us felt that it would be sensible policy to start preparing for that, laying the groundwork for it, and perhaps doing some probing to find out on what terms it could be done. Whereas the official attitude in Washington was that these people were beyond redemption, we couldn't possibly ever consider having relations with them, and that, in addition, we would be betraying our friends on Taiwan.

I think Robertson just discounted the reporting. It didn't agree with his mindset and he just ignored it. But anyway, he thought it was of secondary importance compared to the need to combat communism and to stand by our wartime allies and friends in Taiwan. And then you can't ignore the domestic political aspect of this, that the Republicans and the China Lobby had made such a big thing about our "losing" China—as if it were ours to lose. And so it had become a matter of political orthodoxy.

When I came back at the end of '57, Ralph Clough briefed me on the general situation. I guess I must have misunderstood what he said, because I got the impression that perhaps the department was a little more flexible in our thinking about the future than actually was the case.

I was up in New York on a visit, and my father, who was in Wall Street, asked me to have lunch with a number of his friends and say a few words about China. About a week later I got called into Robertson's office and raked over the coals, because one of the people who had been present had the impression from what I said that our policy toward China was changing. Robertson made it be known in no uncertain terms that it wasn't changing, and that if I wanted to stay on board I'd better mind my manners. I had said something along the lines that, "Well, surely at some point or other we'll have to probably make an accommodation with the mainland."

What about covert operations against the mainland?

KREISBERG: Before I joined the Foreign Service, I was interviewed for the Central Intelligence Agency [and was asked] whether I would be willing to be dropped by parachute into Sichuan. My target would be to organize a group of anti-communist Guomindang soldiers who remained up in the hills in Sichuan and work with them in a number of operations and then exfiltrate myself, if necessary, out through Burma. They looked at me, and they said, "Would you be willing to do that?" And I said, "No." And that was the end of my interview. But there was a very active program involving infiltrating people into China with specific targets—largely military.

Sabotage might have been . . .

KREISBERG: No, I don't think there was sabotage. I think it was largely intelligence. What do the Chinese have? Where do they have it? Is there any indication they are working on nuclear—even at that point, obviously, this was a constant source of concern, nuclear weapons? Where troops are being based. It was a standard semi-war kind of intelligence operation that we engaged in. Some things were run out of Taiwan. There was a lot that was run out of Hong Kong. Hong Kong was a very big station at the time.

LILLEY: They had massive funds, they had a lot of people and no over-sight, none. And it was run by people with very limited experience in that area. And they concocted these huge plans. [But] the big paramilitary programs, the ones in Taiwan had failed, the Western Enterprises. Ray Pierce had headed it, big hero of the [World War II] Burma campaign, but this was different, running guerrilla operations against China. None of them worked and they were being told there were a million guerrillas in China. As Pierce said, "If I ever find a guerrilla, I'm going to stuff him and put him in the Smithsonian [museum]."[59]

TIBET

Chinese control over Tibet dates from the early eighteenth century and passed through periods of tighter and looser overlordship. Tibetan resistance to Chinese control, which occurred sporadically, took official form in 1913 when the thirteenth Dalai Lama declared himself the ruler of Tibet and expelled the Chinese. But British interference and Sino-Tibetan disagreements meant that the issue remained unresolved. Upon coming to power in 1949, the Chinese Communists decided not to invade the territory but compelled the Tibetans to sign the "17 Point Agreement for the Peaceful Liberation of Tibet," which formally acknowledged Chinese sovereignty. During the 1950s, China treated Tibet's religious institutions respectfully, sent in economic aid, and otherwise minimized Chinese influence. In adjacent areas, also populated by Tibetans, however, they launched socialist reforms that provoked a rebellion in 1955–1956. The Dalai Lama took refuge in India in 1956, fearing that Tibet would be next, but when Mao pledged to postpone reform in Tibet the Dalai Lama returned. By March 1959, tensions had again risen to such a level that the Dalai Lama fled, and this time did not return. American CIA operatives supported Tibetan resistance and the Dalai Lama's exile operations. The United States funded groups inside Tibet and paramilitary forces along the border with Nepal.

HOLDRIDGE: In April 1956, the Chinese established what was called the Preparatory Committee for the Autonomous Region of Tibet. They had quite a conclave of senior people. The Dalai Lama made a speech, which was carried intact in the Chinese press. It was also released in English version by the New China News Agency. A comparison of the two showed that there were some very significant omissions in the English version. For example, the Dalai Lama was quoted as saying that the Chinese had built many roads in Tibet, and he was very grateful for this development of his country. He went on to say, "However, in the course of the construction of these roads, many of our people gave up their valuable lives, and we send our sincere condolences to the families of these people." In other words, there was something wrong. There were a number of other spots in that where you could see that the Chinese had overridden religious scruples. They had changed the social system, and there were deep resentments.

I came to the conclusion that the Chinese were having a real problem in maintaining their control in Tibet. If they thought they had it in hand, they were "whistling in the dark." Later on, I saw a British evaluation of my report. They said, "No, no, no. This guy is way off base." But this was three years before the Dalai Lama—the Khambas—revolted in Tibet and the Dalai Lama fled with his whole entourage to India.

1960s

WITH THE END OF THE Eisenhower administration, Americans looked forward, in the words of their newly elected, youthful president John F. Kennedy, to getting the nation moving again. Among the policies that Kennedy appeared to want to change was the way the United States related to China.

Kennedy inherited a mixed legacy. The Eisenhower administration had not advanced toward recognition of the People's Republic of China, even though it had become clear that the communist government would not be a quickly passing phenomenon. Moreover, by the time of Kennedy's inauguration it seemed obvious to many Americans, including large numbers of the nation's diplomats, that a rift had developed between the Chinese and their Soviet mentors—a rift that had significant ramifications for the United States. By the late 1950s, American policies had also proven dysfunctional. The trade embargo against China had frayed, and even Washington's closest allies were exchanging goods with the Chinese. Efforts to keep China out of the United Nations were also running into trouble and the State Department struggled to find new formulas to keep the Nationalists in and the Communists out. On the other hand, by the beginning of the 1960s, American public opinion seemed less belligerent on China and anticommunism, McCarthyism having dissipated. Privately, Eisenhower confided in his advisers that admitting China to the UN and extending diplomatic recognition to Beijing were inevitable developments, although the time was not yet ripe.

China became an issue in the 1960 presidential campaign when, during an interview with NBC's David Brinkley, candidate Kennedy remarked that defense of the offshore islands, undertaken at such cost and peril by the Eisenhower administration, made little sense. Vice President Richard M.

Nixon immediately took up the point during the second televised debate with Kennedy, attacking him for being willing to cede free territory to communism. The perils of dealing with the issue of China may have had a significant impact upon Kennedy. When the new Democratic administration entered the White House there were no bold initiatives on China. There were, however, a series of small measures taken to liberalize policy, and several members of the Kennedy team, as well as Foreign Service officers, anticipated further progress. Some even believed that in his second term Kennedy would open diplomatic relations with Beijing, although little evidence has emerged to substantiate that view.

Of course, changes in U.S. relations with China, even had Washington been eager to make them, would have encountered a succession of problems in China. In July 1960, Soviet Premier Nikita Khrushchev decided to withdraw Soviet technicians assisting China to industrialize and build vital infrastructure projects. Khrushchev had been angered by what he saw as Mao's irresponsibility, stridency, and refusal to accept Soviet guidance. Soviet withdrawal aggravated the turmoil caused by the Great Leap, as did bad weather conditions in the critical years of 1959–1961. Some 30 million Chinese starved to death and possibly another 30 million were never born. China turned toward retrenchment under moderate leaders such as Liu Shaoqi, Mao's heir apparent, which helped deal with the tremendous economic upheaval within the country but increasingly alienated Mao Zedong and the leftists. In 1962, to counterbalance what Mao saw as growing revisionism—the return to Soviet or even capitalist practices—he launched a Socialist Education Campaign that then flowed into the Great Proletarian Cultural Revolution in 1966.

The Cultural Revolution, 1966–1976, became China's most radical and most tragic campaign. The agenda combined revolutionary resurgence with a power struggle as the people of China became pawns wrestling with Mao Zedong's inner demons. Mao had become convinced that China had abandoned the inspirational legacy of the 1940s. He sought to discipline the bureaucracy, eliminate Liu Shaoqi and other "capitalist roaders," rekindle egalitarian ideals, and expose China's youth to the revolutionary experience that had been critical to shaping the character of the founding generation as it had risen to power. To do all this, he set the young against the old, peasants against intellectuals, moderates against radicals, and radicals against fanatics. China plunged into ten years of anarchy with the government and even the Communist Party under assault by Red Guards, some of whom rampaged fully armed and willing to fight bloody battles in the name of Mao Zedong and revolutionary purity. In the process, China's foreign policy also became radicalized. Its Foreign Ministry came under siege, its diplomats were recalled for thought reform and Red Guards rioted beyond China's borders in cities like Hong Kong. At home they burned down the British Embassy and humiliated Soviet diplomats in Beijing. Until countervailing pressures arose toward the end of the decade these radicalized Chinese had no interest in improving relations with the leading capitalist nation in the world. Although the worst of the tumult had passed by late 1969, the Chinese people would have to endure another six years of disorder before the Cultural Revolution truly ended.

Apart from the Cultural Revolution, other factors in the arena of international relations also militated against betterment of Chinese-American relations. Chinese rhetoric and actions in the early 1960s appeared to confirm the picture of China as aggressive and expansionist. During the Cuban Missile Crisis of October 1962, the Soviets blamed Beijing for pushing Khrushchev to take reckless actions in order to prove his zealousness. And then, as if to demonstrate their own militancy, the Chinese attacked India. Although the Sino-Indian Border War had been provoked by India and involved territories long disputed between the Indians and Chinese (a controversy that predated communist control of China), Americans, including the most outspoken advocates of contacts with China inside the Kennedy administration, condemned Beijing. Finally, the United States also confronted the reality of a nuclear armed China. Progress toward development of a Chinese bomb frightened Kennedy and when Beijing finally tested a weapon in 1964, that event further darkened an already highly negative image of China in the United States.

Not all contacts were bleak. In 1962, as evidence of famine inside China grew, the Kennedy administration suggested the possibility of food aid to the Chinese. Further, when Chiang Kai-shek decided to seize the opportunity presented by China's disarray to mount an attack on the mainland, the Kennedy administration stepped in to warn Chiang against rash action and to reassure Beijing, through the Warsaw talks and then in public, that the United States would not support such a venture. Indeed, the ambassadorial talks between the United States and China continued sporadically throughout the decade, providing a channel of direct communication. Growing opinion among the informed public, including scholars and journalists, argued that more contacts ought to be opened. In congressional hearings held in the mid-1960s, witnesses urged the American government to moderate its policies, to think about changing its efforts to isolate China—efforts that were serving also to isolate the United States on China issues—and drop barriers to interaction with the Chinese.

The decline in Sino-Soviet relations also spanned the decade, both worrying and reassuring Washington. Americans approached the whole idea of a rift with trepidation, fearing that the divisions in the communist camp did not really exist but were designed to deceive the West and weaken free world unity. Kennedy dismissed talk of a split, declaring that the argument was simply over how best to bury the West. Gradually, the United States came to acknowledge the obvious: the Sino-Soviet alliance had ceased to function. Americans finally could see that the split between Moscow and Beijing held advantages as well as dangers for the United States. Washington welcomed Soviet interest in détente with the United States, despite Beijing's objections, and celebrated the reduction in Soviet assistance to the Chinese. On the other hand, the State Department worried about the absence of moderating influences over Chinese extremism. Much energy and expertise was lavished on trying to understand what the rift would ultimately mean for the international community. By the end of the decade it became clear that the opportunities opened for the United States were legion.

During the 1960s, concerns about Chinese aggressiveness and radicalism also influenced perceptions of the liberation struggle in Vietnam. The United States initially had become involved in Vietnam at the end of World War II because of the French. Washington worried about the weakness of the French government in Europe and its vulnerability to communism. Thus Americans proved willing to accept the French determination to reimpose colonial control over Indochina and provided considerable aid, especially after the Korean War began. Then in 1954, after the Geneva Conference, when France finally acknowledged its defeat, the United States took over the struggle. To Washington, the contest had increasingly become part of the Cold War confrontation with communism, and in Southeast Asia the primary threat came to be seen as an expansionist China. The Foreign Service officers here talk at length about the U.S. government's efforts to gauge whether China would intervene in Vietnam, whether this would be another Korean-style contest. Lyndon Johnson's obsession with the Vietnam War meant that virtually all policy in Asia during the late 1960s related in some measure to developments in Vietnam.

The Nationalist Chinese government on Taiwan took advantage of the

American commitment to Vietnam, as it did of direct economic and military assistance from the United States. The 1960s became a decade of remarkable growth for the island, with successful land reform and fledgling industrialization beginning to fuel a rapid expansion of the economy. Chiang Kai-shek continued to promote the idea of returning to the mainland, but Washington made clear that it would not support such a venture and risk the possibility of war with China. As a result, Taiwan's involvement in the Vietnam theater failed to serve Chiang's strategic purposes of linking war in Vietnam to a war against China, but did contribute to economic prosperity.

For the Nationalist Chinese leadership one of the central preoccupations of the decade was the fight to retain the seat in the United Nations reserved for China. During the 1960s, support for the Taipei/Washington position on the issue declined, forcing the United States to expend more and more energy to keep a functioning coalition alive. The risks of the effort became clear with the emergence of the Mongolia question. The admission of the Mongolian People's Republic was paired with that of Mauritania. Chiang Kai-shek declared that he would keep Mongolia out because he saw it as part of China—not a legitimate nation—as well as being a communist pawn. But if Taipei cast its veto in the Security Council against Mongolia it would alienate African votes needed for retaining its own seat. Intense American pressure finally persuaded Chiang not to frustrate the admission package, but the effort demonstrated how fragile support for Taiwan had become. Indeed, even though the trend against Taiwan was temporarily arrested by China's outrageous behavior during the excesses of the Cultural Revolution, increasingly American diplomats understood that time was running out.

Thus as the end of the decade approached, the likelihood of change in the United States' China policy seemed to have grown. But few would have imagined that events at the end of the 1960s would utterly transform relations between the United States, China, Taiwan, and the Soviet Union, as well as the rest of the international community. That will be the story of chapter 4.

U.S. POLICY

The early days of the Kennedy administration seemed a period of opportunity with respect to China policy. The idea of change appeared to be in the air. Why that change did not happen has led to speculation regarding

Kennedy's attitudes toward China and has led historians to question whether the resistance toward policy changes rested primarily in the White House or with Secretary of State Dean Rusk. The Foreign Service officers speaking here all thought Rusk comprised a central impediment to liberalization of policy toward China. The historical record is less clear. Warren I. Cohen, Rusk's biographer, remarking upon the secretary of state's convictions about the proper role of a presidential adviser, doubts that Rusk would have thwarted the president had he actually hoped to improve relations with China.[1] During the early days of the Kenndey administration, American officials came to understand that they faced a weakened China where massive famine and social disorder were testing communist control. Whatever initiatives they attempted would be met by leaders preoccupied with internal crisis.

GRANT: [In 1961, at the beginning of the Kennedy administration] we created the Mainland China desk and made it the Office of Asian Communist Affairs, thereby giving it office-level status and beginning to admit that the Chinese Communists existed. That created a place for a focus.[2]

GREEN: It was no longer just CA [Chinese Affairs] controlling China, where almost all the attention of the desk was focused on Taiwan. That meant that all of a sudden the PRC and Mongolia had representation in the State Department, which they had lacked before.

DONALD ANDERSON: The Office of Asian Communist Affairs theoretically covered Communist China, North Vietnam, and North Korea, all the communist countries in Asia. We spent about 98 percent of our time on China, and 2 percent on North Vietnam and North Korea.

GRANT: There was a feeling in the air that Kennedy would like to do something about China, but they hadn't really focused on it, so it was a wonderful time, the sense that people wanted something done, but didn't know quite what they wanted.[3] Anyway, we were trying to bring public policy into line with our recognition of the diplomatic realities. I was out on the lecture circuit, talking wherever I could to TV, radio programs, to national organizations, meetings, and so on, to try to explain what we're about and getting good vibes from them. So there was quite a little operation going.

GREEN: We were making certain moves to allow certain Americans [reporters, doctors] to travel to Communist China. We had under consideration moves to change our foreign access control regulations so

Descending from the aircraft: Ralph Clough at the top of the stairs and below him, Secretary of State Dean Rusk.

that Americans could buy things that came from Mainland China. These things must have been known to the authorities on Taiwan and must have been discomfiting.

LUTKINS: Very early in the Kennedy years, in '61, very gingerly tentative moves were made toward opening up of relations with Outer Mongolia, which then was very much still under Soviet domination. They didn't get very far on this. And part of the reason was that the Nationalist government on Taiwan, of course, had always regarded Outer Mongolia as Chinese territory that had been taken away from China. They and the Chinese lobby made their opposition felt, so that it just wasn't considered important enough by Kennedy to make an issue out of it, and they dropped it.

CLOUGH: Drumright was the ambassador in Taipei when I arrived as DCM [deputy chief of mission]. Averell Harriman had become assistant secretary [of state for Far Eastern Affairs, December 1961-April 1963], and he didn't care much for the position that Drumright took on the Taiwan-China issue. Harriman wanted to see some movement on the China issue.

GREEN: At the chiefs of mission meeting in Baguio [Philippines] in 1962, I made a presentation as consul general, Hong Kong, with regard to what was going on in China and what the implications of this were. It delighted Harriman, because basically what I was pointing out was information that supported the thesis that we should be taking another hard look at what our basic China policy should be. And, of course, Chester Bowles, who was Harriman's superior at that time, being the under secretary, also shared that same point of view.[4] Furthermore, at that Chiefs of Mission meeting, Harriman was really quite dictatorial, and he was very short and sharp with certain people at the conference. The Kennedy Administration was leaning a bit in the direction that was going to make it very uncomfortable for our representatives in Taipei.

CLOUGH: That's right, but the experience on Mongolia had a somewhat chastening effect on the Kennedy administration, because they hadn't realized the strength of the Nationalist views and how it would affect the China Lobby. After all, Kennedy had got in by a rather narrow margin. [Arthur] Schlesinger [Jr.] later said in his book [*A Thousand Days*] that they had a talk about the China issue, and Kennedy said that we haven't got the political support to do very much on China. Let's leave that for the second term. And, of course, he never had a second term.

Did you get any feel for Secretary of State Dean Rusk's attitude toward the PRC?

THAYER: Yes, but my feel was secondhand. I was in his presence from time to time, but didn't have much direct dealings with him. He was pretty hard-line, articulating the line including the PRC threat to Southeast Asia. We were also trying to open relations with Mongolia in those days, and he did not support certain memos that were sent up proposing we do this or that to open negotiations or relations with Mongolia.

Was Rusk calling the shots on China policy? Or was this basically the Democratic Party, having been burned on China in 1952, not willing to get caught again?

DONALD ANDERSON: Dean Rusk played a major role. He had been assistant secretary for Asia, he had been in China, he considered himself a China expert. He was very conservative on China issues. It was very difficult to get any flexibility.

GREEN: Dean Rusk, of course, looms large in all we are talking about. There was a man who was very deeply committed to upholding the position of the Republic of China, diplomatically and otherwise. A man who took a very strong view on the Cold War and also the war in Vietnam. He is not the kind of man who would ever back down. This must have been considerably comforting to Taiwan, to know that Dean Rusk was secretary of state. Probably just gave them the same kind of assurance that they had when Dulles was the secretary of state.

KREISBERG: Rusk was sufficiently closed mouthed, and I was sufficiently junior that I don't have any recollection of Rusk ever giving any hint that he would have liked to have gone further than Kennedy would let him. My most active conversations and dealings with Rusk on this issue were after Kennedy had died. There is a theory, which some people have described as fact in some of the Kennedy biographies, that Kennedy was going to move on China after 1964. I had never seen anything to support that.

During the period 1961–1964, what was happening in China and how did we see developments within China?

GRANT: We were very slow to pick up the changes. In 1961, China had just been through the complete collapse of the Great Leap Forward. Millions of Chinese died. The birth rate just slid down to nowhere. We didn't appreciate any of that. Again, the field probably had a better sense of China than Washington. I, of course, had been working strictly on Taiwan for three years, but was in regular touch with our Hong Kong people; also with Chinese scholars. I was not nearly on target as to how bad things were, but I discovered that CIA was directing a national intelligence estimate which showed Chinese GNP still rising in 1960. I said, "This is absurd!"

It was very clear that a counterattack had been launched by the economic rationalists, if you will, and we were beginning by this time to recognize that China was by no means a monolith. There were these divisions. You could see Zhou Enlai coming back into prominence, and some of the other more conservative leaders. They went back and resurrected the vilified birth control efforts.[5] They shifted their focus first on light industry and industry serving agriculture. But basically, this was a recognition that massive capital-intensive investment was eating up the resources, and they needed to get less capital-intensive solutions out faster. During the early and mid-1960s, there was a quite rational discussion within China, and you could see this in their output, their regular international reports and reports of their meetings and so on, that they were trying in pragmatic terms to deal with their problems— leaving, of course, the ideologues and the old ideologue Mao Zedong more and more frustrated with this descent of the revolution into the practical. It was a period of retrenchment and sanity, and we recognized it as such, and we spotted the Cultural Revolution for the insanity it was, much faster than we had the Great Leap Forward.

Why is it that we had trouble understanding what was happening in China? Were there discrepancies between Foreign Service reporting and covert sources from the Central Intelligence Agency?

GRANT: In that particular instance, that national intelligence estimate, the more optimistic view was coming out of the CIA bureaucracy. In the field, I'm not so sure that there was that much of a divergence. It would depend on the individual. We tended to be in communication and probably think very much the same way. As to why we don't guess right, it's just an opaque society. Now, in fact, we did guess right on their external behavior, which has been much more consistent through all these periods than their internal. We recognized belatedly, by the early 1960s— that the Chinese, despite the rhetoric, were going to be rather cautious in their foreign policy.

The longer I watched them, the more I was aware of this Chineseness. They feel themselves the center of the earth. "Zhongguo" [the

Chinese name for China] means "the central kingdom." They expect respect from others. They thought they should be playing a big role, even when they had no money to give away. They spent a billion dollars U.S. equivalent on the Tanzania-Zambia railway, which was strictly a prestige project.[6] In other words, they were pulled by this image. But there were other things that even the slow reader could read. Take the Portuguese colonies of Macao on the China coast and Goa on the Indian coast. The Indians, whom we always think of as being a major democracy and so on, simply walked in and took Goa.[7] The Chinese did not take Macao, and even kept the overzealous local communists from doing so, partly because they didn't want to rock the boat for Hong Kong. And they didn't want to rock the boat for Hong Kong because they were earning money through Hong Kong.

So there was a very strong strain of practicality, which I began to recognize once we saw the schism with the Soviet Union, and realized it was there, and once we recognized—as a bureaucracy—that the Great Leap Forward had not been a leap at all, it had been a disaster.

You mentioned cables. I've seen Foreign Service officers stay up till all hours to send the cables back to Washington. Do they really matter?

LEONARD: They do. Whether an individual cable is acted on, or has an effect or not, they create the atmosphere and the structure within which decisions are taken. Another very major part of that atmosphere and structure is the reporting in the daily press. Everybody in the State Department reads the [*Washington*] *Post* and the [*New York*] *Times* or finds out one way or another what's in them first thing every day, and maybe some of the other papers as well. One of my jobs that I had a little later was early morning briefer on the seventh floor. This is a small group of three, four, five department officers, usually led by the assistant secretary for INR. At that period it was Tom Hughes, who would come into the department very early in the morning, get briefed on everything that had happened in the previous eighteen hours or so, including the cables and intelligence reports from the CIA, various intercepts, all sources. Then they would go up with these materials and brief the secretary, the deputy secretary, and so on, and end up about ten o'clock briefing the assistant secretaries, the various regional assistant secretaries, and so on. I did that for a while, and found that in fact the people

who were being briefed were very eager to get this. They felt if they did-
n't get it, they were not able to function as effectively in the meetings that
they would then be having with the other senior officials later in the day.
If you were behind one important fact or one key analysis of some event
or other, you not only lost face or prestige, it looked as if you didn't do
your job, you weren't paying attention to it. You also simply weren't
being paid any mind to in the meetings. So the cables have a very important effect on these key officials, and one of the reasons they are surrounded by swarms of junior aides, etc., is because there's far more than
anyone can possibly read and you have to have a system of filtering and
funneling these down so that the facts that really matter, not the texts, are
available to the people who have to then do the policy making.

*What was the impression of the effectiveness of the VOA [Voice of America
radio] in the early 1960s?*

HUMMEL: I'm not sure that we knew. We in the VOA envied "Radio Liberty" and "Radio Free Europe" in their free-swinging, detached ability
   to choose what they broadcast. They would reach people who otherwise were not being reached, with information about their own countries or their own areas that their communist rulers would like to suppress. We couldn't try that. We didn't try to tell the Chinese what was
   going on in China. We didn't know enough about it, for one thing. My
   previous assignment in Hong Kong had convinced me that talking to
   refugees and people who had come out and reading snippets from the
   Chinese press which we could get our hands on did not give us sufficiently reliable information about what was going on. So instead we
   were projecting the United States in what we called a full and fair way.
   It was tilted, obviously, to some extent, by our desire to make the United
   States look good. That is, that we have our democratic processes and the
   things that we were proud of.

*After the Hungarian Revolution of 1956, there was a concern that we were too
active in pushing something approaching a revolt against the communist leadership of Hungary, when we weren't going to do anything about it in a military way. Was this very much of a consideration in our China broadcasting?*

HUMMEL: It had subsided as a major factor, at least in my mind.

NEGOTIATION WITH THE PRC I

During the 1960s, Americans and Chinese continued to meet periodically to try to resolve problems. Most of these encounters proved sterile, but neither side wanted to break the diplomatic contact that the Warsaw exchanges afforded.

GRANT: I had, as were a lot of us young people at that time, been deeply impressed by [George] Kennan's containment policy for the Soviet Union.[8] I remember believing, even from day one when I was in Hong Kong, that in a real world, the only way to deal with a threat like the Chinese Communists is to make foreign adventure against our interests expensive and dangerous, but to make an evolution towards a less unfriendly condition promising—to offer them that possibility.

We ran the preparation of the Warsaw talks from our office. David Dean was the one who actually did the drafting. It was the devil's own time to keep on finding things to talk about every month or two. I forget how often we met. But what we did was constantly pick up little themes. Like there was an epidemic in China. We had an embargo, of course, on trade with China. We said to them, "We are going to lift the embargo so that drugs can be shipped if you'll need them or are interested in having them." We had, of course, an embargo on travel with China. We got this lifted so journalists, if they could get in, could go. We were trying to find as many small ways as we could, just suggesting, "Sure, there's room here for dialogue."

DEAN: I would go to Warsaw every month to advise first Ambassador [John] Cabot and then Ambassador [John] Gronouski in the actual talks with the Chinese and we gradually tried to change the tenor of these talks.[9] When I first got there neither side would acknowledge the other. They'd sit down and start their talks. But when I got there after I'd spoken to Bill Bundy, who was the assistant secretary, we tried very hard to change the atmosphere of the talks, to shake hands at the beginning, to change the language. Instead of referring to their regime we referred to their government. And we took out a lot of other pejorative expressions in an effort to make it a little more civil. I also started to go over to the Chinese Embassy at the end of each talk or the following day to see if there had been any problems with the translation. But it was mostly an ice-breaking type of situation. We tried quite hard to get some agree-

ment on newsmen or on academic exchange and saying that it was difficult to solve the major problems. Why didn't we put them to one side
and get on with more practical ones in the interim.

CLOUGH: The Chinese had now shifted their ground. In the early period,
they were proposing things, and we were saying, "No, not until you
renounce the use of force and release all the American prisoners." In the
'60s, it got turned around, and they began to say: "No, we can't have
any improvement of relations with the United States until the Taiwan
problem is settled." And so they rejected these initiatives that we took
in the early '60s, and the talks became very sterile through the mid-'60s.

GRANT: [Then] the Vietnam problem came to intervene and you simply
could not move very far on China, with us on opposite sides of the Vietnam issue.

SINO-SOVIET SPLIT

Although there had been indicators of Sino-Soviet friction during the
1950s, Americans proved slow to accept the idea of a split. In chapter 2,
some Foreign Service officers noted that they saw the events surrounding
the Great Leap Forward and the Sputnik mission as signs of a growing rift.
Nikita Khrushchev's decision to pull Soviet technicians out of China in
1960 persuaded others, although there remained skeptics for another few
years, including John F. Kennedy.

KREISBERG: I don't think any of us expected [the dispute] to go to the
point of Soviet withdrawal, which it did in 1960. And then, of course,
when the ideological war began in the pages of *Pravda* and the *People's
Daily*, it was clear that the relationship was almost out of control. And
the astonishing thing was, in spite of all that, that for several years, there
continued to be a great reluctance inside the U.S. government to
acknowledge that there was a Sino-Soviet split. There was a widespread
view that it was all a fake. It was a fraud being perpetrated for western
consumption, an argument that drove the professionals out of their
minds, which then went on well into the Vietnam years, with Dean Rusk
being convinced as late as 1963 or '64 that what was going on in Vietnam was simply part of the Sino-Soviet expansion of communist
power.

You're saying we hadn't realized how Chinese the Chinese Communists were.
When did you first see the reflections of the schism?

HOLDRIDGE: This all began with that "Long Live Leninism" editorial
[April 1960], but it got worse and worse.[10] Then it became a personal
diatribe. On the one hand, you had Mao Zedong who, if he didn't write
these editorials, was certainly the one who said that this is what you will
put into them. On the other hand, it was Mr. Khrushchev up until 1964.
Then, when he was replaced by Brezhnev, the Chinese didn't change the
tone one iota. They simply said that the new leaders were even worse
than Khrushchev because they were smarter.

GRANT: As the Chinese and the Soviets seemed to be part of a monolithic
communist movement that was out—as it regularly said it was—to
replace capitalism and us, anybody arguing policy had a very good reason to say, "You've got to do everything you can to make life more difficult for these people, to weaken them." The Hilsman speech [see
below], for instance, the whole slow opening up of U.S.-China policy,
became possible only once we had recognized that that was a false view
of the world and that this was not a monolith.

The Chinese had very grave differences with the Russians over policy. They really were terribly bitter that they paid the price to save
North Korea, and the Russians were the ones who became the tutelary
power because of their ability to provide more aid. But it's an ethnic and
national sense. The Chinese are very proud and do consider themselves
to be the most civilized people on earth, and the Russians not. To have
been, during the early 1950s, in this secondary relationship was terribly
galling to them. We didn't perceive this.

GREEN: When I arrived in Hong Kong in 1961, it was already clear that
this feud was blowing up. The Chinese ability to depict the Soviet
Union in the worst possible language was used. Our translator and our
political officers in Hong Kong soon ran out of language to use, because
it kept intensifying, and the Chinese had ways of describing people in
those scatological terms that we just lacked. We found it impossible to
find words strong enough to convey the tone of Chinese broadcasts
against the Soviet Union and to show that it was getting even worse than
it was yesterday.

LACEY: We made two grave mistakes. First of all, I for one at least, was
inclined because of my earlier NIS [Naval Intelligence Service] expo-

sure in Washington to give the Chicoms too much credit for having more power than in fact proved to be the case. When Khrushchev broke off with Mao Zedong, I didn't appreciate the significance of that development, both in terms of the effect upon China and also the effect on the threatened Sino-Soviet bloc stance against the United States. We should have learned earlier than we did—or at least it should have been built into our briefing earlier than it was—the notion that now the Sino-Soviet bloc is broken up, China became a wholly different kettle of fish or kettle of dragons.

GRANT: I have never had any reason to question that once we recognized the schism, we read it fairly close to the facts. Generally the Chinese behaved toward the Soviets about the way we expected. For instance, in the troublesome Xinjiang province and border problems along the Amur River, the Chinese behaved quite hostile.[11] They weren't about ready to do anything with the Russians to resolve these little issues. The Russians were actually the ones who were probing periodically to see whether they could soften the confrontation one way or another. The Chinese kept saying, "Get your troops away from our border and maybe we can talk."

TAIWAN I

The decade of the 1960s proved to be the last in which Nationalist China could rely upon support from the United States to preserve its controversial status in the international arena. In the Kennedy and Johnson years, interaction between the Taipei authorities and Washington underwent no significant disruptions. In 1960, the State Department began to move Taiwan away from economic dependence upon the United States despite Taipei's reservations. By 1964, with congressional pressure to reduce America's foreign aid commitment and evident prosperity on the island, the Johnson administration declared assistance to Taiwan a success and graduated the Nationalist regime from the program. Taiwan adjusted with no difficulty and American military assistance and cooperation continued.

LEONARD: At the beginning of the Kennedy period, we were all almost without exception in the embassy exhilarated by the victory of Kennedy, and very pleased that there was somebody there who was not in any way a captive of this right-wing Republican ideology on the China question. Most of us were probably critical of the China Lobby. We didn't like our ambassador. He was a very difficult personality, and that may have played a part. His name was Drumright. He was very conservative and most of us felt that there were a lot of things wrong with the way Taiwan was being run, economic as well as political.

DRUMRIGHT: Our economic group, under Wes Harraldson, helped a great deal in establishing the base for the Taiwan we know today. That started during those years, about 1960, with the Chinese establishing programs or inviting foreign investors into Taiwan, establishing laws and regulations to encourage them to come. Now we helped them, but on the whole, most of the credit goes to [Nationalist] China itself and the Chinese for what they did at that time. We had a program there of about $100 million of economic aid and a fairly similar sum for military aid during the four years I was there, and it began to show up very clearly before I left. I left in March 1962, on orders from President Kennedy. He felt I was much too supportive of the Chinese there. There seemed to be an apprehension in Washington that Taiwan would take some step to invade the mainland, which I always decried as nonsense.

GREEN: *What about the troop-community relationship? We had a lot of forces on Taiwan, and we had the Taiwan Defense Command there. We had a lot of men in uniform coming in and out. How did the people on Taiwan view our military and our military presence? Was there a kind of a nationalist reaction against it at all?* [Note: Green is both an interviewer and subject.]

CLOUGH: There was some. The attitude was mixed. Most people felt that they were threatened by Communist China and that the United States had come to the rescue, and that it was necessary to have these American troops around in order to defend Taiwan. And so they were willing to have them. And then various elements of society benefited by running a black market with stuff out of the American PX and commissary and that sort of thing. A lot of people were employed by the American MAAG [Military Assistance Advisory Group] and other American military who were assigned there. We had one of the largest MAAGs in the world; we had 11,000 people in it at one point. But there was a certain amount of friction, because the Americans, of course, were far better off. Their living standards were much higher.

GREEN: And there were red light districts that flourished around a base presence. I would gather from your remarks that there was sufficient feeling of being embattled, of being pretty lonely, certainly up against a great power of Red China, that to have a friend and to have a trip wire, by having a friend there was very important, certainly from the government's viewpoint. But down the line amongst the people there were these [other] feelings.

CLOUGH: Yes, there were personal frictions that you get when any large foreign community is imposed on another, but they weren't very strong. For the most part, the people in general were friendly to Americans.

GREEN: My general impression from meeting Chinese Nationalist officials was that they were pretty decent people to work with, and that it must have been a fairly pleasant experience dealing with the Foreign Office in Taipei. They were reasonable, they were rational.

CLOUGH: That's right, although there were issues on which we disagreed. Most of the people in the Foreign Ministry were Western-trained, they were graduates of American universities, many of them, and they were friendly.

Meanwhile, the standard of living in Taiwan was going up. Was it perceptibly going up while you were there?

CLOUGH: Oh, yes, it had already started, although the real takeoff had not occurred in those years. It was underway in the early '60s.

How did you see the situation on Taiwan with the central government and with relations with the Taiwanese?

THAYER: The Taiwanese did feel exploited. Chiang Ching-kuo was just beginning to have some effect in opening the GMD more and more to Taiwanese. But there was a lot of anti-GMD sentiment, particularly among the Taiwanese intellectuals. There was a good deal of apparent sentiment, nostalgia, for the Japanese. Some of this was phony. Some of this was real. In the '60s I exaggerated the importance of the anti-GMD sentiment in terms of the ability of the Taiwanese, anti-GMD Taiwanese, to turn their antagonism into dramatic pressure against the regime.

As a political officer, I saw a lot of the Taiwanese, sympathized with them, and let myself be influenced, more than a more mature officer would have, by their description of the facts and by their perspectives, although I discounted a great deal of what they said about their economic well-being, because I could see how well they lived compared to how I know they had lived ten years earlier, and the statistics were there also.

How did the political section look upon the GMD as a government, its effectiveness, its value?

THAYER: Well, we thought it was effective. We believed and said in our briefings to newcomers and newspapermen how important it was for the free world to have a strong Taiwan, a viable economy, a military force, Taiwan as a major part of the Pacific chain of democratic or at least non-communist states. We believed in the unpleasant nature of the communist regime. All of us saw the imperfections of the Taiwan regime at that time, as did many in the regime itself. We had a rather healthy attitude. Our embassy was not a spokesman for the regime, although there were times, particularly in the evolutionary period of the early '60s, when, for example, on the issue of Mongolia's seat in the UN [see below], Ambassador Drumright got into a big rhubarb with the Kennedy administration. And there were other times when our embassy as a whole saw things a little more sympathetic to the GMD regime than perhaps Washington did. But I don't think egregiously so. We had some very smart and able people at the leadership of the embassy. Ralph Clough was the DCM, and Ralph was one of our best China language and area professionals. His spoken Chinese is terrific. He's a tremendously wise person and was not going to be anybody's fool. I'm sure that his advice to our series of ambassadors was always good. He was in charge a lot of the time. He was succeeded by Art Hummel, who was a very good DCM, very able with the Chinese, also a very level-headed guy. So we weren't a bunch of patsies for the regime. We very much had our eye on U.S. interests.

We did our first bilateral textile negotiation a few months after I arrived in 1963. We had completed a textile agreement with Japan. The importance of the negotiation, the commercial importance is well understood, the domestic pressures here, perhaps, are well understood.

To me, the really enlightening part of that effort was the problem of coordinating and getting a consensus among U.S. domestic interests as manifested in the various departmental representatives who were there—the Labor Department, the Commerce Department, the State Department. These were all participants in the negotiations.

The relationships with the Chinese seemed to be a lot less acrimonious than the relationships among the American negotiators. As a State Department officer, I was very much a creature of the chief negotiator who was a State Department officer himself. I was quite flabbergasted as a relatively naive Foreign Service officer to find the American side conniving with the Chinese side to bypass one of the American negotiators. Well, this isn't a new idea to older hands, but to me it was an eye-opener.

How did the book piracy issue come up? Could you explain the problem?

THAYER: The problem of book piracy in those days was that the Chinese [in Taiwan] were not only copying without authorization American books, including the encyclopedias, but were exporting these publications back to the United States. It did not sit well with the American publishers to find their prices undercut by, say, *90* percent in their own territory. We were getting a lot of flak, Congress and so forth. I worked with a department director at the Taiwan Ministry of Interior, who, himself, was convinced that Taiwan for its own image had to do something about the problem. Within a year or two, exports to the United States had stopped. And I don't mean it all halted completely, but the Chinese regulations were in place and firmly enough so that the embassy issued strict instructions against any of our personnel taking stuff back as being against both U.S. *and* Chinese laws. I don't know that it was ever implemented properly, but the Chinese customs and the American customs both inspected for pirated books, and pirated books that were attempted to be taken out of Taiwan were confiscated, and there were some penalties imposed.

The language school was not in Taipei, was it?

DONALD ANDERSON: No, it was down in Taichung, at that time a city of 500,000 people, but by Chinese standards it was a very small town. Our teachers were entirely Mainlanders so you did have a rather staunchly anti-communist viewpoint. We did get the *People's Daily* and Chinese communist publications because it was necessary to not only learn the standard Chinese characters, that is, the old-fashioned more complex characters which we used in Taiwan, but also you had to learn the simplified characters which the Chinese Communists had introduced if you were going to read the Chinese communist press.

Among your group was the recognition of Communist China a bone of contention?

DONALD ANDERSON: Among the group that I was with and certainly my own feeling was that we ought to be moving in that direction. It was not a simple matter of simply switching recognition at that point. It probably would have produced chaos on Taiwan, but a lot of the fiction that we maintained for many, many years really gradually became rather silly.

1962 TAIWAN STRAIT CRISIS

After the collapse of Mao Zedong's Great Leap Forward, China plunged into a period of devastating famine and domestic disarray. Always eager for an opportunity to try to recapture the mainland from communist control, Chiang Kai-shek insisted that this upheaval and popular disillusionment constituted a perfect opening for his forces. American diplomats scrambled to deter Chiang and reassure the Chinese Communists while, at the same time, reporting on and coping with the repercussions of the crisis in China.

LEONARD: By 1960, we knew that things were terrible on the mainland, although we had no idea how bad it was. Millions of people literally starved to death in that artificially created famine which followed the Great Leap Forward. That inspired Chiang to think that maybe, maybe he had a chance to overthrow the regime and return to the mainland. He began talking to us about that, and he also began doing things on his own, sort of behind our back, that made us very nervous. Averell Harriman had become the assistant secretary. They replaced Eisenhower's ambassador there with a personal friend of Harriman's, [Admiral Alan G.] Kirk [July 1962-April 1963]. He had been ambassador to Brussels, and ambassador to Moscow, and then had retired. He was in his early seventies at that time. Harriman asked him if he wouldn't go there in order to ensure that the thing didn't get out of hand, because there was a lack of confidence. There was a feeling that Chiang Kai-shek had been pampered by the China Lobby and might misunderstand what would be the American attitude toward an attempt on his part to recover the mainland, to launch any sort of armed action against the mainland. Therefore, Ambassador Kirk was sent out to really talk very frankly to the GIMO and make sure that this was understood. In fact, Harriman himself at one point [March 1962] came out. The State Department and Kennedy personally were all concerned that there might be some sort of dangerous action on the part of the Nationalists.

CLOUGH: Let me tell you about the problem of '62, because this is where the Warsaw Talks and the situation in Taiwan are linked together.

After Drumright had left we began to get these reports about preparations by the Republic of China to do something militarily about the mainland. On the mainland, there was starvation and all kinds of problems that the PRC was having after the collapse of the Great Leap Forward, so Chiang Kai-shek was encouraged to feel that maybe there would be some sort of rebellion on the mainland, and that the time would come for him to move in with his troops. He didn't inform us what he was doing, but we found out. He started getting certain units prepared. He imposed a defense tax to raise money.

Of course, the Communists got word of this, and they moved some additional air units into Fujian Province, opposite Taiwan. And this disturbed our government, so that Kennedy, through the Warsaw Talks [on June 23, 1962], informed the Chinese Communists that we did not intend to back Chiang Kai-shek in a military attack on the mainland.

Or take advantage of their internal problems?

CLOUGH: Yes. And later he made the same statement at a press conference in public. It was a very important statement, and it cooled the ardor of the people in Taiwan.

GREEN: The governor of Hong Kong [Sir Robert Black] called me in one day to urge that I [as consul general] get in touch with our government in Washington and our embassy in Taipei with regard to the way Chiang Kai-shek was using Hong Kong as a launching base for certain covert operations against railroads, kind of spoiling operations. That was kind of a lightning rod that might bring the war into Hong Kong. He was very unhappy. I sent this message on to Washington and never got very much of an answer with regard to it. I went up to Taiwan to urge that some action be taken on this, because it was making for a very bad relationship with Hong Kong and the British. Furthermore, these little needling operations, all they were doing was causing the Chinese Communists to be all the more alert and to bring more forces to bear in the area and stirring up, in other words, a dangerous crisis situation. Meanwhile, China was going through the last toils of the Great Leap Forward. Conditions in China were very, very bad. Refugees were beginning to flow over the border into Hong Kong. That happened in May 1962. There was always this concern that China might lash out in desperation. And that's where that assurance came in. Not only that we weren't going to help Chiang Kai-shek in any of his operations, but we weren't going to try to take advantage of their internal problems.

KREISBERG: My recollection is that the Chinese never really were fully committed, at any point, to taking the offshore islands. Indeed, they saw the disadvantage of taking the offshore islands in terms of severing the link between Taiwan and the mainland.

Since Taiwan had a large role in initiating the incident, did that, in any way, worsen relations between Washington and Taipei?

KREISBERG: Not that I recall. Nothing could worsen negotiations with Taiwan in those periods.

Because it was too important, or because it was so bad already?

KREISBERG: No, they were good. There just wasn't anybody who wanted to see the relationship get worse. It was a very protected relationship.

Do you have a sense of people's opinion of Chiang Kai-shek and the government? Was it a question of overlooking problems, because it was so important? Or the people just didn't see . . .

KREISBERG: There was a great sense of disinterest in what was happening on Taiwan except in terms of stability. The only interest we had was stability.

SINO-INDIAN BORDER WAR

Coming in the midst of the Cuban Missile Crisis, the clash between the Indians and Chinese caught Americans off guard. However, the Kennedy administration had long sought to lure New Delhi out of its posture of neutralism and so reacted swiftly. Washington hoped that Indian Prime Minister Jawaharlal Nehru would become less complacent regarding the threat of communism and, given generous American assistance, align his people with the West.

GRANT: We did guess right, certainly our office did—Asian Communist Affairs—and I did personally, when the dispute flared up with India [in 1962], the Indians having belatedly discovered that the Chinese were in a part of Ladakh that they thought was theirs.

This is up in the Himalayas.

GRANT: That's right. It's the western tip of Tibet and the eastern edge of Kashmir. The Indians claimed it, but they hadn't been there enough even to realize that the Chinese were there and building a road through it. Then they tried to push the Chinese out. The Chinese were not to be pushed, and retaliated by the attack in NEFA [the North East Frontier Agency] territories of India just to the east of Bhutan.[12] I can remember in that instance we said to ourselves, "The way the Chinese have been behaving, they have no advantage in getting too far into NEFA, certainly not in getting onto the Indian plain."

This was November.[13] The winter was coming on. Their supply lines were extremely extended. All they were trying to do was to warn the Indians, "If you won't make a deal that accommodates our interests in the west, we can cause you trouble in the east, where you're very vulnerable." I remember saying, "They'll probably pull out. They don't want to spend the winter in that forward position. They don't want to get dug into it." That was a very wise move on their part. In Jinmen, they had seen the difficulty of how you back off an embarrassing situation if you can't stay there. So they just simply turned around and walked away.

What were the key points of contention in the U.S. government on the whole Sino-Indian border issue?

KREISBERG: Well, the basic issues were, first, who had started it, who was responsible for precipitating the crisis? What we should say to the Chinese about it in Warsaw, what involvement we should have in the conflict? Was it an area where we should become involved? How dangerous was it? And what were the Chinese objectives and motives?

Basically, the INR position through that whole time—which all of us who were involved shared—was that it was unlikely that the Chinese were (a) going to thrust down into the plains of India; (b) try to hold on to most of the territory that they seized in the eastern sector or even a number of the areas in the western sector; and (c) as a result, that we should limit whatever engagement we—some of the people in the department, including Rusk and, I think, Kennedy—were pushing for.

We, of course, ended up in the Harriman mission, in proposing that we provide some substantial assistance to the Indians.[14] But I don't think that anyone at the professional level in the State Department ever believed, ultimately, that the Chinese saw this as a major way of extending ultimate control down into India, which was the line the Indians were trying to push.

HOLDRIDGE: The People's Liberation Army, as a consequence of the Great Leap Forward, was in shambles. No tires for their trucks, no gasoline, no ammunition, shortages of everything, morale stunk. The PLA had hardly recovered from that—if it had recovered—when China attacked India in 1962. Part of the reason the Chinese attacked the Indians in 1962 was to show the Indians they weren't to be counted out. Krishna Menon [Indian defense secretary] thought, we'll just throw these Chinese out of the disputed territory, and the Chinese showed them.

Was there very much conflict between the China desk and the India desk over what all of this meant? Did the India desk feel the threat was more serious than the China people?

KREISBERG: The India people saw it more seriously. They saw it as a political opportunity to strengthen ties with the Indians. It was complicated by the Taiwan Strait Crisis of '62 as well. So there was a question as to whether we were seeing a variety of Chinese moves to push outward. My recollection is that INR did not think that's what we were seeing.

So this was a more isolated conflict?

KREISBERG: That's right. Each one of these as having their own causes. There, obviously, was also the beginning at that time of some question as to whether—particularly as the Soviets backed off from supporting the Chinese—there might be a possibility of moving the Chinese and the Soviets further apart from one other. But my recollection is that that was not a big theme. It was not pursued in any major way.

Did the White House push very hard? You mentioned that you thought Kennedy and Rusk both saw this the same way. Did the White House push this?

KREISBERG: They saw this as more threatening. Rusk's view consistently was that the Chinese were expansionists. I have a less clear picture of what the NSC staff saw. My guess is that Jim Thomson, who handled Asia for McGeorge Bundy at that time, would not have seen it in that way.[15] But Rusk saw every Chinese move as part of a broad conceptual Chinese expansionism.

There was a perception in the United States that communism was an insatiable force. Were you having problems selling the idea that this would be a limited punitive engagement in India to others within the State Department or the government?

GRANT: My counterpart running the Office of Indian Affairs bought this as very possible. I don't remember an argument. For another thing, the Chinese did what we said they were going to do within a matter of ten days or so, so the issue was resolved.

[John Kenneth] Galbraith, who was ambassador in India at the time, this is about the only time I'm aware of that he actually used his old

White House connection effectively.[16] He was just dying to come down on the Indian side of this whole argument. He managed to force through a U.S. government position endorsing the Indian view of the border, whereas our view—and I think the India desk rather shared it—was that this was none of our business, that we should have left that whole question of borders for much longer resolution between them. So in that sense, even though Galbraith was associated with Kennedy and with this whole new school, his instinctive view—probably "localitis"—he simply wanted to take the Indians' position. He wasn't about ready to give a nickel to the Chinese.

We were exaggerating the threat that China posed, and the fact that China was expansionist. When you talk about the attack on India, it was basically because China was trying to settle its border problems with all the countries around its perimeter. They had succeeded in the case of Pakistan and the Hindu Kush, but they came up against the Indians who refused to settle the Aksai Chin [uninhabited desert land in the west that happened to be an important trade route between Xinjiang and Tibet] and the northeast frontier territorial dispute. The Chinese just gave them a lesson or two. Basically, the Chinese were not this kind of expansionist force we perceived [them] to be.

UNITED NATIONS

The struggle over the China seat in the United Nations continued in the 1960s and required countless hours of effort from Foreign Service officers to persuade increasingly skeptical governments to support the American position on representation of the Chinese people by the Nationalists in Taipei. In this battle, Chiang Kai-shek did not always see the issues as did the Americans, and frictions over the UN strained relations between Washington and Taipei, especially during the imbroglio over Mongolia. Secretly, however, Kennedy assured Chiang that the United States would use its veto in the Security Council to keep Beijing out if Chiang would not use his veto on the Mongolian issue. The diplomats speaking here were never told of this private deal.

GRANT: I was very anxious in the UN Chinese representation issue to see us get out of the way of what I thought was an inevitability. That was that the Chinese, despite their rhetoric, were not doing anything, really, to upset other people. Macao and Hong Kong they left there simply out of self-interest. They learned their lesson very quickly about Taiwan. They never have given the Burmese Communists the kind of support they easily could have. Northern Thailand offered opportunities and they didn't exploit them. They did not move into Laos against the Vietnamese, although they were obviously looking at it, even building roads.

The fact that they weren't doing anything meant that more and more countries would leave us on the Chinese representation issue. The Third World was growing, more countries coming into existence who remembered colonialism but didn't have anything against the Chinese and thought of them as Third World. So I figured that we probably were not going to be able to hold our line for very long in the UN. It was anathema to adopt two Chinas, because neither the Republic of China nor the Communists would accept that; both of them would excoriate us. So I was trying to find a way to get others, in effect, to weld [the] Republic of China into its position as best you could do it, while you let the Communists in. One of the techniques I proposed, one of the slogans, was "two contenders." We're not arguing that there are two Chinas; we're just saying that there are two people, both of whom say they're China, both of whom control some land; we're willing to let them both in.

I had resistance to that with some of the more conservative people on the Republic of China desk, but a lot of people liked that idea. It was the German desk at EUR, European Affairs, that objected because of the parallel for East Germany.

The representation issue was complicated early in the administration by the willingness of the Kennedy White House to see the People's Republic of Mongolia enter the UN, wasn't it?

CLOUGH: The question of the admission of Outer Mongolia to the United Nations was linked to the admission of Mauritania. Chiang Kai-shek was threatening to veto this proposal, because they regarded Mongolia as part of China, not an independent state, just a Soviet puppet, and therefore it couldn't become a member of the United Nations.

But the threat to do this was infuriating a lot of Africans, who wanted to see Mauritania get in. Africa was a very important area for the Republic of China. To maintain its position in the UN, it had to have the support of a lot of African countries. They were coming into the UN as independent states in increasing numbers, and we needed their vote on the China representation issue. One of my early chores in the first week or two after I got into Taipei [in July 1961] was to talk to Foreign Ministry people, to persuade them not to take this foolish act.

GREEN: They probably agreed with you, didn't they? It was the old man [Chiang Kai-shek] who was holding out. But they must have tried to convey to him that this was a disastrous policy in terms of upholding their position in the United Nations.

CLOUGH: Anyway, he finally desisted, and that crisis passed. [Upholding the ROC position] took more of the department's time because we had to deal with countries all around the world. Every September, or a few months before, we'd send out these messages and try to line up all the support for the annual vote on the Chinese representation issue. Up until about '61, we were able to get support for not considering the issue.

GREEN: It would have been very important from your viewpoint in Taipei and our national viewpoint that the Republic of China do all possible to maintain its diplomatic standing, and that it certainly maintain the support of countries who had voting powers in the United Nations.

CLOUGH: That's right. They spent quite a lot of money on Africa. They sent out these agricultural technical advisory teams to African countries. They had plots of land in Taiwan to which they invited Africans to come and learn about agriculture. They had a steady, very large-scale interchange. At one point they had teams in 20 or more countries.[17] They did a good job, and this was appreciated by the Africans. This was a way of maintaining this diplomatic link and getting that crucial vote every year.

GREEN: They had the kinds of agricultural technicians that were just needed. They knew how to make proper use of manure and things like that, where we were using chemical fertilizers. Their technology, in other words, was a little bit more applicable to. . .

CLOUGH: And also, as individuals they were willing to go out there for a year or two or three without their families and live under circumstances which were pretty spartan, whereas American aid people wouldn't do that.

GREEN: And they didn't have to have commissaries and other things that tend to create divisions.

Who handled the effort to keep the PRC out of the UN?

FREEMAN: I was assigned temporarily in 1968 to the Office of Regional Affairs in the then Bureau of East Asian Affairs, and worked for Louise McNutt, a great fixture of the department, who, together with Ruth Bacon [longtime UN adviser for Far Eastern Affairs], who had left by the time I arrived, had quite a heroic role in keeping Communist China out of the United Nations. So that was my job, to keep them out of the UN, which involved various shenanigans, including getting the U.S. Navy to pick up the Maldivian delegation and fly them to New York in time for the vote on the Albanian Resolution.[18] We prevailed in this unholy cause.

HONG KONG I

In the 1960s, Hong Kong continued to be the primary listening post for developments inside China. Its reports proved especially useful given China's internal upheavals during these years. The same economic and political troubles upon which the Hong Kong consulate general reported also threatened the security and survival of Hong Kong. Floods of refugees poured into the colony during the famine in China and again during the Cultural Revolution. Tensions also arose over Nationalist spying and sabotage operations run from Hong Kong's protected environs. At the same time, Hong Kong began to emerge as an economic participant in the international system. Although this was good for Hong Kong, it created trade problems for the United States.

LACEY: Julius Holmes [Hong Kong consul general] was a small man who affected height by wearing higher heels than normal. He affected pince-nez glasses and was every word the English gentleman that he purported to be. He had been minister counselor of embassy in London for six years. So he knew the ropes backwards and forwards. Holmes's instructions were "I have four rules. One, I am the boss. Two, I am lazy, and I expect you to do all the work. Three, if anything good goes on around here, I want the credit for it. Fourthly, if anything goes awry, I sure as hell want to know why." That gave me carte blanche to run the show.

My job as deputy principal officer was one of the best jobs I ever had. We had a large consulate general. I think it numbered 145 officers and secretaries. Now of those 145, only a handful were Department of State. The rest were other agencies, and you could imagine which agencies predominated. And, yet, under Julius Holmes's leadership, we had a very effective group of China watchers. That was our main mission. Much of our reporting was regarded as gospel in Washington, at least by some people, as the final word on the China scene. I remember a contretemps that we had with the Department of Agriculture, or maybe the Department of Commerce, over China's food grain production. We had aboard a fine officer by the name of Brice Meeker who guesstimated—not just guesstimated but estimated—that China's production in 1960–61 was on the order of 130,000 metric tons of grain. CIA experts disagreed radically. They felt the figure was much too low. But, as it turned out, we were right; they were wrong.

In January 1960, when I arrived, Hong Kong was a remote outpost of empire, important principally because of the impact of the Colony's textile producers on British industry. But as the momentum of Mao's revolution showed signs of waning, instead of fleeing from Hong Kong, big enterprises like Chase Manhattan were seeking to return and I facilitated those endeavors. Whereas the American business community in Hong Kong numbered at most 200 firms when I arrived, that number rose to or possibly exceeded 1,000 in mid-1964 when I left.

The Hong Kong government itself was being drawn into the international textile market. Hong Kong's textile industries were dominated by Chinese entrepreneurs who with their looms fled Shanghai from advancing Chicom armies. They joined forces with Hong Kong based manufacturers, making some 45 major textile firms. Textiles represented about 50 percent of the colony's exports. As economic section chief I stepped into a heated textile battle between Hong Kong and the U.S.A. Shortly after I arrived—it may have been my very first day on duty—the feisty editor of the *Hong Kong Standard*, K.T. Wu, printed a heated front page editorial that screamed, "Who Stole Hong Kong's Shirt?"

Hong Kong's ire was directed increasingly at the U.S. government as Uncle Sam turned its fangs away from Japan, which was moving into heavier industry, toward Hong Kong. Fortunately for me, the Laceys had become close friends of the Hong Kong financial secretary, John (later Sir John) Cowperthwaite, and he had intimated, despite his fierce belief in laissez faire, that quotas perhaps were not too evil. At least they enabled Hong Kong manufacturers to set garment categories among themselves rather than being subject to New York dealers playing one off against another.

One evening as the textile tensions between the U.S. and Hong Kong were reaching a climax over quotas, I strolled to the Cowperthwaites's. One brandy led to another as our textile discussions became more vague. I left at 3:00 a.m. Next morning I reworked my notes and showed my draft cable to John. I should explain here that one of the several tricks I learned from Julius Holmes was what he called "the art of connivance." The essential purpose of connivance was to establish trust with the host government by first showing contemplated reports to Washington to your counterpart, primarily to insure that your reporting was accurate, but also to establish good working relations with the host government. And that is how the U.S. government signed the first "Long-term Cotton Textile Agreement on the Export of Hong Kong's Products to the U.S.A."

After Julius Holmes left, we were blessed with the leadership of Marshall Green, the ebullient, pun-cracking, wise-cracking, serious officer that he was. Of all the people that I have ever served under, Marshall was the only one who studiously reflected on the past. Another one of Marshall's traits was his ability to handle visiting congressmen. We had untold numbers of VIPs, mostly congressmen, but also generals and admirals and ICA [International Cooperation Administration] directors by the dozens. I remember keeping track of the one month that I was chargé over the Christmas season. My wife and I entertained 142 official parties, not including their wives and friends. Thanks to Marshall Green, primarily, we made it a point of assuming that every single congressional mission, called CODEL, was there to really learn about China and the U.S. mission in the Far East rather than to shop. Of course, we knew better. But nevertheless, we insisted upon briefing every single group that came to Hong Kong. We had worked out a one-half hour top-notch briefing mission in which we gave the political, eco-

nomic, sociological, and strategic information available and our interpretation thereof in terms of the U.S. interests in China.

How were Hong Kong affairs handled from Washington?

DONALD ANDERSON: In those days, we had a Hong Kong-Macao section, and a Mainland China section, and within each of those two sections we had an economic and political unit. I was the economic
defense officer, which was enforcing our embargo on the mainland. It
sort of meant chasing Hong Kong companies around that did business
with China, and trying to prevent them from buying American products.

This was a major effort on our part?

DONALD ANDERSON: Oh, it was one of the silliest I've ever seen. The
consul general himself got in trouble because he had a love for Chinese
export porcelain, and thought that was perfectly acceptable to buy. And
we had a treasury agent in the consulate who warned him that he was
breaking the law.

How good was the work of the Hong Kong Consulate General as a listening post?

LACEY: It was surprising how much direct information came out of
China. There was, for example, in 1962 an extreme drought, a critical
water shortage in the South China provinces. It reached the point where
the government had to erect cordons of barbed wire around the border
of Hong Kong proper to try to hold back the refugees, who nevertheless managed to break through because the situation was desperate.
Those refugees were interrogated both directly and indirectly by officers in the consulate general and by other contacts we had, including the
British.

I can't say enough for the British administration at that time who had
an even more vested interest in what was going on in South China than
did Uncle Sam because the British colony of Hong Kong was dependent upon water, dependent upon food, both of which came from Mainland China. They shared with us much of their information that they
got surreptitiously. So I would say, the Hong Kong consulate general

was probably *the* center of information as far as American interests were concerned.

We had in Hong Kong excellent working relations with the Fourth Estate [the press]. Stanley Karnow was one who was outstandingly good, Bob Elegant another, Stan Rich a third, Fessler a fourth.[19] A small group of us had lunch in the old Foreign Service Officers' Club, which was a former house of a taipan, rich Chinese gentleman. "Love is a Many Splendored Thing" was filmed there.[20] Once a week, a group of us lunched, including people interested in China and including, especially, foreign correspondents. The relationship that we officials had with these foreign correspondents was invaluable. Unlike today, one could say, "This is off the record," and give them the background without fear of being trapped in any kind of news leak. They could be trusted. It was another source of information because it worked both ways. They would also repeat stuff to us based upon their many contacts.

Did you get any feel about CIA operations? Were you getting information, and how did that meld in with your activities?

DONALD ANDERSON: The CIA operation was very important in terms of conditions inside Mainland China. There was a very extensive interview program, and the agency worked very closely with the British, who obviously had a much bigger presence and were screening people coming across the border.

What was your impression of events in China at the time? The Great Leap Forward had . . .

DONALD ANDERSON: It really collapsed, and economic conditions were in terrible shape. This was a period when Hong Kong was just being swamped by refugees coming across the border. There was a terrible drought, and we got down to water for four hours every fourth day. The refugees were streaming across the river that separates China from Hong Kong, and the Hong Kong government was having to cope with these thousands of refugees and began a massive housing program. We were very much involved in that as well because some of them did have claims to go to the United States.

GREEN: Chiang Kai-shek, or the Chinese Nationalists, were using Hong Kong as a base for operations in the areas of Mainland China not too far from Hong Kong, which caused great distress both to the British authorities as well as to the consulate general. We sent messages to Washington about that and to our ambassador in Taipei urging that somehow we put a restraint on this. These little pinpricks, if anything, were being used by the Chinese Communists to steel their people and make them all the more vigilant, driving them more into their little shell.

There was one particular episode at the time of the breakdown of law and order in Guangdong Province in May 1962, when all these refugees came flowing into Hong Kong. The Chinese Communists were trying to get the young people in the cities back into the rural areas, to reconstruct their attitudes. A lot of them refused to go, and they came down to Hong Kong. In this period of inner turmoil in China, there was a kind of an opportunity to be exploited. We were very careful not to do that. I remember putting a staying hand on the wrist of our embassy in Taipei in order to tell them not to stir things up and that it wouldn't do any good. More than that, we wanted to convey to Beijing that this was our position.

HOLDRIDGE: I recall that we took a very dim view of some of the things that the Nationalists were doing. For example, they para-dropped a unit of several hundred men into Hainan [Island]. Of course, the Chinese Communists rounded these people up in short order, and they all were discovered with American equipment still with the U.S. ordinance device stenciled on the outside of the crates. It made our position very shaky. The Chinese would come out from time to time and blast that Hong Kong was being used as a base for espionage by the American imperialists. The British were uncomfortable. They may have withheld some cooperation, as a consequence.

GREEN: I remember you, John Lacey and I, as well as others in the consulate general, were already beginning to see our problems with the Chinese in the long range as involving a first stage of entering into a more civil discourse and relieving them of any kind of fears that we were trying to exploit their internal problems. We were very active in this field, not under instructions from Washington, although we reported our actions to Washington. We were trying to calm down their vicious anti-Americanism. This point was conveyed to their business representatives in Hong Kong. I know it was authorized, because I got the authority from Washington.

HOLDRIDGE: I believe that, in the course of our ambassadorial-level talks, something of this sort was also conveyed. In fact, our conclusion in Hong Kong was that, despite problems such as floods, droughts, or problems generated by the collapse of the Great Leap Forward, China was going to be remaining under the control of the communists. There wasn't anything that anybody from the outside was going to be able to do about it, certainly [not] Taiwan.

GREEN: Don't you think that, in this period of 1962 and 1963, there was a little bit of an opening in the clouds? You talked about the end of the Great Leap Forward. Clearly, it had been a disaster, and the Chinese knew that. Meanwhile, they were more and more concerned with the Soviets and the Soviet threat. In Geneva and Warsaw, as well as in Hong Kong, we were conveying the impression that we are not trying to exploit their internal problems. It seemed to me that there was an opening there. We were trying in the consulate general to make best use of it. We were trying to allow Americans to travel to China, to end our foreign assets control regulations. Obviously, [our restrictions were] a great nuisance and had nothing to do with our overall relations with China. We were creating irritants for American businessmen, for American scholars who wanted to go to China. They couldn't get into China because China wouldn't let them, but it would appear to the world that we were the ones who were keeping them out.

HOLDRIDGE: As a matter of fact, to an extent, we were. We tried very hard, for example, to suggest that maybe some sales of humanitarian items to the Chinese would be in order. We finally allowed American journalists to travel. However, by that time the Chinese were so angered over the whole situation, they refused to give any visas.

GREEN: That's true. We anticipated that might be the reaction, but we generally wanted to have people go in to find out what was going on. In the consulate general, we saw opportunities—not just to engage in a more civil discourse with China, but also possibly to be removing irritants. Governor Harriman, assistant secretary, and Chester Bowles, the under secretary of state, were very interested in a change in our China policy. [Although some people] still saw these things in very rigid, red and white terms, what we were saying in Hong Kong had a very responsive resonance in Washington. President Kennedy was interested in some of the things we were saying and doing in Hong Kong. It resulted in my being asked back to Washington in the early fall of 1963 to take a new look at our China policy.

VIETNAM WAR I

During the Kennedy years American involvement in the Vietnam War accelerated. American servicemen who were on the ground to advise the Vietnamese began to undertake more active roles.

LACEY: The Vietnam build-up, under primarily President Kennedy, was something for which I have ever since felt personally embarrassed and personally ashamed. Then as now, the American people generally, and certainly too many of our officials, were ignorant of what is really going on in Asia. Therefore, our politicians are able to exploit that indifference or ignorance in terms of responding to domestic pressures rather than to developments in Asia.

LEVIN: There were always a couple of Chinese-language officers assigned to the embassy in Saigon because of the importance of the Chinese community in Cholon and its ties all over the country. The reporting based on what the Chinese community was saying, was that the government in Saigon was extremely corrupt, that it was not becoming more effective, that there was a tremendous gap between the urban elite origin South Vietnamese army officers corps and the bulk of the ordinary soldiers of the Vietnamese army, composed of peasant youths from the countryside. Cholon, part of Saigon, was a vast Chinatown. It was the dominant economic force in the country, particularly after the diminution of French interests. These people were involved in rice milling, the movement of crops and commodities around the country, trucking companies, and so forth. The Vietnamese government in Saigon and sometimes the U.S. military would tell the American Embassy that a province was loyal and pacified and completely under their control. The Cholon Chinese would tell the Chinese-language officers that they had to pay enormous taxes to the communists who actually ran the province, or that it was no longer possible to operate in a province where the communists had taken over complete controls and they were pulling out. The Chinese in Vietnam were anti-communist, bourgeois minded, merchant-class Chinese.

The dominant group in the embassy, the ambassador and others in Saigon, often were people assigned from France who were French speakers, because we didn't have enough Vietnamese speakers. They felt that the Chinese-language officers were so intellectually over-whelmed by the recent Chinese historical experience with Communists that they couldn't judge Vietnam on its own merits. They gradually pushed these officers into the consular and administrative sections and then decided that they really didn't need them at all.

Now, your contacts in Hong Kong in the business community there, bankers and government officials, were they supportive of these gradual moves for the U.S. to replace the French in their involvement with the Vietnamese?

LACEY: The word "supportive" is too strong. The business community of Hong Kong—which meant both the Americans and the local people, who were mostly Chinese but also Parsi and Jews—saw this as a moneymaker. They were able to enjoy the prosperity that spun off from our involvement in Vietnam. As our involvement in Vietnam grew to the hundreds of thousands, the recreational programs that the army or the Pentagon sponsored for morale purposes involved many rest and recreation (R&R) trips throughout Asia, including Hong Kong.

KENNEDY ASSASSINATION

The death of John Kennedy was seen by some as arresting movement toward a more liberal China policy. Others denied that Kennedy had made any moves toward a new China policy. In the short term the assassination was followed almost immediately by the Roger Hilsman speech discussed in the next section and no initiatives that had been launched in the Kennedy years were derailed. On July 12, 1966, Lyndon Johnson would, in fact, deliver an address calling for reconciliation in Asia. Neither Beijing nor Taipei particularly mourned Kennedy's passing.

GREEN: I felt that the death of Kennedy in late 1963 put a great damper on all that we were trying to do to bring about a new attitude towards

China. What was the reaction in Taiwan to the assassination of President Kennedy?

CLOUGH: The reaction was shock . . .

GREEN: But in as much as he and his administration seemed to be moving towards a civil dialogue, discourse with China, and beginning to open up travel and trade . . .

CLOUGH: You know, not much of that had happened under Kennedy. That really came later under the early Nixon, those signals.

GREEN: No. No, there were certain moves that were already made at that time. I know, because I was the deputy assistant secretary back there, called back by Kennedy to look at our China policy. I was working with [Roger] Hilsman [assistant secretary]. Therefore, if not Kennedy, certainly people like Harriman and Bowles and others who were working under him, and the new administration in general, wasn't taking at all the rigid views that were taken under the Eisenhower administration. And what I was wondering was, when Kennedy's death suddenly occurred, whether this was greeted with any kind of, even relief, in Taiwan?

CLOUGH: I don't think so. The main reaction was uncertainty as to how this happened, for one thing. And for another, how this would affect U.S. policy. I don't think anyone was confident that a Democratic successor, Lyndon Johnson, would necessarily be any more friendly toward them than Kennedy had been.

HILSMAN SPEECH 1963

The speech made by Roger Hilsman in December 1963 became a landmark in the process of reducing tensions with China. As the Foreign Service officers interviewed here note, the speech actually said little new and could hardly be considered provocative. Nevertheless, it received plaudits at home and abroad for being an initiative toward better U.S.-China relations. It is noteworthy that Hilsman delivered the speech after Kennedy's death. Kennedy never saw the text and it remains difficult to speculate on what his reaction would have been.

GRANT: There was still a so-called Committee of One Million, which was a nongovernmental organization, proclaimed itself a million strong—it

Vice President Lyndon B. Johnson greeted by Vice President Ch'en Ch'eng and, in the middle, Chiang Kai-shek. *Courtesy of National Archives.*

probably was lucky if it had a few thousand—which was diehard pro-Guomindang. You had people like Senator [William] Knowland from California, who was sometimes called "the Senator from Taiwan."[21] There were a lot of redoubtable people who managed to sort of freeze this situation.

It seemed to me that if you could challenge the Committee of One Million and the extreme pro-Guomindang people directly, and they couldn't mount much of a counterattack, that you'd clear the way towards a more realistic policy towards China. The instrument came along. A fellow named Jim Thomson was an assistant to the assistant secretary for the Far East, Roger Hilsman. Jim and I and several others saw it very much in the same light. Jim saw an opportunity in a speech coming up in San Francisco to make the challenge, to throw down the glove, if you will. This was the Commonwealth Club of San Francisco, a good, respectable forum. There had already been a speech prepared, a standard 1950s-type rhetoric speech. We agreed, "Let's deep-six this and see if we can now say something about China." The Hilsman speech was December 1963, and it sounds real timid now. What that speech did was to say, "We don't love the Chinese Communists. We think that they would be happier, and the world would be happier, if they had a more relaxed view of other people's rights to select their own government. But we think these people are going to be around and we're going to be dealing with them."

Now, there wasn't anything really new. Right from 1954, we'd been having ambassadorial-level talks with China. They started at that meeting in Geneva where Dulles refused to shake hands with Zhou Enlai, which has become a part of history. Sure, that was Dulles all over, this dramatic public position, but allowing the opening of ambassadorial-level talks. So we weren't saying anything very new, but we said it publicly. "These guys are going to be around. We plan to deal with them." In a sense, we challenged the conservative lobbies to do something about it, and they couldn't raise a whimper.

There was a pretty good press-alerting campaign under way. A fellow named Allen Whiting—who was actually in the Research Bureau [INR] and shouldn't have been in press contacts at all, but he was quite a wheeler-dealer—got the press alerted to this, so the press was ready and waiting. We got a tremendous reaction.

If you're interested in how decisions are made, by the way, it's rather amusing. We cleared that speech with Governor Harriman, the number three officer in State, under secretary for political affairs, cleared it actually with his special assistant, who didn't spot what was so important in it, and said, "Sure, that looks innocuous enough." We never cleared it anywhere else.

This is very important. This was generated relatively low down within the bureaucracy, using almost boilerplate language, but changing the emphasis.

GRANT: That's right. We started it. Thomson immediately, of course, told Hilsman what we were working on. Hilsman understood it. There was no problem there. We told Hilsman, "We're going to do a speech for you that's going to open it up."

Hilsman said, "Fine. Go ahead and work up the draft." We didn't go over to the White House and say, "We're about to really unload one on

China." What we did do was to create something that flew, and the Committee for One Million was barely heard from. There wasn't a whimper. Nobody complained. Everybody said, "Finally, the United States is getting its act in order."

GREEN: I think the speech gave Dean Rusk considerable agony, because he had not had proper clearance on it. But since the speech had such a good reaction in the American press as a whole and the academic community, Rusk acted as though he was entirely in favor of the speech. But it came as something of a shock to him.

GRANT: It was right in line with what the Kennedy administration liked, I mean Kennedy and his Irish Mafia. This was forward looking, this was new. It was their kind of thing. They were quite happy with it, and we never heard any complaint from the White House of not having checked it out with them.

CLOUGH: That was quite disturbing to the people in Taiwan, where Hilsman intimated that we would keep the door open to possible improvement of relations with Beijing.

HONG KONG II

At the same time as Washington wrestled with the question of opening more channels of communication with China, the American business community expanded its operations on the periphery of China. By the mid-1960s, the United States had become Hong Kong's most important trading partner, outdistancing Great Britain; some 400 American companies did business there.

BELLOCCHI: As chief of the commercial unit, I wound up with quite an accomplishment, getting an American Chamber of Commerce started in Hong Kong.

You mean they didn't have one until then?

BELLOCCHI: No, they didn't have one, and there was great resistance to it. From the policy standpoint we didn't want to raise a high profile in Hong Kong, which I thought patently ridiculous because the Seventh Fleet used to park down in the harbor every day. If we worried about profile, why didn't we worry about all those warships in the harbor? The American business community in those days, they were the old timers, and they operated by the seat of their pants. They represented large corporations in America but they did their business on a personal basis like everyone does in China. And American Chamber of Commerce, that was alien to their kind of thinking. But there were a lot of the new multinationals that were starting to open up offices in Hong Kong and they were the modern managers, and they did want an American Chamber. So during the Cultural Revolution, the Hong Kong government was very much interested in knowing what was the American business community going to do. Were they going to bug out? There was no mechanism to get a good survey quickly as to what was the feeling of the American business community. So I used that as an argument both with Ed Martin, who was then the consul general in Hong Kong, and with the Hong Kong government secretary for commerce and industry. They finally said okay, as long as they didn't raise a high profile, which was no problem at all. The American business community didn't want to make trouble, they wanted to do business. It's become one of the largest AmChams out of Asia.

At that time, you were there, from '68 to '70, why would one want a Chamber of Commerce?

BELLOCCHI: You have to know the atmosphere in those days. There was what was called a foreign assets officer out there, and this guy really took his job seriously. There were not many Mainland Chinese stores in Hong Kong in those days, but there were a few. And this guy would go down there and stand around to see if any American tourists were buying things; that was against the law. The oil company tankers, if they bunkered in a mainland port, it was against the law. So the businessmen were very upset about the restraints that they had, and all their European competitors were making all the money. So when the AmCham opened, the secretary of commerce [Maurice Stans] was passing through Hong Kong and we used that occasion for the grand opening of the American Chamber. Jack Wolfe, who was the Caltex [petroleum company] representative, was the first president of the AmCham. He gives his talk, and boy, he hits Stans right between the eyes with this business. So it demonstrated very quickly why you have an American

Chamber of Commerce. It was not just because they wanted to deal with the Hong Kong government, they wanted to deal with their own government on some of these constraints. And it worked, they got that thing changed eventually.

NEGOTIATION WITH THE PRC II

During the last years of the decade the Warsaw talks continued but accomplished little. The combined weight of the Cultural Revolution and the American war in Vietnam left the negotiators little hope that they might agree on anything. As Donald Anderson, who attended the meetings, reports, "In many ways they were quite sterile."

DONALD ANDERSON: At that point China was in no mood, nor in any position, to entertain very many initiatives, or to take any initiatives. The arrangements for the talks were that each side had four members. There was the ambassador on each side, a political adviser, an interpreter, and a scribe, as he was called—the note taker. We would meet in this meeting room in the Mysliwiecki Palace in Warsaw. We alternated on who spoke first, and each side would deliver a prepared statement running about 15 or 20 minutes. I used to participate in drafting it, and once it was drafted and approved back in Washington I could sit down with my dictionary and translate it into Chinese. I interpreted from English to Chinese, and their guy interpreted from Chinese to English, which is the reverse of normal interpreting situations. After the two prepared statements there was sort of a give and take back and forth, oftentimes working from prepared position papers because we pretty well knew what the Chinese were going to say.

At the conclusion of the meeting—the press almost always came to Warsaw for the meetings, American press, the wire services, etc.—we'd meet briefly with the press, and usually say nothing more than, "We had a useful and productive exchange of views. No further comment."

Then the following day, we had an informal arrangement where the political adviser and the interpreter would meet with their counterparts, usually at the Chinese Embassy, and we would give them an English text of our opening statement, they would give us a Chinese text of theirs, and if there was any confusion about terminology, or what we meant by something, we would try and straighten it out during this informal meeting. I don't know how the Chinese felt about it, but the American side felt it was a useful sort of informal contact where we could talk without the constraints of a formal negotiating session. It also turned out to be useful in other ways. At the first meeting I attended in '66, we went over to the Chinese Embassy. My predecessor, Al Harding, actually did the interpreting. The Chinese gave him a little farewell. It was rather interesting because we noted that in the meeting room where they received us on the wall over the sofa there had obviously been two portraits, there were two light spots on the wall. When we got there there was one portrait of Mao Zedong in the middle, and it was one of the really first conclusive bits of evidence that Liu Shaoqi, the former head of state, had indeed been purged, and was no longer a person.[22] Then as we left the building, on the walls in the halls of the embassy, there were pieces of paper with hand-written slogans, which was the beginning of the big character posters of the Cultural Revolution.

You say a prepared statement. Was this just two people talking past each other?

DONALD ANDERSON: In large part. In the early days we had a number of concerns that we had to address. One thing we talked about was pilots who were flying against North Vietnam but who strayed and went over into Chinese territory and were lost. We were trying to get an accounting for them. Vietnam was a major factor for meeting all the way up toward the end. But at that first meeting in '66, we did use a phrase which was intended, and I think interpreted by the Chinese, as an assurance that we did not intend to invade North Vietnam and told the Chinese in that meeting that "we seek no wider war in Vietnam."

This often was a bone of contention. Was it your feeling, and those with you, that this could really tip things if we landed at Haiphong or something like this? This could bring the Chinese in?

DONALD ANDERSON: Yes. And that's what we were trying to prevent. On the U.S. side we were trying to promote some sort of informal non-official contact. We were trying to get journalists into China for business, and a variety of what we saw as concrete practical steps that one could take to improve the atmosphere in relations and perhaps lower the tension levels between the two countries. The Chinese were not having any of that. It was a very sterile period. They were primarily berating us on Vietnam. For example, we picked up a Chinese boat that had gotten in trouble in the Tonkin Gulf. We gave them food and fixed their ship up, and sent them back. We mentioned this as something we had done as a humanitarian gesture, and they, of course, denounced us for it.

During the Cultural Revolution period all of their diplomats were being called back to China to take part in the Cultural Revolution, so that the senior official on the Chinese side was usually a chargé d'affaires, not the ambassador, and their interpreter would come back and forth. The talks were really pretty dull at that point. The Chinese obviously had instructions that they had to have the last word, so our ambassador would respond to a charge by the Chinese, and the Chinese then felt obliged to answer again. Therefore, the talks sometimes would drag on for three hours or more. One time the chargé on the Chinese side, who was really not a political adviser—their interpreter was far and away the more influential and the brightest of any of the group—the chargé turned to the interpreter after the talk had gone on for about two and a half hours, and said, "Can I stop now?" The interpreter said, "No." So he made another charge about something. So we would usually decide this had gone on long enough, we'd let them have the last word, and then decide on the next meeting.

But the rather humorous thing about it was, the reporters didn't get anything substantive because we would come out and give them a bland statement. In 1970, toward the end of the talks, we really did make some significant progress. In fact, the two opening statements were sufficiently substantive and significant, and meshed in such a way that neither side felt that they could go beyond that particular point without getting further instructions. So the meeting lasted for about a half an hour, maybe 40 minutes, and the press, of course, interpreted it as indicating that our relations had reached the lowest point ever. But it was finally a significant and substantive meeting. So anyway, the talks proceeded through the Cultural Revolution through a very, very difficult period, and then there was a gap of a full year between talks.

The Polish intelligence service was passing everything on to the Soviets at that time. Did you have any feeling that the Chinese were using these meetings to stick it to the Russians from time to time?

DONALD ANDERSON: Not so much to stick it to the Russians, but it was obviously an inhibiting factor.

Were we ready and willing to do a lot of things, but the Chinese were not ready? Or were we stalling and not wanting to get anything going?

DONALD ANDERSON: We were stalling to a degree, and particularly we were not prepared to do much in terms of recognizing the legitimacy of the Chinese government of the People's Republic of China. What we wanted to do was the concrete, practical level of exchanges, and solving problems. They wanted to talk about fundamentals, and that's why we decided toward the end of '69, that if we were to resume the talks we ought to try and address some of these questions. At that point Nixon and Kissinger were in favor of that, and we were able to do things for the first time in terms of formulations on political relationships that we couldn't have done under Johnson, and particularly under Dean Rusk.

CLOUGH: I think that's true. What was happening in the United States in public opinion and in the Congress, was that the kind of almost automatic support for the ROC against the Chinese Communists, which had existed in the early '60s, was dissipating. Congressional hearings were held in '66 at which John Fairbank [professor of Chinese history at Harvard University] and A. Doak Barnett [journalist and scholar] and others testified. What was Doak's phrase? Can't recall, something without isolation [containment without isolation].

VIETNAM WAR II

The key point of intersection between the war in Vietnam and American China policy revolved around the question of whether China would intervene in the fighting. Countless hours of time in Washington were devoted to discussing the steps that, if taken by the United States armed forces, would bring Beijing into the war. Allen S. Whiting, a scholar and former analyst at the Rand Corporation, became a central player in this debate because of the study he had written examining Chinese intervention in the Korean War in 1950.[23] Whiting, who served in the Office of Intelligence and Research in this period, argued that the United States had provoked the Chinese by ignoring their security interests. In Vietnam, the United States, he argued, must take greater care not to venture too close to China's border. Of course, the sense of China as a threat to American troops on the ground in Vietnam militated against improvement of Sino-American relations. In 1965, a Gallup poll showed that 53 percent of Americans blamed China for Vietcong operations, whereas only 26 percent held North Vietnam responsible.

GREEN: It was clear that, not only was the [death of Kennedy at the] end of 1963 a watershed for those of us who were hoping to bring about a modification of the rancor in our U.S.-China relations, it was also our deepening involvement in Vietnam. The new president was totally wrapped up in Vietnam. Those of us who were hoping that we could have some kind of openings to China—I remember this was a real damper.

HOLDRIDGE: I'll tell you why. That was the influence of a predecessor of mine, once removed, as the office director for Research and Analysis for East Asia and the Pacific—Allen S. Whiting. Allen had written a book, going back to the Korean War, which was entitled *China Crosses the Yalu*. He was convinced that, in a situation where China's territorial integrity was being threatened by the approach of hostile forces from the outside—as happened when the U.S. went north of the old DMZ, the 38th parallel, and then China entered the Korean War—the same was going to happen in Vietnam. Here we were, deeply bogged down or beginning to get deeply involved in the Vietnam War. Allen kept telling Averell Harriman that "The Chinese are coming. The Chinese are coming." I can recall watching on television, for example, the then-secretary of state, Dean Rusk, having his innings with [Senator J. William] Fulbright [chairman of the Senate Foreign Relations Committee] on this whole question of China. Rusk kept saying, "Well, the Chinese are going to come in. That's why we have to keep a hard line, keep our guard up." The repercussions of this Vietnam situation really affected our China policy. It put it in a state of semiparalysis for a while.

I can remember Fulbright's reaction to Dean Rusk saying something about the Chinese are coming—"They wouldn't do that." This was said in his best Arkansas accent. In fact, they didn't.

GREEN: This is a very relevant point. I remember Bill Bundy [deputy assistant secretary for International Security Affairs, Pentagon], many years later, looking back and thanking me and John Holdridge for taking a view contrary to Allen Whiting. If only they had listened a little more attentively to this viewpoint. I didn't think that the Chinese would come massing down into Vietnam unless, of course, we carried the war up towards the borders of China. That was different. But to be conducting a war the way we were—raiding parties and that kind of thing against North Vietnam—that certainly wasn't going to bring them in.

The question to me was, how far could you go? I was deputy assistant secretary of state at that time. In 1964, we spent a great deal of time trying to figure out how far we were going to conduct this war into Vietnam. Would we bomb the North? Would we bomb Hanoi? Would we mine the harbors? Would we mine the dikes?

With strong pressure from the press and the Congress critical of our war effort, we kept making self-restrictions—imposing restrictions on our own course of action. We said that we would not bomb Hanoi and Haiphong, we would not mine the harbors, and we would not mine the dikes and flood the country. Every time we did this kind of thing, of course, it gave the enemy assurance. We just bargained ourselves out of the war. Of course, while this was going on, Beijing was getting a clear impression that there were very distinct limits to our actions. Therefore, they were not so concerned about North Vietnam.

DEAN: My feeling was that if we sent ground forces into North Vietnam, the Chinese would respond. And so, of course, the studies [by the Joint Chiefs of Staff that Dean participated in] went further than that. How would we keep the Chinese from responding? Naturally the subject of nuclear weapons came up and I felt that even the use of tactical nuclear weapons would not deter the Chinese. Mao had said on previous occasions that China had a billion people and even if they lost half of them they'd still have 500 million.

HOLDRIDGE: The idea of the Chinese—at a time when they were going through these [Cultural Revolution] throes internally—engaging in some kind of an external war of major proportions was absolutely ridiculous. This is what we were telling people such as Bill Bundy, for example.

DONALD ANDERSON: My stint in the political section in Hong Kong ended up really being devoted in very large part to reporting on the probability of China's entering the Vietnam war. While we were in Hong Kong the Tonkin Gulf incident happened [August 1964], which produced mass rallies in Beijing and a number of very threatening editorials and speeches about the U.S. aggression against Vietnam.[24] There were a lot of people, particularly back in Washington, who still had very fresh memories of the Chinese entry into the Korean War, and there was serious concern as to what the Chinese were going to do, and how far we could pursue the war in Vietnam without provoking Chinese intervention. I was sitting out in Hong Kong reading everything we could get, trying to provide an analysis of the probability of a Chinese intervention.

How could you get any feel for what's going on? It's a controlled press . . .

DONALD ANDERSON: It very definitely was an inexact science. It was almost entirely from content analysis. Looking at the terminology they were using, talking to Chinese about, "What are the implications of this type of language coming from a Chinese source?" Really just gauging whether they were drawing a line and saying, "At this point we will react," or leaving things fuzzy. It appeared to me quite clear that they were trying to leave things fairly fuzzy. And I pretty well concluded that the United States could bomb North Vietnam, but if the United States were to cross the 17th parallel [with ground troops] and start driving toward the Chinese border, then we probably would have gone too far.

HOLDRIDGE: The [Chinese] did their bit as an ally. They did send logistical troops to help keep the roads and railways open. They also sent anti-aircraft units, but they never acknowledged the presence of Chinese forces. They used to talk about the "lips-and-teeth" relationship between China and Vietnam, but this was unacknowledged in terms of actual public announcement of the presence of Chinese forces. The Chinese were being very discreet.[25]

When we would invade what they called their territorial waters or air space, they began this series of serious warnings that they would issue—serious warning number one, number two, violation of Chinese territorial air space on such and such a date over such and such a bit of Chinese or Chinese claimed territory, such as the Paracel [Islands in the South China Sea]. We actually had some aircraft that strayed into China on raids to the north, which were shot down or went down over Hainan, for example. The Chinese really didn't make anything much of it. They played it very carefully, not to bring themselves directly into the conflict. They had their internal situation to resolve. Along comes the Great Proletarian Cultural Revolution, and this threw China into a real convulsion while a lot of the Vietnam War was going on.

GREEN: Don't you think, John, in retrospect, that we tended to regard the Chinese as ten feet tall? /The fact of the matter is that they were far weaker and far more concerned with their internal situation than with any kind of external adventures.

HOLDRIDGE: We did have an intelligence break on that. Do you recall the Tibetan Papers? It turned out that a group of Khambas, operating out of Nepal, crossed the border into Tibet and managed to shoot up a Chinese military convoy, one of the trucks of which contained all of the workbooks of the political officer. When put all together, the upshot of these books was to show that the Chinese People's Liberation Army was in a terrible state. This was as a consequence, primarily, of the Great Leap Forward, and the siphoning off of energies into all sorts of nonproductive things. It was a hollow army.

Was there another side to this? The tremendous antipathy of the Vietnamese to the Chinese gets played up a lot in the post-Vietnam [War] period. They've been fighting them for centuries. Were you talking to Vietnamese experts who were saying that China would not expand this way because the Vietnamese hate the Chinese?

HOLDRIDGE: That was known. I can't recall any specific individual who came up, waving a piece of paper. It was generally accepted that the Chinese and the Vietnamese were ancient enemies and not friends, and that their relationship could hardly be congenial.

GREEN: May I say, though, that this may have been clear to you, John, but it was not clear to me. I was deputy assistant secretary at that time, and later on I was assistant secretary. I never really adequately appreciated the depth of Chinese-Vietnamese animosities. Never.

I had always assumed, even when I was assistant secretary during that period, which was '69 to '73, that the relationship between Beijing and Hanoi was, if not amicable, they both recognized the importance of staying in there together. The idea that any kind of latent hostility could break out between the two of them never occurred to me. Did it to you?

CLOUGH: At some point I began to read some of the history of Chinese-Vietnamese relations.

GREEN: I didn't have the luxury of reading back in history. If one did, one recognized that this was always an underlying possibility.

GRANT: I was very much a dove on Vietnam, but not because of China. It was because I didn't think we could win. I had to take the responsibility for North Vietnam when we created the Office of Asian Communist Affairs. I then began to inquire about what we knew about the table of organization, the basic facts of life in Hanoi, and discovered we knew nothing. I thought this was catastrophic, and I was convinced by other friends that, in fact, we were in a very bad situation.

But I did not think that the Chinese were going to come in overtly. As a matter of fact, there was a very good intelligence estimate, or war game. It had a Greek letter—I think it was Omega—run out of the Pentagon, but with State, CIA, a lot of other participation. They played the game through some time in the mid-1960s, and the way they played it, the Russians and Chinese kept putting in enough to counter our efforts, but just enough, and not moving beyond that, and we kept bogging down. If we had paid attention to that war game, we'd have gotten a very good steer as to how we should have behaved in Vietnam. It would have saved us a lot of heartache later on, because that's exactly what they did.

Assumptions that the Soviets and Chinese were working together in Vietnam, however, did not prove to be accurate, did they?

HOLDRIDGE: The Chinese for a while were actually impeding the shipment of Soviet war supplies across China to Vietnam. They were so jealous of the Soviets for having the inside track, and they were worried about Soviet encirclement of China, as a consequence of this big diatribe between Mao and whoever happened to be in power in Moscow at the time. It began to look to the Chinese as if they were being surrounded, not by the American imperialists, or the Japanese militarists, or the Taiwan revanchists, but by the allies of the Soviet Union—the Soviet Union and Vietnam.[26]

DEAN: So there was really bad blood between the Chinese and the Soviets, and we thought that we could possibly play on this antagonism and deep antipathy. So we tried, Harriman and the others, tried to see if we couldn't exploit these differences.

Exploit them?

DEAN: We wanted both of them to agree to a bombing pause and influence Hanoi to that effect because they were both supplying Hanoi. Our view was that if they could use their leverage on Hanoi that it would be valuable. Now, we thought the Chinese might do it because they didn't want the Soviets to get more influence there. We thought the Soviets might do it because they were angry at the Chinese [for deliberately delaying their supply shipments to Vietnam] and concerned about the growing Chinese power there. But, of course, none of this happened.

With regard to Taiwan and its relationship to the war in Vietnam, did we look to them to be a source of supply or any kind of support of operations?

CLOUGH: Yes, we did. I was present when we notified them, in '65, that Johnson had taken the decision to put in 25,000 ground troops in Vietnam. Chiang Kai-shek's reaction was interesting. He questioned whether American troops would be very effective in the kind of war which was going on in Vietnam. Of course, he had his own ulterior motives. His view was that you don't really solve things in that part of the world until you get rid of the Chinese Communist regime.

GREEN: But basically they must have greeted this American involvement in Vietnam with some relief, didn't they?

CLOUGH: It became clear fairly soon that we were going to have to depend on them to support the military operations. Early on in the '50s, when I was in the State Department, we had appropriated $20 million to improve an airfield near T'ai-chung to accommodate the B-52, the big aircraft, in case we might need it. It didn't become an American base, but we created the facilities there so we could use it. And then, when the Vietnam War came, we did base aircraft there. We had refueling aircraft for the B-52s, which came from Guam, and we had transport aircraft to take things into

Vietnam. Taiwan was also important as a place for repair and maintenance. They had very good facilities at Air Asia, which had CIA
antecedents. They could repair fighter aircraft, overhaul engines, overhaul tanks, trucks and so on.[27] And, of course, Taiwan, Taipei was a very
important R&R place for people coming out of Vietnam, American soldiers. So there were various ways in which Taiwan became important.

GREEN: Did Taiwan benefit economically from the war?

CLOUGH: Yes, sure. It benefited economically, and it benefited diplomatically from this.

GREEN: And in as much as China was giving active assistance, lots of supply assistance and encouragement to North Vietnam, I would think it
would be greeted with some relief in Taiwan to realize that now we saw
that really our enemy was Communist China, and that all this propitiat-
ing of Communist China was certainly something we wouldn't continue in this atmosphere.

CLOUGH: Yes, and that was what happened, actually. I was in the Policy
Planning Council from '66 to '69, and I was responsible for East Asian
Affairs. I came up with a couple of minor things in the field: international relations, dealing with international organizations where we
would soften our position a little bit with respect to Communist China
and Nationalist China. But the International Organizations Bureau was
still dominated by Ruth Bacon and people who still were acting very
vigorously against any slippage at all. During the Vietnam War, I think
Dean Rusk felt that it would be a mistake to divert any attention from
getting that war ended to doing something about China.

KREISBERG: Rusk commented to one of the senior officers in the secretariat of the department back in 1967—'66 or '67—that there are some
young officers in the department of State who are trying to persuade us
to change our China policy, and we are *not* going to do it.

TAIWAN II

The phasing out of American economic aid in the mid-1960s did not slow
Taiwan's economic boom. By 1966, industrial output exceeded agricultural
production for the purpose of earning foreign exchange and the introduction of an export processing zone at Kaohsiung further boosted the government's export promotion strategy. After 1967, under pressure from the

United States Congress, the Pentagon reduced military support as well, but security relations between Washington and Taipei remained strong. Meanwhile, Chiang Ching-kuo consolidated his power on the island. The government remained in the hands of the Guomindang and political expression continued to be suppressed in the name of fighting communism.

What was the political situation in Taiwan from 1965 to 1968?

HUMMEL: It was very much under control. Chiang Kai-shek was in charge, and his son, Chiang Ching-kuo, was minister of defense. I got to know them all extremely well. I had dozens of personal meetings with them, one on one. There was a huge CIA establishment there. It was mostly China watching.

It wasn't concentrating on what was happening in Taiwan?

HUMMEL: Not concentrating, but that was also a target for the CIA station. They did a pretty good job of that, too. We would discover, generally through the CIA chief of station, that the Chinese Nationalists there were training people to use rubber boats to go to the mainland and carry out pinprick raids and so forth and maybe capture some unfortunate sentry, kidnap him back to Taiwan and grill him. This was absolutely forbidden. The United States had insisted, you will not do this. We will not assist you in any way. There will be hell to pay if we catch you at it. But the Nationalists kept preparing operations like this, often with the knowledge and assistance of the U.S. Army Intelligence Unit. We would have to rap knuckles all over the place when we learned of an operation like this.

What was your impression of the Generalissimo, at this period of his long career?

HUMMEL: He was a very old fashioned, authoritarian figure. Not very well educated. Not understanding a whole lot about the dynamics of foreign countries, even the government of the United States, which, I would think, he ought to have known better. How we work, what Congress does, what can be done, and what can't be done. He was very narrow minded and authoritarian. Yet you had to give him credit for holding the country together during the anti-Japanese war. You could see his iron will, assisted by long experience. I would say that there were people who were trickier and maybe smarter than he was around him.

What was the role of Mme. Chiang Kai-shek?

HUMMEL: Well, she was known to be mercurial. I don't think that anybody really liked her. I never liked her. In her disingenuous way she attracted a great deal of American attention during the fight against the Japanese, with her lectures and speech tours, when she spoke to the Congress of the United States, for example. She was a spoiled, ex-beauty who was surrounded by the Soong family, some of whom were very unsavory and corrupt characters. Nevertheless, she was still an important figure. I knew that it would be very important not to make an enemy of her.

What about Chiang Ching-kuo, the Generalissimo's son? What was your impression of him?

HUMMEL: I liked him. He had an unsavory past as a really iron-fisted enforcer of security in Shanghai and on the mainland of China. He was obviously a tough character. However, we got along very nicely. We had a lot of business to handle—mainly Defense Department matters. He was defense minister. His Russian wife was very nice and pleasant.[28] He was smart.

Were you able to play the "Nationalist guerrilla" card with the GMD? The fact that, as a young man, you had been involved with the Nationalist guerrillas—was this something that helped you?

HUMMEL: Yes, it was an asset to me to be known as a friend of Taiwan who had fought as a member of GMD guerrillas. This gave me a certain amount of face. Some of my Chinese Nationalist guerrilla friends were there in Taiwan.

The Chinese Nationalists had a constant desire to do something with Mainland China—conduct clandestine raids or launch balloons, or something like that. I don't think that we did anything to stop them from sending balloons carrying propaganda over Mainland China when the prevailing winds were right. We certainly had to keep the Chinese Nationalists on a short leash for intelligence operations. They, of course, conducted intelligence operations through Hong Kong. Frankly, we never knew a great deal about that. They managed to screen that off from us.

From the point of view of the American military and also the embassy, what was our impression of the Chinese Nationalist military establishment?

HUMMEL: We thought that they were pretty staunch and ready. They were constantly carrying on training exercises and constantly upgrading their equipment and teaching their people how to use the equipment. Hawk anti-aircraft missiles were easily absorbed into their training programs. We thought that they made good use of the equipment that we gave or sold to them. The Chinese Nationalists were good pilots. They maintained their aircraft very well. During my time there most Taiwanese felt, just as the Mainlanders did, that there was a perceptible danger of the Chinese Communists coming over, taking over Taiwan, and doing very bad things to the people.[29]

Taiwan was on a very even keel. My arrival in Taiwan coincided exactly with the end of the last fiscal year in which we gave any AID assistance to Taiwan. Taiwan had graduated. The Chinese Nationalists were very nervous about this. They wanted us to continue the aid program. But we said, "No, you've graduated." Everything went very well. All the AID people left, except one, who was a member of the Joint Commission on Rural Reconstruction (JCRR), which had been extremely successful, first on the mainland, in land reform. They were the ones who helped to spark the land reform in Taiwan, which produced the capital and the impetus for the enormous progress which they have made.

Was there any residue of the old China Lobby from Congress? Did you feel this breathing down your neck?

THAYER: By 1966, the China Lobby had pretty well dissipated, but it was still there, and some of the well-known figures of the China Lobby were around. Because of our dealing with the Taiwan Embassy, the Republic of China Embassy, we saw a lot of these folks—Walter Judd, for example.

BELLOCCHI: [Admiral] Jerauld Wright [USN ret.] was [ambassador, 1963–1965] a conservative. Nothing could be better than Chiang Kai-shek and his people, so one had to be a little careful on how they were criticizing these Taiwanese Chinese, to protect your own career.

DONALD ANDERSON: I remember when I went back to the department—it would have been the mid-'60s—if you used the word "China" without "Communist" in front of it, there were people who would question what you were talking about. There was a long time, for example, that you couldn't use the word "Peking," you had to use the word "Peiping" which was the Nationalist name for the former capital of China. It was a very emotional issue, and the China Lobby was still at that time fairly strong. People still remembered what had happened during the McCarthy period, and the whole issue that we lost China. I had friends who said, "Why do you want to study Chinese?" I guess I took the long view. I figured that I had probably another 20 or 25 years in the Foreign Service and that things would inevitably change.

CHINESE ACTIVITIES IN INDONESIA AND THE THIRD WORLD

The United States government had virtually despaired over the actions of Indonesia's President Sukarno in the early 1960s. Not only had Jakarta mounted an armed campaign against Malaysia, it also threatened to nationalize American companies and it walked out of the United Nations at the end of 1964. Increasingly it shunned American aid and advice and turned instead to the Chinese Communists for support. Fearful that the Indonesian Army would attempt to obstruct growing Chinese influence, the Indonesian Communist Party (PKI) staged a coup against armed forces leaders in September-October 1965. The Army crushed the PKI and eliminated Beijing's power. Tens of thousands of Chinese living in Indonesia were killed by anti-communist elements in the melee that followed.

GREEN: Going back to this period of 1963 and up to 1965, the Chinese clearly had a position of considerable standing and ambition in terms of influence—not military, but political influence—in Africa. They were putting a major effort in Africa. They were also making a major effort in the non-aligned countries of the world. They posed as a non-aligned country. Clearly, they were the biggest and most powerful non-aligned country. They were willing to let [President] Sukarno be their cat's paw. They had these big meetings in Bandung. They made a major effort to make the PKI the dominant party—which it already was by the time I arrived there in 1965—definitely pro-Chinese. The Chinese had a great deal of influence in Jakarta. They were putting up a new CONEFO (the Committee of the New Emerging Forces) complex right outside Jakarta.[30] It was a huge building built with Chinese money. Millions of dollars went into it from China. They were just nearing completion when all this effort of the Indonesia Communist Party, PKI, collapsed in 1965.

The PKI was in cahoots with Beijing to pull off a successful coup that would put up a Nasakom government [an acronym for National-ism, Religion, and Communism] under the titular leadership of Sukarno, who was very compliant and working closely with the com-munists. That failed.[31] It was a tremendous setback to China in terms of its external policies. This, of course, caused something of a breakdown of democratic centralism in Beijing. It sent shockwaves all over the communist world—far more than people have recognized.

HOLDRIDGE: I don't quite agree. I don't think the Chinese were that deeply involved.

GREEN: I think that Sukarno was a willing tool. Whether or not Sukarno was designing to establish a communist government, or thought that he could control such a government, that is beyond my ability to evaluate. There were a series of blows to China at that time, which had a great deal to do with Chinese attitudes and with the problems that we had in our relations with China.

HOLDRIDGE: The Chinese became even more surly and churlish as a consequence of some of these setbacks. The Vietnam War went on for years, and Indonesia was no great plum for the concepts of Mao such as, "Long Live the Victory of People's War." As a matter of fact, the col-lapse of the coup came only a few weeks after Lin Biao had issued this little pamphlet on, "Long Live the Victory of People's War."[32] Along comes the Cultural Revolution, and the whole country went into a con-vulsion. This is precisely the period when we were becoming most deeply involved in Vietnam.

GREEN: This meant the end of Chinese efforts to have influence in the outside world—not necessarily military, but ideological influence in Africa, Southeast Asia, etc. In a way, they were competing against the Soviet Union in these areas, too.

HOLDRIDGE: It was quite plain. Indeed, they were making a deliberate, direct challenge for the leadership of the world communist movement, vis-à-vis the Soviet Union. The Soviets actually resented it, which led to this whole situation. The changes which then occurred, we were wise enough to attempt to exploit.

GREEN: Ideologically, China was out to make marks all around the world.

HOLDRIDGE: But, militarily it was extremely defensive.

CULTURAL REVOLUTION

At the same time as the Americans debated the likelihood that China would intervene in Vietnam, the Chinese argued over whether the escalating U.S. military presence in Vietnam comprised a security threat to China. Apparently Mao Zedong determined that the external danger posed less of a hazard to the PRC than the internal erosion of revolutionary élan and priorities. Thus, even with war on China's doorstep, Mao launched the Great Proletarian Cultural Revolution. For American diplomats, understanding and coping with a China caught up in the frenzy of the Cultural Revolution made the decade from 1966 to 1976 challenging and perplexing. The radical tilt it lent to China's foreign policies in the early years of the movement precluded any real advance in Sino-American relations. American diplomats could only watch from afar as China imploded, relieved not to be experiencing lessons in revolutionary martyrdom directly.

Red China was going through tremendous turmoil at this point in the mid-'6os. Did you think of this as an awesome power or a disintegrating power?

THAYER: China had its first nuclear test in 1964. It had beaten up the Indians in [1962]. We had the Jinmen issue in '58. Communist China was a threat, and we saw it as a threat. We saw—at least I did—the GMD as the only sensible part of China to support. Maybe eventually something else would happen, but in those days there wasn't much doubt as to what we needed to do in our relationship with the GMD. There was a fair amount of discussion of the need for our relationship with the PRC to evolve. So there was a degree of realism, but we didn't see any rapid evolution about to take place.

HOLDRIDGE: At this time, it is conceivable—had it not been for Mao coming out of the wilderness again in August 1966 with the Great Proletarian Cultural Revolution—that there might have been an easing of the tensions, but there wasn't.

CLOUGH: During the Cultural Revolution, for a couple of years there, they practically had no foreign policy. It started in '65, and the worst period was through '67 into '68. By '68, the military was taking over and calming things down. The severe fighting between various groups of Red Guards and troops and so on was ended by '69.

Was the Cultural Revolution Mao Zedong going off in a rampage? Or was this a breakdown in authority? What was causing this as far as we saw it?

DONALD ANDERSON: It was the combination of things. It was a power struggle first and foremost. Mao felt that after the Great Leap Forward had failed certain elements of the leadership—Liu Shaoqi was then head of state, Deng Xiaoping, and a number of others were leading China in a direction of revisionism, or capitalism, which they were. They were trying to put the country back together economically from a very dangerous point.

HOLDRIDGE: These were the ones who wanted to run China in a pragmatic, realistic way, with a diminished ideological content, as opposed to Mao, who wanted to carry the revolution forward to the end, both at home and abroad.

DONALD ANDERSON: Mao felt he was being shunted aside. He had his own vision of what revolutionary China should be and he decided to mobilize the masses, essentially destroy the system, and then put it back together again. And then obviously there were many people who, for their own purely selfish personal reasons, joined into this struggle for their own personal aggrandizement, or power position—notably his wife—and the people around her [the Gang of Four].[33]

What was our view of the Cultural Revolution? I suppose, in many ways, this was your main preoccupation, wasn't it?

DONALD ANDERSON: It was. Well, it was very clearly an unmitigated disaster for China. By that time we were getting a lot of intelligence, mostly through Hong Kong, of what was happening in the provinces. There were a number of places in China where it was nothing short of civil war. They were using artillery, and the factions were engaged in pitched battles. Bodies would come floating into Hong Kong harbor that had been executed. Sometimes multiple bodies all tied together would float into Hong Kong from these factional fights that took place just up in Guangdong province. And, of course, it was a tremendous guessing game as to who was doing what to whom in the upper reaches of the government in Beijing. It was sort of an analyst's dream. So much of the indications of where things were going was done in the press, largely through historical allegories and this kind of stuff. It was great fun to play the game, but it was very, very hard to read.

We did have very good intelligence on the degree of chaos that was going on in China. I remember Bill Bundy during the '60s—during the height of the Cultural Revolution—set up sort of a Wise Men's Group of some academic scholars. They were the best in the United States: John K. Fairbank, Robert Scalapino, A. Doak Barnett. They would come to Washington periodically to discuss "whither China." One of them finally told me, "You know, we're getting more out of this than you are." Because we were assiduously collecting everything we could get by way of intelligence from the provinces, and probably knew about as much as anybody, which certainly wasn't enough.

What was our estimate of Mao Zedong? Was he canny politically? Or was he sort of a bull elephant in a china shop?

DONALD ANDERSON: Oh, no. Mao was a major political thinker, an ideologue, and a truly great leader. Even despite everything he'd done he's still revered by the people of China. He's probably a leader that should have died about 1951. But he brought the revolution to a successful conclusion for the communists, introduced a system which brought a certain amount of hope. There were a lot of excesses, but there was also some hope and a feeling that China was making progress in the early '50s. But really from '57-'58 on, it was just one series of disasters. There was the Hundred Flowers campaign, and then the anti-rightist campaign, and then the Great Leap Forward, then the Cultural Revolution. Basically the Cultural Revolution wasn't really over until Mao died in 1976.

How did we view Zhou Enlai? He always seemed to be a very practical person, but yet he survived under Mao.

DONALD ANDERSON: He was a remarkable individual in that, I really can almost literally say, I've yet to find anyone who doesn't admire the guy. He obviously had to be a magnificent opportunist in the sense of knowing where to land, and when to give and when to attack. But he was universally revered. I was in Hong Kong when he died, and in Hong Kong the lines stretched down the street to pay their respects at the memorial service. It was just tremendous, and genuine. I know Chinese today that have fled China, have been persecuted by the Chinese, and who hate the communist system, but one person they can't say anything bad about is Zhou Enlai. It's amazing. He was always recognized as a pragmatist, and someone who, if there was anybody we could do business with, it was probably assumed it would be Zhou.

HUMMEL: From 1966 to 1976, the Cultural Revolution spilled over into Burma in the same way that it did in Sri Lanka, Nepal, Hong Kong, and other places where, believe it or not, Chinese youngsters and students—and also older people—were stimulated by Beijing propaganda to try to get everybody in the world to wear "Mao Zedong" buttons and to acknowledge Chairman Mao as the leader of everything. This resulted in anti-Chinese riots in quite a few places, and in Burma, in particular, where the Chinese community had a very bad time. Chinese shops all over Burma were burned down. Some people were killed, and a lot of ethnic Chinese were run out of town. The Chinese government in Beijing was so annoyed that they established, right next to China and within Burmese territory, a brand new area of Burma Communist Party insurgents. Up to this time the Burmese government had done an excellent job of maintaining basic peace with the ethnic insurgents—the Kachins, the Shans, and the Karens, who had traditionally been restive. The communist insurgency had virtually been beaten. However, when the Chinese Communists set up their new system, it enabled some of the Burma Communist Party leaders to flee to the Chinese border. They established this brand new insurgency.

This was part of an almost worldwide promotion of national liberation movements. Zhou Enlai toured Africa, proclaiming publicly in the capitals of the various governments that China supported the insurgents. This was an astonishingly stupid performance. The Chinese Communists had a "Pan-Thai Movement" going, with a radio, supporting people of the Thai language and cultural group. So the Chinese Communists were going through a phase of expansionism and support for what they called "national liberation movements." We saw this as contrary to our own interests and also to the interests of all of our friends.

Normalization

NORMALIZATION OF RELATIONS between the United States and China came as a result of a confluence of disparate factors in both countries that served to overcome hostility and emphasize the benefits of reconciliation. Efforts to bridge the divide earlier had confronted barriers in Washington and/or Beijing, falling victim to domestic politics and the Cold War. At the end of the 1960s, however, long-time adversaries discovered salvation in a new relationship.

For the United States, the critical development proved to be the election of Richard Nixon as president. In direct contrast to his reputation as a bitter communist-hater, Nixon made reconciliation an early and high priority for his administration. In pursuing this goal, he was helped by the decline in the influence of the old China Lobby and a gradual growth of interest in "Red China" among scholars, journalists, and businessmen.

The president hoped to secure several advantages. Nixon and his national security adviser Henry Kissinger saw an opportunity to serve large strategic interests by playing the "China card" against the Soviet Union. Reconciliation with China would put Moscow on the defensive, escalate its military costs while lowering those of the United States, and force it to be more cooperative with Washington. Nixon saw the possibility, at the same time, of using China to settle the war in Vietnam. During the Johnson administration signaling had made clear that neither side wanted to go to war over Vietnam. Now Nixon thought that a Chinese leadership working with the Americans on other issues would be inclined to pressure Hanoi to negotiate peace.

Nixon also anticipated that an opening to China would earn accolades internationally and bring significant domestic political benefits. Facing an election campaign in 1972, he relished the idea of being seen as a great peacemaker and celebrated statesman. Moreover, access to the China market might help strengthen business community support at a time when the American economy suffered simultaneous recession, inflation, and unemployment.

China had its own priorities at the end of the decade that spurred interest in accommodation with the United States. Having Washington as a strategic counterweight to Moscow was by far the most compelling. The Sino-Soviet split, which had worsened throughout the 1960s, reached crisis proportions just before Nixon's election to the presidency. On August 21, 1968, Moscow sent tanks into Prague, crushing independent political activity inside Czechoslovakia. The Prague Spring had liberalized Czech politics and economics, challenging the Czech Communist Party and endangering communist control in neighboring states. Although the Chinese did not support the Czech movement and initially sympathized with the ideological dilemma confronted by Soviet leader Leonid Brezhnev, Beijing found his remedy unacceptable. Brezhnev, not only swept away the new order in Czechoslovakia, but declared that the Soviet Union had the right, indeed the obligation, to use whatever means necessary to restore order and preserve socialism, as defined by Moscow, in communist countries.

At a time when China felt especially vulnerable because of Cultural Revolution turmoil, this Brezhnev Doctrine seemed a threat not just to distant East European states, but to Chinese sovereignty as well. The domestic upheaval had not only compromised political institutions but degraded national defenses and frayed the social fabric. Industrial enterprises neared collapse and even in the sensitive domain of weapons manufacture, a shortage of guns and bullets had materialized. On the other hand, the Soviet Union had been massing its forces along the Sino-Soviet frontier. Suddenly national survival dictated having not just a stronger, better prepared military, and domestic unity, but also a powerful foreign friend to deter a Soviet attack.

Of less magnitude in the near term, but ultimately of tremendous importance, China also sought better relations with the United States for access to markets and goods and technology in the West. China had long had trade relations with a variety of American allies, but the United States remained the most desirable potential commercial partner and the source of the most advanced technology. Moreover, once the United States opened economic relations with China, other countries would feel more comfortable in expanding their ties. As the leadership in Beijing began to focus on the need to modernize China, commerce outside the socialist block and a shift away from a policy of self-reliance appeared increasingly crucial.

Finally, China anticipated that better relations with the United States would facilitate its entry into the United Nations. The trend in voting on the UN China seat issue had turned decisively in favor of the People's Republic, but reconciliation with the United States could expedite the process significantly, eliminating the only truly determined opposition to admission. As a result, Taiwan would be forced out of the international forum, and having won that victory, China could accept a more gradual resolution of other aspects of the Taiwan question.

So the Chinese, confronted with danger from the north, began a slow and hesitant process of accommodation with the American imperialists. In November 1968, Zhou Enlai called for resumption of the Warsaw talks, which had been suspended since May because of the Vietnam War. The United States agreed. Then two days before the sessions were to begin a Chinese diplomat defected, giving individuals in the Politburo who remained hostile to Washington an excuse to scuttle the meeting.

The Soviet threat, however, did not diminish, and in March 1969, even without an American connection, Beijing decided to strike. Chinese troops provoked a serious exchange of gunfire with Soviet soldiers on Zhenbao (Damansky) Island in the Ussuri River. The Chinese may have hoped thereby to shock Moscow into retreat, but Mao miscalculated. Instead, the Soviets retaliated with considerable force and a series of bloody confrontations, as well as a war scare, followed. China took the challenge so seriously that it initiated a costly program of tunnel construction under its major cities to act as fallout shelters if the "war maniacs" in the Kremlin fired nuclear weapons. It also returned to a policy of rapprochement with the United States.

This the United States facilitated by its own reaction to the crisis. Washington publicly and repeatedly asserted that it would be deeply concerned if Moscow attacked China, implying that it might actually come to Beijing's assistance. Washington also indicated to China a desire for better relations by easing travel and trade restrictions, downgrading operations of the Seventh Fleet (which had been patrolling the Taiwan Strait since 1953), and actually referring to "Red China" officially as the People's Republic of China for the first time.

As a result, the Warsaw talks finally did resume in 1970. The United States tacitly acknowledged that the Taiwan issue would have to be resolved by the Chinese on both sides of the Strait themselves. China abandoned its demand for an immediate Taiwan settlement before other outstanding problems could be addressed, and both indicated that higher level meetings would be desirable. Again, progress stalled, this time because of the war in Indochina, but Beijing soon gave impetus to the process with its April 1971 invitation to the United States ping pong team to play in Beijing. Soon after "ping pong diplomacy" startled the world, Henry Kissinger secretly flew from Pakistan to Beijing. His private talks there in July 1971 led to Richard Nixon's trip to China in February 1972 and the signing of the Shanghai Communiqué. In the interim, China also secured the long sought UN seat.

The Shanghai Communiqué made reconciliation a firm policy of both governments, aligning them together against any power, that is, the Soviet Union, which might try to assert hegemony over Asia. The most important feature of the agreement proved to be the idea of one China, but not now. In other words, the United States acknowledged, although it did not explicitly accept, the position of Chinese on both sides of the Taiwan Strait that there is only one China and Taiwan is a part of it. In return, Beijing asserted that resolution of the Taiwan problem could be gradual and progress would be made through negotiation, although, in the end, it did not renounce the use of force. Secretly, Nixon and Kissinger also agreed to three other provisions regarding Taiwan: the United States would not support Taiwan independence, it would try to prevent Tokyo from taking Washington's place in Taiwan, and it would accept any peaceful resolution of the Taiwan situation. Finally, they pledged that Washington would move toward opening diplomatic relations with China.

After Richard Nixon returned from China, the United States was swept up in a period of euphoria. The Chinese suddenly appeared to be enormously interesting and engaging people with whom Americans could imagine continuing contact. The stage seemed to be set for closer relations between the two countries. As would become obvious, however, fascination would not be a force powerful enough to overcome the problems generated by domestic politics. The true dawn of a new era would have to wait.

PRELIMINARY INDICATORS

During his years in the wilderness, Richard Nixon gave serious thought to the trajectory of Sino-American relations and concluded that new initiatives would be necessary. In a 1965 conversation with Arthur Hummel in Taipei, he declared that the Nationalists would never recapture the mainland and that the time would come for improving U.S. relations with the mainland regime. He said these things knowing that his room at the Grand Hotel was wired with listening devices. Then, in an article carried by *Foreign Affairs* in 1967, he argued that it was too dangerous for China to continue living in "angry isolation," cherishing hatreds and threatening neighbors. Henry Kissinger also had begun to think about the necessity of a new China policy while serving as Nelson Rockefeller's foreign policy adviser during the 1968 presidential campaign. Even then he posited a triangular relationship in which the United States could improve ties and hopes for peace with both Beijing and Moscow.

NICHOLS: Mr. Nixon came to Hong Kong in the fall of 1965. He was attached to a law firm, but everybody believed he was probably working to run again for president. When he was vice president, he had been in Hong Kong, and somebody had persuaded him to endow a library. On this trip to Hong Kong, the consulate general wasn't too anxious to handle Mr. Nixon. He was not in public office. They didn't know what to do with him, but they knew they couldn't ignore him. So the consul general said, "We've got an out. The Nixon Library and the cultural officer, they make a pair."

I remember the consul general called me in early in the morning and said, "For God's sake, Bob, make sure he understands what's going on, the problems in Hong Kong we have on Vietnam and with Beijing." He was referring to the fact that Beijing was accusing the United States of using Hong Kong as a base for its Vietnam operations. Of course, it was an R&R place for the U.S. Navy, and also the army. The fleet was visiting all the time, and soldiers were flying in from Saigon daily. Just prior to Nixon's arrival, one of the R&R planes had crashed at the end of the runway at Kaitak Airport in Hong Kong. Everybody on board was killed. It was a headline story and also drew attention to the fact that Hong Kong was being used by the U.S. military to send its troops from Vietnam. I was to make sure that Mr. Nixon understood the sensitivities on this score.

My impressions of Nixon prior to his arrival were very negative. My impressions of Nixon the man, based on this experience, were quite positive. He had a tremendous intellectual curiosity. He wasn't telling me anything but rather was picking my brain for everything and anything I could tell him about China and about the attitude of the people in Hong Kong towards China, and the attitude of the Chinese towards

Hong Kong. He never stopped asking questions. What an experience to have a man who had been vice president of the United States and had run for president and was to run again, asking me these questions and paying attention to what I had to say.

Then I warned him about the press. I told him that the American correspondents would try to take over and dominate the press conference, that the Chinese were very passive, and that it would be a good idea if he paid attention to the Chinese questions. And by gosh, he did. He took extra time. In fact, he delayed his departure from Hong Kong.

CLOUGH: The thing that happened that affected the Chinese most with respect to relations with us was what the Soviets were doing. The Soviets began, about '64, to build up their forces on the Chinese border, and this process continued. That disturbed the Chinese, because during the Cultural Revolution, the anti-Soviet polemics became very strong. In fact, they attacked the Soviet Embassy in Beijing.

NICHOLS: At the Voice of America as chief of the Chinese branch, in 1968, I had absolutely no idea that anything was going on regarding a change in our relationship with China, but I was very disturbed because we, as a communications agency—and our main target audience was the people in China, not the people in Taiwan—I was disturbed that we were using language in Chinese that was offensive to the people in China. Our policy at the time required that we call them Communist China, not the People's Republic of China. We had to use the language that Taiwan used in describing the government in China.

Well, I wrote a memo to the State Department about this. It went up to Bill Bundy, who was then the assistant secretary. By gosh, in a week, I got approval to use the proper terms on our broadcast, except when I was directly quoting Secretary Rusk, who always said "Communist China," or another American official. In China people have told me they were listening to VOA then. They heard this difference in language and it was very significant, and people talked about it. I think it probably was used as one of the early signals.

To what extent did the State Department pay attention to the broadcasts?

NICHOLS: They were concerned about them. They didn't control them. They would look over some of the commentaries we were putting out.

I worked with them quite closely, because I had a lot of colleagues in State with whom I had gone through Chinese language training. There was little doubt that the feeling in the Department of State then at the levels below the very top was that we should be moving in the direction of *rapprochement* with Beijing.

HOLDRIDGE: The perceptible change began during movement of the Soviet-bloc armed forces into Prague on August 21, 1968. Under the Brezhnev Doctrine, the vanguard party—to wit the Communist Party of the Soviet Union— because it had been through the revolutionary experience first, was in a position to define the ways which all other communist parties should go through the process of seizing power and building socialism. If they didn't do it the right way, then it was the internationalist duty of all these other good Marxist parties to come and set the errant country or party straight.

The Chinese got the message that the Yugoslavs were way off the reservation at this time, in one direction. They were becoming more capitalist all the time. Here was Mao and company in the other direction, becoming more screwball and extremist. Indeed, Lenin would call it "a left-wing extremist, infantile disorder." This is what the Chinese were guilty of in the eyes of the Soviets. So the relationship became very strained, starting in 1968. Zhou was hosting an Albanian military delegation and announced to the world—to our great interest—that there had been over two thousand violations of China's territory by the Soviet Union.

August 21 was when the Soviet tanks moved in [to Czechoslovakia]. I don't know who the genius was who suggested a resumption of the Warsaw talks, which had been languishing. They sent a letter to the Chinese on September 17, 1968, proposing a resumption of the Warsaw talks. The Chinese responded. A Chinese friend of mine in the embassy said it was 48 hours. It was almost instantaneous for the Chinese. They responded in a rather condescending way. Then they added something which was very significant. It was, "It has always been the policy of the People's Republic of China to maintain friendly relations with all states, regardless of social systems, on the basis of the five principles of peaceful coexistence."

The Chinese had first brought up these five principles of peaceful coexistence with the Indians back in the good old days of "Hindi-Chini bhai bhai"—"Indians and Chinese are brothers." This goes back to the meeting that Zhou had with Nehru which was before the Geneva Conference of 1954.[1]

NIXON, KISSINGER, AND NORMALIZATION

Initiatives on China came from the White House. For the most part, the State Department labored in ignorance, unaware of Nixon's desire to normalize relations, and poorly represented by a secretary of state the president did not respect. Participants from the White House and State Department have subsequently argued over the propriety of the way policy was made and executed, as well as the degree to which the diplomatic establishment proved a barrier to change.

LORD: Nixon and Kissinger each came into office, placing a high priority on making an opening to China. They had independently come to this conclusion. Nixon had indicated this in his article in *Foreign Affairs*.[2] Kissinger felt the same way, primarily because of the Soviet dimension.

Nixon sent Kissinger a memo on February 1, 1969, approximately one week after his inauguration as president, [in which] basically he instructed Kissinger to find a way to get in touch with the Chinese. This was one of the earliest instructions that Kissinger got from Nixon. Of course, Kissinger was all in favor of doing this. You have to remember that we had had 20 years of mutual hostility and just about total isolation from China. We had no way of communicating directly with the Chinese. A lot of Americans were still very suspicious of China, including a hard core of Nixon's conservative base. The American public really wasn't attuned to an opening to China as yet, although there were different attitudes on this possibility. We had allies who would be nervous about such an opening to China. So there were many challenges facing us.

HOLDRIDGE: The study [of China policy] was subsequently followed up by removal of a considerable number of our trade controls, removal of the certificate of origin—which used to be an onus to us in that any item that was brought into the United States had to show that it was not produced in mainland China—as well as the removal of restrictions on travel, provided the Chinese wanted to give visas to Americans who wanted to go.

LORD: This course did not require reciprocity on their part but was designed to show that we were interested in moving ahead. It was also designed to begin to condition our public and our allies that we were moving ahead in this direction. So several things were done, including a toast which Nixon gave to President [Nicolae] Ceausescu of Romania, in which Nixon used the phrase "the People's Republic of China." This sounds unexceptionable now, but at the time no American official and certainly no president ever used that official designation, which the Chinese Communists wanted. We had always said "Red China," "Communist China," "Mainland China," or something like that.

When the Nixon administration came in—obviously Nixon had earned his name as being one of the most vehement anti-communists early on—was there a feeling, "Oh my God, here we're moving farther to the right on this?"

DONALD ANDERSON: No, there wasn't because while Nixon had made his political reputation, as you say, as a vehement anti-communist, he was also recognized as a very savvy and pragmatic international thinker. He had already written in one of the journals saying we had to find a way to improve our relationship with China. So we knew he was inclined in that direction. So there wasn't any worry about the ideological aspect of that particular Nixon anti-communist position.

HOLDRIDGE: The year 1969 was a very critical year for China. In March of 1969 were those very interesting clashes between the Soviets and the Chinese over this little island in the Ussuri River—Zhenbao, as the Chinese called it, or Damansky as the Soviets called it—in which the Chinese came out second best. The Soviets really clobbered that island with one of the most extreme artillery barrages in modern history, leaving it looking like the surface of the moon. That shook the Chinese.[3] In April 1969, they had a party congress. For a period, the Chinese tried to reestablish a better relationship with the Soviets. For about two weeks, all of the polemics seemed to stop. It didn't work.

Then, in the summer of 1969, there was a rapid Soviet troop build-up along the Chinese border. They went from something like 17 divisions up to 20, 30, 40, to a total of 54 over a period of time. There was a very rapid build-up. There was a lot of word floating around to the effect that the Soviets were going to take care of these people who were getting so far off the reservation.[4]

HUMMEL: In 1969, the Chinese were really concerned that the Soviets might pour across the border into China. The Soviets, of course, were also concerned that hordes of Chinese were going to pour across the Soviet border in the other direction. Tension was very high, and at the time the Chinese had ample reason for concern about the Soviet military.

HOLDRIDGE: It did look to me—doing my own analysis and drawing on the resources of the department—that there was probably some debate going on in Moscow over whether military force might not be used as a surgical strike to take out the Chinese nuclear capability.[5]

GREEN: I recall that, in 1969, the CIA considered it a one out of three chance that the Russians would, in fact, try to knock out any Chinese nascent nuclear facilities. The Chinese obviously got wind of this and went underground. That was the time that they started building extensive underground shelters.[6] Also, the Chinese must have remembered what the Soviets did in Czechoslovakia. This must have left a very deep impression of what the Soviets were capable of.

HOLDRIDGE: They hadn't forgotten. In 1956, in Budapest, the Soviets were capable of utter ruthlessness in putting down any form of dissent.[7] The Chinese, of course, [in 1969] were still going through the throes of their Cultural Revolution, and they were in a terrible state—economically, politically, and militarily.

Was there a feeling that things had reached such a point in China that we might be able to open up relations with that country?

LORD: What was clear was that China, because of the Soviet threat, might well be interested in improving relations with us. We also thought that the Chinese might think that, if they could improve relations with us, that might open the door to relations with other countries. Japan was certainly holding back on its opening to China. The French had made some movement toward China, but the British and others, such as the Federal Republic of Germany, were generally holding back in developing relations with China because of the U.S. posture. Not to mention getting into the United Nations and beginning to establish at least unofficial, if not official, relationships and breaking out of various kinds of embargoes and isolation.

When did President Nixon first announce his Nixon (Guam) Doctrine?

HOLDRIDGE: In July of 1969, just a few weeks after I came in [to the NSC], the early changes in travel and trade with respect to China were made. Nixon then took a round-the-world trip.[8] He went to Guam, and made a statement there which caught me by surprise. We had been used to an advanced military posture with respect to East Asia. Nixon came along and said that the security of an individual country was up to that country itself, primarily. He said that we would help with the where-withal, but we weren't going to contribute the manpower.

GREEN: I had written the scope paper for this Nixon Doctrine.[9]

Did anything else happen on this trip?

HOLDRIDGE: As I recall, it was between Jakarta and Bangkok where Henry came back to me on the plane, Air Force One. The NSC had a little enclave just behind the presidential compartment. Henry asked me to draft a cable to the Chinese, proposing that we get together to talk about the improvement in our relations.

I very happily sat down and worked on this thing. I said that we should not look to the past, but look to the future. There were many things that we had in common. There were many issues that were of mutual value, and we should address them, and let's get together. I gave the draft to Henry. He looked at it, gave his characteristic grunt, said nothing, turned around, and went back into the presidential compartment. That is the last I saw or heard of it. I have no doubt that a message, somewhere along the line, was, in fact, sent to the Chinese during this trip. There were two places it could have been done. One was in Pakistan. Yahya Khan was the head of the Pakistani government then. Pakistanis and the Chinese were very close in the wake of what had happened [the war] in India in 1962. The other place was in Romania. I rather suspect that they would have done it through Pakistan. With Ceausescu, in Romania, even though he was not exactly in the best of light with Moscow, there were probably enough guys running around in Bucharest who would have slipped the word to Moscow. We didn't want this information to become public that we were trying to reestab-lish contact.[10]

You have reason to believe that that was the first of the real soundings on the issue?

HOLDRIDGE: Yes.

Had there been any intimations or discussions prior to that with Henry Kissinger?

HOLDRIDGE: No, except that we had seen the developments, since Nixon took office in January of 1969, that he wanted to improve relations with China.

GREEN: I had had many conversations with President Nixon about China. I knew he was interested in it. This is the first time, right now, that I have heard this very interesting fact that Henry asked you to draft this telegram. Assuming that Henry did, in fact, send out the message or a feeler in July of 1969, it would have been a very receptive China that would have gotten that message. At that point, they were pretty terrified by the chances of attack.

HOLDRIDGE: It wasn't that easy. There was a terrible debate going on inside China, going back to 1968, as to the merits of what to do about the relationship with the U.S. Clearly, along about the latter part of 1969, the Chinese were beginning to take a good, hard look at their world situation, quite apart from the ideology of the thing, to wonder about whether it was a good idea to have two major enemies at the same time. By the way, we had already convinced them that we were not going to carry the war in Vietnam up to the point of attacking China.

So were the Chinese Communists playing the "American card"?

HUMMEL: That's right. Another reason for this rapprochement between Communist China and the United States or this exercise in triangular diplomacy as it came to be called, was that President Nixon wanted to get the U.S. out of the Vietnam War. Having a friendlier relationship with China would enable a U.S. withdrawal from Vietnam, hopefully with some prospect of viability for South Vietnam after we left. Of course, this didn't happen.

LORD: Nixon saw advantages in establishing contact with China as the world's most populous nation. Above all he wanted to put pressure on the Soviet Union to get them to be more forthcoming toward us, by showing that we had an option by going to China. This was the so-called "China card," a term which was exaggerated. Nixon wanted to have good relations with Russia as well, but also wanted to try to have better relations with each of these large, communist nations than they had with each other. Nixon also hoped, and here he put more emphasis than Kissinger ever did on this point, that Russia would help him end the war in Vietnam. During the presidential campaign of 1968, Nixon talked about having a "secret plan" to end the war in Vietnam. He didn't really have a secret plan. His main emphasis was that improving relations with the two communist giants, and particularly the Soviet Union, would help to bring pressure on Hanoi to end the war.

HUMMEL: So we had the pivotal position in this triangle. We could have acceptable relations with the Soviet Union, and the Chinese Communists resented that very much. The Chinese could not have decent relations with the Soviet Union. The United States could have good relations with both countries—or decent relations, anyway. At one time, the Chinese Communists publicly accused us of seeking a rapprochement with the Soviet Union, stating that we were "standing on China's shoulders" to get a better relationship with the Soviet Union. This was not too far from the truth.

During your time as deputy assistant secretary and acting secretary, did the Chinese Communists ever seek any support from us against the Soviet Union?

HUMMEL: Only in very nuanced terms. Of course, I don't know what Henry Kissinger told them in those very private conversations. It may be—and I strongly suspect that this was the case—that he went further than the American government as a whole told him to.[11] Congress would have been incensed if the Executive Branch of our government made firm promises of providing military assistance or entering a war without consultation with Congress. However, we came pretty close to it. We said that we would not stand idly by, that there would be serious repercussions on our relations with the Soviet Union, and that we would try to get other countries involved in taking anti-Soviet positions, if such an event would happen. We said that we would do what we could to help China.

HOLDRIDGE: I recall in the latter part of 1969, after his around-the-world trip, Nixon produced a report to the Congress on the foreign policy of the United States. It was the first time that it had ever been done from the White House, not from the Department of State.[12] He got all the NSC staff in there. We sat around in the Cabinet room, and Nixon gave us a little harangue about what our jobs were and how, by God, he was going to run foreign policy. In the course of this he said, "If the Department of State has had a new idea in the last 25 years, it is not known to me."

That was a lot of nonsense, of course, knowing what Marshall [Green] had said to him. Half the people in that room were Foreign Service officers. But Nixon had this thing about the Foreign Service. Those of us who were on detail from the department had to be very cautious. One reason why it might have happened: Nixon preferred one-on-one in his meetings with chiefs of state and heads of government. In Bangkok, the ambassador's deputy went again and again to the mat with Kissinger about the ambassador going in and attending the meeting. There is no reason why the ambassador to the country should have been excluded.

GREEN: It happened in Indonesia, too, where our ambassador spoke Indonesian. He would have done a better job than the Indonesian interpreter they used. He clamored to get into that meeting. Henry took me aside several times and said that, if he once more brings that up, he is out. Therefore, we had no record, except what Henry chose to recall, and what he then chose to tell us he recalled. Increasingly, we in the State Department realized that we didn't know all that was going on. When that happens, you begin to lose confidence.

HOLDRIDGE: Henry would have had a fit if I'd run around and kept the department informed about every little thing which was going on. I would have been fired. The only time he resolved this problem was later in 1973, when he became secretary of state himself, and Brent Scowcroft took over as the assistant to the president for National Security Affairs.

GREEN: I still have quite a bit of correspondence with Henry about various items. They were always very nice letters, nothing nasty. Nastiness was always done behind your back.

What would you say the attitude was in the government, prior to the president's announcement, about relations with the People's Republic of China?

FREEMAN: There were generational differences in the Foreign Service. Those of an older generation who had survived being scourged by the

McCarthy purges, by and large, were true believers in the cause of one China, centered in Taipei. And, of course, right through 1971, we continued the effort to keep the Security Council and General Assembly seat for Taipei rather than Beijing. So there was a very strong bias generally in that older generation in favor of the existing policy of anti-communist confrontation and containment. [Then] there was a generation which had grown up doing China-watching, who had a kind of romantic fascination with the PRC.

LILLEY: There were these terrible fights within the American analytic community about China. [There was a] group that said we have to open with China, it is a bulwark against the Soviet Union. They are not aggressive. Dump Taiwan and go toward China. There was another school of thought saying "Look, these guys had been bastards to begin with. They are always going to be. They have deep anti-foreignism in their makeup. They can sucker you in on these things but they really aren't your friends and they can go back to the Soviet Union in a year if it suited their national purposes." These arguments got very *ad hominem* and bitter.

TAIWAN

In the mid-1960s Taiwan had been confident about its status in the world and its relations with the United States, not just because of its growing prosperity, but also because of Washington's evident anti-communism and the burgeoning chaos on the mainland of China. Taiwan's leaders allowed themselves to believe that the United States might still support their efforts to return to the mainland and ignored signs that more moderate policies toward the People's Republic might be gathering support. Indeed, Washington sought to reassure Taiwan with continued military aid and intelligence cooperation, as well as regular briefings on the Warsaw talks. In 1970, Richard Nixon told Chiang Ching-kuo during a visit to Washington, that "I will never sell you down the river."[13] Such a statement seemed particularly persuasive from a man who had championed the Nationalist cause for much of his political career.

When the Kissinger trip was revealed and the Nixon visit announced, Taipei felt betrayed. The great secrecy with which Nixon and Kissinger had shrouded their moves had worked to prevent Taipei's lobbyists from spoiling the initiative. In fact, the disastrous consequences long predicted and feared in Taiwan did not materialize. No panic engulfed Taiwan, the economy did not collapse, and neither diplomatic nor military interaction with the United States changed significantly.

NICHOLS: It was obvious Mr. Nixon felt that something should change. Very soon we began to see subtle changes taking place. Kissinger would have off-the-record briefings for the press. They'd be given out by the press, quoting a highly placed official of the administration. Well, from the things that were being said by Kissinger, you could see where we were going.

Another thing that happened, we withdrew the Seventh Fleet from the Taiwan Strait. It was announced by Vice President [Spiro] Agnew when he was out there on one of the two trips he made while I was there. Agnew brought the news to Chiang Kai-shek that we were taking the Seventh Fleet out of the Taiwan Straits. [Patrols ended December 1969.]

Bob Clarke, the PAO, and I decided that what we needed to do was prepare our audience in Taiwan for what apparently was coming. We had as much difficulty persuading the embassy to go along with our ideas as we had in persuading the Taiwanese, the people on Taiwan, of what we were saying was happening. We gave monthly press briefings to the Chinese press, and made an attempt to show that U.S. foreign policy was moving away from its hard position, and that a *détente* was in the works.

That must have generated tremendous pressures by the Nationalist Chinese in Taiwan against the American official establishment.

NICHOLS: There was certainly a great deal, and some of it was manifested in rather unpleasant ways. In Taiwan, we had branch offices down-island in Taichung, in Tainan, and in Kaohsiung. In 1970, I was visiting our office in Kaohsiung when we got a telephone call from Tainan, 30 miles from Kaohsiung, that a bomb had just blown up the USIS Tainan office. The office had been almost completely destroyed, and several people had been seriously hurt. This happened at a time when the United States had just given asylum or had helped, supposedly, in the escape from Taiwan of a Taiwan nationalist, a man named

Peng Ming-min.[14] The Chinese government was not happy with us, and strong supporters of this Nationalist regime were not happy with us. Who placed the bomb was never officially acknowledged, but there were very strong suspicions about the source.

What was the attitude of Kissinger and Nixon toward Taiwan? How significant an obstacle to improving relations with China did it appear to be?

LORD: Their feeling was that, in terms of American national interests, you have to take some risks in that relationship in order to move ahead with China. Clearly, Nixon and Kissinger wanted to square the circle. They wanted to open up with China without having to go too far in destroying our relationship with Taiwan and, in the course of doing this, not only hurting our international reputation for steadiness and friendship with our allies, but also stirring up domestic opposition to mistreating an old friend. The strategy was, in effect, and it was effectively carried out, to postpone resolution of the Taiwan issue, try to appeal to Beijing's sense of geopolitics and fear of the Soviet Union and its desire to break out of it isolation, and to try to override their preoccupation with Taiwan. The idea was to keep working on the Taiwan issue, but we would kick it down the road for later resolution.

GREEN: *What were the relations between Taiwan and the Soviet Union then? In view of the growing bitterness between Beijing and Moscow, was there an inclination to try to take advantage of that in some way, by either side, that is, by either Moscow or Taiwan?*

CLOUGH: No. No, there were rumors. I mean, people in Hong Kong were passing around rumors about meetings between people from Taiwan and the Soviets, but I don't think there was anything to that. Our relations with the Soviets in those years were such that if we thought that Taiwan was trying to make some kind of deal with the Soviet Union, we would be very upset. And they were very dependent on us.[15]

GREEN: I recall there was a Soviet merchantman [*Tuapse*] that was seized. It was held indefinitely there.[16]

CLOUGH: Those seamen were held there for years and years.

GREEN: To me, it made absolutely no sense for the Republic of China to hold on to those people, unless they really believed that Moscow and

Beijing were working hand in glove, which seems incredible that they should ever have thought that after '61. But I was thunderstruck when I talked with Chiang Kai-shek in 1969, just before I became assistant secretary, to find him thinking that all this Sino-Soviet split was a lot of propaganda designed to fool the Western world. Now clearly that was not the case, and surely that couldn't have been believed by people in the Foreign Office. Did they feel that the old man was sort of losing his marbles? The Sino-Soviet split was clear from '61 onward, and clear to a lot of us before that time.

CLOUGH: But it wasn't just the GIMO. A lot of people in Taiwan were saying this is just a fake, it's being put on, a show to deceive the West, because it served their interests to get the West to believe that. It would prevent the West from making any move to draw closer to China. In taking this view, there was an element of wishful thinking. There was also an element of calculated policy, to convince the Americans and others that nothing was to be gained by trying to improve relations with Beijing.

At the Taichung language school were you getting any exposure to ideology?

FREEMAN: Well, mainly we were, of course, exposed to Guomindang ideology. The faculty, drawn from the mainland community in Taiwan, included retired generals and professors and all quite committed in one way or another to the Guomindang cause. There were two Guomindang Party cells operating clandestinely in the school, one reporting to the provincial level and one to the national level. There was extensive reporting, by the teachers, of biographic and other information to the authorities. Some of them were dissidents, but subjected to blackmail and forced into this role.

Did you have any impression of how our embassy, particularly the political section, viewed the Guomindang government on Taiwan at that time?

FREEMAN: I once went to the embassy, and sat in the administrative counselor's office while the senior locals, who were Mandarin-speakers from the mainland, would talk in English to the counselor, and then among themselves, in Mandarin, very disparagingly about him and what he was doing. While they were doing that, the Taiwanese locals were talking equally disparagingly, in Taiwanese, about the Mandarin-speaking locals. Then there were two Hakkas who were carrying on a disparaging conversation about the Taiwanese.

The embassy was a strong embassy in terms of political reporting, but, probably inevitably, skewed toward the Mandarin-speaking environment. That was something that was aggravated by Walter McConaughy's tenure as ambassador. Walter McConaughy had made a career, essentially, in China and in Taipei, but never learned a word of Chinese, and was quite, therefore, manipulable by the Chinese authorities there, who are, like all Chinese, very good at manipulating people.

Taiwan has become much more Taiwanese. Did you see that sort of thing developing then?

FREEMAN: It was apparent that the Mainlander hold on Taiwan was a wasting asset, and that Taiwan would emerge, if it remained separate from the mainland for a sufficient period of time, as quite a distinctive, largely Taiwanese-oriented society. But this was in the early stages of happening, and one could make guesstimates about it, but not be sure. Demographically, it was obvious there was a large aging Mainlander population and a much younger and more dynamic Taiwanese one. Industry was largely in the hands of the Taiwanese, and increasingly so. The Guomindang, which had been a majority Mainlander party, began during that period to be a majority Taiwanese party. And the degree of intermarriage, the acculturation of the Taiwanese by the Mainlander-dominated public school system, and other factors were blurring the distinctions between the two, assimilating the Taiwanese into greater Chinese culture, but also assimilating the Mainlanders into something new that was Taiwan culture.

NEGOTIATION WITH THE PRC

Surmounting the legacy of distrust between the United States and China proved to be difficult. The Chinese, in particular, faced substantial hurdles in overcoming factional opposition to dealing with Washington. Both military leaders and civilian radicals attempted to undermine any opening. Mao finally opted for the policy of rapprochement after Zhou Enlai assembled a high-level group of revolutionary heroes to study the issue and they declared themselves in favor of improving relations with the United States.[17] In the United States Nixon had to worry about diverse opinion as well. Some 90 percent of Americans registered negative images of China in the mid-1960s and 70 percent saw China as the greatest threat to world peace. Thus the Nixon administration minimized the potential for interference by carrying on the early phase of reconciliation in secret, not just from the public and Congress, but, as testimony here makes clear, even from the Department of State.

HOLDRIDGE: In early 1969, when we were supposed to have a resumption of the Warsaw talks, the chargé of the Chinese embassy in The Hague defected. He dropped out of a second-story window and ran to the U.S. Embassy, asking for refuge. We, of course, granted it to him. He turned out to be a real dud for any kind of intelligence or political value. He was a psychotic.

LILLEY: The chargé was a very limited man, but he got the cable traffic from Beijing and he knew, he had a feel for the arguments, and we knew a lot about what he was saying. We could factor it against a background that we had. And this British good source that came in added to our knowledge. Plus our own people that were feeding us from inside the Chinese system. You put it all together and you begin to see the outlines of the real power struggle developing in China and what the issues were between the two parties.

HOLDRIDGE: Walt Stoessel [ambassador to Poland], being back [in Washington], was asked by Henry [Kissinger] to convey the message— to make contact with the Chinese in Warsaw. Indeed, he was again to propose a resumption of the Warsaw talks, which Walt did at a Yugoslav fashion show where he caught the chargé [Lei Yang]—the ambassador was out of town. He proposed the resumption. The Chinese chargé said, "I'll come over and discuss it with you at your embassy. How about that?"[18] A few days later, a Hongqi (Red-Flag) limousine, flying the Chinese flag, shows up at our embassy in Warsaw, unmistakably to the great excitement of the press. The next day or so, Walt went back in his Cadillac to the Chinese Embassy, flying the American flag. So we were back on track.

DONALD ANDERSON: By that time it had become the Office of Chinese Affairs, it was no longer Asian Communist Affairs. We shed North

Vietnam and North Korea. Paul Kreisberg was [head of the China desk and] also the political adviser to the talks, so he and I worked very closely together on this. We were told to start drafting a new set of instructions for Stoessel for a meeting with the Chinese. The two of us agreed that we should talk about Taiwan and some of the more fundamental issues between the two countries. I was quite surprised to find that the feeling was that we hadn't gone far enough.

HOLDRIDGE: The proposal was made that there be an exchange of high-level representatives to talk about the resumption of some kind of a relationship, up to and including opening missions of some sort—trade missions, etc.—in each other's capitals. That was presented to the Chinese at the first Warsaw talk in January of 1970. It really took the chargé there aback. The next meeting was in February. There was a sort of a cautious acceptance on the part of the Chinese for this proposal. Now, the department got cold feet the second time around, and they wanted to back away from that business of missions. We in the NSC put it back in again.

DONALD ANDERSON: When we decided to try and resume the talks in 1970, we decided we would have to discuss the issue of Taiwan, and some of the fundamentals of the relationship, and that we couldn't do that in the Mysliwiecki Palace with the Poles and the Russians listening, so we proposed to the Chinese that we change the venue of the talks. We considered several possibilities, one being a third country less under the thumb of the Russians. And the other one, that the Chinese finally agreed on, was to move the talks to our two embassies. So the meeting that resumed the talks after about a year's hiatus in January of 1970 was held in the Chinese Embassy.

GREEN: There were certain differences that existed between Ambassador Holdridge and me with regard to how we should carry on for the Warsaw talks. Should we go in for a high-level meeting, etc.? I remember very well that Henry sent over and asked our views on this, for whatever they were worth. One of the things that I mentioned to him was that I trusted, before we were committed to a high-level meeting, one of our high-level people would have some advance indication that it would result in something that was constructive. Nothing would be worse than to go out there and then get slapped in the face. It would be the end of all that we hoped to achieve in our U.S.-China relations. That kind of thing has been distorted in Kissinger's account in his [book] *White*

House Years. He implies that we were throwing cold water. It was not true at all. All we were saying is that we didn't know all of the pieces in the puzzle.

HOLDRIDGE: This is the first time I had heard of the problems that faced the State Department with respect to having a high-level representative go to Beijing.

GREEN: We weren't in communication with each other. John knew certain things. He was under strict secrecy not to tell us. We knew that we didn't know all of the parts. It created a distrust. Naturally, old friends maintain the same kind of ties we preserve all our careers—John and me—but it put it to the real test, to be dealing with the same problem and for me not to be privy to all the information that he had access to.[19]

HOLDRIDGE: I wasn't always privy, either. You know, Henry would have three different groups working on a problem in the National Security Council. Not one of the members of those groups knew that the others were working on the same problem. That is the way he did it. It was a paranoiac way of doing things, which I hated.

FREEMAN: This was an odd period in American foreign policy, because, in effect, the National Security Council became the bureau for great-power affairs, and the State Department became the bureau for details, relations with lesser states, administrivia, and support of grand enterprises launched out of the NSC.

HOLDRIDGE: The whole question of a high-level emissary to Beijing became moot. In May of 1970, the U.S. military went into Cambodia and Mao Zedong cut off the Warsaw contact with a piece that was signed by Mao himself, on the front page of the *People's Daily*.[20] The whole thing languished. There may have been some efforts by Henry via Yahya Khan or whoever to reopen, but nothing really happened.

Then Edgar Snow visited China in the latter part of 1970.[21] He stood next to Mao on Tiananmen Square for the October 1, 1970, ceremony. Some word came back through Snow that there was some receptivity. In March of 1971, there was an issue of *Life* in which Snow gave some of his accounts of his visit. In this issue, which became almost our Bible, Snow reported how Mao said a visit by Nixon to China would be welcome, and if he wanted to bring his wife and daughters, too, that would be fine.

GREEN: In the latter part of 1970, it must have been a period in which the Chinese were doing some very serious reevaluation of their total strategic position. By the beginning of 1971, maybe by March, when Snow reported his meeting with Mao, they had already made up their minds that they were going to have to change their policy. Of course, we had ping-pong diplomacy shortly after that.[22]

HOLDRIDGE: After a decent interval and after the furor over the Cambodian exercise had died down, the Chinese could once more take a look at their strategic needs, the idea of having one enemy rather than two, and resume the contact with the U.S.

GREEN: There is another interesting point here, which is the Cultural Revolution. It was beginning to peter out in 1971, wasn't it?

HOLDRIDGE: It had already thrown China into such turmoil that even Mao had repudiated the Red Guards and thrown them out of Beijing.[23]

GREEN: In other words, internal events in China were also bringing it to the point of a rapprochement with the United States.

HOLDRIDGE: Yes. The voices of those who preached a less ideological policy and a more realistic one were beginning to be heard again. Zhou was able to save some of his people from purgatory, keeping them out of jails. There was still an intense debate going on in China over the whole merits of this. Nevertheless, the strategic considerations were uppermost at that time.

Could you explain what ping-pong diplomacy was and how it was viewed in the Department of State, in the East Asian Bureau, at that time.

FREEMAN: The Department of State was sort of on a steady-as-you-go course on China. For most people in the department (Al Jenkins was an exception; he had been essentially co-opted by Kissinger and was working with Kissinger directly, behind the back of Marshall Green and the secretary of state, Bill [William] Rogers), ping-pong diplomacy was a minor but interesting evidence, from the Chinese side, of an interest in pursuing a relationship with the United States.[24] In fact, it was the culmination of quite a bit of diplomacy, some of it known to the department, to a few people, and much of it unknown.

There were a great number of other things going on, of course. Part of the business of attempting rapprochement with China was the dismantling of a series of niggling but long-standing trade and investment barriers, resisted fiercely by different elements of the bureaucracy that had acquired a vested interest in these things over the course of more than two decades. I can remember a discussion with the then head of foreign assets control at the Treasury, somewhat later, when the president had made an announcement about doing away with the foreign assets control regulations on China and relaxing various barriers to nongovernmental intercourse with the Chinese, and hearing Stanley Sommerfield [chief of Foreign Assets Control Division, Treasury Department] say to me, "Well, that may be the president's policy, but it's not Treasury's." And that was generally the attitude. Turning the ship of state even a few degrees requires an awful lot of work by the crew, and the crew generally doesn't want to do it. So it's a fairly creaky process.

LORD: During this period, we were trying to improve relations with Russia. We had had a mixed bag of results in this connection in 1969 and up to the summer of 1971. We're talking about July, 1971. We had been suggesting for some time that there should be a summit meeting between President Nixon and Chairman [Leonid] Brezhnev. The Russians were dragging their feet on this proposal, as well as on the issues of Berlin and arms control. So there were instructions for Deputy National Security Adviser [Alexander] Haig to call in Soviet Ambassador [Anatoly] Dobrynin while we were traveling and to make one last suggestion of a summit meeting with Moscow. Haig made the pitch, Dobrynin turned it down. We made a clear decision that we would have a summit with China first, assuming that we could arrange it. Of course, the Russians couldn't know how they were screwing up, because they certainly would have accepted a summit meeting first in Moscow, had they known that we were considering a summit in Beijing. We got the Russians' attention after this secret trip, and things began moving.

How did you approach the idea of a high-level trip to China?

LORD: There were two issues facing us. One was who would go? Also, what would the ground rules be. These were matters which were dangerous for both sides. Their initial position was, more or less: "Send someone over here. We can talk to you, but you must resolve the Taiwan issue before we can do anything else." We wanted to maneuver it so that we were willing to talk about Taiwan. Of course, we would have to do that or we wouldn't get anywhere with them. However, we felt that there had to be a broader agenda as well.

Tell me about the preparations for Henry's trip. What was your role?

HOLDRIDGE: My role was doing the books, position papers [and talking points] on all the issues that would be discussed with the Chinese. Except for Vietnam—Henry wanted to talk about Vietnam himself. First of all, there was a paragraph which indicated the issue involved. Next came the anticipated Chinese position, and then your response.

LORD: One of the criticisms of the secrecy of this whole operation was that we couldn't fully take advantage of the people in the State Department on the China desk; that we didn't have the full advantage of their knowledge. Having said that, I would say that we would often get this knowledge by asking for memos. We didn't have the intimate, day to day exchanges that some of these people might have provided, had they been included.

Kissinger generally liked to meet with Nixon alone, as opposed to having NSC staff people with him. This was both a reflection of Kissinger's ego and his insecurity. Kissinger sought to control access to President Nixon in many ways. This was true in the case of briefings, meetings, or, for example, at decision-making sessions after meetings.

HOLDRIDGE: This brings up a little bit about the surroundings of the Kissinger trip to Beijing in July of 1971. The reason that there was no publicity given on this is—the way Henry Kissinger put it—if it came out, we would be trying to negotiate our China policy, not with the Chinese but with the *Washington Post* and the *New York Times*. He felt that this would be absolutely unacceptable. That is why there was so much secrecy attached to it. Not that we were worried about how people would view it, etc. The question was that advance publicity might have even killed the whole opportunity, because the Congress or the press would have been hanging caveats all over, to the point where we couldn't move. The only way that he saw it was, if you are going to do something like that, you've got to do it in such a way that there are no prior limitations on what you can discuss or how you can go about it.

GREEN: I am prepared to accept that, but I have some caveats, too. I think the assistant secretary of state in charge of that area should be informed. Not to inform me about Henry's trip was almost disastrous. When I was told at a staff meeting in July 1971 that it had just been announced on the radio that Dr. Kissinger had suffered an attack of flu at Islamabad and was taking several days off to recuperate, I told my staff that no one suffering from Delhi belly would ever drive up into the mountains. I just said to my people, "Well, he's probably gone to China." I suddenly realized that maybe he had gone to China. So I swore them all to secrecy about our conversation just in time to prevent the leak. What I was saying in my demure in early 1970 about having a high-level emissary go to China was that there ought to be some kind of advance indication that it succeed. That was exactly what Henry was doing. He was going out there, in secret.

LORD: I don't think that the opening to China could have been accomplished without secrecy. I don't think that the negotiations with Vietnam would have made so much progress toward the end without secrecy. There was the accomplishment of the Berlin negotiations and the SALT [Strategic Arms Limitation Talks] agreements with the Russians. People can disagree whether these would have been possible without secrecy. I'll give you one example, dealing with China. The secrecy certainly cost us in terms of our relations with Japan [the so-called Nixon Shokku, or Nixon Shocks]. The Chinese indicated that they wanted some degree of confidentiality as well, but the emphasis on secrecy was certainly as much from our side as theirs. If it had been known in advance that Kissinger was going to China, first, you would have had the Washington bureaucracy weighing in with specific, and, in Kissinger's and Nixon's view, second level concerns that we had to get this aspect of trade, cultural exchanges, or whatever. Or that we had to be careful about Russian sensitivities. This would have hamstrung the early discussions. Secondly, we would have had our allies weighing in, in advance, trying to bind us, whether this involved our South Vietnamese allies, the Japanese, or the Europeans making demands and limiting us in our discussions with the Chinese. Thirdly, there would have been a firestorm among the conservatives and many of the Republicans domestically in the U.S. about the president's even considering making this dramatic move toward China, causing an uproar and hamstringing him in advance. All of this would also have put off the Chinese.

There have been suggestions in some of the books written about this episode that Kissinger didn't like the Japanese very much and that some of the secrecy involved in this trip was intended to send a message to the Japanese.

LORD: I wouldn't go that far, because Japan is an important ally, and we wouldn't want to disrupt the alliance. It is fair to say, and this continues to the present day, that Kissinger always had a certain suspicion of Japan, even as he had of Russia, versus a predilection to go easier on the Chinese. Kissinger was genuinely concerned about leaks out of Japan, feeling that the Japanese were particularly prone to leaks in their media. He was aware of the Japanese-Chinese "love-hate" relationship, because of World War II and other matters. So it wasn't as if Kissinger wanted to hurt our relations with Japan. He was certainly too calculating in terms of American national interests to go out of his way to annoy Japan. That wasn't the point. However, he was prepared to run some risk of the Nixon shokku and everything else to pull off the China trip correctly and not be pressured, whether by Japan or others, to lock ourselves into a position with the Chinese before he even set out. Now Kissinger would be the first to admit that, as we moved to improve relations with China, we didn't handle the Japan side very well.[25]

Kissinger and Nixon had the feeling that this was totally uncharted territory. Making this trip to China was not without its risks, despite our feeling that the Chinese would be receptive because of their fear of the Soviets and of their isolation. Therefore, we wanted as free a hand as we could get when we sat down with the Chinese. I don't know whether Kissinger would agree with me on this. However, in retrospect, what we should have done, to square this circle, was to have someone, not very prominent or noteworthy, like myself or Holdridge, go to Japan, perhaps a week before the secret trip to China. Such a person could have gone personally to Sato [Eisaku], who was the Japanese prime minister then, and have informed him in advance. In this way, as a minimum, when this news broke, he could have said that he had been informed in advance by the United States. It would have been worth taking that risk of a leak to have done this. I think that Kissinger would have felt that this wouldn't work because Sato would have to tell his cabinet colleagues or be considered complicitous himself in holding back this information. Then it would leak out, and all the down side of advance publicity would have occurred. The fact is that Japan had been holding back in its relations with China, primarily at our insistence. The Japanese were very anxious to move ahead, at least a little bit, in their relations with China.

Was this a matter of any debate beforehand in Washington, when you were making the preparations for the Kissinger visit to Beijing?

LORD: It must have been, but I can't recall any vivid debates, believe it or not. I certainly don't recall myself or anyone else pressuring Kissinger to tell our friends of this trip in advance.[26]

Was there anyone in the NSC or in the immediate circle of people dealing with this trip who was really a Japan expert and who would understand the impact on Japan?

LORD: You wouldn't have to be a genius or a Japan expert to realize that this visit to China by Kissinger would have an impact. I don't think that we fully appreciated this, but perhaps a Japan expert would have brought it home. Certainly, John Holdridge knew enough about Japan to understand this. It's not as if we hadn't been dealing with Japan. We had a recently completed agreement on Okinawa, which was quite significant. We had some sporadic textile negotiations.[27] I want to make clear that Kissinger, whatever his belief that Japan some day may go nuclear or become nationalistic again, certainly, as a friend and ally wouldn't want to go out of his way to cause trouble for Japan. Of course, Kissinger had certain priorities and was worried about leaks. So Kissinger and Nixon probably didn't fully appreciate the totally devastating blow which the announcement of the Kissinger visit to China would be in Japan. They certainly were aware that this announcement was going to break some crockery. They weighed carefully these considerations.

GREEN: When Henry got to China, he didn't know whether this was going to result in a presidential visit, did he?

HOLDRIDGE: Let me say that there had been enough from the Chinese through Yahya Khan in Pakistan to suggest that there would be a positive response. He was not going blindly into outer space. Again, Kissinger was hypersensitive about any leaks on this. In this particular respect, such a dramatic break with the past, I think he was correct.

LORD: Every now and then Nixon would feel a little concerned about the exclusion of Rogers. When Kissinger went on his secret trip to China, Rogers did not know about the trip when Kissinger took off. Nixon made it clear to Kissinger, even though Kissinger was worried about leaks, that Rogers had to know about this trip, as it was taking place. Rogers was told that this invitation had come from the Chinese, sort of at the last minute, while Kissinger was traveling, and Kissinger was going to go on into China. There was the usual duplicity in the treatment of Rogers.

GREEN: As I heard it later on, the Chinese insisted on the secrecy. The fact of the matter is that we insisted on it.

HOLDRIDGE: Henry never intimated that the Chinese laid it on, although they were quite prepared, of course, to accept.

LORD: Kissinger genuinely was concerned about leaking. A good example of one of these leaks is that just before the secret trip to China, the Pentagon Papers [on the Vietnam War] were published [in June 1971, in the *New York Times*], based on selected, secret documents. Daniel Ellsberg, who had been a Pentagon official, put them out without authorization.[28] If anything, these papers were damaging to the Johnson administration, not to the Nixon administration. On purely political grounds you could say that the publication of these papers was all to Nixon's advantage. However, Nixon and Kissinger went through the roof on the principle that you don't leak all of these highly classified documents. They were also concerned that the Chinese, who wanted confidentiality in dealings with the U.S. at that point, would feel that the U.S. government couldn't keep any secrets. [In trying to prevent future leaking, since] Kissinger couldn't say that they could wire tap others but that they couldn't wire tap his staff [he authorized taps on me and others].[29]

Could you talk about Kissinger's trip to China in July?

HOLDRIDGE: We were stepping into the infinite. Getting aboard the airplane around 4: 00 A. M. in Rawalpindi, who should we meet aboard the airplane but Zhang Wenjin, Wang Hairong, Nancy Tang (Tang Wensheng), the interpreter, and the guy from the protocol department.[30] Zhang Wenjin later was ambassador to Washington. He was one of the senior people in the Foreign Ministry in Beijing, and had been associated with Zhou Enlai since the time of the Marshall mission. Wang Hairong was Mao Zedong's grandniece. Zhang Wenjin made it very plain that he had been sent by Premier Zhou to reassure us all that we would be well received, and that there would be no problems about security.

LORD: I've always made a lot of jokes about this, but Kissinger was genuinely upset by the fact that he had no extra shirts with him. He bor-

rowed a couple of shirts from John Holdridge, who stands about 6' 3"
in height. Kissinger is about 5' 9," so he looked like a penguin walking
around in one of John's shirts. Here it was, an historic moment, and he
felt that he was walking around looking ridiculous. And, of course, the
shirts he borrowed from John Holdridge had a label that said, "Made in
Taiwan."

HOLDRIDGE: We were met at the airport by Marshal Ye Jianying, accompanied by Huang Hua, the man who later became ambassador to the
United Nations and then to the U.S. The old marshall, Ye, was the senior man to meet Henry Kissinger.[31] He and Henry got in the first car, a
Hongqi or Red Flag, and drove off. I found myself with Huang Hua in
car number two, also a Hongqi with the usual drapery on the sides.

The first thing Huang said to me was, "You know, in 1954 at Geneva,
your secretary of state refused to shake the hand of our premier, Premier Zhou Enlai." I thought to myself, "Ah-ha! Is this what we're
working up to. They don't want to have a repetition of some silly situation such as that." I hastily assured Huang that we had not come all
these miles, through such a circuitous and secret route, simply to have
this situation recur as had occurred in 1954. It was interesting when
Kissinger was there at the official Diaoyutai guest house in Beijing,
waiting for Zhou, there were a host of photographers around. Zhou
drives up in his limousine, gets out, and extends his hand. Kissinger
extends his hand, handshake, and boom, boom, boom, boom—flash-
bulbs all over the place, videotape, etc. This was an historic handshake.

Your presence in Beijing was all secret?

HOLDRIDGE: Yes. No one knew. We went in a small door in the Great
Hall of the People, underneath the main steps to talk to Zhou. We went
up in an elevator about the size of a telephone booth, all crowded
together. We got there around July 7. We had about two and a half days
there. They were tense, by the way. Zhou would say, after we had had a
long afternoon of conversations followed by a dinner—we would be
sitting just among ourselves—"I will join you at 9:00 when we will
resume our talks." Nine o'clock came, nobody came, nothing happened. Ten o'clock, eleven o'clock, midnight—Henry really was going
through all sorts of paroxysms here, "What is happening? What is
going on?" So we would go out and take a little stroll around the gar-

dens of the Diaoyutai, where we didn't think we could be bugged. He would ask me, and I said, "Well, they are probably debating it."

I had assumed that maybe it was the People's Liberation Army was dragging its feet, but in retrospect it was really the ideologues. These are people who later showed up as the Gang of Four, etc., who challenged this whole idea of an opening to the United States. It was very tense. Finally, we reached an accord. They came out with a communiqué which talked about both sides renouncing and rejecting hegemonism, which could only mean the Soviet Union.

Was there any factionalism? Did you have any sense that Mao and Zhou were doing anything that was dangerous to them?

LORD: We knew that broadened contact with us would be very controversial in China, even as improved relations between the two countries were in the U.S. We didn't know how much they were keeping the fact of our contacts on a close hold basis in their bureaucracy, as we were in ours. We didn't have a particularly sophisticated sense of Chinese factionalism. Whether Lin Biao [Mao's heir apparent] would be opposed to this course, for example, or how Mao and Zhou related to each other, although we probably knew that Zhou had survived by being loyal and always being Number Three in the Chinese Communist hierarchy and not Number Two. We had the general sense that Zhou was more pragmatic and moderate than Mao.

What were the difficult points in the talks?

LORD: The real negotiating, and this went on for hours, was about the following. We wanted to make it look essentially that the Chinese wanted President Nixon to come to China. The Chinese essentially wanted to make it look as if Nixon wanted to come to China and that the Chinese were gracious enough to invite him. Kissinger and I and the others walked around outside, because we knew that we were being bugged, and we couldn't discuss strategy and tactics unless we walked outside. Probably the trees were bugged, too. Who knows? I remember that we waited for hours and hours. The Chinese were probably trying to keep us off balance and were probably working out their own position. The formulation used went something like this: "Knowing of President

Talks during the July 1971 secret trip to Beijing. Participants begin on the right with Henry A. Kissinger, John Holdridge, Winston Lord, Xiong Xianghui, Zhang Wenjin, Ye Jianying, Zhou Enlai, and Nancy Tang. *Courtesy of John H. Holdridge.*

Nixon's interest in visiting China . . ." So it wasn't as if the Chinese wanted Nixon to come to China and were going out of their way. They used the formulation that they invited him because they were nice. On the other hand, Nixon wasn't begging to go to China.

In the midst of this negotiation we also did some sightseeing. The Chinese closed off the Forbidden City of Beijing to tourists so that we could visit it privately and on our own. We had the head of the Chinese Archeological Museum and an expert on the area take us around personally as our guide. I'll never forget it. It was a very hot, mid-July day. I was carrying either one or two of these very heavy briefcases. We had to take them everywhere with us. We didn't dare leave them anywhere for security reasons. Of course, it was dramatic to see the Forbidden City all by ourselves.

After that we had a Peking duck luncheon-banquet. The main topic of conversation was, in fact, the Cultural Revolution. Here we saw just how clever Zhou Enlai was. We know that he, himself, was aghast at the excesses of the Cultural Revolution, which had been unleashed by Mao. At one point he himself had been imprisoned in his office by Red Guards. However, he hadn't survived this long by suddenly being disloyal to Mao on an issue of that importance. The way Zhou recounted this experience was basically as follows. He went through how he had been locked up in his own office. He talked about some of the exchanges he had had with the Red Guards, in a very clinical way. He then used some phrasing like the following. He said: "Chairman Mao is, of course, much more far-seeing and prescient than I am. He saw the need for the Cultural Revolution and all this upheaval and destruction to cleanse the revolution. I wasn't so prescient. I saw the excesses, the problems, and the down side." If Mao read the transcript of what Zhou said, he couldn't have complained. At the same time Zhou was signaling to us that the Cultural Revolution had gotten out of hand, had become rather brutal, and there were excesses. So it was a typical example of cleverness by Zhou Enlai.

What did we think of Zhou Enlai?

HUMMEL: I think that we had an accurate picture of him. He was a survivor. He had done some bad things in the past, on Mao's orders. He was part of the Great Leap Forward and the persecution of the intellectuals. There was very little that he could do to stop the great excesses of the Cultural Revolution, although he did what he could. The quality of his intellect was so obvious to Henry Kissinger and everybody who had a chance to sit down and talk to him. We had a lot of respect for him. There was no doubt that he had to get Mao's approval for—not everything, but virtually so. He would stay up late at night, looking even at the final texts of the stories in *People's Daily*, the Communist Party of China's daily newspaper. He was very meticulous. I saw this during the time that we were visiting Beijing. There would be a communiqué to be issued. He could combine that attention to detail with a very broad and quite extraordinary, sweeping view of geo-strategic thinking. He had an accurate knowledge of events.

FREEMAN: Zhou Enlai was always the urbane, loyal implementer of Mao's policies—implementer in the best sense: he would take broad concepts and translate them into something that could work. I remember a remark that Dag Hammarskjold [secretary general, United

Nations] had made, to the effect that when he first met Zhou, during the Korean War effort to compose a truce in Korea, for the first time in his life he felt uncivilized in the presence of a civilized man. There was this enormous grace and charm about him.

What sort of things did Kissinger and Zhou talk about?

HUMMEL: They were dealing with a wide-ranging tour d'horizon, covering everything, from conditions in the Soviet Union, to Albania, which was China's friend in Europe, to the world economy. Zhou didn't divulge a great deal about China's economy that we didn't know already, but he covered every subject masterfully. And they both loved it.

Richard Solomon, from the NSC staff under Kissinger, has suggested in his writing on negotiating with the Chinese Communists, that Kissinger so much enjoyed talking to Zhou that he would tend to go beyond his talking points and range more broadly.[32]

LORD: Absolutely.

In this particular instance of the secret trip to China, Kissinger may have said some things that, perhaps, would not have been said had they been rehearsed. For instance that it would be good to use the Chinese-American relationship to keep Japan under control. Or that Kissinger gave more ground than he might have on . . .

LORD: There is no question that in the discussions between Kissinger and Zhou they would range widely, on this trip and on subsequent occasions when they got to know each other better. There would be a tendency to sit back and get away from the immediate questions at hand. This was in contrast with the practice when we were negotiating with Zhou's subordinates on specific language. Kissinger would have prepared talking points and positions on all of these issues. At times Kissinger might push the envelope or use ambiguous formulations which might tempt the Chinese. I don't deny that Kissinger did this during these meetings in Beijing, but I don't recall specifically Kissinger's getting out in front on some of these issues. He would say things on certain issues that he would probably be embarrassed if they were shown to the country that he was talking about.

On Japan, for example, Kissinger's basic thrust would have been to tell the Chinese that the U.S.-Japan alliance is in our interest and is in China's interest. So he would have said that Japan has an impulse toward nationalism and re-arming. However, if the Japanese feel secure under the U.S. nuclear umbrella, or our security alliance, then they won't go in that direction. Therefore, Kissinger would say, it is in China's interest for the U.S. to have good relations with Japan. We worked on them in that connection.

In the initial meetings the Chinese attitude was: "We don't like your alliance with Japan. We don't like alliances in general and we also don't like foreign troops on another country's soil. You are just building up Japan and making it more dangerous." We would counter by saying: "If we didn't have this tie with Japan, they might go nuclear and re-arm and be a greater threat to your security. So you ought to be in favor of this alliance."

Frankly, that argument made an impact on the Chinese over the following years. They reached the point where they clearly agreed with us. They have held this position ever since, until the last few years, when they have become more ambivalent about Japan.

HOLDRIDGE: We went public on July 15, after we got back. The only problem was making sure that there was some forewarning to everybody concerned.[33]

GREEN: You wanted to be sure that, when the news broke, that it broke at the same time in Beijing as it did in Washington. That was critical.

SERVICE: By August 1971, the *New York Times* had gotten Scotty [James] Reston into China. Reston had a marathon interview with Zhou Enlai, which was broken by an intermission for dinner. At the dinner table, there was some reference to the obvious fact that attitudes were changing from the former rigidities. It was Reston, apparently, who recalled that a number of Americans had suffered rather heavily because of their early views about the Chinese Communists. Perhaps, Reston suggested, it would be especially interesting to them to see the changes in China.

Zhou seized on the idea with his characteristic alacrity, and spontaneously mentioned four persons who would be warmly welcomed in China. "If they should wish to come." I was one of the four. The other three were John Fairbank, Owen Lattimore, and John Carter Vincent.[34]

The first I knew of this was a telephone call from somebody at the *Times* in New York asking what I thought about "being invited to China." I was very pleased, of course. I wrote to Marshall Green, who was assistant secretary for FE [the Far East] and asked him if the department would have any objection, and got the answer, no objection; to the contrary, they'd be pleased if I were to go. They were obviously fostering contacts.

I then wrote to Huang Hua, an old friend, who was then the Chinese ambassador in Ottawa. Canada had already established relations with China, and he was the first Chinese ambassador in Ottawa. I wrote to him, alluding to the news story and saying that I would indeed be glad to go to China.

When you reported on your trip what was your impression of Kissinger?

SERVICE: He's a very smart, intelligent, quick person. But I made a mistake. There were two other people there. There was [John] Holdridge and a man named Al Jenkins from the State Department. They were present and I thought that they wanted my impressions of China. I'd been in China at this time for over a month. I was talking mostly to Jenkins and Holdridge, because they had some China background. Neither one of them had spent any time in China to speak of, but at least they were so-called China specialists. That was a mistake. I was supposed to talk only to Kissinger. Neither Holdridge nor Jenkins would say a word. They were almost embarrassed by my talking to them rather than directing my talk to Kissinger.

Kissinger asked me at one point, "Were the Chinese serious about Taiwan?" In other words, that they wouldn't have normalization of relations until we broke off with Taiwan. I said, "Yes, they're absolutely serious." He said, "You don't think they're bargaining?" I said, "No, on this question they're not bargaining. It's a symbolic issue. They may be willing to accept some sort of a formula which would still not incorporate Taiwan, unified in the mainland, wholly. We have to recognize Chinese sovereignty, and that means we have to break off diplomatic relations with Taiwan." Kissinger found this very hard to believe. He said, "Oh, my people are always telling me something different. They say they're like the Russians. This is bargaining." I said, "No, this is not a bargaining point."[35]

LORD: The Russians could always be counted on to take anything that they could find in the dictionary that would serve their cause, even if it was a real stretch of what both sides genuinely meant. In this way they were picking up loose change all the time. This is one reason why Kissinger began to prefer dealing with the Chinese, rather than with the Russians. This was partly because the Chinese were always fair on translation issues. For example, in the Shanghai Communiqué, after we issued it [February 1972], and we more closely examined what they had done after we got back to Washington, we found a few instances where the translation of a given phrase could have gone either way. They actually gave us a word that was more favorable to us than it might have been. The other reason that Kissinger preferred dealing with the Chinese was that they were more up front about their basic position. When you got a position from them, it was pretty close to their bottom line, even from the beginning, rather than inflated, as was the case with the Russians.[36]

What was the significance of the February 1972 Shanghai Communiqué?

GREEN: To me, the format of the eventual Shanghai Communiqué was a stroke of genius. I don't recall seeing any kind of communiqué drafted that way, where you were able to get in your independent positions and differences and then show where you agreed.

LORD: [We wanted] to get as much in the communiqué negotiated on [the October 1971 follow-up] trip, so we wouldn't leave it until the last minute and under the pressure of the summit meeting in February 1972. We ended up getting the great bulk of it done, except for the Taiwan issue, where we made some progress but still had some outstanding problem areas. So we had this rather well done, standard, diplomatic communiqué covering a lot of issues and suggesting that the meeting was very friendly, marked by convergent perspectives. At the next meeting it was obvious that Zhou had checked with Mao. He came back and just tore into us with revolutionary fervor, in effect stating that we had given him an amateurish and ill-advised draft communiqué which was basically useless. We had fought against each other in Korea, the U.S. had intervened on the Taiwan question, and we disagreed on many world issues. We had gone through 22 years of mutual hostility and isolation. He said that your people, our people, and our mutual friends around the world are not going to understand this kind of communiqué, which suggests that we are like two, normal countries getting together for a regular summit meeting. He said that this is absurd. Furthermore, some of our allies are going to be nervous. If we are this friendly, this might mean that we are selling them out. In addition, he said that the description of the world situation in the draft communiqué wasn't sufficiently revolutionary from his standpoint. So he said that the whole draft lacked credibility, candor, and, furthermore, couldn't be defended by the Chinese ideologically, in their own party circles, with their own people, and with their friends. By implication he suggested that we might have some of the same problems.

Instead, he suggested, and this was at his initiative, that we have a different kind of communiqué, which was unprecedented in diplomatic practice, in which each side would state its own position. He said that in those areas where we do have some agreement or some parallel interest we can state those as well. However, he seemed to be saying that, having set out our differences, we would each have protected our domestic flanks, relationships with our friends and allies, and made more credible those areas of agreement when we stated them, because we had been honest enough in the rest of the communiqué to make the point. Frankly, this was a brilliant idea. It was unprecedented. I don't know of any other communiqué quite like the Shanghai Communiqué.

I don't recall whether we immediately saw the wisdom in this approach or not, but we had no choice in any event. Certainly Kissinger soon saw it, but at first we were disappointed that we weren't going to have some nice document that would record the major achievements at this forthcoming summit meeting. We were a little bit worried about justifying this visit to our domestic U.S. audience. We spent a fairly frantic night doing a redraft of the Chinese draft to accomplish three things. Tone down the fiery nature of the Chinese rhetoric, without overdoing it, because, after all, it's their view of the world. Then I set out to state our position. We decided to do this firmly and honestly, both to balance the Chinese position to a certain extent, to reassure our friends and allies where that was appropriate, to be firm as a matter of general principle, and also to deal with our domestic audience so that it would look as if we were firm as well. Then we had to have language on Taiwan. We put in principles of international relations on which we felt we could agree, such as non-interference, which they liked, and the view that both sides oppose "hegemony," which was a code word for the Russian threat. We liked this, and they liked it as well.

But basically we were saying that the Soviets are the problem. Is that what they were talking about?

FREEMAN: There was a minor subtext in the Asian context which was that neither of us would allow the Japanese to achieve hegemony, which, of course, they had attempted to do in the '30s and '40s. In other words, what we were endorsing was something rather dear to Henry Kissinger's heart, and to Nixon's as well, and that was the concept of balance of power, very much along the classic European balance-of-power lines, in which any challenge to the existing order can be met by a coalition. No state is so powerful that it can determine the course of events without being opposed effectively by a combination of other states, in which fluidity and maneuver substitute for war.

This was, of course, exactly Henry Kissinger's thesis in his doctoral dissertation, which he later turned into a superb history of Metternich's concert of Europe, which is called *A World Restored*.[37] Kissinger and Nixon intended with China to do much the same as Metternich had done with revolutionary France: namely, to pull the fangs of the revolution and to entangle the revolutionary power in the status quo so thoroughly that it no longer thought of overthrowing it. And strategically it accomplished exactly what both the Chinese and we wished to accomplish, which was to establish an ambiguous relationship that would give pause to the Soviet Union.

The Nixon shokku, the announcement that the United States was talking to the Chinese without having informed the Japanese, caused a real rift in our relations. Did Japan come up in the talks with the Chinese?

FREEMAN: Of course. The Chinese were, and remain, deeply concerned about what they call Japanese militarism, by which they mean unilateral Japanese security policies. At that time, they were torn between their opposition to the American dominance of the Asia-Pacific region, and their desire not to give the Japanese an excuse to follow independent policies and thereby resume an independent role in defense, which would have brought them into conflict with the Chinese. For Bill

Rogers, who had never considered this possibility and who probably saw the Japanese in their post-World War II, rather than their World War II and preceding period, roles, this was a novel and rather incredible thought.

What would you say were the difficult issues in the talks—Japan, Taiwan?

HOLDRIDGE: The difficult point was Taiwan. There was no question about that. The process was involved, and it was complicated in October by the fact that the Chinese had just undergone this reputed coup d'etat against Mao by his formerly designated heir apparent, Lin Biao.[38]

FREEMAN: Lin Biao was the head of the military, and, at various points, had been Mao's sort of right-hand man. For a variety of reasons, having to do with military objections to the Cultural Revolution and the opening to the United States, Lin attempted a coup d'etat, flew out of China, and crash-landed in Mongolia when his plane ran out of fuel.

HOLDRIDGE: It was an eerie situation in Beijing [in October 1971]. The streets were very nearly deserted. I remember we went to a function at the Great Hall of the People, in which Madam Mao was hosting Henry Kissinger. We saw one of these revolutionary dramas of which Madam Mao was so fond—and authored, perhaps. On the way back to the Diaoyutai, which was a distance of some four or so miles, at every street intersection along the main road there, there was a street lamp hanging down. Under every one there was an armed soldier, standing with an AK-47. It was kind of weird. We had wondered whether, in fact, in the light of the reputed coup, which took place just before the Kissinger mission went, the Chinese would actually follow through with it. They did. Zhou seemed his usual self, and there didn't seem to be any problem.

There was no secrecy on this trip?

HOLDRIDGE: No. The Chinese took great care to publicize it, and to show that Ye Jianying, the old marshal and presumed leader of the PLA, was the one that was squiring Henry around.

LORD: On this trip, Kissinger laid the groundwork for the president and him to meet with Zhou to discuss the political issues, including the particularly sensitive issue of Taiwan. Meanwhile, the foreign ministers, Rogers and his Chinese counterpart, would deal with things like trade, cultural exchanges, blocked assets, and economic and other bilateral issues. This was arranged so that they would have parallel conversations and keep the State Department out of really important negotiations. This was nothing that anybody was proud of, but that, I am sure, was part of the consideration.

Was there a concern within the bureau that in the flush of going to China, which was very exciting, that Nixon and Kissinger might give away the store?

FREEMAN: Indeed, there was that concern, embodied most professionally in Marshall Green, but others as well. Of course, grave concern on the part of Taipei and its representatives, and Taiwan-independence advocates, and for their long-standing friends and supporters in the bureaucracy. But the trip had a momentum and strategic logic and drama behind it that swept everything away.

The visit itself is often recalled as a political masterstroke, in terms of domestic politics, by Nixon. But it didn't seem that that was necessarily to be the result when he set out. It was a gamble. I don't believe that he or his political advisors had fully grasped quite what an impact it would have. It was conceived, strategically, as a repositioning of the United States to introduce some uncertainty into Soviet strategic planning. It was understood that this would require some sort of adjustment in relations with Taiwan, eventually, but it was hoped would avoid any immediate deterioration in that relationship. And, of course, there was great interest, as there always is, on the part of the business community, much of it terribly misguided.

My favorite letter, as economic-commercial officer, was from a casket maker in Texas who had heard that the Chinese revered their ancestors, and that people had the habit of preparing for death by buying a casket in advance, all of it true. Of course, modern China uses cremation, but he didn't know that. In any event, he foresaw one-point-something-or-other billion in caskets being sold, over the course of his lifetime, and was salivating at that.

Did you have the feeling that there were forces prowling around, political and media forces, looking for a way to destroy this initiative? That you had to keep it closed, not for tactical reasons with the Chinese, but for domestic political considerations?

FREEMAN: Very definitely, yes. The interest of the media was innocently professional—it's their job to ferret out stories—but inherently destructive. Many enterprises cannot prosper if they are prematurely revealed. And this was a very sensitive diplomatic maneuver, and revelation of details would have been catastrophic.

Politically, Nixon was from the right wing of the Republican Party, yes, but he was not a right-wing populist. He was a strategic thinker and an anti-communist as much out of concern for American interests as from ideological conviction. And, yes, there were efforts being made within his own party, and from some others, a few who were partisans of Taiwan independence, to screw this thing up. Obviously, the Russians were intensely interested, and that was another factor that had to be an argument for strict secrecy.

LORD: The most immediate and the most important impact was with Russia. We had not been making much progress with the Russians. On the whole, we were just treading water. Then, within weeks, the whole Soviet-American relationship started moving forward. This was very concrete evidence that the opening to China would help us with the Russians, which was one of the purposes of the Kissinger visit to Beijing. The Soviets were totally caught by surprise. We then made a breakthrough on the Berlin negotiations, began moving very quickly on arms control, so that we set up the SALT-1 agreement by the time we got to Moscow in May 1972.[39] We began to talk with the Soviets about economic and other arrangements. Of all the reactions to the announcement of the Kissinger trip to China, the most important one by far was the reaction in Moscow.

UNITED NATIONS

The confrontation over the Chinese seats in the Security Council and General Assembly of the United Nations finally was resolved as a result of Sino-American rapprochement. Having abandoned efforts simply to block China, as the votes shifted increasingly toward Beijing and U.S. policies on China changed, Washington sought to promote a dual representation formula that would preserve a place for the Nationalist Chinese. But the Kissinger trip to Beijing, in July 1971, eroded support for Taiwan. Then, coinciding with the crucial October 1971 vote on membership, Kissinger returned to Beijing, thoroughly undermining American lobbying and ensuring China's victory. The Nationalist Chinese representative walked out. Subsequently Taiwan would also be expelled from other international organizations such as the World Bank and the International Monetary Fund.

THAYER: [When] Kissinger's trip to the PRC was revealed, that put the dual representation issue in a new context where the U.S. was trying to preserve a seat for the Taiwan regime at the same time as actively playing footsie with the authorities in Beijing. So that was a complicating factor in the so-called "Chirep" [Chinese representation] issue as it played out in 1971.

The Chinese representation issue had been with us forever, and I can remember, in 1961, Paul Kreisberg, when he was in INR, telling me that INR and others were then exploring some new possibility for a formula for Chinese representation. In 1971, my philosophical context was that Taiwan was a viable entity; I didn't expect Taiwan ever to regain the mainland, but it was a viable entity and a good member of the UN and so forth, and it was appropriate that it continue to be represented in the UN.

On the other hand, the PRC—whatever kind of shambles it was in—it was also, in the end, an entity, a quarter of the world's population and so forth, and it should be represented in the UN, too. So the dual representation issue seemed to me to conform with reality at a certain level, at a logical level. It was not reality at the political level, because the PRC didn't want to put up with dual representation, and the PRC increasingly held the cards. But it was a worthy goal if we could have pulled it off, and we came close—within two votes—on the important question resolution.[40] Now, if we'd pulled it off that year, certainly there's a good chance the next year we would have lost it.

Was there ever any feeling on the part of the Republic of China representation to say, "Okay, the hell with this. We're a separate country?"

THAYER: They never manifested any inclination toward going for a status of an independent Taiwan.

Because that would have probably been much more sellable, wouldn't it?

THAYER: In the end, no, because the PRC was against it, and the majority of UN members recognized the importance of the PRC and were not prepared to cross the PRC. But the leadership of Taiwan and certainly the Mainlanders, who were their diplomatic officers, from the ambassador on down, adhered to a one-China view with their government as being the legitimate government of that one China. We worked very intimately with the Taiwan group and with Japan, as well as a whole group of co-sponsors to preserve their seat. It was the largest lobbying exercise we'd ever undertaken. I was coordinator of this in the New York side. Harvey Feldman, also a Chinese language officer, was in IO/UNP [International Organizations/U.N. Political Affairs]. He was one of the people who had put together this dual representation proposal. We were lobbying like hell in New York, and we were lobbying like hell in capitals abroad. We would lobby, maybe, at the ambassadorial level several countries a day and report to Washington, to the capital, what had been said right through to the vote on October 24th.

I met every day for the last month of this lobbying effort, every evening, with the Japanese political counselor. We would compare notes on what we were doing. We sought their support. And, of course, their relationship with Taiwan was long standing and very close. [Taiwan had been a Japanese colony from 1895 to 1945.] The political leadership, the Liberal Democratic Party, committed itself to going with us on this Chinese representation question. Therefore, in addition to their interest in the dual representation issue and doing their best to keep the faith in their relationship with Taiwan, the Japanese leadership couldn't afford as a domestic political matter to be on the losing side on this issue, and particularly when you throw in the shock, to the Japanese, of the Kissinger visit to China. That had shaken the Japanese government pretty badly, and therefore, they not only sought to coordinate with us but to make damn sure that they knew what the United States was doing. Tokyo was extremely hungry for information on what was happening and for reassurance that the U.S. wasn't dropping the ball or playing any more games or whatnot.

When you say lobby what do you mean? Did talking to an ambassador at the UN have much impact?

THAYER: Well, we operated on the assumption that words do have some persuasive value, that the logical argument carries some weight. We also operated on the assumption that in the real world an argument made by the greatest power in the world has especially significant weight. Therefore, when we would tell a European country or a Third World country who valued the United States' friendship, they would listen with great care. When the United States says a vote in a certain way is of tremendous interest to the Americans, it's not a small matter for another country to say no. But there are other factors involved, too. Neither the Canadians nor the British, for example, joined us in this.

You say you missed this by two votes. Were there any crucial votes that didn't go our way?

THAYER: There were five votes that went differently than we had expected—I mean, differently *against* us than we had expected. There were other surprises the other way. (One of the things you do at the UN at vote time is to make sure the delegates are not hiding out in dark corners or not in the bathroom, that they're in their seats where they can commit themselves to the vote.)

There was some sentiment that we were betrayed by those who changed to vote against us despite promises to the contrary. I was never comfortable with this posture of crying betrayal. History had caught up with us. And having lost the important question resolution, the procedural vote, which required that any vote on Chinese representation was a *substantive* issue and therefore require a two-thirds majority, and everybody knowing that we didn't have a plurality for the substantive issue, the final vote was overwhelmingly for the admission of the PRC and the expulsion of the Republic of China (Taiwan). The permanent representative of the Republic of China—in fact, the foreign minister—was there. He walked out before the final vote was taken once the important question resolution was defeated.

Did you feel any sort of pressure from the China Lobby and Congress that maybe the United States should leave the UN?

THAYER: There were some threats at that time in the Congress. There may have been a sense of Congress, a resolution of some kind, that if Taiwan got thrown out of the UN that the U.S. should stop paying its dues or something. But the fact is that the administration made a tremendous effort to win that vote, and nobody could have asked

Ambassador [George] Bush to have done more, with the exception that there were many who said that the timing of the Kissinger visit in the early summer of '71 undercut our position on the dual representation issue. There are many who said that the second Kissinger visit to Beijing, the announcement of which came just before the final vote in October, also undercut the impression of sincerity on the part of the administration in pushing the dual representation issue. One might say that there's some validity to that argument.

A lot of people whose votes we were soliciting were saying this. And, of course, the Japanese were upset, and the Taiwan group was upset because, on the face of it, it did give the impression of the United States being less than 100 percent behind supporting Taiwan. The fact is that the dual representation did embody letting the PRC in, did incorporate that. So it wasn't totally antithetical for Kissinger to make the trip at the time he did. Although, the second trip coming just before the final vote in the UN, that timing was bad, but I'm not sure it was intentional. It may have been just sloppy. Certainly the UN [mission] wasn't consulted, and it was a surprise to Ambassador Bush.

LORD: In retrospect, and to be honest about it, I don't think that we paid much attention to that. The timing of the secret trip was awkward in terms of the UN vote on Chinese representation. Our objective was to prepare for a Nixon visit to China. That was an embarrassing finale, to say the least, because it drove home the realization that we were causing pain to our friends with this opening to China. I just don't recall whether anybody said: "Do we really want to go to China in the middle of this UN debate?" I just can't recall why we didn't take this matter into our calculations. This was a tactical mistake. No question about that.

I wonder if you could give your impression of how George Bush operated as UN ambassador and impressions of the man.

THAYER: Well, I also served as his deputy in Beijing, so I maintained an admiration for him in both places. In the UN, particularly on the Chinese representation issue, there was no question that Bush was convinced that this was the right thing to do. He was indefatigable in lobbying for this policy. He believed in it. He made a lot of public speeches. He saw a lot of people, shook a lot of hands, entertained a lot of people, gave a lot of his time both at home and in the office to this. And his sincerity was never in doubt.

As an operator at the UN, he was very effective. In the first place, his credibility was very high. He made genuine friends with everybody, and he had a marvelous touch in dealing with the human beings behind the title, invited them out to his home town, Greenwich, to seats at the baseball game, made personal connections with everybody. He's a good politician. But he also had a sincerity that went with this. People believed him. So when he said we, the United States, will do this or believe that and so forth, people believed him. When he asked to see somebody, people would see him. He was terrific on staff morale. He knew everybody. He was very friendly with the hostiles as well as our friends. People had a lot of respect for him.

So what was the fallout? We lost this vote.

THAYER: The immediate fallout was that the PRC came in. And I became the Chinese specialist in New York who was on the spot to coordinate how we handled the new group coming in. And the first thing of importance was getting the new group in safely without being shot. And that was an enormous effort. You can imagine the desk was fully involved in it, getting clearances for a China Airlines plane to fly into La Guardia [Airport in New York], pilots who had never made the trip.

They bought a hotel for their permanent representation in New York. The Chinese sent a very strong delegation. Their "permrep," head of mission, was Huang Hua, who eventually was foreign minister, but very early on—in the revolutionary period—was an America specialist.

Were there any problems from the fact that we didn't recognize them?

THAYER: No, it was not a factor in the multilateral context [in which] we dealt with them. We didn't deal with them on bilateral issues except those having to do with their UN presence. The main thing that distinguished our dealings with the Chinese was that they were a sexy new commodity, and there was tremendous interest in Washington, including by the secretary and the president, that the thing be done right. And so there was a lot of pressure on all of us. There were hostile acts against the permanent mission. One day a mixture of Caucasians and Chinese—I guess Chinese-Americans and ROC citizens—threw rotten eggs against the wall of the Chinese mission. Well, the Chinese mission got appropriately outraged about that, and the U.S. apologized that such an insulting thing had happened to our guests.

You saw the PRC delegates right from the beginning. Did they feel they were in a hostile country?

THAYER: I can't say what was in their minds, but I can tell you what their posture was. Their posture was learning, and they were very cautious and prudent when they came in. They were, I think, unprepared to win the UN vote that year, and so they weren't completely up to snuff. I remember using the metaphor that the Chinese did not, as many people expected, come in breaking up the furniture in the UN. Far from it. They came in very quietly, very politely, very much asking questions and hearing the answers, taking notes and acting upon them.

Where were they learning? In other words, they were not in a position to turn to their old Soviet mentors.

THAYER: Well, they leaned very heavily on the secretariat, and they moved, in due course, to see that some of the more pro-Taiwan elements in the secretariat were replaced by some of their own people, part of the game. They drew heavily on the non-aligned who had supported them and they could ask advice from. But they also drew heavily on our expertise, and if they wanted a briefing on the history of this or that issue or the legal ramifications of this or that issue, they would go to the legal advisor of the UN, but they might also pick the brains of our very excellent legal advisors in New York.

There were other issues on which we were in different camps. One of them was the [division of] Korea question. And another big issue we had during my time was the Cambodia question.[41] On those questions, the Chinese were on the other side, to begin with, anyhow, and they wouldn't come to us for any advice about these, but they were going to their like-minded friends and asking, "How does this work? What is the history of it?"

How did Huang Hua operate? How did he view things?

THAYER: He operated in a low-key, polite way. He's a very complicated guy. He has a long, well-documented involvement in U.S.-PRC relations. He's a student of Leighton Stuart, who used to be head of the [Yenching] university in China and was our ambassador. Huang was quite capable, though, of being outraged at the United States. He's quite capable of being hard-nosed. On such issues as Cambodia, where our position [at that time] was very strongly opposite to the Chinese position, the Chinese were quite capable—and Huang Hua, personally—of attacking us vociferously, even nastily. But his posture toward us generally was quite friendly. But in the end, we felt that he was more of a creature of his mission than a heavyweight politician in his own right.[42]

As the China specialist were there any major issues that you dealt with while you were at the UN?

THAYER: Well, more in the capacity as the Asia person. It's an important distinction because there weren't many China problems in the UN. There were, however, the Korean issue—the perennial Korean issue [of a divided peninsula] was with us—[and] the Cambodia issue for two years was there when Sihanouk was in Beijing and the Lon Nol regime in power in Cambodia. We were supporting the Lon Nol government. There was very heavy lobbying on the Cambodian issue, where we were at loggerheads with the Chinese. We were involved with the Chinese on a variety of Security Council issues. Shortly after the PRC came in, the India-Pakistan war of '71 consumed the Security Council.

In a way, I would have thought that there would have been almost a sigh of relief after twenty-odd years of fighting the representation of China issue.

THAYER: Yes, there was that psychology. I mean, you get caught up in lobbying for the Chinese representation issue. But all of us knew that inevitably the U.S. had to find some relationship to the PRC, some way to deal with the PRC. And the PRC entry into the UN, for all the anomaly it helped contribute to in Taiwan's status, it had the effect of a catharsis. It opened up the possibilities—as the Kissinger visit did, too—of a more normal relationship.

NIXON TRIP TO CHINA

On February 21, 1972, Richard Nixon descended from *Air Force One* to Chinese soil in the climax of a process that revolutionized world politics. Television cameras transmitted images of the Chinese people that Americans had rarely seen, beginning a long and uneven opening up of Chinese society, and recorded the historic toasts that brought greater security and harmony to Asia than had been present there for more than a century. China, which had been a pariah, suddenly joined the world community and aligned itself with the United States to fight an anti-Soviet Cold War. Favorable American opinion of China more than doubled in public polls.

Did you have a feeling that Nixon was trapping himself, not so much in a contest, but in a display of his intellectual virtuosity in dealing with Zhou Enlai?

LORD: That was an element. I mean, any of us, as human beings, when we go up against a heavyweight, want to do our best. However, in all fairness, during those early years of his administration, particularly before the Watergate Affair began to preoccupy Nixon, he prepared very carefully for the major meetings. In effect, Nixon would commit to memory his basic positions. He liked to talk without notes whenever possible, to impress people. He generally did his homework. Foreign policy issues were his primary passion. So there was that element of ego in Nixon's makeup. He knew, from Kissinger's recounting of his conversations with Zhou, that this was a formidable interlocutor and that he had to be up to that. However, this was also an historic trip, and it was very important to Nixon in terms of substance, in gaining Chinese confidence, in projecting firmness, inducing them to cooperate, and pointing out the advantages of cooperation. However, in addition to substance, Nixon also wanted to have a good sense of Chinese culture and history, what he could say in his toasts, how he could work in little Chinese sayings from poetry in his toasts and in some of his remarks at the various meetings. And Nixon was genuinely interested in China.

However, all of this preparation didn't do the president much good when he got to the Great Wall. The press came up to him and said: "What's your reaction to this?" He answered: "It surely is a Great Wall," and that's about all he could come up with.

FREEMAN: We entered China at Shanghai. I was on the backup plane, which arrived first, so I actually saw the arrival of *Air Force One*. I remember I had written some advice for Mrs. Nixon, which was not to wear red, a color associated in China with weddings or prostitutes. Of course, she got off in a brilliant red overcoat. So much for that advice. But it was photogenic, which was the main concern.

LORD: There was a great sense of drama when we went to China with Nixon. I remember that when we landed at Beijing Airport, maybe naively I was somewhat disappointed at what I considered the strained nature of the Chinese reception. We had expected hundreds of thousands of people in cheering crowds, after 22 years of hostilities. There was a very small crowd, including a Chinese Army honor guard. It was a fairly gray day, too. This didn't look like a monumental event, as it ought to have been. Of course, everyone was wondering how the first encounter would go between the president and Zhou, who was at the airport to meet him. They all remembered that Secretary of State John Foster Dulles had snubbed Zhou in Geneva in the 1950s when he refused to shake his hand. Nixon left the plane, walked down the steps, and went over and shook Zhou's hand. This was a famous photograph. Then there was a restrained reception at the airport, with the band playing, the national anthems, the honor guard, and so on. There were not many people there. The reception was very cool. Then there was the motorcade to Tiananmen Square and on to the guest house. There were no crowds in the streets, except the usual ones. No one had been lined up specially.

GREEN: In Beijing, you were in one building and we were in another. In other words, State and NSC were kept . . .

HOLDRIDGE: The sheep were separated from the goats, Marshall, I am sorry to say. How Bill Rogers [the secretary of state] put up with that nonsense as long as he did, I don't know.

FREEMAN: Yes, a man who focused late on the China issue. A very nice man, a lawyer whose proudest achievement was some product-liability suits that he'd engaged in to defend Bayer Aspirin and other miscreants of great renown, and who was intensely loyal to the president on a personal level.

I can remember him, after one of the numerous humiliations that he suffered on this trip—I think it was when he was excluded from the sudden visit to Mao by Nixon, after our arrival in Beijing—saying, "Well, the president needs this, and he can decide who he wants." He was obviously angry, he was humiliated, but he never wavered in his recognition of who was in charge.

LORD: I don't think that Nixon wanted to go out of his way directly to humiliate Rogers. However, the net result was that he did. Nixon wanted to control foreign policy. He wanted to keep it so that it wouldn't be complicated by the bureaucrats in the State Department, and Kissinger, of course, did not resist this, to say the least.

FREEMAN: There was institutional concern in the Department of State, well founded, over this subordinate role, which really was unprecedented, since World War II, when Franklin Roosevelt had run much of foreign policy out of his hip pocket, with results that some question at Yalta.[43] But Rogers himself could not engage intellectually with Nixon and Kissinger on grand strategy, and didn't attempt to do so. He was not an intellectually highly charged man. Some of the more ridiculous moments of my life as an interpreter were interpreting for him and Ji Pengfei, the acting foreign minister in Beijing, and trying to explain the game of golf to Ji, who was a long-standing communist operative who, like most Chinese at that time, had no experience with the outside world and hadn't a clue who Sam Snead, Bill Rogers's great golf hero, was. I could see this was disastrous, but had to go along with it.

You mentioned that you got on the plane at Andrews Air Force Base, not knowing whether President Nixon would meet Chairman Mao?

LORD: Well, we knew in our gut that Mao would meet Nixon. He could do the unthinkable and not meet Nixon, but he didn't. However, when we left Andrews Air Force Base, we did not have an agreed time for the meeting with Mao, and they never promised a meeting. I know that we made unilateral statements that Nixon would, of course, be seeing Mao. There was just that one percent uncertainty, perhaps to keep us off balance, in not confirming the schedule for the president, which was mildly annoying. However, it was typical of the Chinese emperor, indicating that he was the head of the Middle Kingdom and that we were showing obeisance. This was true of other trips that we had. This was partly intended to keep us off balance, and partly to make us feel grateful when the actual meeting took place and that it did take place. The immediate reaction was, rather than being pissed off, that they just sort of said, "come on over and see the Emperor" was an immediate recognition that, whatever the restraint of the initial reception, the fact that Mao was going to see President Nixon within the first couple of hours of his arrival was very significant. It was going to send a clear signal to the world and to the Chinese people that Mao personally was behind this visit and the historic importance of the event. So this was obviously very good news, even if it was a somewhat unorthodox way to proceed with the leader of the Free World.

Nixon asked Kissinger to go with him. Nixon didn't want Secretary of State Rogers along. We somewhat naively thought that there might be more than one meeting with Mao, since this was so early, and Rogers could go to a later meeting. Kissinger, to my everlasting gratitude, asked me to go as well. It was a reward for all of the hard work that I had done. However, it was also in Kissinger's self-interest to have a note taker there, so that Kissinger could concentrate on the conversation.

FREEMAN: Nixon also had a predilection for using the other side's interpreters, because they wouldn't leak to the U.S. press and Congress. At any rate, there were three interpreters. We were an odd group, because Cal Maehlert was rabidly pro-Guomindang and in fact a great personal friend of Chiang Ching-kuo. And right after the trip, he went off on a hunting trip in Taiwan with Chiang Ching-kuo, the son of Chiang Kai-shek, and probably told him everything. Paul Kovenach was a Taiwan-independence advocate.

LORD: Mao had a couple of nurses around him and clearly needed some help. He was an old man but not a dying man by any means. He was just somewhat frail, physically, but not shockingly so. Indeed, he struck us with his presence. It is hard to sort out how much you expect when you see a great man, given his reputation. I say great not in a positive sense but in the sense of impact. Mao was obviously a very bad man in most respects. Both Kissinger and I felt that if we walked into a cocktail party and had no idea who this guy Mao was, his very presence would still have had an impact on us. The meeting lasted for about an hour. I remember distinctly coming out of the meeting somewhat disappointed. It was clear that this man was tough, ruthless, and came from a peasant background, in contrast to the elegant, Mandarin quality of Zhou Enlai. However, I thought that the conversation was somewhat episodic and not very full. Kissinger had sort of the same reaction as I did. Mao was speaking, as he usually did, in brush strokes, whereas we were used to the elegant and somewhat lengthy presentations of Zhou.

Mao would just throw in a few sentences. He went from topic to topic in rather a casual way. We both talked about the danger of the "polar bear," the Soviet Union. Mao certainly said, in one of these meetings, and I believe this was the one, that we could wait to settle the Taiwan problem for 100 years. In one of the meetings, and it may not have been this one, when told that he had made a major change in China, said: "No, I've only changed a few things around." So we had these sometimes rather epigrammatic comments. It seemed at times that he did not quite know what he was talking about. So his comments were somewhat disjointed, not particularly elegant, and a little disappointing.

Obviously everyone was impressed by the meetings with Chairman Mao. However, Mao was a brutal dictator. Was this a factor in your contacts with Mao, or were we all caught up in adulation of Mao?

LORD: Well, it's a very fair question. I agree that Mao might be put up there with Stalin and Hitler as a monster now. However, the official Chinese line is that Mao was "70 percent good and 30 percent bad." They say, and you can reasonably make the case, if you try to be detached, that when Mao was fighting to unify China, his record was fairly positive, in Chinese terms. Then you had the Great Leap Forward, the Cultural Revolution, the starvation, the brutality. Even the Chinese admit that Mao went overboard. We knew that Mao was no Boy Scout. That was true of Zhou Enlai, as well, who was, of course, more elegant. Having said that, we didn't know the full enormity of Mao's crimes at that point. Secondly, we were there on a very hard-headed mission. We tried to serve American national interests. At the time we were concerned about the Soviets, the Vietnam War. We also had the longer range desire to engage with China as an emerging, great country. Thirdly, it was no secret, however, that Kissinger always had and always will put the emphasis on geopolitics, as against human rights. In fairness to Kissinger, he also believes that, over the long run, this makes for a more stable and peaceful world. In addition, there was this euphoria of opening up relations with China. This made the media and virtually everyone tend to downplay the ugly dimensions of contemporary China. No one thought that Mao was a nice person, but for all of these other reasons, this consideration was not uppermost in our mind at the time.[44]

On several occasions you made reference to the practices of the Chinese emperors and that China regards itself as the Middle Kingdom. Was it very much in everybody's mind that the People's Republic of China may be a communist regime, but we're still dealing with something like a Chinese court?

LORD: Well, hopefully not in a subservient or obsequious way, but out of respect, yes. We were dealing with tough, ruthless, Communist Chinese leaders. However, we were also dealing with people who were heading the world's most populous nation which, we were sure even then, would be a major world power in the next century. The combination of arrogance or self-confidence derived from being the Middle Kingdom, and the humiliations and slights by foreigners and xenophobia, has made it particularly complicated to deal with China. Nixon and Kissinger in their toasts and their statements were careful to say, and with genuine sincerity, that China was a great civilization and a great country. Frankly, as a world superpower, much stronger than China, we can afford to be magnanimous. The Chinese are also geniuses at protocol, in making you feel at home. Their whole idea is to inculcate in outsiders coming to the Middle Kingdom a sense of obligation for their hospitality and friendship. In effect, they seek to create ties of alleged friendship. They want us to feel that friends do favors for other friends.

GREEN: *Was there much done in terms of the Shanghai Communiqué's framing and wording during that [1972] presidential trip, or had the document been pretty well done?*

HOLDRIDGE: It had largely been done. I did one little bit while I was there, and that was on exchange of persons—a paragraph that was added about newsmen, scientists, etc. The big problem was the wording of that one paragraph on Taiwan.

LORD: We had really tough negotiations on Taiwan, day after day, right down to the wire. They finally ended on our last night in Beijing, when we were to take off the next day for Hangzhou. Basically, it was a rather historic formulation which has held up to this day. The Politburo of the Chinese Communist Party approved the communiqué that evening. When we got to Hangzhou, Secretary of State Rogers and Marshall

Green saw the communiqué for the first time. That is no way to do business. They said basically that this communiqué was a disaster.

Did they really say that?

LORD: They were very critical, particularly on Taiwan. They said that President Nixon was going to get killed at home and around the world and that we had given in too much to the Chinese. We thought that this view was nonsense, in substantive terms. In fact, we had negotiated the communiqué pretty skillfully and we thought that most of their comment on the communiqué was frankly understandable pique at having been left out of the negotiations. So Nixon had the terrible decision of saying that it was too late now. He pointed out that the Politburo of the Chinese Communist Party had already approved the communiqué. He risked having Secretary of State Rogers and Marshall Green, if not on the record, then leaking out on background, that they had not only been excluded from the negotiations, but that we had also sold out on Taiwan. Or Nixon could have the humiliating experience, which he finally chose, of sending Kissinger back in Hangzhou to reopen the negotiations on the communiqué to get some of these concessions which Rogers and Green had given us on specific language. Some of these were impossible to get. Obviously, they never could have gotten them, but you can't blame the State Department being pissed off. Also, they clearly were going to ask for major changes, both because they'd like to get them, but also because they figured that it would be more embarrassing to us if we didn't get them. Kissinger, of course, was very resistant to this. It was very humiliating. We suggested some changes but didn't try out all of the changes that the State Department wanted, particularly the ones that were really dramatic in their import. Zhou handled the matter very skillfully. He tried to avoid making this situation any more awkward and embarrassing than it really was. He gave in on a few secondary points but didn't touch anything fundamental, nor could he, since the Politburo and Chairman Mao had already approved it.

HOLDRIDGE: The night before the Shanghai Communiqué was issued, we sat up until the wee small hours of the morning at the hotel in Hangzhou. Zhang Wenjin and Foreign Minister Qiao Guanhua were on one side of the table and Henry was on the other side. They were going back and forth about the wording. It was a very tedious thing. You are familiar with the last-minute changes on the morning that the communiqué was issued. We changed [the words] from "all people" to "all Chinese." That was on the morning of the communiqué, just before it was issued. There was a last minute scurrying around. This was because there were many people on Taiwan who do not call themselves Chinese. They call themselves Taiwanese. If we had said, "all people," this would mean that the Taiwanese had also maintained a position of one China and that Taiwan as a part of it, which is not necessarily the case. If you said, "all Chinese," this gets you into something else again.

[The final text read: "The United States acknowledges that all Chinese on either side of the Taiwan Strait maintain there is but one China and that Taiwan is part of China. The United States Government does not challenge that position."]

GREEN: My major intervention had to do with the fact that, in the communiqué, which had already been approved by the president and by Zhou Enlai, that it contained language in which we listed all of our existing commitments, and that America would stand behind them. It left out our commitment to Taiwan [the 1954 Mutual Defense Treaty]. I reminded Rogers, when I saw it, that this would certainly revive in people's memories the fact that Dean Acheson [in 1950] similarly left out Korea as one of the places for which we had a commitment and for which he was held responsible for the Korean War—very unfairly, of course, but there it was. This could really unravel the whole document. It would have been a great opportunity for journalists just to pull the whole document apart at a time when we released the Shanghai Communiqué. It would have riled up the defenders of Taiwan back in the Republican Party—people like Vice President Agnew and the secretary of the treasury [John Connally], who had many reservations about the president going out to Beijing in the first place.

Meanwhile, Henry had worked out—presumably with Zhou or somebody—that same night when we were in Hangzhou, an alternative way, leaving out this language about which security treaties we'd stand by, simply leaving it out. But then he said, in response to a question from the *Los Angeles Times*, that no mention was made there of our commitments to the Republic of China on Taiwan or of our other commitments. These were all covered in the president's state of the world message that he had made earlier on in the year. The way that Henry handled it was brilliant. He did, once and for all, dispose of the problem. I give him credit for it. What I will not give him credit for is the fact that, in his memoirs, he treats my intervention as being lots of silly little, minor nit-picks, very typical of the State Department.

HOLDRIDGE: Henry is a brilliant man, but he is a . . . [expletive deleted by Holdridge] when you really get down to it. He is not the most lovable personality in the world. He is terribly arrogant, and he wants to make sure that nobody else can shed any rays of light on any subject. He does not give credit where credit is due.

How did the Department of State respond to this? What was your impression of Marshall Green, prior to and after the announcement and in the preparations for the trip?

FREEMAN: I had very little personal contact with Marshall Green prior to the trip itself. That was partly because of the delicate role that Al Jenkins had to play. Much of what he did with Kissinger he was enjoined not to share with Marshall. Marshall, of course, was a man of extraordinary charm and wit, a great professional, but not a China specialist or indeed very knowledgeable about China, much more concerned about Japan. He was very much on the sidelines.

Did you have a feeling that our China policy at that time was essentially being run out of the National Security Council?

HUMMEL: Oh, yes, very much so. After Marshall Green left, I was acting assistant secretary for more than a year—maybe almost two years. I learned to like Henry Kissinger, even though he treated us all abominably. (I have seen Larry Eagleburger [a future secretary of state], who was closer to Henry than anybody else, coming out of Henry's office in tears because of the way Henry had savaged him, criticized him, and told him what an idiot he was, that he wasn't doing things right.) At times Henry would just go wild over some issue or another. You are always on a kind of knife edge.

Are we talking about his ego?

HUMMEL: Yes, we are. However, unfortunately, the SOB is so damned bright that, as I look back on these episodes, he was usually right.

LORD: The thing about Kissinger people don't always understand is that the last thing he wanted was yes-men. Very few people survived him as long as I did and [other members of his staff] Eagleburger and [Helmut] Sonnenfeldt . . . and these are people who would talk back to him and who he respected as long as you mounted an intellectually respectable argument.

When Kissinger focused on something, he really knew the subject. However, on peripheral issues involving Africa, Latin America, or Cyprus he would not really know the subject, but he would think that he knew it. With regard to China, he really wasn't a "China expert." Was he knowledgeable about China?

HUMMEL: I had no problem with him on this. He really was a very quick learner. Maybe he expected a little bit more from China than he got. However, this was not a fatal defect, and he was properly cynical about it. He knew that Mao Zedong was fading. I remember that he came back after having seen Mao in Beijing, exclaiming to a very small group of us, "This man is a monster. He is holding himself together by sheer will power. He has a bad case of Parkinson's Disease and can barely stand up. He mumbles so badly that the interpreters have trouble hearing him. Yet there he is. He's a monster." I remember Henry saying that he had appropriate skepticism about him. However, Henry diagnosed American interests very nicely.

LORD: Kissinger was very good at talking to different audiences, using different nuances, so you couldn't catch him in actually contradicting himself by comparing transcripts of interviews and speeches. When people talked to Kissinger, they had the feeling that he empathized with their point of view, even if they were ideologically at different poles. Whether they were conservatives or liberals, each one felt that Kissinger at least understood their point of view and may have been sympathetic with it. This was a tribute to Kissinger's brilliance as well as his deviousness.

In your China diplomacy was the Russian card ever mentioned?

HOLDRIDGE: Yes, of course. We did not do it in ways which brought up the Russians as the bugaboo, but we simply pointed out what the Soviets were doing worldwide, and the problems that this posed for both of us. Therefore, we pointed out the advantages which we could gain mutually by recognizing the problem and working together to resolve it. This was the point from which we started.

To give Henry some more credit, from the very beginning our thought was that, in addition to the strategic elements in this relationship which we hoped to develop, we also wanted to assist China in turning away from its inward-looking positions—its policies which had taken it apart and away from the relationship with the outside world. We thought that maybe by opening up to the United States, this would help to turn China outward, to make it more a normal member of the world community, and something that would be a benefit to the Chinese people as well as to everybody else. This element was there from the very beginning. It was not simply the strategic value.

LORD: Early on we began briefing the Chinese on our relations with the Soviets. We worked on improving relations with the Russians, but we were also using the Chinese to induce the Russians to improve relations with us. With the Chinese, on the one hand, we wanted to reassure them that we weren't being feckless and naive in seeking détente with the Russians. However, on the other hand, we had to spend a certain amount of time letting the Chinese know that we were moving somewhere with the Russians, too, to get them a little excited. So it was a carefully nuanced game here. Basically, we would say: "Look, we want to improve our relations with Moscow. We don't deny that. They have nuclear weapons, and we don't want to get into a war with them. However, we have no illusions. The Soviets are tough and expansionist. And by the way, they are more of a threat to you than to us, given their geography, history, and capabilities. We don't really trust the Russians, but it's in our national interest to try to improve our relationship with them on a hard-headed, pragmatic basis." The subtext to this was: "We are making some progress with the Soviets, and you Chinese should be sure that you keep up with us and improve relations with us, so that we don't get ahead of you in relations with the Russians."

The Russians had tried, at times, to argue to the Americans that they would be better friends of the United States than the Chinese Communists would be.

LORD: That's right. This was a constant pattern with the Russians. They certainly didn't say: "We white men have to stick together." However, you also got the feeling that there might have been a slight cultural and racial undertone to this. They often floated proposals, including an arms control deal which, they thought, would unnerve the Chinese. The Russians made references to their view that the Chinese couldn't be trusted, and so on. Of course, this was always deflected by Nixon and Kissinger.

What was the public reaction to the China opening?

LORD: The trip was heavily televised. It had a tremendous impact back here in the United States. In fact, this coverage led to the almost instant romance and euphoria that was overstated. After all, horrible things were still going on in China. We swung from one extreme to another, from picturing China as an implacable enemy to a new friend.

SOLOMON: John Scali, who was Nixon's director of communications, and the politicos in the White House were very much on edge about Kissinger gaining so much of the limelight from the China opening. They wanted to make sure that the credit went to the president, who had indeed taken the initiative.

FREEMAN: The Nixon administration had been essentially unable to send any speakers to campuses, because of Vietnam protests and the like. Suddenly, however, China became an acceptable topic, a politically correct topic on campuses, and I found myself doing a great deal of public speaking. In the first year after the Nixon trip to China, I did more than a hundred public appearances. There was so much ignorance. It's hard to recapture that moment, but the spectacle of this Red-baiting president going off to China and then to Russia was quite difficult for people to understand. It intrigued them greatly. So I tried to concentrate on putting the events and the various issues, which had been, if not resolved, at least addressed with creative ambiguity in the Shanghai Communiqué, into some sense of perspective, rather than to talk about the internal workings of Chinese society.

What about the China Lobby?

LORD: You have to remember that the NSC staff, and particularly myself, in my position as a special assistant to Kissinger and close to being responsible for this particular portfolio, had very little contact with the outside world. I rarely got out of the damned office to attend dinner parties, for example, in the Georgetown area of Washington, including with Kissinger and some of the movers and shakers in social settings. Otherwise, I had no contact with the Congress, no contact with the press, no contact with foreign diplomats unless I was sitting in on meeting, for example, with Soviet Ambassador Dobrynin or going up to New York with Kissinger for a UN contact. So I wasn't personally exposed to this. I don't recall any tremendous pressures from the right-wing lobby. I'm sure that there was some concern expressed to Nixon and Kissinger. Certainly, the overwhelming reaction from the media was positive. American public opinion and Congress were an easier sell politically than, we thought, would be the case. I'm sure that Nixon, in particular, was somewhat nervous about public reactions as we went along. This initiative did take some courage. Kissinger genuinely believed that Nixon deserved lots of credit for the successes that were achieved and his courage in making lonely decisions on major issues. Nixon sent Kissinger into China without anybody else knowing about it, risking a tremendous backlash from our allies and, above all, from his conservative base in the Republican Party and elsewhere at home.

FREEMAN: [After the Nixon trip], the American right wing began to go to China. They discovered a society in which students sat straight upright in their chairs and had short hair and respected their elders and adhered to family values of a sort that were then already nothing but a matter of nostalgia in the United States. They found no theft or significant crime. There was order and what appeared to be a measure of progress, although terrible poverty. And there was this sudden, strange fascination by the American conservatives with this really very conservative society, which Mao had attempted to radicalize, but had failed to radicalize.

SOLOMON: I was involved in the counterpart talks which focused on the effort to expand cultural and other exchanges. Our side, at Kissinger's guidance, proposed trying to begin to develop some economic exchanges, and the [Chinese negotiator] sniffed, and said, well, China had no interest in economic exchanges with other countries. Later we learned that he had been severely criticized by Zhou Enlai for not understanding that China wanted to expand relations with the United States. So you could see that the officials were operating in a complex political environment where they didn't fully understand exactly where Chairman Mao and Zhou were taking the relationship with the United States.

1970s

AFTER THE BREAKTHROUGH of the Nixon trip to China both sides anticipated that diplomatic relations would soon follow. The central obstacle to
progress appeared to be the Mutual Defense Treaty that the United States
had negotiated with the Nationalist Chinese authorities on Taiwan in 1954,
but Nixon was willing to abrogate it for full diplomatic relations with
China. To facilitate relations in the interim, in 1973, Washington and Beijing agreed to establish liaison offices to conduct routine business. The
United States and China also found that their policies on developments in
Korea and Cambodia coincided, with an equal emphasis on seeking peace
and stability, and that with the end of American involvement in Vietnam
they could imagine coordinating actions in such sensitive areas. The
United States even managed to convince Chinese leaders that the U.S.-
Japan alliance relationship, rather than being simply a threat to China, was
a useful mechanism for keeping Japanese militarism under control. Of
course, both sides saw cooperation against the Soviet Union as a key element in the relationship. Thus they shared intelligence information, with
the United States turning over hundreds of intercepts and photographs,
and China agreed to let the Americans use Chinese soil for monitoring
operations.

In the areas of economic and cultural intercourse, the early 1970s also
saw halting progress and innovation. Washington loosened trade regulations to allow for an expansion of commerce and China permitted American businessmen to attend the semiannual Canton Trade Fair, the vital
center of Chinese foreign business arrangements. Trade exploded,
mounting from $5 million in 1971 to $900 million in 1974, although it subsided thereafter. Delegations of American professionals and entertainers
traveled to China, but their tours remained tightly scripted and contacts

with ordinary Chinese virtually impossible. News organizations could finally report from China, but news bureaus could not be maintained. Scholars could make brief research forays, but no sustained academic exchange was possible.

In both China and the United States, domestic politics proved to be the key restraint to rapid movement on establishing official diplomatic relations. In the United States the Watergate scandal erupted, undermining Richard Nixon's political strength and forcing him to listen to the most conservative, anti-China elements in the Republican Party. When his abuses of power finally forced his resignation in August 1974, Nixon turned the presidency over to Gerald Ford, who became an even weaker president, unable to carry the Congress with him on anything so controversial as recognition of China. Increasingly, he had to worry about conservative critics, particularly Ronald Reagan. The California governor, who sought to wrest the Republican nomination away from Ford in 1976, staunchly supported Nationalist China and decried Nixon's sacrifice of U.S. allies in Taiwan.

These problems and delays discouraged the Chinese. Neither Nixon nor Ford severed the unpalatable defense relationship with Taiwan. Worse, evidence accumulated that contacts between Washington and Taipei were multiplying as Taipei opened new consulates in the United States, while Americans launched a new trade center, dispatched a new ambassador, and concluded new arms sales to Taiwan. The relaxed attitude toward the recovery of Taiwan voiced by Mao Zedong in his early encounters with Kissinger and Nixon evaporated. Beijing rejected the idea that Washington might retain any high-level official contact with Taiwan, even a liaison office as Kissinger proposed in 1974, and Chinese officials flatly refused to renounce the use of force to resolve the cross-Strait standoff. In 1975, Deng Xiaoping declared that full diplomatic relations between the United States and the People's Republic of China could not be realized until political and military ties between Washington and Taipei ended.

Chinese leaders found American decisions on issues other than Taiwan similarly distasteful. They objected to American policies on arms control and détente with the Soviet Union. If opening to the United States could be justified as a way to protect the Chinese people from Soviet aggression, then American understandings with Moscow and Washington's unwillingness to contest Soviet hegemonic behavior in Europe and Asia rendered reconciliation worthless, and possibly dangerous should the United States barter Chinese safety for Russian good will.

The potential for betrayal and exploitation seemed apparent to radical factions in Beijing, among them the Gang of Four (which included Jiang Qing, Mao's wife). The Gang of Four attacked Zhou Enlai's moderate policies and, after his death in January 1976, blocked Deng Xiaoping's ability to carry on Zhou's initiatives, accusing him of capitalist sympathies. Thereafter they maneuvered to control the succession, engineering the purge of Deng in April as mass demonstrations in Tiananmen Square commemorated Zhou and condemned the Cultural Revolution. Mao's health, already poor, rapidly deteriorated, and in September he too died. But Mao's passing did not produce the entrenchment of radical politics. Instead the Gang of Four was itself purged and Deng Xiaoping reemerged to pursue Zhou Enlai's legacy of internal reform and relations with the United States.

Deng's agenda spanned the political and economic landscape, including efforts to eradicate the remnants of Cultural Revolution practices, to introduce economic reforms that moved China away from socialism toward modified capitalism, and to establish new relations with the West that would provide opportunities to expand trade and acquire technology. Thus in 1978, almost at the same moment that he eliminated communes from the Chinese countryside, he consolidated diplomatic relations with Washington.

In the United States it took the inauguration of Jimmy Carter in 1977 to overcome inertia in U.S.-China relations. Although the Carter administration put passage of the Panama Canal Treaty and revival of détente with the Soviet Union ahead of reconciliation with China, Carter committed himself to recognition early in his presidency. He also accepted the argument that the United States would have to agree to Beijing's conditions regarding Taiwan before normalization could be attained. When his secretary of state Cyrus Vance, who sought to calibrate progress so as not unduly to alarm Moscow or jeopardize détente, angered the Chinese with his caution, Carter overruled him. Indeed, solicitude for the Soviets won fewer proponents as Moscow pursued aggressive policies in Ethiopia and west Africa at the same time as it refused to make deep cuts in strategic arms needed to conclude an arms control agreement. Disenchantment with Soviet behavior was shared by Chinese leaders who had tried to improve relations in the wake of Mao's death but had been rebuffed. Thus Beijing proved responsive when Carter authorized his national security adviser Zbigniew Brzezsinki to take the initiative and move forward vigorously to reach an understanding.

Negotiations proceeded on several fronts at once as the testimony here indicates. The Chinese finally conceded much of what the United States demanded because Deng wanted to complete the normalization process quickly. Not only did this mesh with his consolidation of power and inauguration of economic change in the countryside, but it freed him to launch an attack on Vietnam to punish Hanoi for its intervention in Cambodia. So the Chinese overlooked American insistence on continuing arms sales to Taiwan and accepted a one-year postponement of the abrogation of the Mutual Defense Treaty. Of course, the United States had already given up the idea of retaining formal relations of any kind with Taipei and agreed to a one-year moratorium on weapons sales. The final declaration also contained a unilateral American statement calling for peaceful resolution of differences across the Strait and a Chinese statement that the future of Taiwan remained an internal Chinese affair. Thus on December 15, 1978, Washington and Beijing declared that they would establish formal relations as of January 1, 1979.

Reaction to opening diplomatic relations with Beijing proved largely positive throughout the United States. The one area that troubled people, particularly members of Congress and the remnants of the old China Lobby, was the fate of Taiwan. Although there had long been an understanding that recognition of the People's Republic would force some down-grading of ties with Taipei, critics denounced the Carter administration for agreeing to abrogate the Mutual Defense Treaty, abandoning efforts to retain a liaison office in Taiwan, and not extracting a pledge from Beijing to renounce the use of force in the Strait. Members of Congress complained about the lack of consultation. During 1978 they had passed, on a bipartisan basis, the Dole-Stone amendment, which enjoined the White House to keep Congress apprised of proposed changes in the Mutual Defense Treaty. When the administration moved ahead independently, it provoked angry denunciations. Thus, it was not surprising that Congress rejected a weak administration bill to provide for continuing unofficial contacts with Taiwan. In its place members passed the Taiwan Relations Act, with explicit provisions, which the Carter people had not deemed necessary, to insure the security of the island. The TRA also strengthened Taiwan legal status and access to the U.S. market. No one could be certain what the future would mean for Taiwan, but no imminent demise would be likely under the umbrella of the TRA.

LIAISON OFFICES

Because the process of normalization remained controversial and complicated, after years of hostility, neither Washington nor Beijing could move
toward diplomatic relations immediately. Initially they tried to use their
embassies in Paris for routine diplomatic exchange and a CIA "safe house"
in New York for sensitive communications. By early 1973, this awkward
procedure clearly was not working and they turned instead to a new structure to facilitate contact and to work toward settlement of larger outstanding problems.

DONALD ANDERSON: The lead-up to the Nixon trip and the continuing
    contacts had been conducted in Paris through General Vernon Walters
    who was the military attaché, and the Chinese ambassador [Huang
    Zhen]. After the Nixon trip the contact in Paris sort of went public and
    the president announced that this would be the point of contact between
    the Chinese and ourselves, and that Ambassador Arthur K. Watson
    would represent the U.S. side.

FREEMAN: Paris had been a point of contact with the Chinese, primarily
    on the Vietnam War. Kissinger had found it convenient during his con-
    tacts with the Vietnamese there to also maintain contact with the Chi-
    nese. So there was a certain logic to that.

DONALD ANDERSON: Ambassador Watson was flying back to the United
    States on one of his fairly frequent trips and, according to the story that
    appeared in the press, he got rather intoxicated and by way of apologiz-
    ing to the stewardesses attempted to stuff $10 bills in their blouses,
    which one of the stewardesses duly reported to the press. Of course, the
    press was all over the State Department and the White House asking,
    "Is this the guy that's going to be handling our contacts?" "Yes, he's
    going to do it, but we'll have somebody there with him who is a China
    specialist." That is why I was suddenly transferred to Paris. Jack
    Kubisch, who was the DCM, appeared in the hall on our way down to
    the ambassador's office, and said in an absolutely remarkable way,
    "Whatever he says, agree." It was sort of a panicky advice that I should
    be terribly cautious. I went down and met with the ambassador and he
    was an absolutely charming man. We had a session, just the two of us,
    and he said he considered the China contacts one of the most important

jobs that he had in Paris, that I was his man for those contacts, and I had access to him anytime I wanted to. So I left thinking this was going to be great.

The ambassador didn't take part in many of the routine things that we did, but I saw the Chinese maybe a couple of times a week. At this point there were delegations going back and forth between China and the United States. The first Boeing [aircraft] sale was made, and the Boeing people came through to meet the Chinese who were en route to [corporate headquarters in] Seattle.

FREEMAN: As trade began to become possible with the Chinese, there began to be a proliferation of trade promoters and associations. And it was quite apparent that, left untended, this field would eventually be filled by some sort of Chinese front group, which would be an advocate not for American interests, but for Chinese interests. So I had the idea, and a young man at Commerce [Department, China desk] named [George] Driscoll worked with me very hard, to produce a proposal whereby the U.S. government would sponsor, but not fund, the creation of a prestigious business council that would preempt the field, the National Council for U.S.-China Trade [later the U.S.-China Business Council].

DONALD ANDERSON: This was the point at which the National Council for U.S.-China Trade was designated as the umbrella organization for trade. The National Committee on U.S.-China Relations and the Committee on Scholarly Communications with the People's Republic of China were designated as the educational and cultural umbrella organizations. We were expecting to get these two commercial and educational packages to present to the Chinese. I handed the ambassador the two papers, each maybe ten pages long. He glanced at them, and tossed them back in my lap, and I believe his words were, "This is crap. I'm not going to talk about this penny-ante stuff." He said, "I'll leave that to you to take care of with your counterparts." And while we were riding over to the Chinese Embassy he said, "What I really want to do today is just talk about global issues, sort of a tour d'horizon." I had been specifically told by the NSC that I was not to do that kind of thing, that this was basically a mail delivery program.

But we did sit down with Ambassador Huang Zhen, who was an interesting individual, and Ambassador Watson did indeed proceed to indulge in a tour d'horizon. The most memorable moment of which I remember—this was 1972—he said, "Mr. Ambassador, the one thing that I think both of our countries have to worry about the most is Germany and Japan." Ambassador Huang looked rather surprised at this statement, but we carried it all off. Ambassador Watson left on vacation very shortly after that and resigned.[1]

You were a mailbox operation, simply transmitting messages.

DONALD ANDERSON: The instructions were really that we were a mailbox, and I can remember one instance when Marshall Green came through—he was the assistant secretary at the time—and I told him that I was going to try and use these contacts to broaden the discussion. And he said, "That's fine Don." And the first time I wrote a cable back based on a discussion with my counterpart on his views on Sino-Soviet relations, I got a very fast phone call from Washington saying, "Dr. Kissinger does not want you doing that. Deliver the mail, and that's all."

When did the idea of the U.S. Liaison Office in Beijing arise?

FREEMAN: The Paris channel, as 1972 proceeded, became more and more overloaded. In the State Department, many people argued for the establishment of more regular contact directly with decision makers in China. We clearly couldn't have an embassy, because we had one in Taipei. We could have had a consulate, but that would have been complicated because it had a precedent in international law. There had been a proposal, which had been floated before the Nixon visit, for something called a liaison office, but nobody knew what that was and it hadn't been defined.

The two authors of this were Roger Sullivan and myself. Roger Sullivan was then the deputy director of the Asian Communist Affairs Office. I think Al Jenkins was initially quite skeptical. The basic idea was, no one knows what a liaison office is; there's never been one. It doesn't imply anything. We could allow events to define it, rather than worrying about it setting a precedent or raising questions of diplomatic recognition and the like.

Kissinger was against it, because he thought he would lose control of the relationship if the State Department had its own people [there]. And so the initial effort to persuade him was quite soundly rebuffed by him. It was not until early 1973 [February] on his last trip prior to the Gang of Four seizing control in China and Nixon getting bogged down in Watergate, that we were able to persuade him to advance the cause of a liaison office to the Chinese.[2]

LORD: That sounds like nonsense. Kissinger and the NSC wanted direct communications with the Chinese. Kissinger wanted to have the most ambitious arrangement that we could get away with, without calling these offices embassies. I clearly remember that he and I felt that a liaison office was a trade off which was better than other possibilities. Any office that you would set up was going to have State Department people in it, although I knew that Kissinger might be suspicious of other bureaucrats. Kissinger wanted to have negotiations and direct contact with the Chinese, not to mention the signal it sent around the world, including the Russians and the Vietnamese, that we were advancing in our relationship with China. It's absurd to say that we didn't want a liaison office.

HOLDRIDGE: We had managed to have a number of visits to China, subsequent to the president's visit. There was one in June of 1972. There was another in the fall when I recall Henry spent some time in Japan. Japan was feeling deeply hurt, having been left out of all of this situation. In January of 1973, we began to talk about the future relationships between us and the advantages of having a mission. I personally thought that maybe the Chinese would balk at going too far. It was my thought that maybe something in the nature of a trade mission might be more acceptable to them. To my astonishment, it was Zhou who proposed going on up to the level of a liaison office which, of course, we immediately accepted. To all intents and purposes, we were a diplomatic mission.

HUMMEL: It was a very interesting gimmick. It had been one of a series of conceivable options in study papers dating back to several years before. However, nobody thought that the Chinese Communists would agree, as long as we had an embassy in Taipei.

GREEN: It was really justified in the eyes of the Chinese on the grounds that this was a stepping stone to full recognition. We had to go through the antics of liquidating our relationship with the Republic of China on Taiwan and having a new relationship there. That would take time. During that time, it was important to have a continuation office.

HOLDRIDGE: We opened [the Liaison Office] in May 1973, in time to read (in the Chinese press) that, as of May 1, Deng Xiaoping had been brought out of hiding and had reappeared on the scene, resuscitated.

FREEMAN: At the last minute, a CIA person was added [to the staff], at the insistence of the White House, to establish a White House channel of communication. The Chinese made quite a point of sort of snickering about the CIA turning up. The purpose of this was to give Kissinger a private channel outside the State Department. He appointed John Holdridge as a second DCM, also with the title of DCM, to serve as the NSC representative in Beijing.

LILLEY: State wanted no part of this, they wanted no USIA, they wanted no attachés, and the last thing they wanted was a CIA creep. Henry did, Henry and Jim Schlesinger, who was then director, wanted somebody from CIA. The State Department objected violently to this, but Henry said Chairman Mao wants it. Exchange. They send their guy to us, we send our guy to them and he's declared. That means you go to the Chinese and say Lilley is a CIA man under State cover.

When you declare does that mean you refrain from doing certain things?

LILLEY: The idea was that we would not engage in any operations that were against China. That means you won't go out and recruit Chinese agents in Beijing and start running them against China. What you do in a CIA sense is you do passive work for the day when you need dead drops, you need signal sites, you need this sort of thing. Did I have any links with the Chinese service? No, the Chinese weren't ready for this. That came later.

HOLDRIDGE: The Chinese were working overtime to finish up a mission for us. It was intended for somebody else, but the Chinese redid it to our specifications, which meant extensive remodeling.

FREEMAN: The Chinese offered us a small cement residence with a quaint cupola, rather an odd octagonal room at the top, which they explained was for signals. Well, our communications gear isn't put in such places and requires special handling. I can remember going over to the Diplomatic Services Bureau one afternoon with Bob Blackburn [administrative officer] and explaining that we needed more office space on the compound. The Chinese, in the true Soviet style, had established an office to manage and control and staff the offices of foreign barbarians in their capital, and everything—the buildings, electricity, car registration, and, of course, local staff—came through this office. And I drew a building and explained that the top floor should have no windows, and that this should all be built to vault specifications and whatnot. Two hours later, they called us back and showed us a completed architectural drawing. They broke ground about six o'clock that evening, and they built that structure. I've never seen anything like it. They worked around the clock. They basically used workers and threw them away when they were exhausted. They built the whole thing in sixteen days, and most beautifully. The upper story, where the communications were to be, had false windows, so it looked perfectly normal from the outside. And inside, it had beautiful walnut paneling.

Of course, the first act that we committed when we got into it was, for security reasons, to rip out all this beautiful paneling. We were so embarrassed by the desecration of Chinese craftsmanship that we sawed up all the pieces of walnut and sent them out in the diplomatic pouch, rather than bring them out of the building where the Chinese could see what we were doing. We never found any evidence of bugging or anything of that sort in that area.

HOLDRIDGE: They were very cooperative, going out of their way to be accommodating. That didn't last too long. After a while, we were catching the backlash of differences within the leadership of the Chinese Communist Party about the merits of opening up to the United States. Our relationship would blow hot and blow cold.

FREEMAN: The first days in Beijing were spent in introductory meetings with senior Chinese officials. We ended up spending a great deal of time with Qiao Guanhua, who was, in effect, the acting foreign minister (and the brains in the Foreign Ministry);[3] Ji Pengfei, who was the nominal foreign minister; Zhang Wenjin, who was the assistant minister in charge of American and Oceanian Affairs, an extraordinarily able diplomat; and Han Xu, who was the acting chief of protocol. This was during the Cultural Revolution and no one had formal titles. It was interesting, there was cordiality and cooperation from these people.

DONALD ANDERSON: The Gang of Four, Jiang Qing and her group, were still very much a force to be reckoned with. Mao was still alive, but failing, and Zhou Enlai was very much managing the U.S.-China relationship. But he was failing too. Basically we didn't know that when we got there, at least I didn't. When we set up the Liaison Office, Kissinger came out again in November [1973], and Zhou appeared in pretty good shape and was at the banquet for Kissinger in the Great Hall of the People. That visit went very well, and Kissinger went away quite pleased.

LORD: [During this November 1973 visit] we were summoned on short notice to a simple residence in Zhongnanhai. Inside there was a ping-pong table and then Mao's study with a semicircle of armchairs, with books all over the place, behind him, on the floor, and on tables. This meeting with Mao lasted for three hours. Mao seemed to enjoy talking to Kissinger. We thought that it showed confidence and that it was important. Mao made some jokes about problems with the Soviets. The Chinese expressed some concern about U.S. "steadfastness" in facing the Soviet threat. During the meeting with Mao, he was noticeably more frail. Mao mentioned the "Watergate Affair." He compared it with "breaking wind." He could be a little crude. He made the point that, in Chinese eyes, this was nothing and clearly wondered why everyone was so excited about it. There was no evidence that they thought that this had anything to do with China. It plainly puzzled them because they just didn't understand our system. They wondered why a third-rate burglary could bring President Nixon down, particularly when he had done great things, such as achieving the opening to China. The Chinese were somewhat baffled by it and were somewhat contemptuous of American puritanical attitudes.

SOLOMON: Of course in their own internal politics they were well aware of factional conflict. But at the same time they viewed Nixon as in a very strong position domestically. After all, he had won a tremendous victory in 1972, and they told themselves that Nixon's opening to China was one reason that the president had done so well. So they couldn't understand what Watergate was all about. In early '73, we began seeing intelligence reporting that said the Chinese thought that Nixon was under attack because of his opening to China. And interestingly enough, the Russians were interpreting Watergate as reflecting Nixon's pursuit of détente with them. So both these foreign governments were interpreting the evolving Watergate scandal as a foreign policy-relevant issue rather than a domestic political [one], which shows how insular they were.

LORD: On Taiwan Mao was relaxed. He basically said that China could do without Taiwan "for a hundred years." We made it clear during this trip that we couldn't accept the Japanese formula for the normalization of

Mao Zedong remarks to Winston Lord in 1973 that he seems very young.
Courtesy of Winston Lord.

diplomatic relations. The Japanese had "leap frogged" us after we surprised them in 1972. Then they went ahead with their own process of
normalization of relations with China. They broke diplomatic ties with
Taiwan and normalized ties with the PRC. We said, in effect, that perhaps we could normalize relations if we could do it short of the Japanese formula, so long as we recognized the principle of "One China."
There was a somewhat more tentative mood in the discussions.[4]

Did access depend upon high-level visits?

HOLDRIDGE: Sometimes we would be doing very well, indeed. We
would see Qiao Guanhua, the foreign minister, who helped to draft the
Shanghai communiqué. He would be very congenial. Then we would-
n't see him for a long period, and we would only see the deputy director of whatever office we were working with in the Foreign Ministry.
We would be summoned from time to time. The phone would ring, and

one of the little voices at the other end of the line from the Foreign Ministry would say that so-and-so would like to see you. This always meant that we were going to be hit between the eyes with some sledgehammer blow. They were going to discipline us for something.

DONALD ANDERSON: At the same time, of course, they were bugging us, and restricting our travel. It was difficult. We had the normal relationship with the Foreign Ministry. When I say normal, it was a pretty sterile relationship. They were always willing to see us, and they were always pleasant when we went to see them, but in terms of a dialogue, we had very little. After about the first year, David Bruce left as head of the liaison office to become ambassador to NATO, and George Bush arrived as the second head of the Liaison Office. I think the fact that there was very little dialogue was one of the reasons why David Bruce lost interest very early on. Given his background in London, Paris, and Bonn, he visualized an on-going dialogue with Zhou. If my memory is correct, he may have seen Zhou twice after his arrival, but after that he was relegated not even down to the foreign minister, but often times being called in by the head of the American and Oceanian Department, who is about the equivalent of an assistant secretary, and at that time not a very pleasant fellow, and basically, Mr. Bruce decided this was beneath him. David Bruce obviously was one of our premier diplomats. He was a very, very decent fellow, and his wife Evangeline was a very nice person. I don't really think that they were probably well suited to the job.

But the Chinese were not alone in downgrading the Liaison Office.

LORD: I kept trying to encourage Kissinger to bear in mind that the heads of the Liaison Office had to know what was going on. However, there is no question that whenever there was heavy lifting on really important and sensitive issues, this would be handled by Kissinger himself and not by the head of the Liaison Office in Beijing.

Appointment of David Bruce was a gesture that we're putting a top level person there?

DONALD ANDERSON: Yes, exactly. The Chinese did the same thing. They sent Huang Zhen, the ambassador to France. It was a gesture to show how important this relationship was and how important the Liaison Office was.

What were your duties in the Liaison Office?

DONALD ANDERSON: We did a lot of China watching, which consisted of reading the newspapers, periodicals, and trying to figure out what the historical references were, the implications of rather arcane philosophical discussions that appeared in the newspaper from time to time, getting out on the streets and walking around. It was very difficult to talk to people, but occasionally someone would talk. There was a period during that time when big character posters were put up, a form of expression that the Chinese permitted from time to time. We would go out and literally spend hours just standing in front of a wall reading the big character posters, then exchanging notes with western journalists who were out doing the same thing, and collecting as much information as we could that way. The journalists were much more open about photographing, so we worked out a deal to acquire those. And then visiting with people who came through—western businessmen, and Chinese-American scholars who would come through oftentimes had better access than we. One of the things we did is attach ourselves to any major delegation, or any delegation at all that we could, that was traveling around China and go with them as escorts. A lot of it was show and tell. We were shown what they wanted us to see and given the standard propaganda line. Then there was a great deal of gullibility in that.

Is it true that Americans tend to have a rosy view of, or keep thinking that things will work out in China?

DONALD ANDERSON: Actually, the problem is not exactly that way. It's a two-sided problem. We tend to swing to both extremes. China is either, as you say, this wonderful place with its 4,000 years of culture, and panda bears, and rosy cheeked little kindergarten children that we all love. Or it's the other extreme, the Chinese and the Korean War, and brain-washing, and torture. We do have a difficult time getting ourselves positioned in the middle where we recognize this is a marvelous country with incredible history, but they're also a bunch of bad guys and they can do very nasty things.

I can understand the euphoria of the politicians, because, if you're Nixon, you get a lot of credit for opening up and doing this great thing. But Kissinger has a reputation of being much more analytical, cold-blooded. Was he saying that maybe we better damp this down, let's not go to extremes?

FREEMAN: He remained relentlessly realistic, although he was much charmed by the Chinese. The Chinese have a political culture that puts an emphasis on strategy and the long-term view. Once, after interpreting for him at a meeting in New York, when he was secretary of state, I can remember him commenting afterwards that if these people ever become powerful, they will bury us, because of the adroitness of their strategic thinking. He was aware of the need occasionally to correct the admiration that one tended to feel in the presence of very able men, on the Chinese side.

How did you find the Chinese bureaucrats? I'm told that they're one of the most difficult to deal with.

DONALD ANDERSON: In the liaison office period, they were difficult to deal with, particularly if you got into substantive issues where they would have to go out on a limb and make a statement about a political issue. They were very, very cautious. On the other hand, I find their diplomatic service very, very able, and they were a very bright bunch of people. If they're not telling you something, it's not because they're stupid. They're not telling you because they're protecting themselves. And at times they could be very skillful in finding ways to accomplish what you wanted to do.

I remember one case when Henry Kissinger was coming and I was handling the press. It would have been '73. Henry had a friend with the *New York Times* who was traveling in China, and we got this cable from Kissinger saying, "Please arrange to have this guy included as part of the press corps." So I went over to see Mr. Ma, who was head of International Liaison, and he said, "Mr. Anderson, you must understand that our rules are that only the people traveling with the secretary on his plane are considered part of the press corps, and that those are the only ones that can be included." He said, "You understand now our principled position." I said, "Yes." And he said, "Now as a practical matter, since this fellow is a friend of Henry Kissinger's we will include him in all of the banquets, all of the briefings." And I discovered that the Chinese often times follow this approach. They have a position in principle, which if you understand that, and agree with it, then in terms of practical implementation of that principle, they can do the exact opposite.

HOLDRIDGE: Another problem which we dealt with in the early days was the Chinese exhibition of archeological articles dug up during the Cultural Revolution. It was quite an exhibition, including jade body suits, Tang dynasty figurines, all really beautiful things. It was making a tour of the world, and it was going to come to the United States. One of the things we were negotiating with the Chinese was the terms, the agreement, that we would have between our two countries on this exhibition.

The Chinese presented us with an agreement which they had used in every other country worldwide where this thing had been visiting. Lo and behold, when we sent it back, the people in the legal division of the department objected strenuously. There was not enough protection, etc. We had to go back to the Chinese to try to change certain paragraphs. Each time we suggested a change, the Chinese would toughen up, until the terms were stiffer than ever before. Ultimately, the exhibition came to the United States and was a great success. But the Chinese had, meanwhile, used this little episode to teach us a lesson—Chinese love to teach lessons.

Looking back, have you seen the Chinese become much easier to deal with? Do you feel that their exposure to us developed a greater mutual understanding and trust?

HOLDRIDGE: Yes, to an extent. Starting with normalization, the Chinese had begun to function as normal members of the world community. They joined the International Atomic Energy Agency, the World Bank, the International Monetary Fund, applied for the General Agreement on Tariffs and Trade, and began to function just like any normal country. They sent 40,000 students to the United States. People were accessible at various levels of the government—you could talk to them as individuals and not as ideologues.

During the time you were assistant secretary for East Asian Affairs [1976 to early 1977], were there any difficulties in getting the Chinese Communists "set up" in the United States or our getting "set up" in Mainland China?

HUMMEL: Not very much. They had a lot of friends here. They were annoyed that they couldn't get their hands on the lovely residential property, called Twin Oaks, that had been occupied by the Chinese Nationalists [as their embassy].

The whole idea of the separation of powers, the prerogatives of Congress and those of the Executive Branch. They had to start from scratch, because they had grown up with stereotyped, Marxist ideas of what the Americans were like. We'd have to explain what Congress could and could not do and what the prerogatives of the Executive Branch were.

When they first showed up as a liaison office here in Washington, we had not settled the "claims and assets" problem on both sides. We had done a lot of work on it and we continued to work on it—collecting information from Americans who had claims against China for expropriated property. We asked the Chinese to tell us what they thought that we owed them—in sequestered bank accounts and so on. We were preparing for—and I was very conscious of this—a time when we would switch diplomatic recognition from Taiwan to the mainland. One of the major considerations was the danger that anything that the Chinese Communists sent to the U.S., such as a Chinese ship or airplane, might be attached by a court order, with a view to settlement of some company's claim against China.

The Chinese Nationalists saw this whole thing as a zero sum game, which it probably was. Any benefit that the Communist Chinese or Beijing got was detrimental to the interests of the Nationalists. So the Chinese Nationalists loved to make trouble between the United States and Beijing. They held demonstrations with the Nationalist flag near the PRC Liaison Office and they threatened legal action against the Liaison Office.

Was there concern over Chinese Nationalist intelligence operations in the United States?

HUMMEL: Yes, but I would say frankly that we were also conscious of Chinese Communist intelligence operations. We did our best to penetrate them in various ways. I don't want to go into too much detail on this, but I may say that the Chinese Communists were also doing their best to penetrate various aspects of our society, including economic and technological secrets. They were setting up Chinese-Americans for recruitment. This was the same thing that the Chinese Nationalists had been doing for a long time. The Chinese Nationalists had an advantage in that they had so many friends, particularly in the Pentagon, that they could just walk in the front door of the Pentagon and talk to their friends, who were highly anti-communist and somewhat opposed to State Department policy on accommodation or at least coexistence with the PRC. So we had people within our own government who were not marching to the same tune as the Executive Branch.

STALEMATE

High hopes for rapid progress on normalization stalled after 1973. China had thought that alignment with the United States meant cooperative opposition to the Soviets. Instead, the United States tried to use its new relationship with China to promote détente with the Soviet Union. Beijing deplored the 1975 Helsinki Accords on European security and the 1976 Sonnenfeldt Doctrine, which accepted the Soviet sphere of influence in Eastern Europe, as indications of American weakness. Beijing also objected to evidence of continuing close ties with Taipei, especially arms sales, and accused Washington of trying to follow a one China, one Taiwan policy. As political frictions surfaced, trade and cultural exchanges slowed as well. Similarly, negative images reemerged in the public mind on both sides, with the Chinese fearing Americans as dangerous and unreliable, whereas the Americans assailed the oppressiveness and rigidity of Chinese society.

There was a criticism during the campaign when Bush was running for president that as head of the Liaison Office, 1974–75, he passed through, but did not take control. Was that accurate?

THAYER: Well, to be explicit, no. I had the impression of somebody who took the job very seriously. He really worked hard on his spoken Chinese language when he was there. When he traveled, he learned. When he attended meetings he took notes, and he would come back and faithfully, much to our gratitude, report to the staff. Deng Xiaoping liked Bush, and he gave a farewell lunch for Bush. In the charming way the Chinese have, they gave the lunch in the "Taiwan Room" of the Great

Harry Thayer and George Bush at the U.S. Liaison Office in Beijing in 1975. *Courtesy of Harry Thayer.*

Hall of the People. But Bush wasn't a patsy for the Chinese. I was going to illustrate this in a very modest way by recalling an episode involving one of our officers from Hong Kong, whose wife was of Vietnam-Chinese origin. They had both come to Beijing, visiting there for a few days. The wife came to the front gate of the liaison office compound to visit the office, as any Foreign Service wife would do, and showed her American passport to the Chinese Army (PLA) gate guard. But because she had an Oriental face—the Chinese have a very hard time thinking of Americans as anything but white-faced Anglo-Saxons—the guard refused to let her in. She insisted, and the guard continued to refuse. Ambassador Bush heard about this, and was clearly outraged. He decided to unleash the political counselor, who just raised holy hell about the guard's performance, the principles involved, and so forth. The result was that the woman was let into our compound within about thirty seconds. But the point to be made here was about Bush, who was often accused of not being able to stand up for himself, being a wimp, he was prepared to pull out all the stops and be as hard as necessary.

We learned later of a humorous denouement of that episode. A senior Chinese representative in Washington visited the White House a day or two later. He was to meet his wife separately at the White House. For some reason, the guard initially refused to let the wife of the representative into the White House. We understood at the time the Chinese were convinced that this was a swift American retaliation for the episode at our gate in Beijing.

DONALD ANDERSON: George Bush didn't really have the same cachet [as David Bruce had had] as having been ambassador to London, Paris, and Bonn. On the other hand, in many ways politically, he was better plugged in, and probably had more clout in Washington with the Nixon administration and ultimately later the Ford administration, than Bruce. He's a very energetic guy, and sort of a go-go-go type of approach. He arrived running; I think he gave a reception for the entire liaison office staff the day he got off the plane. One of the first things he did was go out and buy a ping-pong table and move it into the formal dining room of the residence so that the kids could go over and play ping-pong, and he would go over at lunch time and play with them.

But again, he was frustrated by the lack of communication and dialogue with the Chinese. At that time we were dealing very frequently with a lady by the name of Wang Hairong, who was Mao's niece and at that point was an assistant minister of Foreign Affairs. She was really noteworthy for her clamlike approach to dialogue, and it used to drive George Bush up the wall, because he would go over and we would have a message to deliver from Washington on whatever issue. Quite literally, most of the time the message would take five minutes, and then Wang would sort of sit there, and George Bush would be damned if he was going to arrive at the Foreign Ministry and leave ten minutes later. So he would sometimes tend to launch into discussions of issues, political issues that I wondered about occasionally at the time, because we got no response. Wang, or whoever was his interlocutor, would sit and listen, but we got very little in response.

Do you have any feel for how the policy apparatus worked at that time?

DONALD ANDERSON: The way it worked, Washington would send us a message, we would go over to the Foreign Ministry, deliver the message, and they would say, "Thank you, we will inform the appropriate offices." And then maybe a week later we would get a phone call saying, "Would you come in?" We would go in, and they would read from their prepared position paper. So we got answers, but it was a process that had to go through particularly the party machinery to get the right answer, or to get an approved answer. In a normal diplomatic situation you could go in and do that, and there is conversation and some back and forth in dialogue on the issue. But there was very little of that. Basically, everyone was scared to death. It was a time when the power struggle in Beijing was very intense, so no one was going to stick their neck out.

Was the Gang of Four, the radical left, able to intrude on the process?

DONALD ANDERSON: At that time, they seemed to be cooperating with the whole process. It was a very strange time. I mean, Jiang Qing, Mao's wife, hosted the Boston Symphony, which was one of the big cultural events of the initial period of exchanges. She was very charming, of course, when Nixon was there. She was pushing her revolutionary operas and ballets. Jiang Qing, for all of her anti-Western attitudes, had a fascination with Western movies. We very quietly worked out an arrangement with Jack Valenti, for example. He would send us movies . . .

He was president of the American Picture Association.

DONALD ANDERSON: He would send us out films that she wanted to see, and we would deliver them to Jiang Qing and her friends, and they would return them. We would return them back because the American Picture Association was very, very sensitive about copyrights, and piracy, and this kind of thing. Some of the choices of her movies I found rather interesting. The first movie she asked for was *Day of the Jackal*, which deals with assassination. We didn't really sense any attempts to obstruct the relationship, although there was a power struggle going on at that time between the followers of Zhou Enlai, a more pragmatic group, and the leftists. As long as Zhou was alive, it seemed, the U.S.-China relationship was contained.

FREEMAN: China was in a period of lull. Mao was failing. Jiang Qing, his wife, was using her nominal position as his wife and her access to him, along with a number of other women who were around him, to build her own political authority.[5] The street in front of the former American Embassy in the old legation quarter was named Anti-Imperialist Street; the one in front of the Soviet Embassy was named Anti-Revisionist Street. But there was no overt unrest. There were no demonstrations. The Red Guards were a thing of the past. There was lingering political tension and a sense of oppressiveness from ideology. It turned out that this period was indeed the moment at which the Gang of Four began to emerge as the de facto leadership of China. So that, by the fall of 1973, early 1974, U.S.-China relations began to become much more tendentious.

Of course, Watergate was going on in the United States, and Nixon was in the process of falling from power. There was something similar going on, Zhou Enlai greatly hampered, in China. Both sides, for strategic reasons, in subsequent visits by Kissinger to China, continued to put much the best face on the relationship, but inside, it was rotting, because of the ideological struggles in the United States and in China.

DONALD ANDERSON: Kissinger came back to Beijing in November of 1974, and by that time I was head of the political section, so I was the sort of overall control officer for that visit. Kissinger saw Zhou in the hospital. He'd already been diagnosed as having cancer. I don't think anybody knew exactly what the diagnosis was, but he was ill. By that time a discussion with Mao had to go through two interpreters: one who spoke his native Hunan dialect, and then someone who could speak Mandarin. It was therefore screened through two female interpreters, one of whom was his niece, and the other was a lady by the name of Nancy Tang, who was one of the finest interpreters I have ever met, but who got involved with the Gang of Four and eventually got into trouble with them. So the visit in '74 did not go nearly as well as the earlier visits, and it was partially a reflection of the power struggle that was going on in Beijing. Of course, we had our own problems back in Washington with the Nixon resignation [August 8, 1974].

LORD: On this trip Deng Xiaoping was the host. Deng had made a come-back, went down again, and then made another comeback later on. The first time that we ever met Deng was when he headed the Chinese Del-egation to the UN General Assembly in New York. I recall that at the time we didn't know much about Deng. Initially, we were not particu-larly impressed with him. We just felt that, after Zhou Enlai, he was a let down.[6] Of course, the times had changed. Specifically, we began to probe on the possibility of making further progress on Taiwan. How-ever, Deng stuck to a hard line on Taiwan. We were not overly gener-ous ourselves, either. By then the Watergate Affair was behind us, so this was our first trip to China after Nixon had resigned and [Gerald] Ford had become president. Deng himself was in a vulnerable position, trying to deal with the Gang of Four.

Did you feel any particular change in the work you were doing, and our rela-tionship with China with the Ford administration?

SOLOMON: Once Ford was in office, the issue for the Chinese became whether Ford and Kissinger would carry through. They viewed nor-malization as a commitment and an obligation to complete during what remained of the Nixon second term. During the two or three Kissinger trips to China before the Ford summit trip in December of 1975, the focus of all interactions was the effort by the Chinese to pressure Kissinger into completing normalization. My job was to shepherd through that process, and we were still writing memos to Kissinger on the assumption that the effort would be made to complete normaliza-tion. But the message we were getting from the White House political people was that the conservative Republicans would not support Jerry Ford in completing normalization. It led to some very interesting and very tense exchanges with the Chinese as they tried to strong-arm Kissinger. I remember, in particular, the October '75 trip, which was the one just before the Ford summit trip in December. The Chinese, Deng Xiaoping in particular, put a variety of pressures on Kissinger, trying to get him to deliver President Ford to the Nixon normalization finale. That did not happen, and our relations with the Chinese were very strained for a period.

LORD: This [October 17–24, 1975] was the most unpleasant, frosty trip of all of the trips I made to China from 1971 to 1976. The Chinese were very "cold" on substance, at meetings, and in their public toasts. They were very tough on détente and alleged that we were being naive about the Russians. [Mao] first made the allegation that we were, in effect, standing on their shoulders to reach toward Moscow. Mao was very sick by this time. He spoke in grunts and wrote things down. I used to joke that Mao would speak in a grunt for 10 seconds. Then his interpreter would hold forth for two minutes. I used to say that he would attach a number to each policy formulation: Number One was Taiwan, Number Two was Russia, and Number Three was South Asia. I thought that Mao would whisper the number, and then the interpreter would give the standard policy line.

Was any thought given to canceling Ford's trip to China?

LORD: There was no thought of canceling it. However, we were very unhappy when we left China because we saw this as a trip without any results. As we got back to Washington, James Schlesinger was fired as secretary of defense. He had just returned from a visit to China. The Chinese really liked him because he followed a particularly hard line on Russia and was friendly toward China. Kissinger lost his job as national security adviser [although he remained secretary of state]. At the time there were long discussions between Kissinger, Scowcroft, Eagleburger, and myself about whether or not Kissinger should resign, since he had lost his NSC hat. He felt that in the eyes of leaders around the world and of his own prestige, this was really a put down. Of course this was an overreaction [he didn't resign].[7] Ford was worried about his flank. He didn't want Reagan to get the Republican nomination.

SOLOMON: In this situation of Chinese pressure on Kissinger to complete normalization, they were suddenly faced with what looked to them like a political coup or a purge. They suddenly panicked, fearing that all their supporters and those who took a hard line against the Soviet Union—Schlesinger in particular—were now on the political outs. In that context, they almost overnight took the pressure off and proceeded with the Ford summit meeting, realizing that they had reached their limit of progress on normalization; they saw they couldn't pressure Kissinger and Ford to complete the process at that point in time.

LORD: We decided to get tough with the Chinese. The original Ford trip was supposed to be for several days and to include visits to Beijing and to four or five other cities in addition. We informed the Chinese, politely, that President Ford would only be able to go to Beijing. He would just spend a couple of days and we were not only going to China but to Indonesia and the Philippines, to make it an Asian trip. We did get the attention of the Chinese. They immediately began to warm up.

Mao had about an hour's meeting with President Ford. Mao agreed with Ford on most issues. At the very beginning, and this is a semi-amusing story, Mao repeated his comment that he would soon receive an invitation from God. President Ford looked a little puzzled at this. He didn't seem to understand that this was Mao's elliptical way of referring to his forthcoming death. So, when we left the meeting, Ford went up to Mao and said something to the effect: "I'm going to overrule Kissinger [who had earlier demurred] and make sure that you get that invitation from God very soon." Kissinger and I were aghast. However, the interpreter fielded the comment and said: "The president wishes you 10,000 years of life," or something like that.

THAYER: Two high points of my service as DCM out there were the visits of Henry Kissinger in October of 1975 and of President Ford in December. In a situation where symbols are in some ways the substance of the relationship, a visit by the secretary of state to Beijing was an important event in itself. But there were various issues to be settled that weren't settled by the Kissinger visit or, for that matter, by the president's visit, because the Chinese were so tangled up in their own domestic problems that it was very hard for them to make any decision that was favorable to the relationship. This was before Mao's death, but the Gang of Four was riding high. President Ford's visit helped balance off his earlier meeting in Vladivostok with the Soviets. But there were no great advances substantively. Then Bush himself left China almost immediately after the Ford visit, on December 7, 1975, to go back and run the CIA.

What was Kissinger's role once he established this relationship? Did he move on to other things? Did you feel that he was on top of China relations all the time?

DONALD ANDERSON: Pretty much, yes. He retained a very direct interest in China, and at a minimum Kissinger set a tone that really shaped the way we dealt with China for a very long time. Essentially Kissinger saw the opening to China as part of a global strategic move, and was very much interested in the triangular relationship. At the same time he was very affected by China. He was obviously very impressed with Mao and Zhou Enlai, and with their intellectual capabilities, their strategic thinking. They were people he felt he could commune with. Then there was very definitely an atmosphere in the U.S. government as long as Kissinger was running the show that basically in dealing with China you looked at the big picture and the strategic relationship, don't bother with details, which led to a lot of people—not necessarily myself, but a lot of people—feeling that we were giving away things that we didn't need to give to China. In other words, if the Chinese said, "We want this," in terms of a negotiation, the inclination was to say, "Okay," rather than have a show-down, and quibble over details, which may or may not have been wise.

THAYER: The Chinese invited Nixon to come to Beijing in the middle of the 1976 New Hampshire primary on his first foreign foray after his resignation, and there was a good deal of speculation in the American press at the time that somehow the Chinese were trying to interfere with that primary. I think Chinese motivations in inviting Nixon were two-fold. First, they really do make a big point of being true to their old friends, and they considered Nixon an old friend. But there was a political point to be made, too. And that is that the relationship after Nixon left the presidency (starting before Nixon left, in fact) was not moving forward as well as the Chinese perhaps had hoped. So it was a way of sending a message to the Americans.

How were we reading what was happening in China?

THAYER: Mao was out of it, but he was still there. The Gang of Four was riding high. There were the riots or demonstrations at Tiananmen and at the Martyr's Shrine subsequent to Zhou Enlai's death in April of 1976. People were going up and people were going down, but most of this was obscure to us. The Chinese were just themselves tied in knots. How we discerned this was the way people would speak to us, the jargon they would use in briefings, toasts, what was printed in *People's Daily* and in other publications. But we didn't really understand a lot that was going on very deeply behind the scenes.

How about Thomas Gates, the next ambassador? What was his background,
and did he make any changes?

THAYER: Gates [1976–1979] made no change in the basic policy. There
was no change to be made. Gates was selected after a long delay. He was
a secretary of the Navy, and then secretary of defense under Eisenhower. He was chairman and CEO of Morgan Bank in New York. Ford
had confidence in him, he was a noncontroversial political figure; that is,
a nonprofessional. We wanted to have a political figure for symbolic
purposes in China. He didn't have any background in China.

What other developments were there during the 1970s?

HOROWITZ: There was a limited commercial opening; they were interested in beginning to sell some things to the West and they were interested in American wheat and some other products, but they were still
rather skittish about it. The Chinese officials were not very open; they
were afraid to be in many ways. What we learned was mostly what our
businessmen would tell us. We would digest it and then give advice,
without revealing any secrets, to other businessmen. There were so few
business visitors to Beijing in those days—that's where businessmen
wanted to go because it was the headquarters of the state trading companies—that they would come to see us. We would tell them what to
expect and how to conduct themselves and very often they would come
back later and give us a report. So we were able to build up a body of
knowledge on doing business with China at that time.

We did a similar thing at the Canton Trade Fair, a twice a year vehi-
cle.[8] That is where the Chinese did most of their selling, but also a lot
of their buying too. The Canton fair was an important first step for an
American or other foreign businessman in dealing with China. If they
could get a visa to go to the Canton fair they might have some hope of
developing a relationship and later on maybe traveling to Beijing or
other parts of China. What we did was to take a suite at the hotel opposite the Canton fairground to serve as a mini-office. We would man it
through the whole month of the fair with one or two people. We would
give advice and help, and learn from the experiences of American businessmen. The Chinese still published no data and gave you very little
information.

FREEMAN: Generally, the process of opening trade relations went rather smoothly. Of course, we were dealing with a society in which there was essentially no commercial code, no legal system to enforce contracts. There were great adjustments to be made. The Chinese essentially had the attitude of Henry Ford: "You can buy a shirt, any shirt, as long as it's white and it's got our label on it." The Americans, obviously, specialized in going in and buying things for the American market, which meant that the shirts had to be specially designed and had to have the Bloomingdale's label. So the process of persuading the Chinese not to insist on their brands and their designs was a very difficult one.

And there were wonderful jokes about Chinese brand names that had a different connotation in English than they did in Chinese. For example, elephants are powerful beasts, and those that are white are pure. So the largest-selling brand of batteries in China was the White Elephant brand. Shoes in Chinese are *pee-shyeh*, and in the Chinese romanization, that comes out as *pixie*. So we had Pixie brand shoes for men. It had its moments.

Did you feel at all the problems that plagued us serving in the Soviet Union where the KGB was trying to entrap you? Were there any of these games or were there just restrictions on you?

HOROWITZ: We always felt watched, but so did other foreigners. I don't think we felt more watched than other people. They listened, we were positive our apartments were bugged, and to the extent that they could bug our offices they probably did that too. We finally moved into some apartments. The elevator operator must have been the head party cadre, because she seemed to be the font of all information. We were watched quite carefully, what we did and where we went. We had to request permission to travel outside of Beijing—we learned the technique of asking to visit five places and hope they'd approve two. When you went to another place you had to check in with the police when you arrived and you had to check in when you left. That was true for all foreigners. So they kept close touch, but I didn't sense they were trying to entrap us.

Some of the politics did get into the trade things. I remember very vividly that one of the problems we had was the Chinese complaint that in American wheat which they bought there was a type of wheat smut which they didn't have in China and they were afraid that this would contaminate their wheat. We had to bring experts in from the Department of Agriculture to look into this and explain that there was no danger. The issue was more political than it was economic, because at that time the Shanghai papers, and in Shanghai the radicals had a dominant voice, were criticizing Chinese officials who bought poisoned wheat from abroad. There was a political conflict going on and it impinged on our commercial operation. At the liaison office we did not have much contact with the radicals of the party, the Gang of Four crowd. Most of the people we saw and had dealings with in the government were the pragmatists, the ones who were trying to get the country back on the road again and working to get the economy improved.

Were we concerned about the transfer of technology? Not just military technology but also that they might get our techniques and copy them.

HOROWITZ: Yes, but it was not a serious problem then. We visited factories where there would be one piece of Western machinery, very old, and then several more that were copies. At that point we still had very stringent controls on export of technology to China, as well as other communist countries. Their economy was not very advanced at that time.

FREEMAN: It came up primarily in the context of concern by the export-control community about reverse engineering of what would be sold to China. Indeed, there were attempts to do this. The Chinese took the Boeing 707, studied it carefully, and built something that we dubbed the "Boeing 708," which turned out to be a rather awkward flyer and never went anywhere.

They were famous for copying things generally. There was a story that when the Russians shipped some MiG-21s to Vietnam, by rail across China, the rail cars somehow got lost, and the MiG-21s didn't turn up for quite a while. When they did turn up in Vietnam, some of the dials in the cockpit were upside down. Obviously, the whole thing had been disassembled. Indeed, the Chinese began to produce an aircraft quite similar to the MiG-21 a couple of years later.

But the general answer to this was that Chinese technical capabilities were so limited that, by the time a commercial product had been reverse engineered and they were in a position to produce it themselves, one or two further generations of technology would have been introduced in the United States, and it wouldn't be a threat to the market position of companies.

What about intellectual property problems, basically copyrights and that type of thing?

HOROWITZ: Not a serious problem then because they had total control over publications. Very, very little material had been published in China in any language since before the Cultural Revolution. There was no free market anywhere, so it was a totally controlled situation. To illustrate the atmosphere: there was an international club, which was designed for foreigners—tennis courts and swimming pool. There was a very nice room that was called the library; it had a lot of windows, easy chairs, a lot of shelves, most of which were empty. The only books on the shelves were Mao's works and three or four communist publications, that's all.

FREEMAN: That issue, which had been at the center of our relationship with Taiwan for many years, is one that is typical of the relationships between advanced societies and developing ones. In the nineteenth century, the greatest violator of copyright was the United States.

Oh, yes. Gilbert and Sullivan had long stories about the problems.

FREEMAN: And Charles Dickens. It's normal for developing societies to regard intellectual products as the common heritage of mankind, rather than as entitled to protection for the benefit of their originators. But this wasn't an issue with the Chinese at that time. It became an issue later, largely because we did succeed, as Taiwan became an exporter of technology, in persuading Taiwan to clamp down, at which point they simply relocated all of their factories to the mainland.

How were we reporting on political events? How were we getting our information?

HOROWITZ: Conversations with other people, impressions—there was always a big exchange among people in the foreign missions—some little bits and pieces that the Chinese would tell us, what we would see in the newspaper. It was limited. We knew when there was a big meeting in the Great Hall of the People from the number of limousines that would be pulling up, and one or the other of us would bicycle by a few times to see what was doing. It was frustrating. The Chinese were very uptight in those days, very reserved; they would not speak in a relaxed way or off the record. Relations were not so good. As a matter of fact, the second year we were there there was a drop in the U.S. trade with China; instead of an increase, it fell. Our relationship with the Chinese was in many ways tied to what was happening in China and the political struggle that was going on.

Did you have any contact with the Soviets when you were there?

HOROWITZ: Oh, yes. The Soviets in Beijing felt very isolated; they wanted to be friends with us because they knew it would aggravate the Chinese if we were friendly. Frankly we wanted to keep the Soviets a little bit away; if we got too close it would harm our relations with the Chinese. The Soviets had magnificent embassy grounds and they would open up their place—they had a pond—for ice skating and hockey on the weekends, invite our kids to go there, invite us to films. They wanted to be our pals in the worst way. They were helpful too in that they would explain to us how Sino-Soviet trade was carried out. Also the other East Europeans who were there were friendly; we heard a lot about the trade patterns of China and the rest of the communist world. To the extent that we could, we would compare notes with them. The Soviets were very anxious to be friendly.

LORD: At times, particularly in the mid-1970s, the Chinese would say: "You Americans are getting a little naive with the Soviets. Détente is really an illusion. You're getting too soft and you're trying to stand on our shoulders to reach the Soviets. You're trying to use us and you're being naive with the Russians." We got some of that flavor, particularly from Deng Xiaoping later on, and not so much from Mao and Zhou.

We began to share intelligence reports with the Chinese, and I would go off and brief the Chinese on Russian troop deployments. We would also give them information on Soviet capabilities, both to show that we were friendly and that we were trying to share information that might be useful to them. And also, frankly, to make the Chinese a little nervous about Soviet intentions.

Was there a sense of confidence on the part of the Chinese that you were telling them everything?

LORD: Well, it was not in the style of the Chinese to tell us that they did-
n't think that we were telling them everything. Nor would they show
gratitude at our being forthcoming in briefing them. They listened to us
with interest. I don't recall that they probed us with a lot of questions to
show their eagerness. I don't recall whether this began with the trip in
June [1972], but certainly by February 1973, we began to brief them on
Russian deployments [on the Chinese border]. They did not reciprocate
greatly in terms of their relations with Russia. On the other hand, they
did not have much to offer. Relations between Russia and China were
pretty frosty at this point.

At what point did they begin to provide us with information as well?

LORD: Well, whether it was Russia, the Middle East, or Vietnam, for a
long period of time we generally gave them a lot more than they gave
us. We didn't consider the intelligence exchanges as a zero sum game.
First of all, we thought that we knew more than the Chinese did on most
of these issues. Secondly, we hoped to get more out of them, and we
encouraged them. However, we felt that even the unilateral intelligence
briefings would give them a greater stake in the emerging relationship
with the United States which, after all, was still somewhat fragile after
some 22 years of hostility between our two countries. We hoped that
our efforts would show them that we regarded them as a more friendly,
strategic partner. Specifically, if there were any arguments in the Chinese Politburo about the opening to the U.S., we hoped to help those in
favor of such an opening, like Mao and Zhou. We also hoped generally
to indicate to the Chinese that we were not naive about the Russians but
were willing to share information about the Russians with the Chinese.
Furthermore, we also made it clear that we wanted to improve relations
with Russia as well. We made it clear that we would not do this at Chinese expense but that it was in our national interest as well. We said that
we were not about to form a tight, anti-Soviet alliance with China, any
more than we would gang up with Russia against China. We wanted to
strike a balance. This was to give the Chinese an incentive to improve
relations with us. This was the usual triangular game.

SOLOMON: When Deng Xiaoping was rehabilitated after 1974, the argument between Deng and Kissinger was whether the Soviet threat was
greater to China or the United States. The Chinese, Deng in particular,

resisted the notion that they (the Chinese) were afraid of the Soviets and that the Soviets were gearing up to attack China. The phrase that the Chinese bandied about was that the Soviets were feinting towards the East but preparing to attack in the West—that Soviet pressure on China was really a distraction from their real plan, which was to put military pressure of one sort or another on the NATO alliance, or on the United States. Kissinger argued the opposite, and this became a matter of not only debate, but of ultimately some distrust because the Chinese came to feel that Kissinger was distorting the information about Soviet deployments that he was giving to them as a way of trying to scare them, and thereby influence their approach to dealing with the United States. At several points, we picked up some diplomatic reporting in which Deng would tell visiting American congressional groups that he wasn't sure he could believe everything that Kissinger was telling him about the Soviet threat. So that issue ultimately became a matter of debate and distrust because each side saw that the other was trying to constrain its options by painting the immediate threat from the Soviets to the other as greater than the other side was willing to admit.

Did you also discuss other foreign policy problems?

LORD: One area where we did make progress over several trips to China concerned our alliance with Japan. During the early talks with the Chinese, their basic line was that we were helping Japan to re-arm by our alliance with them and that we were making them dangerous. We pointed out that this was an illogical position. Our alliance with Japan and our troops stationed in Japan, plus our nuclear umbrella over Japan, meant that Japan didn't really need to re-arm or go nuclear. We said that it was in the interests of China and of the East Asian region that Japan feel that its security was taken care of by close ties with the U.S. In fact, that argument had an impact on the Chinese over time. They never came right out and said so, either publicly or even privately. However, they clearly got the point and were much more restrained.

We also talked about the Middle East in these discussions. The Chinese were clearly pro-Arab and were not willing to do much with Israel. This situation changed later on when the Chinese began to get military help from Israel.[9] On these trips there was often discussion of Europe. China always wanted us to have strong relations with Europe. They wanted to make sure that Russia had to worry about its western flanks and could not focus all of its energies on China and East Asia. In some of these meetings with Zhou and Mao there was discussion regarding the Central Eurasian pivot area from Turkey around to Pakistan. Of course, the Chinese had a particular friendship with Pakistan vis-à-vis India. The Chinese were suspicious of India [see chapter 3]. Occasionally, there were conversations about Cuba and Africa, but these were not areas for major discussions.

TAIWAN

Taiwan thrived despite the initial rapprochement between Washington and Beijing, but Nationalist authorities feared further erosion of their position as the United States moved toward diplomatic relations with China. In fact, in 1975, Beijing set forth conditions for normalization of relations with the United States that impinged directly on Taiwan's future. There were three points: Washington must terminate official relations with Taiwan, it must abrogate the 1954 Mutual Defense Treaty, and it must remove all American troops from the island. The stalemate that developed in U.S.-China relations, therefore, was good news for Taipei. Nevertheless Taiwan's representatives found as the 1970s progressed that their access in Washington decreased, that the Chinese liaison office preoccupied American officials, that American officials were less interested in visiting Taiwan, and that the American troop presence on the island declined steadily. All this proved uncomfortable and humiliating during the Nixon and Ford years but would become desperate when Jimmy Carter assumed the presidency and began to review American China policy in preparation for formal recognition.

SOLOMON: [In April 1972] I was assigned to escorting the Chinese ping-pong team around as the eyes and ears of the White House. It occurred about a month and a half after Nixon's triumphal visit to China in February of '72. Taiwan was very nervous about the Nixon initiative, and while they didn't overtly oppose the ping-pong trip or normalization, they saw themselves as extremely vulnerable. At the University of Maryland, Taiwan turned out a huge claque of their supporters who, in effect, were enticing the Chinese ping-pong players to defect to Taiwan.

Richard Solomon participates in a session of "ping-pong diplomacy" in Beijing in June 1972. *Courtesy of Richard Solomon.*

[Senator] Barry Goldwater [R-AZ], a great friend of Taiwan, was not happy about the ping-pong tour, and indeed about the normalization process. I was there to make sure that there were no foul-ups, and the government delegation that went along included FBI and CIA types. We were very concerned about security, and there were reports of some security threats to the delegation at one point.

Here was a government with which we had been a very close ally, with strong congressional support. They were being cast adrift. What were the dynamics?

FREEMAN: The most important was an instruction from Kissinger, who was secretary of state by then, not to speak honestly to Taiwan representatives about what the future might hold. This was an unspoken instruction, of which I learned when I had lunch once with the Republic of China ambassador and said to him, "I don't know when it's going to happen, but there will be a switch in relations. And you need to think about how to handle various problems, because the United States will not wish to see you damaged by this." And I talked to him about a number of things that I was pushing on the Desk, such as trying to reduce the visibility of arms sales by shifting, to the extent possible, to technology transfer and local manufacture, trying to make this issue more manageable, recognizing that normalization with China would not come for years, and that we should use those years to try to reduce the impact on the ROC, since none of us knew what the details of the normalization agreement might be.

I was roundly chastised for talking to him about this. Of course, I then followed discipline and did not. But I felt that it was improper, with a government that was a friend, not to help them to come to grips with emerging realities and to adjust themselves so that they would not be adversely affected by what was going to come.

The Taiwan government must have known this was coming. Did they have a head-in-the-sand attitude?

FREEMAN: There was deep denial in Taiwan. It was unacceptable to question the heritage of Chiang Kai-shek. I can remember, in December 1970, having a conversation with Ch'ien Fu (Frederick Chien), who later became the foreign minister of the Taipei government, in which I said to him, "You know, you will lose your UN seat eventually, and maybe it will be next year." (As it turned out, it was.) And I said, "Or it'll be the year after. But you will eventually lose. And the reason you will lose is not because people don't like and don't believe that you are a political entity, it is because you are impersonating a great power, sitting in the Security Council. Why don't you recognize the inevitability of loss, and adjust to it by withdrawing voluntarily from the Security Council, but retaining your General Assembly seat?" And I got the predictable response from him, several Chinese sayings: "The righteous and unrighteous cannot live under the same sun," and "I'd rather be a piece of broken jade than a whole brick." And this was very much the atmosphere in Taipei, which was still, at that time, a very ideological, benevolent dictatorship. So unpalatable realities were not welcome and were not discussed.

Even by diplomats on informal occasions here in Washington?

FREEMAN: Oh, there were younger diplomats with whom one could have candid conversations. What they were able to do with them, in terms of reporting, I can't say. There was certainly awareness in Taiwan of the peril of their position.

You went to Taipei as political counselor from '75 to '78.

BURNET: It was really a hand-holding operation to ease the Republic of China government into accepting what was inevitable even at that time: U.S. recognition of the communist regime on the mainland. We didn't know when, of course. But our main job then was to say: Look, it isn't going to be that bad. You aren't going to fall apart. The sky isn't going to fall when we shift our recognition to the mainland.

But it was clearly understood that this was going to be happening sooner rather than later?

BURNET: It was understood by us, and we tried to make it clear to our counterparts. Sometimes the ambassador didn't talk that directly—he couldn't, really—to *his* counterparts.

What was your impression of the Chinese officials on Taiwan you dealt with?

BURNET: I, of course, had most to do with the Ministry of Foreign Affairs and the head of the American desk there. I felt that they were professionals and that they were doing their job. I wished, many times, that they could have let their hair down and leveled with me a little bit more than they did. They kept up a pretty good front of official policy. Of course, their views were pretty orthodox, that China was one, and that eventually they hoped to regain the mainland, although that was quite remote at that point. We didn't have an awful lot to do (after all, Washington's focus was elsewhere), as long as we kept things quiet and made sure that the two Chinas didn't get involved over the Straits of Taiwan. That turned out to be one of my major tasks, to keep an eye on the Chinese Air Force and their activities, and to monitor our military's relations with the Chinese Air Force.

Tell me, how does one keep an eye on an air force?

BURNET: Well, you have this island of Taiwan just a hundred miles or so off the mainland which had its own air force. They were flying daily patrols over the Taiwan Straits. And the People's Republic of China had its air force and *they* were flying patrols too. Occasionally these patrols met. We didn't want any flare-up or any exchange of fire, so there were places that we thought these patrols shouldn't be going, and that they should observe a certain restraint and caution.

When there was a contact of some sort, this had to be reported to Washington in great detail: how it happened, who did what to whom, what the upshot was and what steps needed to be taken to prevent a repeat performance. Of course the military would make its report, but naturally the ambassador wanted his own complete report of what happened that day in the air over the China Sea.

This was just about the time Chiang Kai-shek died, wasn't it?

BURNET: As a matter of fact, Chiang Kai-shek died in the spring of '75, shortly after I arrived. Reminds me, when he died one member of the political section thought of a short, one-sentence telegram to report this grave event back to Washington. I don't know whether you remember the period in W.W. II under Stilwell in the China-Burma theater. Stilwell's word for the Generalissimo was the "Peanut." We wanted to send a two-word telegram: "Peanut planted." But we decided the ambassador wouldn't appreciate this, even in jest, so we never sent it in for him to sign. But we kicked it around a while for fun.

Anyway, he had a vast, very fancy state funeral, which the entire diplomatic corps had to attend. We were taught how to go up by threes to the podium and bow from the hips to his portrait in a gesture of sympathy or respect. The whole diplomatic corps was lined up and had to go through this: click, click, bend at the hips, bend twice, and move off. And from then on it was Chiang Ching-kuo, Chiang Kai-shek's son, who was running the show.

What was the impression of him at that time?

BURNET: It was a very good feeling. A feeling that here's a good, pragmatic, businesslike Chinese who was going to take over from the doddering old man, and that things would be a lot easier for us and a lot easier for our relationship under him. Everybody felt the same way—people in the agency, people in the economic section, my section, the Trade Center—we all felt good about it.

In your section, were you all pretty much of one accord as far as our change to the People's Republic of China, or did you have some who felt we're selling out?

BURNET: Fortunately, we did not. Everybody was of more or less the same mind. Everybody thought that it was inevitable and that it was just a matter of time.

FREEMAN: The other major issues we had during that period? Well, for example, Taiwan has something called the Chung-shan Institute. Chung-shan was the political nickname of Sun Yat-sen. This is the military research and development facility in Taiwan. They had a cooperative program with the Israelis in which they were producing a version of the Gabriel anti-ship missile. They also had a program to develop longer-range short-range ballistic missiles and medium-range ballistic missiles that could hit Shanghai and other places on the mainland.

We discovered that they had, very cleverly, one by one, inserted their entire missile-design team into M.I.T., one student applying, apparently with no connection to the others, to study nose-cone design, another one doing guidance, another one doing rocket fuel, another one doing metallurgy for fuselages, and so forth. So, from nose cone to afterburner, they had it covered.[10]

HUMMEL: We discovered that Taiwan and South Korea had made a beginning on nuclear programs which could, eventually, have led to nuclear weapons. We stamped on those with great vigor. When this kind of information comes up, it calls for quick and unequivocal action.[11]

FREEMAN: There was also quite effective espionage going on from Taiwan. They were not asleep; they were alert. And this probably was stimulated even more by the official lack of candor that characterized our relationship.

What about the China Lobby? There were many people within Congress who had strong ties to and feelings for Taiwan. What role did that play, from your perspective?

FREEMAN: There was some aftermath of McCarthyite innuendo, repression, and intimidation from the political right. But essentially, during this period, the American body politic was confused about China, including Taiwan. Conservatives who had supported the anti-communism of Chiang Kai-shek saw the utility of China as a counterweight to the Soviet Union, which was the enemy. And that silenced all but the most ideological. Those with any strategic sense saw the merits of what Nixon had done. The liberals could hardly sympathize with Taiwan, because Taiwan was, at that time, a dictatorship, with labor reform camps and the like, a society in which the Taiwanese identity was suppressed by the Mainlander ruling class.

HUMMEL: There were some die-hards, such as former Congressman Walter Judd, also a former medical missionary in China of China Lobby fame, Ray Cline, a former CIA officer [and CIA station chief in Taipei] who made a lot of his income from Taiwan after he retired. They would keep up a drumfire of criticism that we had too close relations with the Chinese Communists and had abandoned our old friend and ally Nationalist China. However, the majority sentiment was that all of our efforts were good things to do. It was in the American interest.

SOLOMON: I escorted the first group of congressional leaders to China [in July 1973], headed by Warren Magnuson on the Democratic side [D-WA]. The congressional leaders—many of them—did not understand what was behind this policy, much less its nuances. Zhou Enlai received this delegation, gave a dinner for them, and during the dinner Senator Magnuson said to Zhou that he didn't understand why Taiwan shouldn't be independent. Al Jenkins of the State Department started kicking Magnuson under the table, trying to get him to shut up because it was such a disastrous opinion to articulate. And, of course, we didn't know whether the Chinese would see this as a provocation or as something that was just Magnuson's personal point of view.

CARTER

Jimmy Carter became president in part because of the Vietnam War. When he was inaugurated in 1977, he sought to begin a new era in Asia and tried to deal with the region for itself and not as a Cold War problem. But when Carter established diplomatic relations with China it was in part the result of an anti-Soviet turn in policy. He also sacrificed improvement of relations with Hanoi to solidify contacts with the more strategically important Chinese.

THAYER: Things didn't really start to change until the Carter administration, and that was partly because the situation in China changed then. A leadership came into place with the demise of the Gang of Four, the death of Mao, the rise of Deng Xiaoping and others who saw the value of an improving Sino-U.S. relationship.

LORD: In 1976, both Mao and Zhou Enlai died. There was a temporary elevation of Hua Guofeng. Mao said that with Hua in charge, he was at ease. The Gang of Four was arrested and tried. Hua was gradually pushed aside by Deng over the next year or two. The reforms didn't really take hold until Deng came back to power for the third time. We realized even then that Hua was not a dominant figure.

THAYER: The team of China specialists working on U.S.-China relations was led by Bill Gleysteen, one of the ablest Foreign Service officers of his day, who came in as senior deputy assistant secretary under Dick Holbrooke, who was Vance's assistant secretary for East Asia and Pacific. Dick was vigorous, aggressive, intellectually very alive, clearly anxious to make his mark. So there was no doubt who was running the East Asia Bureau in the policy sense. Dick took a very strong interest in developing U.S.-China relations. Mike Oksenberg in the NSC was very high on and instrumental in moving the relationship along. We had some very good people. Burt Levin and Harvey Feldman on the Taiwan desk. Paul Kreisberg, the deputy head of policy planning staff at that time, had a role also. Mort Abramowitz, originally a China specialist, was deputy assistant secretary for International Security Affairs over in Defense. Later, on the China desk, Don Anderson and Lynn Pascoe were valued players, as was Chas Freeman, who was a key player on the task force set up after December 15, 1978, to coordinate the follow-on actions, including the Deng visit. There were some extremely able, highly motivated people involved in putting together a China policy as the Carter administration began to get in gear. Incidentally, there was a national security decision memorandum [regarding the recognition question] which ended up on the front pages of the *New York Times* because of some dispute allegedly going on about arms sales to the Chinese.[12]

Can you give a little feel for the atmosphere of the change-over from adminis-trations from your particular point of view in the China field? Was this a hos-tile takeover?

HUMMEL: During the transition from me to Dick Holbrooke as assistant secretary for East Asian Affairs in January 1977, when President Carter came in, I was in close touch with the transition team. We prepared all kinds of papers, we conducted oral briefings, outlining a host of posi-tions in the East Asian area, including the China situation, on which I personally briefed the new ambassador, Leonard Woodcock. During all of this time and after, when I was still in Washington, Holbrooke would never meet with me at any time. He didn't want to talk to me. Appar-ently, he didn't want his image to be sullied by fraternizing with the Republican team. We would set up a lunch, and his secretary would can-cel it. We never met. It was peculiar.

THAYER: Dick Holbrooke was an exceedingly able, controversial but able—I consider him a good friend—advocate of moving on U.S.-China relations, and he arranged, before inauguration, for a group of us to brief Secretary [Cyrus] Vance on U.S.-China relations and made cer-tain proposals to him before Carter took over, about where we should go on U.S.-China relations.

FREEMAN: Dick Holbrooke has the most brilliant policy mind that I have ever encountered. He is someone with enormous quickness to see the political realities of Washington and understand how to use those to create results. So he's a very driving personality, with acknowledged brilliance. He has succeeded then and subsequently because of that bril-liance, not because of his charm. He began his tenure, before my time, in the East Asian and Pacific region by throwing out a great number of older people and bringing in people with whom he felt more comfort-able. He paid a great deal of attention to personnel. He created a more dynamic bureau by doing that, but he broke a lot of rice bowls and made a lot of enemies. And he's infuriatingly distracted always. He would often have a meeting, with two television sets going, on different chan-nels, and while he was reading a newspaper, he would be discussing a policy issue. He has a notoriously short attention span, but somehow the sheer power of his intellect compensates for all of that.

THAYER: I never hesitated to disagree with Holbrooke, and did so in handwritten notes, in more formal memoranda, on the telephone, in person. Dick had the self-confidence and the open-mindedness never to take offense. He didn't feel his rank being challenged at all. He liked the intellectual give and take. And the result of this facet of his personality was that he picked brains and made creative people more creative.

U.S.-China, U.S.-Vietnam, and U.S.-Soviet policy all were entangled there, and this made the policy aspects of Holbrooke's job a lot more complicated than one would ordinarily think, because to some extent these three strands of policy were crossed, occasionally short-circuited, or blocked each other, and that was an important element.

Can you give some illustration of the types of things that were working to effect your operations vis-à-vis China?

THAYER: Well, I'll be a little cautious here, but just to say that often the [Zbigniew] Brzezinski [NSC] agenda was not the same as the Vance agenda [at State]. And, therefore, the Oksenberg [NSC] agenda was frequently not the same as the Thayer agenda or the Holbrooke agenda. So oftentimes not all the cards were on the table between NSC staff and the East Asia Bureau, and it took quite a lot of extra effort to keep track of what Oksenberg, on his own or on Zbig's behalf, was up to at any given time. To some extent the problems were almost endemic in that kind of a situation.

Why would the two people responsible in the NSC and in the State Department be moving in different directions?

THAYER: It's fair to say that there were differences between Vance, Holbrooke and Brzezinski, for example, on how fast we should move on U.S.-Vietnam relations, and that had some impact on how we perceived the pace of U.S.-PRC relations. Nayan Chanda covers this to some extent in his book *Brother Enemy*.[13] Because of differences in perception of the desired pace of these respective relationships, there were various tactical things that went along with that, differences between what the NSC would like to do and what the East Asia Bureau would like to do.

Brzezinski was of Polish extraction and renowned for hating the Russians. Did you find that Brzezinski had the same abhorrence for the Chinese, or was this pretty much a Polish-Russian thing?

FREEMAN: Brzezinski was viscerally anti-Russian, and his anti-Russian sentiment led him to be quite pro-Chinese. In other words, his concern about the Soviet Union was a geopolitical concern, not primarily an ideological concern. During his visit to China, he remarked to his Chinese hosts, when he went to the Great Wall, "Last one to the top gets to fight the Russians in Ethiopia." He had a sort of schoolboy-like, almost appealing, naive enthusiasm for sticking it to the Russians. And he liked the Chinese for that reason. I'm sure the Chinese found all this entertaining. They are a very sober-minded people, and I'm not quite sure what their reaction to Mr. Brzezinski was. On the other hand, they clearly knew that Mr. Brzezinski was a very strong supporter of the U.S.-China relationship.

THAYER: So it was a matter of working from a common bias, a shared vision of what we wanted to achieve. The real differences were in how we best go about it, and that was a natural and healthy process. The first part of this process, incidentally, was to analyze the many, many hours of conversations between Henry Kissinger and Zhou Enlai and Mao dating back to the first 1971 visit. The State Department had not had access to the records of those conversations until the Carter administration. So when Carter came in, one of the first things we were able to do was to get access to these records, which were held by the White House, and analyzed them to give us the platform from which we could then figure out how to move ahead. These records of the Kissinger meetings, we kept extremely carefully, double locked, and double sign-in and sign-out, read only in one room with a light off, etc. We were determined also that it was important to keep the confidence of the Chinese that we were serious in our purpose and not going to use these historic records loosely.

Was President Carter at the time a player on the China issue?

THAYER: President Carter was very much a player. Memoranda that we drafted went to the president, he read them, marked them. It was his personal decision—at least he was one of those who made the decision—that the access to the facts of the normalization negotiations, knowledge of that, be extremely restricted. And we restricted it within the State Department in 1978, kept it entirely in the East Asia Bureau, knowledge of negotiations, handled the paper extremely carefully. So the way we handled the Congress and the public side of normalization, the president was very much aware of and in favor of—encouraged it.[14]

DONALD ANDERSON: One big problem at this particular time was that the normalization negotiations, and some of the moves that were being made, were so highly restricted, so highly classified, that a lot of the other kinds of lower level measures that needed to be taken to prepare for it were not being taken because you couldn't tell the people that had to do it. For example, the legal adviser was called upon to perform heroic service when we were starting to move toward normalization and had to have some form of legislation to take care of Taiwan. Because of the relationship we had with Taiwan, we couldn't just simply say, "Good bye," and walk away. The Japanese had led the way with their arrangement that they had developed with Taipei after they normalized with Beijing, and we more or less followed some aspects of the Japanese model where we created in effect an embassy, but declared it a private, nonprofit, entity. That was all done through the Taiwan Relations Act [1979], and of course, this all had to be done in the context of the normalization negotiations. And much of it was very difficult to accomplish because the people you needed to do it couldn't be told why they were doing it. In early December '79, Ambassador Woodcock, who had been meeting with the Chinese foreign minister, had two meetings, or maybe three, with Deng Xiaoping. That was where the last pieces fell into place. I'm sure it took Deng Xiaoping himself to say, "All right, we will do these things." Then it was decided that they were going to do it.

Was the reason for such secret negotiations concern that American politics might intrude?

DONALD ANDERSON: Yes. There were several problems. One, there was concern about Taiwan. Taiwan actually got treated rather shabbily in terms of notification. They did not want Taiwan to know that we were about to make this move because Taiwan at that time had quite a strong lobby on the Hill. I don't think they wanted the Hill to know too far in advance. They did brief, but a very, very short time before it actually became known. And there was a good deal of resentment about that in the Congress as well. But they did not want a big political brouhaha blowing up with Congress passing emergency resolutions, and the top people on Taiwan going to their constituencies.

BELLOCCHI: Oh, the sad tales we would hear from Taipei on that. I've always been affected quite frankly by the very crude way we handled that situation in Taipei. The decision, of course, was almost inevitable that we were going to be recognizing China, but the way we handled even our own people! Our own people practically became the enemy, they cut off communications, they weren't getting their pay. There was no rational reason why we should consider just because they're in Taipei, that they should be treated that way. We decided to lower the boom, bang, everything had to be stopped immediately, leaving all those people out there high, wide, and dry. It was awful.

LILLEY: When [Warren] Christopher [deputy secretary of state] goes out [to Taiwan to begin negotiations on new diplomatic arrangements, there were] riots where they got hold of his car and tipped it and threw eggs on it. This is in Taiwan in December of '78. [The Americans] felt it had been contrived [by the government and GMD] and done by collusion in Taiwan. Perhaps it had been. This got people very angry. It got the State Department very angry.

DENG XIAOPING VISIT

Deng Xiaoping's whirlwind tour of the United States in January 1979 captured the imaginations and the hearts of many Americans. Pictures of this tiny Chinese leader, the first ever to visit the United States, riding around in a miniature stagecoach at a Texas rodeo wearing a ten-gallon hat ran in newspapers everywhere. Less remarked upon were his belligerent anti-Soviet statements and his muted hints that China would soon mount a campaign to teach Vietnam a lesson for its invasion of Cambodia.

THAYER: As we moved toward normalization, there began to be, partly by accident, partly nurtured by the Carter administration, a feeding of the American tendency to display a special emotion toward China. This was most illustrated during the visit of Deng to the United States. In a gala at the Kennedy Center, Deng came onto the stage and greeted a bunch of small children who had just done a dance of some kind. [Movie actress] Shirley MacLaine got up and made an absolutely inane speech about what a great people the Chinese were, and she also had the ignorance to say what a terrific thing the Cultural Revolution was.

Chas. W. Freeman, Jr. shaking hands with Deng Xiaoping as President
Jimmy Carter looks on. *Courtesy of Chas. W. Freeman, Jr.*

In any event, there was this euphoria about Chinese. American business was crawling all over each other to get a piece of the China action.
Bloomingdale's had its China-style furniture and its China days, and
China was really a sexy item in the United States. I felt at the time that
the administration was overselling China to the American public. It was
important that we help contribute to an atmosphere of increased
warmth in the relationship in order to bring both sides of the normalization equation up to the point of willingness to regularize the relationship. But China was oversold in 1978–79, just as we had oversold

Chiang Kai-shek in World War II. Americans were especially upset by Chiang Kai-shek's corruption because they expected something different. Americans were offended by the fact that in the post-'79 period, as the '80s moved along and then climaxed by the Tiananmen massacre, the Chinese turned out not to be saints and perfect partners after all. This is a long-standing problem in the relationship.

HUMMEL: Right after the visit by President Nixon in 1972, there was a huge flood of euphoria. It was absolutely unrealistic, both on the Chinese and on the American side. The Chinese became disillusioned that we weren't pouring lots of aid money in there, lending capital at low interest rates. So there was a kind of dip in the value which the Chinese attached to the American relationship.

At the time that full diplomatic relations were established, there was another wave of euphoria in our bilateral relations. We signed very quickly some 20 agreements of all kinds: trade, scientific relations, technology, exchange of persons, a Fulbright agreement, and various others. There was also an agreement on textile quotas. We introduced the Chinese to quotas at an early stage. That set off another wave of euphoria on the part of the Chinese. However, once again, the capital never materialized to the extent that the Chinese expected. On our side we were seeing the unlovely, unpleasant aspects of Chinese society in the draconian hand of the Communist Party of China and the fact that laws didn't mean very much. If a very high party official wanted something done, it was done—whether it was a good or bad thing or whether it would hurt American businessmen.

What were our concerns at the time of the Deng Xiaoping visit?

FREEMAN: There was considerable concern about the prospects for U.S.-China relations, in terms of congressional shenanigans on Taiwan, which centered on the Taiwan Relations Act [see below]. There was the Jackson-Vanik freedom of immigration issue to address.

HUMMEL: When Deng Xiaoping himself visited the U.S. in 1979, after the change in recognition, it was explained to him—and he finally grasped the idea—that we had legislation called the Jackson-Vanik Amendment. This was designed to promote, persuade, or force the Soviet government to allow Jews to emigrate from the Soviet Union. However, in that amendment there was a provision that, to have most favored nation tariff treatment, which we give to virtually everybody, a country with a communist or nonmarket economy would have to demonstrate that it had free emigration.[15] This was explained to Deng. He is supposed to have said, "Oh, that's easy! How many do you want? Ten million, fifteen million?"

FREEMAN: And that rather disposed of that issue.

REUTHER: Right. He did it with such a straight face that the Americans really did not know how to respond. In fact, after getting this promise from him we had to go around and say don't you dare do such a thing. This sort of illustrates that when you are dealing with China on its own, all the stereotypes from the Cold War, all the anti-Russian stuff, all the anti-Chinese Communist stuff really gets in your way.

FREEMAN: There was a mad scramble to get a series of basic framework-setting agreements for cultural exchange and other things in place. We had to do an enormous amount of administrative work to upgrade the embassy. There was the issue of who the ambassador was going to be, although it was fairly much a foregone conclusion that Leonard Wood-cock, having been the liaison office chief, would be the first ambassador, as indeed happened. At any rate, this work on the China working group was essentially completed by the middle of February 1979.

What was your impression of Leonard Woodcock? He came out of the American automobile union, an unlikely figure to head the Liaison Office or be ambassador, yet automobile union people are pretty tough, and we were up against some pretty tough people in China.

FREEMAN: Leonard Woodcock is a man of strong will and excellent, seasoned judgment, and personable. He was very much in charge, presiding over the Liaison Office. He had the respect and admiration of his staff, in part because he didn't pretend to expertise on China that he didn't and couldn't develop, not speaking Chinese and not having studied it. What he was was an excellent judge of character and a fine negotiator. He deferred on most questions to Stape [Stapleton] Roy, who was the deputy chief of the Liaison Office and later DCM in the embassy. He had a very fine staff of officers, quite gifted, reporting on China, and he used them well.

When we were preparing to host the Chinese vice premier, Deng Xiaoping, how did we view his position within China, and what were we trying to do?

FREEMAN: Deng Xiaoping had, at the age of 23, been secretary general of the Chinese Communist Party. He had been purged for anti-Soviet sentiment. He was purged a second time, during the Cultural Revolution, for anti-ideological sentiment, for pragmatism. He had arisen again, and he seemed to be in an increasingly unchallenged position. There had been, in 1978, a plenum of the Communist Party that basically embraced his aspirations for reform of the economy and an opening up of China.[16]

I suppose the White House, in looking at this, had several considerations. In terms of foreign policy, wanting to consolidate the China relationship and give it some momentum, thereby increasing leverage on the Soviet Union and on others, such as Vietnam, to whose activities, both internal and in Indochina, we strongly objected. There was, as always, some aspiration by the administration for the business opportunities that a normal relationship with China, especially a China that was opening its doors, might bring. In domestic terms, Deng Xiaoping's visit was seen by the administration as something that could turn the atmosphere, excitingly, in the direction of a favorable American view of relations with China.

DONALD ANDERSON: His visit was a tremendous success, and he was very popular everywhere he went. I accompanied the Deng party on that trip around the United States. Everywhere he went there was a degree of tension because there were the Chinese Nationalists and some people were out with the Chinese Nationalist flag, etc. But by and large his reception was very warm, and he handled himself very well.

Did he understand the Chinese Nationalists element in the United States? Was he surprised?

DONALD ANDERSON: I don't think he was surprised. I mean, they're pretty sophisticated on that subject, and they follow it extremely closely themselves. It was obviously one of their concerns, and one of the things they talked to us at the working level about. "We understand there's been a few demonstrations here, and what are you going to do about them? Will you make sure that they are kept at a certain distance," etc. So they were expecting it, and it was managed I think in a way that satisfied them.

TAIWAN RELATIONS ACT

In order to maintain American ties with Taiwan after formal diplomatic relations ended, substitute structures had to be created and a new legal status introduced for diplomatic, cultural, and economic exchanges. The Carter administration submitted legislation to Congress early in 1979, but members angrily rejected the proposed law as too weak and unresponsive to Taiwan needs and American interests. Over the following weeks the Taiwan Relations Act (TRA) emerged. It specified a security agenda, including the continuation of arms sales, an injunction that resolution of the Taiwan Straits stalemate be peaceful, and the warning that any use of force would be viewed with grave concern by the United States. Members of the administration were sufficiently worried about provoking China with this bill that they contemplated a presidential veto, but the overwhelming support for the legislation in Congress suggested that the White House had no real choice. Carter explained to the Chinese that he would interpret the act in ways consistent with their normalization accord, and Deng agreed to be mollified.

THAYER: There were surprisingly little differences within the government, within the executive branch, relating to Taiwan. There wasn't a manifestation of the China Lobby in my office or in the East Asia Bureau or in the legal advisor's office. At least it wasn't an important factor. Every one of us were convinced that we had to retain some kind of relationship with Taiwan, that the continuation of arm sales was important and that American businesses must have access and so forth—even though these things were not all covered fully in our initial presentation of the Taiwan Relations Act. But there was a unanimity about the overall project. The project was to normalize relations with the PRC, to retain some kind of relationship between the people of the United States and the people of Taiwan, because it was pretty well understood we would have to break diplomatic relations with Taiwan.

On something as sensitive as changing our relationship with Taiwan, did you keep Congress informed? Did you have a dialogue with staff members?

THAYER: Dick Holbrooke is very much a political animal and worked hard to maintain and develop personal ties on the Hill. For example, he invited the head of the East Asia and Pacific Affairs Subcommittee of the House

Foreign Affairs Committee—Lester Wolff, in those days, Congressman Wolff of New York—to sit with us at a weekly East Asia staff meeting.[17] So he was very sensitive about the need for congressional support and consulted carefully with a whole range of people on both sides of the Hill. Our consultations on China were informal, and we talked often, at all levels, with individual members of both houses, Republican and Democrat, and their staffs. We also testified in informal committee sessions. But State did not have what the Congress felt was appropriate consultations on China. And the Hill raised holy hell with us and with the president when he announced the normalization of relations with China, explicitly accusing that we had not consulted Congress adequately.

In fact, we had told them virtually everything in substance, but we hadn't said, "And we plan to do this so-and-so at such-and-such a time, and we are negotiating these things right at this very time." But to any reader of the newspapers, it was obvious that there was a lot going on in the relationship, a lot of signs of progress in the relationship. Brzezinski visited China in May 1978. Others in the Executive Branch went. And also there were congressional visitors, a lot of them, going to Beijing at the time. We encouraged a lot of this. So there was no question that the Congress could get the message, but formal consultations, consultations that the Congress felt were adequate, no.

Congress has all kinds of people in it, and there were plenty of people in Congress who were very strong supporters of Chiang Kai-shek and Taiwan. There was obviously a lot of resistance to any break in relations with Taiwan. We did not want to derail the normalization negotiations by tipping our hand too much on the Hill in terms of timing or details of an agreement.

FREEMAN: There was a lawsuit, by [Senator] Barry Goldwater [R-AZ] and others, to set aside the president's termination notice for the mutual defense treaty with the Republic of China, and to claim that the Senate, having consented to the making of the treaty, had to consent to its unmaking. That ultimately produced a Supreme Court decision that reaffirmed the president's power.[18]

Were we keeping the Taiwan side informed of what we were doing?

THAYER: We had, in earlier years, informed the Republic of China Chinese Embassy, about the outlines of progress or lack of progress in the

Warsaw talks. But we were then in a different mode with the PRC. By 1977, we were not keeping Taipei fully informed about our discussions with the PRC.[19] By 1978, we were not even keeping State's policy planning staff informed.

Did you have the feeling that the Republic of China government had braced itself for a new type of relationship, as long as there was a solid relationship with the United States?

THAYER: Well, the Chinese from Taiwan saw our peaceful relations with the PRC probably as constructive, but they certainly were never in favor of U.S. breaking relations with the Republic of China. However, they were aware that plenty was going on. Any reader of the newspaper would know. The signals were there, but we were not spelling it out for them.

In the end, we sought, as part of the normalization plan, to establish a relationship with Taiwan, something along the so-called "Japanese model," which was an unofficial relationship but carrying out pretty much the same functions as in an official relationship. And so the Japanese model, which we examined very closely, was the basis for our approach. As it turned out, we needed—much more than the Japanese had needed—to do a lot more U.S. internal legal adjustments to be in a position to carry on a relationship with Taipei. We needed laws to make it possible for Foreign Service officers to be separated from the Foreign Service and work unofficially in Taipei, because we were determined, among other things, to be as good as our word. That is to say: our relationship with Taiwan was going to be conducted on a non-official basis. Well, we put together the Taiwan Relations Act, which would establish the American Institute in Taiwan and its legal structure. We sent a draft Taiwan Relations Act to the Hill after the president's announcement on December 15, 1978.

FREEMAN: While at the Harvard Law School I wrote a series of papers, basically for policy planning, which dealt with the question of Taiwan. And the legal research I did became the basis of the Taiwan Relations Act. I worked hard on the major issue of how to deal with Taiwan in a political-legal sense, and the details of how to manage an Export-Import Bank relationship with a noncountry, and how to ensure that Taiwan's foreign-exchange reserves in the United States were secure, and how to deal with the issues of embassy and consular property, privileges and immunities, and how to ensure that full faith and credit was given to court decisions by a place that didn't legally exist, and so forth.

The [drafters of the TRA] essentially cut the gordian knot by inserting a provision that said that, notwithstanding any other provision of U.S. law, Taiwan would be treated like a country even if it wasn't one, and by handling the defense treaty with a one-year termination notice.

THAYER: The reception to the Taiwan Relations Act on the Hill was outrage. What we did was to send up a package which covered the legal requirements of establishing this unofficial relationship but did not have the political elements such as security concerns that the friends of the Republic of China, in particular, but also many others of a more neutral stance, thought was appropriate for the circumstances. The administration badly underestimated what the Hill reaction was going to be to this skeleton of a Taiwan Relations Act. It wasn't broad enough for the Congress. We didn't present it in the best possible way. And we got torn apart by the Congress for this.

From your perspective, did Congress strengthen it, harm it, skew it?

THAYER: Well, Congress took our skeletal Taiwan Relations Act designed for specific operational purposes and made it into a political document which went far beyond what the administration had intended. But the administration was able to avoid the most troublesome aspects being proposed that would tend to re-officialize the U.S. relationship with Taiwan. For example, we did not want in the Taiwan Relations Act any reference to the Republic of China, for perfectly obvious reasons. We didn't recognize the Republic of China; therefore, it would be inappropriate to refer to it by that name.

One of the things that we did in normalization was to give a one-year notice of abrogation of our mutual security treaty. We sought to not have any formal security commitment introduced into the Taiwan Relations Act. So there was a lot of dispute over this, a lot of very hot, heartfelt, outraged dispute with many of those opposed to the administration policy absolutely convinced that the administration was engaging in an immoral act by breaking relations with Taiwan. The administration was equally convinced that what we were doing was very much in the national interest, entirely appropriate, and moral, as long as we maintained these people-to-people relations with Taiwan. But there was a lot of blood on the floor in the process.

Usually, Congress is a burr under the administration's saddle, but sometimes it can use Congress to do what has to be done, and then say my hands are tied. Was this what happened?

FREEMAN: It was a bit of both, actually. The administration would have preferred to have been less forthright about the American interest in peace and security in the Taiwan area, and certainly would have preferred less definitive language on arms sales to Taiwan. But, in the end, faced with congressional demands for language that might have queered normalization, it was necessary to compromise.

How did the PRC react?

THAYER: Well, we had made clear to the PRC Chinese all along that there would be certain legal steps we'd have to go through. They didn't like that, but we hadn't explained to them the kind of Taiwan Relations Act that there would end up being because we didn't know. The Chinese were not happy about what was produced by the Congress.

What was your impression of how the People's Republic of China was dealing with Congress? Were the leaders pretty well informed about how the system worked?

THAYER: The Chinese liaison office was staffed by people who were pretty competent. Some of them had been educated in the States. Others had served for a long time in the liaison office. The liaison office had quite good relations with and access to the Hill. I'm sure they were surprised by the amount of activity for continued support of the Republic of China on the Hill, and they didn't expect the kind of Taiwan Relations Act they would get.

It's pretty damn hard for any country to understand how our political system works, and it's particularly difficult for a China that had been so out of touch with the U.S. for so long. But they had people following U.S. affairs in Beijing over the years, and they had their American experts and so forth. But it's quite a different thing in understanding the dynamics of Congress. After all, the Carter administration misread the strength of the Congress's reaction.

You're saying the State Department, even the Carter administration, really misjudged the vehemence which Congress would react to this.

THAYER: Well, it seems to me we did and so did the PRC. But the PRC consistently made it clear that it was our responsibility to keep our own house in order, and the PRC quite understandably did not want to take responsibility for the way the U.S. Congress behaved.

Did you have the feeling that at any time our new establishment of relations was being jeopardized by the Congress as we worked on the TRA?

THAYER: There were risks there if some of the language proposed by the—for want of a better term—right wing in Congress, if some of the language proposed had stayed in the Taiwan Relations Act, it would have violated certain specific and implicit undertakings to the Chinese.

FREEMAN: I was the one who drew up the list of potential names of the Taiwan organization here. They picked "The Coordination Council for North American Affairs." The idea was to avoid any geographic reference to China or Taiwan, and to avoid the words "United States" or any implication of what they called "officiality," a word that they invented. Elements of officiality were what the Nationalist Chinese were seeking in the negotiations.

Taiwan's negotiations were run by one of the most distinguished and able diplomats I have ever had the opportunity to observe, Yang Hsi-k'un. He was, of course, castigated for achieving less than Taipei wanted. But he came to the negotiating table with virtually no cards, and he manufactured cards. It was an extraordinarily skillful performance: on the level of rhetoric, tugging at the American heartstrings; at the level of practicality, devising solutions; at the level of tactics, integrating intelligence with negotiation.

Taiwan, it turned out, had a mole in the Situation Room at the White House. And the most infamous example of Ambassador Yang's ability to use this came one day when Roger Sullivan, who was heading the U.S. negotiating effort, was to have met, I believe at 10:30, with Yang, to present a specific proposal that Jimmy Carter had personally reviewed. There was a handwritten note from Jimmy Carter to Roger Sullivan that instructed him what to say. As it happened, that meeting was postponed by the State Department until 11: 30. At eleven o'clock, Senator Dick Stone of Florida called Roger Sullivan and protested what he had just said to Yang, though, of course, he hadn't said it yet. This handwritten note, in one copy, had somehow found its way from this mole in the Situation Room directly to the Republic of China Embassy, and had been promptly acted upon in terms of invoking congressional opposition.

It sounds very much like the situation with Israel in the United States, where you have strong partisans, with good political credentials.

FREEMAN: There certainly are some similarities. There was a strong ideological bond with Taiwan. Years of cooperation had created personal bonds of some importance. Taiwan has an intelligence service that was initially trained by the Russians, later by the Nazis, and then by us, which has its own competence, and which has worked very effectively in the United States, and which, when this crunch came, had people in the right places to do what had to be done. I later discovered (this is jumping ahead a bit, to when I was country director for China from July of '79 to July of 1981) that my weekly written reports to Dick Holbrooke were being read in Taipei. A friend in Taipei sent me a copy of one of these highly classified reports, after urging me to tone it down, because I was sometimes quite flip. The FBI never was able to identify who it was who was providing this and getting it into Taiwan's hands.

Taiwan is comparable to the case of Israel in the sense that the partisans of Taiwan, like the partisans of Israel, believe that they have the right to act to protect the interests of their second homeland or their much-admired foreign counterpart, and that they can exercise this judgment independently of the rest of the government because there is a higher cause involved. Taiwan makes very few enemies and many friends, because it relies on patient cultivation of relationships, and does not overburden those relationships, except at moments of dire need.

Taiwan's sources of sympathy are multiple. They may be people who have studied in Taiwan and come to have an affinity with that Chinese culture. They may be anti-communist ideologues. They may be people who, simply out of venality, have accepted a financial relationship with Taiwan's intelligence service. Taiwan, moreover, now has forty, fifty years of experience lobbying in the United States. Taipei got increasingly sophisticated about lobbying, publicity, public relations, and the courtship of interest groups.

In 1980, U.S. trade with the Chinese mainland was booming. In fact, in that year, the Chinese were buying one out of every seven bales of cotton produced in the United States, and had emerged as a major factor in some key American economic sectors. But no one was aware of this. It was as though the Chinese found this embarrassing and they wished to keep it secret. I knew it, as country director, and presumably the Board of Trade in Chicago knew it, and the cotton traders knew it, but no one else knew it.

But if Taiwan bought a Q-Tip cotton swab, that little bit of cotton would be trotted out by a congressman, who would say, "I have with me my dear friend Mr. Lee, from Taipei, who has just bought this bit of cotton. This was grown in our district, and it will increase employment. And you can see how important this relationship is." Taiwan, of course, very cleverly understood that allowing a congressman to announce that sort of deal, however small it might be, ingratiated the congressman, who then owed one to Taiwan. This helped the congressman's re-election. It gained publicity for Taiwan, of a favorable nature, in the district. And no official had to be there. So they did this with great skill.

They courted governors. President Clinton, prior to becoming president, when he was governor of Arkansas, was in Taiwan four times. The lure, to a governor, of being able to take a trade delegation over to Taiwan, do some business, and get some publicity back home as a promoter of state exports, was simply irresistible.

They had a really very subtle and effective publication, which I have always enjoyed looking at, both for what it contains and for the technique that it embraces, called *The Free China Weekly*, which is a sort of tabloid that comes out every week, with a bit of information about Taiwan and cross-Strait relations (Taiwan Strait), Taiwan versus the mainland, and interaction between all of the above. It very skillfully flogs three to five different themes in each issue, written in colloquial American English. They have a very slick publication on trade that they put out.

They have by far the most professional and skilled congressional-relations staff of any foreign regime represented here. They are much better than the Israelis, who are usually regarded as the best, because, whereas the Israelis gain their way by threatening political retaliation through Jewish or right-wing, Christian, pro-Israel supporters, Taiwan threatens no one. Everything is done by inducement. In the long run, courtship is more effective as a tie that binds than ultimata and threats.

So Taiwan has brought to bear on diplomacy all of the skills of interpersonal relations that Chinese culture embodies, and they've done it supremely well because, as a small place overshadowed by the rest of China, they've had to try harder. The PRC, by contrast, is much more similar to the pre-modern China of the Emperor Qianlong, who told George III to take his trinkets and buzz off, because China had no need for intercourse with barbarians.[20]

As Taiwan's economic prosperity has advanced and its democratization has proceeded, it has had an easier and easier task of selling itself in the United States, since it has, in fact, become increasingly admirable as a society, and its natural affinities with Americans have grown, rather than diminished.

How about the human rights situation at that time? How did you see the political situation evolving when you were there?

BURNET: Washington let us know that they were not *just* interested in the annual human rights reports which were just getting going in those days. The record of [the] Republic of China was not very good in this area. Arrests of the opposition, throwing people into the poky for a long period of time and virtually forgetting about them, were going on all the time. So we had to burrow into the political opposition among the Taiwanese, which wasn't hard to find, and they were always glad to talk to us. They knew what was going on. They knew who was in jail, and where, and how long they had been there, and what they had done to get there, and what happened at their trial.[21]

Was the Taipei government responding?

BURNET: Yes they were. We were effective and our pressure helped. And all other kinds of outside pressure helped, too. Somebody would lean on Washington about a certain individual, and then we'd go to the Chinese and say: Look, we hear he's not well, he's not getting proper food and medicine. How long is he going to be there? And can you see your way clear to make things easier on him or even release him? We'd do it, and we'd get responses from them. We got results, slow, but we got them.

RELATIONS WITH THE PRC

Even before full diplomatic relations had been established between the United States and China a range of contacts flourished. Trade grew and cultural exchanges multiplied. Strategic and military cooperation proved possible, with the United States easing restrictions on advanced technology exports and declaring that, although it would not directly sell weapons to Beijing, it would no longer object if its European allies did so. But real collaboration in the security arena followed recognition when the Soviet Union invaded Afghanistan. After that, the United States placed monitoring stations on Chinese soil, authorized nonlethal military sales, and worked with China to support the Afghan resistance. Increasingly Chinese and American policies on a range of issues, from Cambodia to NATO, coincided.

FREEMAN: The normalization of relations set off an avalanche of American official travel to China. For a period, the relationship was trip-driven. That is, it was driven by the requirement of senior officials, on both sides, but especially in the United States, to produce results from visits that they made.

But these trips were mainly for people who wanted to go see the other side of the moon, weren't they?

FREEMAN: They were motivated by many factors. There was serious business to be done. There was a scramble by bureaucracies to establish relations with their Chinese opposite numbers. There were people like Mike Blumenthal, the secretary of the treasury, who had been born in Shanghai and who wanted to go back. There was a natural curiosity. There was an element of tourism. There was prestige associated with a visit, and publicity and public prominence. And there was the possibility of achieving things—which is not the case on every trip—because the United States and China suddenly faced the requirement to establish, in short order, the sort of relationship we might have developed over decades had we had relations. State governors, congressional delegations, business delegations, and scientific delegations crossed the Pacific between China and the United States and began to really build a deep and cooperative relationship, and to explore the potential for trade and investment, although investment was not yet really possible directly, and for cooperation on science and technology.

HUMMEL: There was a flood of Chinese students to many countries, but mostly to the United States. So there was a very substantial flow of Chinese out of the PRC and American students into the PRC, quite often for the purpose of teaching English. They were welcome everywhere and were scattered all over China. Quite often they were studying Chinese on the side. Some of them were going to special language schools around the country. But the American presence was everywhere in China.

FREEMAN: Another current was knitting the two bureaucracies together, the bureaucracies in Beijing and in Washington. They had two motives. One, the Chinese record and Chinese achievement in some areas provided unique data and insight. For example, in the area of astronomy, Chinese records are the longest and most complete on astronomical events. Access to these records was very important to astronomers and physicists studying interstellar events. If you look at the public-health area, there are records in China of very large populations that have been subjected to consistent environmental stress (for example, elements in the drinking supply), which allow you to study the impact of the environment on the human body in a way that can't be done easily elsewhere. In the two years that I was there ('79-'81), we were on a bit of a roller coaster. I either personally negotiated or oversaw the negotiation of some 36 treaties and agreements.

But I have to say that, politically, the motivation for doing all this was very clear, and that is that those of us charged with promoting U.S.-China relations wished to ensure that the relationship was sufficiently broad and engaged a sufficient number of bureaucracies and special interests on both sides so that it would be insulated, to some extent, from political cross currents.

HUMMEL: Another thing that happened that turned out to be unexpectedly beneficial was the formation of the Foreign Commercial Service. When this subject was first raised, I was dead against it. I think that most Foreign Service officers were. We felt that our Economic Sections could and should be able to be staffed to do this kind of thing. As it turned out, there is now a good demarcation between economic reporting and negotiations, and assisting American firms to take advantage of bidding opportunities, to give them advice when they come to the country for the first time, and so on.

How did the Chinese respond to the Afghan coup in December 1979 and the subsequent Soviet invasion of Afghanistan?

FREEMAN: Their initial reaction, rather similar to ours, was quite panicked, for several reasons. China and the United States have long shared a relationship of alliance, or at least patronage, with regard to Pakistan. In the case of the United States, that relationship's been quite erratic and had its good and bad moments. In the case of the Chinese, it's been very steady. And the Afghan invasion was an obvious threat, immediately, to Pakistan, to its territorial integrity, stability, and perhaps to its very existence, especially given the Indian-Soviet collusion on many matters. But the Chinese, rather quickly, within a matter of a month or two, concluded that, in fact, the Soviets were more likely to become bogged down and regret their Afghan adventure than to use it as a springboard for further advance.

U.S.-China cooperation, conducted primarily through intelligence channels, with money from many sources, was absolutely central to creating the Mujahedin resistance to the Soviet invasion. And that program cemented relationships between the United States and China in yet another dimension.[22]

VIETNAM

Among Richard Nixon's major motives for reconciliation with China had been settlement of the Vietnam War. Although it is not clear that China did much to facilitate the Paris Peace Talks, it did not try to prevent them, either. Once the United States and Vietnam reached their agreements, the Sino-Vietnamese relationship quickly began to unravel. China refused Vietnamese requests for increased economic assistance, and when ethnic tensions flared between Vietnamese and Vietnam's Chinese population leading to expulsions, China suspended aid and technical support. Soon Hanoi turned to the Soviets, concluding an alliance with Moscow in 1977.

THAYER: In the period of '68 to '70, we were looking for opportunities to improve our relationship with the PRC and did everything we could to keep the Vietnam thing from interfering with that.

LILLEY: [The idea of opening to China] became more attractive in the Vietnam War. They had 80,000 troops supporting the Vietnam effort. They were building roads and sending in supplies. And we had not really picked up the signs of dissension between the Chinese and Vietnam which were there. Our [intelligence] penetrations really weren't good enough to expose this.

FREEMAN: In fact, we were phasing down; we were in the Vietnamization period. The president had given his speech at Guam, the Guam Doctrine, which was welcome to the Chinese, because it clearly implied the United States was pulling back into a support role, not just in Vietnam, but generally in Asia, playing more of a balancing rather than active and aggressive role.

In the talks with Bill Rogers [in 1972], which I interpreted, Vietnam and the whole question of Indochina figured very prominently. We spent hours and hours on this, to no particular avail. The Chinese had the position that they were not a direct party. They obviously agreed with the Vietnamese and not with us. I don't believe that much was accomplished except perhaps explaining to them a bit more about our reasoning, such at it was.

LORD: It's hard to judge now how nervous the Kissinger trip made Hanoi. It certainly didn't make the Vietnamese communist leaders immediately flexible. However, we figured that the combination of the announcement of both of these summit meetings was certainly going to put pressure on Hanoi to be more reasonable. We hoped, of course, that this would give an incentive to both Beijing and Moscow to put such pressure on Hanoi because, for example, with Beijing there was an ideological embarrassment in negotiating with the U.S., which was fighting with their compatriots. We didn't realize fully at the time the extent of the Sino-Vietnamese hostility, either. We assumed at the time that, if they were not like lips and teeth, as they had once likened their relationship, at least the Chinese and Vietnamese communists were friendly.[23]

Nixon had hoped that Beijing would help the United States extricate itself from Vietnam. Did China intervene with Vietnam?

LORD: I don't think that the Chinese ever leaned heavily on Hanoi. They were helpful to us in their own self interest. The North Vietnamese position for years was that the U.S. not only had to withdraw unilaterally but, as we left, we have to overthrow the government of Nguyen Van Thieu and replace it with a coalition government. We made our position clear as early as the fall of 1969, that we could live with a unilateral withdrawal as well as a cease-fire, a return of POW's [prisoners of war], and international supervision. However, we made clear to the Chinese that it is one thing to have a military settlement. It's another thing to ask us to overthrow an ally and to decide for the Vietnamese people themselves their political future. We said that we're not going to do that. We said that if you want us as a balancing force in Asia, and particularly against the Soviet Union, as well as a restraint on Japan, you should support us. If the Japanese felt insecure, they might feel a need to remilitarize and develop nuclear weapons. We said that if the Chinese want us to play this role, which is in their interest, they can't have us humiliated in Vietnam, making all of our allies and friends around the world think that we are totally untrustworthy.

What was your perspective on the Vietnam peace talks?

DONALD ANDERSON: We kept the Chinese very well informed on positions that we were taking. Again, I was something of a mailman. I was the guy that Bill Sullivan would send out to the Chinese embassy at night to deliver papers and messages, and talk to the Chinese about what our positions were going to be. Basically the Paris peace talks were a means for the United States to exit Vietnam. I mean it's a very controversial agreement, but at the time, viewed with a great deal of relief by most of the people that were involved.[24]

We saw Vietnam and China as being part of one big communist conspiracy. When did we notice the split?

FREEMAN: It really developed over the course of 1978. The relationship between China and Vietnam was always a great deal more complex and nuanced than what we perceived. First, it is an article of faith for many American specialists on Vietnam that the Chinese played a minor role in the war. On one level, that's correct; on another, it isn't. For example, I have spoken with Chinese generals, including one who was present in Da Nang when the Marines landed in 1965, and watched the battle with the Vietnamese, as an advisor. There were Chinese all over the place, intermingled with the North Vietnamese, not with the Viet Cong. There were Chinese in Cambodia. And, of course, there were Chinese defenders of the railway system in North Vietnam. So the Chinese were strong backers of Vietnam, in terms of advice and support and providing a sort of secure rear area for the Vietnamese.

On another level, of course, there was no affection between them at all. Vietnam's main partner was the Soviet Union, not China.[24] China and the Soviet Union were in a virtual state of war, so it was an uneasy relationship. Ideologically, the Vietnamese were Soviet-oriented, not Chinese-oriented. China had little appeal to anyone, except the Khmer Rouge, in the middle of the Cultural Revolution. The Khmer Rouge, who had a connection with the Chinese Gang of Four and who fell out of favor with China after the fall of the Gang of Four, were in a terrible relationship with the Vietnamese. I know some Chinese military men who were with the Khmer Rouge, who described firefights with Vietnamese units even back in the '60s and '70s.

In the spring of '78, as events in Cambodia took their course, and as Vietnam began to become more and more threatening to Cambodia, and as the Vietnamese lock on Laos got stronger, the Chinese-Vietnamese relationship began to deteriorate substantially. And it was very clear, that, after the Vietnamese invasion of Cambodia, the Chinese would react. Which indeed they did, shortly after Deng Xiaoping left Washington.[25]

It was clear that China was about to administer a lesson (actually an entire curriculum) to Vietnam, in response to Vietnam's invasion of Cambodia. Indeed, one of the motives for Deng Xiaoping's compromises with the United States on normalization was to clear the American flank before addressing the issue of Vietnamese imperialism and the occupation of Cambodia. At one level [in the United States], there was a malicious delight in some quarters about the prospect of the Chinese administering a drubbing to the Vietnamese, which they did, though at a huge cost to themselves. On another level, there was apprehension about the implications of this sort of Chinese activism in Southeast Asia.

That Sino-Vietnamese interaction is poorly understood. The purpose of the use of force is not to avoid casualties on your side, and not to inflict damage. It is to make a political point. The political point the Chinese wanted to make to Vietnam was that they could take Hanoi, if they wished. They demonstrated that. It cost them more, and it revealed more weaknesses in their armed forces, than they anticipated. Indeed, it provoked a thoroughgoing reform of the Chinese military, as those lessons were digested. But the Vietnamese themselves, in talking about these battles, describe a level of ferocity and level of casualties on their side that was vastly greater than anything they experienced at the hands of the Americans. The political point was made.

LILLEY: In '75, '76, '77, the Chinese military was really in bad shape. They had been somewhat discredited in the Cultural Revolution. They had to move in and restore order after the Red Guards went wild. They had no modern equipment since the Russian equipment in the '50s. So they were pretty backward. Our military didn't have any people in China until after normalization in '79, [but] wanted to reach out to them. But they were sort of kept away, although there were some subterranean contacts between the two. I suppose one of the breakthroughs came when we took the trip out there in '78 with Jim Schlesinger, who was then secretary of energy. Energy controls all of our nuclear weapons. So he wanted to get into all of these discussions with the Chinese, particularly since the Vietnamese were getting ready to clobber Cambodia. You were seeing the fall of the Shah [in Iran] right then and there [at the end of 1978]. Oh, things were changing. Carter was trying to move in the direction of making up to Vietnam and the Chinese were turning against Vietnam, and the Vietnamese were getting ready to invade Cambodia. It was a very messy time. And I remember Li Xiannian, who was then president of China, really dumped on the Vietnamese, and he said, "How can you Americans, after what they did to you, go back and cultivate these guys? They took money from us. They are the worst, lying, hypocritical people." And then, of course, one year later China was moving in on them [February 17, 1979]. And we sort of stood back from that and gave them some encouragement on this because they were moving in to hit Vietnam after the Vietnamese had moved in and taken out Pol Pot.[26]

Then the Chinese get hit themselves very hard and this really showed Deng how bad the army had become. Deng had known this back as early as '75. We've got some Chinese secret documents that Deng was fed up with the Chinese military. He said they're fat, and they're lazy, and they're disorganized, and then this Vietnam thing almost proved it.

FREEMAN: The Chinese, for a long time thereafter, in what we would consider to be a remarkably cynical fashion, used the Vietnamese border as the live-fire training ground for their troops. It was real live fire. They rotated entire divisions through there on a regular basis, to give their military a taste of combat. The Vietnamese obviously are a very skilled infantry, perhaps the best in the world, and they were used by China to good effect. The basic point was to demonstrate to Vietnam that it could not afford a hostile relationship with China, and it could not exercise a regional imperialism in disregard of Chinese interests. And that point was made.

Do you think this was understood by the China watchers at that time?

FREEMAN: Oh, I believe so. I believe so. At any rate, this issue was, in public perception, a background issue, but in official perception in Washington, it was very much a central issue during the Deng Xiaoping visit.

HONG KONG

The decade of the 1970s proved a peaceful and prosperous one for Hong Kong. Concerns that U.S.-China rapprochement could undercut the status of the British colony did not seriously destabilize local politics even though, immediately upon its admission into the United Nations, China removed Hong Kong from the list of colonial territories entitled to eventual self-determination.

What was the business climate like in Hong Kong at the time you were there?

BELLOCCHI: This was in the '70s, when they really started to take off with a lot of industries. First of all, it was a transition from the old seat of the pants Shanghai-types who represented all these large corporations, to the professional managerial class coming in. And electronics were just beginning in those days.

Who were you talking to about China?

BELLOCCHI: It's funny, maybe its changed now, but in my time the Americans and the British community weren't all that close. I mean it wasn't an adversarial relationship, but they had their friends and we had ours. There was much more mix with the Hong Kong Chinese than there was with the British.

The Hong Kong people were not looking towards Taiwan, but looking towards . . .

BELLOCCHI: The outside world. Taiwan, that could have been in Mars as far as the people were concerned. Someone from Taiwan would come down and speak Mandarin, they would assume he's from the mainland, and they didn't want anything to do with him. They didn't think about Taiwan at all, it was just off their radar scope.

Did the Vietnam War have any impact on operations in Hong Kong?

BELLOCCHI: There was a lot of R&R in Hong Kong, so it was commercially quite a boon to Hong Kong with all these troops coming in. In Hong Kong, as long as they were making money they were happy. There were demonstrations in which some of our [younger] officers actually went out with the demonstrators. It was peaceful demonstration, they weren't throwing eggs or anything. But that was appalling.

SHOESMITH: At the same time as the Hong Kong government was receiving Vietnamese boat refugees, giving them first asylum, they were returning people who fled the mainland of China into Hong Kong.[27] They would be rounded up from time to time and sent back to the mainland. Of course, some of those people who came in had relatives in Hong Kong. So the relatives and other persons who were sympathetic took exception to the fact that the Hong Kong government was giving this asylum and receiving these refugees while it was turning away the people coming in from China. The difference, of course, was that the Hong Kong government had a commitment that these refugees would not be permanent residents in Hong Kong. They would be resettled [primarily in the United States, Canada, and Australia], whereas those who came in from the mainland were seeking permanent residence.

In the period you were there, were people beginning to feel concerned, particularly the wealthy Chinese merchant class, about the mainland claim on Hong Kong?

DEVLIN: Yes, they were. Every year that that came closer, there was something of a decline in their willingness to reinvest in the economy, more apprehension of what would happen, a greater desire to ensure that their children would be able to get to the United States, get to England or Australia. The United States, Canada, and England were the major objectives. It was difficult to get into Australia.

Hong Kong was the preeminent China watching place for years, all of a sudden we open an office in Beijing, so what's Hong Kong doing?

DONALD ANDERSON: The two brought two different kinds of attributes. In Beijing you have the ability to talk to people, you can get out on the streets, you're interacting with the Foreign Ministry and other ministries in the government. There is a large political relationship to be managed, which requires an on-the-spot presence of an embassy. Hong Kong, on the other hand, has a number of advantages. One is resources. There is a Foreign Service national staff there, a local Chinese staff, many of whom have worked for the consulate for 20 or more years, who have followed these developments and have a historical memory that is invaluable. And being Chinese they can get through Chinese materials twice as fast as any American regardless of how good his language is. And then there is the international press, and a whole China watching community there. And a very substantial intelligence operation [at least until reversion in 1997]. There are intelligence resources there that you don't have anywhere else. And its been very interesting that over a long period of time you get a different perspective from Beijing and Hong Kong. Usually, when events are breaking, Hong Kong tends to be more on the pessimistic side that things are going wrong, or that there is a power struggle going on. And in Beijing, living right in the community, the inclination is to see things as being more normal than they look from the outside.

1980s

DIPLOMATIC RELATIONS BETWEEN Washington and Beijing did not solve all problems between China and the United States, but considerable progress became possible in the decade following the decision officially to recognize one another. In China a reform era began in December 1978, with Deng Xiaoping's innovations at the third plenum of the Eleventh Central Committee, where the CCP agreed to reemphasize Zhou Enlai's Four Modernizations of agriculture, industry, science and technology, and military affairs. This plenum proved a watershed event, even though change in various sectors, such as the elimination of communes, had begun on a local level before the meeting. Deng initiated reform primarily to remedy internal deficiencies, of course, but eagerly sought American markets and technology to give impetus to change and found relations with the United States easier to legitimize as a result of the reform movement.

The effort gained momentum during the 1980s, and the opening to the United States did, as hoped, provide economic benefits. Trade between the United States and China rose rapidly, climbing from just over $4 billion in 1983 to some $13.5 billion by 1988. American investment also climbed steadily from a mere $18 million early in the decade to $1.5 billion at the end of 1988. So too did the flow of Chinese students to the United States rise where, by 1988, some 40,000 studied in American universities. A tourism industry also emerged, with roughly 300,000 Americans traveling in China in 1988.

Of course the new exposure to Americans did not always prove easy for the Chinese Communist leadership, particularly in the post-Cultural Revolution era when ordinary Chinese insisted upon expanding the boundaries of political expression. Growing American and Western cultural and political influences prompted efforts to retrench. Thus there were campaigns against bourgeois liberalization (1980–1981), spiritual pollution (1983–1984), and, in the early 1990s, peaceful evolution (the specter of Secretary of State John Foster Dulles was revived to warn against Western subversion). Not all political upheaval could be blamed on Americans. The Democracy Wall Movement (1978–1979), during which posters and periodicals called for political reform, flourished as a result of a power struggle between Deng Xiaoping and Hua Guofeng (Mao's designated heir). The subsequent crackdown (1979–1980) led to the imprisonment of Wei Jingsheng, the man who became China's most internationally recognized dissident. After a period of repression, political radicals resurfaced with new demands for dialogue and liberalization in 1986–1987, prompting demonstrations in central China and Beijing, followed by a crackdown early in 1987 that toppled the general secretary of the CCP, Hu Yaobang. And finally, there would be the Beijing Spring of 1989, discussed in chapter 7, which combined domestic and foreign pressures for change into a national movement whose demise had a devastating impact on U.S.-China relations.

Early in the 1980s, in the United States a revolution of sorts also occurred, but this was in the mind of the American president and in the interests of the Republican Party. Ronald Reagan had been a vigorous anticommunist, as well as a domestic political conservative, for decades, and in that guise had promoted the cause of Chiang Kai-shek and the Nationalist Chinese government on the island of Taiwan. During the election campaign of 1980, he made clear that he did not approve of Jimmy Carter's decision to establish diplomatic relations with Beijing at Taipei's expense. His rhetoric nurtured expectations in Beijing and Taipei that there would be a drastic change in American policy were he to win the White House.

But the realities of international affairs and the hard work of critical members of the administration prevented Reagan's sympathies from undermining national policy. In 1983, the president declared he would rather adopt the young tennis star Hu Na than send her back to Communist China. But by 1984, he was off to China himself and was heard to declare that the Chinese were not communists at all. As the decade wore on links proliferated across economies and cultures, producing an era of good feeling for China among Americans. Although some critics began to voice concern over human rights abuses inside China, problems such as forced abortion, religious repression, and political disenfranchisement grew only gradually in importance as Americans and other foreigners built their relationships with the Chinese.

More disturbing, early in the decade, to the burgeoning relationship between Beijing and Washington than human rights was the confrontation over Taiwan. From the first days of the Reagan era, when representatives of Taiwan were invited to the inauguration, through negotiation of the August 17, 1982 communiqué, China found reason to object to American policies concerning the Guomindang regime. Tension over whether Americans encouraged the idea of Taiwan's independence were given impetus by changes on the island. During the 1980s, Taiwan turned from autocracy to democracy under the guiding hands of Chiang Ching-kuo and Lee Teng-hui. Coupled with its flourishing economy, democratization made relations with Taiwan more appealing and more important to Americans.

Significant changes also came to pass in Hong Kong, where the United States had long maintained a large diplomatic, intelligence, and commercial presence. Early in the decade Hong Kong's prosperity appeared to be at risk, in part because of the uncertainty of the colony's political future. Although London was bound by treaty to return portions of the territory to China in 1997, no provisions for this event had been made. Therefore, the British launched often acrimonious negotiations with Beijing over Hong Kong's future. The result was the 1984 Sino-British Joint Declaration in which London and Beijing agreed on general policies for retrocession. The renewed stability this brought to the territory bolstered American confidence and expanded trade and investment.

At the same time, profound differences between Moscow and Beijing began to be addressed in the 1980s, with unpredictable implications for the United States. Several factors, including Reagan's views on Taiwan and growing Soviet hostility to the Sino-American connection, led Beijing to reexamine its international posture and decide that it had positioned itself too close to Washington. Moscow, it was feared, might launch a preemptive attack on a China too much a part of the Western camp. Instead, during 1982, the Chinese began to follow a more independent foreign policy and sought to improve relations with Moscow. Nevertheless, the Chinese demanded that three obstacles be removed before serious progress could be made: (1) that the Soviets pressure Vietnam into withdrawing its troops from Cambodia, (2) that the Soviets pull their own forces out of Afghanistan, and (3) that there be a substantial reduction in troop levels along the Sino-Soviet border.

When Mikhail Gorbachev took the reigns of power in the Soviet Union in 1986, the Chinese finally got what they had long sought. In July 1986, at

Vladivostok, Gorbachev declared that he would remove Soviet forces from both Afghanistan and the border, particularly Mongolia. Skeptical Chinese leaders hesitated to move forward, however, so in 1988, Gorbachev revisited the issue and removed additional troops from East Asia while also persuading the Vietnamese to set a date [September 1989] for their own departure from Cambodia. As this reconciliation materialized, Americans worried about the impact it would have on U.S.-China relations. Even if there were no overt anti-American alignment, the alleviation of the Soviet threat to China would weaken the strategic rationale for close cooperation between Washington and Beijing. Chinese officials, recognizing American discomfort, however, worked hard to reassure the United States. In the end, as it happened, a triumphal summit in Beijing between Gorbachev and Deng was overshadowed by dissident protests in Tiananmen Square almost on the eve of the collapse of the Soviet Union.

ELECTION CAMPAIGN

During the 1980 presidential campaign, China policy became an issue between Ronald Reagan and Jimmy Carter. Reagan was not opposed to the China opening per se. In fact, he had been critical of Gerald Ford during his years in the White House for allowing the momentum of the relationship to slow, when, as Reagan saw it, China comprised a handy counterweight to the Soviet Union. However, Reagan wanted better relations with Beijing without abandonment of Taiwan. Therefore, he declared that upon entering office he would create a liaison office in Taipei, providing, once again, an official link between the two old allies. In response to vigorous Chinese protests, George Bush, Reagan's running mate, went to Beijing to clarify these statements. But while still on Chinese soil, the Bush mission was undermined as candidate Reagan reiterated his support for Taiwan. Eventually Reagan had to face reality and relinquish his rescue effort, but in the interim he caused considerable distress in Washington and Beijing.

FREEMAN: Ronald Reagan essentially proposed, over the course of 1980, to reverse two elements of the normalization understandings with regard to Taiwan, encouraged by Jim Lilley, who was at that time principal advisor to [George] Bush. First, he felt that an official relationship of some sort should be reestablished with Taiwan. Second, he did not agree with the formulation that the Carter administration had carefully preconcerted with the Chinese on arms sales to Taiwan. That formulation was that the United States would continue to sell carefully selected defensive weapons to Taiwan, and there would be overall restraint in the level of sales. And he objected to that.

Subsequently, Reagan thought better of this, when he began to realize the importance of China to our overall international strategy, and specifically the things that the Chinese were doing with us with regard to Afghanistan—the collection of intelligence on the Soviet Union and the like.

HUMMEL: To upgrade our relations with Taiwan was a move which could have destroyed our relations with the PRC. Because the statements made by Reagan during the campaign upset the PRC a great deal, the Reagan people sent George Bush on a quick trip to Beijing [in August 1980] to try to explain. He, of course, had been the head of the U. S. Liaison Office in Beijing, 1974–75. The Chinese Communist leaders knew him very well. They liked him. However, he failed to mollify or calm the fears of the Chinese Communists as to what the Reagan administration might be up to.

LORD: There was a great deal of apprehension by the Chinese and others about what would happen to our China policy as President Reagan took office. I remember distinctly on various occasions with the Chinese in New York and Washington, reassuring them, saying that any president when he gets into the oval office tends to have a different view of geopolitics. This president would be no exception, particularly because he had chosen Al Haig as secretary of state, who had been heavily involved in the China opening and was very pro-engagement with China.

HOLDRIDGE: In 1980, our friends in Taiwan saw their great and good friend Reagan come along. Remember, Nixon sent Reagan to Taiwan to explain what was happening after the Shanghai Communiqué. Later on, to keep things on track, especially over the whole question of the United Nations' membership, Reagan was sent by Nixon to reassure Chiang Ching-kuo that we would stand firmly behind Taiwan and its position internationally. In comes President Reagan, and Taiwan thought that it was going to have it home free.

HUMMEL: At the time of Reagan's inauguration, Anna Chennault, the widow of General Claire Chennault,[1] was mixing her sticky fingers into all kinds of things. She was a member of the Republican National Committee. She was very actively involved in planning for the inauguration. Without consulting anybody, as far as I could find out, she decided to invite representatives from Taiwan to come to the official inauguration.

HOLDRIDGE: The governor of Taiwan, the secretary general of the Guomindang Party, and the mayor of Taipei were all included to represent Taiwan, the Republic of China, at the inauguration. Chai Zemin, the Chinese ambassador let it be known that if these people showed up, he wouldn't. The last thing we needed in the world to start the Reagan administration off with was a big fuss over China policy.

The way I resolved that one was first to go to Anna and tell her she had made a dreadful mistake, and that she should do what she could to pull back on the reins. I then made an international phone call in the clear, assuming that ears would be listening all over, to Chuck Cross, the head of our American Institute in Taiwan.[2] During that telephone call, I told him what dreadful consequences would ensue in the relationship with Taiwan if we started out the Reagan administration with a big brouhaha over China policy. The word got through, and the secretary general of the Guomindang Party, who was here, got a diplomatic illness. Jim Lilley, who was in the CIA at the time and was our AIT representative later on, and I went over and called on the poor, ill gentleman in his hospital room. This was to show that our hearts were in the right place.

HUMMEL: Anna's stock, of course, dropped sharply, both in Beijing and in many circles in Washington.

The Reagan administration came in with more ideological baggage than most. What impact did that have?

DONALD ANDERSON: Reagan scared us all to death before the election, and really immediately after the election. The transition team that he sent over to State was pretty shocking.

FREEMAN: The transition was a somewhat bizarre experience, because it went in two phases. First, there was a group of congressional right-wing types who landed in the State Department. They were ostensibly representing the president, before he had really selected a new secretary of state officially, although Al Haig was rumored. This group arrived, and they were hostile. I was told that Senator [Jesse] Helms had a list of 17 people who had to be purged, and that I was on that list. So there was a very nasty atmosphere. These people went around and interviewed the different desks, including the China Desk, and tried to get some sense of what the state of play on the relationship was.

But the instant Al Haig was named as secretary, he thanked all these people for their good work, sent them packing, and brought in his own people, who were a great deal more strategically sensible and less ideological. So there was a sort of sigh of relief. It was a difficult transition, although it was a friendlier takeover than the one between Reagan and Bush in '88-'89, which was a very unfriendly thing indeed, as different wings of the Republican Party succeeded each other.

Secretary Haig was a strong supporter of a good relationship with China, and had maintained close contact with the Chinese when he was at SHAFE [Supreme Headquarters Allied Expeditionary Forces] as SACEUR [NATO Supreme Allied Commander, Europe], and had, of course, been involved with the opening of the relationship with China as Kissinger's deputy back in the early '70s. He did gradually gain ground with the president on these issues, and convince him that the enemy was the Soviet Union, not China, and that there were merits to maintaining a good relationship with China, and that that meant that we had to go through a certain level of contortion in our relationship with Taiwan to demonstrate that it was unofficial.

He did something extraordinary, early in the Reagan administration. He brought Ji Chaozhu, who was at that time still a mid-ranking Chinese official, but who had gone to Harvard and was actually on the ship of Chinese students who returned to China at the time of the Chinese Revolution and the Korean War, and who had served as Zhou Enlai's interpreter, in to spend some time with the president.[3] Ji was a very personable, fluent English speaker, a very glib spokesman for Chinese views, in terms that Americans can understand and relate to. Haig's motive was very clear, and it worked, and that was to show the president that the Chinese might be communist, but they were also decent human beings, and that you could talk with them. Reagan had entered office with an ideological stereotype of China really untempered by any human contact with the Chinese. Haig did everything he could to try to help President Reagan get a more sophisticated understanding of China. This began to break down a bit of the stereotype in Ronald Reagan's mind. So that all worked, thanks to the genuinely heroic willingness of Al Haig to impale himself on this issue.

On this battle for the "soul" of President Reagan on China, George Bush was vice president but had actually been Reagan's opponent for the Republican nomination for president. Bush had also been our representative in Beijing. Did you feel that he was playing much of a role, or was he not yet comfortable with Ronald Reagan?

HUMMEL: He was very much out of it. I am quite sure that George Bush, whom I got to know quite well, simply didn't want to have to argue with Ronald Reagan about China policy. He saw that Secretary of State Al Haig was doing the heavy lifting on this and that he was doing the right thing. Why should George Bush strain his own, personal relations with Reagan when he didn't have to?

DONALD ANDERSON: Haig kept the China thing on the trolley and prevented it from taking a real lurch. And once he had stabilized it, and the bureaucracy that was built up around the president, after that there were relatively few problems. We had a tougher bunch than we did in the early days. Paul Wolfowitz was the assistant secretary, and there was less empathy with the Chinese. He was more interested in other issues, and he didn't see why we were pandering to the Chinese. They took a more pragmatic attitude, and were willing to risk offending the Chinese more so than, say, during the Carter period.

SIGUR: I felt very deeply that we had not as strongly emphasized the U.S.-Japan relationship, that we had been somewhat mesmerized by China, with the opening to China under Nixon and Kissinger, and continuing on with that through the Ford and Carter administrations. I support fully the opening to China and the way in which we pursued our policy. But I thought that in some ways we had tended to neglect the Japan relationship, which, it seemed to me, was becoming more and more significant to us certainly in the trade area, but also in the security side as well, and that we therefore had to take some rather special steps. Not to say that in any way we diminished the China relationship, that is not true, but at the same time, we emphasized and tried to build up the Japan relationship.

HUMMEL: In the spring of 1981, Secretary of State Al Haig decided that he wanted to push me to be ambassador to Beijing. What Haig wanted in Beijing was somebody who would vigorously, and at probable risk to his career, oppose, in official communications, any stupid things that might be done by the White House. It was not only President Reagan who wanted to be nice to old Taiwan friends, whom we had treated rather shabbily. It was also Richard Allen, who was then the national security adviser, who was also very vociferous about this issue.

Haig clearly understood the problem of China which had been created by Reagan's own personal proclivities and also by Richard Allen. Among other things, Haig made his own trip in June 1981, to the PRC to mollify the Chinese—or to promise them that he would do his best to keep the relationship on a reasonable track. Haig persuaded President Reagan to make some mollifying statements during the spring of 1981, saying that our relationship with the PRC was governed by two communiqués—the Shanghai Communiqué and the communiqué related to the switch of recognition from Nationalist China to the PRC. The main thrust of this was that there was only one China and we would not promote two Chinas—one in Taiwan and one in Beijing. Reagan publicly reaffirmed those principles.

TAIWAN ARMS SALES ISSUE

When the United States and China opened diplomatic relations in 1978, they did not seek final resolution of the issue of Taiwan because they could not agree on policies toward the island. Washington, as we have seen, did abrogate the defense treaty, withdraw its military forces, and sever formal relations. But Congress refused to drop the sales of weaponry designed to keep the island free. The Chinese objected from the first, and, by 1981, had concluded that continually expanding sales of advanced equipment would make it more and more difficult to bring about reunification. So Beijing decided to take action to try to stop the sales.

FREEMAN: On the arms sales issue, Reagan persisted in his view. It found expression, over the course of 1981, in the so-called FX issue, the FX being a fighter aircraft, that the Carter administration had authorized.[4] This would have been the first such major weapons system produced by the United States specifically for export, rather than for acquisition by our own armed forces.

This issue was a very political one. There were two companies competing for it: Northrop, which was based in southern California, and General Dynamics, which was based in Texas. The General Dynamics aircraft was a downgraded version of the F-16. The Northrop aircraft was a newly designed aircraft, in effect, major re-engineering, based on the old F-5.

Which had been our principal export fighter.

FREEMAN: Exactly. That competition was left open during the campaign, because, of course, Carter wanted to appeal to the voters of both southern California and Texas, and didn't want to alienate one or the other. And he bequeathed this decision to Ronald Reagan. In the event, Reagan, solomonically, decided not to tear the baby in half, and to let both of them compete [further]. It meant that Northrop, which had put a huge amount of money into developing the F-20, as they called it, their version of the FX, was going to be in deep financial trouble if it couldn't make a sale to Taiwan.

HOLDRIDGE: Taiwan had been told earlier at some stage in the process that they would get an aircraft which would be an upgrade of the F5E/F series, which they had. It was known as the F5G, and it was carefully designed by Northrup so that it did not have a kind of a range or a loiter time capability which would allow it to be an offensive weapon against the mainland. It would be a fighter interceptor and useful for defensive purposes. Taiwan begins to talk about it all over the place. The Chinese fired back their responses. They could live with what was there—the F5E/F—but they could not accept an upgrade.

FREEMAN: So there were powerful economic interests and political interests involved. The conjunction of Ronald Reagan's sympathy for Taiwan and his gut feeling that it was wrong to deprive a former ally and a friend of access to this very potent weapons system with the economic and political muscle that was behind it from Texas and California meant that he strongly favored selling this aircraft to Taiwan.

HUMMEL: In China in June, Haig exceeded his instructions by saying publicly that we would now begin to sell selective, defensive armaments to the PRC. This matter had been discussed and studied, but he did not have the authority to make that statement. Al is pretty much of an unguided missile. On China he was very good, but in other ways he is kind of flaky.

Then, in July and August 1981, just as I was preparing to go out to Beijing as ambassador, there were press stories emanating from the

Arthur W. Hummel, Jr. with Zhu Rongji. *Courtesy of Arthur W. Hummel, Jr.*

White House—which were all true—that Richard Allen had developed the idea that we would sell some military equipment to Beijing, just enough to keep them satisfied. Then we would radically increase our sales of military equipment to Taiwan. The PRC leaders, of course, read all of this. They had planned to send their vice chief of staff, an admiral named Liu Huaqing, on an exploratory trip to the United States, to arrive in August 1981, with a considerable list of things that we might be able to sell to the PRC and which we would discuss. We had an advance copy of this list. When the stories appeared in the press about this plan to entangle the PRC with a few purchases of military equipment, leaving us free to sell a great deal to Taiwan, the PRC decided that it had to react. First of all, they canceled Admiral Liu's visit. That was quite a shock to those of us who were working on China.

FREEMAN: These developments were a clear challenge to the normalization understandings with Beijing. As the summer proceeded, I began to get signals from Chinese contacts of two things. First, a renewed effort by them to engage Taiwan in peaceful reunification. I was able, in fact, on the basis of those contacts, to predict pretty accurately, well in advance, the statement that Ye Jianying [chairman of the National People's Congress Standing Committee] made to what he called "Taiwan compatriots" [on September 30], a very detailed proposal on reunification, with major new elements of flexibility in it. And I anticipated, but not adequately, that this indication of flexibility by the Chinese on the Taiwan question would be accompanied by a ratcheting up of the pressure on the United States to re-adhere to the commitments that we had made at the time of normalization.

HUMMEL: The next move was much more serious. The PRC Prime Minister [Zhao Ziyang] and President Reagan met in Cancun [Mexico] at the time of a meeting of the Group of Seven Industrialized Countries [in October]. During the half-hour or 45-minute meeting that they had, the prime minister didn't have time to say what he wanted to say. So he sent the foreign minister, Huang Hua, on a separate visit to Washington. He presented a very tough ultimatum. He said that unless the United States agreed to set a date for ending all arms sales to Taiwan, there would have to be a downgrading of diplomatic relations between the PRC and the United States. The PRC wanted to see an end to what they saw as encouraging Taiwan's independence. In a way, that was true.

The Reagan administration was reviving the TRA legislation, not only as an excuse, but treating it as a mandatory obligation in law passed by Congress, as opposed to communiqués, which are only documents approved by the Executive Branch. The Reagan administration was using the TRA as a reason for acceding to the very sharp demands of the people in Taiwan, who at that time were still quite concerned over military readiness and the eventual possibility, down the road, of a PRC invasion of Taiwan. All of this led to the PRC ultimatum. We were told that we had to set a date for termination of arms sales.

HOLDRIDGE: Al very strongly resisted that idea, but said across the table that we would be willing to accept limitations on quantity and quality— keep it at an existing level. We had a big problem about what Taiwan's actual needs were. Various government agencies labored long and diligently to come up with the idea that Taiwan did not need an upgrade. The F5E/F was perfectly adequate for anything which China, at that time, was able to put into the air.

LILLEY: I was the guy at the NSC. So I said do a study on it. Get Defense to do a study. I don't think CIA will give you an objective account. So

Defense did the study and came back and said they don't need them. Haig loved it. It went up the line and Haig leaked it to the press, and the *Washington Post* picked it up. And eventually Bush and the president decided they weren't going to do it.

HUMMEL: At the time John Holdridge was assistant secretary for East Asian Affairs. I had come back to Washington to attend a crucial meeting on the PRC ultimatum. Of course, downgrading diplomatic relations would mean that I would lose my job as ambassador to the PRC, so this matter had my full attention.

FREEMAN: By the early part of 1982, we were engaged in intense negotiations. The first phase of these was really quite memorable, in that we were thundered at by the then Chinese vice foreign minister, Pu [Shouchang]. In the best Mandarin tradition, he lectured and hectored and put us in our place, seated in a high seat, with us in low seats, in the room. When it was clear that that was going nowhere, the Chinese then switched interlocutors, and we got Han Xu, who was assistant minister for American and Oceanian affairs, who had been in Washington and was very well known.

HUMMEL: The 10-month process of negotiations, which I carried on in Beijing, was done in very desultory fashion at first [beginning in February 1982]. Nobody quite knew how to approach this issue. I had very good, almost fortuitous support from Democrats. Walter Mondale came through Beijing. Harold Brown, a former secretary of defense [in the Carter administration] came through. I urged them—and they readily agreed—to tell the PRC leaders that no American president, Republican or Democrat, could set a date for terminating arms sales to Taiwan under the existing circumstances. The PRC leaders at the very top level did not understand the political nuances that made it impossible for any American president to do what they were demanding. However, the people further below in the PRC government had a more sophisticated agenda. Their agenda was simply to get the full attention of President Ronald Reagan, which they succeeded in doing.

Al Haig insisted on seeing President Reagan privately, and often. Over a considerable period of time, Al was able to persuade President Reagan that we had to work our way out of this impasse and that we could not, at that time, sell unlimited military equipment to Taiwan. In effect, we decided on a unilateral moratorium on all arms sales to Taiwan while negotiations were going on. This was a very difficult thing for President Reagan to agree to do, but it is greatly to Al Haig's credit that he was able to persuade Reagan on this issue. His clinching argument with Reagan was, "We Republicans cannot have, in our first year in office, a foreign policy disaster like a rupture with the PRC. This would hurt us, domestically." It was the domestic aspect, then, which caught Reagan's attention, which was rather ironic, instead of the strategic and foreign policy damage.

Were there forces within the Republican-dominated Senate—or elsewhere, besides Allen—who were basically trying to hurt our relations with Communist China?

HUMMEL: Oh, yes, Senator Jesse Helms [R-NC]. And people around the edges, who had been involved with China for a long time in the China Lobby. I refer to Ray Cline, a former CIA official who was actually on the Taiwanese payroll, and Walter Judd, a former Congressman who had been a medical missionary in China and was very active in the China Lobby. There were a lot of people who were strongly urging— and who were being strongly urged by the Taiwan people, who were very deeply entrenched in and around Washington—to do something for Taiwan.

　　At that time the Taiwan people saw this as a zero sum game and did a lot of things around the edges to try to spoil the relationship between Washington and Beijing. Demonstrations in favor of the Guomindang political party were held at a time when PRC government officials were visiting here. There were damaging newspaper stories. There were all kinds of little things—and some not so little—to promote and support the cause of Taiwan, because advocates of Taiwan could see that support for Taiwan was eroding, as Americans became more and more involved in trade and negotiations of all kinds with the PRC.

FREEMAN: As the negotiations proceeded, they developed effectively two tracks: first, a series of formal meetings, chaired by the ambassador; and, second, far more productive and detailed, a series of informal lunches at my house, with two of the senior but subordinate members of the Chinese delegation, Zhang Zai and Zhang Wenpu, in particular, with some others, and the political counselor from the embassy, Jay Taylor, talking ostensibly totally on an ad referendum, off-the-record, trying to explore the basis of a compromise, on a sort of what-if basis—

What if we said this, what would you say to that? What about this set of words, would that do it? Although informal, these discussions were very closely controlled from Washington. The president was personally reviewing every account of these discussions, and they were conducted with meticulous care on both sides.

We kept in extraordinarily close contact with Washington. We actually communicated mainly in Chinese, written in Roman letters, in order to keep prying eyes from being able to read the comments that we were making about the state of play, and it produced candor. There were huge battles going on back in Washington, the precise details of which I didn't entirely know. But this resulted in very, very specific instructions with regard to wording changes and different approaches that we might take. Now we in Beijing made many of the suggestions that resulted in those instructions. We were occasionally overruled on our suggestions, but often they were accepted, although not without a battle.

Just to get a flavor for this, when you were doing the negotiating and you got somebody lecturing you, trying to put you in your place, what was the American riposte?

FREEMAN: The American reply to this, through Art Hummel, who is a consummate diplomat, was tough, but not strident, reasoned, and refused to allow us to be put on the defensive, as Mr. Pu was attempting to do. But this exchange of set-piece statements clearly wasn't going to go anywhere. The informal discussions were conceived, by both sides basically, as a kind of off-conference method of producing something. There actually were very, very few formal meetings, until the precise end. I think the Chinese had not been accustomed to this kind off-site, informal session. They, however, quickly grasped the ground rules and played very fair in the course of this rather intense and often quite unpleasant set of exchanges. People on both sides came to have increasing respect for each other. That helped subsequently in rebuilding the relationship, once we were able to get past this bad moment.

HUMMEL: The negotiations continued, with growing intensity, through the summer of 1982 and finally culminated on August 17, 1982, with a communiqué. The necessary shape of the communiqué had been pretty visible to everybody for a good many months. The PRC leaders just couldn't bring themselves to agree to it until the very last minute. The PRC leaders like to stretch things out to the deadline. The shape of the communiqué was determined by the fact that we had to persuade the PRC leaders to link a continued diminution of our arms sales to Taiwan, in both quantity and quality, to a peaceful situation in the Taiwan Straits. We had a little escape valve there in terms of quality because I made sure that we said that we could not always match the quality of seven-year-old weapons, because we no longer would manufacture them. The effect of this, of course, was that if there was no peaceful situation, if the PRC decided to try to invade Taiwan, which we thought was very unlikely, then all bets were off. We could then sell or give anything we pleased to Taiwan. Also, we brought this communiqué into conformity with the TRA, which required us to sell things which are necessary for the defense of Taiwan. So the more necessary the defense, the more we could sell.

The negotiations were quite excruciating for several months. George Bush came over to the PRC. He carried letters from Ronald Reagan, which were later made public, reaffirming our fundamental policy of one China and also reaffirming that we would continue to have what we called unofficial relations with Taiwan.

HOLDRIDGE: The problem was the August 21 date. By August 21, 1982, the Air Force was going to have to notify Congress of the continuation of the F5E/F [production] line. If we didn't have a joint communiqué to resolve this whole question of arms sales to Taiwan by this time, our whole relationship could have been plunged into chaos.

Al Haig admits in his book that the best thing he did for his country at this time [June 1982] was to take himself out of the position of secretary of state.[5] He was so disliked in the White House—the suspicions were so intense—that anything that Al would have sent over would have been thrown back into the teeth of the Department of State. Time would have been wasted. In fact, Al actually opposed the visit of Vice President Bush to China in May of 1982, which happened to cut the Gordian knot. Maybe this is some explanation for why Bush was willing to send [National Security Advisor Brent] Scowcroft [after Tiananmen (see chapter 7)]. Somebody has to take an initiative. He went and was able to convince the Chinese that we were absolutely sincere in trying to find a resolution. We weren't trying to do them in, but we had our own domestic problems to take care of, as well.

HUMMEL: There were also other items of military equipment which we owed to the PRC, and many to Taiwan, which had already been paid for. There were several deadlines which we simply could not postpone any further. We persuaded the PRC leaders that, if we did not have an agreement on their ultimatum, the terms of which were public knowledge, we would then have to go ahead and make these sales to Taiwan, and the whole world would believe that we were just spitting in the eye of the PRC and ignoring their ultimatum. We pointed out that that would not be good for the PRC and not good for the United States, either.

FREEMAN: The break point in these negotiations was a personal communication from President Reagan to Mr. Deng, saying, "I just can't go any farther." That was the essence of it. And that came in about July. Mr. Deng and President Reagan both decided to hold their noses and call off the fight. We had a series of rapid plenary sessions between the ambassador and Han Xu that wrapped up the communiqué text in mid-August.

The core of the compromise was that the Chinese had to accept that U.S. arms sales would continue to Taiwan, something which stuck in their craw, thus making the United States the only country that had Chinese permission to sell weapons to what they regarded as a province in rebellion against the central government. We, for our part, had to agree to cap the quality of the weapons we transferred at existing levels and to reduce the quantity of sales progressively, with a view to ultimately reaching some complete solution of this problem and ending arms sales entirely.

LILLEY: They [the Reagan administration] worked in what they called the Six Assurances to Taiwan and these basically boiled down to the United States will not pressure Taiwan to negotiate, the United States will not serve an intermediary role, the United States will not terminate arms sales to Taiwan.[6] These were all worked into a statement that John Holdridge made subsequent to the communiqué. Reagan said his interpretation as relayed through Gaston Sigur was, "Listen, this thing hit me at the last minute. I don't like it. And I want you to understand that my understanding of this communiqué is that we will maintain a balance. And if China becomes belligerent or builds up a power projection capability that brings insecurity, instability to the area, we increase arms sales to Taiwan regardless of what the communiqué says about quantity and quality."

LORD: In 1982, I testified backing the Reagan administration on the third communiqué that was negotiated with respect to arms sales to Taiwan. We couldn't actually get the Chinese to renounce force, but we felt there was a strong enough indication along with our commitment and arms sales in the same communiqué to give us sufficient linkage and therefore we could always provide for Taiwan's defense as long as they had a security problem. We would only reduce their arms sales as the situation got more peaceful.

SIGUR: In the accompanying statement by the president, he made that very clear that he would never have agreed to the communiqué without what we considered to be the Chinese acceptance that there would be no use of force. Now sometimes they'd quibble on this one, but we believed the Chinese acquiescence not to use force.

FREEMAN: The intelligent policy always had been rather than to make arms sales, to transfer technology, so that Taiwan, admittedly at somewhat greater expense, could produce major weapons systems in Taiwan. And there would not be the visible export and all of the debates in Congress and publicity that we uniquely generate when we transfer weapons to some foreign purchaser. In fact, that was attempted, and it was the genesis of the so-called IDF (indigenous fighter) program in Taiwan, as a substitute for the F-20 (FX). It was also attempted with other items, such as patrol boats and the like.

SIGUR: When we signed the communiqué, in August of '82, the opposition to the signing of it, from the side that felt we were in fact capitulating to the demands of Beijing and that we were not adequately providing for the security and future safety of our friends on Taiwan, it came from the Congress, and it was all over the place. It wasn't just . . .

You didn't feel this was the right wing of the . . .

SIGUR: No, sir. I don't want to go into names here, but it was people who you would not think of that way at all, who would give me phone calls and say, "What have you done? How dare you do something like this?" I'm talking about one of the leading Democratic senators. Yes, I got it from all sides. However, the fact that Reagan had done it in some ways muted some of the critics up there from the more right wing of the Republican Party who would have, if it had been another president, really been much more loud than they were. And, during the course of the time of finalizing this communiqué, I and others really made a tremendous effort to explain what we were doing on the Hill. And we would try to tell them that in no way were we abandoning our friends on Taiwan. Quite the opposite. What we were trying to do was to create a more stable atmosphere in which we could continue to maintain good and close relations, unofficial, with Taiwan, and at the same time, build up the ties with Beijing, which was essential in our terms. And the president was perfectly behind this dual track policy. He went over it line by line and comma by comma in terms of what was being done.

You said earlier that these were excruciating negotiations. Could you talk a bit about your experience at that time with the Chinese style of negotiation?

HUMMEL: Frankly, I don't think that there's anything particularly unique about the Chinese negotiating style. Any clever negotiator—and many American lawyers—knows all of these tricks as well. One of them is to shame the other side, pulling out some ancient statement that you made two months before and pretending high indignation because you were now saying something else. Another one is trying to get matters of principle established before the negotiations start and, buried in these principles, of course, are the elements that they want to insist on. There have been books written about Chinese negotiating style.[7] There is a long list of their tactics, but none of them are unique to China.

FREEMAN: Both sides, frankly, postured. The Chinese would say that they could not ignore the feelings of 1.1 billion Chinese—by which they meant that they couldn't ignore the feelings of the handful of people who really mattered in China. We would cite congressional sentiment, on our side, as a constraint on what we could do. I'm sure both sets of statements did reflect some sort of reality, but both of us were aware that we were posturing.

Sometimes you get into one of these negotiating situations where everything has to be referred to someone else. The people you are negotiating with are nothing more than a "letter box." Did you find this to be the case?

HUMMEL: Well, yes. However, very frankly, this was true on both sides. I was a letter box, too. Now, I could—and did—make many strong suggestions back to Washington and obtained approval of those suggestions. However, I couldn't break new ground with the Chinese without obtaining permission from Washington. This makes one long for the sailing ship days when there was no radio and no undersea cable. Ambassadors were sent out with six months' worth of "Extraordinary and Plenipotentiary" powers to commit the United States government.

CHINA IN THE 1980s

The early days in Beijing proved to be difficult, but probably less dispiriting than some Foreign Service officers had feared. The Chinese kept tight controls, spying on Americans in the Middle Kingdom, but they also were happy to have them there. For the Americans, the challenge of operating in this sometimes oppressive communist dictatorship was matched by the exhilaration of witnessing the dramatic changes taking place almost on a daily basis.

HUMMEL: We had a considerably substandard embassy in terms of housing when I arrived [in 1981]. The office and the residence were squeezed together in a small compound, as well as the USIS office, too. The reason for this is that when we first came there to establish the U.S. Liaison Office, it was below the status of an embassy. Then, when we switched recognition to Beijing, the large estate which was the residence for the Chinese Nationalist ambassador in Washington was sold off so we could not turn over that residence to the PRC, which was very unhappy about it.[8] So because the PRC did not get preferential treatment in Washington, we couldn't get preferential treatment in Beijing. It took a lot of very hard work and wrangling with the PRC authorities to get better premises. In the beginning, Beijing was really a tough post. We had an average of, say, 20 to 30 new staff members living in hotel rooms with their families at any given time. Those hotels were not very good. The PRC authorities dragged their feet, trying to get us to do more things for them in Washington.

China is a country in the exotic Orient. Was there a problem with either male or female staff getting involved with a Chinese national more than would have happened elsewhere?

HUMMEL: In those very early stages of our relationship with the PRC, Chinese men and women who might have become involved with Americans would have been severely penalized if they were caught having sexual relations with foreigners. It was the PRC government attitude which prevented it. We had quite a few cases of this among the non-official American community.[9] That's another aspect. The non-official community was burgeoning—teachers, students, resident business people, and lawyers. All kinds of Americans were moving in, in great numbers. We had some nasty cases there where the Chinese authorities would pretend that they had information in their possession—so-called Chinese classified, internal documents. A lot of people, including journalists, had access to such documents. Anyway, they would use these excuses to expel someone—or even put them in jail.

What were the Chinese after in such cases?

HUMMEL: They were trying to separate the two societies. First of all, they had a paranoid attitude about security and national secrets, including economic statistics. Secondly, there was a genuine desire to prevent contamination of Chinese society with American social habits. The Chinese Residential Block Committees exercised very close control over the personal lives of everyone living in their area. If they went to bars and got drunk, they would be punished when they returned. All of this began to break down during the period from 1981 to 1985. The level of personal and social freedom improved substantially. Not, of course, political freedom.

KURZBAUER: Fox Butterfield's China was challenging, exciting, and stressful. So my image of China from his book [*China, Alive in the Bitter Sea*][10] and others was dark. I had just read about the Cultural Revolution and the great dislocations and the terrible traumas. If somebody asked me how I imagined China, I would have said regimented, everybody in lock-step, everybody wearing the same clothes, everybody reading same book—or turmoil or anarchy! These two kinds of extremes. I know that is an emotional image, not a scholarly or professional image, but that was my view. So at first when I was assigned to Beijing, I didn't know what to expect and I didn't think it was going to be an easy assignment. I thought it would be isolated, difficult materially, but more importantly emotionally isolated. So my view was cautious, nervous, and uncertain.

HUMMEL: This leads to something else—the fact that we were quite sure that our houses and offices were bugged by the Chinese. This meant that a certain number of subjects—and you'd be surprised at how few they were—would have to be discussed in a special room. This was the so-called bubble, classified conference room. A room built of plastic inside another room, no windows, just drapes, and with fans blowing to make "white noise" so that you can't be overheard. This room was not supposed to be buggable. These subjects included future negotiating positions, anything relating to the CIA, and that kind of thing. However, there was no harm in letting the Chinese monitors know what our basic attitudes were about Chinese actions, about our routine operations, and most of our problems and work.

LORD: We had the constant reality that everything was bugged, including our entire household, so we were always careful whenever we spoke in the house, even in our car, unless we wanted to make a point like "I hope we aren't having sea slugs at the next Great Hall banquet." You felt, obviously, that you and your people were being followed. In my case, they probably did it out of security reasons. They wanted to make sure nothing would happen to me [the American ambassador]. Of course, you feel more secure ironically, in a communist-controlled society. You won't get hurt by criminals or other elements because the [security forces] are always around and they have got things under control.

What was your impression of the Chinese ruling apparatus?

HUMMEL: They had some quite good people. Deng Xiaoping was already somewhat in the background. He was not the head of the Communist Party of China and he was not the head of the government. However, he was the head of the Military Commission of the Party, which was still a very powerful position. Whatever he wanted to have happen would happen—in those days.

The prime minister, Zhao Ziyang, was a really first-class administrator and a nice person.[11] The top-level Chinese leaders never really grasped the complexities and difficulties of the American political system. We have an Executive Branch that can make promises and a Congress that can then refuse to carry them out. But the working levels understood this—the people in the ministries.

After we solved the problem of Taiwan arms sales, there was a year's period, nevertheless, when we continued to have abrasions and difficulties. I would be called in, roundly criticized, and urged to change American policy on all kinds of issues. But these were all manageable. They did not always go up to the highest level of government, as they previously had.

All during this period, from 1981 to 1985, the Chinese economy was booming and the farmers were making fabulous amounts of money for the first time. The government was beginning to allow private enterprise and small collectives. Everybody's standard of living was going up. There were no appreciable political frictions. The American side was not hammering away on human rights, the way we did later, after the Tiananmen incident.

You have a whole series of U.S. government agencies operating in the embassy. Could you, as ambassador, control them?

HUMMEL: The NSA [National Security Agency] have a completely insatiable desire to capture every damned thing that's possible to capture from air waves, telephones, and microwave relays. They would say that they needed to have three people with their "black boxes" inserted into a six-man consulate in China. I would just say, "Hell, no, you're not going to do it. Over my dead body, because it will instantly be obvious to the Chinese what these people are up to, and our whole access at that post will suffer." They might produce some reports that we or Washington might find useful, but I could never get them or CIA to show me precisely what interesting and important information they fed back to me out of all of this collecting. That was a common complaint, all over China. Sometimes, they do marvelous things, tracking shipments of nuclear weapons. But as far as political or economic information related to my interests are concerned, I didn't get anything useful.

I was often disappointed in the quality of the military attaches. The Defense Intelligence Agency, DIA, was invented by Robert McNamara, secretary of defense in the early 1960s. The purpose was to strip down the separate intelligence organizations of the various military services and centralize them, so that there would be less duplication. The purpose was not achieved because the separate services did not really downsize their own Navy, Army, and Air Force intelligence systems. Furthermore, because they had to staff their own intelligence organizations, the services didn't send their best people to DIA. The DIA is responsible for sending defense attaches abroad. This two-step process resulted in not sending the best intelligence people to the field.

There is also the problem that intelligence is not the way to the top in the military services. The intelligence function has some very good people, but it's still not a desirable assignment. How much of a burden was all this on the embassy?

HUMMEL: The department left very little time for voluntary reporting or think pieces. I resented the manipulation by Washington and the monopoly exercised by Washington on the kind of reporting we did.

As the deputy chief of mission, how did Arthur Hummel use you?

FREEMAN: He was an absolute model manager. He's a laconic man, very taciturn, and very quick to decide. Excellent judgment. Delegates easily. A typical encounter between him and me was brief. I would go in and describe a problem. He'd ask a question or two. He'd say, "Well, what do you think the choices are?" I'd give him some options. He'd either say, "Well, there's another option," or he'd say, "Of those, I think we ought to do this. Go do it." He never looked back on a decision. If he had made a mistake, against my advice, or with my advice, he accepted full responsibility for the decision.

As a negotiator, one of his merits indeed was his ability to maintain silence. Unlike many Americans, he's not bothered by a couple of minutes of sitting silently, looking at someone. Some recent studies have shown that the average American can only tolerate about 17 seconds of silence. Not Art Hummel. He would sit there, poker-faced, and wait for the other side to say something.

He's very personable, a warm person. His wife [is] very charming and very much in the old Foreign Service den mother mode, not excessively demanding on the women of the embassy, but very supportive of them.

Stape Roy (J. Stapleton Roy), [who became ambassador in China 1991] had been the chargé in Beijing, following the departure of Leonard Woodcock. Stape has a very controlling style. One of the first things I did when I got there was to change things around. I don't believe that the job of the DCM or chargé is to edit other people's work. If it was a purely analytical piece, with no real policy implication, I just told people, "Send it out. I'll read it afterwards. You have to take responsibility for what you write." Stape had been approving even visa cables, and I just cut all that off. So I tended to delegate a great deal and to try to use my time to direct and inspire, working with the different reporting and analytical offices.

Second, there was a staff meeting that went on for about an hour, and I used a technique there, which I subsequently used elsewhere, just saying, "This staff meeting is going to last twenty minutes, and after twenty minutes, I will get up and leave. So you've got twenty minutes to say what you need to say."

Art Hummel very much was the same way. He looked to me to do the long-range strategic planning papers for U.S.-China relations. Art Hummel let me be CEO of the embassy, and he was chairman of the board. He set the broad policy, he made the major decisions, but he looked to me to not just bring problems to him, but bring solutions.

Was there much cooperation with other embassies?

FREEMAN: I continued a tradition, organized by my predecessor, of having a five-power lunch with the deputy chiefs of mission, or equivalents, from Britain, France, Germany, and Japan. Once a month, we would meet to talk about the situation in China and international relations as they affected China.

We also had very close relations with the Yugoslav Embassy. They had an advantage over others, because they had a party-to-party relationship with the Chinese, and tapped into the International Liaison Department, which had a whole different set of insights and focuses than the Foreign Ministry. They often were very knowledgeable about goings on within the Chinese Communist Party, or at least more knowledgeable than those of us who were not communists.

What about the management of relations with the Chinese?

FREEMAN: I tried very hard to broaden dialogue with the Chinese. I set up a series of regular luncheon discussions with the leadership of different geographic bureaus, at the Foreign Ministry, for example. I continued a practice, which Stape Roy had very wisely initiated, of meeting with some of the party ideologues and think tanks, editors of *People's Daily* and *Red Flag*, which was the ideological journal, and members of different institutes. This was quite innovative, in the Chinese context, because China, even though it is not a world power, thinks like a world power and expects to be a world power, and the United States was unique in that we were interested in what the Chinese were thinking about Africa, even though we weren't African. So the African Department over at the Foreign Ministry saw Africans and us, and that was about it. Once in a while, a European would go over and say hello.

What was your impression of these bureau heads that you were talking to in the Chinese Foreign Ministry? They had come out of the Cultural Revolution, in which you had to tread a very careful line or you were off to Mongolia.

FREEMAN: There were several exceptions, but by and large, these were really quite sophisticated people; as you say, very cautious because of the experiences they'd had. But suddenly confronted with an embassy that talked to them in Chinese, rather than demanding that they go through interpreters or speak a foreign language, they opened up quite a bit. We even got a discussion going, for example, with the Korean Desk, even though, at that time, Korea was the great symbol of the Cold War in Asia.

There were a couple of exceptions. We had major legal difficulties with the Chinese over antediluvian, literally antediluvian, railway bonds. Some railway bonds had been issued in 1911, which actually had a role in provoking the 1911 Sun Yat-sen Revolution, to build a railway in south China, between Hunan and Guangdong. These so-called "Hu-Guang" railway bonds had been bought out by someone in New York at half a penny on the dollar. And they were planning to attach Chinese property to get these things.[12] The Chinese equivalent of a legal advisor, Mr. Huang, a very charming, Soviet-educated lawyer, was absolutely aghast at the American legal system, and refused to believe that it really could operate the way we described it. This issue went all the way up to Deng Xiaoping, who at one point angrily stated, "How many governments does the United States have? Let's see, you've got the Executive Branch, which doesn't pay any attention to the Congress, which doesn't pay any attention to the Executive Branch. And then you have this other thing, the courts. I can only deal with one government." He was exasperated by all this.

And the third sort of frustrating Chinese official, really quite aggravating, was the leadership of the Diplomatic Services Bureau. The Diplomatic Services Bureau at that time controlled virtually every element of our daily lives. It provided (or, rather, didn't provide) apartments to American officers and their families. It was the source of all of the local employees, who were actually employees of the DSB, not ours. Frankly, an outrageously exploitative organization. We would pay them hundreds and hundreds of dollars a month for the services of the Chinese; they would then turn over ten dollars a month to him or her. They were part of the Beijing municipality, not really responsive to the Foreign Ministry. They couldn't find land to build apartments. They didn't have the capital. They weren't terribly interested in learning anything about how Westerners wanted apartments designed.

Did you find a contrast in dealing with the Shanghai authorities? One gets the feeling that they really are a different breed than the people up in Beijing, much more aware of the world, and looser, and easier to deal with?

DONALD ANDERSON: There is a certain amount of that. As a matter of fact, up in Beijing in the Foreign Ministry you'll find an awful lot of Shanghainese. I used to kid them about the Shanghai mafia that used to run the American and Oceanian Department. Shanghai in many respects at that time was kept on a tighter leash by Beijing than many other parts of China because really the Gang of Four and this whole Maoist clique that attempted to usurp power, their power base was Shanghai. Jiang Qing herself had been an actress in Shanghai.

So Shanghai for a long, long time was viewed with a certain distrust, and there were a lot of hangovers and holdovers from the earlier period that were still in jobs; frequently not doing much but they had not been dislodged. So that it was a different atmosphere, but Shanghai people are generally much more friendly, and effusive, and sophisticated, than in Beijing.

Shanghai was one of the more popular places for American businesses to come. Nike Shoes came in and tried to set up a joint venture. McDonnell Douglas was just beginning what became a major co-production operation building commercial jets. So we had the beginning of a business community, and we had regular meetings of this community to brief them and get their reactions. That grew into the Shanghai-American Chamber of Commerce.

How about the relations with the embassy? Any problems.

DON ANDERSON: No, we had quite good relations actually. We set up a courier system—it was illegal, but we used to send a diplomatic pouch up with our classified stuff. We'd send up an officer, so we got back and forth as frequently as possible.

RASPOLIC: When I was in Guangzhou, I regarded the Guangzhou operation as entirely independent. I would pick and choose which issues I wanted to inform Beijing about or to keep them informed if I thought they might be interested in it, or if I thought it might be precedent-setting, you know, contribute to consular operations in general in China. But I felt that we were the largest post in the country in terms of manpower and IV [immigrant visa] caseload, and we dealt directly with the department. Beijing did not visit us and was totally unaware of what the hell we were doing, so therefore I felt no strong allegiance to the consular section in Beijing.

Once I transferred to Beijing my opinion of Guangzhou is, "What the hell are they doing? Don't they know that they can't do that? Didn't they read our last directive? Why are they not acknowledging that this is not new ground? Why are they going directly to the department? Why aren't they asking us first? Why aren't they giving us the option of speaking for all posts in the country, rather than negotiating with the department independently?" Your perspective is quite different.

Can you talk a bit about the effort of reporting on China?

FREEMAN: China is a vast country, somewhat larger than the United States, including Alaska, with a huge population and an exceedingly primitive transportation network. I took the view that if the consulates were reporting purely on events and trends within their consular district that didn't have any clear national analog, they should just report directly and they didn't have to clear it with us. This led to a bit of friction with the reporting officers, because I also insisted on, and we got a budget for them to do, quite a bit of traveling around the country. Jay Taylor, in particular, who was the political counselor, a very gifted writer and manager, insisted that his reporting officers be out of the office a certain amount of the day. If he found them in the office, he'd really kick them out. He said, "If you don't have an appointment, go sit in the park and talk to people. What makes you valuable is that you're here, not in Washington."

Of course, China was undergoing really kaleidoscopic change. All of the old givens were being undermined and overturned, as the reform process proceeded. Even the economic officers were astonished, and forced to continually upgrade their projections for the Chinese economy, as the reforms began to liberate labor power and produce more efficient use of capital assets and, therefore, astonishing growth rates in this period.

So from an intellectual point of view, it was an exciting time. And the reporting officers were, by and large, excited. There were one or two and they were probably useful correctives, and often they tended to be people with a background in the Soviet Union, who just couldn't believe what was going on, and who were always darkly pessimistic about it: It wouldn't work. It was all a fraud. What seemed to be happening couldn't really be happening. After all, this was a communist country. But for most officers, there was a sense that, as difficult as life was in China, and as constrained as politics were, and as hampered by socialism as economics were, the country really was opening up and moving in interesting directions.

There are two subjects that could always cause a problem: human rights and corruption. You want to be truthful, yet you don't want to give too much food to enemies.

FREEMAN: Yes, you're quite right to point to those dilemmas. On human rights, the principal exercise, of course, was the production of the annual human-rights report, where we did try to be very scrupulously honest and straightforward, but also to put things a bit in perspective. Things always look different from the field than they do from Washington.[13] Corruption, at that time, was not that serious a problem, in the way that has subsequently become a problem. The point being that if bureaucrats buy and sell commodities, people buy and sell bureaucrats. That's just a law of nature. I can remember one case that was fairly typical. All housing and benefits for workers came from the so-called work unit.[14] So the Ministry of Posts and Telegraphs built housing, high-rise apartment buildings, for its workers. And then they sat vacant for a long time. What had happened was that the electric company said they wouldn't provide electricity unless twenty apartments were turned over to their people. And the water company said they wouldn't provide water unless a certain number of apartments were turned over to them.

Were you seeing, at this time, any signs of a breakdown of central authority at the provincial level?

FREEMAN: No, but certainly you got a very, very vivid sense of the differences between different regions and provinces and cities throughout the country. It was almost a joke. We would send out every two weeks a cable in which we would say, "In the next two weeks we're going to be looking at this issue, especially in light of this policy statement that was printed in the *People's Daily* on such and such a date in an editorial which represents the thinking of the Communist Party on this matter. We would like to have your analysis of what the local reactions to all this are."

Invariably we would get, from Shanghai, "The people are aware of this. They're talking about it. They disagree with it. They're angry. They think this is apostate." Or "They endorse it." Strong opinions and active debate. And we would get, from Shenyang, something that said, "The people up here are aware of it, but they're not really terribly concerned about it. We can't find anybody who really gives a damn about it." And we would get, from Guangzhou, "They never heard of this policy down here, and they could care less. Nobody down here reads the *People's Daily* anyway." So you began to get a sense of the diversity of the country. I'd always had an of image of China as centrally directed. But when you looked at it more closely, you realized that it was centrally coordinated, not centrally directed. That each province was essentially self-sufficient economically. In fact, they even had nontariff trade barriers on the borders.

When Deng Xiaoping's revolution began, he took advantage of this. He very, very deliberately fostered experimentation at the provincial and city level, with different ways of doing things. Then he would go out and have a look at the six or seven ways that people had tackled Problem A, to see what lessons might be drawn for a national system. He fostered differentiation. To the extent that there is a serious problem in center-province relations, it's partly the result of that. But it's also just expression, in new form, of something that was always there—a lot of autonomy for provinces.

Did this autonomy extend to local dealings with foreign governments or businessmen?

KURZBAUER: Every provincial government has a *Waiban*, a foreign affairs office, that is suppose to facilitate and assist foreign activity in that area, but also keep an eye on it and make sure that what is being done is not contrary to the perceived interests of China or the provincial government. The cultural and educational and scientific and media institutions in Northeast China with whom our consulate had relationships had to report to their provincial government or at least their institutional foreign affairs office the contacts they might have with us, or the plans that they might have to do some program with the American consulate.

In light of what happened within a few years to the Soviet empire where the nationalities split it up, did you wonder whether China would hold together?

LORD: We knew and we reported on tensions between the provinces and Beijing about taxes, about foreign exchange, about autonomy, about joint ventures, so there was already tension on the economic front between central control and the provinces. We felt this was in a safe framework of unity within the country. There was no real evidence or prospect that it was going to split apart. They have advantages in holding together that the Soviets and Russians did not have [when the Soviet Union collapsed in 1991]. First of all, 93 percent of the Chinese are Han, whereas in the Soviet Union they were 50 percent Russian and 50 percent non-Russian. Secondly, Russia was an empire, whereas, on the whole the present territory of China, most people would argue, has been Chinese for a considerable period of time. Thirdly, the Chinese have always had a tremendous advantage in overseas investment [and remittances] in helping their economy, and the Russians never had that. Fourthly, the Chinese are more self-confident. Furthermore, those who are taking power at the center were generally coming from the provinces or cities and therefore they had some of the perspectives of the outlying areas they could bring to Beijing and some empathy and sensitivity on how to handle this. Having said that, there were considerable tensions between Beijing and the provinces. A good example was Shanghai, where in those days you had to pay very heavy taxes to Beijing. They felt they were the most dynamic part of China; Beijing was reaping the benefits and they weren't.

What about the prospects of warlordism?

FREEMAN: I did not believe that China was in danger of breakup, or that the military, which is a strong, centralized, national institution, would develop warlordism. There is still, after the past 150 years of tortured Chinese history, a strong sense among Chinese that the country cannot be allowed to fall apart, that unity is all important, and that the maintenance of social and political order has to take priority over virtually everything else. The Chinese have this conclusion because, literally, over this period, something on the order of one hundred million of them have died in disorders either caused internally or by foreign invasion. So I believed that these psychological and political factors would outweigh others.[15]

REAGAN VISIT TO CHINA

Ronald Reagan had never before visited a communist country when he arrived in China in April 1984. During his five-day stay, he emphasized American values of freedom and democracy, particularly in a rousing speech at Fudan University in Shanghai, but also highlighted areas in which the United States and China shared interests, including trade and resistance to aggression from the Soviet Union. During briefings for the trip, Reagan

David and Mary Dean with President Ronald Reagan. *Courtesy of David Dean.*

met with scholars and the president of the Council on Foreign Relations, Winston Lord, who had been active on China policy during Henry Kissinger's White House and State Department years. According to Secretary of State George Shultz, Bette Bao Lord made such an impression on the Reagans that it contributed to Lord's subsequent appointment as ambassador.

HUMMEL: What state visits like these do is to give an unmistakable signal to the bureaucrats on both sides that the relationship is stable. This is very valuable. It means that routine business between the two countries is conducted more smoothly. It is a signal that it is better to be nice to the other side. Regarding our very cumbersome export controls on technological exports to China, for example, the Department of Defense always dragged its feet hard on these things. Well, you could sense a little loosening up every time we'd have a high-level exhibition of the value of this relationship. The same effect was perceptible on the Chinese side. Visits like these are a hell of a burden on the staff of the embassy, temporarily, but it's "do-able," and the effects are noticeable in the relationship. In fact, it's almost essential in some respects.

How did Reagan respond to the visit? What was your impression?

HUMMEL: He was a trooper, in the sense that when he was briefed, he remembered his brief and did what he was supposed to do. I don't think that there was a great deal of gray matter there. He was more hard of hearing than I had realized. I frequently had to raise my voice in briefing him. I had breakfast with him and his top people each of his three mornings in Beijing. We would discuss what was likely to happen and who was who. He didn't absorb background very much, like the personal background of Deng Xiaoping. However, he did know what he was about and he did it. Down in Shanghai he put on a performance which nobody could have bettered at a Chinese university. Most of the questions were agreed on in advance. He was absolutely superb. This was his showman or trooper side. He did extremely well, including the meetings with high-level officials. He knew what he wanted to say, he didn't deviate or give away things, and he was not sloppy in his presentation.

DON ANDERSON: It was a major trip, but there was not major substance. There were not too many people that wanted any new breakthroughs or any major substantive changes. So it was a big photo operation. It was a chance for the great communicator to go to China, and communicate to the Chinese, but there was a very strong element of a desire to communicate really over the heads of the Chinese to the American people as well. And there was incredible television and press coverage of that trip, and he did it extremely well.

FREEMAN: When Reagan actually came to China, he suddenly discovered very warm, reasonable human beings, who spoke in pragmatic, non-ideological terms. And he drew the extraordinary conclusion, which he voiced in a statement that he made during a stop in Alaska en route back to the United States, that the Chinese really weren't communists at all, which was news to those of us who were dealing with them. What he meant by that was that they were decent human beings, rather than ideological fiends.

His visit was fascinating. First of all, this kind of thing puts an enormous strain on an embassy. In his case, the entourage was over a thousand. Given his responsibilities as commander-in-chief in a period of the Cold War when every president was mindful that a submarine-launched missile attack on the United States meant that warning was down to seven minutes, when he traveled in China, he had to be within range of earth satellite stations. We actually installed these at intervals along the route.

Anyway, concern about security was pathological on both sides, and the city of Beijing was essentially shut down. The ill will that was caused was less due to the Secret Service than to the Chinese acceding easily to American security requirements, which meant that the whole rush hour was stopped for two hours—people outside, unable to move, bicycles everywhere.

George Shultz, who was the secretary of state by then, was along, and had very good talks with the Chinese.[16] Caspar Weinberger, the secretary of defense, also came out in what was a very important meeting, because, unlike Harold Brown's earlier travel, it was not in a condition of crisis.[17]

Did you find that you were having to peel off the layers of euphoria that the Chinese were wrapping around the presidential and congressional delegations? China is very exciting. Did you have to bring them back to reality?

FREEMAN: Yes, but also, quite honestly, I saw my role in accompanying these delegations as building a bit of enthusiasm for the relationship. There were a lot of things that the congresspeople might not have asked about, which I put them up to asking about, precisely because I wanted them to have their stereotypes shaken and to get a more accurate view of China. But, yes, they were often prone to very misguided positive over-interpretation of things that were going on, and they did have to be brought back to earth once in a while.

HONG KONG

The 1970s had been a peaceful decade along the Sino-British frontier as the Chinese Cultural Revolution and the war in Vietnam ended. With stability and peace came the expansion of the Hong Kong economy, particularly the service sector, including financial institutions linked to regional economic development. But at the beginning of the 1980s, this burgeoning prosperity abruptly stalled. The political uncertainty of retrocession to Chinese control in 1997, which affected contracts and leases, had become a palpable reality. In response to the anxieties of the business community, in 1982, London sought to initiate talks with Beijing regarding the future of the colony. Hopes that China might leave the enclave in British hands vanished quickly and a prolonged period of uncomfortable negotiations ensued. Under the provisions of the resulting 1984 Sino-British Joint Declaration, China guaranteed that Hong Kong would retain its economic, legal, and social structure for a period of 50 years after July 1, 1997. Apart from Beijing's control over foreign relations and military affairs, Hong Kong would also enjoy a "high degree of autonomy." During all these diplomatic exchanges the United States played a largely peripheral supporting role even though extensive American holdings in the territory made the outcome extremely important to Washington.

You went back to Hong Kong as consul general from '86 to '90. Was there any change in being in Hong Kong at that time?

DONALD ANDERSON: There were lots of changes, but not as many as many people might have expected. The assumption was at the time of normalization that Hong Kong would gradually shrink, would diminish, and in some respects it did. I mean the political section and economic section were considerably smaller. But strangely enough the consulate was at least as big, and maybe a little bigger, than I had ever known it to be. We had 12 or 13 different government agencies represented there, and there was constant pressure to increase. The big thing, of course, that had changed substantively was that in the 1984 Sino-British Joint Statement a time certain had been set for Hong Kong's reversion to Beijing, which affected a whole range of things in Hong Kong, and the attitude of the Hong Kong people. There was great fear and uncertainty, prior to the statement—in the period '82, '83, and into early '84. Property values were affected, people were beginning to make arrangements to get out, and there was a high degree of uncertainty.

Then came the Joint Declaration in 1984, and the document was a very good document. There was a great collective sigh of relief. But the next phase in the process, as agreed, was to begin the preparation of the basic law for Hong Kong, in effect a miniconstitution. That process was just beginning in 1986 [and would not be completed until 1990]. There was again something of a deterioration of confidence, in part because of the negotiations over the basic law and a growing sense that the Chinese really weren't going to leave Hong Kong alone. And, of course, Tiananmen occurred, which was a terrible shock.

CHINA IN THE LATER 1980s

During the second half of the 1980s, Sino-American relations, as well as the domestic Chinese economy, experienced a period of rapid growth. As Ambassador Winston Lord makes clear, military and trade links were diversified and strengthened. Many observers in the State Department believed that the relationship between Americans and Chinese had matured so far that no problems were likely to cause serious disruptions in the future. This was an optimistic time.

Although China was embarking on reforms, there were those in the U.S. Congress who were still very critical of China. What impact did this have on your confirmation hearings in 1984–85?

LORD: My nomination [was] pretty bloody. Helms' opposition ostensibly turned out to be on the abortion/population issue, but he had other reasons not to welcome my appointment. He didn't like the China opening. The media paid a lot of attention to this, and there were editorials across the country, including lead editorials in the *New York Times* and the *Washington Post*, calling me a hostage and putting pressure on Helms. The population issue was a matter of funding for UN programs, which Helms didn't want to do. We pointed out that we were not funding abortion, and the UN programs were, in fact, for areas like education on contraception, which would lower the need for abortions if you looked at them sensibly. Helms' position was that all these funding operations were fungible. Helms won somewhat of a victory. There was a crimping of our funding much to my dismay.[18]

Was there much difference between the period of your ambassadorship and that of your predecessor Art Hummel?

LORD: My timing, from November 1985 to April 1989, really was quite fortunate. I got there when things were really starting to move forward again after having been tense early in the administration. I left just after the first week of the Tiananmen Square demonstrations, the week of April 22 [see chapter 7]. So I was in a period which was probably the most positive period in U.S.-Chinese relations since the opening. There were a tremendous increase in exchanges and high-level visits in both directions and agreements even in trade.

We had some clandestine cooperation with the Chinese in the intelligence area. This included, on the positive side, working with them on monitoring Soviet missile tests and deployments, working with them to provide arms to the Afghan resistance against the Soviet invasion of Afghanistan, and sharing intelligence on other parts of the world. At the same time, of course, it still was a communist country. There was mutual suspicion on each side of spying like mad on each other, so it was a complex intelligence relationship. We had begun during the Kissinger-Nixon days sharing intelligence with the Chinese, but really began in earnest under Brzezinski and Carter when we began to monitor Soviet activities and provide joint aid to the Afghan resistance. Even when there was tension in the relationship on other issues or across the board, this aspect of the relationship was never really affected. We could go forward in good times and bad and build on a solid foundation, not known by the public and only by a few in the Congress, but it was important for both sides in times of tension that we had this overall strategic interest to work together as well as we could.

I also was interested over this period and had some success in expanding our military to military contacts. The military always had and always would play an important political role in China, so we wanted to reach that constituency. It would give us a chance over time to get a better sense of Chinese strategic and military intentions and capabilities. It would send useful signals to the Soviet Union and other potential adversaries. The military was important with respect to the export of dangerous weapons, which we didn't like. We had some modest arms sales.

The issue of arms sales arose initially during the Carter years, and there was a very controversial article by Michael Pillsbury in Foreign Policy[19] recommending that sales be used to get the relationship back on track. By the time you were ambassador, was it still controversial?

LORD: It was still controversial but less so.[20] There were some things in the works, which included working with them on the avionics for their rather dated but important F-8 fighters. It included radar for their artillery, which is relevant to Vietnam, and some upgrading of their ships. We certainly weren't going to do anything that was going to be a threat to Taiwan in our view or to military balances in general. Most of the technology or help we are talking about was 20 years old, give or take a few years. We felt this limited attempt was useful politically and psychologically without causing any undue controversy.

How satisfied were you with transparency? There have been complaints that we show the Chinese everything; they don't show us much.

LORD: There hasn't been a particularly good balance. We always tried to get more access to what they were doing, and we would visit, some staged visits, some of their units and facilities. When the secretary [of defense] or the chiefs of staff would come, they were probably embarrassed by how far behind us they were. So there is no question we consciously knew that in terms of technology and access, that they were getting more. You couldn't see this as something you could balance off exactly. For example, if they see more of our bases and capabilities, we figured that would impress them about how strong we were militarily and how far behind they were. We had the same thing on the intelligence side. Generally we would tell them more about what was going on than we would get from them. Partly if it would advance our interests, if it would make them a little nervous about the Russians or concerned about some of their partners in the Middle East that we thought were not helpful elements to regional stability, partly to try to get more information out of them.

What were our military people saying to you about the Chinese capabilities?

LORD: Well, they were way behind us. When you visited their ships or saw their aircraft or even their elite ground units, you could see just how far behind they were. They were a major big army, but it was not that strong. They were just then beginning to cut down the size of the army. They were trying to begin to modernize, and that is, of course, where they had an interest with us in getting technology. They had an unfortunate experience with Vietnam: when they invaded in 1979, they really got a bloody nose from the Vietnamese. If they couldn't handle the Vietnamese, who could they handle?

We were concerned about nonproliferation, although most of the issues we had with the Chinese in that period were on missiles, Silkworms to Iran and some other missiles to Saudi Arabia. They did that to earn money for the PLA, as well as to gain friendship and influence in other countries.[21] On the nuclear side, they had a fledgling capability then for deterrent purposes, only regional in nature; they certainly couldn't reach us at that point. At the time they were obviously relaxed about proliferation; they were helping Pakistan with their program.[22]

How did you go about dealing with the Chinese on the very difficult issue of missile proliferation in the Middle East?

LORD: On the Silkworms to Iran, we finally got them to agree not to send any more. They claimed they never had sent any, but we got them to agree that they wouldn't do it again. Shultz worked hard on this. Then when their foreign minister was visiting Washington in the late '80s, we got reports of their sending missiles to Saudi Arabia, and we got them to clamp down on that.[23] There was still ambiguous activity with Pakistan with respect to the nuclear program. The other issue that has some resonance [in 1998] is Chinese rockets launching American satellites.[24] While I was there the Challenger blew up.

It was a manned orbital U.S. shuttle.

LORD: That was a tragedy obviously in personal terms, but also a setback for our whole launching capabilities. Our satellite industry wasn't able then as today to have enough launches of American capability. Plus we felt the general orbiting satellites for communications purposes would feed into the whole communications information revolution and it would have a positive impact on China. Above all, we wanted to help our satellite makers. This was a major agreement we worked out when Secretary [of Defense Frank] Carlucci visited China in 1988. We had several conditions we worked on even after the Carlucci visit. One was the number of launches so they wouldn't unfairly hurt our own satellite launchers. Another was tight controls and inspections so there wouldn't be any security breach.

What kind of arguments did you make to the Chinese to try to persuade them not to engage in proliferation?

LORD: You use a combination of sticks and carrots. The Chinese were interested in getting more technology, including dual-use technology. For commercial reasons we were interested in this as well, so we would use that, saying, in effect, if you behave yourself on missile proliferation, we can do more on exporting dual use-technology. So there was that trade off. We also tried to appeal to their geopolitical interests, saying instability in the Near East and the Persian Gulf was not in their interest either. Now that argument has much greater weight in the 1990s when they have to import oil themselves. They want stability. We also made the point that arming Iran with Silkworm missiles that could hit American ships was a serious problem for U.S.-Chinese relations in terms of American domestic congressional opinion. Now, that had to be balanced off with their need to make money, the PLA in particular, and their desire to have an influence in the region. It was not easy going. There was a lot of tough work over many months by us at the embassy and in Washington, but we did make progress.

Was it more difficult to argue the case about Saudi Arabia since that is an American ally? Did you have to approach it differently than Iran?

LORD: I guess it was somewhat more difficult. I remember we hit them when Foreign Minister Wu [Xueqian] was in Washington [in March] '88. Shultz had a barbecue at his house in Washington. Wu got this from the national security advisor, Colin Powell as well. We thought it was destabilizing to have missile proliferation in the Middle East generally, and of course, we had the Israeli connection.[25] It was mostly with the Saudis we had to appeal to instability in the region and the impact on American opinion.

Did you have any trouble at that time with dual-use technologies?

LORD: These are technologies that could be used for either military or civilian purposes, and the issue is that if you export it, you have got to make sure that it is used for the reasons it is supposed to be used for. I do recall that we were constantly trying to expand the list of exports we thought we could safely export to make more money for Americans and more jobs without endangering national security, including a looser definition of computers, because computers have advanced so far that we felt that some could now be safely sent to China.

SIGUR: Within certain elements of our government there were always differences of view. Toward China in the economic area, there was opposition to [the sale of high-level technology] from the Department of Defense—or from some elements in the Department of Defense. (I have to be careful about labeling one department, because it wasn't quite that simple.) But during the course of this time, the NSC and the State Department always pushed toward greater opening and trying to do what we could with the Chinese.[26]

What was the role of the ambassador in trade issues?

LORD: I felt that ambassadors and country teams had a distinct obligation to American businesses to help American jobs and exports. It would also help to strengthen the overall relationship with China. I spent as much time, if not more, on our economic relationship than any other aspect during my years there, seeing Chinese on investment or trade matters, opening exhibits, promoting deals, lobbying for American companies, reporting on economics back home, devising strategies to improve the investment and trade climate. As a result, I had very good relations with the American business community.

I can understand why for strengthening the overall relationship, the more American investment we had in China the better, but what is in it for the United States economically, the United States per se, to have a lot of McDonalds?

LORD: Well, it means increased earnings for American companies, increased jobs in America, increased exports to America, as well as the effect of American business practices and interactions loosening up the political and cultural restraints in China.

Were American jobs being lost because American firms were using cheaper Chinese workers rather than American labor?

LORD: This was really not an issue at the time. Prison labor hadn't really reared its ugly head at the time, although even [in the 1990s] it doesn't involve American businesses, or at least hopefully not. At that point we even had modest surpluses with the Chinese. Trade was growing strongly while I was there, but it was modest. It was a constant battle to get the Chinese to relax their investment climate so that we could get in there.

In the 30's there was a book called Oil for the Lamps of China,[27] talking about millions of customers. This has been a theme throughout the history of Sino-American relations. It has usually turned out to be a myth. China has not been as profitable or as easy as was hoped. Can you talk about the attitude of business, the capabilities of American business, and any problems or maybe examples of what you had to deal with?

LORD: This was still relatively early. Already there were frustrations for American business because some had been there for a couple of years and weren't getting anywhere, but on the whole there was a feeling, a recognition that they had to have some patience. They were anxious to be in there for the long run; if they got in early and earned some credit with the Chinese they would have the inside track when things got a little looser vis-à-vis their competitors. A lot depended also on local leadership. For example, in Shanghai, there was a tremendous contrast between the two mayors I dealt with. The first was a guy named Jiang Zemin, and he was not very helpful. The climate was not very good for investment in Shanghai when I first went down there in late '85–86.

He became general secretary of the CCP in 1989, and later president.

LORD: And the American business community was very frustrated. Then Zhu Rongji, who is now the prime minister of China, took Jiang's place as mayor and there was an immediate change. For example, rather than have to go to a dozen different places to get permission to start a joint venture or public transaction, you started one-stop shopping where they were all consolidated in one place. When I went back to Shanghai in '87–88, the American businessmen were very pleased at the progress that was being made. The biggest problems were transparency, red tape, delays, ability to have access to the Chinese market as opposed to being pressured just to export or to provide technology. Also the hiring of the Chinese staff, the ability to get the best Chinese workers and keep them. Often they would get them, train them well, and the government would take them back and send them elsewhere. So there was control by the government over personnel working in American joint ventures

Was there much business community interest?

REUTHER: One of the first things we did was to commission our in-house [State Department] Intelligence and Research Bureau to conduct some studies for us. I remember one of the questions put to them was, if China had a telephone network equivalent to Italy or Spain, midlevel European, what would it require? The answer was that it would require the world's production of copper for the next five years to wire China. Fortunately, satellite technology was at hand, but if the stringent export control laws scared away U.S. business, we would have no commercial relationship, a weak Chinese economy, and potential supply and price problem in the international economy.

Of course, such an effort collided with the encrusted export control laws that applied to China. Over the previous 30 years, many a freshman congressman demonstrated his anti-communist mettle by sponsoring anti-Chinese legislation. The result hardly left any room for any significant trade.

At the time of normalization, our export control laws placed China and the Soviet Union in one category. The law assumed that the Chinese would potentially divert any purchase to Moscow, and that any sale to China became a precedent for a sale to the Soviet Union. One of the most acrimonious aspects of interagency implementation of the new relationship with China was overcoming these presumptions. In time, because of our interagency delays, the Chinese realized little was coming out the pipeline and at high level meetings we began to receive queries from the Chinese as to this project or that computer. To State, China's economy was so needful that diversion to non-economic purposes was a remote chance we were willing to take. Defense fought us well into the next administration.

How else did you go about building a relationship with China?

REUTHER: The second element was to demonstrate to the Chinese that the U.S. sought a full and productive relationship. So one of our objectives was to look for areas in which we could engage our two countries in responsible, normal, commercial, diplomatic endeavors.

Were you involved in negotiating agreements?

REUTHER: At that moment, Chinese commercial aviation was in its infancy, few planes were in the air. When the Chinese were going to New York in those days, they had no experience in heavy traffic and the requirement to circle, waiting one's turn to land. Normally, New York air traffic controllers create two stacks of airplanes to safely separate the aircraft and prioritize landings. Apparently it got to the point that, when the Chinese aircraft arrived, the air traffic controllers pulled all the stacks away from New York, brought him down, and then returned to normal procedures. This story, however, isn't about safety. Its about Chinese inexperience with a commercial economy. We believed it was to our advantage to expose them to how we handled these kinds of problems.

The civil aviation negotiations were interesting because the Chinese brought with them their standard bilateral civil aviation agreement. It was quite inadequate because it assumed both countries had national airlines. During our initial meetings we explained at great length that there was no U.S. national airline. We had numerous airline companies. We described how we allocated routes through a bidding process. The Chinese were absolutely flabbergasted. How could a country like the United States not have a national airline? In their lobbying effort, the Pan Am representatives took advantage of the Chinese presumption, saying, in essence, "Don't listen to what the government guys tell you, we are the U.S. national airline. Remember we served China in the '20s . . ."

Pan Am actually participated in the discussions?

REUTHER: As with many of these negotiations, there is an official delegation and industrial representatives. On the one hand, the industrial representatives acted as resources for our delegation, but did not participate
in the bilateral discussion. On the other, they had full access to the
opposite delegation. They hosted some of the meals, privately met with
the Chinese delegation, and made their own presentations to them. It
would be interesting to get the Chinese to tell us what they thought of
that whole thing.

What about Chinese business practices?

REUTHER: What we found out was that the National Science Foundation
and the educational establishment in China opposed IPR [intellectual
property rights].[28] They opposed it on the basis that since China had no
patent or copyright legislation of its own, and it was un-Marxian to be
paid for the results of your own intellectual endeavors, they saw no benefit in it. We also found out that the R&D [research and development]
sections of industrial enterprises practiced what might be called reverse
engineering.

Figure out how something works and is put together.

REUTHER: Exactly. On the other hand, when we talked to MOFERT
[Ministry of Foreign Economic Relations and Trade] officials, they
were very eager to obtain some agreement on intellectual property
rights because foreign investors had come to them and said, "I am not
going to bring my plant here until you can protect my industrial
process." We tried to explain how we looked at patents and copyrights
and why we deemed it important, why it was important to our trade,
how much of our trade involved IPR issues. We argued how unfortunate it would be for them if they were unable to take advantage of the
IPR gateway to technology by paying a few royalties. We pointed out
that the industrial world would not be favorably disposed if China continued to violate these patents. For the Chinese ministries that had intellectual rights offices, and not all of them did, we learned that there was
another major input into Chinese thinking on IPR negotiations. These

offices were very much aware of the status of our negotiation with the Japanese and Taiwanese on some of these same issues. During my ministry interviews, one of the very sharp comments I received was from a senior cabinet secretary who supervised economic ministries, who said, "You cannot expect China to get ahead of what you have gotten out of the other governments."

Across the straits, we had been seeking IPR agreement from the government of Taiwan for years. When I was in Taiwan, 1983–85, the Taiwan authorities finally agreed to some basic IPR protection, after almost 15 years of discussion, for American authored books. For years American manuscripts were pirated in Taiwan. The Taiwan publisher would mark the front page "for sale in Taiwan only," or something like that, but then sell throughout Asia. Everybody went through Taiwan to buy their copies of the American classics, academic volumes, book of the month volumes—the range of pirated books was significant.

What was happening in the domestic economy in the mid to late 1980s?

HOROWITZ: The Chinese were fully involved in the program of economic reform. There was more openness; it was easier to travel. Chinese officials had titles and they had calling cards; in 1973 to 1975, an official might be identified as "a responsible person"; they had no phone books, no rosters. Now, they would speak more openly. We just had a lot more contact all up and down the line. There was no question that the economy was improving; compared to the '70s, there was much more food in the market, more clothing and things to buy. They were making good strides, but there was still a certain amount of political reaction from time to time.

As part of the reform efforts one of the first things that the Chinese did was to try to remove some of the stringent controls in the rural areas. The communes in effect had been taken apart; it became possible for people not to own land, but at least have land that was theirs [to use according to their own priorities]. Incentives were built in and agricultural production went up, and along with that a tremendous growth in small-scale local industry. It is one of the things that is different about China from Russia and East Europe; when there is food in the market and clothing to be bought and there is not a serious inflation situation in the economy, then you can begin to experiment with other reforms.

What impressions did you have of China's leadership?

LORD: I had really very good access to Chinese leaders in the sense that we had so many visits and high-level visits during my period, and they would always see most of the top Chinese leaders [and include the U.S. ambassador in those meetings]. Deng Xiaoping was pretty consistent. First, very self-confident and lively. Not as stiff as many Chinese leaders. He would smoke a great deal and occasionally use a spittoon. He was very short, you know, hardly reach the floor, but he was a commanding presence. He always wanted to talk about big issues, geopolitical as well as the bilateral relationship. He would never get down into details. He felt that was not consistent with his position. He was already phasing down some of his active involvement. Generally at most of the meetings where you had a visiting cabinet official like the secretary of state or defense or economic agencies, he would come toward the end and would usually be the good cop. If there were mixed messages to be sent in the course of a visit, some of the tougher ones would be sent by the premier or the foreign minister, whereas Deng generally would emphasize the positive. Also he was very much dedicated to U.S.-Chinese relations. He had a lot to do with improving it and clearly wanted to keep that moving ahead despite tensions. In almost every meeting there were cracks by him against the Russians and usually against the Japanese as well. His formulations on human rights would be minimal but emphasizing, as all Chinese leaders did, the need for stability, which was a code word for them for political control or even repression.

His general pattern was one of pretty firm control on politics. After all, he sacked Hu Yaobang, the party secretary general, in the early '80s [January 1987], partly because he felt that Hu was too liberal on political reforms, perhaps too liberal on issues like Tibet. Maybe he didn't like his freewheeling, self-confident style. There was also an element of feeding him to the conservatives who were upset about the student riots in Shanghai in December-January of 1986–87.[29] After all, Deng Xiaoping had been the henchman for Mao in the anti rightist campaign way back in the late '50s.[30] With all his positive aspects on economic reform and opening to the world and U.S.-Chinese relations, you get a consistent trend of political conservatism.

Hu Yaobang was unpredictable. He was somebody who really was spontaneous and he wasn't scripted. A very active and very small person. I think he was the only one who was smaller than Deng. Clearly, he was for a looser political system. I have talked to many Tibetans who felt he was very enlightened on Tibet, and indeed he was trying to loosen up the repression in Tibet. There is documentation for that. Clearly he felt the need for political reform as well as economic reform. He was pushing the envelope. The reason he was sacked by Deng was the feeling among the conservatives that he was encouraging these trends.

Zhao Ziyang now looks very good to reformers and those of us who want to see a better political system in China. He was in the Tiananmen Square arguing for restraint, not using the army, meeting the students halfway, when he was sacked for it. He has kept up carefully from his house arrest his drumbeat for the need for political reform. He has come out dramatically twice in 1997 and 1998 on the eve of summits with letters to the leadership calling for a reversal on the official verdict on Tiananmen Square. He was, when I was there, trying to separate the party from the government, trying to loosen up the political system. Not dramatically, but pushing the envelope. So you would have to put him on that side of the spectrum along with Hu Yaobang. Very intelligent, very impressive in his meetings, generally on the friendly side in dealing with Americans, private citizens or official visitors, but gave a sense of great confidence. He was a good example of the new kind of leadership in China where they earn their leadership credentials as technocrats, economic experts, pragmatists.

Li Peng, who is everyone's convenient scapegoat, deserves a negative verdict from Americans in the sense that he clearly has been in his demeanor, the way he has acted in meetings, from intelligence reports, and from reports from other Chinese, he is generally more suspicious of the U.S., more conservative on economic reforms, certainly very tight on political issues. Probably tougher on Taiwan than some others. Clearly he not only declared martial law, but believed in putting down the students. He has not been a positive force in U.S.-China relations. On the other hand, he is enough of a pragmatist to recognize that China needs the U.S., particularly for technology, trade, investment, etc. He is an engineer by background and clearly wanted to forward the relationship for those reasons. Nevertheless, with his Soviet background and his general suspicion of the U.S., particularly our human rights policy subverting their political system he was a restraint on U.S.-Chinese relations. He was not one for conceptual discussion, geopolitical discussion.

Now, having said that, the man obviously had more staying power than I gave him credit for. After his direct negative involvement in Tiananmen Square in 1989, I didn't think he would last very long. He clearly is head of the conservative camp and, with Jiang Zemin and Deng's general approach to a more collective leadership and the need for balance, plus his own bureaucratic alliances, he maintained his position, much to my surprise.

Jiang Zemin is obviously the most important in 1998. He was not that important when I was there, as mayor of Shanghai. He did not strike us then as a man of tremendous gravitas. He was friendly, he was jolly, and he would like to show off his English and his affinity for some Western culture classics, but didn't seem entirely serious. I would not have picked him as the future leader of China. He has balanced off the conservatives and the moderates. He has been very impressive, but none of this I would have predicted.

Doesn't he get launched in part because of how well he handled Shanghai during the Tiananmen period in '89 [see chapter 7]? Also maybe you could comment on the importance of Shanghai for producing political leaders.

LORD: That is a good point. Jiang certainly gets the credit for having defused very tense and large demonstrations in Shanghai without the kind of bloody put-down that you had in Beijing. That did capture people's attention. It also protects him somewhat about a reversal of the verdict [on Tiananmen], although it may not happen anytime soon. It will happen in my view. Clearly Shanghai had been a source of Chinese dynamism and leadership for good or for ill for many decades. That is where the Cultural Revolution started. You have, of course, Jiang Zemin from Shanghai, the number one guy. Now the number two guy, Zhu Rongji from Shanghai. The Foreign Ministry for decades, not so much in the '90s, but certainly when I was there during the '80s, dominated by key people from Shanghai, at least the American handlers.

You and the embassy were looking at how all these people fit together. In other words, a little bit like Kremlinology. How were decisions reached? How effective was the government at that time?

LORD: Well, on the whole we thought the government was pretty effective in the sense they were moving ahead on economic reform. Most
of the time you had the feeling that the envelope was being pushed on
political and cultural reform. Some lively journals like the *World Economic Herald* in Shanghai, which was subsequently shut down. People
pushing the envelope like Liu Binyan, the reformist reporter, in covering corruption. You even had in some of the universities people
beginning to speak up for political reform. On the whole we felt that
things were moving in a generally positive direction. We were still
very concerned, particularly about Tibet and the continuing holding
of dissidents and repression. We knew that Deng was rather ambivalent. You would have attacks on spiritual pollution, on liberalization,
even as the envelope was being pushed. Deng was falling into a pattern of dumping his successors. He got rid of two, both of whom were
more liberal in a political sense than he was. On the economic front
we felt we were making progress, and we thought the leadership was
generally quite effective. They were beginning to promote people
now based on merit and economic performance rather than revolutionary credentials or military expertise. Now in decision making, it
was clear that Deng was calling the shots on any important issues,
U.S.-Chinese relations, U.S.-China-Russia relations, relations with
Japan, basic economic reform decisions, Taiwan. These were determined by Deng pretty much on his own. Day to day operations,
details, and secondary issues including running the economy on a
detail basis, he would delegate.

*Did you have any sense whether some of this decision making on Deng's part
was a result of negotiation with Li Peng or others who might have been more
hard-line or liberal, or was he really just making up his own mind?*

LORD: The honest answer is you can't be sure, because it was still a fairly
opaque society and system. We had much more contacts and reporting,
but an area that we were not strong in despite all our best efforts was
decision making. Certainly our impression was that Deng had an
absolute veto. There was no important policy that could be promoted if
he opposed it.[31]

What was your impression of revolutionary Marxist fervor?

LORD: None of the fervor. Still a lot of the people didn't want to talk about it, a lot of bitterness about the Cultural Revolution. Also people, whether officials or non-officials, were cautious in their conversations. In the 1990s, people can't get up and make speeches that are unsettling to the Party, and they can't organize opposition or distinct parties, but at least they speak quite freely to you on their own. In the late '80s this was clearly the exception, not the rule. Ideology was pretty dead. Even then people were worried pretty much about economics.

HUMAN RIGHTS AND POLITICAL REFORM

The growing economic prosperity in China and exposure to foreign ideas helped to spur anticipation of political reform as well. The decade had begun with the crackdown on the Democracy Wall Movement, but by the mid-1980s, a resurgence of activism and greater flexibility on the part of the leadership produced a brief era of openness and experimentation.

LORD: On the whole, during the period I was ambassador [1985–1989], China with fits and starts was moving to become somewhat more open politically and culturally as well as economically. There were obvious tensions and some periods of setbacks. Partly as a result of that, Hu Yaobang was ousted, and indeed a period of some retrenchment on political and cultural freedoms set in. Not only was Hu kicked out as party secretary, many of his friends and intellectuals either were repressed or rounded up. There was a campaign against bourgeois liberalization, emphasis on the four cardinal principles.[32] Other incidents occurred at this time. Some overseas Chinese student had come home for the holidays and was arrested. Some Shanghai writers, some officials at the universities, and the Chinese Academy of the Social Sciences were all sacked.

All this at a time when Gorbachev was beginning to gain momentum and international reputation for reform, including on the political and cultural side in Russia. Of course, this was the classic Chinese dilemma. The leaders wanted to have economic reform without political reform, ambivalent about foreign influence, needing outside help but worrying about spiritual pollution. How do they get Western technology without Western influence?

What was the approach on human rights at the time?

LORD: I raised human rights lots of times, but I don't want to pretend we pushed it stridently or hard. We took it seriously, we raised it. It was a problem, but it was not a dominant issue.

Beyond that, we tried to have an impact by having philosophic and relatively candid discussions with Chinese officials on the need for political reform and loosening up. In addition, we personally and the embassy generally spent a lot of time with intellectuals, artists, academics, reformers, etc. My wife [Bette Bao Lord], her background and knowing the language, being Chinese of course, and knowing the culture, she was a tremendous advisor to me informally on how to deal with the Chinese culturally, psychologically, and even interpret their positions. She had an instinct no barbarian could have. She had a tremendous circle of contacts for both me and the embassy, as well as herself, and there was a whole area of Chinese society that would not have been possible without her and the fact that she was a well-known authoress[33]—academic circles, cultural circles, intellectual circles, artistic circles. She worked with Charlton Heston to put on a Chinese production of the *Caine Mutiny*, which was an extraordinary success. She was extremely well-known and popular in China. Chinese leaders probably had some concerns because she knew too much. They always liked to think they could fool the barbarians, but they knew they couldn't fool her.

Also, we were pushing the envelope in terms of political freedoms in China, seeing semi or outright dissidents. We wanted to do this partly to report to Washington what was going on in those areas and partly to push the envelope. We could do that culturally in some ways more than we could politically of course. Partly [we sought] to establish ties with what we felt would be future Chinese leaders, also people in think tanks, many of whom reported directly to Zhao Zhiyang or Hu Yaobang with ideas on reforms both economic and political. People already in positions of power although young, in their thirties and forties, in terms of ideas and the debates going on in China on the need for more political reform.

For the last couple of years [that we were there], I decided that we would make a more concerted effort to get out to Chinese universities and think tanks in Beijing, Shanghai, and other cities, to have more interaction with the younger generation, to show the flag, to get their mood, and to try to modestly encourage reform efforts. Bette and I were invited to come out to Beijing University to meet with the students outdoors on the lawn. I don't know if it was [called that] then, but in retrospect, it was known as democracy salon. The students, among whose leaders was Wang Dan, the famous dissident that got out of jail with U.S. efforts and was exiled to the United States [in 1998], invited various people to come and speak to them about China and its future, including political reform and concerns of young people, in informal settings. Not speeches but to sit on the grass and hold conversations. It turns out we were the fifth in a series. One of our predecessors had been Fang Lizhi. Frankly, at the time, perhaps naively, we would have done it anyway, we didn't realize just how sensitive this was for the leadership. We made no attempt to hide that we were going out. You couldn't anyway because you were bugged all the time and people following you anyway. Of course, no one ever complained. So we had the biggest audience they had ever had. It started between 300–500 and kept growing while we were there. We arrived at 6: 45 and we went on until it got dark at 9: 30. A very agitated, excited, enthusiastic crowd. Many of the questions were personal. What is it like to have an inter-racial marriage in China? How did you two meet? How does your marriage work? Some on foreign policy and U.S.-Chinese relations, but a considerable amount on the domestic situation. I was very struck at the degree of unhappiness, impatience, frustration of the students and by the openness and the fervor of this group. There was a lot of cynicism among the Chinese students including corruption, backdoor influence, inflation, future control of their lives. They wanted their leaders to be more accessible and engage in the kind of exchange that they did with us. I, of course, knew there would be security people in the crowd hearing every word. Partly for that reason, partly as ambassador, you shouldn't be overly provocative, partly out of conviction because I thought on the economic and opening front, Deng Xiaoping was doing positive things, and partly so the students wouldn't get in too much trouble, I was very careful. I found myself almost defending Deng against the students.

By a very unfortunate coincidence, the next day [June 2] a student was murdered by hooligans. As far as we know it was totally unrelated to any of this, [but] demonstrations broke out at Beijing University. It spread to meetings and to wall posters and a march on Tiananmen

Square that was aborted. This was quickly controlled by the security with warnings to the students, plus it quickly died out because many of them realized the '86–87 protest hadn't helped. In fact, although they were in favor of reform, they wanted to go faster, they realized that if they got too out of control, they would give the conservatives ammunition. They [knew the leaders] would always be concerned about the students and the workers linking up. It is one thing in a communist society to have students and intellectuals unhappy, but if you have in a Marxist society, the workers unhappy, then you really have a problem for social stability. Clearly they had been watching what had been happening in Poland and Hungary and Yugoslavia, lots of unrest even then in the USSR. There had been a heavy Reagan emphasis on student rights in the late May, June Moscow summit.[34]

So then you began to get warnings about meeting with students.

LORD: The country director for American affairs suggested in friendly fashion that in the future I notify the authorities in advance so that they could make proper arrangements for meetings like this. In Tianjin on June 9, a new vice mayor made a friendly warning about a visit to Nankai University that afternoon. Then during the following week we got reports of displeasure over the Beijing University appearance at a politburo meeting. On Sunday night, June 12, the ambassador to America Han Xu said the chairman, Deng Xiaoping, respected me greatly, and in a very friendly and private way he suggested I be more prudent with students. I went back very tough. I said I was astonished and upset. I wasn't rude, but I made clear I was mad. I had said nothing negative and behaved myself with the students. Someone was misinforming the chairman. I think Han was a little taken aback. Washington's comment a couple of days later was, it is great you guys are getting out and talking to all the students. Thanks and we applaud this, but do we really need to have such a high profile at this point?

When you are talking at think tanks were you getting good solid questions?

LORD: It would vary. There were times when you'd go to think tanks, and you could have very good discussions on international issues, you know the Middle East or Russia. Taiwan you'd get the party line. You wouldn't raise that yourself unless they did, and they usually didn't. When it came to Chinese domestic scene, not much problem, even some debate on economic reforms. But I never felt there was much loosening up either in these joint sessions or even one-on-one on political issues. People were still very cautious, including my best friends in the government, as well as think tankers, certainly about talking in front of others with any degree of candor about political issues and even alone. Occasionally we'd have working dinners at our house with a mixture of officials, semidissidents, reformers. We were always trying to keep this debate going and hear about it and participate. The only frank discussions would take place when some of our embassy contacts who could speak Chinese were alone with people at times, and certainly Bette and her conversations in her circle.

Did you feel that you were alone in what you were doing or were the French ambassador, the British ambassador out there pushing these same themes?

LORD: Pretty much on our own. Certainly in any official government policies on human rights we were generally on our own. The others gobble up the contracts and hold our coat so to speak, while we take on the tough issues. The Japanese partly because of the guilt feelings of what they did in Nanjing in W.W.II,[35] partly because they worry about making money; the Europeans because of money. There were some exceptions—the Australians, occasionally the Canadians, sometimes the British or the Europeans—would weigh in. With respect to ambassadors, I can't be sure, but I don't know of any that were getting out to the students or the think tanks like I was.

What were conditions like for American journalists in China?

LORD: Journalists during this period generally had problems. John Burns who was a *New York Times* correspondent, although he was a Canadian citizen actually, had been detained by the Chinese [in the summer of 1986] because he had traveled in areas that he didn't have permission to travel in.[36] My instinct told me this was a possible bombshell. I immediately dropped my vacation and raced back to Beijing. It was very tense because there was some concern they might actually charge him with trespassing or violating security. In the Chinese so-called justice system, once you are charged, you are guilty. So he probably would have been jailed. We worked extremely hard, much harder than the Canadians did. We finally got Burns expelled. In the process, of course, we lost a tremendous observer of the scene. Ironically he was writing an article for the *Times* that was positive about Deng's reforms in the countryside.

What arguments were you using with the Chinese authorities?

LORD: The main argument was of course the impact. You take the premier American newspaper, you jail that reporter, it is going to have a devastating impact. Secondly, he clearly wasn't spying. The journalists generally were always frustrated by the surveillance they had in China. The longer they stayed there, the more cynical they got about the Chinese and human rights in general. In fact, they were nervous about making contact with students or dissidents or intellectuals because they might get them in trouble. The fact their phones were bugged, and they always had to get permission to travel places. It was a tough place to do business, even though it was fascinating in terms of substance.

Could you talk about one of the most widely covered newspaper stories of the period, the Bush visit and Fang Lizhi?

LORD: President Bush's trip to China in early 1989 was in the home stretch of my tenure as ambassador. Bush I had known for a long time. I had played tennis with him on occasions. I had seen him almost every time I went back to Washington, talked to him about China when he was vice president. I briefed him on behalf of Nixon and Kissinger when he went out to head up a liaison office early in his career. I had what I thought was a very good relationship. He was going to Japan to see the emperor, and going to come to China on an official visit, but not on a full state visit. As an old friend of China, one who had worked on the relationship, he was looking forward as was Mrs. Bush to return and see all their old friends. The Chinese had gone out of their way to make this a friendly visit. The Chinese agreed to have him go on live television. The first time I believe any foreign leader, certainly the first time any American president had addressed the Chinese live.

As part of the trip, there was to be his return banquet for the Chinese in the Great Wall Hotel. We had instructions from the White House to make it a big banquet, include all walks of life, old Chinese friends but all parts of society, reach a broad audience. They asked us for guest lists. Mao Zedong once said that a revolution is not a dinner party. Well, this turned out to be a dinner party that turned out to be a revolution. We came up with a full list, which included all kinds of people, officials, American business people, Chinese, academics. It also included a few dissidents, one of which was Fang Lizhi, who was outspoken on political reform. He had lost his job at Hefei University [the Chinese University of Science and Technology, in Hefei, Anhui province], but was still an official research worker for the Chinese government in Beijing. He was not some wild-eyed radical trying to overthrow the government. We said the Chinese won't like this, but frankly we did not expect an explosion in the reaction, and we said we thought it was important that the president demonstrate his overall concern with human rights as part of our engagement with the Chinese, both out of principle, also to try to help the situation and protect himself with his domestic audience and Congress back home. If we had a separate meeting with dissidents—after all, Reagan had done this in Russia—this we felt would be overly provocative to the Chinese. We finally got White House and State Department clearance on the guest list, including Fang.

Then at an advance team banquet, a protocol guy complains. It wasn't a huge complaint but it was the first warning we got. We said relax, big crowd, diverse. Don't get so upset about this. We immediately alerted Washington. Meanwhile, somehow the French press runs with something in Taiwan about how we invited Fang Lizhi and some idiot in our embassy on background said yes we did this to make a statement. Of course the Chinese, they would have reacted anyway, I'm sure. Throughout this, however, very warm friendly media coverage continued to go forward. Then at 9: 00 on February 24 we had the roughest meeting I have ever had with the Chinese. I went through all the arguments about how they shouldn't blow this out of proportion. It is just one person at a banquet. I immediately sent a message to Korea and Air Force One. It was less than 20 hours before the president's arrival. Basically because there was so little time, I didn't want the Chinese to have any illusion that we were going to back away. I said I would report to Washington, of course, but I said I doubt very much whether we are going to change the list.

Then at 12: 30—the president is landing four hours later—there is a message from President Yang Shangkun to President Bush saying if Fang Lizhi comes to the banquet, he is not coming and nobody else is coming from the leadership. By now I know I have a disaster on my hands. I went up in the plane to greet the president, which you usually do. He was distinctly unfriendly. To have a return banquet and no Chinese leaders there would not have gone unnoticed by the press. Throughout the Chinese are keeping us hanging. It is a very productive, good trip, with warm public coverage, but this thing is hanging over us. Finally we get a note that the Chinese leaders have now agreed to come to the banquet. So we made sure Fang's table wasn't in direct line sight of the leaders. I'm feeling great. I can't see from where I am sitting at the head table, Fang Lizhi's table. I'm just assuming he is there. It turns out that Perry Link [an American scholar] was with Fang Lizhi. They had gone to the banquet hall and were turned away by the Chinese security and weren't allowed to attend. None of this we knew until I got into the car. My economic counselor lets me know that Fang Lizhi is at the embassy. My heart stopped. I figured the press were going to get a hold of this, but it turned out to be a disaster beyond my wildest dreams. That's all the press cared about, nothing else about the trip. It was all down the drain. It was a low point in my career.

After a short while we were making some progress; this thing was quieting down, and then there was a backgrounder in the press that was given by [Brent] Scowcroft [the national security adviser] saying the embassy had screwed up the president's visit and they hadn't kept the Washington team informed about the Chinese being upset, and that we had invited Fang Lizhi on our own. All of which is totally untrue, of course. My embassy was about ready to lob nuclear bombs on Washington. Over the next two days, with the help of [Peter] Thomsen [the DCM] and my wife, I decided to do a secret message to Scowcroft with a copy to [Secretary of State James] Baker. I said I'm a professional, I have been around for 30 years. There are times when you need a scapegoat for the national interest or the president, and an ambassador should take a fall. I don't have any problem with that principle. But what has this backgrounder done besides being totally inaccurate? Number one, it revived the whole issue. Number two, it looked weak to the Chinese, having the president look defensive and embarrassed. It is the Chinese who should be on the defensive. Thirdly, it was wrong. Fourthly, it was discouraging for Chinese reformers and dissidents. Fifthly, he undercut all his credit with the human rights and congressional types by making clear that he was sorry this guy [was invited] to the banquet and hurt the Chinese feelings. Finally, he had destroyed any possible influence I could have in my remaining tenure as ambassador. I sent this message to Scowcroft, whom I had known for 15 years, was a relatively good friend and working colleague, who had praised the trip. To this day, I never had even an acknowledgment of the message or explanation. Not one.

What bothers me the most is the president didn't get mad at the Chinese for ruining his trip. He got mad at his own team. Now, I don't think it reveals a lack of experience in foreign policy, but frankly a clear softness on human rights, and a feeling that we shouldn't do anything to ruffle the Chinese. The president, in fact, did not raise human rights in his meetings with the Chinese at all. He got Baker to do it.

Bush considered himself somewhat of a China expert because of his experience in the Liaison Office in China. Were there any other people at the very top who had any interest in China, or were they mostly Europe oriented?

LORD: That is a good question. Scowcroft was more arms control and Russia. He had been national security advisor under Ford after all, so by definition he was a generalist including China. Baker hadn't had much dealings with Asia generally I believe, or with China. There were plenty of good people like Stape Roy [deputy assistant secretary] and others back there working on it.

Were there other key policy issues Bush was trying to resolve during the visit?

LORD: Resolve may be too strong a word. He was a brand new president, so the purpose was not to make breakthroughs, but to establish a positive tone to the beginning of the relationship as he came in. Secretary Shultz visited China a couple of times during my tenure, as did almost every other cabinet official. It was a sign of the times. We had three different CIA directors coming in black hats. We had a couple of secretaries of defense. Congressional delegations, which I encouraged. High-level visits from everyone from the Stock Exchange to President Carter to Billy Graham to Kissinger to Gregory Peck, Charlton Heston. A great variety. Probably the single most positive visit and the most important one, leaving aside President Bush one way or another, in the spring of '89 [was] Secretary Shultz's trip from March 1 to March 6, 1987. It was an important time, because of the Hu Yaobang sacking and some tightening up. On our domestic scene, we had the Iran Contra issue flaring up.[37] The strategic purpose of the trip was to make sure that we moved forward again in our relationship and to have in-depth discussions on the international issues, which included Russia, Afghanistan, Indochina, Korea, the Iran-Iraq war. Then a lot of emphasis on the economic agenda and a careful declaration on Taiwan which in effect said we would welcome any progress between Taiwan and Beijing. The secretary did reference human rights themes publicly. I thought perhaps the touch was too light, but the references he did make in his toasts and speech got very good media reporting, and perhaps he judged the level he needed about right. So I felt this trip did provide new momentum in the relationship. We agreed with the Chinese on new contacts with the North Koreans through our respective embassies in Beijing, trying to encourage North-South dialogue. We began to preview how we might begin to liberalize some exports of technology. Again, if Beijing behaved itself in other areas. We agreed to a PRC consulate in Los Angeles. We got some movement in reciprocity issues of interest to us.

TIBET

The American public rarely paid a great deal of attention to Tibet after 1959, when the Dalai Lama fled Chinese forces and took up residence in exile in northern India. American policy recognized Tibet as a part of China and officials resisted being drawn into the issue of independence or autonomy after early covert activities in the area failed. But as human rights questions grew in importance in the later half of the 1980s, the plight of Tibet emerged as a salient issue in the United States. Tibetans began actively to seek support from American public opinion and Congress to put pressure on the Chinese. The Chinese themselves provoked greater outside scrutiny when in the autumn of 1987, they brutally suppressed a series of demonstrations in Lhasa.

FREEMAN: The background on Tibet is that, in the 1950s, the CIA spent a vast amount of money to produce a rebellion in Tibet. And that rebellion was the precipitate cause of the Dalai Lama's flight over the border to India. That is, we attempted, as part of our general policy of desta-bilizing China, to destabilize Tibet and, if possible, detach it from China. We were all very sensitive, in the 1980s, to the way in which American maneuvers on Tibet might be viewed in Beijing, given this history.[38]

Subsequently, the issue of Tibet has been embraced by quite a range of people in the United States: some are simply drawn to exotic cultures and favor primitive peoples out of some sentimental impulse; others, for one reason or another, as the United States has become more anti-scientific, are more drawn to mysticism. There is a significant portion of the American public now that is avowedly dedicated to what is, in my view, superstition.

[In this period] there were some fairly promising exchanges going on between the Dalai Lama and the Chinese. At one point, it looked as though the Dalai Lama and the Chinese were about to do a deal, and that he was coming back. That was sabotaged by militant members of the Dalai Lama's entourage, rather than the Chinese.

In fact, this was a period of continuing liberalization in Tibet. The Cultural Revolution sacking of monasteries and libraries and the like was being repaired at the expense of the Chinese government. Large amounts of money were going into Tibet for reconstruction. The Chinese had reversed the Red Guard mentality. Although many of the Red Guards in Tibet were Tibetan, not Chinese, they had made an all-out effort to destroy both the relics and the reality of Tibetan culture. The Chinese had turned 180 degrees and were trying to restore and protect Tibetan culture.

LORD: The Tibet issue flared up a couple of times while we were in China. In 1987, particularly in the spring, there was a clamp down on political and cultural expression in China. Whether or not related, things began to heat up in Tibet. The Dalai Lama went to the U.S. in the middle of September 1987. On September 27, and the next few days, there were considerable riots and demonstrations in Tibet. There were about 20 deaths and hundreds injured. The Congress passed a resolu-tion 98–0. Tom Brokaw had just been there for NBC and did a piece and said some nice things about the Dalai Lama. The Chinese weren't too happy about that. They were making it hard for us to have access, but we smuggled out reports.

Some American specialists on Tibetan affairs have suggested that one of the things that was happening was the Tibetans becoming more sophisticated on how to play to American public opinion. Was this a concern in the embassy that there was an effort to circumvent the diplomatic corps and get to Congress directly?

LORD: No, I don't think we had that feeling. [But] there was some synergy between the Dalai Lama's visit in the United States and the demonstrations taking place a few days later. Our reaction was not one of how dare the Tibetans express their views. We were really upset about the Chinese reaction. Now obviously without suffering from clientitis, we didn't want the Tibet issue any more than any other one issue to wreck our whole relationship. I pushed the Chinese on it, but we would also try to keep the overall relationship going. I went to Tibet, the first American ambassador to ever go there, from August 4 to August 10, 1988, both to convey our concerns to the officials running Tibet as well as back in Beijing. Show the American flag for whatever that might do for the morale of Tibetans and to show the congressional and domestic audience that we cared enough. I had the most comprehensive talks up to then on Tibet of any American official ever had with the Chinese. I can't say I got very far. I pressed the human rights situation there generally, the suppression of Tibetan culture and people. [They made] their familiar defense of how Tibet had been a feudal enclave before, of slavery under the Dalai Lama. How much better off the Tibetans were now. I did get more consular visits and some journalists in there. On prisoners all I got were some numbers.

Did you have the feeling that Tibet served as a good rallying flag for particular conservatives who detested our China policy, or did Tibet run deeply in your opinion in the consciousness of the American public?

LORD: Well, the province of Tibet is so remote it is hard to get coverage of it and know what is going on and conveying that to the American people generally. I do think people in Congress and other human rights groups were absolutely sincere in their concern for Tibet and the extinguishing of Tibetan culture, the treatment of nuns and monks, the roundup of prisoners and the put down of demonstrations. Clearly those who were suspicious of China for human rights generally would also highlight this issue for that reason, but it was born out of a genuine concern for what was a genuine problem. I would say it probably had a higher profile in human rights than anything else while we were there.

SIGUR: The problem of human rights, particularly as it involved Tibet [was one] we had to continually raise with China and keep close touch with the Congress. Some people in the Congress didn't think we were strong enough with the Chinese. But I thought we were. I thought we handled that fairly well. We did get some communication going between their officials dealing with Tibet and members of our Congress and their staffs, who had discussions back and forth on it.

EXCHANGES BETWEEN CHINA AND THE U.S.

Among the most significant aspects of the growth in contacts between the United States and China was the flourishing of cultural and scholarly exchanges. During the 1980s, access to universities in both countries broadened and students and researchers took advantage of opportunities in increasing numbers. Among American diplomats this development seemed especially welcome, because they believed that exposure to American life would have a lasting impact, helping to make China and the Chinese more enthusiastic about the free market and democratic reform.

The Soviets tended to want to have ballet and jazz orchestras exchanged, but as far as students going, they wanted mainly students who would learn everything they could in the field of mathematics or physics, and they wanted our Americans to go look at icons. What was the Chinese attitude?

SOLOMON: Well, in the early period, the exchange programs were tightly controlled, highly structured. They involved primarily the exchange of established professionals in the various science disciplines, or musical or other entertainment groups. There was almost none of the free-wheeling exchanges of students that began in China in the spring-summer of 1978, when Deng Xiaoping opened the door to very active exchanges. At that time exchanges were designed to gradually turn public opinion in each country in a more positive direction. Later on, when the exchanges did develop, the Chinese students came over in tens of thousands. They did tend to focus primarily on the sciences and engineering, some in the business management area, very few in the social sciences. There was a tremendous imbalance in the numbers exchanged; that is, not all that many American students went to China to study in contrast to the tens of thousands of Chinese who came to the U.S.

DONALD ANDERSON: I have always pushed [scholarly exchange] because Chinese that have come to the United States now, and it's growing every year, will be a tremendously important factor in our bilateral relations and in China's modernization. I was struck by that when I was consul general in Shanghai. After the Gang of Four period was wound up, many of the older people who had been in prison or had been under house arrest, or whatever, were coming back and getting responsible positions. Many of these people had been trained either in the United States, or at places like St. John's University in Shanghai, which was an American-run missionary university. Dealing with them was just marvelous because they understood, even after an absence of 35 years, what we were talking about.

FREEMAN: Over this entire period, beginning with normalization, there was an extraordinary trend in progress in which the children of the Chinese elite came to the United States to study. There are very few members of the Chinese Communist Party Central Committee or senior officials in ministries who have not had one or more children graduate from American universities. Even Deng Xiaoping's children came here to study, and, in one case, to serve as a wife of a military attaché in the Chinese Embassy.

Up to this point had there been a dearth of foreign education or were they switching from the Soviet Union to the United States?

FREEMAN: In the 1950s, there was significant exposure to the Soviet Union, but in far smaller numbers than later occurred with the United States. The Soviet system was just a lot less accommodating and much more controlled than the American one. That was the early period of restoration of full sovereignty under the communists, and there was suspicion of foreigners. So that the people who tended to be trained in the Soviet Union were being trained as specialists either for the Foreign Ministry or, in some cases, as engineers. Li Peng, the former premier, for example, studied in the Soviet Union [in the late 1940s and early

1950s]. He's an electric-power engineer, who has come to specialize a bit in nuclear power.

This enormous flow of young people, middle-aged people, many of them, whose education in China had been interrupted by the Cultural Revolution and domestic turmoil, to the United States has given a younger generation of Chinese an extraordinary familiarity with the United States. The effects of this were rather interesting. There was enormous regard for the American economic system, the openness it has to new ideas, the way in which ideas can move from the university laboratories or company laboratories into innovative production technologies. Probably the Chinese reforms were inspired in no small measure by the discovery of this whole new way, for them, of doing business and managing technology.

On the political level, there was a mixture of admiration and distaste for what the Chinese discovered here. No Chinese that I have met seems to want to emulate either the U.S. federal system or the constitutional democratic presidential system that we have.

So there was certainly an admiration for the intellectual freedom that the U.S. provides, but at the same time, a great distaste for what many of the Chinese see as the inevitable results of excessive acquisitive individualism and First Amendment rights. The Chinese tend to tie social disorder in the United States—high rates of teenage pregnancy, drug use, the extraordinary crime rate, the lack of personal security on the streets, some of the things that we Americans also find least admirable about our society— to our political system.

Over time, some of these ideas might well be adapted to China. But, in fact, a more potent example for the Chinese, one that they cite themselves frequently, is Taiwan, which evolved in an earlier period in which there was a greater sense of optimism and confidence in the United States than there is now, and many of the social problems hadn't emerged in their current virulent form. So the Chinese look for models that get on with the business of economic reconstruction, building prosperity first, and then deal with some of the political problems of the system later, in a gradual way.

The dominant sentiment for the Chinese, and the reason they react the way they do to some of the untidy aspects of American life— pornography and crime and addictions—has to do with the searing experience of Chinese history. Disorder in China can have catastrophic consequences, and you don't have to be very old, if you're Chinese, to have actually experienced some of those. So that, while people would like to see human liberty expand, they're very cautious about how authoritarianism is to be relaxed.

But the expansion of student exchange was quite something to observe. And the management of this, just from an embassy technical view, was very difficult. First of all, we had visa forms that were deeply offensive to the Chinese, because they asked whether you were a communist, pusher, prostitute, or whatever, all in the same section, and the Chinese, who were rather proud to be communists, didn't see why these other affiliations should be associated with their political philosophy. Most of the Chinese who came here were communists, and every one of them required a waiver from the attorney general to get in. This added inordinate delay to travel, and complicated things. We began to press hard for a simplification of procedures, because we had to send a telegram on every visa applicant and wait for a name check and so on.

Taiwan had notorious levels of nonreturn (at one point, about 80 percent didn't go back), but the vast majority now do go back, although they may delay for a few years, to work in the U.S. In China, I was more surprised by how many did go back than by how many didn't, because living and working conditions in China in the early '80s, were really pretty awful, and you had to be fairly dedicated to want to go back. The Chinese seemed to take a very relaxed attitude about whether people came back or not.

But we had a number of notorious defections, not particularly by students. There was the Hu Na incident, a woman tennis player from Sichuan, who had been a sometime tennis partner for Wan Li, who was vice premier, and for Deng Xiaoping. Her defection was contrived by the immigration lawyer for the Guomindang in San Francisco, and I suspect was contrived in part for political effect. But whether that was the case or not, she did defect [in 1982, and was granted asylum on April 4, 1983], and all holy hell broke loose, and we lost our cultural exchange agreement.

Were you there at the time?

FREEMAN: Yes, I was. Because of Deng's personal involvement in the case, this became really quite a nasty matter. And Ronald Reagan got personally involved and made various defiant statements about how she could move into the White House. The problem was that this sort of stuff got so easily bound up with Taipei's rivalry with Beijing. I remember arguing strenuously with friends in the Foreign Ministry that these things become causes célébres only to the extent that you make them such.

At the same time China was opening up, allowing its citizens to go abroad, people in the overseas Chinese community, including many who had fled the mainland, began to come back in very large numbers, to look at their old homes, to meet their old schoolmates, to see the Great Wall. This overseas Chinese connection, although at various points it's been attenuated, is one of the great differences between the Chinese Revolution and the Russian Revolution, in an earlier era. The Chinese seem to be very willing to forgive and forget, not make terrible demands on émigrés. They haven't had a history, for example, of going out and killing émigrés.

The old GMD group in Taiwan had a very effective apparatus in the United States, looking after émigrés, public relations, and spying. What was your impression of that of the Mainland Chinese?

FREEMAN: Much less effectively managed, on many levels, than comparable work from Taipei. Also less overtly demanding. Taipei really demanded positive loyalty from people. Beijing was much more tolerant and willing to have broad contact, perhaps because it was starting from a very low base and needed to appear flexible and accommodating. This sort of work was not done terribly well by Beijing during that period. To some extent, this kind of activity came at the expense of the sort of efforts that Beijing should have made to cultivate Americans with no close connection with China.

For example, they monitored very carefully Taiwan's activities with the overseas Chinese in Chinese. They didn't monitor Taiwan's activities with non-Chinese in English. So, in terms of Beijing's interactions with Taipei on this overseas Chinese battlefront, it seemed that Beijing was treating this more as an extension of the Chinese civil war than as something really involving the United States.

Did you have problems on the consular side with Americans getting into trouble?

RASPOLIC: American Citizen Services is very busy in Beijing because most American tourists who come to China visit Beijing. We had the traditional gamut of problems, a lot of deaths, a lot of people suffering from the "Peking duck syndrome." Death by duck. The elderly person, because a tourist in China generally is elderly, because they're the ones who have the money and the time to afford to go to China. They go, they're taken out at 6: oo in the morning, they're off to see the Great Wall, then tromping through the Ming tombs, and they stop off at the Forbidden City. Then they go back to the hotel, shower and change, and go out for a banquet. By the time they get back to the hotel, it's 10: oo or 11: oo at night. You're 75 years old and you had a bypass 15 years before, and bingo!

How did you find the Chinese as far as helping you with the death cases?

RASPOLIC: Very helpful. We had very good relations with the major hospitals in town. We had two or three hospitals with foreigners' clinics that we dealt with extensively, both for death and illness cases. Tourism is an important business to them, it is their main industry, and they certainly don't like seeing tourists die.

On the cultural side, here is the ancient Chinese culture, and the very aggressive American culture, were there problems?

DONALD ANDERSON: The problems weren't between an ancient Chinese culture and a modern American culture. The problems were in the degree to which the Communist government wanted to maintain control. And the degree of openness that they were prepared to permit. We were always pushing for more and more open exchanges, more frank discussions, and the Chinese were always just a little bit nervous.

LORD: Basically the Chinese strategy was to get Western technology and Western money without being subverted by Western ideals, culture, and ideas. We would have reminders of their repression. I remember one example where we were going to send to China an exhibit from the National Portrait Gallery. Just before it was about to come over, the Chinese said there are two portraits that cannot be included in this. One is Golda Meir from Israel, the other is [General Douglas] MacArthur, because of the Korean connection. There were some in my USIA section that wanted to bend on this. I thought this was absolutely wrong. It would be bad generally as a principle and secondly setting a precedent for future cultural exchanges, and also it would set off an uproar in the United States where there is still understandably great suspicion of China not only its human rights but its cultural backwardness. So we hung very tough on this, but the Chinese wouldn't give in and the portrait exhibit didn't take place. This was an example of their idiocy.[39]

TAIWAN

Efforts to codify the new U.S.-Taiwan relationship proved difficult in the early 1980s, largely because Nationalist Chinese officials continued to try to restore a measure of officiality to contacts between Washington and Taipei. On the other hand, as time passed, Taiwan's leaders came to recognize the harsh reality of the international arena and to adapt. As a result, Taiwan moved from authoritarian control toward democracy. It also began to reach across the Taiwan Strait to initiate new contacts with China.

LILLEY: [In 1982, when I arrived] Taiwan was on an upswing economically. They were developing the high-tech electronics industries. They had been in food processing, and textiles, and shoes. Then they started moving into semiconductors, transistors, electronic consumer goods, computers. They were in this transition period.

Politically it was still fairly stiff. They did not allow an opposition party. They only called the opposition Taiwanese group the *dangwai*, outside the party they called them. But they allowed them to publish. They closed down if they went too far, the magazines and the newspapers. But they did allow them to say things and they begin to allow them to come into the political process.

REUTHER: Members of the opposition would register a number of magazine names. When the Garrison Command closed one title, for some article mentioning Chiang Ching-kuo's secret fortune or Chiang Wei-kuo's activities, the opposition would return the next month under a new name.

LILLEY: A couple of things happened at that time that begin to change things. The first was Chiang Ching-kuo—he was a brilliant man, a real visionary—and he had early on told me indirectly but prophetically,

"I've got a four point program for Taiwan: (a) I'm going to democra-
tize, (b) its going to become a Taiwan process, (c) I'm going to maintain
prosperity because I have to, and (d) I'm going to open up to China."
This was passed to me in '82. He did every one of them in his own sort
of chessboard way, very careful moves. He took his old hard-line men-
tor Wang Sheng, who ran the political department in the military, sent
him to Paraguay as ambassador, got him out of there. He brings in a
Taiwanese governor, unelected governor, Lee Teng-hui to be his vice
president in '84. He makes sure that I get to meet Lee [as AIT director]
and spend time with him. Get to know each other. Nobody else would
be there. He begins to allow more and more Taiwanese to come out, to
have meetings etcetera, etcetera. He impresses people like [Congress-
man] Steve Solarz [D-NY] that he is beginning to release the bonds on
these people.

REUTHER: Congressmen Solarz from New York visited Taiwan and publicly identified himself with the opposition. His attention assisted their
cause and gave them some cover. I recall accompanying him to a speaking engagement at a Taipei hotel. His address was not as remarkable as
the opportunity for the opposition to meet without being arrested.

*How did the Taiwanese enter the political arena instead of being limited to
making money and doing business?*

REUTHER: Chiang Ching-kuo was an absolutely fascinating personality.
He first came to Taiwan as a strict enforcer of the security system. Chiang, however, may have realized that the army, and then the party, in
time would exhaust the pool of Mainlanders. This realization probably
led to the Taiwanization of the upper reaches of the GMD and government. When a cabinet shuffle would occur, when the Guomindang
would have a standing committee election, Chiang would add one or
more Taiwanese, generally balanced by Mainlander appointments, but
slowly resulting in increasing numbers of Taiwanese in positions of
influence. Explaining the significance of creeping Taiwanization, we
would add that our interlocutors characterized the Taiwanese
appointees as younger, Western educated, and more talented. Young,
American-educated Mainlanders suggested they and their Taiwanese
counterparts were the group Chiang increasingly relied upon.

The GMD, which needed a mechanism to legitimize itself and extend to the grass roots, had held elections on Taiwan since the early 1950s. These elections allowed them to fan rivalries among local Taiwanese factions. The GMD would support one local faction one election and another local faction the next election. But the older hard liners had always believed that the GMD should always win an election by a landslide. The people returning to the island, the moderates, the modernizers, were saying, you could win an election with 51 percent of the vote, your manhood was intact and you were still in power. That was a revolutionary idea and it took years before the older members of the party agreed that the only thing you had to do was to win the election, not overwhelm it.

How strong was the opposition?

REUTHER: In fact, one of the key things that was going on in Taiwan at that time was a consequence of the January 1979 change in diplomatic relations. The political opposition saw derecognition as damaging to the ruling party's claim to power. It argued that even the Americans have walked out on the GMD; that Taiwan was isolated, weak, and in danger of being turned over to Beijing because of GMD claims to be the government of all China. The end result of increased opposition pressure and derecognition was the Kaohsiung demonstrations on Human Rights Day in December 1979. The entire leadership of the opposition was in Kaohsiung on that day. The government trapped the opposition into a street riot and used that circumstance to crush it. One individual, because he was ill and couldn't make the rally, was the only *dangwai* leader not rounded up.[40] Also swept up in the government crackdown and tried in military court was the leadership of the Presbyterian Church of Taiwan. So from 1979 on, the worst aspects of the authoritarian government that had been in place since 1949 exhibited itself. Underlining the significance of these events, on the anniversary of the February 1947 massacre of Taiwanese protesting GMD rule, the family of one of the defendants [Lin Yi-hsiung] was slaughtered in its home.[41] When I arrived everyone was in jail, the family was murdered, and little incidents denoting pressure on the opposition happened from time to time. You know, a Chinese American visiting tripped and fell off a five-story building while in police custody.[42]

Was this Henry Liu?

REUTHER: No, that was Chen Wen-chen. Henry Liu was a GMD-trained political warfare officer, who worked as a journalist, had fallen out of favor with the GMD, and was in the process of writing a biography of Chiang Ching-kuo. The biography was supposedly very critical. He was living in the United States. A group came to the United States in 1984 and assassinated him in his garage in a town outside of San Francisco.

What is interesting about this event is that it appears to have become a turning point in the way the GMD governed Taiwan. It is my impression that the younger, American-educated members of the Guomindang—those who had been pushing for elections and similar procedures to keep the party in power rather than strong-armed tactics—were quite upset that they were a party to this murder. They were not willing to see the Taiwanese opposition come to power, but they thought different tools were available to the GMD; that it could base its legitimacy on its success in economic policy.

THAYER: The responsibility for this murder lay with one of the intelligence branches of the Taiwan government. There were a lot of discussions between us and our friends in Taiwan, a lot of American outrage about the murder. It eventually surfaced that this was connected to officially connected people, and three of them were, in fact, convicted in Taiwan court and jailed.[43]

Was this sort of a rogue elephant operation?

THAYER: The responsibility was at a fairly high level in the intelligence branch, and the key guy, as far as we know, was convicted; and justice, as far as we know, was done.[44] But we had to express our outrage—forcefully and at high levels—before action was taken.

Did you find the native Taiwanese leaders less confrontational than the GMD?

FREEMAN: The Taiwanese, with 50 years of Japanese occupation and 25 years of really brutal repression by the Chinese Mainlanders behind them, do have a different mentality. But far from being less confrontational, they are perhaps more fiery of temperament than the Mainlanders who came over, and really quite cocky. Taiwan is a wonderful success story. It's the first Chinese society that has successfully modernized, both politically and economically. It is, in many respects, the most admirable society that has ever existed on Chinese soil. The achievements that people in Taiwan have made give them a kind of self-confidence that sometimes verges on obstreperousness and genuine rashness in their approach to the mainland.

What about Taiwan's relations with the United States?

LILLEY: There was steady movement on the United States' part to take care of their defensive needs. Secondarily, they wanted access to government officials and they had been frozen out [under Carter]. They thought immediately when Reagan came in they could walk right into State Department, right into the White House. They couldn't. But what we did was to discreetly meet with them. We began to meet with them at high levels. And we worked with them. They'd send over the foreign minister, the premier, the minister of finance, the chief of the general staff, the minister of defense. We met with them all.

Was there any trouble with the Mainland Chinese protesting?

LILLEY: Oh yeah. They would get wind of one of these things and they would throw a fit. But we could tell it was—you have to tell the difference between rhetoric and the real thing. [In Taiwan] I didn't meet them at the Foreign Ministry. I met them at a guest house, although I went to the Foreign Ministry once or twice. And I went into the presidential office too, sub rosa. The [Taiwan authorities] had a sense that we were inhibited by the rules but that we knew how to get around them.

You became the third director of the American Institute in Taiwan [AIT], following Chuck Cross and Jim Lilley. How did that work?

THAYER: None of the AIT staff is legally an official employee of the American government. All of us who were Foreign Service officers were legally separated from the State Department.

REUTHER: We needed an administrative device which allowed Foreign Service officers to resign their commissions, take a job with this private company—AIT—and still be eligible for reinstatement as a commissioned officer without the lost of benefits. Let me tell you, it took a lot of legal thinking to turn that light on, and in the end we were never able to apply that system to our own military. AIT Taipei had a military section, but there is no way in our legislation, or via the regulations the uniformed services followed, for a military officer to resign his commission and then return to duty.

So they were all retired military?

REUTHER: They were all retired military who had had full military careers, retired, and then were picked up as private hires.

THAYER: But the American Institute in Taiwan, which is modeled after the Japanese equivalent entity that they established when they broke relations with the PRC, is set up to conduct relations with Taiwan in very much the same way as an embassy conducts relations. We were broken down into the same kind of sections—political, economic, and so forth. But we called them by different names. The political section was called the General Affairs Section [GAS], for example.

The point being that we wanted to remove all the symbols of government-to-government relations and all the symbols of an embassy, while still being able to carry out the substantive work. We had no American flag flying in Taiwan. I was not known as ambassador; I was known as director. I did not call on officials of Taiwan in their government offices. If I wanted to complain to the minister of economic affairs, as I did more than once, to get some trade problem straightened out, I would have to ask him to meet me either in a hotel room or a restaurant. I technically didn't deal with the Foreign Ministry. I dealt with the head office of the Coordination Council for North American Affairs [CCNAA], which was my counterpart.

REUTHER: The authorities on Taiwan spent all their time trying to prove to themselves and their public that we had an official relationship. For two years [1983–1985], we engaged in a running game of thrust and parry with the local authorities. For example, Taiwan's unofficial counterpart to AIT was the CCNAA. It had an office in Washington (and other American cities) and one in Taipei, with which we conducted liaison as if it were the "Foreign Ministry." Publicly we were seen working with CCNAA, which was housed in a separate building a few blocks from the Ministry of Foreign Affairs. In fact, we worked closely with talented and patriotic officials at the Ministry of Foreign Affairs, but in unofficial venues. At one point, for their domestic reasons, the authorities on Taiwan told us that they would move CCNAA into offices on the backside of the building that housed the Ministry of Foreign Affairs. This would create a situation where, if you will, the address for the ministry is 1500 Third Street, but the address for the opposite side of the same building was 1500 First Street. Despite their arguments of efficiency, their intent was to impart the appearance of officiality to the relationship. We begged them not to tinker with the symbols of unofficiality, and they finally dropped this idea. Our objective was not to put Taiwan down. The reality was that we could have as robust a relationship with Taiwan as we desired, as long as we kept it unofficial, meaning out of the public eye. A public event would force Beijing to notice; otherwise Beijing would turn a diplomatic blind eye. At issue for the authorities on Taiwan was their domestic legitimacy, which they had tied to their claim to be the government of all of China.

FREEMAN: The unofficial representatives of Taiwan throughout the country, and their many, many offices, were constantly engaging in petty moves to demonstrate the officiality, as they put it, of the relationship. This would include arranging with local officials to fly the flag of the Republic of China over the mayor's office, or, in some cases, to acquire consular license plates from the local officials, since there's no federal regulation of this, or to list themselves, as they did in many telephone books, including in Washington, as the Embassy of the Republic of China. They took out ads in the *Yellow Pages*, portraying themselves as an embassy, and stressing that they were the Republic of China, and so on. All of this entirely understandable from their perspective, but enormously irritating to the State Department and to the PRC, as they were endlessly ingenious in the way in which they sought to score these political points.

Where was the American Institute in Taiwan located? How did this work?

FREEMAN: There was a small Taiwan coordination staff in the Bureau of East Asian and Pacific Affairs, which I eventually succeeded in having moved down adjacent to what was then the Office of Chinese Affairs. There is an internal corridor connecting the two (called the Taiwan

Strait, of course). That move greatly facilitated cooperation within the department.

The American Institute in Taiwan has its Washington offices [across the Potomac River] in Rosslyn, Virginia, and it is responsible for day-to-day contact and providing a venue for meetings, of an unofficial character, with officials from Taiwan. It is also the body that is responsible for the post—management and other administrative support functions for the American Institute in Taiwan offices in Taipei and Kaohsiung, in Taiwan. So if a delegation from Taiwan came here, it would be received by AIT, and AIT would arrange appropriate meetings with American government officials, outside of U.S. government offices, in appropriately informal settings.

Well, it turns out, of course, that appropriately informal settings are far more productive than the usual formal settings, and that to insist that all business must be done over a working lunch or over a drink in a hotel lobby produces far better results than making people come to your office. So I don't think Taiwan lost, in any respect, by this, and maybe even gained.

THAYER: When the relationship was first established, there was little confidence, or certainly not full confidence, on the part of our friends in Taiwan that we could have an unofficial relationship that really worked.

SHOESMITH: As a matter of fact, it's worked so well that other governments have adopted that system for maintaining relationships with Taiwan.

REUTHER: Part of the change of relations in 1979, of course, was a much less intimate relationship with the elite, the Guomindang. AIT had good relations with the economic and the commercial offices of the government and the business community, but not with the ruling party. So my job was to reestablish the relationship with the Guomindang.

What were the major issues that you had to deal with between the United States and Taiwan?

LILLEY: When I got there it was probably 90 percent security, and we began to get this behind us, and by the time I left [in 1984] we were spending 40–50 percent of out time on our issues, which were trade.

This included the problem of intellectual property and the fact that Americans were getting ripped off?

LILLEY: Taiwan was the capital of the world. Encyclopedias for what, 20 bucks? Rolex watches, Gucci bags, it was all there.

THAYER: The major issues we had [after 1984] that I can discuss here were in the trade area. Taiwan was targeted by the USTR, United States Trade Representative's office, for a number of negotiations—and Section 301[45] actions were threatened more than once. We had some very heated times with the authorities in Taiwan over trade matters. The most unpleasant was, for me, the American effort to get Taiwan to open its market to American cigarettes. Taiwan wasn't the only place where we've done that. This was an issue in Korea, Thailand, and so forth. The tone of this debate on cigarettes got to be quite nasty. We brought a lot of pressure. The trade issue thus became a big *political* issue, with overtones of pushing opium on the Chinese.

The fact is that Taiwan has a tobacco monopoly bureau and Taiwan makes its own cigarettes, and a good deal of revenue was earned by this. Their market was closed, relatively speaking, to American cigarettes, closed to American cigarette advertising, but open to Taiwan advertising. The American tobacco companies wanted it open. We at AIT failed to anticipate what should have been obvious. We had the papers just flooded with reports about bringing this huge pressure on poor innocent Taiwan, Americans pushing poison, cancer-inducing substances, on the people of Taiwan. The fact is that the Taiwan monopoly was pushing their cigarettes as hard as they could. So a lot of this was, of course, hypocritical posturing on the part of our Taiwan interlocutors.

In the mid-1980s, to what extent was there interaction between Taiwan and the mainland? Was there investment by Taiwanese entrepreneurs in China?

REUTHER: The Taiwan Garrison Command watched Mainlander and Taiwanese alike. In those days it was recognized that it was the Mainlanders, brought to Taiwan in the last days of 1949, who longed to visit the mainland. The Taiwanese did not like the Mainlanders they knew. One *dangwai* stalwart at the time told me that Taiwanese were always worrying about a sell-out; that, as the Mainlanders aged, they might turn to Beijing in their twilight years and turn Taiwan over. After all, the GMD and the CCP were of a single mind that Taiwan was just a Chinese province.

For the Mainlanders, despite Garrison Command, there was a safety value. One could go to Hong Kong and once in Hong Kong one would disappear and visit mainland relatives. There were rumors that, because the people in Fujian Province spoke the same language as people in Taiwan, Taiwanese business people could sneak back to Fujian and do a little business. Such travel was easily monitored by the security forces. But the GMD couldn't cut it off because that would damage Mainlander support.

KOREA

In the 1980s, the Democratic People's Republic of Korea remained a client state closely associated with Beijing. But although Kim Il Sung, North Korea's leader, still called his friendship with Beijing "invincible," Beijing had begun to expand its economic relations with South Korea and to think about ways to resolve hostilities on the peninsula that threatened the peace vital to Chinese modernization and development.

FREEMAN: [In the early 1980s, the Chinese] grossly misperceived Korea through ideological blinkers. The South Koreans were fumbling around with the Chinese, through the Korean CIA in Hong Kong. Koreans are very direct and tough people, and they were making quite a hash of this. They tended to demand things up front, and to use very blunt and insulting bargaining techniques, and to misunderstand the difference between things that needed to be done with a wink and a shrug and things that could be done explicitly. And so they were getting nowhere.

Over the spring of 1983, I had quite a number of discussions with the Chinese, arguing with them that they should find a way to have an opening to South Korea, which was something the South Koreans desperately wanted and which we supported, in general terms. This culminated during [Caspar] Weinberger's visit to China in the summer of '83.

He was secretary of defense.

FREEMAN: Deng Xiaoping actually proposed to Weinberger a meeting in Beijing between the South and North Koreans, with the U.S. in attendance, all hosted by the Chinese. I was astonished. That evening, after he left, as we got the reporting cable done, we confirmed with the Foreign Ministry that indeed Deng had said this, that indeed it was very important, and that indeed he was making a major policy initiative. And we sent off a cable saying that, only to discover that Paul Wolfowitz [assistant secretary of state for East Asian and Pacific affairs] had edited this comment out of the conversation, alleging that he hadn't heard any such thing. Then he denied adamantly that it had been said, and accused us of having put words in Deng's mouth. Washington was mystified by our cable reporting a Chinese initiative in Korea.

During George Shultz's visit to China with President Reagan in the spring of '84, the Chinese again raised the issue of meetings with South Korea, the U.S., and North Korea. Shultz agreed, talking to [Ambassador] Art Hummel. Between Beijing and Shultz's arrival in Seoul, Paul Wolfowitz again reversed this.[46]

Again, we were talking about opening relations at that point?

FREEMAN: We were talking about a Chinese proposal to host a South Korean-North Korean meeting, with the U.S. in attendance, in Beijing, which would have involved, inevitably, U.S. and Chinese mediation between South and North Korea, and which, frankly, was a pretty creative and useful suggestion. It followed up on Deng Xiaoping's earlier suggestion.

And then there was a very nasty leak in the Periscope section of *Newsweek*, accusing Art Hummel of having manipulated George Shultz on the Korean issue. I later discovered that there was a notation made in my personnel file to the effect that I had put words in the Chinese mouths on Korea. Very nasty stuff.

Korea was a very ideological question for us as well as for the Chinese, and evidently, by the middle of '83, the Chinese were thinking a little more creatively and less rigidly on this than we were. The point here was that the United States and China share an interest in maintaining peace and stability in the Korean Peninsula. And this issue had a history of which the Reagan administration was blissfully unaware. Dick Holbrooke, in his last days [in office] had begun a discussion with the Chinese on parallel moves by China toward South Korea, and by the U.S. toward North Korea. That, of course, was killed by the defeat of Jimmy Carter in the 1980 election. Probably, therefore, I was one of the few people left in the government who was aware of that. They then began to do things with South Korea, but we did nothing. From their perspective, this was puzzling backtracking by us. But this was a very controversial issue in Washington, very dear to certain elements of the right wing.

The Chinese also were absolutely disgusted when, right in the middle of their efforts to broker some contact between the U.S. and North Korea with the South Koreans, Kim Jong Il, Kim Il Sung's son, evidently inspired and directed the bombing in Rangoon of the Korean Cabinet, which resulted in the deaths of many able people.[47] The interesting thing to me was that, having spent a lot of time talking to the Chinese about Korea, I got a sense of the extent to which they maintained a stiff upper lip about their alleged allies in North Korea, but really regarded them with a mixture of contempt and derision.[48]

At any rate, the North Koreans, by their own actions, ended up obviating any possibility of an opening to either South Korea or the United States. And maybe that was what they tried to do. Still, we had some opportunities that we missed, because of people not hearing what they didn't want to hear.

Why didn't Paul Wolfowitz subscribe to the idea of having a meeting with China, North Korea, and the United States?

FREEMAN: I'm not entirely sure, but I would speculate that there were several reasons. First of all, Mr. Wolfowitz took a very jaundiced, rather ideological view of China, and was inherently suspicious of any initiative that originated with the Chinese. Second, with regard to contacts with North Korea, he was apprehensive about the political reaction from the Republican right, which he has courted and from association with which he has benefited, and that therefore he saw such a development as politically unattractive. And he might also have been concerned about the adequacy of prior consultation with South Korea. On the other hand, he must have been aware that South Korea itself was conducting a whole series of maneuvers intended to get the Chinese to put forward just exactly this sort of proposal.

Could you explain how we felt about North Korea in the late 1980s?

SIGUR: We were particularly concerned about what they might do to upset things in South Korea during the changeover of power from Chun

[Doo Hwan] to a civilian.[49] This was something that was of great concern to us. We were also very much concerned about the [1988 summer] Olympics and the possibility of the North trying to upset the games. So during this time of crisis in South Korea, we made it as clear as we could to the North that any efforts on their part to try to take advantage of disturbances in the South would lead to American reaction. And we made this clear to the Soviet Union and to China, and urged them to make this clear to their North Korean clients, so that they wouldn't misunderstand here, that the United States would not sit by. I'm not saying that the United States was the mover and shaker in all this; it was the Koreans themselves.

SOVIET UNION

Chinese efforts to better relations with the Soviet Union during the 1980s were slow and hesitant, but ultimately successful. After the Chinese had been satisfied regarding Soviet troop deployments, it appeared that no further barriers would exist to re-establishment of close ties. In fact, in May 1989, Gorbachev traveled to China for a summit judged by all to be a triumph for Deng Xiaoping and a significant advance for peace in Asia. Indeed, Americans increasingly viewed improvement of Sino-Soviet relations as a positive factor, enhancing rather than undermining triangular diplomacy.

SHOESMITH: There was speculation about the possibility of a warming of China-Soviet relations, but at that time it seemed very remote. As of 1981–1983, the Cambodian issue was still very hot, as well as Afghanistan. On both of those issues the Chinese and the Soviets were at loggerheads. There were still problems along their own border. The Soviets were building up their military presence in East Asia. None of these things seemed to augur any improvement in Sino-Soviet relations. On the contrary, although it was regarded as a possibility, if not a near term probability, those who thought it was a possibility would always add the caveat that it will never get back to where it was prior to 1960, at the time of the Sino-Soviet split. That both countries—and particularly China itself—had moved to a degree that any sort of full rapprochement was unlikely. There would still be suspicions on the Chinese side. There would still be conflicts of interest between the two.

How about the Soviets at this time—were they trying to find out what we were up to, still feeling frozen out, or were things beginning to relax for them?

HOROWITZ: By the mid-80s, the Chinese had moved to a situation where they had a more independent foreign policy—not lining up again with the Soviets but trying to have more normal relations with the Soviets and a more normal range of contacts with them. They were interested in the changes that were beginning to take place there; they were watching it closely. They were not anymore so much worried about imminent Soviet attack as they had been in the '70s. That had all disappeared— back in the '70s they would show you the air raid shelters they had been digging in the villages.

How were the Chinese, during this period, looking at the Soviet Union?

FREEMAN: The Soviet Embassy was essentially isolated; no one would speak with the Soviets. They had extremely limited access to the Chinese government. Some of them were really quite fine Sinologists, and genuinely, personally distressed by this situation. But while there was some minor movement, there wasn't anything too much going on.

At one point, we used to talk about the China card. Were we, at least from Washington, trying to manipulate China in any way vis-à-vis the Soviet Union?

FREEMAN: We were trying to give the Soviets the impression of their being effectively encircled, and the idea that the U.S. and China could, if provoked, respond together to the provocation. This was part of the general policy of keeping the pressure on the Soviet Union and containing it. It did contribute rather directly to the ultimate collapse of the Soviet Union, so it was a successful policy.

The shift in Chinese emphasis was illustrated in the wrangling we had in the August 17 communiqué negotiations over how the Chinese would state their opposition to hegemonism and whether they would recognize common strategic interests with us. They frankly didn't want to be quite so closely associated with us, by 1982, as they had in 1972. The Chinese didn't want to state flatly that they did not want an intimate strategic connection with the United States, but they clearly didn't.

What was the nature of Sino-Soviet relations in the mid-to-late-1980s, at a time where the Soviets were still involved in Afghanistan and the Soviet Union was the Soviet Union, not yet Russia?

LORD: [The Soviet Union] was still [China's] primary concern. Now they were already easing relations with the Russians during this period. Gorbachev gave a speech in Vladivostok on Asia [July 1986] that I considered very significant at the time.[50] Clearly that was a pitch for better relations with China. The Chinese felt if they could ease relations with Russia, it would help them in terms of their military deployments and expenditures.

Did you use the Soviet card or did you let the Chinese figure out what the Soviets were up to themselves?

LORD: We kept telling the Chinese we hope you can improve relations. In fact, our view was, and it was sincere, we wanted a Sino-Soviet relationship that was not tense or hostile but certainly wasn't an alliance. The situation that had existed in 1969, the border clashes, we genuinely thought were too dangerous and too tense. It could lead not only to a conflict between them but a wider conflict in the region with others and even perhaps the nuclear dimension. Even if you could crudely say it is nice to have these two guys fighting each other, we didn't want that kind of hostile, tense relationship between these two major powers. Now, we obviously didn't want them to go all the way back to the 1950s and be solid allies again. We wanted to have better relations with each one than they had with each other. You don't want to make them feel that they are getting you nervous with their relations with the Russians. We felt that the Russians and the Chinese each needed us more than they could possibly use each other. Similarly on the geopolitical front, no matter how much they patched up their relations, there would be this suspicion.

We knew that they were suspicious of what Gorbachev was doing and had real ambivalence. They liked the fact that he wanted to improve relations with China, and they worked with him on that, but they were very concerned about what Gorbachev was doing on the domestic political front in terms of freeing up that society, both because it might have a contagion effect in China and unleash similar currents there and because they felt, and they were correct in a way, that this would lead to lack of control by the Communist Party in Russia and even loss of their empire.

Crisis Years—Tiananmen and the 1990s

THE OPTIMISTIC DECADE of the 1980s in U.S.-China relations ended in one of the most traumatic crises in China's history, a crisis that produced equally sharp repercussions for Chinese-American understanding. During the spring of 1989, the death of Hu Yaobang, formerly general secretary of the CCP, sparked massive demonstrations in the heart of Beijing. Traditionally political activists, including students and intellectuals, used mourning rituals to raise issues of popular dissatisfaction with government officials. Hu Yaobang, although no liberal, had been purged because he had advocated a vigorous reform agenda and some modest political change. In 1989, several impulses in Chinese society came together to trigger a nationwide protest movement, nominally in Hu's memory and sustained initially by young people. Gradually, they were joined by people from all walks of life. Some called for greater freedom of expression, an end to arbitrary government, and a remedy for growing corruption, as well as demanding improvements in education. Others, with equal passion, objected to the costs of reform in the loss of social welfare support, including erosion of guarantees such as lifetime employment.

What made these events extraordinary, however, was the presence in China of the international press corps that had descended on the capital to cover the visit of the Soviet leader Mikhail Gorbachev. Officialdom, eager to suppress the embarrassing protests that were getting more attention than the summit meeting, ineptly tried to discredit the movement by impugning the motives of participants. Instead they fueled continuing upheaval. On the night of June 3–4, 1989, Deng Xiaoping and his government allies deployed military force to clear Tiananmen Square and end demonstrations across China. The ensuing chaos and bloodshed not only shook the Chinese people, but also horrified the world community.

In the aftermath, various nations applied sanctions. Tourism, trade, and investment slumped, and human rights became central to political intercourse with Beijing. Among those seeking to punish China's leaders, however, none acted as sternly or applied constraints as broadly as the United States. Fueled by Congress, American indignation and disgust replaced the national consensus that good relations with China should be maintained despite offensive internal government practices and occasional differences over international issues. The hostile new attitude toward China would last well into the 1990s, threatening many of the fragile links built with great effort during the first decades of normalization. Fearful that the crisis could, in fact, undo the Sino-American strategic relationship, President George Bush secretly sought to keep lines of communication open, sending top diplomats to Beijing to further cooperation in various areas. When these efforts became public they caused a widespread outcry and a perception that Bush was "soft" on China.

It came as no surprise, therefore, that during the American presidential election campaign in 1992, Democratic candidate Bill Clinton used China as one of several grounds upon which to attack the Republican administration. Accusations that Bush had coddled the butchers of Beijing took a toll. In the process, however, Clinton boxed himself in on China, taking a position on human rights that directly contradicted his emphasis on domestic economic revitalization with its heavy dependence upon expanding trade. Once elected Clinton would have to back away from his threats to reconsider Chinese access to most favored nation (MFN) treatment.

Clinton's retreat proved gradual. He attempted first to place conditions upon renewal of MFN but discovered that, although the Chinese had more to lose than Americans, they would not make even minimal concessions to meet Clinton's requirements. Humiliated, Clinton reversed his position and delinked MFN from human rights.

Meanwhile in China, the impact of world obloquy paled next to the need to stabilize the government in the wake of such wide-ranging domestic political turmoil. Dissidents were hunted down and imprisoned and the pace of economic reforms slowed. Within the leadership those who had lost the struggle over how the demonstrations should be interpreted and handled had to be replaced. Out of these changes emerged a new central figure, former mayor of Shanghai and Deng Xiaoping protégé, Jiang Zemin. Perceived by American officials as a weak reed, lacking his own political base and links to the military, estimates in Washington suggested a brief interregnum until some new strongman would emerge. But in fact, Jiang proved to be more politically astute than either Americans or many of his own people guessed. Before the end of the decade, he appeared to have consolidated his position. Deng Xiaoping's death in 1997 caused barely a ripple at home or abroad.

The events that proved most disturbing centered upon relations between China and Taiwan. At the root of the frictions between them lay the changed nature of the political system and social climate on the island. After losing the diplomatic recognition of the United States and most other nations at the end of the 1970s, Taiwan's leader Chiang Ching-kuo unexpectedly accelerated democratic reforms and vigorously pursued economic ties with the international community. Slowly he allowed opposition elements to become more active and eventually to coalesce in a political party, the Democratic Progressive Party, which had as one of its founding principles advocacy of independence from China. At the same time, Chiang brought members of the Taiwanese majority into a government and party, the Guomindang, that had been dominated by Mainlanders since 1945. These innovations frightened China's political leadership, which viewed Taiwan as a rebellious province destined to be reunited with the motherland under Beijing's control.

The Chinese Communists had reason to be worried. In 1989, as they confronted popular demands for liberalization and chose instead to crack down, Taiwan drew international attention for its intensifying democratization. Long neglected because China had greater strategic importance in the cold war, Taiwan, freed from its autocratic past, suddenly seemed a more desirable place. While people disparaged the People's Republic, they praised Taiwan.[1]

Moreover, the Cold War ended with the collapse of communism in Eastern Europe late in 1989 and then the fall of the Soviet Union in 1991, removing the strategic rationale for overlooking Chinese behavior. The peaceful transitions that took place in other communist regimes made the willingness of communist dictators in China to commit atrocities in the name of regime preservation seem even more repugnant.

As a result, Taiwan emerged from its decades of isolation and began to tap renewed interest in its economy and culture to raise its status in the world. Part of that effort was a pragmatic diplomacy practiced under the guiding hand of Lee Teng-hui, president of Taiwan after Chiang Ching-kuo's death in 1988. Lee, a Taiwanese and a technocrat, educated in Japan and the United States, had been brought into the government as part of Chiang Ching-kuo's liberalization effort. As president he traveled abroad, lobbied for membership in international organizations, and successfully convinced governments to expand their ties to Taiwan even as they maintained their official relations with Beijing. Lee ended the state of war between Taipei and Beijing and furthered the growth of cross-Straits relations begun by Chiang.

China's leaders saw all these changes and recognized that they presented a serious challenge to Beijing. They undermined arguments that Chinese culture precluded democratic practices, they gave impetus to the differentiation of Taiwanese society from the mainland, diminishing the appeal of reunification, and they threatened to reverse China's successful campaign to cut Taiwan off from the international community so that it would eventually weaken and collapse into waiting Chinese arms. Beijing's strategy followed two lines. First, it began a series of appeals to ethnic and national pride, hoping to make unification appear to be the natural and most beneficial solution. Whenever the moderate approach appeared not to be making progress, however, Beijing turned to coercion. As former ambassador to China Winston Lord explains, the events of 1995–1996 that swirled around the China-Taiwan stalemate brought U.S.-China relations to the brink of war.

As it happened, although the Taiwan Strait crisis ranked as the most dramatic event in the decade, other problems also drove Washington and Beijing apart in the 1990s. Foreign Service officers reported on intellectual property rights violations, proliferation and, of course, the chronic abuse of human rights. At the same time, China experienced a growth of nationalism, with Western, and especially American culture being attacked as immoral and decadent. Among the most popular books of the decade in Beijing was *China Can Say No*, which expressed disgust with American values and institutions and argued that China could follow a different path.[2] Commentators on both sides worried about the development of a new cold war.

TIANANMEN

In 1989, the Chinese leadership faced a crisis of legitimacy. Protesters poured into the streets of China's major cities and demanded that the government be more responsive to their needs whether those were economic, political, or social. The leaders lacked the skills, wisdom, and flexibility to accommodate. Instead, they visited harsh oppression on Chinese citizens, from intellectuals to workers. Weeks of peaceful demonstration collapsed in a night of brutality and bloodshed. In this single act, Deng Xiaoping discredited many of his achievements, stunning the people who had rallied around his reform effort. In the aftermath, China paid a significant price at home and abroad.[3]

LORD: When people think of students in Tiananmen Square, what they forget is there were seven weeks without a single incident of violence, without a single death. If anything, the traffic ran better than ever. It was the most orderly, responsive, disciplined crowd. Not one accident, not one incident in seven weeks with a million people sometimes in the square, absolutely extraordinary. Furthermore, it was not just students. It was journalists, academics, party members, military, business people, farmers, peasants, workers, all kinds of people demonstrating.[4] Now it wasn't just about democracy. It was about inflation, corruption, nepotism, poor conditions physical and mental at the universities. There were a lot of different sources of angst, including the people's preoccupation with having a better economic existence, a better life, and getting away from the horrors in the past.

How much connection was there between economic reform and political events such as student involvement in the spring and early summer of 1989?

REUTHER: Well, here you have the Chinese population in the spring of 1989 with this economic expansion that was being throttled in their eyes by corruption, and their answer was to call for a dictator to clean up the corruption. They didn't see any other method of reinvigorating reform. From our point of view, the spring of 1989 was not a democracy movement. We went down to Tiananmen Square and talked to demonstration leaders. They did not have a sophisticated understanding of democracy. Remember the demonstration leaders at first were students from the premier universities, meaning they were sons and daughters of ranking party members. When government put out an editorial that said the students were being disruptive, student leaders took offense. In addition to their policy complaints was added the issue of face.

Did the Fang Lizhi experience influence in any way what the embassy reported about the students who gathered in Tiananmen Square just a few weeks later? Was there a concern that there was an unwillingness in Washington to hear about this?

LORD: No, and I'd have trouble admitting if it did. We didn't pull our punches on reporting. We clearly were made even more aware than we had been how sensitive Deng and the leadership was to the human rights question. Frankly, we did not predict Tiananmen Square, I don't think anybody did in terms of the massive demonstrations that did take place. It was in over 200 cities—not just Beijing—which was extraordinary. I left the day of the first big demonstration on April 22, 100,000 people at Hu Yaobang's funeral. He had died on the 15th. In the intervening week there had been posters and wreaths to Hu.[5]

REUTHER: The whole thing starts off in a very Chinese way. A demonstration for the funeral for an honored leader [Hu Yaobang] was the excuse to get out into the streets. Once they were out on the streets you couldn't lock the barn door afterwards.

LORD: Hu Yaobang had always been known as someone unpredictable and spontaneous, feisty, unlike most stodgy Chinese leaders, and had been liberal on political reform and Tibet and related issues. In retrospect, he was built up as even more of a liberal hero than was actually the case. In any event, Chinese intellectuals and students saw him as someone who was hopeful. They were unhappy to say the least about his having been sacked a couple years earlier, as well as the continuing lack of real political reform in China. Thus, starting relatively slowly but building up quickly, people reacted to his death by circulating poems and posters and wreaths to his honor, and people began to demonstrate in Tiananmen Square in relatively modest numbers.

We really are talking about something that a moderately capable leadership should have been able to deal with, aren't we?

LORD: Absolutely. One reason I was so outraged by the massacre was that it was unnecessary. Particularly in the early part of this, the first couple of weeks, the actual requests by the students and others were very modest, essentially to have a dialog with the government. They were not asking for anything revolutionary. There were occasional signs that were insulting, but basically it was obviously very peaceful. A leadership that had its act together and was moderately inclined could have defused this thing.

FREEMAN: The only thing that surprised me about it was that the government did not move quicker to put this down. And I wish, in retrospect, that they had, because the loss of life would have been far less if they had been more resolute early on, rather than allowing the students to, in effect, get out of control and pose a direct challenge to their authority.

LORD: Obviously there was debate in the Politburo. They were paralyzed as to how to respond. There were those, probably Li Peng and some of the military, who felt that any demonstration, however peaceful, in the center of Tiananmen Square with all its history was either inherently dangerous or symbolically dangerous. They ought to squash it right away. There were others like Zhao Ziyang and some other generals including a former secretary of defense, who wrote to the leadership saying, don't use force.[6] When [Mikhail] Gorbachev [the Soviet leader] came [in May 1989], they couldn't greet him at Tiananmen Square. What was supposed to be a major rapprochement with Russia was overshadowed by the demonstrations. That made them mad. They held off until Gorbachev left because they didn't want to make a big incident beforehand. They began to tighten the screws after that.

SOLOMON: There was an element in the leadership that wanted to use political means to diffuse the opposition, but the situation by late May had become quite polarized. The students were playing to the mass media and they became uncompromising, and the leadership basically split down the middle. And as we saw shortly after Tiananmen, Zhao Ziyang—who was then the prime minister—was purged for being too "soft," and the hard-line element around Li Peng emerged and took responsibility for suppressing the demonstration.

REUTHER: Finally the authorities declared martial law [May 20]. Now that was a significant event. We had established an office in the Beijing Hotel, which is right up from Tiananmen Square. From the hotel the embassy dispatched two officers at a time to chat with demonstrators in the square. We could talk to people, see who they were and see what was going on. The authorities declared martial law, responding in large part to labor and business people becoming sympathetic to the students.

To what extent did the embassy become directly involved in these events?

REUTHER: The Chinese [always house] the foreign diplomatic community in compounds. The main compound is on one of the main streets that exits out of Tiananmen square. From time to time, to keep their morale up and connect with the public, the students marched out of the square and around the internal beltway. That would bring them by the embassy and housing compound. I don't think the Rose Bowl parade or the Macy's Thanksgiving Day parade was ever as exciting as sitting up on the roof watching just miles and miles and blocks and blocks of people—ten across—marching down the road.

Such parades were very stirring and obviously got people quite involved. In fact, the positive public response was the reason the authorities became worried and the hard-liners saw things as spinning out of control. What is remarkable about Tiananmen Square is the push and pull between the hard-liners and the moderates right up to the end. We heard rumors that the PLA was divided. The conservatives said to the liberals, "Okay, let's see if you guys can get them to stop demonstrating." So, troops were sent in unarmed without their officers, and the Beijing public stopped them from getting to the student center. The moderates in the government failed, the moderates in the student demonstration slipped away with martial law.

What happened on the night of June 4 was that the hard-liners moved armed troops into Beijing and, like the Paris Commune of 1848, the population of Beijing rose up. The students were a minor focus of what happened that evening. The Western press missed a good story by creating a students versus government story. Forgotten in that storyand part of the legacy for the Chinese-was the city of Beijing rose up in revolt. All the destruction, all the death, was caused by the troops fighting their way into Beijing. By the time the PLA arrived at Tiananmen Square, the students surrendered and were marched off very easily.

Was there some sort of shooting incident near or at the American Embassy?

REUTHER: Obviously on the night of June 4 there was shooting all over the place. Beijing was full of tourists and business people. It became obvious that the situation in Beijing was very unstable. So all the embassies in Beijing evacuated their nationals. We ultimately evacuated about fifteen hundred Americans, tourists, business people, our own embassy staff. The Japanese evacuated 4,000 out of all of China. All the embassies slimmed down their missions. There were probably fewer foreigners in Beijing on June 6, 1989, than in the last 500 years. Think about it. The point is that the dream of any nationalistic Chinese for the last 200 years, since the first Opium War [1839–1842], is to get the foreigners out of China, because it is the foreign influence that corrupted and weakened China. So there were conservative elements in the Chinese structure that were very pleased to see these departures. To them the departure of all the embassies was a next logical step.

Someone acted on that impulse. Across from one of the diplomatic compounds that faced Jianguomen Street was a Japanese hotel under construction. By virtue of the way housing was allocated, the Chinese knew apartment assignments among the compound buildings. In the morning of June 6, or two days after Tiananmen Square, a group of soldiers who were walking along in front of the diplomatic compound suddenly started shooting up from the street into the building. They said they had received sniper fire from the roof of the building. More to the point: the platoon hidden in the building across the street simultaneously poured fire horizontally into building number one. Given a 10-floor building, if you are shooting from the street, bullets will lodge in the ceiling the first six inches or so from the window. In this case, however, you had horizontal fire poured into the apartments of the American, British, Japanese, and German military attachés, those same embassies' security officers, one American economic officer, and one Brit. They just trashed those apartments with automatic weapons fire. Later the American attaché told me that he received a phone call from somebody he knew in a central military unit who said don't be home at 10: 00, click.

So it was planned?

REUTHER: Something was known in advance. Something whose objective was to scare us away, to make us close all of the embassies.

Were there casualties?

REUTHER: No. All the apartments were empty except for one. The American security officer's kids were still there and the maid got them below the windowsill in time. This shooting had a great impact on us—being shot at tends to do that to you—but we were quite determined that we would not break off relations with China, they were stuck with us. We would stay engaged and not be scared out. In fact, we presumed the perpetrators were a small cabal of people and that there would be others who were not supportive of this kind of thing. But if we left, if we did what the shooters wanted, then we would also leave the reformers naked to them.

What is interesting about this is that the Tiananmen Incident reintroduced China into American domestic politics. American politicians expressed the outrage we all felt. But after a while, moralistic statements about China became just another jab at one's American partisan opponent. So a situation developed where some in Congress were calling for a break in relations with China. And you have the Bush administration saying, "No, we have to stay engaged with China because we can't let them break it off and go their own separate way." In fact, the advantage at that time of having Bush as president was that, because he had been head of the earlier Liaison Office, he understood how important the whole issue was and secondly how crucial it was to maintain contact with the Chinese so that we didn't lose contact with the reformers.

SOLOMON: Right after the shooting to repress the students, the president himself knew that the relationship was in a deep crisis. He, together with [James] Baker, the secretary of state, said we've got to impose some sanctions, because if we don't do it Congress will make things even worse. Baker, unfortunately, phrased one of the sanctions in terms of a cut off of high-level visits. What he had in mind was canceling the visit of then secretary of commerce Robert A. Mosbacher, who was scheduled to go to China in July as head of the U.S.-China binational commercial commission. Baker didn't [mean to] imply that all high level contacts would be cut off; it was just these regular, "business as usual" exchanges. But the press didn't view it that way. So suddenly the impression was created that the administration was going to cut off all high-level contacts with the Chinese leadership. My understanding is that the president got very upset at that implication. Baker dropped management of the China relationship as a hot potato. I think he felt that he had mismanaged the response in terms of what the president wanted. As Baker subsequently would say, "the desk officer for China works in the White House." Baker, at that point, was delighted not to have to deal with China, which he saw as a political loser. So, basically the State Department was out of the China business. The link between the State Department and the White House on China policy became [Lawrence] Eagleburger [deputy secretary of state] dealing with Brent Scowcroft as [national] security advisor.

It was in that environment that Bush was urged by former President Nixon and former Secretary of State Kissinger not to let the situation lead to a breakdown in our dealings with China. As a consequence, Bush arranged for the secret Scowcroft trip in July '89 to try to keep a dialogue going and to tell the Chinese frankly what was required to try to repair the damaged relationship. Then there was a second, public trip in December '89. Those trips were an effort to keep a dialogue going. But they elicited a domestic firestorm of criticism, particularly from the Democrats, who felt that Bush, as they said in the election campaign of '92, was "coddling dictators," the butchers of Beijing, by maintaining these high-level contacts. After Tiananmen the China relationship became a great political liability for Bush.

GREEN: [The protest] was whipped up all the more by the presence [in the United States] of tens of thousands of Chinese students from the Chinese mainland.

HOLDRIDGE: There were 40,000 Chinese students. The president vetoed a congressional bill which would have allowed these people to stay on indefinitely, pending some kind of a return to normalcy on the mainland. The president was quite correct in vetoing it. He [could] handle this problem administratively.[7] The same thing was true about sanctions. If you codify into law measures which are regarded by the Chinese as hostile to them—anti-Chinese, which interfere in their own internal affairs—the Chinese are bound to take note and respond vigorously.

How did the people of Hong Kong react to the demonstrations at Tiananmen?

DONALD ANDERSON: The democracy movement in China had a tremendous impact in Hong Kong. One Sunday there were at least 800,000 people marching peacefully down the main street of Hong Kong. There was an interesting change that took place during that period because they were demonstrating for "our compatriots in China,

our brothers in China." This was a whole new attitude, because generally Hong Kong Chinese have looked upon people across the border, in
the mainland, as sort of country bumpkins. "We're the smart guys,
we're the wealthy, we're the ones who know how to do it, and all those
people up in the mainland are kind of dummies." And when the democracy movement started, there was all of a sudden in Hong Kong a feeling of being Chinese, of being part of the thing that they were seeing
in Beijing. In fact, there was a lot of support, monetary and material
support that went from Hong Kong into China during that period.
Practically all of those tents that were on television in Tiananmen came
from Hong Kong.

When the crackdown came were people looking to the United States to do
something? How did they feel about how we reacted?

DONALD ANDERSON: Everybody watched in horror. I personally felt
like I was watching a tragedy. They recognized there wasn't anything
we could do in the short term in the sense of changing things. In the
short term we did take actions to provide shelter and help for people
who were escaping who had been involved in it. We cooperated with a
group of about five other countries to help some of these young people,
and some not so young, to get through Hong Kong and get on safely to
the United States or to Europe.[8] And, of course, the president immediately announced economic sanctions, etc.[9] Actually, the United States
probably took as strong measures as anybody, and kept them in place
longer than anybody else. One of the very interesting things about the
post-Tiananmen reaction was that probably the people who were back
in doing business more or less as usual, were the Chinese from Taiwan
and from Hong Kong.

DEAN: The Chinese on Taiwan were shocked by Tiananmen like everybody else, and dismayed by it like everybody else. Disappointed by it.
But they weren't really taken by surprise as we were because they knew,
through harsh experience, that the communists would use force to preserve their power and to knock down dissent. They expected them to
use force to do this. So when they did, it wasn't the same as in the U.S.
where we thought that Humpty Dumpty had fallen off the wall and it
was the end of the world. There was only a brief pause in Taiwan before
they resumed all of their increasing number of visits, increasing num-

bers of factories moved over to the mainland to establish themselves there, and increasing number of investments.

Was there a certain amount of satisfaction in Taiwan, seeing the United States being disappointed in what happened?

DEAN: They would say something like this: that the U.S. didn't realize the true nature of the communists and now they were seeing it for themselves, whereas we knew it all along and we weren't taken aback by this. We knew that they would do something like this, whereas the U.S. foolishly thinks that they can get a nice chummy relationship and they don't take the true nature of the communist beast into effect.

At the time you left China in the autumn of 1989, on the economic side, had things begun to return to the way things were before or would that take quite a while?

REUTHER: Such a destructive event as Tiananmen Square makes people who need security and stability and predictability in their relationship hold back, and nobody wants stability and predictability more than business people do. The first few months after Tiananmen Square were quite telling. We began a series of economic reports discussing the economic price China paid for Tiananmen. I recall one report on the tourist industry, in which we compared all international flights coming into China in the pre-Tiananmen Square period versus what was happening after Tiananmen. Literally everyone just stopped coming to China. Tourism collapsed and most airlines simply did not fly their posted schedules. Hotels—two major Hong Kong invested properties had just opened— had enormous vacancy rates. Some airlines still flew. Lufthansa had a joint venture with the Chinese airlines, so they could not terminate all flights. They came in once a week instead of four times a week. And they came in empty. Cathay Pacific was doing good business because all the businessmen took refuge in Hong Kong and then flew up for a day or two to maintain their contacts and fly back. Hotel occupancy scraped along at maybe 5 or 10 percent. We calculated that in tourism alone Tiananmen cost China millions of dollars in lost revenues.

FREEMAN: Part of the reaction to Tiananmen was a freeze on all military interaction and contact. Some limited contact continued. Members of the so-called Capstone Course [for the U.S. military], a commissioning course for colonels about to become brigadiers, or captains about to become rear admirals, continued to visit China for a class visit. But essentially there was no military contact and no high-level political dialogue to speak of.

DONALD ANDERSON: There is this love-hate relationship. When things are going well with China, and China is being good, Americans think China is wonderful. It's all panda bears, and rosy-cheeked kindergarten children, and people going to banquets, and delivering stupid speeches. And then when China does something bad, like Tiananmen, then China can do no right. There is this overwhelming desire on the part of the United States people to somehow punish and correct China. Harold Isaacs wrote a book quite a long time ago called *Scratches on Our Minds*.[10] where he makes this very clear. We have this problem, partially on the part of Americans because there is this affinity to sort of change China, to make it over into what we think should be the image of China.[11]

U.S.-CHINA RELATIONS IN THE 1990s

During the early 1990s, the responsibilities of those dealing with U.S.-Chinese relations consisted almost entirely of trying to resolve difficult problems in ways that would not weaken an already fragile relationship in a highly incendiary atmosphere. As Chas. W. Freeman, Jr. observes here, the coming together of Tiananmen, the fall of communism in Europe, and the growth of democracy in Taiwan reduced China's appeal to Americans. At the same time, these events served to increase Beijing's nervousness and sense of vulnerability. All this lessened the room for maneuver and produced continuing frictions. George Bush ran into condemnation for his determination to retain ties seemingly at any cost. But even as Americans rejected his sympathetic approach to Beijing, they divided amongst themselves regarding the proper degree of sanction to place upon such a populous nation growing at such a rapid pace. The battleground became the annual renewal of the most favored nation trade treatment after Chinese students in the United States and members of Congress identified it, in early 1990, as a key to keeping Congress interested in China policy.[12] In the end, partisan and commercial pressures triumphed.

James Lilley with President Jiang Zemin in 1991. *Courtesy of James Lilley.*

FREEMAN: There were three events in 1989 that affected the development of U.S.-China relations. First, and most important in strategic terms, was the collapse of the Soviet empire. The Berlin Wall came down in November 1989, and with it any credible Soviet threat. So the U.S.-China relationship, which had been premised on the idea of a strategic triangle, or balance, between Washington and Moscow, with Beijing as the swing factor, suddenly was left with no strategic rationale. There was no obvious impulse to cooperate.

Somewhat earlier, on June 4, 1989, the Chinese government brutally crushed a student rebellion in Tiananmen Square—and did so in the full glare of the television cameras. That seared a negative image of China firmly into the minds of most Americans. An American distaste for a politically incorrect China, American disillusionment with a China that it probably had had illusions about, really dominated the relationship.

And so the two things coming together meant that the previous policy of setting aside ideological differences in order to pursue practical cooperation between the United States and China effectively came to an end, symbolically, with the ill-fated December 1989 visit of National Security Advisor Brent Scowcroft to Beijing. It was not until the summer of 1996, seven years later, that a national security advisor from the United States again visited Beijing.

That brings me to the third problem that came to a head in 1989. That was the beginning of Taiwan's democratization and its move out of the framework that had successfully managed the Taiwan problem for the United States and China, and for Taiwan, in earlier years. By the early 1990s, Taiwan was well advanced in the process of democratization, and by about 1995–96, had emerged as a robust democracy, maybe one of the most robust democracies in the world.

Always in the past we had managed to handle the Taiwan problem on the basis of the common understanding of people in Taipei and Beijing that there was only one China, that Taiwan was part of China, and that the only issue was: Where was the capital of China? Was it in Taipei or in Beijing? For 21 years, we successfully, if fraudulently, insisted at the U.N. that the capital of China was in Taipei, not in Beijing.

This One China policy, which Taipei and Beijing had agreed about, began to fall apart as Taiwan democratized and the native (that is, pre-1949) Chinese population on the island began to express its own sense of separateness from other Chinese.

What was your view of using MFN renewal as a tactic to influence Chinese behavior?

LORD: I felt that, on the one hand, we should not revoke MFN status for China. MFN status is available to most countries. More importantly, there was much substance to the argument that you can encourage a society by engagement and by opening up our relations. If we cut off MFN status, we would be cutting off the performers and business people who were working in the direction we wished. This would hurt American business interests and legitimate concerns, both in terms of our exports to China and imports from China of cheaper goods for our blue collar people who buy textiles, shoes, sneakers, and toys. This would also hurt innocent bystanders, particularly Hong Kong and also Taiwan. Cutting off MFN status would be too blunt an instrument to express our displeasure with what China had done. Such action would put us in confrontation with China, when I still believed in engagement. On the other hand, I was increasingly frustrated with what I thought was the overly soft approach toward China by the Bush administration and the fact that we didn't seem to have any leverage with China.

Where did you feel that the thrust for this sort of business as usual attitude or policy on the part of the Bush administration was coming from? Was it because Bush had been the chief of the U.S. Liaison Office in Beijing?

LORD: Directly from President Bush himself. This was proven to me in connection with the Fang Lizhi incident [see chapter 6]. It was clear to me, in view of President Bush's supine reaction to the Fang incident, that this kind of attitude toward the Chinese was coming from him. And I figured that Brent Scowcroft shared Bush's view. Secretary of State James Baker was more politically attuned and kept his head down on China, because he knew it was not popular in Congress and among the public more generally, although he got more involved later on. So Baker was a little bit more nuanced in his approach. Bush and Scowcroft were soft on China. It's phony to debate isolation versus engagement. You can have engagement of a hard-headed nature. You can be firm with the Chinese but also have a broad agenda of positive things to accomplish.

SOLOMON: After the Iraqi invasion of Kuwait [August 1990], it was evident that if we were going to have a UN coalition, or at least the UN sanction of some collective effort to deal with Saddam [Hussein]'s aggression, we would have to work with the Chinese, given their veto position on the Security Council. The Chinese basically took a passive position. They were very anxious to avoid setting a precedent on the use of force, or seeming to cooperate with us too closely. It was in that environment that the State Department reactivated its [post-Tiananmen] dealings with the Chinese, at least at the assistant secretary level.

You were in the Republican camp for a long time. How did your meeting with President Clinton come about?

LORD: I'm what you might call a liberal Republican, which is almost an oxymoron these days. In the course of July or August 1992, I was asked if I would meet with Governor Clinton, who was the Democratic candidate for president. [Tony] Lake and I had worked on the NSC [National Security Council] staff under Kissinger and Lake was in charge of foreign policy issues in the Clinton campaign. Clinton wanted to be briefed on Japan and China, so Lake assembled a group of people which included me, Dick Holbrooke, and two other people who were more expert on Japan. During the presidential election campaign, I received calls on a couple of occasions for my advice specifically on China policy, including the MFN issue.

Could you talk about China as you described it to candidate Clinton?

LORD: I was, of course, a strong believer in engaging China. When I was younger and working with Kissinger, my overwhelming emphasis then was on geopolitics. I don't recall that I cared much about human rights, trade, and other matters. I continue to share Kissinger's view of the strategic importance of the relationship between China and the United States. However, frankly, and he would admit this too, we had somewhat of a parting of the ways, not so much personally but conceptually, since the Tiananmen Square incident [of 1989]. I assign a higher priority to human rights than Kissinger does, not only because of the virtues and values of human rights and idealism, and the need to maintain congressional support, but also because it is in China's self-interest to emphasize respect for human rights. China cannot develop its economy without a freer society, because this is the age of information. If there is unemployment and other pressures, there may be instability in China. For all of these reasons, the protection and promotion of human rights should be an important part of our policy.

I came out in favor of what I considered modest conditions for an extension of MFN status for China. The point here was to lay out some objectives, sufficiently concrete to be meaningful, but not so specific and detailed that we would box ourselves in. We would have some leverage on the Chinese because of their trade surplus with the U.S. and because of the importance of trade to them.

How did China come up as an issue during the 1992 presidential election campaign?

LORD: In the course of the presidential election campaign of 1992, candidate Clinton used very strong language. He was tough on President Bush's position on China because Bush had allegedly "coddled" a dictator. I was not consulted on the language he used in his speeches. I thought that it was excessive, although I can't say that I was leaping up and down in protest.

Do you have a sense that Clinton used this attack on President Bush as an important part of his campaign?

LORD: In fact, foreign policy was never as big a deal as other issues. Clinton's basic campaign was that President Bush ignored domestic policy. However, in the foreign policy area, it's fair to say that China was one of the three or four topics that Clinton touched on.

Clinton had been to Taiwan when he was governor of Arkansas. However, he had no real experience with, or interest in, China as such. So were his remarks on China part of his basic view or were they obtained from someone else?

LORD: These views were part of his own convictions. In the first place, Governor Clinton was friendly to Taiwan. However, he wasn't being propelled by a pro-Taiwan outlook. He understood that China was important. He didn't want to swing all the way over to isolation and containment. He genuinely was concerned about China on human rights grounds. Surely, there was a partisan element. Clinton saw that Bush was vulnerable on this issue, and it might play well before the American people. I'm sure that that was another factor.

In fact, during the campaign Bush tried to win votes by selling advanced fighter aircraft to Taiwan.

FREEMAN: The [August 17, 1982 communiqué] agreement [see chapter 6] survived until August 1992, when George Bush, ironically, given his connections with the PRC, in order to appeal to the voters of Texas, authorized the largest arms sale in U.S. history, in this case 150 F-16s, made in Texas, to Taiwan. That totally destroyed both the cap on quality and any restriction on quantity, and, in effect, shredded the communiqué. It released the Chinese from their undertaking to tolerate arms sales to Taiwan, as well.

China, then, had become a domestic political issue. Did this effect your confirmation hearings for the position of assistant secretary for East Asian and Pacific Affairs where you served from 1993 to 1997?

LORD: When I was nominated to be ambassador to China [in the 1980s], Senator Jesse Helms [R-NC] held me up for several months. This time the process was quite easy. I was approved more or less right away. I worked very hard on my opening statement for the confirmation hearings. The [State Department] congressional people didn't want me to make a major statement. They preferred bland opening statements, such as that I was happy to be here, that the appointment as assistant secretary of state was a great honor, that I looked forward to working with Congress, and that I thought that the Clinton administration was terrific. Instead, I prepared a broad-ranging speech, including my view on how we should deal with China. I had to fight to give it.

Why?

LORD: You don't try to make policy before you're even confirmed. I wanted to get out of the starting gate in a hurry and lay out an Asian policy that I was sure the administration was comfortable with. I had no illusion that I was opening any fresh ground. I wanted to give my presentation a conceptual framework and demonstrate to the Senate and House of Representatives that I knew what I was doing. I wanted to elevate Asia in our foreign policy, because throughout our history we have usually been Eurocentric in our orientation.

The Clinton administration came into office in 1993, not really well focused on foreign affairs. There seemed to be a certain amount of drift.

LORD: Yes, that is fair. This was the view on the outside of the administration and also a fair view from the inside. The administration had to deal with Bosnia, Somalia, and the Haitian problems, for example.[13] There was backing and filling on the extension of MFN status for China. This left something to be desired and tended to be inconsistent.

So both in terms of perception and reality, it's fair to say that the Clinton administration didn't do well at the beginning. This was partly due to the process of shaking down a new administration. It was partly due to the fact of the president's overwhelming focus on domestic issues. There was the election slogan, "It's the economy, stupid." However, you pay a price for this. You can't run foreign policy without the full involvement of the president and the White House.

A good example of this is the strategy paper [written] at my initiative, which was finally approved in September 1993. The basic policy toward China which we are following [in 1998] was laid out in that memo. We said that we had to be firm on human rights. However, the elements of constructing a broad agenda included trying to find positive elements on which to work with the Chinese, as well as how to deal with specific problems and the importance of China and the U.S. working together in the next century. It took a long while to get White House approval of it, not because of opposition to it. It was a hell of a good paper. The delay in obtaining White House approval was just due to inertia.

It was important to have the strategic approach to China laid out to the public in a broader framework, so that these constant problems that we had on human rights, nuclear nonproliferation, trade, and Taiwan wouldn't be the only thing that people noticed. These issues could be put in a broader context of the need for engagement in some of the more positive aspects of the agenda. I literally spent four years trying to get President Clinton to give a speech on China. In fact, I wasn't able to get the president to give a speech on China during the first Clinton term. Even Secretary of State Christopher didn't speak out solely on China for a couple of years.

It was partly the fact that we were never able to get President Clinton's attention. This was due, very frankly, to some of his political advisers. If the president gives a speech on China, you know that it's going to be controversial. This was a delicate, sensitive matter. First, because it involved campaign positions and then, as time wore on, and the president changed his position on the extension of MFN, he would make statements around the general subject of MFN, but these would be 10- and 20-minute statements.

What were the early developments regarding policy toward China?

LORD: At that point some people thought that President Clinton might recommend revoking MFN for China. There was a lot of sentiment for revoking MFN or attaching conditions to extending it in Congress. It seemed to me, and, of course, Secretary of State Christopher agreed, that I should get out to China and sort of test the waters in April or May 1993. Chinese officials had sort of ambivalent feelings toward me, all the more so since my wife had been even more critical and outspoken [see chapter 6]. They knew that they would have to deal with me for four years. They basically listened to my presentation, which included a heavy dose of comment on human rights. However, I was careful to cover a broad agenda, including regional and global issues, as well as bilateral problems. I was honestly concerned about the looming deadline on MFN extension to China for another year. Therefore, I made a pitch for progress on that front. The discussions I had were workmanlike, but I didn't expect immediate progress.[14]

In the course of May 1993, we had to start figuring out what our decision would be. Congress was controlled by the Democratic Party. I handled the key negotiations with Representative Nancy Pelosi [D-CA] in the House of Representatives and Senator George Mitchell [D-ME] on the Senate side. Of course, we consulted other agencies of the U.S. government. However, it's fair to say that the economic agencies didn't feel that they had had a fair enough crack at the process. What people now forget is that what we worked out at the time was, on the whole, hailed as a very good outcome. The president changed his position on MFN and later was criticized for it. Now, I want to make clear that the economic agencies of the U.S. government would have preferred no conditions on MFN extension. They don't like sanctions, they don't like any uncertainties in trade. Further, they advanced legitimate arguments on what might result from losing on the extension of MFN status to China. The business community in general didn't want any conditions on MFN extension. So they were not happy. However, even the people in the business community and former colleagues of mine like Kissinger were somewhat pleased over how moderate the conditions on MFN extension ultimately were.

There were plenty of people on the other side of the argument who wanted much tougher conditions on MFN extension or even outright revocation of MFN status. Therefore, when we came out with what were really moderate and realistic conditions, this was hailed in most quarters at the time as a significant success. Specifically, we came up with two mandatory conditions. First, there was the Jackson-Vanik amendment language, which related to free emigration from China. The other was connected with goods produced by prison labor. We had five other conditions, which dealt with prisoners, Tibetan culture, and other matters. In dealing with these conditions we had to be specific enough to make it possible to figure out what we were trying to do. However, we had to avoid being so specific as to put us in a box, by saying something like: "You must release 28 prisoners." So we just said that there must be "significant, overall progress." It wasn't even put in terms that there must be overall progress in each of the five categories. The feeling was that, with the Chinese stake in this bilateral relationship, there would be enough progress, so that, a year later, we would not have to revoke MFN status for China.

The Bush administration had been castigated for being too soft on China. Were there any significant number of Republicans or conservative Democrats who were in favor of doing something to China?

LORD: There were some people like Senator [Jesse] Helms [R-NC] or Congressman [Gerald] Solomon [R-NY] who either wanted to revoke MFN status for China or attach very heavy conditions on MFN extension. Then there were some Democratic and Republican members of Congress and a lot of Republicans, like former Presidents Ford and Bush, who favored MFN extension. The fact that Representative Pelosi and Senator Mitchell agreed to much less than what they had said that they wanted made the job easier. They were very statesmanlike. Frankly, one reason that I received personal praise, as did the Clinton administration at the time from most quarters, was that we were able to have Representative Pelosi and Senator Mitchell give us the necessary cover . . .

Senator Mitchell was the Democratic majority leader in the Senate. However, Representative Pelosi . . .

LORD: She was a member of the House Foreign Affairs Committee. She is from San Francisco, represented a lot of Chinese in her district, and always has been very outspoken in favor of Chinese dissidents and scholars. She had regularly urged President Clinton to be firm with the Chinese authorities.

Over the next few months, in fact, thanks to the extension of conditional MFN and just engaging the Chinese, we made some progress. I don't want to exaggerate it. However, until we got to the trip to China by Secretary of State Warren Christopher, in February 1994, we were beginning to make some progress. There were a few releases of prisoners, somewhat better accounting of the number of detainees, and an agreement to talk with the Red Cross about prison conditions. Chinese formulations on Tibet were less bellicose. The Chinese agreed at some point to a regular and formal dialogue on human rights with John Shattuck, the assistant secretary of state for Humanitarian Affairs.

However, we encountered serious problems. First, there was general Chinese resistance to pressure. This was public pressure, even though we tried to implement these arrangements in private, as much as we could. The Chinese remained preoccupied with repression and political control. This related to the fact that Jiang Zemin himself had not yet solidified his position as Chinese political leader. Above all, Chinese concern about human rights became an internal issue in China.

On top of these matters, all of which might have been manageable, there was disarray on our own side, which totally undercut our leverage on this issue. First, there was the U.S. business community, which didn't want to have any conditions placed on MFN renewal and which, at the end of the road, doesn't care a damn about human rights at all, although there are some exceptions. The business community doesn't realize why a politically more open society is in their own interest. Anyway, the U.S. business community, instead of lobbying the Chinese to improve human rights practices in China, so that MFN could be renewed on its own merits, was lobbying the Clinton administration to drop any conditions, and was very vociferous in that respect. That is, perhaps, understandable and certainly legitimate.

What was not legitimate was the behavior of our economic agencies, particularly the Treasury, the Department of Commerce, and the USTR [Office of the U.S. Trade Representative]. Sometimes they would put themselves on the record expressing half-hearted support for the president's policies. However, very purposefully and on background [to reporters], they were attacking the president's own policy.

This came to a crescendo in the winter and spring of 1994, but this pattern of behavior was already evident from the very beginning of the Clinton administration.

President Clinton, to his detriment, didn't rein in these economic agencies. Therefore, we had splits in our position, which the Chinese could see and which totally undercut our leverage. The Chinese could say to themselves: "Why should China make concessions?" I'm not saying that this is the only reason that we ran into trouble. I am saying that it sure as hell hurt us. If the president disciplined his own administration, we might well have pulled this off.

President Clinton met the president of the PRC, Jiang Zemin, in November 1993. This was his first meeting with Jiang. At Seattle, when we lifted the APEC meeting to the summit level . . .

APEC means?

LORD: The Asia Pacific Economic Cooperation forum. This is a grouping of major economic powers in the Asian and Pacific region to promote free trade and investment. It now meets annually. In Seattle in 1993, we lifted this meeting to a summit level to underline our interest in Asia and the importance of Asian trade, as well as Asia's political significance.

[The Clinton-Jiang encounter] was frankly a poor meeting. They spent about an hour or an hour and a half together. Jiang didn't have full confidence in himself. He was still consolidating his position in China. President Clinton asked Jiang a question about economic reforms and Chinese economic policy, as an easy way to get a conversation started with him. President Clinton was then treated to about a 45-minute monologue in which Jiang cited statistics. It wasn't a hostile meeting by any means. It was just wasted time during this first meeting. Then they touched on other issues briefly and to no great consequence. So very frankly, although of course we went out and said what a wonderful meeting it was, President Clinton was disappointed with it.

In these early meetings on the edge of an international conference a lot of the agenda focused on problem areas, including human rights, the trade deficit, and nuclear nonproliferation. On the Chinese side, the issues they raised included Taiwan. We tried to talk about other, positive aspects of the agenda. We probably should have tried harder. However, people have to understand that if you are having a strategic dialogue with the Chinese, it isn't all that easy.

Warren Christopher was seen by many China watchers in the United States as being largely uninterested in China. Was that your assessment?

LORD: Christopher has been accused of not spending enough time on China. It has been reported that Christopher went to Syria "9,000 times" and to China twice. The fact is that he met his [Chinese] counterpart [Chinese Foreign Minister Qian Qichen] 12 times in four years. So, on the average, this was about once every three months. Christopher made two trips to China. The first trip to China [March 12–14, 1994] turned out to be very unfortunate.

Christopher had been deputy secretary of state during the Carter administration. What was your impression of any baggage which Christopher carried to China, when you first were getting acquainted with him?

LORD: I would say that he had a pretty balanced approach. There were two elements which certainly made him somewhat more skeptical and hard-headed on China than, say, Secretary Baker during the Bush administration. The main element was that Christopher had always been strong on human rights and had a lot to do with implementing President Carter's human rights policy. Christopher had a human rights background as a lawyer, and he was genuinely concerned about this issue. So he had some distaste for the Chinese political system. Having said that, I would add that he was obviously a very experienced international operator. He understood the importance of China in our foreign policy. Christopher had spent most of his life in California, had a Pacific orientation, and believed in the importance of the Pacific Ocean area. Indeed, I got a lot of support from him in elevating Asia in our foreign policy. Again, like me, he didn't advocate holding the whole Chinese-American relationship hostage to the human rights issue.

He had also delivered the bad news to Taiwan about full normalization of our diplomatic relations with Beijing. In Taipei [in December 1978] his car was rocked back and forth by Taiwan demonstrators. However, he didn't hold that against Taiwan. He understood their emotions, and this incident didn't make him anti-Taiwan or affect his view toward Beijing.[15]

Why then did Christopher's first trip to China go so badly?

LORD: The Chinese, in advance of Christopher's visit, began rounding up dissidents. This reflected their general nervousness. The Chinese authorities figured that these dissidents would speak out, try to meet Christopher. Then, literally when we were flying to China and to our own surprise, Assistant Secretary of State for Humanitarian Affairs John Shattuck met privately with Wei Jingsheng, the most famous Chinese dissident. Shattuck had gone to China ahead of Secretary Christopher and his party to try to make more progress on human rights as part of our formal dialogue. Shattuck consulted with Ambassador J. Stapleton Roy, but not with Secretary Christopher. So we were blind-sided by this development. The fact is Shattuck had every reason to meet with Wei. Wei was an heroic figure. He'd been let out of jail, at least on a temporary basis. This was one of the things that we managed to accomplish. I will say that for about 24 hours the Chinese authorities failed to react, even though, with their surveillance system, they knew that Ambassador Roy and Assistant Secretary Shattuck had met with Wei. However, Wei made some public remarks, and the Chinese authorities, in effect, felt forced to react. The Chinese authorities blasted the hell out of everybody because of the meeting with Wei. Something this sensitive should have been checked out in advance with the Chinese authorities. In this atmosphere, there were some calls in the United States to cancel the Christopher visit to China. So we had debates on this issue within the delegation before we got on the airplane to go to China and on the airplane itself enroute to China. However, if we canceled the visit, we weren't going to get the MFN extension through and we would have to make the horrible decision to cut off MFN extension. Then, whatever we did, the whole Chinese-American relationship would come to a standstill.

So we recommended that Secretary Christopher should get on the phone, from the plane, to some key senators and congressmen, to deflate any pressures to cancel the trip and assure them that we would press strongly on these issues. All that Secretary Christopher could do was to be firm in public before he got to China. This was to justify going ahead with the trip and to show the Chinese that he wasn't just a pushover. However, he should not be critical of the Chinese on Chinese soil but should see whether we could make progress, have our cake, and eat it, too. We reached China and had a frosty reception from [Prime Minister] Li Peng, who was extremely rough and tough.

In what way?

LORD: He was very dismissive of Christopher, accused him of meddling in China's affairs, and criticized Assistant Secretary John Shattuck's manner in dealing with Wei. We didn't make progress on other issues, either. Li Peng was always tough on human rights issues. So it was just a very nasty atmosphere. President Jiang Zemin wasn't particularly friendly, either, but he was a lot less vitriolic. This was in his style, anyway. He's always been more tempered in dealing with our relationship than Li has been. However, Jiang was also less than cordial.

The press was already saying that the visit had been a disaster. People back in the U.S., including the representatives of the economic agencies, were giving background interviews with reporters. They were directing their attacks at Secretary Christopher, and not the Chinese. This was really a disreputable performance by our government. Of course, it was important to get a White House statement backing up Secretary Christopher. This had to be a presidential statement, saying that Christopher had represented American interests firmly. A statement which said that we wanted good relations with China, but the Chinese had to behave themselves better. We never got such a statement from the president, who remained silent.

What was the impact of this ill-fated trip on the MFN issue?

LORD: Rather than just getting mad at the Chinese, Christopher felt that we had to re-think whether we were on the right course on the MFN issue, however modest the conditions were and whether the MFN issue wasn't too blunt an instrument for dealing with the Chinese.[16] So we returned to Washington. It was pretty clear now by March 1994, that we weren't going to make it over the hump and get an extension of MFN status for China by May, because of the lack of progress on this trip and the disarray in our own government. During the spring of 1994, we went through an agonizing reappraisal. We did a lot of computer runs, working with the Department of Commerce, to see whether it was possible to come up with an MFN arrangement affecting only those Chinese exports that were from Chinese military industries or were derived from military sources. In other computer runs we considered to what extent we could hurt China if we applied higher tariffs on Chinese exports in the event that we revoked MFN status for China, but wouldn't hurt Hong Kong or Taiwan. We just couldn't find any way of doing this. There was no way to sort out the Chinese structure of military versus civilian companies. The only thing that we could identify was Chinese arms exports of handguns to the U.S.

Well, as we got down to the wire, we found that we had three choices. First, we could say that the Chinese hadn't met the conditions, however modest, for the extension of MFN. Therefore, we were revoking MFN status for China. We didn't want to do that. The negative impact on Chinese-American relations and on our business and exports, as well as the impact on Hong Kong and Taiwan, were generally things that we wanted to avoid.

Why would whatever we did with MFN status for China have an effect on Hong Kong and Taiwan?

LORD: Well, the great bulk of Chinese exports to the U.S. go through Hong Kong. Many of them are reprocessed and given a higher value in Hong Kong. This is one reason why we have disputes in our trade. The Chinese think that we exaggerate the deficit in our trade with China, because a large part of this trade with the U.S. really comes through Hong Kong. So by hitting Chinese exports to the U.S., we were going to hit the economy of Hong Kong very heavily. A large number of jobs in Hong Kong would be affected. We would be raising tariffs on goods of Chinese origin, if China lost MFN status, to a level which would be prohibitive in many cases. Hong Kong would have been severely affected, and Taiwan somewhat less so.

Was Taiwan also reprocessing Mainland Chinese goods destined for the U.S.?

LORD: A large part of our trade deficit with China was caused by Hong Kong and Taiwan production [relocating] into China. So our trade deficit went down with Taiwan and Hong Kong but went up with China. There were mixed feelings in Taiwan, because the government there didn't like Beijing. However, the Taiwan government did not lobby Congress to cut off MFN status for China. The Taiwan government just stayed neutral on this issue.

Another choice was to say: "Well, China already has MFN status. We're not happy with Chinese behavior. However, based on how we define it, the Chinese have met enough of our goals, and we will renew MFN status for China." We rejected that course because it would have lacked credibility.

On the two mandatory conditions, emigration was an easy call. Generally people could get out of China without any great difficulty. Prison labor involved somewhat of a stretch, but in good conscience, taking into account the views of the lawyers, we could say that we already had a prison labor agreement and we had some inspections provided for to ensure that they were not exporting the products of prison labor. However, in terms of overall, significant progress in the other five categories, for example releasing prisoners, there wasn't much to point to. The Chinese authorities let some people out, but they were also beginning to round up others. Nothing had happened in the case of Tibet. We could have tried to stretch what had happened, but we would have had a fire storm in Congress. Probably this would have resulted in having the president overridden by Congress, anyway. In any event, it would have made the president look so eager to stretch the truth that he would have done anything to renew MFN status for China. We would have lost credibility in Beijing because the Chinese government would have concluded that the American government was so desperate to renew MFN status for China that they were calling our bluff. The third choice, which we eventually selected, was the least bad alternative, but it was very embarrassing. It meant a reversal of policy. I still feel, to this day, that if we had had a united administration, we might have pulled it off.

In initiating this policy, to what extent, if at all, did you consider that you were giving leverage to the Chinese? In many ways the renewal of MFN status for China could only work with Chinese good will. So the initiative for making the Clinton administration policy work was in Chinese hands. Was that a consideration?

LORD: Yes. However, we felt that the Chinese had enough of a stake in the Chinese-American relationship in general, and the export and trading part of it in particular, to have Chinese good will. After all, we were taking one-third of their exports, and they had a huge surplus in their trade with the U.S. Therefore, in this view the Chinese had an incentive to cooperate with us, if not out of good will, at least in their own self-interest. However, that depended on China's concern that there was a real danger of their losing MFN status. However, between the business lobbying and what the economic agencies were saying, that clearly was not the case. Surely there was always the danger that we might reach the point, a year later, where we had made no progress on the conditions for MFN extension. We thought about this, but we took this choice as the best available alternative when we started out, particularly given the pressures in Congress and what President Clinton had said during the 1992 election campaign. So, in June 1994, President Clinton made some explanations in the White House press room, in discussing our reversal of policy. The president said that he wasn't going to pretend and he wasn't going to lie to the reporters. He said that we considered that conditional MFN renewal had been a useful instrument up to now, but we had used up whatever utility it had, and we couldn't make any further progress on this front.

We stressed that we would continue to consider human rights a very important part of our policy and that we would do it through resolutions passed in Geneva and through the human rights dialogue.[17] We began to mention legal reforms in China at that time. We mentioned that we would work through Radio Free Asia and other programs involving nongovernmental organizations. We also said that we would try to work with the business community on the adoption of good business principles to promote human rights. We made very little progress on human rights. The Chinese called off the dialogue with Assistant Secretary John Shattuck after a while.

What issues were there other than human rights?

LORD: We had the famous case [in 1993] of the ship [bound for Iran] with the chemicals on it, the *Yinhe*. We received poor intelligence from our people. The ship wasn't transporting dangerous chemicals. We stopped the ship, boarded it, and examined it. We got egg on our face, as a result. What happened was that our intelligence people had proof, from the cargo manifest of the ship, that it was scheduled to load certain dangerous chemicals on board. Either the Chinese snookered us in a kind of con game and took these chemicals off at the last minute to embarrass us or, in fact, they unloaded it in time.[18] It didn't have any dangerous chemicals on board at the time we inspected it. [The United States never issued an apology to China.]

Many questions have been asked in Congress about whether the administration should have sanctioned China and/or Pakistan about transfers of missiles and missile technology from China to Pakistan. The administration insisted that these transfers had not been clearly demonstrated. However, intelligence sources suggested that the administration did know about these transfers of missiles and missile technology and that there were such transfers.

LORD: There have been a lot of issues during the last several years regarding transfers of technology from China to Pakistan and others in the nuclear, missile, chemical, and biological areas. These reports have reflected varying degrees of precision and severity, sanctionability. We did invoke sanctions against China on two occasions, in 1993 and 1995. The specific area to which you refer is whether we had evidence to prove that they shipped missiles to Pakistan. The general feeling was that we were right on the edge, but we never had a smoking gun. In effect, without getting into classified material, we saw suspicious crates and heard chatter about unpacking these crates. We were able to see some signs of training by Pakistanis on how to use certain equipment. However, this would have been a real hammer if we had invoked the sanctions. I admit that people were not anxious to do this.

They link their proliferation of missile technology with our providing arms to Taiwan and possibly, in specific terms, Theater Missile Defense equipment.[19] However, in the nuclear area they were making progress throughout this period. There were those, certainly in CIA and maybe in DIA [Defense Intelligence Agency], who felt that the evidence was sufficient and that we should invoke it.

There were different sanctions for different reasons. Whatever their noble purpose, they were generally not well crafted, leaving aside a debate on whether sanctions are effective at all. Most of the effect of sanctions is to cut off our exports. So it hurts our economic interest and has very little impact on Chinese imports.

Have the Chinese cooperated on any of these sensitive issues?

LORD: The PRC joined the NPT [Non-Proliferation Treaty, 1992] and the Comprehensive Test Ban Treaty [1996], even though the Chinese have done much less testing than anybody else. They agreed to cut off the export of fissile materials. They made this agreement on non-safeguarded facilities after the ring magnet episode with Pakistan [May 11, 1996]. They agreed not to ship any more missiles. If the missiles were shipped in the past, we would [not] ex post facto sanction them for something they had done some time ago. They have behaved much better ever since. China also joined the Zanger Committee [on nuclear export control, October 1997] and has helped us with regard to North Korea. On the whole, they've moved forward on the nuclear front.

That was shown by the decision of President Clinton to [announce during] the visit of President Jiang Zemin in October 1997, implementation of the agreement [on nuclear energy cooperation] which we reached in 1988 when I was ambassador to the PRC.[20] We never sent this agreement to Congress for ratification because we couldn't say, in good conscience, that the PRC had ended its unhelpful activities with Pakistan. We encouraged the PRC successfully, when I was ambassador in Beijing and since then, to cut off all nuclear cooperation with Iran, even though it's legal. Iran is a member of the NPT and is subject to supervision under that treaty. We just said that such nuclear cooperation was unwise, even though it wasn't illegal. China has also agreed to cut off sending any conventional missiles to Iran, so we have made further progress in this area.[21]

The Chinese were somewhat helpful on North Korea and became increasingly helpful in this connection. On Cambodia [in 1990], the Chinese halted their aid to the Khmer Rouge [the Cambodian communists]. They were more helpful there and supported the UN operation and the elections.

Could you say something about the relationships within the American administration? One of the things that has often been talked about is the growing role of Ron Brown, secretary of commerce, in defining foreign policy. To what extent was Secretary Christopher as important a player as previous secretaries of state might have been?

LORD: Secretary Christopher was the most important player short of President Clinton, despite criticism of him. Now Tony Lake, the national security adviser, got into this picture constructively, toward the end [of the first term]. Having said that, there was no question that Christopher did not control foreign policy as Kissinger did. So there was in some people's eyes, and probably in the eyes of the Chinese, some varying degrees of emphasis which were different, if nothing else. Whenever there was an economic cabinet member, like Ron Brown, or the secretary of the treasury, or the USTR going to China, we would work with them. After that change in MFN policy, we had a much more united and disciplined administration. So we began to get a more cohesive policy, partly because with no conditions standing in the way of MFN renewal, the economic agencies were comfortable with the policy. The economic agencies were important, but they didn't dominate foreign policy. [The State Department] had very good relations with the White House and the NSC with regard to policy toward East Asia. It is fair to say that, although the White House became more involved, the Department of State was still in the lead on China policy.

Were we not only in front but virtually all by ourselves in dealing with human rights in China, compared to the British, the French, and so forth?

LORD: The answer is yes. Our friends would hold our coats when we raised some of these tough issues with the Chinese, whether it concerned human rights, nuclear nonproliferation, or even trade negotiations, and then take the trade contracts. It's another good reason why the conditional approach on MFN renewal did not work. No other country tried to put on sanctions or conditions on trade status. Other countries didn't press the Chinese on human rights. There were modest exceptions to this, like Great Britain and Australia. So the Chinese, of course, were very adept at saying, "Well, you people may want to place conditions on MFN renewal or keep bugging us on human rights, which are our internal affair, but our European and Japanese friends don't do this. We'll just give them the contracts."

Did people concerned with the China portfolio have opportunities to meet with President Clinton and brief him? Did Secretary Christopher go on trips with him?

LORD: Well, early in the first Clinton term foreign policy was not the president's major preoccupation. However, we would meet with President Clinton before he met with Chinese President Jiang Zemin, perhaps a week or so in advance. Then we would meet with Clinton again just before he would go into the meeting. Most of the interagency meetings on China policy were at the level of Sandy Berger [deputy national security adviser], Peter Tarnoff [undersecretary of state for Political Affairs], and myself, at the Department of State level. Joe Nye [assistant secretary of defense] would sit in, representing the Department of Defense. These meetings did not involve the president. I don't recall a full-scale, NSC meeting on China alone during the first two or three years of Clinton's first term, if, in fact, such a meeting ever occurred. There were a couple of sessions at which we briefed the president, attended by outside experts in addition to ourselves. Generally, briefing President Clinton was a little hair raising because he was usually late. I'm talking about the briefings just before he would go into a meeting. These are supposed to begin an hour in advance of such a meeting. The president would show up for his briefing with only about 15 minutes to go before the meeting. Several people would be standing around in the Oval Office in Washington or some hotel, wherever we were, shouting last minute advice at him. We would be pretty nervous. We didn't know how much homework he had done and whether he could absorb all of this advice.

I know that, on occasion, President Clinton met with former Secretary of State Kissinger and with General Al Haig. Often, businessmen would weigh in on U.S. policy toward China. We know now, of course, that even campaign contributors could do that.[22]

Was the lack of serious debate on China policy reflected in China? Was this situation at all dangerous?

FREEMAN: After Tiananmen, the United States has had a very outdated image of a rapidly changing China. The Chinese have not correctly interpreted American actions and feelings. And so mutual suspicion grew. In fact, by the time I was in the Pentagon in 1993–94, the general staff department in Beijing was beginning to plan for a possible war with the United States, and the Joint Chiefs were beginning to think in the same terms about China. Both sides, in effect, finding the other a convenient substitute for the Soviet Union as an enemy.

This is a budgetary thing, too.

FREEMAN: It's got all sorts of dimensions to it. So I thought it was essential, and Bill Perry [deputy secretary of defense, 1993–1994] thought it was essential, and Les Aspin [secretary of defense, 1993] was less ardent, but agreed, that we reestablish a military dialogue between the two countries, in order to mitigate the problem of a conflict by inadvertence or avoidable misunderstanding. I began to argue for this with the help of the China desk officer at DOD, Eden Woon. But the White House wanted nothing to do with the Chinese, who were egregious violators of human rights, the so-called butchers of Beijing. And, in fact, when the North Korean nuclear issue arose, in March of 1993, when Les Aspin, at a meeting in the White House Situation Room, suggested that we should talk to the Chinese about the problem, he was brushed aside by Tony Lake on the grounds that China was politically unacceptable and we could not have such a dialogue.[23]

At any rate, by August-September, with the Korean issue helping to clarify American interests to some extent, there was greater understanding of the need to establish dialogue with China. And so in November of 1993, I flew into Beijing, and held two days of official meetings with the deputy minister of defense, and saw the senior people in the Central Military Commission and the defense minister. And we agreed that the United States and China would resume military dialogue and conceivably look toward conducting a variety of concrete military activities, including some very modest joint-exercise activities.

[But] the Taiwan issue, which has always been a problem in U.S.-China relations, reemerged with a vengeance in 1994 and again in '95 and '96, to derail for a time the reopening of dialogue between Beijing and Washington in the military area.

Did you have any feelings when you were talking to the Chinese officials that some of them were also concerned about how both sides are beginning to use the other as the Evil Dragon?

FREEMAN: Oh, indeed, very much so. I found a real community of interest on that.

LEE TENG-HUI AND THE VISA ISSUE

The democratization of Taiwan accelerated in the 1990s, bringing with it both advantages and disadvantages from the American perspective. Washington and its diplomats had labored over decades, along with American economists, missionaries, educators, and others to further the growth of democratic practices in Taiwan. As the evolution of the island's political system finally became apparent many Americans felt considerable gratification. But U.S. diplomats also discovered that the predictability and reliability of Taiwan decision making had ended. An active electorate placed demands upon Taiwan leaders that endangered national security and threatened to drag the United States into armed conflict in the Taiwan Strait.

LILLEY: [The DPP], the party of the Taiwanese, began to win more and more. As they moved up, Lee Teng-hui, the president [after Chiang Ching-kuo's death in 1988], began to coopt their issues and began to speak out for a separate identity, for leading the Chinese out of the Pharoah's land like Moses did the Jews. You'd get things being said that "I feel strongly toward Japan," and "Taiwan deserves to be independent. We should be in the UN." All of this rocks China.

LORD: [In 1993] we launched the first, systematic review of our Taiwan policy since the passage of the Taiwan Relations Act [1979]. This review went on for a good year or so, including debates on how bold we could be. There was never any feeling that we were going to revolutionize policy toward Taiwan in one way or another. We weren't going to go backward and resume having official relations with Taiwan. That would really have hurt ourselves with Beijing, as it was one of the most sensitive areas from Beijing's point of view. Nor were we going to flip over, do the bidding of the PRC government, and hurt Taiwan in any significant way. So this review was constrained from the beginning, and correctly so. However, within that framework we wanted to see whether we could strengthen ties with Taiwan without hurting our China relationship.

Natale Bellocchi with President Lee Teng-hui. *Courtesy of Natale Bellocchi.*

Many anomalies had grown up since we passed the Taiwan Relations Act in 1979. These have turned out to be awkward in terms of how we deal with Taiwan, because this relationship has to be unofficial. A lot of things were rather hurriedly thrown together in 1979 to compensate for normalization of relations with the PRC and to keep our ties with Taiwan. So not only did we want to strengthen relations with Taiwan, but we wanted to simplify relations in a way that wouldn't have major substantive impact but which would just make it easier to work the Taiwan side of the issue.

BELLOCCHI: The system works fine except in policy matters. The U.S. government must maintain complete control over policy, so the State Department laid down the policy. AIT implements it, but does not have a role in the decision making. It may be, of course, they will try to draw on all the expertise they can get, especially in Taiwan, what our views are, and what the reactions would be, and I contributed. But the decision itself is made over there in government.[24]

AIT headquarters is more the administrative headquarters which the money comes into. We have public affairs activity because the State Department doesn't conduct public affairs on behalf of the people in Taiwan. [As director] I went around the country speaking largely to Chinese-American associations. And then probably more important than anything is liaison with the Taiwan representative here, which I did on almost a daily basis. I was the liaison with State, with Commerce, with Agriculture, Treasury, all the others.

LORD: [The Taiwan Policy Review] took a long time, and Taiwan kept bugging us in terms of what was going to happen. The results were modest, but helpful. We changed the name of the Taiwan office in Washington to Taipei Economic and Cultural Relations Office [TECRO]. Now what was it called before?

It was called the Coordination Council for North American Affairs.

LORD: The Coordination Council for North American Affairs is a real mouthful, and I'm not saying that TECRO is a big improvement. It certainly didn't make this office more official. We wouldn't do that, but it gave more sense of what this office was up to. We did approve, in principle, cabinet-level official business with Taiwan, which was the most significant thing. However, such business had to be related to specific goals. Such contacts wouldn't be frequent, but they would be acceptable when they could help us, particularly in the cultural and economic areas. The only U.S. cabinet-level official who has ever gone to Taiwan was Carla Hills [in 1992], at the end of the Bush administration.[25] She was U.S. trade representative. We said that Taiwan officials who have economic functions could meet in U.S. government offices, even though we said that they couldn't meet U.S. officials in the State Department in Washington, because this would suggest diplomatic overtones. We decided that we would vigorously support Taiwan membership in international organizations which didn't require statehood. However, even in the case of those which required statehood, we would press to make sure that their voice could be heard in some fashion, perhaps as observers. In the case of those organizations which didn't require statehood, such as APEC, WTO, and other economic agencies, we would push for some Taiwan presence more strongly.

At the APEC meeting in November 1993, we also worked out that

Taiwan could attend the summit meeting that year. That was also very tough and delicate. Taiwan had already become a member of APEC during the Bush administration, but it was not a foregone conclusion, when we lifted the level of representation from foreign ministers to heads of state or heads of government, that Beijing would settle for Taiwan being present. We arranged for Taiwan to send a representative at the economic cabinet level. This got Taiwan into the APEC summit meeting but at a slightly lower level.

In any event, we did all of these things for Taiwan. Of course, it was less than Taiwan had hoped for, but we felt that we had cleaned up a lot of the anomalies, maintained our basic policy, avoided really annoying Beijing all that much, and modestly pleased Taiwan. The outcome wasn't dramatic.

Why did it take so long?

LORD: Essentially because people disagreed. Also, frankly, this was a result of inertia in the White House, particularly when there was sensitivity on this issue. It was hard to get meetings scheduled and decisions made.

Were there people arguing that this was going too far, that we were going to hurt Chinese feelings, and this was a bad move?

LORD: I don't remember that there was a lot of passion in the discussions, to be honest, because it didn't mark a dramatic departure. I don't recall anybody in the Clinton administration pushing for much bolder moves in support of Taiwan. I don't recall anyone saying very passionately that this was going to hurt our relations with Beijing.

I ask because, from the outside, the feeling always was that if movement had been faster on this issue, it would have been seen as a really positive administration effort. However, it took so long that everybody's expectations were raised.

LORD: That's a very good point. This package of measures involving Taiwan was not revolutionary by any means. We did not review or change our policy on arms sales to Taiwan and the basic policy of unofficial and friendly ties with Taiwan. If we had done all of this, say, in three or four months, people would have said: "It was a pretty good job." However, the economic and academic experts on the outside were watching this situation, wondering what the hell was going on. Taiwan, of course, was working with Congress to try to put a little pressure on the administration to undertake some bolder moves forward. They had their expectations raised, although, through careful backgrounding of the press, we tried to keep those expectations down. By the time these changes came out, a lot of people probably thought that we had produced a mouse. Having said that, we didn't pay a price of any significance in Beijing. We got modest kudos from Taiwan. On the whole, Congress thought that we should have gotten more, but members of Congress grudgingly said that we at least did something.

DEAN: President Lee felt himself sort of deserted by the U.S., or ignored. So instead of maintaining this low-keyed foreign policy that had been so productive he decided to embark on a new high visibility policy which he called pragmatic diplomacy. It was going down to southeast Asia and playing golf with heads of states. It was making more visits abroad to countries that did recognize Taiwan, mostly in Central America. It was pressing very hard to be the host of the Asian Games. It was pressing very hard to be invited as a head of state to the APEC meetings, which President Clinton elevated to head of state meetings. But he wasn't able to do any of these things. Then he sort of coopted the oppositionist parties' slogan of rejoining the UN and he did get the countries that had diplomatic relations to raise the issue of Taiwan before the UN rules committee to try to get it on the agenda, but unsuccessfully. And then finally this visit to the U.S. to raise Taiwan's international visibility and persona. To persuade countries that Taiwan had a right to international representation. As much right as most of the members of the UN.

LORD: In the course of 1994, there was the episode of President Lee Teng-hui of Taiwan wanting to visit the United States in transit to Central America, where he was making a state visit. Up till then we hadn't had transit visits due to opposition by Beijing, which had a tremendous, double standard in this regard. They accepted that President Lee could play golf and have official meetings with the leaders of Southeast Asian countries, and Beijing would hardly say anything about it. In any event, in 1994, Lee wanted to have a stopover somewhere in mainland U.S. We split the difference. You couldn't fly directly from Taiwan to Central America. So on grounds of logistics, convenience, and courtesy, you could make a case for approving this transit visit through the U.S. We knew about Beijing's sensitivities and we decided to have the transit take place in Hawaii. President Lee would come into the VIP lounge while his plane was refueled. I sent out the head of our Taiwan office in the State Department to greet him as a matter of courtesy.

The problem is that this solution didn't work. The Chinese government in Beijing was mad and beat up on us. President Lee, wanting a more high-profile visit, said that he wanted to spend a couple of days in Hawaii and play some golf. Instead of Taiwan being grateful that for the first time its president had set foot on American soil, it turned out that it was not satisfied. Lee decided that he would play up this incident and magnify it by not getting off the airplane. Taiwan put out a statement that we wouldn't let Lee off the plane in Hawaii. We never caught up with that allegation. I was blue in the face, telling every newsman on the record, and every congressman and senator that I could get my hands on that this allegation was not true. Of course we wanted him off the plane.

What was the impact of this episode?

LORD: In early 1995, Lee started pressing again for a working visit. He knew that he couldn't come as a head of state for a State visit. The excuse he used was that he wanted to receive honors from Cornell University. The idea was that he would go up to Cornell, give a speech, and be feted by his former university [from which he had earned a Ph.D. in agricultural economics]. Taiwan already had strong lobbyists on Capitol Hill, of course. Taiwan was in second place, just behind Israel and just ahead of Greece in its lobbying effort in Congress. Taiwan also hired a PR [public relations] firm. My own view is that Taiwan would have been able to mount a lot of pressure for a visa or, rather, just a travel permit, even without the PR firm, whose name escapes me.

It was Cassidy and Associates.

LORD: Cassidy and Associates. They had $4 million available for this campaign. There were some people in the Taiwan government who argued against this trip, saying that they should not annoy the Americans. There were various factions in Taiwan behind this project, pushing it, including Ding Mou-shih, who had been the Taiwan representative in Washington. In any event, the pressure was intense for us to allow Lee to come to the U.S. and give a speech at Cornell University.

To compel the administration to grant the visa, the lobbyists engineered a vote early in May 1995 calling upon the president to allow Lee to travel to Cornell. It passed in the House of Representatives 396 to 0 and 97 to 1 in the Senate. Bill Clinton, however, may not have needed that much persuasion given his anger at the Chinese for not improving their human rights record and his positive experiences in Taiwan while he was governor of Arkansas. How important was the lobbying?

BELLOCCHI: Chas. [Freeman] made a speech out there in Hong Kong that said the [Taiwan government] bought the vote. That's absurd, really, I'm sorry, it's absurd. Buying certainly helped. There's a lot of lobbying that goes on. But there's no question about Taiwan's effectiveness. There are people that support them because they are a democracy, and they have turned their human rights thing around so completely, so they have a very broad spectrum of support up on the Hill.

LORD: This particular episode, along with the reversal of our policy on MFN extension, were the two key events for which the Clinton administration has been criticized on specific aspects of our policy, as well as the general policy toward Taiwan.

The fairly generally held view [in the administration] was that, even though the Chinese government was being somewhat unreasonable by objecting to an unofficial, private visit by President Lee, the turbulence that would be caused in our relations with Beijing wasn't worth granting a travel permit to Lee. The way we phrased it was that our basic policy was not to allow visits by high-level Taiwan officials. I remember going up on Capitol Hill on several occasions and just getting lambasted. I was asked: "Are you going to let these 'pirates' in Beijing pressure you? This guy Lee is a democrat and a friend of the U.S. What the hell is going on here?"

In April 1995, Secretary Christopher had [a meeting] with PRC Foreign Minister Qian Qichen, at which he said that our fundamental policy was still not to allow visits to the U.S. by high-level Taiwan officials. However, Christopher also said that we were having a difficult time convincing the U.S. Congress that this was the right course, and the pressure was building up. Understandably, Qian Qichen reported the first part of Christopher's remark back to PRC President Jiang and others that the U.S. continued to oppose such visits. Either he didn't report the second part of Christopher's remark or didn't give appropriate weight to these congressional pressures. Maybe Qian thought that, whatever these pressures, we would just ignore them. In the event, the PRC authorities were caught by surprise. Jiang looked as if he had been outflanked by Taiwan. This was a very sensitive issue, particularly when Jiang was trying to consolidate his position, which was embarrassing both for President Jiang and for Foreign Minister Qian, who, after all, was a great hero of their foreign policy because he had been able to deal with the fallout from the Tiananmen Square incident. It was one of the reasons why Foreign Minister Qian was so hard line [later] during the Taiwan Straits missile crisis. He needed to show that he could be firm on Taiwan and so protect his flank. Anyway, Congress voted.[26] These were "sense of the Congress" resolutions without legal effect. However, the votes were overwhelming and were a clear message to the administration. We felt that Congress would be so outraged if we held out on this issue that it might tamper with the Taiwan Relations Act and might enforce other things with respect to Taiwan which could really hurt our policy toward Beijing. We also felt that the PRC government was over reacting. The president just changed his mind. He put emphasis on the freedom of travel and other considerations when he announced his decision. Of course, we tried to package this decision for the PRC government as best we could. What we told them, and what we told Taiwan at the same time that we did this, was that this visit was going to be at the lowest key possible. So we worked out that President Lee would hold no press conferences. He would go directly to Ithaca, N.Y. [where Cornell University is located], and not even go through New York City. He would not be met by any U.S. government official, although we would have my Taiwan country director accompanying him, partly to keep Lee under control, work with their people, and make sure that he didn't do something that would be awkward. There were Congressmen and Senators who wanted to go up to Cornell and meet Lee. We couldn't do anything about that.

In retrospect, we should have agreed to grant Lee a traveler's permit from the beginning. We would then have avoided the flip flop in the eyes of the PRC government, although they still would have been outraged at the decision. However, on the merits, Lee Teng-hui should have been allowed to make a private, unofficial visit, and then we should have been prepared to tough it out with the PRC. Another thing that we should have done, we should have been much more air tight on the speech that Lee was going to give at Cornell University.

We were assured by Benjamin Lu, the Taiwan representative in Washington [head of TECRO], that Lee's speech would be nonpolitical, and would cover economic reforms in Taiwan. We attempted very vigorously to get details of the speech from the Taiwan representative in Washington, but without success. This should have made us suspicious. The PRC government was going to scream and shout, even without the speech. They did not react all that strongly even during the first couple of days. Then Lee gave his speech. In his speech he had something like 27 references to the Republic of China on Taiwan. He totally double crossed us. Of course, the PRC Chinese went ballistic. I went ballistic as well. After all, on this issue President Clinton had stuck his neck out, risking our relationship with the PRC. I refused to receive Benjamin Lu, the Taiwan representative. For a few months he had absolutely no access to me. I was the highest level official in the State Department that he was allowed to see. He was finally recalled to Taiwan. I would like to think that I had something to do with it. He is a nice man but ineffectual. He was either weak or disingenuous.

Also we went back to Beijing on it, but the damage was done. The PRC government cut off some trips and exchanges. They withdrew their ambassador from Washington, and relations got very frosty, just when we had been making some progress. The PRC began its first military exercise [in the Taiwan Straits] in July 1995, not long after the Lee visit. I can't remember whether they fired any missiles or, at any rate, not particularly close to Taiwan during this first military exercise.

There were missiles, but they were not aimed very close to Taiwan.

LORD: We reacted to this, saying that these exercises were not helpful, but I don't recall any formal protest, since they were not particularly provocative. During the rest of 1995, we tried to get MFN status renewed for China by a fairly significant majority despite the controversy that came up every year.

TAIWAN STRAIT CRISIS

Beijing's decision to test missiles in the waters around Taiwan in the summer of 1995 proved to be just a preliminary exercise for the main show in the spring of 1996. As Taiwan prepared to hold the first direct presidential elections in Chinese history, Beijing decided to try to intimidate the voting public. Whether Chinese leaders hoped to turn Lee Teng-hui out of office or just to weaken him, the missile firings so close to Taiwan had just the opposite effect. Lee did better in the elections than expected and China shocked the whole region with its reckless behavior.

LORD: As we reached the beginning of 1996, it looked as if we faced a real nightmare. This was before the Taiwan Missile Crisis heated up again. We discovered that there was a whole minefield ahead of us. The PRC Chinese were sending ring magnets to Pakistan, which helped Pakistan develop their nuclear capability. Consequently, we slapped on sanctions because of that.[27] We had very tough negotiations on intellectual property rights. American business interests were losing billions of dollars each year because of pirating [unauthorized copying] by the PRC Chinese of CDs [compact disks], VCRs [video cassette recordings], computer software, pharmaceutical products patented in the U.S.[28] In March 1996, we had the Geneva human rights resolution tussle coming up. This was always a source of irritation between us and Beijing. The MFN extension came up right after that. [And] there was still the chill left over from the withdrawal of the PRC ambassador from Washington. So the relationship between the U.S. and the PRC Chinese was not in very good shape early in 1996.

In late 1995 or January 1996, we began a process of intensive, strategic reviews, both in the State Department and at the White House. We tried to think of ways that we could do things the PRC might find positive, in addition to pressing them on things that they would find difficult. We also agreed that we really would try to make a much more aggressive effort to engage in a strategic dialogue with the PRC. Secretary Christopher chaired most of the key sessions.[29]

At this time Liu Huaqiu was Tony Lake's equivalent within the Chinese hierarchy as national security adviser, although not as powerful. He was also vice foreign minister, reporting directly to Li Peng. He had also been an America hand for some time, including when I was in

Beijing as ambassador. Anyway, Liu was coming to visit the PRC Embassy in Washington in March 1996, to talk to all of the consuls general and the ambassador. So, with close coordination between the State Department and the White House, we arrange[d] a day-long retreat to have a strategic dialogue with him. Lo and behold, on the day Liu arrived in Washington, Friday, March 7, 1996, the PRC fired missiles that landed on either side of Taiwan. One missile landed off one port in Taiwan, another one landed off a second port.[30] This incident greatly escalated the tension in the Taiwan Straits. So that particular moment was clearly the low point in U.S.-China relations during the first Clinton term.

We had already arranged for Liu's visit to begin on a Friday night with an informal dinner at the State Department, hosted by Secretary of State Christopher. This was to make clear, as Liu went off the next day for a full day's meeting with Tony Lake [and myself], that the State Department was still heavily involved in U.S. foreign policy. When we got word of the PRC missile firings, we decided to add Secretary of Defense [Bill] Perry to the discussions. The strategic dialogue had now been overtaken by the PRC missile firings, which we had to address first. Perry said that what Beijing had done could result in grave consequences. This was a pretty heavily loaded term. He said that this could lead to a possible conflict with the United States. He likened what the PRC had done, firing missiles north and south of Taiwan, as a kind of bracketing artillery fire, where you fire to one side and then to the other side so that you can zoom in on the actual target. He used that image, which was strong language. (Secretary Christopher and Tony Lake weighed in strongly.) Our clear impression was that Liu was totally surprised by the timing of the missile firings, if not the missile firings themselves. Liu, of course, was firm. He is always firm. He can be jovial at times. However, he can be very feisty in his discussions in defending Chinese interests and attacking the U.S. He clearly felt awkward about this situation, although he didn't say that. We indicated that we thought that this was a hell of a way to start important discussions.

On the next day there was a lot of snow on the ground, and it was cold. We drove down to Pamela Harriman's estate in Virginia.[31] There were four of us on our side, including Tony Lake, Bob Suettinger of the NSC staff, Jeff Bader [China country director at State], and myself. Lake hadn't played that much of a role on China policy. Now he was getting more involved on some of these Asian issues, and specifically on China. The discussion lasted roughly from 9: oo a.m. to 4: oo p.m. First, we had to repeat the warnings. Tony Lake also made references to words we heard from Chas. Freeman about a potential Chinese [nuclear] threat against us, if we had a nuclear confrontation [see below]. Then the presentation became more conceptual, philosophical, and strategic, describing two great powers heading into the next century, that is, how we could work together, why that is important, and how we see China. We said that we want to see China as a strong, stable, prosperous, and open society. We weren't out to contain China, divide it, or subvert it. However, we would defend our interests. We would maintain our force levels and our alliances. We would be firm in negotiating. We had interests and would stand up for our values. We sketched out some areas where we could work more effectively together and give some content to this approach. Some of the areas involved ranged from Korea to Cambodia, regional security dialogues, APEC, economic questions, Chinese admission to the WTO, and environmental questions, including crime and narcotics.

Then in the second part of the day we planned to take on the tough issues. We covered human rights, trade, nuclear nonproliferation, Taiwan. Then we ended up by indicating suggestions on how we could make progress and some foreshadowing, without locking ourselves into it, of a possible summit meeting.

How serious do you believe the nuclear threats were that Xiong Guankai made in his talks with Chas. Freeman?

LORD: Basically the Chinese were alleged to have said more or less as follows. They said, "Look, we're not worried if we get into some tension and potential conflict with the United States. By the way, we have nuclear weapons, too. In the event of a real confrontation we don't think that the Americans are going to 'give up' Los Angeles in exchange for Taiwan." Chas. Freeman likes to think that these discussions were of fundamental importance. I think that that's baloney. It was vague, at least the way we heard it at the time. It seems to have gotten more precise since then. We all felt that there was enough there so that we had to respond and take note of it. We didn't want to inflate its importance.

Xiong reportedly put this in the context of the 1950s and 1960s, when it was possible for the United States to eliminate China with nuclear weapons. However, he noted that times have changed.

LORD: On the very next day [after the retreat with Liu] we met in Secretary Perry's office, Saturday, March 8. Those present were Perry, Christopher, and myself, John Deutch, the Director of Central Intelligence, General [John] Shalikashvili [chief, JCS] and either Tony Lake or Sandy Berger from the National Security Council staff. The question was what, if anything, we could do to deter Chinese use of force. Neither we nor the Chinese Nationalists had any intelligence that the PRC was going to use force at that time against Taiwan, beyond firing a few missiles and using intimidation. We had no evidence that the PRC was going to hit even an uninhabited island with a missile or harass shipping. Certainly the PRC was not going to attack Taiwan if they didn't even have the capability to attack one of the offshore islands. Our best judgment was that the PRC wanted to engage in psychological and political warfare to intimidate Taiwan and send a signal about the sensitivity of this issue, from the PRC point of view. Taiwan intelligence agreed with that view.

Having said that, it was agreed that there was a 5 or 10 percent chance that we were wrong. The PRC might take aggressive action at a lower level. Namely, for example, seize an uninhabited offshore island or lob a missile at some uninhabited territory. There was a danger that our intelligence was wrong and that the PRC might just do something which would be very humiliating and which would make it very difficult for us to decide what to do in response. Or, through miscalculation, the PRC might stumble into action. Either a missile misfire which would hit a populated center, or harassment of shipping could result in a collision. Or something could happen just inadvertently. Our choices after the Chinese had done something would be much more difficult, even after an accident, however modest it was, than if we deterred that from the beginning.

So the feeling was that we had to have a demonstration, beyond the rhetoric that we had been applying, both privately, through diplomatic channels, and publicly, when we said that we didn't like what the Chinese were up to. Furthermore, we wanted to show our allies and friends in the East Asian region that we were reliable partners. We also, of course, wanted to reassure Taiwan about its security concerns. And, of course, we were concerned about our domestic front in Congress. For all of these reasons there was a unanimous view in this group which met in Secretary Perry's office that we needed to do something quite significant.

We had the usual aircraft carrier deployed in the region, the USS *Independence* with its accompanying battle group [which was based in Japan]. We made sure that it moved close to the region of the Taiwan Straits. This key decision, by itself, would get some attention from Beijing, but it was not particularly dramatic. So we decided to deploy another aircraft carrier [the *Nimitz*], along with its accompanying escorts, to the area, which would really make our point. This would marshal the biggest fighting force in the Western Pacific for a long time [since Vietnam].

What was Taiwan's reaction to U.S. policy?

LORD: With Taiwan, of course, the deployment of the carriers was reassuring and a great boost to morale. In addition, we told China that we found what Beijing was doing was unacceptable. However, we told Taiwan that we also didn't like Taiwan's being overly provocative in its diplomacy, because this might drag the U.S. into a conflict and would not serve Taiwan's security or the economy of Taiwan. Specifically, we had Peter Tarnoff, the undersecretary of state for Political Affairs, and Sandy Berger, deputy national security adviser, meet secretly at a hotel in New York with Ding Mou-shih, who had been the Taiwan representative in Washington during the early part of the Clinton administration. He was now a direct adviser to the Taiwan government on national security affairs. We knew that he had a direct pipeline to President Lee and was also an able guy, unlike Benjamin Lu. We didn't even tell Benjamin Lu that this meeting was taking place. We delivered both the reassurances to Taiwan and the request that they not be provocative at the same time.

What was the impact of China's actions in Taiwan?

BELLOCCHI: Missile firing was a rather crude way of reminding the Taiwanese to behave. But the other side of that coin is that it's a unifying experience for the people on Taiwan, and strengthened the differences between the people on Taiwan, and the people on the mainland.

LORD: This shows how little the PRC leaders understood about democracy. All they did was to increase Lee's margin of victory in the Taiwan presidential elections and make many people on Taiwan very angry.

BELLOCCHI: The political leadership on Taiwan has got to put the welfare and security of the people on that island first, or they won't stay in power. And that's the change. Not unification first, the people on Taiwan first. The last time I heard the figures they say a total of 300 out of 7 million [Taiwan visitors] have stayed [in China]. These are people that were old, and wanted to die in their old village. Nobody will stay over there. "The PRC, that's great, it's interesting, its got a big wall, big statues, big buildings, but I wouldn't want to live there."[32]

China, of course, has changed a great deal, but nothing compared to the way Taiwan has changed. Nobody has been killed by this revolution that's taking place, so people haven't noticed it as much. But if you could feel it when you go to Taiwan the people that you're dealing with now, it's like a big breath of fresh air. They want to talk independence. They want to oppose the leadership simply because they can do it now, and weren't able to do it before. It's that kind of thing that the leadership has to live with. They have opened the doors and opened the windows, and everybody wants to shout, and boy their politics are as vigorous as you can find anywhere. So we worry that they should really be thinking about their relationship with the mainland. The only time they think about it is how much money can I make over there.

And this constrains what the leadership can do?

BELLOCCHI: You cannot do in a democratic Taiwan what you could do in an authoritarian Taiwan. If you're a political leader and depend on votes—the people have opinions over there—they're one of the most widely traveled people in the world, 20 percent of the people on Taiwan travel abroad every year. They're really very conscious of what goes on in the world, so that makes them extremely sensitive to the fact they have no status. They're getting more and more proud, or nationalist. And that isn't given enough weight [in the United States], and it absolutely is not given enough weight over in the PRC. And a political leader has got to be responsive to it, or he's going to lose power. And the president of Taiwan no longer has that carte blanche power, no matter how popular he is, that the old leaders of Taiwan used to have.

What was the impact of the United States actions in the Taiwan Straits on opinion in the rest of Asia?

LORD: We got lots of credit in Asia. Many Asian governments patted us on the back and were very happy, although not many said so publicly. The East Asian countries were concerned about the episode of China creating mischief in 1994 in the South China Sea and China's buildup of their military.[33] Even though nobody wanted a confrontation with China, the East Asian countries were concerned about Chinese power. That was one of the reasons, along with keeping Japan under control, that these countries welcomed the U.S. military presence in East Asia. These actions were also applauded in Congress and in the U.S. press.

What was the impact on U.S. China policy?

LORD: We were annoyed with what Beijing had done but we weren't going to change our policy on one China. We were urging Taiwan to cool it. We were encouraging Beijing and Taiwan to have direct talks across the Taiwan Straits [talks that had been suspended in 1995 because of the Lee visit]. The deployment of carriers to the Taiwan Straits helped to cool things down. From then on our relationship with Beijing started to improve.[34]

By the time Secretary Christopher went to China in November 1996, we had developed considerable momentum. We went to China just before going to Manila, where the annual meeting of APEC was taking place, and President Clinton would meet PRC President Jiang Zemin. It was agreed that the two presidents would announce mutual summit meetings. This was a happy note to close off Clinton's first term.

Regarding the crisis caused by the PRC firing missiles near Taiwan, during the Cold War we deployed Patriot missile batteries in Israel. The Patriot missiles were designed to shoot down just the type of missiles that the PRC had. Did we consider doing anything of that nature?

LORD: We had already provided Patriot missile equipment to Taiwan. It was called MAD. This did not mean Mutual Assured Destruction but something else called Modified Air Defense. I don't remember that we rushed this equipment to them during the middle of the Taiwan Straits Crisis. Maybe we provided it to them afterwards. Can you recall the timing?

We had promised to provide Patriot missiles to the Chinese Nationalists at some time before the Dole-Clinton election campaign of 1996. Senator [Robert] Dole spoke about providing Theater Missile Defense to Taiwan, while Clinton said that we were going to speed up the delivery of Patriot missiles to Taiwan. Was Taiwan, then, safe because of these missile defenses and China's lack of amphibious capabilities?

LORD: In effect the PRC sent a message to Taiwan that, although they can't attack Taiwan in an amphibious way, they can lob in a few missiles. They can affect the Taiwan stock market, investment, and so forth. So the PRC didn't lose totally on this. I'm sure that the PRC rationalized it in their own mind that their tough muscling around had some positive impact.

Our policy toward Taiwan has basically been one of strategic ambiguity, in what we would do regarding the Taiwan Strait. How much discussion has there been of changing that policy? Do you think that President Lee Teng-hui made an assumption that Taiwan would have American support, regardless of what happened?

LORD: Of course, we didn't want Taiwan to think that they had a blank check from us. That was why we were telling Taiwan not to be provocative, just because we were deploying the two carriers to the Taiwan Straits. There was some discussion of the question of strategic ambiguity, but I don't recall that there was any view that we should be more precise. First of all, the Taiwan Relations Act itself states that the administration has to consult the Congress before taking any specific actions. So I said to congressmen that it was rather ironic that they seemed to want the administration to get out in front of them. [Then] it is prudent generally that you don't state in advance what you will do in specific situations. And most fundamentally, if we get away from ambiguity and go in either direction, we're in trouble. If the PRC thinks that we won't come to the defense of Taiwan in a crunch, they're going to be aggressive and they're going to press Taiwan. In that case we're likely to run into a difficult situation and possibly a conflict. If Taiwan thinks that we're going to come to their defense, no matter what happens, they're going to be provocative, knowing that they're going to have a free ride, no matter how angry Beijing gets. Therefore, we can't be precise. Having said that, we've got to use the right kind of adjectives and send aircraft carriers at the right moments to make clear that it's dangerous for Beijing to think that they can act aggressively. So there wasn't much debate within the administration on this crisis. Frankly, I didn't feel too much pressure from Capitol Hill. The merits of the case were pretty persuasive.

JAPAN

Continuing friction between the United States and Japan on trade issues and tensions over the basing of American forces on Okinawa increasingly obscured the significance of the strategic relationship between the two allies. This fact became distressingly apparent during the North Korean nuclear crisis in 1993–1994 and again during the disturbances in the Taiwan Strait 1995–1996, when the limits of Japanese support for American operations in Asia proved unclear to Washington and Tokyo. Both to arrest the erosion of the alliance and to clarify responsibilities in times of crisis, American and Japanese officials engaged in a review of cooperative policies and devised a new approach to collaboration.

LORD: I worked very closely with Joe Nye to insulate the U.S.-Japan security relationship and our overall ties from the trade disputes that we had with Japan. Then we got into the [U.S.-Japan] Defense Guidelines, on which Bill Perry [then secretary of defense] took the lead, and Secretary Christopher and I worked with them. These guidelines came out around the time of the president's trip to Japan, which was in the spring of 1996.[35] It was a very successful trip. It had been postponed from November 1995, because President Clinton said that he had to stay home because the budget had not yet been passed. We also felt that with the end of the Cold War and the passage of 15 or 20 years it was time to update the guidelines on U.S. policy toward Japan.

Some people have said that the Japan Guidelines document was strengthened because of the Taiwan missile crisis. The answer to this is, "Yes." Japan again began to become worried about an aggressive China. It was kept ambiguous whether the Japan Guidelines document applied to Taiwan. Neither we nor the Japanese have either confirmed or denied it. We were not about to deny that it applied, because it might well have applied. However, it was provocative to say that it does apply because Beijing considers Taiwan part of the territory of China. The phrasing of situations surrounding Taiwan . . .

Situations in areas surrounding . . .

LORD: Surrounding Japan, so it doesn't mention Taiwan. So we effectively stonewalled the Chinese on what the guidelines document really means.

In your experience has it been difficult to get Japan to talk about China? Have there been continuing consultations between the Japanese and American governments on China problems?

LORD: There have been no difficulties at all. I went out of my way on this subject myself, because of my own, personal experience in the 1970s, the Nixon Shocks [see chapter 5]. On almost every Asian trip I would drop in on Japan, either at the beginning or the end. We would maintain a constant dialogue on China policy and make sure that there were no surprises in this regard. The only rift between us was on human rights. Japan just wouldn't put any pressure on China. Partly this was natural, anyway, because Japanese commercial instincts probably overrode everything. It was also partly because of their guilt feelings about World War II and the rape of Nanjing. The Japanese didn't want to look as if they were lecturing China, when . . .

The Japanese weren't the right people to do that.

LORD: They weren't the right people. They haven't been exactly forthcoming in confessing their sins in China. The Japanese have sort of said that, because of their history, it's awkward for them to discuss human rights abuses, even though they don't admit to anything.

The Japanese always seem to be uncomfortable, both when our relations with China are bad and when our relations with China are good.

LORD: A very good point. If our relations with China are bad, then the Japanese get nervous about tensions in the Taiwan Straits, because they might have to choose between the U.S. and China. If U.S. relations with China are good, the Japanese wonder if it will be at Japan's expense. So the phrase which they have been using is that we may either bash Japan or may by-pass Japan.

BELLOCCHI: The Japanese are more cautious than ever. I mean, they've got more at stake, they're much closer to China than we are. They've got problems, and they're growing problems. They've got a lot of business with Taiwan; they have more business with the PRC than we do. They also have a democracy that's increasingly aware of the democracy in Taiwan. So Taiwan's support in Japan is actually growing. It was very high at first because the Japanese appreciated that old Chiang Kai-shek didn't demand reparations for World War II. Well, that crowd has sort of died away. But now the newer group is coming up. They're doing business with Taiwan. They respect democracy in Taiwan. So the Foreign Office in Tokyo is beginning to feel the same kind of pressures that our State Department feels on the issue of Taiwan—in a much lesser degree now, because their inclination to be more wary of the PRC is much greater than ours because of geography more than anything else.

TIBET

In the 1990s, as American disenchantment with China became evident on a variety of issues, the question of Tibet also caught the popular mind to an unprecedented extent. Tibetans drew graphic parallels between the brutality Americans had witnessed at Tiananmen Square and Chinese repression in Tibet. They mobilized American sympathizers in positions of broad influence, most particularly the motion picture industry, where film stars and movie producers highlighted religious and political persecution. U.S. government policy remained firm, recognizing that Tibet is a province of China, but diplomats were often confronted with the need to justify that policy at home even as they had to parry suspicion of American motives in

China. The U.S. government did make repeated efforts to encourage dialogue between the exiled Dalai Lama and Beijing. For instance, during his 1998 visit to China, President Bill Clinton publicly called for a more open Tibet policy.

FREEMAN: There is, of course, in the post-Soviet-collapse era, a sense that, well, if the Soviet Union broke up and various nationalities that had been incorporated into the Russian Empire flew out of it, why shouldn't Tibet do the same? This has been a cause of considerable friction between the United States and China, because every Chinese, whether he is a dissident who participated in the events in Tiananmen Square in 1989 and is in jail or has been in jail, or whether he is a high official of the government, agrees that Tibet is and always has been and always will be part of China. There is absolutely no sympathy for separatism, or any willingness to tolerate it. Therefore, gestures that, in terms of American politics, seem innocent and noble and perhaps are seen as free shots in the political arena, like congressional resolutions proposing the recognition of Tibet and independence and the sending of an ambassador there, are seen by the Chinese (and technically they're correct) as justifying a declaration of war in response, since the initiatives proposed to sever a portion of the country from central control, and promote rebellion and secession. Well, of course, Americans don't see that, and therefore are somewhat puzzled by the strength of the Chinese reaction to all this.

Finally, Tibet is a very different issue from what is often presented in the United States. It is not so far the case that China is deliberately populating Tibet with Han Chinese. To the extent there is economic opportunity in Tibet (and that is not a wide extent), Chinese who want to make money will and do move there. But most Chinese find it an exotic but very harsh, environment. It's a nice place to visit, but they don't want to live there.

The Tibetan population is quite distinct, quite resentful of Han economic and political dominance, very much devoted to the Dalai Lama, and chafing under Chinese rule. All that is true. But it is also true that Tibetan culture was a primitive and remarkably unsuccessful culture, in terms of producing a decent lifespan or state of public health or economic opportunity or engagement with the outside world by Tibetans. And Tibetan association in the broader Chinese family has brought the

Tibetan people all of those benefits. Tibet is not viable as an independent country in the modern era. It is viable as an independent country only if it is prepared to live at medieval standards of living, which I don't believe anyone is.

So it's a complex situation. And because Tibet is so far away from the United States, it's a blank screen on which you can project your own mystical fantasies with great ease. We were better served when we dealt, as we did in the '80s, with that issue with some caution and some sense of the inflammatory potential that appearing to sponsor secession by a part of China from China might have. Generally speaking, countries, including the United States, are well advised not to sponsor causes that are hopeless. Tibetan independence can only succeed if there is massive foreign intervention. In other words, a war with China. And I don't see the United States or the American people being willing to make that sort of sacrifice for that cause.

Concluding Thoughts

As the twentieth century experiences of imperialism, victimization, revolution, war and chaos recede into a past millennium, relations between the United States and China, as well as between these two and Taiwan, are uncertain and unsteady. In the twenty-first century, China is more likely to play an important international role than it did in the five decades examined here by the veterans of America's China service. Barring a catastrophe, China will be stronger, more unified, and more prosperous than at any time in its post-imperial history. At the same time, the United States will be, at least in the early years of the new millennium, the dominant global power, with responsibilities and influence that have a worldwide reach. Whether the rising state of China and the status quo politicians in Washington will be able to handle their conflicting priorities and goals so as to avoid direct conflict must be one of the most crucial questions for international relations practitioners and analysts in the years ahead. The U.S. and China will have to deal with continuing disputes over trade imbalances, human rights, and military modernization. And they will be forced somehow to manage the incendiary problem of Taiwan, which threatens not only their ability to sustain constructive ties, but also the peace of the region and the world.

Among the diplomats who have spoken in these pages about their experiences dealing with Chinese affairs are those who look ahead to a new era in Asia with anticipation but also a measure of alarm. John Holdridge, for instance, worries that "The Chinese are very much in the mood that Japan was prior to World War II. The Japanese had this terrible chip on their shoulder. They felt that they were being looked down on by others. They were in a very bellicose and belligerent mood. If [the Chinese] were confident of themselves and of their own system and situation, they wouldn't be so difficult to deal with." This is a feeling shared by Winston Lord, who points to China's "combination of arrogance, xenophobia, and national-ism." Part of this grew out of the "bad century or, say, 150 years when [the Chinese] were humiliated by foreigners," followed by the difficulties of adjusting to a new status. It is not entirely surprising, he contends, that:

> This gives the Chinese a certain desire to flex their muscles and also to be treated as equals. On top of that the Chinese have a certain smugness vis-à-vis the Soviet experience. They figure that Gorbachev and other Russian leaders allowed too much political freedom without making economic progress. So the Soviets lost their empire, and the Communist Party lost control of the country. They think that they're not going to make the same mistake.

Internal change—economic and political—inevitably will remain at the top of the agenda for both the critics and defenders of the Chinese system in the early years of the twenty-first century. China's communist leaders recognize the inevitability and appreciate the benefits of economic reforms. Since 1978, the new economic order has made China's prosperity and growing influence possible. But the political effects have not been nearly as welcome.

Anxiety about the political future touches officials, intellectuals, and businessmen. The government opposes democratization, but tolerates a degree of liberalization, particularly in such venues as village elections. Ordinary life in China became much freer in the 1990s, with increased mobility and a considerable scope for free expression. The impenetrable barrier continues to be political organization and direct opposition to the Chinese Communist Party, all of which the leadership considers intolera-ble. But, Chas. Freeman asserts, reservations about political change exist even among those not vested with power. "No Chinese that I have met seems to want to emulate either the U.S. federal system or the constitutional democratic presidential system that we have." Much of this sentiment, he believes, has stemmed from the mixture of

> admiration for the intellectual freedom that the U.S. provides, but at the same time, a great distaste for what many of the Chinese see as the inevitable results of excessive acquisitive individualism and First Amendment rights. The Chinese tend to tie social disorder in the United States—high rates of teenage pregnancy, drug use, the extraor-

dinary crime rate, the lack of personal security on the streets, some of the things that we Americans also find least admirable about our society to our political system. The dominant sentiment for the Chinese, and the reason they react the way they do to some of the untidy aspects of American life—pornography and crime and addictions—has to do with the searing experience of Chinese history. Disorder in China can have catastrophic consequences, and you don't have to be very old, if you're Chinese, to have actually experienced some of those. So that, while people would like to see human liberty expand, they're very cautious about how authoritarianism is to be relaxed.

Although the degree of discomfort with political freedoms might be less than Freeman contends, it does seem likely that political change will come slowly. Freeman speculates that "the Chinese [will] look [to Taiwan and South Korea] for models that get on with the business of economic reconstruction, building prosperity first, and then deal with some of the political problems of the system later, in a gradual way." Meanwhile, dissidents will continue to be repressed and imprisoned.

Of course, the challenge will not only be China's internal development and its place in Asia, but also the nature of future Sino-American relations: cooperative or contentious? constructive or destructive? wary or warm? Again, American diplomats who continue to worry about the interaction, even though they have left their official posts, think about issues that will certainly complicate the ability of their successors in Washington to adopt a clear and productive China policy. Among these "were Chinese suspicions of the United States," which Winston Lord encountered and which are not likely to dissipate easily:

Some of these were allegedly for tactical reasons to put us on the defensive. Some of the Chinese leaders genuinely felt this. The most extreme Chinese view of the United States is that we're keeping them down, and we don't want another superpower around. So in this view, we are trying to restrain, contain, and isolate them. This is allegedly proved by our maintaining our military presence in the Pacific Ocean area and by our strengthening our relations with Japan. Allegedly, the U.S. is trying to control China's exports of military materials and military sales. Another allegation is that we are trying to keep China out of the WTO [World Trade Organization].[1] Then we are allegedly trying to divide up

China's territory, with pressures on Hong Kong, Tibet, and Taiwan. On top of that we are allegedly trying to subvert China politically by pushing human rights and democracy, so that the PRC Government will lose political control of the country. If you put all of these allegations together, I would argue that that's a fairly difficult mood to deal with.

One crucial element will clearly continue to be the triangular relationship among the United States, China, and Taiwan. Creative solutions for that difficult conundrum remain few and far between. David Dean has proposed an approach that has had some currency among scholars, if not the leadership, in all three places:

> A close friend of mine, the publisher of the *China Times* in Taiwan, wrote an article just about exactly the same time I did, about the prospects or possibilities of a confederation or a commonwealth. Subsequently even the former chairman of the oppositionist party, the DPP advocated a situation for Taiwan and the mainland like the British Commonwealth of Nations. It's an idea that probably would be accepted by [the United States] and other countries and, in the final analysis, by Taiwan, since it would give them their independence in everything but name. The only objections probably would come from China. They have touted their "one country two systems," which they are using for Hong Kong.

As Dean notes, however, the "one country two systems" proposal Beijing has made to Taiwan "is much broader than the Hong Kong model and its not impossible for me to see in some future period, 10, 20 years from now that their definition of 'one country two systems' is suspiciously like the definition for a commonwealth or confederation." After all, Dean adds, and others emphasize, the leaders in Beijing "don't want to be forced into confrontation over Taiwan."

On the other hand, so long as Taiwan remains a symbol of political legitimacy, no government in Beijing can easily let Taiwan make its own decisions. And an obstinate Beijing faces an increasingly apprehensive Taipei. To date the population on the island has been cautious, consistently favoring preservation of the status quo over either reunification or independence. So long as Beijing can live with that situation, time may bring the two Chinese entities closer together as their economies are integrated and political change on the mainland renders its institutions more palatable to people in Taiwan. But whether Chinese leaders have the political latitude to be patient is unclear. Furthermore, there are those who would argue that time may not work in Beijing's interests as a younger generation in Taiwan thinks of itself less and less as Chinese and more and more as Taiwanese. As Winston Lord notes, "The Chinese military are demanding more of a role. In the South China Sea and the Taiwan missile crisis, they showed that they can be more aggressive." The future could well be very dangerous, a reality that bodes ill for a United States, which will be hard pressed to avoid involvement.[2]

There are, of course, a series of other issues that destabilize Sino-American relations. These may be less likely to lead to war than confrontation in the Taiwan Straits, but they demand enormous energy and attention from diplomats. The mounting trade deficit that the United States has been running with China, second only to that with Japan, disturbs Congress and fuels the conviction in the business community that China has not done enough to open its market to American goods and services. Because businessmen have been China's most fulsome supporters and lobbyists, their disenchantment with the China market would be devastating to the relationship. Of course, China, confronting the dual imperatives of reforming its banking sector and its state owned enterprises, has resisted dramatic change in its policies on foreign trade, investment, and licensing for service industries. The result was prolonged and difficult negotiations for its entry into the World Trade Organization. With the extensive concessions finally made by Beijing in the autumn of 1999, accession seemed certain, but implementation still appeared likely to produce friction.

There have also been problems surrounding China's determination to modernize its military. Great powers, the leadership is convinced, have great military forces. Furthermore, the Chinese endured a humiliating lesson about inadequate training, defective equipment, and inferior logistics when they invaded Vietnam in 1979. As Jim Lilley observed, they were aware that eventually they must embark upon reform, Deng Xiaoping having concluded that the Chinese military was "backward and stupid." However, China has only had the resources for serious improvements in recent years. Although the United States actually encouraged "the Europeans to sell weapons systems to the Chinese because we ourselves couldn't" in the 1970s, recalls Lilley, the eagerness with which elements of the military have today sought to make up for lost time has worried the United States. The issues have involved proliferation of weapons of mass destruction, acquisition of high-tech weapons systems from the former Soviet Union, and possibly through espionage in the United States, and the deployment of military assets in or against areas important to Washington. China's attitudes toward the maintenance of American forces in the Pacific have also been in flux. Questions have been raised regarding the need and appropriateness of such a large contingent of U.S. troops in the region (100,000). Beijing has further opposed the introduction of Theater Missile Defenses into Japan and Taiwan, which could imperil its own missile capabilities, and protested aspects of the U.S.-Japan Defense Guidelines negotiated in the late 1990s.

Among the most troublesome areas of contention in Sino-American relations, human rights will remain at the top of the agenda in the twenty-first century. Although it has become a central element, it has actually been a relatively recent component of diplomatic discourse with the Chinese. Winston Lord was quick to concede that when normalization first occurred, Richard Nixon and Henry Kissinger put far more emphasis on strategic concerns than on human rights abuses. But with the Carter administration, human rights became more prominent. Frank Burnet recalls that "at either the ambassador's or Washington's suggestion, to make an impression on the staff (to get us thinking in that direction), they had us set up a seminar on human rights in general. I organized it, and held it at my home, wives were invited. It was really a good exercise." The inauguration of regular human rights reports to Congress meant that, for the first time, Foreign Service officers had deliberately and routinely to collect relevant data for the annual exercise, assessing behavior in areas such as religious observance, political dissent, and prison labor. Then, with the massacre at Tiananmen Square in 1989, human rights temporarily crowded out all other considerations. That high tide receded in the late 1990s, but human rights issues continued to command much attention from policy makers, members of Congress, and the public. China, of course, gives that preoccupation impetus by persisting in the arrest and incarceration of political and religious figures whose offenses appear inconsequential or non-existent to the outside world.

Hope for progress is possible in part because China no longer is the "pariah" that Richard Nixon warned would endanger American security when he began in the 1960s to justify his desire to reach out to Beijing. John Holdridge notes that, "Starting with normalization and now more recently, the Chinese began to function as normal members of the world community. They joined the IAEA, the World Bank, IMF, [and] have applied for the GATT [now the WTO]." So long as Beijing wants to be part of an advanced, industrial international society that subscribes to universal values, adheres to trade regulating organizations, and observes arms control agreements, the People's Republic must be less defiant and more willing to compromise than it was in its early revolutionary days.

Nevertheless, the actual remedies for the difficult disputes between the United States and China remain elusive, making it all the more obvious that all sides will have to take responsibility for provocative actions and work harder to avoid incitement. Secret assurances such as those in 1982 to Taiwan's leaders by Ronald Reagan that agreements with Beijing will be evaded are no more constructive than the firing of missiles across the Taiwan Strait by Beijing in 1996. There will have to be more sober efforts at maintaining smooth and productive ties.

For this the China service of the new millennium will be critical. The American diplomats who work in China or deal with Chinese affairs in Washington have been the fulcrum of the relationship in decades past. Today, because contacts between the societies have multiplied and diversified, the Foreign Service no longer plays as central a role and much diplomacy occurs through private channels whether business, cultural, or scholarly. The Department of State has also increasingly been forced to share its power and initiative with other government agencies such as the National Security Council, the CIA, the Defense Department, and the Department of Commerce, as well as the U.S. Congress.

The participation of groups and individuals who become competitors in crafting a viable China policy complicates the job of State Department officials. It has often been a point of contention for diplomats who, as Arthur Hummel complained, can loose control of their embassies abroad or, as Marshall Green bitterly comments, can be circumvented through secrecy and deception, or as Winston Lord notes, must expend considerable time and energy mediating among conflicting interests at home. When, as in the cases of Presidents Bill Clinton and Richard Nixon, the White House does not stand solidly with the State Department, the effort can be arduous indeed.

Gaston Sigur recalled that problems would also arise when legislators questioned the executive branch's grasp of or motives in making policy toward China. On the August 1982 communiqué, for instance, there were efforts on the part of certain members of Congress to say, even to [President Reagan], that "we wonder if you fully understand the import of what you have done, that perhaps elements in the State Department or the National Security Council have talked you into something that you don't. . . . " And at that, the president would get furious. He would say, "What are you talking about? This is mine. This is my document. This is what I want to do." So he took the full responsibility for it, which was essential.

To ameliorate tensions, Sigur tried to build bridges between the executive and legislative branches of government. He would

have leading senators and congressmen come over to the State Department for breakfast with me and the deputy assistant secretaries. Then we'd go to a staff meeting in EAP, where I'd bring in the country directors, and we'd sit around and everybody would talk about what was happening in their area. This was something that the Congress loved. It was just terrific. Then, as a consequence, before resolutions would be written up on the Hill or presented to the Senate or to the House, we would always be checked with, and asked about it, and what did we think about this and how did this fit in.

Sigur may have exaggerated the effectiveness of courting Congress, but there is no doubt that the State Department lavishes considerable attention on the members in hopes of moderating their demands and interference.

Despite all these rivals, the diplomatic corps will remain at the center of the relationship. The individuals who have testified here to their role in shaping the history of Sino-American relations are but a small portion of the corps who participated in and witnessed the great events of the last five decades. They and their successors have much to teach the rest of us about the realities of international affairs. Those lessons are not always easy, but they are well worth learning.

INTRODUCTION

1. The Northern Expedition had begun in 1926 under the leadership of Chiang Kai-shek and the Guomindang to wrest power from warlords who, since the collapse of the Republican government under Yuan Shikai, had dominated China. Chiang successfully reunited the country in 1928.

2. There has been a long debate over whether the Communists or the Nationalists fought harder against the Japanese. Suffice it to say, the Communists waged costly campaigns against the Japanese through conventional and guerrilla warfare, which helped to keep the Japanese bogged down in the China theater. On the Chinese Communist war effort see Chalmers Johnson, *Peasant Nationalism and Communist Power* (Stanford: Stanford University Press, 1962). On the Chinese Nationalist war effort see Ch'i Hsi-sheng, "The Military Dimension, 1942–1945," in James C. Hsiung and Steven I. Levine (eds.), *China's Bitter Victory* (Armonk, NY: M.E. Sharpe, 1992).

3. Wang Bingnan, *Nine Years of Sino-U.S. Talks in Retrospect,* (Washington, D.C.: Joint Publications Research Service, August 1985) (JPRS-CPS-85-069). David Shambaugh has also focused attention on Chinese America watchers in his *Beautiful Imperialist: China Perceives America, 1972–90* (Princeton: Princeton University Press, 1991).

4. See the highly perceptive work of Paul A. Cohen in *Discovering History in China* (New York: Columbia University Press, 1984) and the seminal study *Orientalism* By Edward Said (New York: Vintage Books, 1979).

5. For lists of the interviewers consult the Association for Diplomatic Studies and Training at the National Foreign Affairs Training Center, Arlington, Virginia. I was directly involved only in the sessions with Winston Lord and Paul Kriesberg. The large majority of the interviews were conducted by Charles Stuart Kennedy, himself a retired Foreign Service officer. I have made no distinction in the text regarding the particular interview from which any given material was derived.

CHAPTER ONE

1. Actually, Chiang Kai-shek knew about, and approved of, Roosevelt's concessions, which he hoped would secure Moscow's support for his struggle against the Chinese Communists. See Odd Arne Westad, *Cold War and Revolution* (New York: Columbia University Press, 1993). That, however, does not make the Yalta bargain less of a betrayal of the Chinese people.

2. On Patrick Hurley, see Russell D. Buhite, *Patrick J. Hurley and American Foreign Policy* (Ithaca: Cornell University Press, 1973).

3. The Soong family dominated the Nationalist regime and shaped much of China's history in the mid-century. Three sisters married powerful men: Qingling became Sun Yat-sen's wife; Ailing married the powerful banker H.H. Kung; and Meiling was the wife of Chiang Kai-shek. One brother, T.V., served in various government posts, including that of prime minister and two other brothers were financiers. See the controversial family portrait in Sterling Seagrave's *The Soong Dynasty* (New York: Harper & Row, 1985).

4. See the essay by William C. Kirby, "The Chinese War Economy," in Hsiung and Levine (eds.), *China's Bitter Victory*, 185–212.

5. Established in 1939, it mediated between the GMD and CCP. Its leaders were drawn from several minority parties and its followers included university students. It sought to appeal to the United States with its message of democracy in contrast to the authoritarian and communist programs of the major parties.

6. On John Leighton Stuart, see Shaw Yu-ming, *An American Missionary in China* (Cambridge: Harvard University Press, 1992). Stuart wrote his own memoir, entitled *My Fifty Years in China* (New York: Random House, 1954).

7. Huang was an associate of Zhou Enlai and would become foreign minister of the People's Republic of China from 1976 to 1982. On the role of missionary educational institutions, see Jessie Lutz, *China and the Christian Colleges, 1850–1950* (Ithaca: Cornell University Press, 1971), and Philip West, *Yenching University and Sino-Western Relations, 1916–1952* (Cambridge: Harvard University Press, 1976).

8. Marshall made clear that it had not just been the fault of communist irreconcilables, but also the Guomindang's "dominant group of reactionaries who have been opposed, in my opinion, to almost every effort I have made . . . [who], interested in the preservation of their own feudal control of China, evidently had no real intention of implementing" political reforms or peace. Statement by Marshall, January 7, 1949, in Lyman P. Van Slyke (intro), *China White Paper, August 1949* (Stanford: Stanford University Press, 1967), 686–689.

9. The literature of the civil war period and Sino-American relations is rich and varied. Among the most useful works are Dorothy Borg and Waldo Heinrichs (eds.) *Uncertain Years* (New York: Columbia University Press, 1980); Westad, *Cold War and Revolution*; and my own *Patterns in the Dust* (New York: Columbia University Press, 1983).

10. In the midst of growing anti-American sentiment on the part of those who believed that the United states was perpetuating the civil war by propping up the GMD, two marines assaulted a Peking University student on Christmas Eve, 1946. Students organized anti-American protests at Beida and other Beijing universities, as well as in other cities, including Shanghai and Tianjin. See Suzanne Pepper, *Civil War in China* (Berkeley: University of California Press, 1978).

11. The comprador system had grown up around the unequal treaties launched by the Opium War treaty settlement in 1842. These licensed merchants were permitted to do business with foreigners, but were also held accountable for their behavior in China. Many became very wealthy and all were, to varying degrees, tainted in Chinese eyes by their contacts with the foreign communities.

12. Peking University (colloquially known as Beida) was the premier institution of higher learning in China. It had been established to help modernize China during the 1898 Hundred Days of Reform. Although the other reforms introduced at the time were rolled back, the university survived and trained China's elite throughout the twentieth century.

13. For Melby's extended examination of the period, see John F. Melby, *The Mandate of Heaven* (Toronto: University of Toronto Press, 1968). Possibly the most astute analyst of the Nationalist era in China was historian Lloyd Eastman. See his *The Abortive Revolution* (Cambridge: Harvard University Press, 1990), covering 1927–1937, and *Seeds of Destruction*, (Stanford: Stanford University Press, 1984) covering 1937–1949.

14. On the civil war in Manchuria, see Steven I. Levine, *Anvil of Victory* (New York: Columbia University Press, 1987).

15. Chang Chun-mai (Carsun Chang), *The Third Force in China* (New York: Bookman Associates, 1952).

16. China's government was divided among a host of political factions competing for power. As a result, government policies often had to follow elaborate negotiation and Chiang was able to have his way through skilled manipulation. Nevertheless, in 1948, the Guangxi Clique, foremost among the anti-Chiang factions, managed to make Li Zongren vice president in a contest against Chiang's candidate for the post. Li and Chiang did not work smoothly together. In 1949 Chiang resigned and Li became acting president, but Chiang thoroughly undermined his authority. He ultimately fled to the United States. For Li's perspective see Li Tsung-jen. *The Memoirs of Li Tsung-jen* (Boulder, CO: Westview, 1979).

17. The American missionary community in China constituted the largest and wealthiest portion of the foreign missionary presence, numbering some 62 percent of the Protestant missionaries. They ran 236 schools, 248 hospitals, 13 colleges, and 50 theological institutes, and operated activities related to the Young Men's Christian Association in 40 urban areas. American Protestant property in China was valued at $70 million in 1949. The American share of Catholic holdings in China was also large.

18. Bishop James E. Walsh was released from prison in the People's Republic of China in 1970 after 12 years in captivity. He was 80 years old.

19. In the summer of 1947, Wedemeyer was sent to China to evaluate the military situation and make recommendations regarding what the United states could do to prevent Chiang's fall. Wedemeyer's report called for a huge commitment of economic and military assistance contingent on Chiang's agreement to undertake reforms. The Truman administration, however, had already decided that Chiang was unwilling to reform, and that to be effective, military aid would necessitate American ground forces. Marshall decided to suppress Wedemeyer's report rather than engage in a public discussion of the merits of Chiang's regime. Later the administration would be attacked for this decision. Wedemeyer discussed China in his book, *Wedemeyer Reports!* (New York: Devin-Adair, 1958).

20. On the role of the China Lobby during the civil war years, see Ross Y. Koen, *The China Lobby in American Politics* (New York: Harper & Row, 1974). The book was originally printed in 1960, but pressure from the China Lobby stopped its distribution after only 800 copies had been released.

21. Luce had put the Generalissimo and Madame Chiang on the cover of *Time* magazine during World War II and continued to support them in the following civil conflict. See W.A. Swanberg, *Luce and His Empire* (New York: Scribner's, 1972), which condemns him, and Patricia Neils, *China Images in the Life and Times of Henry Luce* (Savage, MD: Rowman and Littlefield, 1990), which tries to rehabilitate him. More persuasive is Robert E. Herzstein, *Henry R. Luce* (New York: Scribner's, 1994) and T. Christopher Jespersen, *American Images of China 1931–1949* (Stanford: Stanford University Press, 1996).

22. The U.S. Navy ran the unit to collect intelligence beginning in 1946. When the Communist victory became inevitable, the ESD provided Chinese agents with secret codes and radio transmitters. The Chinese Communists discovered the group almost as soon as they took over Mukden and shut it down, arresting eight operatives. Other ESD units continued working elsewhere in China.

23. Wu represented the People's Republic of China at the United Nations from November 14, 1950, to December 30, 1950, during the Korean War, to participate in debate on a Chinese-sponsored Draft Resolution on U.S. Aggression Against Taiwan. This was offered at the same time as the United States sponsored Draft Resolution on Chinese Aggression Against Korea. Washington secured the adoption of the latter and blocked the former. Wu served as vice minister of foreign affairs from December 1950 to January 1955.

24. The attitude of the Chinese Communist authorities on issues of international law were different than American diplomats hoped or expected. The CCP announced in September 1949 that it would analyze, reject, or maintain all treaties entered into by the Nationalist regime on the basis of whether they inflicted imperialist burdens upon China. Similarly, the CCP rejected the customary practice of

accepting the diplomatic credentials of foreigners until the issue of recognition of a new government could be resolved. Instead, they treated all foreign diplomats as individuals without official titles or functions. Of course, the Americans also refused to use official titles in dealing with the Communists, lest this impart any presumption of diplomatic recognition.

25. In fact, embarrassed apologies were given Stuart by high level officials.

26. In the 1920s, Du had governed the Green Gang alongside Huang Mapi (Pockmarked Huang), who was also chief of detectives in Shanghai's French concession. It was said that Huang first brought Chiang into the Green Gang.

27. The two major incidents were the Olive and Ward cases. There were several other lesser confrontations, including the occupation of the consulate in Shanghai by ex-Navy employees demanding severance pay, the detention of U.S. servicemen in the Qingdao area on charges of espionage, and the refusal of an exit visa to an American military attaché in Nanjing and a consular officer in Shanghai. But at the same time, the CCP repeatedly assured the foreigners they and their property would be protected, and Americans were aided in a variety of conflicts with local officials. Secretary of State Dean Acheson took note of the fact that foreigners were treated surprisingly well, given that they were caught in the midst of a revolution and civil war.

28. The Department of State publishes a series entitled *Foreign Relations of the United States,* in which telegrams, memoranda and other policy documents are reprinted. The particular volume that Holloway mentions here is U.S. Department of State, *Foreign Relations of the United States, 1949,* vol. 9: *The Far East: China* (Washington, D.C.: Government Printing Office, 1975) (hereafter, *FRUS).*

29. The Committee of One Million Against the Admission of Communist China to the United Nations was established in 1953. For more discussion of its activities, see subsequent chapters and see also Stanley D. Backrack, *The Committee of One Million* (New York: Columbia University Press, 1976).

30. A variety of books have been written about the travails of the China officers, including E.J. Kahn, *The China Hands* (New York: Viking, 1972); Robert P. Newman, *Owen Lattimore and the "Loss" of China* (Berkeley: University of California Press, 1992); and Gary May, *China Scapegoat* (Prospect Heights, IL: Waveland Press, 1979).

31. O. Edmund Clubb served as the last consul general in Beijing, 1950, and then as the director of the Office of Chinese Affairs in the State Department from 1950 to 1952. He was forced to retire in 1952. See O. Edmund Clubb, *The Witness and I* (New York: Columbia University Press, 1974). Tony Freeman was acting deputy director of the Office of Chinese Affairs in 1949. He never again served in Asia but did rise to be ambassador to Columbia and Mexico. Philip Sprouse was director of the Office of Chinese Affairs in 1949 and was appointed ambassador to Cambodia in 1962. Jack Service endured the most difficult censure, being arrested for espionage in the *Amerasia* case in 1945, and being dismissed from the State Department in 1951. He

was reinstated in 1957, but given only safe assignments and retired in 1962. Service reflected upon his crisis years in *The Amerasia Papers* (Berkeley: University of California Press, 1971). John Paton Davies, who, like Jack Service, had been born in China of missionary parents, was dismissed by Secretary of State John Foster Dulles in 1954. In 1969, the State Department, after reviewing his case, restored his security clearance.

32. The Sino-Soviet Friendship Treaty of 1945 exchanged Stalin's promise to deal only with the Guomindang in China for concessions in Manchuria on Port Arthur, Dairen, and the Manchurian railway lines. For a detailed discussion of the prolonged negotiations, see Westad, *Cold War and Revolution*. The 1950 Treaty of Sino-Soviet Friendship allowed the Soviets to sustain their presence in Manchuria, and although providing a security guarantee, gave relatively low levels of economic aid.

33. In fact, in March 1949, the National Security Council, with the approval of the president, adopted a policy designed to lure China away from the Soviets with liberal trade terms. The decision to maintain American diplomatic posts in China behind Communist lines also attested to the hope that the bloc was not monolithic. NSC 41, "U.S. Policy Regarding Trade with China," March 3, 1949, U.S. Department of State. *FRUS, 1949*, vol. 9: *The Far East: China*, 826–834.

34. This was an anti-Manchu, anti-foreign secret society uprising in 1900 that was co-opted by the government to drive the foreigners out of China. It failed and in the Boxer Protocol China had to agree to allow foreign troops to be stationed in the capital to protect the foreign community. Paul Cohen. *History in Three Keys* (New York: Columbia, 1998)

35. Early in 1947, the Guomindang had announced that the new constitution promulgated on the mainland would not apply to Taiwan and that there would be significant budgetary cutbacks as well. Thus on February 28, a minor confrontation with police flared into an uprising that was then brutally suppressed by Nationalist troops secretly transferred from the mainland. Thousands died and the local Taiwanese population was deeply alienated from the regime. See Lai Tse-han, Ramon H. Myers, and Wei Wou, *A Tragic Beginning* (Stanford: Stanford University Press, 1991).

36. Chiang stepped down from the presidency, under pressure, on January 21, 1949, turning his office over to vice president Li Zongren. He continued interfering in government affairs, however, sharply circumscribing Li's authority, and in the summer of 1949 established an alternate government in Taiwan.

37. Philip C. Jessup, an internationally respected professor of law at Columbia University, was asked by his close friend Dean Acheson to serve as ambassador-at-large. During 1949, he conducted a review of American China policy as head of a consultant group including Everett Case, president of Colgate University, and Raymond B. Fosdick, former president of the Rockefeller Foundation.

38. On January 5, 1950, Truman announced that the United States would not again involve itself in the Chinese civil war and would not intercede if the Communists attacked Taiwan. Secretary of State Acheson reiterated the point at the National Press Club on January 12, 1950.

39. The JCRR had begun its work, less successfully, on the mainland in 1948. In Taiwan it had three Chinese and two American commissioners and a highly skilled technical staff largely educated in the United States. The reform program revolutionized landholding by reducing rents for tenant farmers, confiscating and selling land formerly held by the Japanese, and in 1953 implementing the Land-to-the-Tiller Program. This last effort made land available to tenants and launched the former landlords into efforts to industrialize the island economy. See T.H. Shen, *The Sino-American Joint Commission on Rural Reconstruction* (Ithaca: Cornell University Press, 1970).

CHAPTER TWO

1. The term Taiwanese is used in various ways. Here I am referring to the 85 percent of the population that descended from immigrants who fled Fujian and Guangdong in the eighteenth and nineteenth centuries, rather than the tiny number of indigenous inhabitants. The remaining 15 percent of the people represent those who left the mainland after 1945 and are generally referred to as Mainlanders. That number is today in decline as generational change and assimilation reduce the community, which identifies itself as different from the Taiwanese.

2. General Douglas MacArthur, commander-in-chief of American forces in Korea and Japan was a staunch proponent of the Chinese Nationalist cause. He supported the idea of using Guomindang troops in the Korean theater, which Truman rejected, and took an unauthorized visit to Taiwan in July 1950, announcing that he had arranged a coordinated American-Chinese defense of the island. He also sent a survey mission to Taiwan, despite the Secretary of State's fierce opposition, to assess military capabilities. This mission then recommended massive assistance.

3. After February 1949, the administration slowed arms deliveries. In March, Acheson opposed efforts by Congress to appropriate $1.5 million in military aid. The State Department initially decided not to request more aid for the Nationalists as part of the 1949 Mutual Defense Assistance Act, but in July, fearing Republican attacks, it included a provision for money to be used in the general area of China at the President's discretion. In fact, it avoided expending those funds in China's war effort, although various types of economic assistance continued.

4. On the revolution in the countryside, the classic work is William Hinton, *Fanshen* (New York: Random House, 1966); see also his later book, *Shenfan* (New York: Random House, 1983). Among the memoirs by missionaries recounting their experiences, see F. Olin Stockwell, *With God in Red China* (New York: Harper, 1953).

5. The Chinese decision to enter the war has been carefully studied by Chen Jian in his *China's Road to the Korean War* (New York: Columbia University Press, 1994).

6. Zhou asked Panikkar to transmit the following message on October 3, 1950: "The American forces are trying to cross the 38th parallel and to expand the war. If they really want to do this, we will not sit still without doing anything. We will be forced to intervene." Chen, *China's Road*, 180.

7. MacArthur was not alone in this. The CIA concluded, even after UN troops had crossed the 38th parallel, that "a consideration of all known factors leads to the conclusion that barring a Soviet decision for global war, such action is not probable in 1950." Quoted in Burton I. Kaufman, *The Korean War* (New York: Knopf, 1986), 89.

8. The campaign ran through the summer of 1950 and was designed to overcome pro-American feeling among the Chinese people, suppress opposition to the CCP, and mobilize the population for internal reconstruction.

9. The Americans nicknamed him "panicky Panikkar."

10. The Soviets, however, did not want to become involved directly and encouraged Chinese intervention. See Kathryn Weathersby, "The Soviet Role in the Early Phase of the Korean War: New Documentary Evidence," *The Journal of American-East Asian Relations*, 2 (Winter 1993): 425–458.

11. Arthur Dean was a former law partner and close friend of John Foster Dulles.

12. Rhee actually orchestrated the release of some 25,000 North Korean POWs on June 18, 1953 in order to undermine the armistice negotiations. On the talks, see Rosemary Foot, *A Substitute for Victory* (Ithaca: Cornell University Press, 1990).

13. The meeting of foreign ministers in Berlin was held from January 24 to February 18, 1954, and included representatives from the United States, the Soviet Union, France, and the United Kingdom. The subsequent Geneva conference took up issues surrounding Korea and Indochina. The Korean discussion began April 26, 1954 and was adjourned on June 15, 1954, having accomplished nothing. The Korean and Indochina aspects of the Geneva Conference are covered in U.S. Department of State, *FRUS, 1952–1954*, vol. 16: *The Geneva Conference* (Washington, D.C.: Government Printing Office, 1981).

14. Matthew B. Ridgway, *A Soldier's Story* (New York: Harper, 1956).

15. The Chinese Nationalist government ran a semicovert operation in northern Burma, with CIA support, designed to destabilize the Chinese Communists. Rather than evacuating Nationalist soldiers who had fled China with the Nationalist collapse in 1949–1950, Chiang resupplied them and conspired in repeated abortive invasions of Yunnan province, as well as continuing border harassment. General Li Mi led some 20,000 men in the early 1950s. Later there were several supposed evacuations, but operations continued into the mid-1960s. Nationalist Chinese responsibility was, of course, repeatedly denied, as was American complicity. Nancy Bernkopf Tucker, "John Foster Dulles and the Taiwan Roots of the 'Two Chinas' Policy," in Richard

H. Immerman (ed.), *John Foster Dulles and the Diplomacy of the Cold War* (Princeton: Princeton University press, 1990), 235–262.

16. U. Alexis Johnson, U.S. Coordinator for the Conference and ambassador to Czechoslovakia 1953–1957. He later wrote about his experience in *The Right Hand of Power* (Englewood Cliffs, NJ: Prentice-Hall, 1984).

17. Wang was head of the Chinese delegation and ambassador to Warsaw. He recorded his impressions of the continuing dialogue he conducted with the Americans in *Nine Years of Sino-US Talks in Retrospect*, a work translated by the Joint Publications Research Service, JPRS-CPS-85–069, August 7, 1985.

18. This became a famous insult that the Chinese later highlighted in Henry Kissinger and Richard Nixon's trips to China in the 1970s; see chapter 5.

19. At the time, there were rumors in the Chinese community that if people identified themselves as wanting to return to China they would be shipped off to Taiwan instead. That presumably kept some individuals from declaring their true preferences.

20. This was the first conference of Afro-Asian nations. Washington worried that it would boost Chinese prestige in the Third World and tried, unsuccessfully, to convince its friends not to attend. Zhou's statesmanship was clearly demonstrated. Coming in the midst of the 1954–1955 Taiwan Straits crisis, Bandung gave Zhou a platform to call for talks to prevent the crisis leading to war.

21. Osborn here is referring to several significant developments. Internally China had just weathered the 1956–1957 Hundred Flowers Campaign, during which Mao Zedong's invitation to criticize the CCP, "letting a hundred flowers bloom and a hundred schools of thought contend," was taken literally and the outpouring of complaints shocked the leadership. Mao's hope was to address tensions between the Party and China's intellectuals before there was an upheaval comparable to the 1956 Hungarian Revolution. But the depth and breadth of criticism horrified him, and he struck back with a devastating anti-rightist campaign. Sino-Soviet relations were also strained in 1957. Beijing had dismissed the dire consequences of a nuclear war, whereas the Soviets worried about the fate of mankind and thought the Chinese unrealistic and irresponsible. The Soviet Union successfully launched the first man-made satellite, Sputnik, demonstrating its technical superiority over the United States. The Chinese wanted to capitalize on this development, rejecting the notion of peaceful coexistence, whereas the Soviets were more interested in developing détente with the United States. See John Wilson Lewis and Xue Litai, *China Builds the Bomb* (Stanford: Stanford University Press, 1988).

22. The September 4th occasion was a news conference that followed a well-publicized meeting between Dulles and Eisenhower, who was vacationing there. Eisenhower had agreed to a memorandum saying that the fall of Jinmen might lead to the capture of Taiwan and warning Beijing that all this would produce a volatile situation. Eisenhower was somewhat distracted at the time as he confronted a critical civil

rights crisis in Little Rock, Arkansas, where Governor Orval Faubus ordered troops to prevent a dozen black students from entering a local high school.

23. Beam wrote about his experiences in Jacob D. Beam, *Multiple Exposure* (New York: Norton, 1978).

24. A. Doak Barnett held a variety of positions in the early 1950s in Hong Kong. He was a fellow of the Institute of Current World Affairs, 1947–1950 and 1952–1953, a correspondent for the *Chicago Daily News*, 1947–1950 and 1952–1955, a Foreign Service officer with the Hong Kong Consulate General 1951–1952 and with the American Universities Field Staff, 1952–1956

25. The Great Leap Forward, 1958–1961, was one of many campaigns through which Mao Zedong hoped to speed China's socialist development and ensure its ideological purity. In this instance, the campaign sought to use mass mobilization of the population and resources, particularly in the countryside, to leap over stages of development. Among the highlights were expansion of agriculture into arid areas, production of steel from backyard furnaces, rampant exaggeration of crop and industrial production, and nationwide communization of land holding, as well as massive starvation. See Roderick MacFarquhar. *The Origins of the Cultural Revolution*, vol. 2: *The Great Leap Forward, 1958–1960* (New York: Columbia University Press, 1983).

26. Eileen Chang (Chang Ai-ling), *Rice Sprout Song* (Hong Kong: Dragonfly Books, 1955). It was reprinted in 1998 by an American publisher.

27. In the wake of China's entry into the Korean War, the United States declared a trade embargo against the PRC and persuaded the UN to go along. This lasted until the mid-1950s, long after the Korean armistice, when even close American allies began to defy the restrictions. Throughout, Hong Kong suffered particularly. To begin with, the United States insisted upon treating Hong Kong the same as China, but, even after the most drastic prohibitions were lifted, U.S. pressure on Hong Kong authorities remained intense.

28. In fact, in 1949, Chiang shipped the assets of the Bank of China to Taiwan despite the contrary orders of the then-president, Li Zongren. In the subsequent withdrawal from the mainland, many businessmen, scientists, and government bureaucrats, as well as soldiers, fled to Taiwan. Although U.S. advisers were essential, Chiang was not without his own resources. For an interesting view of the struggles within the GMD, see the oral history and diaries of the Nationalist ambassador to the United States, V.K. Wellington Koo, in the Butler Library Manuscript Division, Columbia University, New York.

29. The idea of using Nationalist Chinese troops in Korea was promoted by Generals Douglas MacArthur, Matthew Ridgway, and Mark Clark.

30. Actually, MAAG personnel had been at much higher levels. MAAG advisers first arrived in May 1951, and quickly numbered some 250. By the end of 1952, there were over 700 attached to the mission, and that number expanded dramatically during the Taiwan Strait Crisis, 1954–1955 to reach some 2,000.

31. Sun was not freed until 1965 by Lee Teng-hui. He died in 1990.

32. Sun Yat-Sen, considered the father of the Chinese revolution that overthrew the Qing Dynasty in 1911 and created a republican government in 1912, formulated the Three People's Principles: nationalism, democracy, and people's livelihood. These principles became the basis of Guomindang ideology.

33. See Robert Accinelli, *Crisis and Commitment* (Chapel Hill: University of North Carolina, 1996); Thomas E. Stolper, *China, Taiwan and the Offshore Islands* (Armonk, NY: M.E. Sharpe, 1985).

34. At a meeting between Eisenhower and Dulles on March 6, 1955, the two agreed that the secretary would state publicly that the United States would use nuclear and conventional weapons interchangeably. He did this March 8 and again March 15, followed on March 16 by Eisenhower's own public affirmation.

35. Dulles met with the UN secretary general on September 27, 1958.

36. The text of the joint communiqué is available in U.S. Department of State, *FRUS, 1958–1960*, vol. 19: *China* (Washington, D.C.: Government Printing Office, 1996), 442–444.

37. The slogan of "rollback" emerged in the 1952 Republican presidential campaign and became associated with John Foster Dulles. The idea was that the Democrats under Truman had been soft on communism, having been willing just to contain it rather than liberating people from its grasp. In actuality, the Truman administration had also practiced rollback.

38. This discussion occurred on October 22, 1958. According to the memorandum of conversation drafted by Marshall Green, Dulles asked Chiang whether he wanted the United States to use nuclear weapons, and Chiang replied that he didn't believe it would be necessary. On the other hand, "the use of tactical atomic weapons might be advisable." Cautioned by Dulles that these would cause the loss of millions of lives, Chiang noted that he did not want to see a world war begin and did not fully understand nuclear technology. But he did think it essential that Communist artillery be silenced. Dulles authorized a military briefing for Chiang. At other times, foreign service officers reported that Chiang denied any interest in using nuclear weapons against other Chinese. Green memorandum in FRUS 1958–1960, vol. 19: 430.

39. In fact, Mao would oust Peng in July 1959 as a result of his criticism, at the Lushan Plenum, of Mao's policies in the Great Leap Forward. Mao promoted Lin Biao to take his place as minister of defense and head of the People's Liberation Army.

40. Kenneth T. Young, *Negotiating with the Chinese Communists* (New York: McGraw Hill, 1968).

41. Mao delivered his speech during a visit to Moscow in November 1957, a month after the launch of the Sputnik satellite. In a second speech, during the same visit, he was more explicit, saying, "socialist forces are overwhelmingly superior to the imperialist forces."

42. The first message to Eisenhower was sent September 6, and the intemperate

letter was sent September 19, 1958. The gist of these communications was to warn the United States not to attack China, but rather to deal with the Chinese reasonably. The second message was so abusive Eisenhower refused to accept it.

43. From 1950 to 1965, the United States provided an annual average of $100 million in nonmilitary assistance. This exceeded the per capita contribution to any other government.

44. McCarran's interest in China stemmed in large part from the silver industry in Nevada. He became a leading proponent of congressional investigation of the administration's China policy and pushed for increased aid to Chiang Kai-shek to be given in silver bullion because the Chinese used silver coins. Under the provisions of the Internal Security (McCarran) Act of 1950, the Senator held hearings to uncover communists, spies and saboteurs in the United States.

45. Other reports put the crowd at 25,000 and suggested that there were successive waves of attacks on the Embassy.

46. NSC 162/1, "Review of Basic National Security Policy," October 19, 1953, was amended and adopted by the president as NSC 162/2 on October 30. It built on the work of Project Solarium, a series of meetings among top level administration officials held in the White House sun room, to explore containment policy toward the Soviet Union. The resulting paper became the central component of the Eisenhower administration's New Look Policy, i.e., a national defense relying upon nuclear weapons in order to save money.

47. The Eisenhower administration New Look called for reduced conventional forces and an increased dependence on nuclear weapons, so as to reduce the defense budget. According to Dulles, it also entailed having "a great capacity to retaliate instantly by means and places of our own choosing."

48. The Hukbalahap insurgency in the Philippines started in the late 1940s as an anti-Japanese resistance movement under communist/socialist leadership. Having been built on an older agrarian movement, it also targeted landlords and in the postwar years, when avenues to legitimate power were closed, the Huks rebelled. The popular defense minister, Ramon Magsaysay, finally was successful in suppressing the revolt in 1950–1951. Remnants of the Huks remained in operation for some years thereafter.

49. Joseph Alsop, "Shocking New Strength of Red China," *Saturday Evening Post*, 226 (March 13, 1954): 19–21.

50. As early as 1949, the United States had applied economic sanctions on the new regime in China. With the Korean War these became a total embargo that not only the United States, but all its allies also observed. After the war enforcement became more difficult. The mechanism used to restrict trade with China was the China Committee (CHINCOM), a subcommittee of the Coordinating Committee for Multilateral Export Controls (COCOM), which had been established to deny the Soviet Union and the Warsaw Pact countries of eastern Europe access to equipment and technology that could be put to military use.

51. Gao Gang, leader of the northwest region, expected to be named premier in 1952. When he was appointed to the State Planning Commission instead, he tried to rally other base area leaders like Deng Xiaoping and Chen Yi to oppose Zhou Enlai and others at the center. Mao, however, backed the center and Gao was purged and committed suicide. His closest collaborator Rao also fell and was imprisoned.

52. Mao was actually in Moscow for an extended period from December 1949 into February 1950 to negotiate the Sino-Soviet treaty of alliance, which was finally signed on February 14. It afforded China protection against Japan and any nation allied with Japan, i.e., the United States, and provided some economic assistance, but that proved relatively meager. Mao later recalled the stay as extremely unpleasant and demeaning.

53. Zhou visited Poland, East Germany, and Hungary in January 1957 to stress the crucial nature of intra-bloc unity, equality, and Soviet leadership. This came in the wake of the Hungarian revolution in 1956 which was smashed by Soviet tanks in November. Mao sought to preserve Marxism-Leninism and the Warsaw Pact, which, China's leaders believed, helped to protect Chinese national security.

54. The article actually appeared in the CCP theoretical journal *Red Flag* on April 16, 1960. It was *the* major ideological statement of the Sino-Soviet dispute. See William E. Griffith, *Sino-Soviet Rift* (Cambridge: MIT Press, 1964); G.F. Hudson, Richard Lowenthal and Roderick MacFarquhar (eds.), *The Sino-Soviet Dispute* (New York: Praeger, 1961); and Donald S. Zagoria, *The Sino-Soviet Conflict* (New York: Antheneum, 1966).

55. Mao declared the atomic bomb "a paper tiger which the U.S. reactionaries use to scare people. It looks terrible, but in fact it isn't." This was in 1946. See "Talk with American Correspondent Anna Louise Strong," *Selected Works of Mao Tse-tung*, vol. 4 (Peking: Foreign Language Press, 1969), 100. Nikita Khrushchev found Mao's attitude "incredible" and it contributed to the Sino-Soviet split. On these and related issues, see Lewis and Xue, *China Builds the Bomb*.

56. The U.S. government had repeatedly tried to persuade Chiang to reduce his vulnerable forces on the offshore islands to a token contingent, changing from a major base, whose loss would be catastrophic, to an outpost. Dulles followed up personally with Chiang in Taiwan during his October 1958 visit. Chiang consistently refused.

57. It is true that Dulles became a stronger critic of the Nationalists during his years as secretary. It is also interesting to note that in 1950 he had written in his book *War or Peace* (New York: Macmillan, 1950) that the Chinese Communists should be brought into the United Nations.

58. Famine in the countryside meant some 30 million children and elderly Chinese starved to death and another 30 million who under normal circumstances would have been conceived in these years were not born. In recent years reports have come out about the horrors of the period that include tales of cannibalism. Jasper Becker, *Hungry Ghosts* (New York: Free Press, 1997).

59. Western Enterprises was a commercial operation specially created to disguise covert operations. It trained agents and provided logistical support as well as carrying out overflights for espionage and leafleting. It ceased to function in 1954, but by then there were 600 CIA personnel in Taiwan. The effort was taken over by the Naval Auxiliary Communications Center.

CHAPTER THREE

1. Warren I. Cohen, *Dean Rusk* (New York: Cooper Square, 1980). On Rusk, see also Dean Rusk, *As I Saw It* (New York: Norton, 1990); and Thomas W. Zeiler, *Dean Rusk: Defending the American Mission Abroad* (Wilmington, DE: Scholarly Resources, 2000).

2. In fact, the Office of Asian Communist Affairs was established effective November 27, 1963. It included mainland China, North Korea, North Vietnam, and South and Southeast Asia, and had a Sino-Soviet specialist on the staff. Prior to this, the mainland China portfolio belonged to three Foreign Service officers who were housed in the Office of East Asian Affairs, which also had responsibility for Taiwan, Korea, and Japan. No one dealt full time with either North Korea or North Vietnam.

3. Biographers and chroniclers of the era all talk about the atmosphere of new beginnings. See David Halberstam, *The Best and the Brightest* (New York: Penguin, 1972); Arthur Schlesinger, Jr., *A Thousand Days* (Boston: Houghton Mifflin, 1965); and Roger Hilsman, *To Move a Nation* (New York: Delta, 1967).

4. See Howard B. Schaffer, *Chester Bowles: New Dealer in the Cold War* (Cambridge: Harvard University Press, 1993); and on Harriman, Rudy Abramson, *Spanning the Century* (New York: William Morrow, 1992).

5. Birth control programs were first launched in urban areas in the mid-1950s, but were derailed during the Great Leap, when Mao advocated a larger population as a resource for accelerated economic growth. People, he urged, should be seen as hands, not mouths. Given the traditional desire for sons, many Chinese, particularly in the countryside, welcomed this view. But as the reality of food shortages and economic disaster struck, birth control activities resumed in 1962. During the Cultural Revolution, access to information and birth control supplies was unpredictable, but a national program for limiting births remained in place. Late in the 1970s, the central government opted for a harsher approach of restricting families to one child. William L. Parish and Martin King Whyte, *Village and Family in Contemporary China* (Chicago: University of Chicago, 1978).

6. In Africa, the People's Republic of China competed for prestige and influence against the Nationalist Chinese. It formed close relations with Zanzibar in the early 1960s and with Tanzania after Zanzibar and Tanganyika merged in 1964. Its assistance for the railroad project, beginning in 1965 after the World Bank had declared the railway uneconomic, formed the most costly part of its continuing courtship of

the East Africans and made Tanzania the second largest non-communist Chinese aid recipient after Pakistan.

7. The Portuguese colony of Goa, on the west coast of India, had been under pressure for some time. The Indians tried peaceful demonstrations to speed retrocession to no avail. In 1961, under criticism for weakness against China, the Nehru government took action where it could be more immediately effective and sent troops into Goa. This initiative, even though it violated the government's nonviolent posture and was criticized abroad, was very popular at home.

8. George Kennan's containment policy grew out of his so-called "Long Telegram" of 1946, and his famous article "The Sources of Soviet Conduct," *Foreign Affairs* 25 (July 1947): 566–582. The containment doctrine has been the subject of many studies, including John Lewis Gaddis, *Strategies of Containment* (New York: Oxford University Press, 1982). Kennan has also merited many books, including Walter L. Hixson, *George F. Kennan: Cold War Iconoclast* (New York: Columbia University Press, 1989); and Wilson Miscamble, *George F. Kennan and the Making of American Foreign Policy, 1945–1950* (Princeton: Princeton University Press, 1992).

9. For Cabot's reflections, see John M. Cabot, *First Line of Defense* (Washington, D.C.: School of Foreign Service, Georgetown University, 1979).

10. This April 1960 editorial was the first of Beijing's public diatribes against revisionists. Although Beijing's indictment was against Moscow, it would be more than another year before the Chinese and Soviets named each other explicitly in their criticisms.

11. The Chinese made the border friction public in March 1963, in *People's Daily*, but it had been building since 1958. In Xinjiang, conflict over territorial possession was aggravated by ethnic friction between Chinese and local Kazakh and Uyghur populations. The Soviets were seen by Beijing to be complicit in local uprisings. The presence of oil and uranium deposits raised the stakes for both Beijing and Moscow. In the Amur River region, the issue was simpler, i.e., disputed islands. Griffith, *The Sino-Soviet Rift*.

12. Chinese troops were significantly better equipped and trained, with substantially better logistic support. The Indians seemingly deluded themselves into believing that they out-classed the Chinese and clearly were the provocateurs. For a comprehensive history of the Sino-Indian border war see Neville Maxwell, *India's China War* (New York: Pantheon, 1970). See also Allen S. Whiting, *The Chinese Calculus of Deterrence* (Ann Arbor: University of Michigan Press, 1975).

13. The initial Chinese attack came in October. The Indians ineptly counterattacked in November, met devastating opposition and, in the process, left much of northern Indian open to Chinese attack. In a state of panic the Indian government appealed to the United States for assistance on November 19, 1962. On November 20, however, the Chinese began their voluntary withdrawal. See Robert J. McMahon, *The Cold War on the Periphery* (New York: Columbia University Press, 1994).

14. The mission led by W. Averell Harriman, assistant secretary of state for Far Eastern Affairs was dispatched in November 1962 with the objective of assessing India's military needs, assuring Pakistan that American assistance to India would not be used against Pakistan, and urging Nehru to negotiate with Karachi.

15. James C. Thomson, Jr. worked hard at trying to change Washington's hard-line policy on China and move toward diplomatic relations. He believed Kennedy supported such measures and would have recognized the PRC in his second term. James C. Thomson, Jr., "On the Making of U.S. China Policy, 1961–9: A Study in Bureaucratic Politics," *China Quarterly*, 50 (April/June 1972) or "Dragon Under Glass: Time for a New China Policy," *Atlantic*, October 1967.

16. Galbraith had been one of JFK's earliest and most vigorous supporters. He was also a friend of McGeorge Bundy, Kennedy's national security adviser, from the days when they had both been on the faculty at Harvard University.

17. The Vanguard Project, launched in 1961, sent teams of agriculturists to Africa, Asia, and Latin America to advise, particularly on rice cultivation and animal husbandry. The project also brought technicians to Taiwan for training. Funding came from the United States through the Agency for International Development; the overseas operations were assisted by the CIA.

18. The Albanian Resolution would have expelled Taiwan and admitted the People's Republic of China to the UN by a simple majority vote.

19. Stanley Karnow was serving as the bureau chief for *Time* magazine and would also work for the *London Observer* and the *Saturday Evening Post* beginning in 1963 and the *Washington Post* beginning in 1965. Robert Elegant wrote for *Newsweek* and then the *Los Angeles Times*. Stan Rich freelanced and would later work for USIA. Loren Fessler worked with Karnow. He was more of a China specialist than the others, having served with the OSS during World War II and being fluent in Chinese. In 1998 he was living in Macao.

20. A 1955 film starring William Holden as a war correspondent who falls in love with a Eurasian doctor, Jennifer Jones, in Hong Kong during the Korean War.

21. Actually, Knowland was called the Senator from Formosa because in the 1950s and 1960s those sympathetic to the Nationalist Chinese cause used the Portuguese name for the island rather than the Chinese name Taiwan.

22. Liu Shaoqi had been Mao's putative successor but had collaborated during 1961 and 1962 in trying to deradicalize Chinese politics in the wake of the disastrous Great Leap Forward. In 1966, with the beginning of the Cultural Revolution, Liu became one of Mao's primary targets. He was labeled "China's Khrushchev" and accused of "taking the capitalist road."

23. The study was later published as *China Crosses the Yalu* (Stanford: Stanford University Press, 1960). Whiting's work has proven unusually durable.

24. On August 2, 1964, the USS *Maddox* was fired on by North Vietnamese torpedo boats while on an electronic espionage mission. When a second incident was

alleged on August 4, President Lyndon Johnson secured the Tonkin Gulf Resolution from Congress. The text, which authorized "all necessary measures" to repel an attack, had been prepared long before the incident. It would be used to legitimate a sustained bombing campaign against North Vietnam beginning in 1965.

25. China had sent 50,000 soldiers into North Vietnam by spring 1966; a total of 320,000 Chinese soldiers served in Vietnam between 1965 and 1973. Although China did not publicize this action, Chinese troops did wear uniforms so that U.S. surveillance would know they were present. Lyndon Johnson kept most of these developments secret from the Congress and the American public.

26. On Soviet involvement in Vietnam, see Ilya V. Gaiduk, *The Soviet Union and the Vietnam War* (Chicago: Ivan R. Dee, 1996).

27. Air Asia, the largest aircraft repair and maintenance facility in Asia, was a wholly owned subsidiary of Air America, which flew for the CIA, State Department, and AID.

28. Chiang Ching-kuo had been sent to the Soviet Union and educated there. He returned to China in 1937.

29. During the late 1960s, Taipei put more money into its military forces than did any nation not actively at war and fielded the largest standing army, proportionate to its population, in the world.

30. CONEFO was an anti-Western coalition organized by Sukarno in 1963.

31. Marshall Green wrote about the problems of his ambassadorship in *Indonesia: Crisis and Transformation, 1965–68* (Washington: Compass Press, 1990).

32. Lin Biao, who became heir apparent after the purge of Liu Shaoqi, delivered his talk "Long Live the Victory of People's War" in September 1965. It declared China's support for national liberation struggles against the West. It was greeted with much consternation in Washington, where some State Department officials likened it to Hitler's *Mein Kampf*.

33. Jiang Qing headed a radical leftist faction during the Cultural Revolution made up of the former head of cultural affairs in Shanghai, Zhang Chunqiao; Wang Hongwen, a labor organizer; and Yao Wenyuan, a newspaper editor. When Mao died in 1976, his successors immediately purged the Gang of Four. The intrigues around Mao Zedong are luridly detailed in a book by his physician Li Zhisui, *The Private Life of Chairman Mao* (New York: Random House, 1994).

CHAPTER FOUR

1. The Geneva Conference ran from April 26 to July 21, 1954. During the course of these difficult weeks, Zhou traveled to India to meet with Jawaharlal Nehru. Initially the Five Principles of Peaceful Coexistence were limited to the Sino-Indian arena, but, at the Bandung Conference of Third World states in April 1955, Zhou applied the principles more broadly.

2. Richard M. Nixon, "Asia After Vietnam," *Foreign Affairs* (October 1967).

3. Zhenbao Island is on the Chinese side of the main channel of the Ussuri (Wusuli) River, which marked the border between China and the Soviet Union. The first serious clash occurred on March 2, and the provocation seemingly came from the Chinese. The motivations remain unclear, but it appears that China's leaders hoped to deliver a sharp warning against further encroachment on Chinese territory, much as they had done with the Indians in 1962

4. According to a high-level official, Arkady N. Shevchenko, in *Breaking with Moscow* (New York: Knopf, 1985), 164–165: "The Politburo was terrified that the Chinese might make a large-scale intrusion into Soviet Territory. . . . A nightmare vision of invasion by millions of Chinese made the Soviet leaders almost frantic."

5. By the autumn of 1969, after the Chinese had shunned Soviet efforts to reconcile, Soviet leaders began to examine the possible use of nuclear weapons in a preemptive strike on China. They had already carried out sufficient reconnaissance to know that Chinese military facilities would be vulnerable and even the recently constructed shelter system in Beijing was not nuclear bomb-proof. Meanwhile, Moscow had completed its own antiballistic missile defense system against the Chinese. At this juncture, the United States rebuffed Soviet suggestions of cooperation in dealing with Chinese nuclear weapons through a strike on its nuclear installations and warned against independent Soviet action.

6. The construction of tunnel systems under several of China's major cities proved very costly, but reflected the anxiety in the government over the Soviet threat.

7. The Soviet Union sent tanks into Hungary in 1956, to crush demonstrations calling for greater autonomy within the socialist camp. The United States had encouraged these assertions of dissent through Voice of America broadcasts, but at the time of the uprising and Soviet intervention, it took no action. Not only was it distracted by a crisis over the Suez Canal, it also had no ready access to Hungary, situated deep within the Soviet sphere of influence in Eastern Europe.

8. The public announcement that there would be relaxation of the trade embargo against China came on the eve of Nixon's departure, July 21, 1969.

9. The Nixon (Guam) Doctrine was articulated initially by accident at a press conference before the policy had been thoroughly discussed in the government. Nixon reaffirmed America's willingness to extend a nuclear umbrella over its allies and other states important to the national interest, and to live up to other defense commitments. But he said that in instances of other types of aggression, each country must stand up for itself, although the United States would provide equipment and support. The doctrine alarmed governments all over Asia. Robert Litwak, *Détente and the Nixon Doctrine* (Cambridge: Cambridge University Press, 1984).

10. Sources suggest that Nixon took advantage of both stops on his trip and asked both Yahya Khan and Nicolae Ceausescu, president of Romania, to convey messages to the Chinese. In both cases he made it clear that the United States opposed Soviet

efforts to isolate China. Nixon also prevailed upon President Charles de Gaulle to let the Chinese know he wanted to open a dialogue.

11. Although some of the negotiating record remains classified, new insights have become available in William Burr, (ed.), *The Kissinger Transcripts* (New York: Norton, 1999).

12. This was the first in a series of such annual reports grouped under the title *U.S. Foreign Policy for the 1970s*. The first volume for February 1970 was subtitled *A New Strategy for Peace*.

13. James C.H. Shen, *The U.S. and Free China: How the U.S. Sold Out Its Ally* (Washington, D.C.: Acropolis Books, 1983), 51.

14. Peng, a professor of law and international relations at National Taiwan University, served briefly with the Republic of China's UN mission. While in New York, he became converted to radical independence sympathies, and upon his return to Taiwan involved himself in dissident activities. After advocating the ouster of Chiang Kai-shek, he was imprisoned. When he was released, he managed to flee Taiwan and seek refuge in the United States. Peng Ming-min, *A Taste of Freedom* (New York: Holt, Reinhart & Winston, 1972).

15. The Soviets were shopping for friends. In the immediate wake of the news of Sino-American rapprochement, Moscow dispatched Foreign Minister Andrei Gromyko to Japan. Territorial disputes, however, prevented Soviet-Japanese reconciliation. See Andrei Gromyko, *Memoirs* (New York: Doubleday. 1989).

16. The Soviet tanker was seized on June 23, 1954. The Soviets presumed American complicity because they discounted the Nationalist Chinese ability to carry off such an operation. In fact, according to scholar Robert Accinelli, the U.S. authorities had notified Taipei of the location of the ship. Washington, however, was surprised and alarmed when Chiang refused to release the ship or its crew. Robert Accinelli, *Crisis and Commitment*, 150–151.

17. At some time in March or April, Mao also instructed four trusted, top military men to study the international situation. These four—Chen Yi, Ye Jianying, Xu Xiangqian, and Nie Rongzhen—had all held high government posts and had been criticized during the Cultural Revolution. Their reports, delivered in July 1969, made a strong argument for rapprochement with the United States. Chen Jian and David L. Wilson, "All Under Heaven Is Great Chaos," *Cold War International History Project Bulletin* (Winter 1998): 155–175.

18. According to Henry Kissinger, Zhou Enlai told him that the chargé had no orders regarding such a situation and had tried to evade Stoessel. Henry Kissinger, *The White House Years* (Boston: Little, Brown, 1979), 188.

19. Holdridge and Green both related their own versions of the events. See Marshall Green, John H. Holdridge, and William N. Stokes, *War and Peace with China* (Washington, D.C.: Dacor Press, 1994); and John H. Holdridge, *Crossing the Divide* (New York; Rowman & Littlefield, 1997).

20. The Cambodian government under Prince Norodom Sihanouk was overthrown in March 1970 by a pro-American group under Lon Nol. This cleared the way for an American incursion against North Vietnamese base areas inside Cambodian territory because the elimination of the prince also overturned the country's neutralism. Nixon hoped to buy time for Vietnamization and to bully Hanoi into a peace settlement. Although the venture may have temporarily reduced pressure on South Vietnam, it also widened the war and ultimately led to a disastrous communist takeover of Cambodia. On the Cambodian role in the Vietnam War, see Arnold R. Isaacs, *Without Honor* (New York; Vintage, 1984); on the aftermath, see David P. Chandler, *The Tragedy of Cambodian History* (New Haven: Yale University Press, 1992).

21. The journalist Edgar Snow had written probably the most popular and influential book about the Chinese Communists, entitled *Red Star Over China* (London: Gollancz, 1937 and picked up by Random House in 1938). Its inspiring characterization of Mao and his supporters impressed a worldwide audience, as well as being the first positive account of the CCP to reach many Chinese.

22. In April 1971, while the U.S. table tennis team was competing in Japan in the World Table Tennis Championship, its members received an invitation from the Chinese team to visit China. The American Embassy in Tokyo approved the idea, and the Americans flew to Beijing, where they were welcomed by Zhou Enlai. The trip proved a sensation and this ping-pong diplomacy became a key link in improving Sino-American relations.

23. Mao began to crack down on his revolutionary rebels in July 1968, when it became clear that the unity of the People's Liberation Army was being jeopardized. In the autumn, he reinvigorated an old campaign designed to disperse labor forces and sent the young Red Guards into the countryside to learn from and assist the peasants. By the end of 1970, more than 5 million had been "sent down." See Thomas Bernstein, *Up to the Mountains and Down to the Villages* (New Haven: Yale University Press, 1977), and Peter Seybolt, (ed.), *The Rustication of Urban Youth in China* (New York: M.E. Sharpe, 1975).

24. Alfred LeS. Jenkins was a foreign service officer assigned to Kissinger's staff. Kissinger, however, did not have a State Department person at the NSC in order to involve the department in his China policy. Kissinger explains in his memoir, *The White House Years*, 775, that Jenkins "was an expert in the bilateral issues that had been the staples of Sino-American discussions for two decades; my task was to give him a sense of participation without letting him in on key geopolitical discussions, especially the drafting of the communiqué."

25. See Nancy Bernkopf Tucker, "U.S.-Japan Relations and the Opening to China," in Robert Wampler (ed.), *Power and Prosperity* (Cambridge; Harvard University Press, forthcoming).

26. U. Alexis Johnson, at that time undersecretary for Political Affairs, contends

in his memoir that there had been a plan to send him, a former ambassador, to Japan, to see Sato before Nixon publicly announced his trip to China. Nixon, afraid of leaks, cancelled the trip. Johnson, *The Right Hand of Power*, 554–555.

27. In 1969, the United States conducted negotiations with Japan over the issue of Okinawa reversion and over reducing textile exports to the United States. On Okinawa an accord was reached in November at the first Nixon-Sato summit in Washington. Okinawa would return to Japanese control in 1972. The United States would retain use of its military bases and it obtained Sato's agreement to renew the 1960 security treaty. On textiles, an understanding proved more elusive. Nixon thought he had extracted concessions, but Sato did not follow through and this produced continuing tensions.

28. The release of the Pentagon Papers by Ellsberg triggered the break-in at the Watergate, where the Nixon White House was trying to steal Ellsberg's medical record from his psychiatrist's office. This Watergate episode eventually led to Nixon's resignation from the presidency.

29. White House wiretapping was initiated on May 9, 1969, with Kissinger's alleged declaration to FBI director Herbert Hoover that the White House "will destroy whoever did this if we can find him, no matter where he is." Taping of Winson Lord was initiated May 12, 1970, and lasted nine months. Seymour M. Hersh, *The Price of Power* (New York: Summit Books, 1983), 87, 197.

30. Nancy Tang was born in Brooklyn, New York, and later went to China and attended the Foreign Languages Institute in Beijing. She served as Mao's English language interpreter.

31. Ye Jianying (1897–1986), one of the legendary old marshals of the revolution, a senior PLA leader and Politburo member, was also a political moderate and critic of the Cultural Revolution. He was promoted to the Politburo Standing Committee in 1973 and served there until 1985.

32. Richard H. Soloman, *Chinese Political Negotiating Behavior, 1967–1984* (Santa Monica, CA: RAND Corporation, 1995).

33. These warnings consisted of telephone calls and State Department meetings in the final hours before the trip and the agreements were announced.

34. All four had been victims of McCarthyism in the 1950s. John S. Service and John Carter Vincent had been Foreign Service officers and Owen Lattimore and John K. Fairbank had occasionally been advisers to the government, as well as scholars and writers. See chapter 1.

35. Kissinger's assumption that the Chinese were not all that serious about Taiwan was perhaps a reflection of his own attitudes toward America's ally. Kissinger moved toward the abandonment of Taiwan with relatively little concern. See James Mann, *About Face* (New York: Knopf, 1999), and Patrick Tyler, *A Great Wall* (New York: Public Affairs, 1999).

36. For a discussion of Chinese negotiating style, see Solomon, *Chinese Political*

Negotiating Behavior; Alfred D. Wilhelm, Jr., *The Chinese at the Negotiating Table* (Washington, D.C.: National Defense University Press, 1994); and the earlier Arthur Lall, *How Communist China Negotiates* (New York: Columbia University press, 1968).

37. Klemens von Metternich of Austria and Viscount Robert S. Castlereagh of Britain were the subjects of Kissinger's doctoral thesis, which explored their establishment of a balance of power in Europe as they dealt with the rise of a revolutionary France in the early nineteenth century. The book was published in 1957 by Houghton Mifflin.

38. For the Lin Biao story, see the work of one of the key interpreters of the Cultural Revolution Roderick MacFarquhar, "The Succession to Mao and the End of Maoism, 1969–82," in MacFarquhar (ed.), *The Politics of China, 1949–1989* (New York: Cambridge University Press, 1993), 248–339.

39. In 1971, Leonid Brezhnev guaranteed Western access to Berlin in exchange for West German recognition of Eastern European boundaries disputed since World War II. SALT I, the Strategic Arms Limitation Treaty, stopped development of ABM (antiballistic missile) systems and froze the number of missiles (although not the inventories of warheads, which were quickly expanding with the introduction of MIRVS i.e. multiple independently targeted re-entry vehicles).

40. This formula was devised in 1961, when the United States was beginning to lose influence in the UN because of the influx of newly independent nations from the Third World. To continue to exclude Beijing, the United States made the issue of its entry an "important" rather than a procedural question which meant that it required a two-thirds vote for passage. This bought the United States several more years of UN membership for Taipei.

41. In March 1970, Prince Norodom Sihanouk was ousted by Lon Nol, a general supported by the United States. But Lon Nol's administration did not prosper, fighting continued, and there was increasing involvement by the United States, South Vietnam, North Vietnam, and China. In contrast to their later alignment, in the early 1970s, the United States and China aided opposing groups and disagreed strongly on developments in Cambodia.

42. The United States and China sought quite different outcomes in Cambodia in the 1960s and 1970s as Beijing supported communist forces that Washington sought to suppress. After Vietnam invaded in December 1978, and ousted Pol Pot and his murderous Khmer Rouge regime, however, U.S. and Chinese interests came together in opposition to Vietnamese aggression. They both supported the Khmer rouge in the UN and in a covert war in Cambodia during the 1980s.

43. At the Yalta Conference in February 1945, shortly before his death, Roosevelt allegedly made unnecessary concessions to the Soviet Union for which the Democratic Party was later pilloried.

44. On Mao as tyrant, see Philip Short, *Mao: A Life* (New York: Holt, 2000);

Jonathan Spence, *Mao Zedong* (New York: LipperViking, 1999); and the review of both books by Ian Buruma, "Divine Killer," *New York Review of Books*, February 24, 2000, 20–25.

CHAPTER FIVE

1. Huang Zhen was serving as China's ambassador to France when Donald Anderson first encountered him. Huang would subsequently be sent to Washington, D.C., as the first head of the Chinese Liaison Office.

2. Chinese sources allude to discussion in the Politburo of some form of representative office as early as May 1971. Nevertheless, during Kissinger's October 1971 visit, when Kissinger raised the concept, the Chinese rejected any such interim step, calling it "unrealistic." It may have come up again during Kissinger's June 1972 trip, but was not agreed upon until February 1973.

3. Freeman comment taken from elsewhere in the oral history transcript.

4. Nixon wanted to preserve official diplomatic relations with Taipei even after establishing diplomatic relations with Beijing. The Japanese, in normalizing their relations in 1972, agreed only to have unofficial ties with Taipei.

5. Roxane Witke, in her *Comrade Chiang Ch'ing* (Boston: Little, Brown, 1977), produced an authorized biography of Mao's wife that deviated from history but provided interesting insight into the mind of this critical figure. A less controversial perspective comes in Ross Terrill, *Madame Mao: The White-Boned Demon* (New York: William Morrow, 1984).

6. On the career of Deng Xiaoping, see Richard Evans, *Deng Xiaoping and the Making of Modern China* (New York: Penguin, 1997); and Maurice J. Meisner, *The Deng Xiaoping Era* (New York: Hill and Wang, 1996).

7. In the so-called Halloween Massacre, Ford fired Schlesinger, replacing him with Donald Rumsfeld (White House chief of staff). He replaced Kissinger as national security advisor with Brent Scowcroft (Kissinger remained secretary of state), and William Colby as director of Central Intelligence with George Bush, who was recalled from his post at the Liaison Office in Beijing. Ford also dropped Nelson Rockefeller from the Republican ticket for 1976. Kissinger's view of these events is in his *Years of Renewal* (New York: Simon and Schuster, 1999), 834–844.

8. Before the Opium War fought between the British and the Chinese, 1839–1842, all trade between China and the Europeans was channeled through the southern city of Canton [Guangzhou]. This Canton system was revived in 1957 through the semiannual Canton trade fair as China embarked on an effort to be self-sufficient and minimize the importance of foreign trade. Merchants could only attend if invited and the trade was primarily export-oriented. By the late 1970s, participation had climbed to as many as 30,000 foreigners.

9. Israel recognized the PRC in January, 1950, but the Chinese delayed opening

formal diplomatic relations and, once the Korean War erupted, Israel felt unable to act without angering the United States. By 1954–1955, when Israel altered its position, China had committed itself to close relations with the Arab states and rejected Israeli overtures. From then until the 1970s, little formal diplomatic contact occurred between Israel and either Beijing or Taipei. During that decade, however, Israel launched lucrative clandestine programs of arm sales and technical assistance to both militaries. When the United States refused to supply Taiwan with the short-range Harpoon and Sidewinder missiles it wanted, Israel not only sold Taipei substitutes, but also licensed local production. In January 1992, Israel and the PRC finally opened diplomatic relations, but, ironically, Israel-Taiwan contacts also accelerated. See Jonathan Goldstein (ed.), *China and Israel, 1948–1998* (Westport, CT: Praeger, 1999).

10. The 15 specialists pursuing training at MIT had already been in the program for 18 months when it was discovered that they were Taiwan government scientists. Experts believed that they had learned enough, by the time the U.S. government told them to leave, to assemble missiles in five to 10 years that would be able to hit within a one-mile radius of a target at a distance of 1,000 miles.

11. The Chinese Nationalists had had a research reactor since 1961, and an unsupervised Canadian reactor since 1973. By 1976, they had trained 700 nuclear scientists in the United States. Only under intense pressure from the Gerald Ford administration did Chiang Ching-kuo promise to stop development of nuclear weaponry. A second effort was arrested in the late 1980s. A CIA spy ,Colonel Chang Hsien-yi, who had been serving as the deputy director of Taiwan's institute for nuclear research, turned over critical information to the United States that allowed American officials to pressure Lee Teng-hui to stop these activities. Sources indicate that the program ended but the relevant records were not destroyed. David Albright and Corey Gay, "Taiwan: Nuclear Nightmare Averted," *The Bulletin of the Atomic Scientists* (JanuaryFebruary 1998): 54–60. The South Koreans also embarked on their development of nuclear weapons during the 1970s until pressured by Henry Kissinger to stop the program.

12. *New York Times*, June 24, 1977, A1, A3. The document was actually presidential review memorandum 24, commissioned by the National Security Council in April 1977, and completed in May. It examined presidential options regarding relations with China and policy toward Taiwan, and argued for renewed emphasis on normalization of relations with Beijing. The issue of arms sales to China had been hotly debated since the mid-1970s. In PRM-24, the more conservative posture advocated by Secretary of State Cyrus Vance, opposing sales because of the negative impact on the Soviet Union, dominated over the view of National Security Adviser Zbigniew Brzezinski and Secretary of Defense Harold Brown, which favored security cooperation, technology transfer, and arms sales by European governments to China.

13. Nayan Chanda, *Brother Enemy: The War After the War* (San Diego: Harcourt Brace Jovanovich, 1986). See also the relevant memoirs: Zbigniew Brzezinski, *Power and Principle* (New York: Farrar, Strauss, and Giroux, 1985) and Cyrus Vance, *Hard Choices* (New York: Simon and Schuster, 1983).

14. Jimmy Carter, *Keeping Faith* (New York: Bantam Books, 1982).

15. The Jackson-Vanik amendment to the 1974 Trade Act was aimed at the Soviet Union, but covered other communist states and required that the president certify that a government granted free emigration or that the extension of most-favored-nation treatment would encourage the government to do so.

16. The CCP held a month-long central work conference followed by the third plenum of the Eleventh Central Committee from November to December 1978. Deng seized the initiative and elevated Zhou Enlai's four modernizations of agriculture, industry, science, and technology, and national defense to the government's top priority.

17. Wolff's vocal criticism of Carter's approach led to publication of Lester Wolff and David L. Simon, *Legislative History of the Taiwan Relations Act* (Jamaica, NY: American Association of Chinese Studies, 1982).

18. The lawsuit filed by seven senators and eight representatives in federal court charged that the administration did not have the unilateral right to abrogate the defense treaty with Taiwan. They won an initial judgment in October 1979, saw it overturned in November, and then finally denied by the Supreme Court. In the interim, the Senate proved unable to agree on whether a resolution to prevent a president from taking such actions could be applied retroactively to the Taiwan case.

19. The ROC ambassador in Washington complained bitterly about his treatment in Shen, *The U.S. and Free China: How the U.S. Sold Out Its Ally*.

20. The emperor's edict in 1793 to the British king declared that China had no need of foreign commerce and therefore would not agree to having a British representative reside in the capital, fix fair tariff rates, or open new ports for trade as London had requested. The communication was presented to Lord George Macartney, who had led a mission to the Chinese court to improve relations with the Chinese. An important reexamination of the Macartney Mission has been written by James Hevia, *Cherishing Men from Afar: Qing Guest Ritual and the Macartney Embassy of 1793* (Durham, NC: Duke University Press, 1995).

21. On the political turmoil, see Douglas Mendel, *The Politics of Formosan Nationalism* (Berkeley: University of California Press, 1970); and Mark J. Cohen, *Taiwan at the Crossroads* (Washington, D.C.: Asia Resource Center, 1988).

22. For a discussion of the importance of Afghanistan, see Odd Arne Westad (ed.), *The Fall of Détente* (Boston: Scandinavian University Press, 1997); and Raymond L. Garthoff, *Détente and Confrontation* (Washington, D.C.: Brookings Institution, 1985).

23. Zhai Qiang, *China and the Vietnam Wars, 1950–1975* (Chapel Hill: University of North Carolina Press, 2000).

24. On the peace talks and efforts to end the war, see Allan E. Goodman, *The Lost Peace* (Stanford: Hoover Institution Press, 1978); Gareth Porter, *A Peace Denied* (Bloomington: Indiana University Press, 1975); and Nguyen Tien Hung and Jerrold L. Schecter, *The Palace File* (New York: Harper & Row, 1989).

25. The Chinese incursion into Vietnam lasted 17 days. Withdrawal began March 5, 1978. The United States provided the Chinese with satellite information regarding the positioning of Soviet forces to China's north.

26. The Socialist Republic of Vietnam invaded Cambodia in December 1978, and the Kampuchean (Cambodian) National United Front for National Salvation, created by the Vietnamese, formed a new government on January 8, 1979, with Heng Samrin as president.

27. The first of the Vietnamese boat people arrived in May 1975; the numbers peaked in 1979, with 73 percent of the 66,000 arriving in the first six months of the year being of ethnic Chinese background. Under such massive pressure, the Hong Kong government persuaded Great Britain, Australia, Canada, and the United States to sign a burden sharing agreement in 1979. In 1982, the government tried to close the refugee camps and deny the boat people work permits. Repatriation was not begun until much later because of American opposition.

CHAPTER SIX

1. Claire Chennault headed the American Volunteer Group, the Flying Tigers, in China during World War II. After the war he lobbied in Washington for the Guomindang. Anna proved able to turn her marriage to the general into access to the Republican power elite. See Claire L. Chennault, *Way of a Fighter* (New York: G. Putnam's Sons, 1949).

2. Cross recalls the problems of the period in Charles T. Cross, *Born a Foreigner* (New York: Rowman & Littlefield, 1999).

3. Some Chinese students sought asylum, others returned to China to support the revolution. A third group, numbering 129, was not permitted to leave because they were said to be privy to sensitive scientific knowledge. Among them, Qian Xuesheng and Guo Yonghuai later contributed significantly to China's nuclear and missile programs when a repatriation agreement was reached between Washington and Beijing in 1956.

4. On the FX controversy, see A. Doak Barnett, *The FX Decision* (Washington, D.C.: Brookings Institution, 1981).

5. This book is Alexander M. Haig, Jr., *Caveat* (New York: Macmillan, 1984).

6. The other three assurances were that there would be no prior consultation with the PRC regarding arms sales, that there would be no revision of the Taiwan Rel-

tions Act, and that the United States had not changed its position regarding the sovereignty of Taiwan.

7. Solomon, *Chinese Political Negotiating Behavior, 1967–84*; Wilhelm, *The Chinese at the Negotiating Table*.

8. Twin Oaks, a 26-room Victorian mansion located in northwest Washington, was "sold" to the Friends of Free China.

9. Stories of early involvement between Americans and Chinese would include the book by Liang Heng and Judith Shapiro, which tells of his experiences during the Cultural Revolution and their meeting and efforts to secure permission to marry. *Son of the Revolution* (New York: Knopf, 1983).

10. Fox Butterfield, *China, Alive in the Bitter Sea* (New York: Times Books, 1982).

11. He was prime minister, September 1980 to April 1988, and general secretary of the CCP January 1987 to May 1989.

12. These bonds had been issued by the Qing dynasty to finance railway construction in south China. Speculators wanted the Chinese government to pay principal and interest on the bonds and managed to get a court judgment in Alabama, in 1982, asserting that Beijing should redeem the bonds. Ultimately, the Chinese authorities were forced to hire lawyers in the United States who successfully got the decision reversed in 1986. The Supreme Court refused to hear an appeal in 1987.

13. The State Department's Country Reports on human rights had been mandated by the Foreign Assistance and Related Programs Act of 1976, and the first set of reports were presented to Congress in March 1977. Initially, they only covered countries to which Washington gave military aid, but were almost immediately broadened to cover the world. The reports accordingly grew from 137 pages to 1,140 by the end of the Carter administration.

14. The work unit (*danwei*) grew out of the 1961–1962 effort to force peasants out of the cities where the food supply was shrinking alarmingly. To prevent future migration into the overburdened cities, people were locked into a system of residency requirements in which nontransferable coupons entitled them to specific goods only in their home jurisdictions. Further, the job mobility of urban workers ended, but in exchange they obtained guaranteed lifetime employment in state-owned enterprises, and these enterprises became responsible for providing housing, education, health care, recreation, etc. The so-called "iron rice bowl" lasted until economic reforms took hold under Deng Xiaoping.

15. The debate over whether the unity of China could be sustained continued into the 1990s. See Jack Goldstone, "The Coming Chinese Collapse," and Huang Yasheng, "Why China Will Not Collapse," both in *Foreign Policy*, 99 (1995): 35–68.

16. For the secretary of state's view, see George P. Shultz, *Turmoil and Triumph* (New York: Charles Scribner's Sons, 1993).

17. Harold Brown, defense secretary, traveled to China in January 1980. Because

of the Soviet invasion of Afghanistan, the Chinese proved willing to set aside the Taiwan issue and enter into a military exchange and intelligence sharing relationship. Brown also announced that the United States would be willing to sell nonlethal military goods to China, including helicopters and communications equipment.

18. China's birth control program came under attack in the early 1980s for its use of forced abortion and sterilization, as well as the growing problem of female infanticide. At the time, the United Nations Fund for Population Activities operated in China, and critics of family planning insisted that UNFPA was complicit in these criminal procedures. The Reagan administration, which opposed abortion as a form of birth control, decided, beginning in 1984, to withhold 50 percent of the American contribution to this organization. Not satisfied, members of Congress, notably Senator Jesse Helms, pressed the issue, delaying Lord's confirmation five weeks. Finally, the Reagan administration terminated UNFPA funding.

19. Michael Pillsbury, "U.S.-Chinese Military Ties?" *Foreign Policy* (Fall 1975): 50–64. The argument was that weapons sales, joint exercises, and contingency planning, as well as exchanges of attachés, would return momentum to a flagging relationship and strengthen Washington's position against Moscow.

20. In 1984, China became eligible for the U.S. Foreign Military Sales program, which meant that Beijing could obtain U.S. financing to buy American weapons. Several purchases and technology transfers resulted in the following years, including avionics for 50 Chinese fighter aircraft, radars, and joint production of an antisubmarine torpedo. The avionics project, Peace Pearl, was the most controversial because of the potential threat upgraded aircraft posed to Taiwan.

21. During the Iran-Iraq war, China sold weapons to both sides, earning billions of dollars in the process. After the United States had decided to reflag Kuwaiti oil tankers in the Persian Gulf in 1987, Chinese supplies of Silkworm anti-ship missiles to Iran became a major issue. Under extreme pressure from Washington, the Chinese halted their sales and the United States lifted export restrictions on advanced technology in March 1988.

22. Reports to this effect surfaced in the news media in June 1984. Beijing agreed to join the International Atomic Energy Agency in 1984, and pledged privately not to assist Pakistan. It took longer for China to adhere to the Nuclear Non-Proliferation Treaty and probably considerably longer actually to stop its aid to the Pakistanis.

23. Sales to the Saudis of C-SS-2 intermediate-range ballistic missiles were objectionable to the United States because they introduced a new class of weapons to the region. These missiles could carry nuclear payloads and had a range sufficient to hit Israel. The Chinese tried to comply with American demands by imposing certain conditions on the missiles once in Saudi Arabia, but the Saudi government refused to permit international inspections.

24. During 1998, stories broke in the American press regarding possible theft of

highly sensitive information as a result of Chinese launches of U.S. satellites. In one case, suggestions were made that classified circuit boards were removed from a crash site. In another, more credible instance, American technicians were said to have passed information to Chinese scientists to improve launch reliability.

25. Wu met with Reagan as well as Shultz and discussed trade and missile proliferation. The United States lifted sanctions originally imposed in October 1987, in response to Silkworm missile sales to Iran. The sanctions had barred sales of high-technology goods to China.

26. The contest over licensing reached a climax in the Clinton administration when the president abruptly shifted from State to Commerce to speed approvals and promote business. After the Cox Committee reported on Chinese espionage in 1999, however, the White House was compelled to return the power to a more cautious State Department.

27. Alice Tisdale Hobart, *Oil for the Lamps of China* (Indianapolis: Bobbs-Merrill, 1933).

28. Intellectual property rights (IPR) afford protection for proprietary materials of economic value such as patents, brand names, copyrights, and trade marks. International practice anticipates that governments will guard against illegitimate use of someone else's intellectual property. Piracy hurts innovation, eliminating the willingness of business to take risks and invest heavily in something that will quickly be purloined.

29. Astrophysicist Fang Lizhi made a series of provocative speeches on Chinese university campuses in 1985 and 1986, urging students to seek greater freedom of expression and to oppose corruption. In Shanghai, he even declared that "complete Westernization" was China's only hope. Student demonstrations began on December 5, 1986, and ended abruptly with arrests in Tiananmen Square on January 1, 1987. See Richard Baum, *Burying Mao* (Princeton: Princeton University Press, 1994).

30. The Anti-Rightist Campaign of 1957 had followed the Hundred Flowers Campaign and was designed to eliminate dissent. Deng took a large role in the repression. See Roderick MacFarquhar, *The Origins of the Cultural Revolution,* vol. 1: *Contradictions Among the People* (New York: Columbia University Press, 1974).

31. On decision making, see Carol Lee Hamrin, Zhao Suisheng, and A. Doak Barnett (eds.), *Decision-Making in Deng's China* (New York: M.E. Sharpe, 1997), and A. Doak Barnett, *The Making of Foreign Policy in China* (Boulder, CO: Westview Press, 1985).

32. Deng put forward the four cardinal principles in spring 1979. They stressed (1) Marxism-Leninism Mao Zedong thought; (2) the socialist road; (3) continuation of the people's democratic dictatorship; and (4) absolute political control by the CCP.

33. Bette Bao Lord wrote three books based on her Chinese roots and connections: *Spring Moon* (London, Sphere Books, 1982); *Eighth Moon* (New York: Avon,

1983); and *Legacies* (New York: Ballantine, 1990). She did not perform the traditional role of an ambassador's wife and her cultural outreach was controversial in the American diplomatic corps as well as in China.

34. Reagan arrived in Moscow May 29, 1988, for a largely symbolic summit with Gorbachev. He addressed students at Moscow State University in his most significant address of the trip on May 31, 1988.

35. During the brutal rape of Nanjing in 1937, some 200,000–300,000 were killed and 20,000 women, of all ages, raped and mutilated. The Chinese feel that Japan has never sincerely apologized for its brutality. In January 2000, for instance, a conference on the 1937 Nanjing Massacre in Osaka, Japan, called it "the biggest myth of the 20th century." Such Japanese denial has been very provocative. See the controversial book by Iris Chang, *The Rape of Nanjing* (New York: Basic Books, 1997); and John Rabe, *The Good Man of Nanking* (New York: Knopf, 1988), translated by John E. Woods.

36. John F. Burns, the Beijing bureau chief for the *New York Times*, was taken into custody July 17, 1986, while on a motorcycle trip through an area off-limits to foreigners. He was charged with espionage and expelled July 23, 1986.

37. This scandal revealed by the press in the autumn of 1986 involved a White House trade of arms for hostages being held by pro-Iranian Islamic fundamentalists in Lebanon. At the same time, the White House was defying a congressional ban and providing secret military support to the Contras, anti-government rebels, fighting the left-wing Sandanista regime in Nicaragua. These two actions became linked when the administration diverted profits from the arms sales to support the Contras.

38. On U.S. involvement with the Tibetans, see John Kenneth Kraus, *Orphans of the Cold War* (New York: Public Affairs, 1999); and on Sino-Tibetan relations, see Melvyn C. Goldstein, *The Snow Lion and the Dragon* (Berkeley: University of California Press, 1997).

39. The exhibit, entitled, "Then and Now: American Portraits of the Past Century from the National Portrait Gallery, Washington, D.C.," traveled to Hong Kong, Hokkaido, and Tokyo in 1987 and 1988. The United States cancelled the China showing in the summer of 1987.

40. John Kaplan, *The Court Martial of the Kaohsiung Defendants* (Berkeley: University of California Press, 1981).

41. Lin's mother and twin daughters were killed on February 28, 1980, in their home, while the Guomindang was supposed to be guarding it. In 1998, Lin was chosen to be head of the increasingly influential Democratic Progressive Party.

42. Professor Chen Wen-chen from Carnegie Mellon University was picked up for questioning by the Taiwan Garrison Command in 1981, regarding his political activities in the United States. His body was later discovered on the campus of National Taiwan University; the government denied involvement in his demise.

43. Henry Liu, an undercover agent probably for both the FBI and the Taiwan Intelligence Bureau of the Ministry of National Defense, journalist, and author of a critical biography of Chiang Ching-kuo, was assassinated in front of his home in California, in 1984. Although the killing was carried out by gangsters (the United Bamboo), evidence pointed to members of the government as having ordered the murder. On Liu and other Taiwan intelligence activities, see David E. Kaplan, *Fires of the Dragon* (New York: Antheneum, 1992). An important English-language biography of Chiang is Jay Taylor, *Chiang Ching-kuo and the Revolutions in China and Taiwan* (Cambridge: Harvard University Press, 2000).

44. The high-level intelligence official was Admiral Wang Hsi-ling, but it appeared reasonably certain that he had been acting under orders. Who gave the orders was never established. Lee Teng-hui granted those who were imprisoned early releases, including Wang, who was pardoned in 1991.

45. In 1988, as part of the Omnibus Trade and Competitiveness Act, the United States initiated a system by which countries with barriers to American trade could be identified. Section 301 also prescribed procedures for retaliation.

46. In fact, Reagan even mentioned the idea during his remarks to the South Korean National Assembly in November, 1983. See Don Oberdorfer, *The Two Koreas* (Reading, MA: Addison-Wesley, 1997).

47. The bombing on October 9, 1983, followed only a month after the destruction of a passenger plane, KAL 007, by Soviet military aircraft as it strayed off-course over Soviet territory. This second event, which killed four high South Korean officials, narrowly missed murdering President Chun Doo Hwan. Nevertheless, Chun resisted the temptation to take retaliatory action against Pyongyang.

48. Deng was so angered by the bombing, which occurred the day after he had broached the idea of three-way talks with the Americans at North Korea's request, that he refused to meet with the Koreans for weeks thereafter.

49. Chun, who had come to power in South Korea by means of a coup, had pledged he would serve only one term as president. As his term drew to a close, he began maneuvering to preserve his influence and was opposed by street demonstrations. The Reagan administration interceded to encourage Chun to hand power to a civilian government, and that pressure helped reinforce Korean protests. Chun stepped down early in 1988.

50. Gorbachev's July 1986 speech at Vladivostok was notable for its concession on two of the three obstacles the Chinese had identified to the improvement of Sino-Soviet relations. Gorbachev announced that he would withdraw six regiments from Afghanistan and remove a significant proportion of the Soviet forces stationed in Mongolia. He also suggested negotiations regarding Sino-Soviet border defenses. The speech was initially greeted with Chinese skepticism, particularly because Gorbachev did not address the third obstacle, having to do with Soviet aid to Vietnam.

CHAPTER SEVEN

1. There is an extensive literature on democratization in Taiwan, including: Bruce J. Dickson, *Democratization in China and Taiwan* (New York: Oxford, 1997); and Linda Chao and Ramon H. Myers, *The First Chinese Democracy* (Baltimore: Johns Hopkins University Press, 1998).

2. Song Qiang, et. al., *China Can Say No—The Political and Emotional Choice in the Post-Cold War Era* (Zhonguo keyi shuo bu—Lengzhanhou shidai de zhengzhiyu qinggan jueze) (Beijing: Zhonguo gonshang lianhe chubanshe, 1996).

3. A number of good books have been published on the events at Tiananmen, including narratives such as Scott Simmie and Bob Nixon, *Tiananmen Square* (Seattle: University of Washington Press, 1989) and Mu Yi and Mark V. Thompson, *Crisis at Tiananmen* (San Francisco: China Books and Periodicals, 1989). An insightful analysis of why the government used force can be found in Timothy Brook, *Quelling the People* (Oxford: Oxford University Press, 1992).

4. Actually, the peasantry tended not to participate because they had been among the greatest beneficiaries of Deng's reforms.

5. On the democracy movement and Hu's role in it, see Merle Goldman, *Sowing the Seeds of Democracy in China* (Cambridge; Harvard University Press, 1994).

6. On May 21, 1989, the two surviving field marshals of the PLA from the civil war era, Nie Rongzhen and Xu Xiangqian, declared on TV that the demonstrations were a patriotic event. This was followed by a letter sent directly to Deng Xiaoping by seven senior generals, reportedly including retired Defense Secretary Zhang Aiping, retired chief of staff Yang Dezhi, and retired naval commander Ye Fei. They protested the use of martial law tactics and asserted that the people's army should never fire on the people. Some 100 other officers signed the letter. Richard Baum, "The Road to Tiananmen: Chinese Politics in the 1980s," in MacFarquhar, ed., *The Politics of China, 1949-1989.*

7. The students had been working with Congresswoman Nancy Pelosi (D-CA) and others on legislation allowing them to stay in the United States after expiration of their student visas. The Pelosi bill passed 403 to 0 in the House and by a voice vote in the Senate, but Bush vetoed it. To ensure that his veto would stand, he granted the students comparable terms by executive order. As a result, the president angered both Congress and Beijing.

8. The arrests in China began June 6. Warrants named individuals involved in leading the protests, as well as others who had simply been outspoken critics of the regime. By late June, perhaps tens of thousands had been arrested and some 35 workers had been executed after summary trials. Escapees numbered more than 40 student leaders and intellectuals.

9. The sanctions imposed initially included suspension of high-level military exchanges and military sales, and warnings against American travel to China (which struck hard at China's tourist industry). These were supplemented by measures to

persuade international financial institutions to deny Beijing loans, to suspend financing under the U.S. Trade Development Program, to suspend investment guarantees by the Overseas Private Investment Corporation [OPIC], to deny export licenses for American satellites intended for launch on Chinese rockets, and to prevent implementation of a 1985 nuclear cooperation agreement. Some of these sanctions were also imposed by European governments and Japan.

10. Harold Isaacs, *Scratches on Our Minds* [also called *Images of Asia*] (New York: Capricorn Books, 1962).

11. See Jonathan Spence, *To Change China* (Boston: Little, Brown, 1969).

12. The annual MFN decision was customarily made in the spring, and until the Tiananmen events had been a routine event. The president declared he planned to renew and Congress took no action to block this. In 1989, following the June 4th crisis, there were proposals in the Congress to revoke MFN for China, but no such initiative was included in the comprehensive sanctions bill that was passed. Disagreement over the idea, it was thought, might have slowed down passage of the legislation. Pressures to revoke or put limitations on MFN, however, began to be felt in 1990 and in every year thereafter.

13. These issues inherited from the Bush administration burdened the new foreign policy team. In Bosnia they faced civil war and genocide as the Serbs tried to eliminate competitor populations. In Somalia, efforts at remedying a humanitarian crisis ended with the deaths of American soldiers. And finally in Haiti, the administration confronted both the issue of boatloads of Haitian refugees and the effort to restore the democratically elected president to power after a coup.

14. Lord traveled to Beijing with a package of 14 principles for the improvement of relations, but found the Chinese unwilling even to discuss some of them.

15. For the secretary of state's views, see Warren Christopher, *In the Stream of History* (Stanford; Stanford University Press, 1998).

16. According to Barton Gellman in the *Washington Post*, "Christopher never quite got over his indignation over that trip." Barton Gellman, "U.S. and China Nearly Came to Blows in 1996," *Washington Post,* June 21, 1998, A20.

17. Each year, at the annual meeting of the United Nations Human Rights Commission, the United States attempted to pass a resolution condemning China for its human rights abuses. American diplomats never succeeded in this effort.

18. A spokesman for the U.S. Department of State suggested that the crew had dumped the chemicals overboard, despite the U.S. Navy's monitoring efforts.

19. Theater Missile Defense systems are designed to destroy attacking missiles before they hit targets. Such systems operate at various altitudes and with different equipment, but China has opposed Taiwan's possession of all such systems. The Clinton administration did provide Taiwan with Patriot missiles, but more sophisticated defenses remain largely experimental and very expensive.

20. Presidents Ronald Reagan and Li Xiannian signed an agreement on July 23,

1985, allowing the sale of American nuclear reactors and nonmilitary technology to the People's Republic.

21. New indications of Chinese proliferation activities with Iran surfaced subsequently. For instance, Acting Undersecretary of State John Holum, on a November 1998 trip to Beijing, reportedly expressed concern about technology transfers to Iran that violated the MTCR addendum. But China has consistently refused to adhere to the restrictions in the addendum, because China has not been an actual MTCR signatory.

22. Here Lord is alluding to the campaign finance scandals that disrupted the second Clinton administration. Businessmen with interests in China were able to gain access to the president to argue for amelioration of restrictions on trade. This included key figures in such major companies as Hughes Electronics, which wanted to use Chinese rockets to launch their satellites.

23. The nuclear crisis began March 12, 1993, with North Korea's announcement that it intended to withdraw from the Non-Proliferation Treaty because of intrusive International Atomic Energy Agency inspections and accusations that the North was conducting illegitimate activity at Yongbyon. Pyongyang also insisted that the United States and South Korea were conducting provocative military exercises (Team Spirit). On the Korean crisis of 1993–1994 see Oberdorfer, *The Two Koreas*.

24. Different AIT directors had different degrees of involvement with policy determination. The early directors tended to be more influential. Then, in the late 1990s, a new head of AIT, Richard Bush, again asserted considerable weight in policy circles.

25. Hills was the first. Subsequently Frederico Peña, secretary of transportation, also traveled to Taiwan in December 1994. In November 1998 Energy Secretary Bill Richardson attended a conference in Taipei and met with President Lee. In response to the Peña visit, the PRC canceled a long-planned Peña trip to China scheduled for January 1995.

26. The House of Representatives voted 396 to 0 on May 3, and six days later, the Senate voted 97 to 1. The Clinton White House changed its position on May 22, 1995.

27. These specialized magnets were designed to be installed in high-speed centrifuges at the Pakistani Abdul Qadeer Khan Research Laboratory in Kahuta. Once in place, they would be employed in the process of enriching uranium for incorporation into nuclear weapons. U.S. officials contended that the shipments occurred in three parts between December 1994 and mid-1995. The story broke in the *Washington Times* in February 1996. The CIA had discovered the sale late in 1995, and the State Department reportedly concluded that the evidence uncovered warranted sanctions. Under the 1994 Nuclear Proliferation Prevention Act, all Export-Import Bank assistance was supposed to be cut off. U.S. companies, for which disruption of loan guarantees totaling $10 billion presented a problem, included Boeing, Westing-

house, and AT&T. Chinese Vice Foreign Minister Li Zhaoxing claimed that the sale of 5,000 magnets was "peaceful nuclear cooperation."

28. At the same time as the administration faced the ring magnet issue, it was also threatening China with more than $1 billion in trade sanctions.

29. A contrary view that Tony Lake was the crucial actor can be found in Barton Gellman, "U.S. and China Nearly Came to Blows in 1996," *Washington Post*, June 21, 1998, and "Reappraisal Led to New China Policy," *Washington Post*, June 22, 1998.

30. The summer 1995 missile firings splashed down 90 miles north of Taiwan, but the 1996 tests were much closer. On the south, the target area was 32 miles from the coast, threatening the port of Kaohsiung; on the north, the zone was only 22 miles offshore, jeopardizing traffic into Keelung.

31. Pamela Harriman, widow of Averell Harriman, and influential Democratic Party personality, served as American Ambassador to France from July 1993 to her sudden death in February 1997.

32. At the beginning of 2000, some 2 million people from Taiwan were visiting China annually, and some 200,000, mostly businessmen, were living there. John Pomfret, "Taiwanese Conflicted over China," *Washington Post*, March 6, 2000, A15.

33. Several parties—China, Taiwan, the Philippines, Brunei, Vietnam, and Malaysia—have claims to part or all of the South China Sea area, focusing on the 230 islets, rocks, and reefs of the Spratly Island group. These territorial claims have been complicated by the assumptions that some of the area may be rich in oil or natural gas. The Chinese have called it the "second Persian Gulf." Military clashes occurred between China and Vietnam in 1974 and 1988. In 1994, the PLA Navy targeted Mischief Reef, building shelters and stationing guards on an area previously used by Filipino fishermen. China's actions at Mischief Reef provoked ASEAN into a more unified stand for some months thereafter, but evident anger from the Southeast Asian states did not convince China to leave the reef. See Scott Snyder, "The South China Sea Dispute: Prospects for Preventive Diplomacy," Special Report, United States Institute of Peace, 1996.

34. A good analysis of the crisis in the Taiwan Strait and its impact on China, Taiwan, and the United States is found in John W. Garver, *Face Off* (Seattle: University of Washington Press, 1997).

35. Clinton and Hashimoto announced the strengthening of the alliance in the spring of 1996 but the guidelines were not made public until the autumn. On the relationship between Washington and Tokyo, see Michael J. Green and Patrick M. Cronin (ed.), *The U.S.-Japan Alliance* (New York: Council on Foreign Relations, 1999); and Ralph A. Cossa (ed.), *Restructuring the U.S.-Japan Alliance* (Washington, D.C.: Center for Strategic and International Studies, 1997); and Yoichi Funabashi, *Alliance Adrift* (New York: Council on Foreign Relations, 1999).

CONCLUDING THOUGHTS

1. The United States and China finally reached an accord on entry into the WTO in September 1999.

2. See Nancy Bernkopf Tucker, "China-Taiwan: U.S. Debates and Policy Choices," *Survival* (Winter 1998–99): 150–167.

Meehlert, Cal, 271

Meeker, Brice, 185

Meir, Golda, 419

Melby, John: on Beijing, fall of, 47–48; biography, xix; on Madame Chiang, 34–35; on China Lobby, 39–40; on China White Paper, 61–62; on communists, 27; on GMD, 26–27; on Marshall Mission, 24; on Shanghai, evacuation of, 36–37; on John Leighton Stuart, 25–26

Menon, Krishna, 179

military assistance advisory group (MAAG), 117, 512n30 (117)

Ministry of Foreign Economic Relations and Trade (MOFERT), 396

Ministry of Posts and Telegraphs, 380

missionaries: 36–37, 505n17 (36); detained in China, 96; evacuation of, 72; eviction of, 85

Mitchell, George, 458–59

Moceri, James: biography, xix; on Drumright's appointment to ambassadorship, 133–34; on riots at USIS Taiwan, 140–41; on Taiwan land reform, 135–36; on Taiwan/mainland differences, 138

Mongolia: Kennedy recognition of, 161–62; link to Taiwan-UN question, 159, 173, 182

monolithic communism: 144, 344–45; end of belief in, 161

Mosbacher, Robert A., 446

most favored nation (MFN) status: 450, 456, 457–59, 463, 535n12; conditions for, 458–59, 466; effect on Christopher's 1994 China trip, 464–65; effect on Clinton administration, 470; effect on Hong Kong, 465–66; and human rights, 438, 467; and prisoner releases, 459; as tactic, 452–53, 466–67; effect on Taiwan, 465–66; and Taiwan Straits Crisis, 481; U.S. reversal on, 479

Moyer, Ray, 76

Mukden Incident, 12, 13

Mukden: 506n22 (41); communist arrival in, 41; house arrest of U.S. embassy staff, 42–44

Mutual Defense Assistance Act, 509n3 (84)

Mutual Defense Treaty, 81, 275, 281, 284, 314; abrogation of, 334–35, 527n18 (332)

Nanjing: 492; embassy in, 23, 24; rape of, 406, 532n33 (406)

National Committee on U.S.-China Relations, 286

National Council for U.S.-China Trade (U.S.-China Business Council), 286

Nationalist Chinese: 5–6, 7, 16, 17, 22, 139; in Africa, 516–17n6 (165); aid efforts for, 19; attack Shanghai, 53, 56, 60–61, 71; blockade, 56, 60, 71, 125; in Burma, 93, 510n15 (93); and civil war, 16, 19, 52; corruption, 119; create government on Taiwan, 80; in Hong Kong, 111; espionage in Hong Kong, 184; intelligence gathering, 297–98, 337–38, 485; irregular troops, 118–19; Manchuria, invasion of, 22; morale, 149; and Peking, 46–47; on Sino-Soviet relations, 66; and reclaiming the mainland, 15; retreat to Taiwan, 18, 53, 73; treatment of civilians, 20, 21; as true government of China, 130; and